# EXTERNAL AUDITING AND ASSURANCE AN IRISH TEXTBOOK

Published in 2018 by
Chartered Accountants Ireland
Chartered Accountants House
47–49 Pearse Street
Dublin 2
www.charteredaccountants.ie

ISBN: 978-1-912350-03-2

Typeset by Datapage
Printed by GRAFO, S.A.

MIX
Paper from
responsible sources
FSC® C116691

# EXTERNAL AUDITING AND ASSURANCE AN IRISH TEXTBOOK

3rd Edition

Martin Nolan and
Christine Nangle

CHARTERED
ACCOUNTANTS
IRELAND

# Contents

# Introduction

## RECENT DEVELOPMENTS IN AUDITING AND ASSURANCE

### The EU Audit Regulation and Directive

The publication in May 2014 of the EU Audit Regulation and Directive (ARD) was the catalyst for significant and wide-ranging change in the auditing profession. The implementation of the ARD resulted in:

- The appointment of the Irish Auditing & Accounting Supervisory Authority (IAASA) as the "competent authority" in the Republic of Ireland, replacing the Financial Reporting Council (FRC). The IAASA is now responsible for issuing auditing standards for use in the RoI (previously, the FRC's standards having been adopted).
- A requirement for the competent authorities to carry out regulatory reviews of the audit of public interest entities (PIEs).
- Revision of the auditing standards, including the Ethical Standard, to reflect the detailed requirements of the ARD.
- Revision of the *UK Corporate Governance Code*.
- New rules relating to auditor rotation for PIEs.
- Restrictions on the provision of non-audit services, including caps on certain non-audit services and bans on others.
- Reduced ethical provisions are now permitted for the audit of smaller entities.

To comply with the ARD, in June 2016 the FRC completed its revisions to the *UK Corporate Governance Code* and to its auditing standards, and issued updated guidance on audit committees. These changes took effect for financial years commencing on or after 17 June 2016.

At the same time, the IAASA, in its new role as the competent authority in the RoI, obtained a licence from the FRC to tailor its audit framework for use in the RoI. These newly tailored standards were adopted on 31 January 2017 and are mandatory for use in the audit of Irish financial statements for periods beginning on or after 17 June 2016, for which audit opinions are signed after 1 February 2017. The figure below depicts this new development. Note the new naming conventions – previously the FRC's International Auditing Standards were referred to as ISA (UK and Ireland) reflecting their application in both jurisdictions; now we have ISA (UK) as issued by the FRC, and ISA (Ireland) as issued by the IAASA.

## AUDITING STANDARDS IN THE UK AND IRELAND

E.g. ISA (Ireland) 230 *Audit Documentation* – **ISSUED BY IAASA**

***Note***: IAASA obtained a licence from the FRC to use ISAs as revised by the FRC at 17 June 2016 and made amendments to these to reflect Irish legislation but otherwise they are largely unchanged from FRC's versions. New IAASA standards are used by RoI for audit of financial statements of periods beginning on or after 17 June 2016.

E.g. ISA (UK and Ireland) 230 *Audit Documentation* – **ISSUED BY FRC** and updated 17 June 2016 to reflect final changes required under EU audit reform.

**Used by RoI for audit of financial statements of periods beginning before 17 June 2016.**

E.g. ISA (UK) 230 *Audit Documentation* – **ISSUED BY FRC**

Following IAASA's adoption of their own version of the FRC's standards, the FRC, no longer needing the standards to be relevant for two legislative jurisdictions. made amendments to the ISAs (revised 17 June 2016) to include specific references to UK legislation.

For audits commencing **before 17 June 2016**, the FRC's Ethical Standards 1–5, the provisions available for smaller entities (ES – PASE) and its ISAs (UK and Ireland) continue to be the appropriate standards.

### Revisions of Auditing Standards

The FRC's overhaul of the standards (in June 2016) to comply with the requirements of the ARD largely reflects the additional requirements relating to the audit of PIEs, in particular, the inclusion of a new report to the audit committee. ISA 260 *Communication with Those Charged with Governance*, paragraph 16R-2, outlines the auditor's responsibility with regard to this additional report for the audit committee and identifies the minimum information expected to be included in the report. Other standards have been updated to cross-reference this new reporting requirement within the respective audit areas.

Other specific changes to standards include:
- ISA 320 *Materiality in Planning and Performing an Audit*, paragraph 20, was expanded to better emphasise the need for the auditor to consider disclosures in the substantive procedures;
- ISA 510 *Initial Engagements – Opening Balances*, paragraph 21D-1, reinforces the importance of the application of the auditor's professional scepticism, particularly when reviewing management's estimates relating to fair values, the impairment of assets and provisions;

- ISA 230 *Audit Documentation*, paragraph 6, asserts that audit documentation shall include all documents, information, records and other data required by ISQC 1, and applicable legal and regulatory requirements.

The Ethical Standard underwent a complete revision and restructure and now includes a series of alternative provisions and exemptions for smaller company audits. The ISQC 1 was revised and now calls for audit quality through the application of strong policies and procedures within the audit firm at both the firm and audit engagement level.

Changes subsequent to the 2016 revisions are in general relatively minor, such as updating for legislative terms. Some standards have had more specific revision, including:

- ISQC 1 is revised with further provisions around group audits, the auditor ceasing to hold office and audit documentation retention and, in turn, ISA 220 *Quality Control for an Audit of Financial Statements* is also amended.
- ISA 250 Section A—*Consideration of Laws and Regulations in an Audit of Financial Statements* is updated around the communication of key audit matters and communication relating to entities that report on application of the *UK Corporate Governance Code* (and the Irish Corporate Governance Annex for the RoI).
- ISA 450 *Evaluation of Misstatements Identified During the Audit* is updated to improve the representations around management's response to identified misstatements.
- ISA 700 *Forming an Opinion and Reporting on Financial Statements* now requires the auditor to not sign the audit report earlier than the date on which all the other information contained in the annual report has been approved by those charged with governance and the auditor has considered all necessary available evidence.

**Table A** and **Table B** below is a list of the extant auditing standards in issue as at 1 January 2018 in the RoI and UK, respectively.

## Table A: Extant List of Auditing Standards – Republic of Ireland

The IAASA's Ethical Standard and Auditing Standards in issue at 1 January 2018.

| Standard | Full title | Primary Chapter Refs. |
|---|---|---|
| | Ethical Standard for Auditors (Ireland) 2017 | 2 |
| ISQC (Ireland) 1 | International Standard on Quality Control (Ireland) 1: *Quality Control for Firms that Perform Audits and Reviews of Financial Statements, and other Assurance and Related Services Engagements* – Updated July 2017 | 2 |
| ISA (Ireland) 200 | *Overall Objectives of the Independent Auditor and the Conduct of an Audit in Accordance with International Standards on Auditing (Ireland)* | 1 |

| | | |
|---|---|---|
| ISA (Ireland) 210 | *Agreeing the Terms of Audit Engagements* – Updated July 2017 | 5 |
| ISA (Ireland) 220 | *Quality Control for an Audit of Financial Statements* – Updated July 2017 | 5 |
| ISA (Ireland) 230 | *Audit Documentation* | 6 |
| ISA (Ireland) 240 | *The Auditor's Responsibilities Relating to Fraud in an Audit of Financial Statements* – Updated July 2017 | 3 |
| ISA (Ireland) 250 | *Section A—Consideration of Laws and Regulations in an Audit of Financial Statements* – Revised July 2017 | 3 |
| ISA (Ireland) 250 | *Section B—The Auditor's Statutory Right and Duty to Report to Regulators of Public Interest Entities and Regulators of Other Entities in the Financial Sector* | N/A |
| ISA (Ireland) 260 | *Communication with Those Charged with Governance* – Updated July 2017 | 3 and 18 |
| ISA (Ireland) 265 | *Communicating Deficiencies in Internal Control to Those Charged with Governance* | 8 and 18 |
| ISA (Ireland) 300 | *Planning an Audit of Financial Statements* | 5 |
| ISA (Ireland) 315 | *Identifying and Assessing the Risks of Material Misstatement Through Understanding the Entity and its Environment* | 7,8 and 10 |
| ISA (Ireland) 320 | *Materiality in Planning and Performing an Audit* | 5 |
| ISA (Ireland) 330 | *The Auditor's Responses to Assessed Risks* | 7 |
| ISA (Ireland) 402 | *Audit Considerations Relating to an Entity Using a Service Organisation* | 10 |
| ISA (Ireland) 450 | *Evaluation of Misstatements Identified During the Audit* – Updated July 2017 | 18 |
| ISA (Ireland) 500 | *Audit Evidence* – Updated July 2017 | 6 |
| ISA (Ireland) 501 | *Audit Evidence – Specific Considerations for Selected Items* | 6 |
| ISA (Ireland) 505 | *External Confirmations* | 6, 13, 14 and 16 |
| ISA (Ireland) 510 | *Initial Audit Engagements – Opening Balances* | 6 and 11–17 |
| ISA (Ireland) 520 | *Analytical Procedures* | 5, 7 and 11–18 |
| ISA (Ireland) 530 | *Audit Sampling* | 6 |
| ISA (Ireland) 540 | *Auditing Accounting Estimates, Including Fair Value Accounting Estimates, and Related Disclosures* | 6 and 11–17 |
| ISA (Ireland) 550 | *Related Parties* | 18 |

| | | |
|---|---|---|
| ISA (Ireland) 560 | *Subsequent Events* | 18 |
| ISA (Ireland) 570 | *Going Concern* | 18 |
| ISA (Ireland) 580 | *Written Representations* | 18 |
| ISA (Ireland) 600 | *Special Considerations – Audits of Group Financial Statements (Including the Work of Component Auditors)* | 20 |
| ISA (Ireland) 610 | *Using the Work of Internal Auditors* | 10 |
| ISA (Ireland) 620 | *Using the Work of an Auditor's Expert* | 10 |
| ISA (Ireland) 700 | *Forming an Opinion and Reporting on Financial Statements* | 19 |
| ISA (Ireland) 701 | *Communicating Key Audit Matters in the Independent Auditor's Report* | 19 |
| ISA (Ireland) 705 | *Modifications to the Opinion in the Independent Auditor's Report* | 19 |
| ISA (Ireland) 706 | *Emphasis of Matter Paragraphs and Other Matter Paragraphs in the Independent Auditor's Report* | 19 |
| ISA (Ireland) 710 | *Comparative Information – Corresponding Figures and Comparative Financial Statements* | 19 |
| ISA (Ireland) 720 | *The Auditor's Responsibilities Relating to Other Information* | 19 |

## Table B: Extant List of Auditing Standards – UK

The FRC's Ethical Standard and Auditing Standards in issue at 1 January 2018.

| Standard | Full title | Primary Chapter Refs. |
|---|---|---|
| | Ethical Standard for Auditors 2016 – Integrity, Objectivity and Independence | 2 |
| ISQC (UK) 1 | International Standard on Quality Control (Ireland) 1: *Quality Control for Firms that Perform Audits and Reviews of Financial Statements, and other Assurance and Related Services Engagements* – Revised June 2016 (Updated July 2017) | 2 |
| ISA (UK) 200 | *Overall Objectives of the Independent Auditor and the Conduct of an Audit in Accordance with International Standards on Auditing (UK)* – Revised June 2016 | 1 |
| ISA (UK) 210 | *Agreeing the Terms of Audit Engagements* – Revised June 2016 (Updated July 2017) | 5 |

| ISA (UK) 220 | *Quality Control for an Audit of Financial Statements* – Revised June 2016 (Updated July 2017) | 5 |
|---|---|---|
| ISA (UK) 230 | *Audit Documentation* – Revised June 2016 | 6 |
| ISA (UK) 240 | *The Auditor's Responsibilities Relating to Fraud in an Audit of Financial Statements* – Revised June 2016 (Updated July 2017) | 3 |
| ISA (UK) 250 | *Section A—Consideration of Laws and Regulations in an Audit of Financial Statements* – Revised December 2017 | 3 |
| ISA (UK) 250 | *Section B—The Auditor's Statutory Right and Duty to Report to Regulators of Public Interest Entities and Regulators of Other Entities in the Financial Sector* – Revised June 2016 | N/A |
| ISA (UK) 260 | *Communication with Those Charged with Governance* – Updated July 2017 – Revised June 2016 (Updated July 2017) | 3 and 18 |
| ISA (UK) 265 | *Communicating Deficiencies in Internal Control to Those Charged with Governance* | 8 and 18 |
| ISA (UK) 300 | *Planning an Audit of Financial Statements* – Revised June 2016 | 5 |
| ISA (UK) 315 | *Identifying and Assessing the Risks of Material Misstatement Through Understanding the Entity and its Environment* – Revised June 2016 | 7,8 and 10 |
| ISA (UK) 320 | *Materiality in Planning and Performing an Audit* – Revised June 2016 | 5 |
| ISA (UK) 330 | *The Auditor's Responses to Assessed Risks* – Revised June 2017 | 7 |
| ISA (UK) 402 | *Audit Considerations Relating to an Entity Using a Service Organization* | 10 |
| ISA (UK) 450 | *Evaluation of Misstatements Identified During the Audit* – Revised June 2016 (Updated July 2017) | 18 |
| ISA (UK) 500 | *Audit Evidence* – Updated July 2017 | 6 |
| ISA (UK) 501 | *Audit Evidence – Specific Considerations for Selected Items* | 6 |
| ISA (UK) 505 | *External Confirmations* | 6, 13, 14 and 16 |
| ISA (UK) 510 | Initial Audit *Engagements – Opening Balances* – Revised June 2016 | 6 and 11–17 |
| ISA (UK) 520 | *Analytical Procedures* | 5, 7 and 11–18 |
| ISA (UK) 530 | *Audit Sampling* | 6 |

| ISA (UK) 540 | *Auditing Accounting Estimates, Including Fair Value Accounting Estimates, and Related Disclosures* – Revised June 2016 | 6 and 11–17 |
|---|---|---|
| ISA (UK) 550 | *Related Parties* | 18 |
| ISA (UK) 560 | *Subsequent Events* | 18 |
| ISA (UK) 570 | *Going Concern* – Revised June 2016 | 18 |
| ISA (UK) 580 | *Written Representations* | 18 |
| ISA (UK) 600 | *Special Considerations – Audits of Group Financial Statements (Including the Work of Component Auditors)* – Revised June 2016 | 20 |
| ISA (UK) 610 | *Using the Work of Internal Auditors* – Revised June 2013 | 10 |
| ISA (UK) 620 | *Using the Work of an Auditor's Expert* – Revised June 2016 | 10 |
| ISA (UK) 700 | *Forming an Opinion and Reporting on Financial Statements*– Revised June 2016 | 19 |
| ISA (UK) 701 | *Communicating Key Audit Matters in the Independent Auditor's Report* | 19 |
| ISA (UK) 705 | *Modifications to the Opinion in the Independent Auditor's Report*– Revised June 2016 | 19 |
| ISA (UK) 706 | *Emphasis of Matter Paragraphs and Other Matter Paragraphs in the Independent Auditor's Report* – Revised June 2016 | 19 |
| ISA (UK) 710 | *Comparative Information – Corresponding Figures and Comparative Financial Statements* | 19 |
| ISA (UK) 720 | *The Auditor's Responsibilities Relating to Other Information* – Revised June 2016 | 19 |
| ISA (UK) 800 | *Special Considerations – Audits of Financial Statements Prepared in Accordance with Special Purpose Frameworks* – Revised | N/A |
| ISA (UK) 805 | *Special Considerations – Audits of Single Financial Statements and Specific Elements, Accounts or Items of a Financial Statement* – Revised | N/A |

## TECHNOLOGY AND AUDITING

In many industries technology is fundamentally impacting on the traditional roles and responsibilities of the workforce. Accounting and auditing is no different – the appearance of blockchain and advances in artificial intelligence (AI) are seen by many as the greatest advancements in accounting since Luca Pacioli invented double-entry bookkeeping nearly 525 years ago.

Technology can be a double-edged sword. Blockchain is a good example. On the one hand it offers a new platform on which to base accounting, one that is more resilient, secure and resistant to unauthorised changes (fraud); one that offers the potential for an automated audit of all transactions, where all transactions are authenticated as one company transacts with another. On the other hand blockchain could be seen as a threat, that the need for accountants and auditors will be removed, or the profession downgraded to merely data-crunching. A similar story is heard with AI. According to Google, robots will achieve human intelligence levels by 2029.

Whether it is blockchain, AI, or some other technology still in embryonic form, it is fair to say that the *traditional* tasks of the accountant and the auditor will, at some point, likely be replaced. Yet, before blockchain and AI we had 'electronic data interchange', cloud computing and 'big data'. They too changed the way the accountant/auditor worked – new methods and techniques were devised, but the *purpose* of the accountant/auditor remained the same or, if anything, became (arguably) more prominent. The important point is that the 'basics' of accounting are not forgotten, that the accountants and auditors of the future understand the route of transactions and do not become complacent or reliant on the power of technology. To do so would ignore a vital component of accounting and auditing – the ability to apply professional scepticism, the human sense that something doesn't add up, which isn't always a tangible factor. As technology increasingly automates the audit process, the auditor has the opportunity to free themselves from the more mundane and laborious tasks and to devote their time and expertise to understanding the business and moving towards a more advisory and value-adding role.

Technology has changed the face of accounting and auditing, and it will continue to do so. It offers enhancements and efficiencies, but it challenges the traditional role. The auditor will have to embrace all it has to offer, and in the process create new ways to add value to the services they provide.

## ABOUT THIS TEXTBOOK

*External Auditing and Assurance: An Irish Textbook* sets out to overcome a perennial difficulty that students of external audit and assurance experience – putting the audit process into a clear and understandable context. In general, textbooks on auditing do not seek to relate the audit process specifically to an organisation's financial statements. The approach taken here is to treat the audit process as a continuous discussion related directly to the final outcome (the end product), i.e. the auditor's report and the financial statements to which it refers.

To encourage this approach, a fictional *Directors' Report and Financial Statements* for a large company, Large Company Limited, are included (**Appendix B**). Throughout the book Large Company Limited is referred to and extracts shown to illustrate specific areas or ideas. The purpose of this is to simulate the actual activities of the auditor and to provide a more practical learning experience, particularly to help focus on the typical assertions and disclosures that need to be addressed as part of the audit process.

In general, students study financial accounting and reporting under the IFRS Framework. Although IFRS is mandatory for public limited companies, the FRC and IAASA frameworks apply to the vast majority of companies (private) at present. The terms used in the text are as per IFRS. As accounting students are aware of the interchangeable terms, there should be no difficulty arising from this approach.

## Overall Structure

This textbook is divided into four Parts, grouping the audit process into its key constituent elements. The four Parts are:

### Part I – The External Auditing and Assurance Environment

In these first three chapters we set the scene – giving an outline of the evolution of external auditing and assurance, defining the basic terms and explaining the objectives of the auditor. The regulatory and legal environments in the RoI and the UK/NI are explained and an overview of the key legal cases that have shaped the auditor's legal liability. Also within the audit environment are the related topics of ethics and corporate governance. Finally, any discussion on auditing and assurance must consider the issue of fraud and the role it plays in shaping the auditing profession.

### Part II –The Audit and Assurance Process: Planning and Controls

Having set the scene, we can now begin to look at the audit process. In Chapters 4–10, we initially outline the audit process, providing an overview to place each area of the process in its wider context. The focus of this Part is to understand the planning and control stages of the audit. Risk assessment is fundamental to an audit, governing as it does the decisions of what to test and how to test it. The differentiation between controls testing and substantive procedures is introduced in this Part, along with the concept of "sufficient and appropriate audit evidence" – concepts that recur throughout the entire audit process.

### Part III – The Audit and Assurance Process: Substantive Procedures

Chapters 11–17 are dedicated to a detailed analysis of the substantive procedures as they relate to each financial cycle – revenue and receivables, property, plant and equipment and so on. Each chapter includes worked examples of the specific audit procedures and techniques and outlining audit programmes and working papers for each cycle. To give a better practical understanding, the *Directors' Report and Financial Statements* of Large Company Limited (**Appendix B**) are referenced throughout.

### Part IV – The Audit and Assurance Process: Completion Procedures and Reporting

In this final Part, the concluding procedures of the audit are explained, culminating in the issuing of an audit opinion and the requirements of the audit report itself. A chapter on group audits is included here, highlighting the specific issues around the group audit process.

At the end of each Part, there are a number of **Challenging Questions** designed to test the student's understanding of all of the material covered in that Part. These challenging questions use a case-study approach and require the student to integrate and apply what they have learnt. Solutions to Challenging Questions are made available to lecturers to share with their students.

## EXTERNAL AUDITING AND ASSURANCE: TEXT STRUCTURE

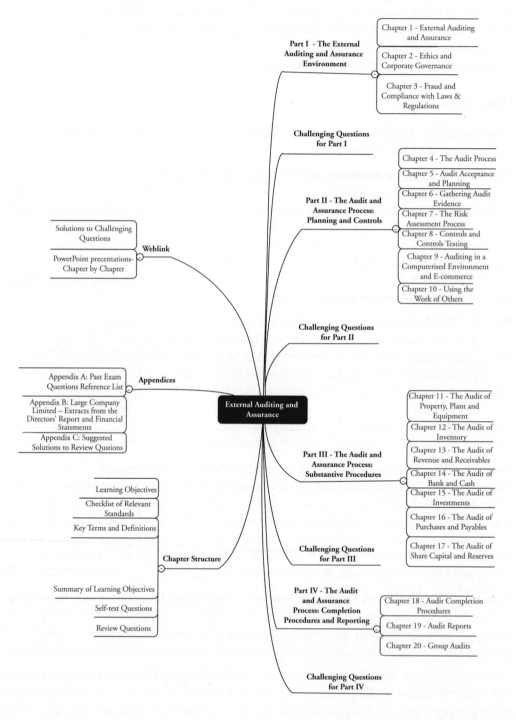

## Chapter Structure

Each chapter has a consistent structure, with the following features:

- **Learning Objectives** – outlining at the outset the objective of the chapter.
- **Checklist of Relevant Standards** – to guide the reader towards further technical study of the topics contained in the chapter.
- **Key Terms and Definitions** – those terms most relevant to the chapter are defined as a quick reference guide and to prepare the reader for the discussions that follow. These terms are shown in purple bold within the chapter. The Glossary towards the end of the book contains a more complete listing of the key terms encountered.
- **Conclusion** – a brief summary of the main points discussed in that chapter.
- **Summary of Learning Objectives** – at the end of each chapter to bring the chapter full circle and ensure that the reader understands each of the learning objectives.
- **Self-test Questions** –focusing on a basic understanding of the key topics arising in the chapter.
- **Review Questions** – more detailed questions requiring application of the material covered in that chapter. Suggested solutions are provided in **Appendix C**.

For any student of auditing and assurance, the volume of knowledge required can be daunting. However, the fundamental challenge is about making sound judgements based on all the available information in a given set of circumstances. Such skill is acquired over time and through practical experience. In exam situations, students are often required to make judgements as if they were experienced auditors – this textbook seeks, as much as possible, to narrow the gap between theoretical knowledge and practical experience.

## RECOMMENDED FURTHER READING

Wide reading is essential to gain the fullest understanding of auditing and assurance. Accordingly, the following sources are recommended.

### Journals

- *Accountancy Ireland* (published by Chartered Accountants Ireland, see www.accountancyireland.ie Students of Chartered Accountants Ireland can subscribe to the Accountancy Ireland Extra enewsletter, with access to the updated digital edition)
- *Economia* (published by the Institute of Chartered Accountants in England and Wales, see www.economia.icaew.com)
- *Accountancy Age* (see www.accountancyage.com)
- A good daily and Sunday newspaper.

### Other Textbooks

- Louise Kelly, *Advanced Auditing and Assurance*, 2nd Edition (Chartered Accountants Ireland, 2018).

- Brenda Porter, Jon Simon and David Hatherly, *Principles of External Auditing*, 4th Edition (Wiley, 2014).
- Iain Gray, Stuart Manson and Louise Crawford, *The Audit Process: Principles, Practice and Cases*, 6th Edition (Cengage Learning, 2015).
- Andrew Brown, *Corporate Fraud* (Chartered Accountants Ireland, 2010).

# Acknowledgements

In the first edition, the authors received valuable contributions from: Gary Comiskey CISA, Marie Keogh ACA, Bernadette Lea ACA, Patricia Morris FCA, Alan Pitts ACA, Sarah Quirke ACA and Umesh Rana CPA. For the second edition we received valuable contributions from Gary Comiskey CISA in updating the complex area of computer auditing and the new developments in e-commerce and cloud computing affecting auditors.

A special word of thanks to Keith Quigley, BBS (Accounting & Finance), a graduate of the Institute of Technology Tallaght and now a qualified Chartered Accountant, who dedicated considerable time to providing a student's perspective on the contents of the second edition.

We would also like to thank the publishing team at Chartered Accountants Ireland, particularly Liam Boyle and Michael Diviney for their work and dedication in preparing this third edition for publication.

Finally, we would like to thank the lecturers from the various universities and institutes of technology for their feedback which has been invaluable in shaping this textbook.

# PART I

# THE EXTERNAL AUDITING AND ASSURANCE ENVIRONMENT

# 1

# EXTERNAL AUDITING AND ASSURANCE

## LEARNING OBJECTIVES

Having studied this chapter on external auditing and assurance, you should:
1. understand what is meant by the term 'assurance engagements';
2. understand the objective of an external audit of financial statements;
3. be able to explain why and how the auditing profession has evolved;
4. be able to demonstrate a detailed understanding of the legal and regulatory frameworks that govern external audits in the Republic of Ireland and the UK/Northern Ireland;
5. be able to demonstrate an understanding of the setting and use of International Standards on Auditing in the Republic of Ireland (RoI) and the UK/NI; and
6. be able to demonstrate an understanding of the case law shaping the legal liability of auditors.

## CHECKLIST OF RELEVANT STANDARDS

The relevant standards, in both the RoI and the UK/NI, covered in this chapter are:
- ISA 200 *Overall Objectives of the Independent Auditor and the Conduct of an Audit in Accordance with International Standards on Auditing*

Note, in general when referring to ISAs, it should be understood as referring to the UK and Ireland versions, unless otherwise specified as either ISA (UK) or ISA (Ireland). See the Introduction for an extant list of auditing standards for the RoI and the UK/NI.

## Key Terms and Definitions for this Chapter

**Assurance**   A statement that inspires confidence in the subject matter.

**Audit**   An audit (in the context of a financial audit) is an independent examination of an entity's financial statements in order to determine if they are reasonable and in accordance with applicable accounting standards.

**Audit Opinion**   An expression of opinion on the truth and fairness of a company's set of financial statements.

**External Audit**   A formal examination of a company's financial statements, with a formal conclusion on their truth and fairness in the form of an audit opinion expressed in an audit report. For the purpose of this textbook, the term 'audit' will refer to **external audit** unless otherwise explicitly stated.

**Financial Statements**   The financial statements of a client entity represent a compilation of individual reports and statements that show how it has used the funds entrusted by its shareholders and other stakeholders. A set of financial statements normally includes a directors' report, auditor's report, a statement of accounting policies, and primary financial statements with notes, such as the statement of comprehensive income, statement of financial position, statement of cash flows, etc.

**Material Misstatement**   In simple terms, a material misstatement is said to occur when an erroneous item's inclusion or omission in the financial statements could affect the economic decisions of the users of the financial statements.

**Public Interest Entities (PIEs)**   In general terms (in both the RoI and the UK), a PIE is an entity "whose transferable securities [i.e. stocks, shares and debt] are admitted to trading on a regulated market" (ISA 220, paragraph 7(m)-1).

**Reasonable Assurance**   Providing a high degree of assurance but not an absolute assurance.

## 1.1 INTRODUCTION

Auditing is one of the key accounting disciplines and forms the backbone of many accountancy practices. For the purpose of this text, where we refer to the 'audit firm' this can relate to 'an accountancy practice'. Furthermore, the terms 'auditor' and 'audit firm' are used interchangeably, reflecting the fact that the audit firm may in fact be a sole practitioner.

In very simple terms, an **audit** involves an independent audit firm/auditor examining financial information prepared by a client entity in order to provide assurance on its authenticity and accuracy.

ISA 200 *Overall Objectives of the Independent Auditor and the Conduct of an Audit in Accordance with International Standards on Auditing* defines, at paragraph 3, the objective of a financial statement audit as follows:

"The purpose of an audit is to enhance the degree of confidence of intended users in the financial statements. This is achieved by the expression of an opinion by the auditor on whether the financial statements are prepared, in all material respects, in accordance with an applicable financial reporting framework."

The term 'audit' refers to the process undertaken by the auditor to gather and assess a range of audit evidence that will enable such an opinion to be formed and expressed by the auditor. Evidence is gathered in a number of forms and using a wide variety of methods, which will be discussed in more detail in **Chapters 4–17**. The topic of forming an audit opinion will then be covered in **Chapters 18** and **19**, while group audit considerations are covered in **Chapter 20**.

**Chapter 2** deals with the ethical requirements imposed on the auditor and outlines how corporate governance impacts on an audit, while **Chapter 3** asks what responsibilities the auditor has with regard to the detection of fraud and non-compliance of the client entity with laws and regulations.

Before one can appreciate what is to come in these chapters, it is important to understand the foundation of the auditing profession and **Chapter 1** is intended to provide the reader with that understanding.

**Section 1.2** first considers the role of **assurance engagements** and how it relates specifically to **external audit**. This section introduces two important concepts – '**reasonable assurance**' and '**material misstatement**' – and also discusses the **limitations of an external audit**. Having clarified assurance engagements as they relate to external audits, we then consider the historical development of auditing and assurance in **Section 1.3**. This discussion centres on '**agency theory**'. The agency theory relates to the separation of owners and managers of companies and the potential mismatch between shareholders' expectations and management's decision making. The term 'management', for the purpose of this text, shall include directors and management charged with governance of a client entity. Within the auditing standards the term 'those charged with governance' is also used to describe the directors and management collectively.

In **Sections 1.4** and **1.5** we consider the **legal and regulatory environments** that govern external audit, focusing on the Companies Acts, enforcement authorities and regulatory bodies that issue regulations, guidance and monitoring with respect to auditors and the performance of external audits. Additionally, we introduce the regulatory standards that govern the performance of external audits.

Having set the legal and regulatory scene in which external auditing operates, in **Section 1.6** we further explore the role the recognised accountancy bodies (RABs) in the RoI, and their equivalent in the UK/NI, the recognised supervisory bodies (RSBs) play in regulating, monitoring and supervising their members. **Section 1.7** reflects on the rights and duties of the auditor with regard to appointment, removal and resignation.

Finally, in **Section 1.8** we discuss the **legal liability** of the external auditor by introducing some key legal terms as they apply to external auditing and by considering some of the landmark cases that have shaped the external auditor's legal liability.

Following the introduction of assurance engagements in general, the focus of this textbook is on external audit engagements as they relate to the audit of financial statements. Hereafter the word 'audit' shall mean 'external audit' unless explicitly stated otherwise.

## 1.2 THE NEED FOR AUDITING AND ASSURANCE

### Introduction

**Assurance** can be defined as a statement that inspires confidence in the subject matter (i.e. 'he assured me he would be here on time'; 'he assured me that the calculation is correct'). The effect of an **audit** is that stakeholders interested in a set of financial statements are given a level of assurance as to their accuracy.

Auditing is a specific discipline that exists within the wider discipline of assurance reporting. The International Framework for Assurance Engagements, as issued by the International Auditing and Assurance Standards Board (IAASB), provides the following definition for an **assurance engagement**:

"An engagement in which a practitioner expresses a conclusion designed to enhance the degree of confidence of the intended users other than the responsible party about the outcome of the evaluation or measurement of a subject matter against criteria. The outcome of the evaluation or measurement of a subject matter is the information that results from applying the criteria."[1]

The above definition is broader and less specific than the definition of an audit. The subject matter is not confined to financial statements and, in practice, can involve any number of different things, including both financial and non-financial information. However, common to all assurance engagements, including financial statement audits, is a number of core elements:

- a subject matter, e.g. set of financial statements;
- users of the subject matter, e.g. shareholders;
- a set of criteria, e.g. International Financial Reporting Standards (IFRSs) or the Financial Reporting Standards (FRSs) issued by the Financial Reporting Council (FRC), such as FRS 101, FRS 102 and so on. In the UK and the RoI, the majority of companies use FRSs in preparing their financial statements; and
- an examination and conclusion, e.g. audit procedures leading to an audit report.

**Table 1.1** below provides further examples of assurance engagements, demonstrating that assurance can be provided in a wide variety of instances and not just external audit.

The provision of assurance is most commonly associated with the annual statutory audit of a company's financial statements (statutory requirements are discussed in more detail below). In this case, the examiner (the external auditor in the case of external audit) gathers evidence on the items included within the company's financial statements and then expresses an opinion on how these statements were prepared. External audit is the most

---

[1] International Auditing and Assurance Standards Board, *Handbook of International Quality Control, Auditing Review, Other Assurance and Related Service Pronouncements* (2015 Edition), Volume 1.

TABLE 1.1: ASSURANCE ENGAGEMENTS

| Assurance Engagement | Subject Matter | Users of the Subject Matter | Set of Criteria | Examination and Conclusion |
|---|---|---|---|---|
| External audit and assurance | Financial statements | Shareholders/stakeholders | Companies Acts and applicable financial reporting framework | Audit opinion on the financial statements |
| Audit of pension schemes | Pension plans | Pension-holders | Legislation and pension plan rules | Auditor examines evidence to support pension plan and pension plan movements and issues a report concluding on their accuracy |
| Forensic audit to uncover fraud | Alleged events of fraud | Company against whom alleged fraud was undertaken/the State | Legislation | Practitioner examines evidence to conclude on alleged fraud – issues a report providing assurance as to whether or not fraud occurred |
| Internal audit assurance | Assignments can vary, e.g. assessment of controls within the revenue and receivables cycle | Audit committee/directors/'those charged with governance' | Laid down in client entity's policies and procedures | Internal audit opinion on efficient and effective operation of internal controls within the revenue and receivables cycle of the client entity |

common form of assurance engagement in practice and, as such, it is the most closely regulated, with guidance and requirements to be found in auditing standards issued by accounting bodies (e.g. International Standards on Auditing (ISAs)) and within government (national and EU) legislation. Such regulation adds a degree of uniformity to procedures applied and reports produced in the financial statement audit, and will be discussed in more detail below.

### Reasonable Assurance

The external auditor provides **reasonable assurance** that the financial statements are free from **material misstatements**. The assurance is **not a guarantee** – it provides a high degree of assurance, but not absolute assurance, that the financial statements are fairly presented. For this reason, the term '**true and fair**' is used when concluding on the opinion: 'In our opinion the financial statements: give a true and fair view, in accordance with …'

The auditor's assessment of true and fair is based on their opinion that no **significant errors** (**misstatements**) exist in the financial statements. Significance is measured by the auditor with reference to **materiality**. As such, the auditor's assessment of true and fair is based on their belief (due to the collection of evidence) that the financial statements are free from **material misstatement**. The terms 'misstatement' and 'materiality' are defined below in **Table 1.2** and are discussed in detail in **Chapter 5**.

TABLE 1.2: MISSTATEMENT AND MATERIALITY

| Term | Related Auditing Standard | Definition |
|------|---------------------------|------------|
| Misstatement | ISA 450 | "A difference between the reported amount, classification, presentation or disclosure of a financial statement item and the amount, classification, presentation or disclosure that is required for the item to be in accordance with the applicable financial reporting framework. Misstatements can arise from error or fraud." |
| Materiality | ISA 320 | "Misstatements, including omissions, are considered to be material if they, individually or in the aggregate, could reasonably be expected to influence the economic decisions of users taken on the basis of the financial statements." |

The reason that the concept of reasonable assurance exists is due to the inherent limitations of an audit. The limitations of an external audit are set out in **Table 1.3** below.

TABLE 1.3: LIMITATIONS OF AN EXTERNAL AUDIT

| Limitation | Limitation Explained | For further reading see: |
|---|---|---|
| Judgement | Auditors must use their judgement throughout the audit in areas such as:<br>• setting materiality;<br>• deciding on the number of items to test;<br>• assessing risk;<br>• extrapolation of errors in a sample. | <br><br>Chapter 5<br>Chapter 6<br>Chapter 7<br>Chapter 6 |
| Accounting and internal controls | Inherent limitations exist in accounting and internal controls in the:<br>• existence of non-routine transactions;<br>• possibility of human error;<br>• possibility of collusion;<br>• possibility of management override of controls;<br>• omission of some controls on grounds that they do not justify their cost;<br>• need for estimates in accounting. | <br><br>Chapter 8<br>Chapter 8<br>Chapters 7 and 8<br>Chapters 3 and 8<br><br>Chapter 8<br>Chapter 6 |
| The audit report | The audit report itself has inherent limitations, in that:<br>• it has a prescribed standard format, which can be restrictive;<br>• it contains auditing jargon that may be difficult for the reader to understand. | <br><br>Chapter 19<br><br>Chapter 19 |
| Sampling risk | For practical reasons, not all items in the set of financial statements are tested. The auditor performs sample testing and extrapolates on the results, which naturally means that some misstatements may go undetected. The results of the sample will indicate what is likely to exist in the rest of the population, but it does not provide a guarantee. | Chapter 6 |
| Timing of the audit report | The audit report is generally issued a long time after the balance sheet date, so even if it does provide a warning (in the way of a modification of opinion), the users may well have made poor decisions in the intervening period which, had the report been available earlier, may have been avoided. | Chapter 19 |
| Audit evidence | The auditor attempts to collect sufficient appropriate audit evidence to support the balances and transactions in the financial statements, but this evidence is often persuasive rather than conclusive. | Chapter 6 |

## 1.3  HISTORICAL DEVELOPMENT OF AUDITING AND ASSURANCE

The need for audit has essentially been driven by the increasing separation of the ownership from the management of companies. Although some form of auditing existed in Greece as long ago as 500 BCE, it was only with the Industrial Revolution and the growth of publicly owned companies in the 19th Century that the need for auditing really developed. The premise of a publicly owned company is that it is funded by capital raised from the selling of shares to the public. Together the shareholders own the company, but they are not responsible for its day-to-day management, which is performed by a team of directors/managers employed by the company (the '**management**'). As such, management act as the *agents* of the shareholders and are responsible for the stewardship of the company.

Management should run the company with the aim of maximising the shareholders' wealth. However, there may exist a conflict between the personal interests of management and the interests of the shareholders. For example, management may seek to pay themselves a considerable end-of-year bonus, thereby extracting resources from the company for personal gain. As a result, shareholders seek to monitor management by requiring them to prepare accounts detailing how they have used the company's resources, and shareholders gain assurance over the accuracy and legitimacy of these accounts by having them checked by an independent source, i.e. through the annual financial audit. The **independent audit report** provides the shareholders with a degree of confidence (**assurance**) that the contents of the financial statements are **true and fair** and can be relied upon to make decisions about their investment.

FIGURE 1.1: AGENCY THEORY

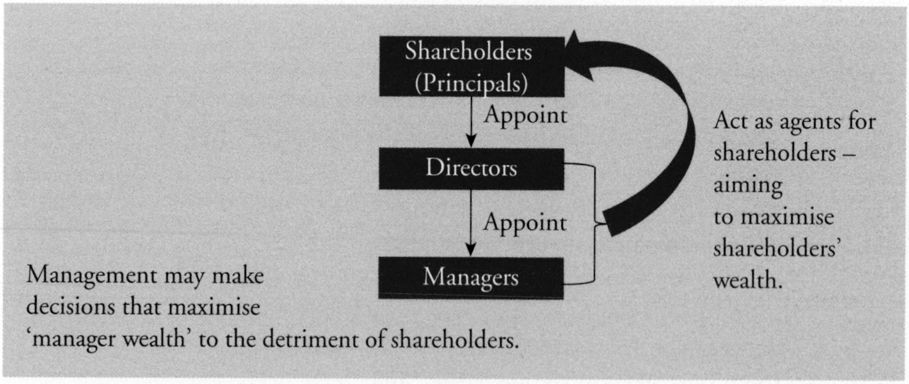

Agency theory highlights a concern for the shareholder: how can they be sure that management (those charged with governance) are acting in their best interests? It would be impractical for all shareholders to have a role in the company (and they are likely to lack the expertise to do so). Capital markets are designed to give people access to markets and to make profits (through dividends and capital growth) without intervention in the actual running of companies. Over the years, the need for audit services has increased as the numbers of users of financial statements (and other information produced by companies) has increased. **Users of financial statements** (often referred to as 'stakeholders' due to their common interest in the company) can include the following groups:

- shareholders;
- financial institutions;
- suppliers;
- customers;
- employees;
- governments; and
- the general public.

It would not be possible to provide access to books and records to all stakeholders, so the independent audit report offers an unbiased opinion to increase the credibility of the financial statements for all users/stakeholders.

All of the above groups now look for the independent audit report as a means of gaining assurance over financial statements. As the number of users of financial statements has increased, so too has the debate over the issue of whether or not the auditor is liable for negligence to all of these users. Where the audit opinion is found to have been incorrect as a result of negligence on the part of the auditor, to which of these users of the financial statements should the auditor be held accountable? This debate continues to evolve on a case-by-case basis. In essence, auditors are **generally not liable to any parties other than the direct client** (i.e. the shareholders), unless there are very specific circumstances in which the auditor was expressly aware of the intentions of another user to place reliance on the audit report (see **Section 1.8** and **Appendices 1.1** and **1.2** where landmark legal cases are discussed).

In the last 20 years there have been a number of high-profile instances of accounting irregularities, including, most famously, Enron and WorldCom in 2001, Lehman Brothers in 2008, Autonomy in 2011, Olympus and Barclays in 2012, Mobily in 2013 and Tesco in 2014. These cases have resulted in a considerably increased focus on the need for a robust audit of financial statements, and there has been a number of changes in statutory and regulatory guidance over the past number of years to attempt to address these concerns.

Standard-setters strive to update accounting standards, and to introduce new ones, prompted by the lessons learnt from various scandals over the past two decades as well as by the ever-changing business environment, which increasingly involves complex economic transactions (driven largely by e-commerce). Naturally, auditing standards are in turn updated to reflect changes in accounting standards and, more recently, to respond to the growth in the use of fair values and narrative reporting.

The public perception of the auditor and the auditing profession continues to be compromised by frequent corporate failures as a result of poor corporate governance culminating in fraudulent financial reporting. The role and responsibilities of the auditor are considered in more detail in **Chapter 2** in relation to ethics and corporate governance, and in **Chapter 3** in the context of fraud.

## 1.4  THE LEGISLATIVE FRAMEWORK

### Introduction

In general, company law in both the RoI and the UK/NI sets out requirements and responsibilities for businesses in terms of filing annual accounts, the preparation of financial statements and so on. Central to this is the requirement for companies to have their annual financial statements audited (albeit there are some exemptions depending on the size and nature of the business).

The key legislation in the RoI is the Companies Act 2014 (CA 2014) and the Companies (Accounting) Act 2017; in the UK/NI it is the Companies Act 2006 (CA 2006). A significant overhaul of both CA 2014 and CA 2006 was necessitated by the publication in May 2014 of the EU Audit Regulation Directive, with new rules on statutory audits becoming applicable. These changes are discussed in more detail in **Section 1.6**.

As well as the requirement for audit, CA 2014 and CA 2006 also set out requirements with respect to directors' and auditors' responsibilities in relation to the preparation of financial statements and the audit of those financial statements. When producing a set of financial statements, the directors essentially accept responsibility by the inclusion of a **directors' responsibility statement**. This statement summarises the directors' responsibilities in relation to the preparation of the financial statements. The directors generally include this statement within the **directors' report** or immediately following it. Directors' responsibilities are dealt with in more detail below.

With regard to auditors' responsibilities, company law in both jurisdictions lays down a number of requirements that set out the scope of audits that extend beyond those required by **professional standards**. The International Standards on Auditing (ISAs) are the auditor's professional standards. They are set by the International Auditing and Assurance Standards Board (IAASB) and implemented and regulated in particular jurisdictions by the relevant **competent authority**. Previously, the UK's Financial Reporting Council (FRC) was the competent authority for both the RoI and the UK/NI. In 2016, however, the Irish Auditing & Accounting Supervisory Authority (IAASA) was appointed the competent authority for the RoI, and is now responsible for the issuing of ISAs in the RoI; the FRC remains the competent authority in the UK/NI. The IAASA have licensed the FRC's audit framework, tailoring the standards as necessary to reflect Irish company law. The standard-setting and regulatory framework is discussed in greater detail in **Section 1.5**.

**Figure 1.2** below depicts the broad legislative and regulatory landscapes in which external audits are carried out.

FIGURE 1.2: LEGISLATIVE AND REGULATORY ENVIRONMENT GOVERNING EXTERNAL AUDITS

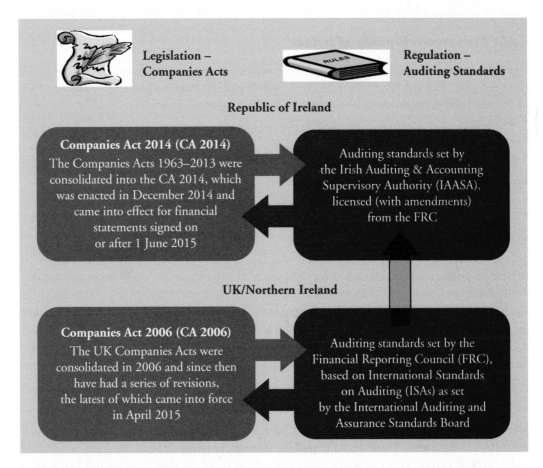

There are significant differences between the legislative frameworks in the RoI and the UK/NI. We will therefore look at each separately in greater detail.

### Legislative Framework in the Republic of Ireland

In the RoI, the Companies Act 2014 (CA 2014) consolidated the previous Companies Acts 1963–2013 and introduced reform into Irish company law. CA 2014 was enacted on 23 December 2014 and applies to financial statements signed on or after 1 June 2015. Part 6 of CA 2014 comprises 23 chapters dedicated to the requirements to prepare the financial statements, including the directors' report, annual return and audit report. The Companies (Accounting) Act 2017 commenced on 9 June 2017 and applies to financial years beginning on or after 1 January 2017. It mainly impacts the form, content and filing of annual and consolidated financial statements. In particular, it facilitates the introduction of FRS 102 Section 1A for small companies and FRS 105 for micro companies. In this section we explore some of the provisions as they relate to the requirement for the external audit of a company's financial statements.

Section 360 CA 2014 outlines circumstances under which companies can apply for an audit exemption, which are determined by reference to the type and size of the entity.

## Audit Exemptions: Republic of Ireland

Not all entities are required to have their financial statements audited. In the RoI, for financial years beginning on or after 2016, **small private companies** who meet any **two** of the following criteria are not required to have an external audit:
- an average of 50 or fewer employees;
- assets not in excess of €6 million;
- an annual turnover not in excess of €12 million.

The entity cannot take up the exemption if:
- its Articles of Association state that it must be audited; or
- a shareholder (holding at least 10% of shares, by value or by number) specifically requests that the entity be audited. This request must be sent by the shareholder in writing and must be received at least one month before the financial statement year end.

Where an entity takes up the audit exemption, it must include an 'audit exemption statement' on its statement of financial position, stating that it was entitled to exemption from audit under section 359 CA 2014 relating to small companies and that the members have not required the company to obtain an audit of its accounts. If a company's annual return is filed late, the company loses their entitlement to claim an audit exemption in the current year and in the following year.

Dormant companies and companies limited by guarantee are also not required to have their accounts audited, assuming they meet the exemption criteria.

Some companies are specifically **excluded** from being able to avail of the audit exemption regardless of their size. These include **public interest entities (PIEs)**, banking and insurance entities, certain types of investment entity and listed entities (companies listed on a regulated European market).

## Auditor's Responsibilities: Republic of Ireland

The Office of the Director of Corporate Enforcement (ODCE) was set up in the RoI to enforce compliance with the Companies Acts. The following are some of the specific responsibilities of the auditor outlined in CA 2014.
- **Duty to provide an audit report** The principal duty of the auditor is to report to the members of the company on the financial statements examined by them (section 391 CA 2014). Section 336 sets out what should be included in the statutory audit report and is covered in more detail in **Chapter 19**.
- **Duty to report failure to maintain adequate accounting records** Where auditors form the opinion that the company being audited is contravening, or has contravened, its obligations to maintain adequate accounting records, they are obliged to serve a notice on the company informing it of that opinion (section 392 CA 2014). Under sections 281–285 CA 2014, a company is required to maintain adequate accounting records for a period of not less than six years.

- **Duty to exercise professional integrity** Auditors are under a duty to carry out audits with professional integrity (section 390 CA 2014). In preparing their report, auditors must exercise the skill, care and caution of a reasonably competent, careful and cautious auditor.
- **Duty to report to the registrar and director – Category 1 and 2 offences** Where, in the course of carrying out the audit, the auditor becomes aware of Category 1 or Category 2 offences, they are required under section 393 CA 2014 to report the offence to the ODCE, with particulars of the grounds on which they have formed that opinion.

  Section 871(1) defines a Category 1 offence as one that could give rise to either:
  - ◆ a summary conviction, a Class A fine or a prison term not exceeding 12 months or both; or
  - ◆ a conviction on indictment, a fine not exceeding €500,000 or a prison term not exceeding 10 years or both.

  Section 871(2) defines a Category 2 offence as one that could give rise to either:
  - ◆ a summary conviction, a Class A fine or a prison term not exceeding 12 months or both; or
  - ◆ a conviction on indictment, a fine not exceeding €50,000 or a prison term not exceeding five years or both.

- **Duty to furnish evidence of approval** Under regulation 51 of the European Communities (Statutory Audits) (Directive 2006/43/EC) Regulations 2010 (S.I. No. 220 of 2010), an auditor must be able to furnish the ODCE with their approval to act as auditor should they be requested to do so.
- **Duty to explain reasons for resigning** Should the auditor resign before completion of their term, or should they not wish to be reappointed, they must inform the Companies Registration Office (CRO) of the reasons for doing so.

The final **audit report** is required to include a paragraph under the heading 'Auditor's responsibilities for the audit of the financial statements' (see **Chapter 19**, Example 19.1 for an example).

### Directors' Responsibilities: Republic of Ireland

Company directors also have a number of responsibilities under company law, some of which are summarised below:
- to maintain proper accounting records;
- to prepare annual accounts;
- to have an annual audit performed (subject to exemptions);
- to maintain certain registers and documents; and
- to have a compliance statement (for certain large companies).

When producing the financial statements, the directors are required to provide a summary of their responsibilities in relation to the preparation of the entity's financial statements. This is referred to as the 'directors' responsibilities statement' and should either be included as part of the directors' report or alongside it.

In the final audit report, the auditor may refer to the directors' responsibilities under the heading 'Responsibilities of directors for the financial statements' (see **Chapter 19**, Example 19.1 for the suggested wording).

## Legislative Framework in the UK/Northern Ireland

All companies are required to appoint an auditor under section 485 of the Companies Act 2006 (CA 2006). Additionally, all companies are required to have their annual accounts audited under section 475 CA 2006. There are some allowances, however; sections 477–481 CA 2006 allow certain exemptions from the audit requirements.

### Audit Exemptions: UK/Northern Ireland

Not all entities are required to have their financial statements audited. In the UK/NI, for financial years beginning on or after 1 January 2016, **small private companies** that meet any **two** of the following criteria are not required to have an external audit:
- an average of 50 or fewer employees;
- assets not in excess of £5.1 million;
- annual turnover not in excess of £10.2 million.

The entity cannot take up the exemption if:
- its Articles of Association state that it must be audited; or
- a shareholder (holding at least 10% of shares, by value or by number) specifically requests that the entity be audited. This request must be sent by the shareholder in writing and must be received at least one month before the financial statement year end.

Where an entity takes up the audit exemption, it must include an 'audit exemption statement' on its statement of financial position, stating that it was entitled to exemption from audit under section 477 CA 2006 relating to small companies and that the members have not required the company to obtain an audit of its accounts.

Some companies are specifically **excluded** from being able to avail of the audit exemption regardless of their size, including: **public interest entities** (PIEs), banking and insurance entities, certain types of investment entity and listed entities (companies listed on a regulated European market).

### Auditor's Responsibilities: UK/Northern Ireland

In the UK/NI, the principal duties of the auditor, as laid down in section 498 CA 2006, are to:

"carry out such investigations as will enable him to form an opinion as to—
(a) whether adequate accounting records have been kept by the company and returns adequate for their audit have been received from branches not visited by him, and
(b) whether the company's individual accounts are in agreement with the accounting records and returns, and
(c) in the case of a quoted company, whether the auditable part of the company's directors' remuneration report is in agreement with the accounting records and returns."

The auditor reports on these matters by exception, i.e. if not satisfied with any of these requirements then this is stated in the audit report. Furthermore, section 498 states: "If the auditor fails to obtain all the information and explanations which, to the best of his knowledge and belief, are necessary for the purposes of his audit, he shall state that fact also in his audit report."

The auditor is also required to report if the disclosure of directors' benefits, (remuneration, pensions, etc.) does not comply with the legislation and are not adequately disclosed in the accounts. If this is the case, the auditor must include in their report, "so far as he is reasonably able to do so, a statement giving the required particulars".

A description of the auditor's responsibilities is required to be included either:
(a) within the body of the auditor's report;
(b) within an appendix to the auditor's report (referenced in the auditor's report); or
(c) by way of reference in the auditor's report to a website location.

The final **audit report** is required to include a paragraph under the heading 'Auditor's responsibilities for the audit of the financial statements' (see **Chapter 19**, Example 19.2 for an example).

### *Directors' Responsibilities: UK/Northern Ireland*

Similar to the requirements in the Republic of Ireland, directors have a diverse range of responsibilities under company law, which they are required to acknowledge in the directors' responsibilities statement (included in the entity's financial statements, either as part of the directors' report or alongside it).

In the final audit report, the auditor may refer to the directors' responsibilities under the heading 'Responsibilities of directors for the financial statements' (see **Chapter 19**, Example 19.2 for the suggested wording).

## 1.5 THE REGULATORY FRAMEWORK

### Introduction

Having established the legislative responsibilities and duties of the auditor, let us now consider the regulatory environment of external auditing. The regulatory framework includes the standards that govern the performance of audits as well as the many bodies involved in setting standards, approving membership of those permitted to carry out an audit and ensuring high-quality audits through guidance and monitoring.

### The Audit Regulation and Directive

On 17 June 2016, new EU rules on statutory audit became applicable throughout the European Union. This new audit reform legislation, the Audit Regulation and Directive (ARD), is intended to address the inadequacies being observed in the audit market. Following the large number of corporate failures over the last decade alone, it is clear that investors lack confidence in **public interest entities (PIEs)** and, by extension, in the reliability of audited financial statements. This issue is compounded by the fact that there is perceived to be an excessive familiarity between client entities and their respective audit firms, which naturally impacts on perceived independence. There is also a fear that the larger accountancy practices are dominating the audit market leaving a lack of choice of audit firms. In this context audit reform aims to restore investor confidence and improve audit quality in an attempt to nurture future investment and economic growth. In order to achieve this, audit reform aims to: bring about greater transparency of financial information; issue stronger directives regarding the need to be independent and exercise a greater degree of professional scepticism; improve the regulatory supervision of statutory auditors as well as the co-ordination of audit supervision by competent authorities; and contribute to a more dynamic audit market in the EU.

The ARD effects all areas of audit regulation, including the oversight of auditors, quality and standard application, competition in the market, auditor selection and the independence of the auditor.

Amendments to the ethical standards, along with statutory regulation, took effect on 17 June 2016 for both general requirements and for audits of financial periods where those periods commenced on or after that date.

Audit reform uses two legislative instruments:
1.  Amendment to the European Communities (Statutory Audits) (Directive 2006/43/EC):
    • sets out duties of statutory auditors/audit firms; and
    • introduces the requirement for public oversight of the audit profession and co-operation between regulatory authorities in the EU.
2.  New regulations setting out specific requirements for the statutory audit of PIEs.

The first set of measures applies to all statutory auditors/firms, regardless of whether or not they are auditing a PIE, and include:
• the introduction of stronger independence requirements at an organisational level;
• the enhancement of the audit report to make it more informative to investors;
• the strengthening of the competencies and powers of the competent authorities responsible for the public oversight of the audit profession within the Member States;
• the establishment of a more effective sanctioning regime by harmonising the types and addressees of sanctions; and
• the renewal of the competence of the European Commission to adopt the International Standards on Auditing (ISAs) at EU level.

The second measure applies only to the audit of PIEs. Before we consider these new requirements, we must be clear on what a PIE is and how it is defined in legislation. ISA (Ireland) 220, paragraph 7(m)-1, refers to PIEs, as defined in Irish legislation, as:
"(i)  entities governed by the law of a Member State whose transferable securities are admitted to trading on a regulated market of any Member State [as defined by EU Directives];
(ii)  credit institutions [as defined by EU Directives];
(iii) insurance undertakings [as defined by EU Directives]."

In the UK, the same paragraph of ISA (UK) 220, defines a PIE, in UK legislation, as:
"(i) An issuer whose transferable securities are admitted to trading on a regulated market;
 (ii) A credit institution within the meaning [as defined by EU Directives];
(iii) An insurance undertaking within the meaning [as defined by EU Directives]."

When auditing PIEs the following, more stringent, measures now apply:
- increased audit report requirements, including the introduction of a new, more detailed report to the audit committee;
- the introduction of a mandatory rotation of statutory auditors and audit firms;
- the introduction of a list of non-audit services that cannot be provided by the statutory auditor or audit firm to the client entity;
- the imposition of limitations on the fees charged for non-audit services;
- enhancement of the role and competences of the audit committee, giving it a prominent direct role in the appointment of the statutory auditor or the audit firm, as well as in the monitoring of the audit; and
- establishment of a dialogue between the statutory auditor or audit firm of a PIE on the one hand, and those charged with governance of that PIE on the other.

The most significant change affecting the regulation of audit was the requirement for each EU Member State to appoint a single competent authority. The competent authority is tasked with the oversight of the auditing profession. The Irish Auditing & Accounting Supervisory Authority (IAASA) has been appointed the competent authority in the RoI; the Financial Reporting Council (FRC) is appointed in the UK. Below we examine the role of the differing parties who contribute to the Irish and UK auditing profession, starting with the international body.

### *The Role of the International Auditing and Assurance Standards Board (IAASB)*

The IAASB was set up to serve the public interest by setting high-quality international standards in the areas of auditing and assurance and other related standards. It aims to enhance the quality and consistency of auditing practices throughout the world and, in doing so, to strengthen public confidence in the global auditing and assurance profession.

The IAASB sets the International Standards on Auditing (ISAs), as well as other guidance on auditing and assurance, for adoption in local jurisdictions by a competent authority.

### *The Role of the Competent Authority*

Following the enactment of domestic legislation brought in to implement the Audit Regulation and Directive (ARD), IAASA was appointed the competent authority for audit in the RoI, and the FRC the UK competent authority. As the competent authorities, IAASA and the FRC are responsible for the regulation and oversight of the audit market in the RoI and UK/NI respectively, which includes:
1. the setting of auditing and ethical standards;
2. the regulation of the statutory audit environment; and
3. the monitoring and enforcement of the statutory audit environment.

**Standard Setting**    Previously the standards issued by the FRC were applicable for use in both the UK and the RoI. On 16 June 2016 the FRC updated its International Standards on Auditing (ISAs) to complete its responsibilities with regard to the ARD. IAASA, as the competent authority in the RoI, then obtained a licence from the FRC to adopt these updated standards. Changes were made by IAASA to the FRC's standards to reflect legislative differences within the RoI. Under IAASA, the International Standards on Auditing are referred to as ISA (Ireland), while the FRC's standards are now referred to as ISA (UK). **Figure 1.3** below depicts the adoption of auditing and assurance standards in the RoI and the UK/NI.

ISAs are accepted as best practice by professional accountancy bodies. An auditor who does not apply these standards to an audit engagement leaves themselves open to regulatory action. The ISAs contain objectives for, and requirements of, the auditor, including application and other explanatory material.

The International Standard on Quality Control 1: *Quality Control for Firms that Perform Audits and Reviews of Financial Statements, and Other Assurance and Related Services Engagements* (ISQC 1) deals with an audit firm's responsibilities for its internal system of quality control for audits and reviews of financial statements.

FIGURE 1.3: AUDITING AND ASSURANCE STANDARDS ADOPTION IN THE ROI AND UK/NI

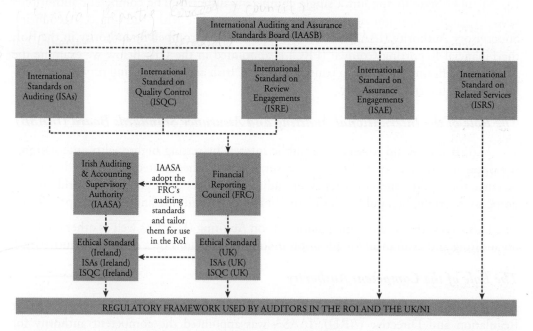

The ISQC 1, whether the Ireland or UK version, should be read in conjunction with the Ethical Standard for Auditors (Ireland) 2017 or the Ethical Standard (2016), respectively. Both versions are discussed in greater detail in **Chapter 2**.

Failure to apply these standards in practice could leave the auditor open to accusations of negligence should the **audit opinion** they express subsequently prove to be incorrect. Reference to the fact that the audit has been carried out in accordance with ISAs is generally included within the auditor's report (see **Chapter 19**).

**Monitoring and Enforcement**    The ARD requires the competent authority to implement a system of investigations and sanctions to "detect, correct and prevent inadequate execution of the statutory audit". This responsibility can be delegated to a RAB or RSB (see below) for audits other than on public interest entities (PIEs). Both the IAASA and the FRC have exercised this right, so that the Institute of Chartered Accountants in Ireland (in its capacity as a RAB and a RSB) is the body responsible for monitoring and disciplinary functions in the RoI and NI (see also **Section 1.7**).

The ARD also requires the competent authority to publish on its official website details of any sanctions it has imposed. The details must remain on the website for a minimum of five years.

### The Role of Recognised Bodies

The supervision and monitoring of the audit profession and the issuing of appropriate accounting and audit qualifications is conducted by recognised bodies. In the RoI, a **recognised accountancy body (RAB)** is responsible for both the supervisory/monitoring aspect and for the issuing of qualifications; in the UK/NI, these functions are split between a **recognised supervisory body (RSB)** and a **recognised qualifying body (RQB)**.

Prior to the adoption of the Audit Regulation and Directive (ARD), RABs and RSBs/RQBs were designated in Irish and UK/NI company law as the competent authorities. The implementation of the ARD, which transferred the status of competent authority solely to the IAASA and the FRC, involved the revocation of the legislation governing this area. However, RABs, RSBs and RQBs continue to have a role within their specific regulatory framework, as delegated by the competent authority (IAASA and FRC respectively).

The Institute of Chartered Accountants in Ireland is appointed as a RAB (by IAASA), but is also a RSB and a RQB as appointed by the FRC. In the UK, the Institutes of Chartered Accountants in England and Wales (ICAEW) and in Scotland (ICAS) are appointed RSBs and RQBs.

In guidance issued collectively by the three institutes, the matters delegated to them by the relevant competent authority are as follows:
- "the approval of firms as registered auditors;
- the approval of individuals as responsible individuals [a 'responsible individual' is a partner or employee of the firm who is responsible for audit work and designated as such under the audit regulations];
- setting procedures for maintaining the competence of responsible individuals;
- in relation to audit work other than that of public interest entities or as retained by the Competent Authority:
  - monitoring the conduct of audit work;
  - investigating possible breaches of these regulations; and
  - disciplining and sanctioning breaches of these regulations."[2]

---

[2] Institutes of Chartered Accountants in England and Wales, Scotland and Ireland, *Audit Regulations and Guidance 2017*, paragraph 5.

In general then, audit firms must be registered with, and are subject to supervision by, a RAB or RSB; and persons responsible for company audit work at a firm must hold a recognised qualification from a RAB or a RQB.

In the quote given above, the wording "to audit work *other than that of public interest entities*" refers to the fact that both the IAASA and the FRC (as the competent authorities) have **not** delegated the regulation or supervision of the audit of PIEs to the recognised bodies, and are themselves responsible for the supervision of these audits. In addition, the FRC also retained the supervision of audits of certain companies listed on the Alternative Investment Market or the ICAP Securities and Derivatives Exchange. The FRC can choose, should it so desire, to issue licences to audit firms or to move licences from one body to another.

Finally, while RABs and RSBs continue to issue enforcement sanctions, the IAASA and the FRC can also apply enforcement sanctions directly to audit firms if they see fit.

### *Summary of the Regulatory Framework in the RoI and the UK/NI*

**Figure 1.4** and **Figure 1.5** below illustrate how company law and the powers assigned to the competent authority, IAASA and the FRC respectively, work together to regulate the audit profession from standard-setting to membership and the monitoring of auditors.

FIGURE 1.4: SUMMARY OF THE REGULATORY FRAMEWORK IN THE RoI

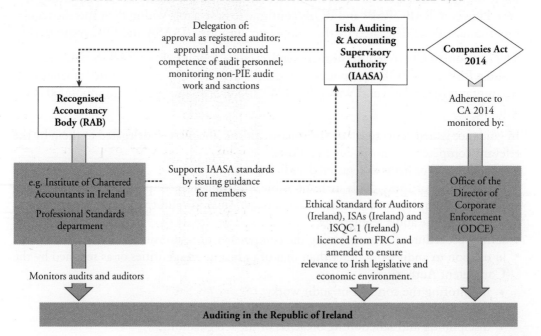

FIGURE 1.5: SUMMARY OF THE REGULATORY FRAMEWORK IN THE UK/NI

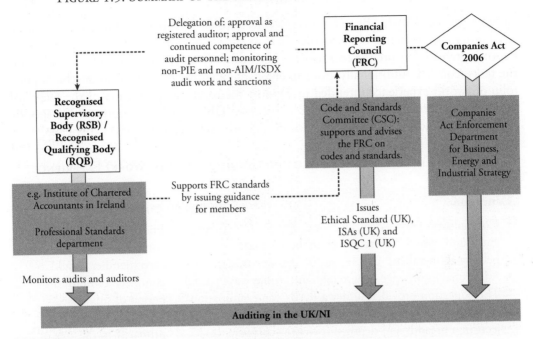

## 1.6 REGULATION, MONITORING AND SUPERVISION OF AUDITORS

Having established the legal and regulatory environment that governs auditing, in this section we will take a closer look at the specific requirements for the individuals and firms wishing to act as auditors.

As we have already established, the competent authorities (the IAASA and the FRC) have delegated responsibilities to recognised accountancy bodies (RABs) and recognised supervisory bodies (RSBs), respectively. Notably, audit firms must be registered with, and are subject to supervision by, a RAB or RSB; and persons responsible for company audit work at a firm must hold a recognised qualification.

Both RABs and RSBs operate stringent entrance requirements, a strict code of ethics and **mandatory** continuing professional development (CPD) for members in order to maintain a level of professionalism and competence. They are responsible for ensuring their members:
• have the requisite education and work experience;
• meet the eligibility criteria; and
• that their audit work is supervised and monitored.

We will now look in detail at each of these areas.

## Education and Work Experience

In order for the RABs/RSBs to have confidence in their members' abilities, they insist on strict entry requirements, obliging members to engage in education supported by examination suitable to ensure the member has the necessary technical knowledge to carry out the tasks required. Additionally, prior to entry, the member is required to develop a portfolio of (work) experience intended to support the practical application of the technical knowledge gained during the education process. **Table 1.4** below outlines the specific requirements under the 'Three Es': education, examination, and (work) experience.

TABLE 1.4: THE THREE ES – EDUCATION, EXAMINATION AND (WORK) EXPERIENCE

| Education | Examination | Experience |
|---|---|---|
| • Compulsory knowledge (accounting and audit-specific) is required to be held by all members.<br>• Additional knowledge, where relevant. The education provided under a RAB or RSB should cover additional subjects in a breadth and depth sufficient to enable its members to perform their duties to the expected standard. | Each member should demonstrate that they have passed an examination of professional competence: theory and practical application. | Practical application is considered key; therefore each member should complete a minimum period of supervised practical experience, primarily in the area of audit and accountancy (in a suitable professional environment). |

## Eligibility

Eligibility to practice as a statutory (registered) auditor is written into company law in both the RoI and the UK/NI,[3] the principal requirement being membership of a RAB or RSB. In turn, the competent authority (the IAASA or the FRC) is required in law to set the criteria by which membership to a RAB/RSB is governed. The eligibility criteria are set out in the *Audit Regulations and Guidance 2017*, produced by the Institutes of Chartered Accountants in England and Wales, Scotland and Ireland.

The criteria for a firm to be eligible are:
• "be fit and proper", which is taken as "complying with the fundamental ethical principles";
• have professional indemnity insurance (PII); and
• that it is "controlled by individuals who hold the appropriate qualification".

---

[3] In the RoI: S.I. No. 312/2016, European Union (Statutory Audits) Regulations 2016 and enforced by the Office of the Director of Corporate Enforcement (ODCE). In the UK/NI: sections 1212–1225 Companies Act 2006 and enforced by the Department for Business, Energy and Industrial Strategy (BEIS) through the Insolvency Service.

Regulation 2.02 expands on these core criteria, setting the necessary conditions to be met for a firm to be registered by the RAB's/RSB's Registration Committee. In addition to being "fit and proper" and having PII, it specifies that an individual be a "responsible individual". That is, the individual:

"a    has an appropriate qualification;
 b    is competent to conduct audit work; and
 c    is allowed to sign audit reports in their name on behalf of the firm."

A registered auditor firm can be a body corporate, a partnership or a sole practice. If a firm is not a sole practice there are additional requirements as set out in Regulation 2.03. These include that each principal has the appropriate qualification and is either: a member of the Institute (meaning the ICAEW, ICAS or ICAI), a member of the Association of Chartered Certified Accountants, an "audit affiliate" of the Institute, a registered auditor or "an EEA auditor" (one registered in a country of the European Economic Area).

In addition, if a firm is a corporate practice, its Articles of Association must also meet certain specific criteria.

Once eligible, there may be events that occur that render the individual ineligible:
- Failure to meet eligibility requirements at any point, resulting in the RAB's/RSB's registration committee cancelling or withdrawing registration.
- The existence of any situation that would be seen to be in breach of the RAB's/RSB's code of ethics or the competent authorities' ethical standard.
- Bankrupts cannot act as auditors while their debts remain unpaid or until debts are excused by a court.
- Individuals who have been found guilty of fraud or serious misconduct (i.e. on indictment under criminal law).

Furthermore, the competent authority also has the right to withdraw registration under its sanctioning powers.

### Sanctioning Powers of the RAB – Republic of Ireland

Under Part 4, Chapter 3, regulation 52(3) of S.I. 312/2016, the recognised accountancy body (RAB) shall withdraw approval of an auditor if:

"(a)    circumstances arise (involving acts or omissions on the part of the auditor) from which the RAB can reasonably conclude that the auditor's good repute is seriously compromised; or
 (b)    any of the conditions specified in Regulation 24 are no longer being complied with in respect of the auditor."

To apply such a withdrawal the competent authority must be able to demonstrate procedural fairness and have served any notices required by its own investigation and disciplinary procedures.

Under S.I. 312/2016, regulation 52(6), if the RAB is to withdraw approval it must serve notice in writing on the auditor, stating the circumstances that have arisen; or such non-compliance has occurred on the part of the auditor. Said notice should give the auditor not less than one month to take steps to restore his or her repute to good standing, or comply with the condition concerned. Should the conditions not be complied with within the specified timeframe, it shall then withdraw the approval of the auditor. Subsequent paragraphs outline the RAB's responsibilities with regard to the process for appeals of such withdrawal decisions. The RAB is required, under Part 4, Chapter 3, to withdraw the approval under those regulations of the person concerned as a statutory auditor or audit firm, where withdrawal of the approval is mandatory under the foregoing regulations.

Regulation 55 of S.I. 312/2016 requires the RAB to inform the supervisory authority and the Registrar of Companies of the decision to withdraw approval of an auditor "as soon as possible, but not later than one month after the date of withdrawal of approval". The RAB is also required, under regulation 56, to notify the relevant competent authorities of the host Member States, where the statutory auditor or audit firm is also registered and entered in the public registers of those states, of the withdrawal and the reasons for it. Regulation 56(3) shall apply if the approval of a statutory auditor or audit firm is withdrawn by the supervisory authority.

### Sanctioning Powers of the Competent Authority – UK/Northern Ireland

Under regulation 5 of the Statutory Auditors and Third Country Auditors Regulations (SATCAR) 2016, if the competent authority, i.e. the FRC, considers that a person eligible for appointment as a statutory auditor has contravened a "relevant requirement" (as described under paragraph 11 of regulation 5) it may apply a sanction to that person, which may include:
- notice to cease the conduct giving rise to the contravention; or
- prohibiting the person permanently or for a specified period from carrying out statutory audits; or
- prohibiting the person from acting as director of a public interest entity (PIE) for a period of up to three years; or
- excluding the person from membership of one or more RSBs.

Furthermore, regulation 6 requires the competent authority to publish details of sanctions it imposes under regulation 5, while regulation 7 permits the competent authority to enforce the sanction through the High Court.

### Supervisory and Monitoring Roles

As noted in **Section 1.5**, it is the responsibility of the competent authority (the IAASA or the FRC) to monitor and enforce the conduct of statutory audits, but that this responsibility can be delegated to a RAB or RSB. In the RoI and NI then, this responsibility has been delegated by the IAASA and the FRC to the Institute of Chartered Accountants in Ireland (ICAI), in its capacity as both a RAB and a RSB. This responsibility is reflected in legislation and in the ICAI's own bye-laws and regulations. Within the ICAI the Professional Standards department, along with relevant compliance and disciplinary committees, is charged with these obligations.

To fulfill these obligations the RAB/RSB must appoint a "monitoring body" to monitor its members with respect to their continuing professional development (CPD) and their competence to carry out audits of financial statements.

This monitoring must be carried out by inspections, and conducted by persons with appropriate professional educations, with experience in statutory audit work and having adequate training in the conduct of inspections. They should also be sufficiently independent of the subject under investigation.

The RAB/RSB should include within its regulations provisions relating to:
• admittance and expulsion;
• investigation of complaints; and
• compulsory professional indemnity insurance.

With regard to their competence to carry out an audit, the monitoring body should find evidence of:
1. a properly structured audit approach;
2. commitment to quality control procedures; and
3. commitment to ethical guidelines.

Each registered audit firm is required to complete a firm's annual return (FAR), which is risk-assessed with regard to its compliance with the regulations. This is done by way of a 'desk top review', which could lead to further follow-up correspondence or, in certain circumstances, a monitoring visit.

Similarly, all members are required to complete an individual annual return to evidence their compliance with CPD regulations and with the RAB's/RSB's code of ethics, in particular with its fundamental principles.

## 1.7 APPOINTMENT, REMOVAL AND RESIGNATION OF AUDITORS

Having established in **Section 1.6** who can act as the auditor of an entity's financial statements, let us now consider how auditors are appointed to the role of auditor for a specific company or **client entity**. We will also address the removal and resignation of auditors from their role.

### Appointment of Auditors – Republic of Ireland

In the RoI, the shareholders of a private company appoint an auditor annually by ordinary resolution, in accordance with section 383 CA 2014. A vacancy to cover the period prior to the first annual general meeting (AGM), or prior to the next AGM in instances where the auditor has resigned, or where a casual vacancy arises, may be filled by the directors pending approval by the shareholders at the next AGM. However, once appointed, the auditor is in place until the next AGM.

All **public interest entities (PIEs)** are required to have an audit committee (except in limited circumstances – see S.I. 312/2016, regulation 115). Section 167 CA 2014 requires that if an audit committee is established, any proposal of the board of directors of a large company (being either a PIE or 'large company' as defined within CA 2014 (see **Section 1.4**)) with respect to the appointment of **statutory auditors** to the company shall be based on a recommendation made by the audit committee.

The statutory auditors shall report to the audit committee of a large company or PIE on key matters arising from their audit, in particular on material weaknesses in internal control in relation to the financial reporting process.

### Appointment of Auditors – UK/Northern Ireland

In the UK/NI, the shareholders of a private company appoint an auditor annually by ordinary resolution in accordance with section 485 CA 2006. A vacancy to cover the period prior to the first annual general meeting (AGM), or prior to the next AGM in instances where the auditor has resigned, or where a casual vacancy arises, may be filled by the directors pending approval by the shareholders at the next AGM. However, once appointed, the auditor is in place until the next AGM.

Similar to the RoI, all PIEs are required to have an audit committee. With regard to PIEs not subject to audit by the Auditor General, the audit committee, following a selection procedure (as laid down in Article 16(3) of the Audit Regulation), is required to make a recommendation to the directors of its first- and second-choice candidates, with reasons for its decision and a statement that its recommendation is free from influence from any third party. The directors are then required to propose to the shareholders an auditor/auditors for appointment. If the directors' proposal is a departure from the audit committee's recommendation, they must state their reasons for doing so. These requirements relating to PIEs are laid down in section 485B CA 2006.

### Mandatory Rotation of Auditors – Republic of Ireland

Articles 16 and 17 of the Audit Regulation and Directive (ARD) introduced mandatory rotation of audit firms in all EU Member States. In the RoI, this was implemented by S.I. 312/2016, which requires mandatory rotation of audit firms after 10 years for each PIE. In practice, many PIEs rotate auditors more frequently than this to demonstrate an increased level of corporate governance.

The transition arrangements depend on the length of the existing relationship – specifically, relationships that have been established for longer than 11 years as of June 2014 have longer to transition. The competent authority, i.e. IAASA, may, however, grant an extension on this 10-year rule for up to two years in exceptional circumstances. Audit reform rules also set out requirements for running audit tenders and require PIEs to have a tender process in place for the selection of new auditors, the responsibility for which lies with the audit committee.

Contractual terms written between the audit firm and the client entity will not apply where they contravene implied maximum terms under the ARD.

## Mandatory Rotation of Auditors – UK/Northern Ireland

In the UK/NI, the mandatory rotation of auditors was implemented by SATCAR 2016[4] (amending section 490 *et seq* CA 2006). As with the RoI, this now requires the appointment of a new firm of auditors every 10 years. However, the UK has also taken up a Member State option to extend this maximum period to 20 years, provided the audit is publicly tendered at least every 10 years. Previous to this legislative requirement, the *UK Code of Corporate Governance* required all FTSE 350 companies to retender every 10 years on a 'comply or explain' basis. The competent authority, i.e. the FRC, may, however, grant an extension on this 10-year rule for up to two years. In practice, many PIEs rotate auditors more frequently than this to demonstrate an increased level of corporate governance.

Contractual terms written between the audit firm and the client entity will not apply where they contravene implied maximum terms under the ARD.

## Removal of Auditors

In both the RoI and the UK, auditors are generally removed due to:
1. **Tenure** – the length of time for which the auditor has held the **audit engagement** with the client entity. As will be discussed further in **Chapter 2**, Section 2.5, **long association** between the audit firm and the client entity can develop into a close relationship between the staff of the respective organisations. When one becomes overly familiar with an individual, it can create a sense of obligation towards that individual, which may be in conflict with one's duty as the auditor. As per the discussion above on mandatory rotation of auditors for PIEs, tenure is a more regulated area.
2. **Incompetence** – where doubts exist over the auditor's continued competence to carry out their duties.

Ultimately, the removal of the auditor must be subject to a majority vote at the client entity's AGM. However, the auditor should be given a notice period. The grounds for removal must either be connected to the conduct of the auditor in the performance of their duties, or be seen to be in the best interests of the company. Differing opinions on accounting treatment or audit procedures will not, however, be viewed as justifiably in the best interests of the company.

The auditor has a statutory right to make representations at any meeting held where their removal or non-reappointment is to be proposed.[5] Additionally, where a statutory auditor has been removed, the Companies Acts in both jurisdictions give them the right to attend the next AGM of the company.

## Resignation of Auditors – Republic of Ireland

An auditor can resign from the audit of a client entity for a number of reasons, such as: an inability to work with the management team of the client entity; the identification of ethical issues; concerns over management integrity as a result of **limitation of scope**

---

[4] S.I. No. 649/2016, The Statutory Auditors and Third Country Auditors Regulations 2016.
[5] In the RoI: section 397 CA 2014; in the UK/NI: section 513 CA 2006.

(see **Chapter 19**, Section 19.4), breach of laws and regulations, senior management fraud, etc. When an auditor acting within the RoI does resign, they must comply with certain rights and duties laid down under sections 400–403 CA 2014. These require the auditor to serve notice on the company stating their intention to resign from the office of statutory auditor to the company. This is known as the **Statement of Circumstances**.

The notice from the auditor is required to contain either:

"(a)  a statement to the effect that there are no circumstances connected with the resignation to which it relates that the statutory auditors concerned consider should be brought to the notice of the members or creditors of the company, or

(b)  a statement of any such circumstances as mentioned in paragraph (a)."[6]

The auditor is further required to send a copy of the notice to the Registrar of Companies within 14 days of serving the notice. In turn the company shall, where the notice contains a statement, send a copy of the notice to every person who is entitled under section 338 CA 2014 to be sent copies of the documents referred to in that section. This should be sent not more than 14 days after receipt.

Where the auditor includes a statement in such a notice he may, under section 401, request the convening of a general meeting of the company. Where such a request is received the company should send notice to its members not more than 14 days following the auditor's request and hold the meeting not more than 28 days from date of that notice to members.

Where, for any reason, the auditor ceases to hold office between the conclusion of the last AGM and the next, the auditor shall, within 30 days of receiving/giving the notice, notify the supervisory authority, i.e. IAASA. This notice should be accompanied by:

"(a)  in the case of resignation of the auditor, the notice served by the auditor under section 400(1), or

(b)  in the case of removal of the auditor at a general meeting pursuant to section 394, a copy of any representations in writing made to the company, pursuant to section 397(2), by the outgoing auditor in relation to the intended resolution except where such representations were not sent out to the members of the company in consequence of an application to the court under section 397(4)."[7]

Similarly, the company must also inform the supervisory authority (IAASA).

## Resignation of Auditors – UK/Northern Ireland

As in the RoI, resignation of auditors in the UK/NI can occur for the same reasons as given above. If an auditor acting within the UK/NI does resign, they must comply with certain rights and duties laid down under sections 519–525 CA 2006. Section 519(3A) requires the auditor to: "where there are matters connected with an auditor's ceasing to hold office that the auditor considers need to be brought to the attention of members or creditors of the company, the statement under this section must include details of those matters."

---

[6] Section 400(3) CA 2014.
[7] Section 403(2) CA 2014.

Any such statement, the Statement of Circumstances, must be sent to the client entity:
"(a)  in the case of resignation, along with the notice of resignation;
 (b)  in the case of failure to seek re-appointment, not less than 14 days before the end of the time allowed for next appointing an auditor;
 (c)  in any other case, not later than the end of the period of 14 days beginning with the date on which he ceases to hold office."[8]

Where the statement relates to a PIE, a copy of the statement must also be sent to the registrar. ISA (UK) 250 Section B – *The Auditor's Statutory Right and Duty to Report to Regulators of Public Interest Entities and Regulators of Other Entities in the Financial Sector*, paragraph A4, also calls on the auditor of a regulated entity to "assess whether it is appropriate to bring any matters of which the auditor is then aware to the notice of the regulator" (the "regulator" being those empowered by CA 2006 to regulate the entity, and includes the Financial Conduct Authority, the Prudential Regulation Authority and such other bodies as may be so empowered in future legislation).

ISQC (UK) 1, paragraph A22, outlines policies and procedures on withdrawal from an engagement and the client relationship. The auditor must inform the appropriate audit authority if they cease to hold office as auditor before the end of their term of office. This will include the respective RAB/RSB and competent authority in their jurisdiction (the IAASA or the FRC). The auditor should also notify the Companies Registration Office in the RoI and Companies House in the UK.

**Table 1.5** summarises the duties and rights of the auditor on resignation in both the RoI and the UK/NI.

TABLE 1.5: AUDITOR'S RESIGNATION – DUTIES AND RIGHTS

| Auditor's Duties | Auditor's Rights |
|---|---|
| • To notify the shareholders in a Statement of Circumstances, outlining the circumstances giving rise to the resignation. | • To request the directors to send the written Statement of Circumstances to the members of the company (shareholders) prior to the convening of a general meeting. |
| • To notify the respective RAB/RSB (should the resignation be during a term of office).<br>• To notify the supervisory authority (IAASA or FRC) within 30 days of the Statement of Circumstances. | • To request the company to circulate notice of the holding of a general meeting and the circumstances relating to the auditor's resignation (to be convened by the directors not more than 28 days following date of request to convene). |
| • For RoI: to notify the Companies Registration Office (CRO) or the ODCE. For the UK/NI: to notify the Registrar of Companies (Companies House). | • To speak at the general meeting. |

---

[8] Section 519(4) CA 2006.

## 1.8 AUDITORS' LEGAL LIABILITY

**Introduction**

The auditor has certain duties laid down in legislation. In both the RoI and the UK/NI, the main duty of the auditor is to form an opinion as to the truth and fairness of the financial statements examined by them. This opinion must be supported by the audit evidence gathered by the auditor throughout the course of the audit, and delivered in the form of an audit report addressed to the members of the client entity (the shareholders).

The Companies Acts (UK 2006 and RoI 2014) also require the auditor in their audit report to report on failure to maintain proper accounting records. Indictable offences, those serious enough to be tried before a judge and jury, should be reported directly to either the Office of the Director of Corporate Enforcement (ODCE) in the RoI, or to the Department for Business, Energy and Industrial Strategy (BEIS) in the UK/NI.

In carrying out these duties, the auditor must do so with professional integrity. The auditor has a duty to exercise reasonable care, and failure to do so may result in being held liable for damages to the company/client entity or, in particular, to its members (i.e. the shareholders).

Essentially, should the auditor provide an incorrect opinion that causes financial loss to the client entity or to its shareholders, and they are found to have not acted with professional integrity or with the expected reasonable care, they may be sued for damages. Any loss, however caused, will ultimately have to have a financial measure for damages to arise.

It is important to understand the legal terms used with regard to auditors' legal liability. **Table 1.6** below explains some of the key legal terms, along with landmark legal cases relating to the legal liability of the auditor.

TABLE 1.6: KEY LEGAL TERMINOLOGY AND ITS RELEVANCE TO AUDITING

| Legal Terminology | Explanation and Case Law (where applicable) |
| --- | --- |
| **(Law of) Tort** | Tort is a civil wrong independent of contract arising from a breach of duty created, not by agreement, but by operation of law. |
| **Due professional care** | Consideration is given to the relevance of professional standards, i.e. whether or not the auditor applied auditing standards in determining the adequate performance of audit work; and whether the relevant financial reporting framework was used in determining the basis for expressing an opinion as to the truth and fairness of the financial statements. |

*Re Kingston Cotton Mill Co.* (1896)
- A manager exaggerated stock values for years to fraudulently over-state profits. It eventually came to light when the company could not pay its debts.
- The auditors relied on a certificate from management to confirm the stock value.
- The auditors did not attend the physical inventory count nor attempt to validate the opening balance of inventories or cross-reference to sales and purchases, which would have high-lighted the issue.
- The judge held that the auditor must rely on some skilled person (i.e. the manager) for the materials necessary to enable them to enter the stock in trade at its proper value in the statement of financial position. The auditor has to perform with the skill, care and caution of a reasonably competent, careful and cautious professional. **The auditor is a watchdog, but not a bloodhound.**
- This case laid down some fundamental auditing principles, such as the 'watchdog' rule and the concept of the reasonable skill and care of the auditor.

*Re London & General Bank* (1985) also deals with auditor responsibility. In this case the auditor, while having adequately informed the directors of insufficient security obtained in relation to loans and overdrafts guaranteed to customers, **failed to ensure that the financial statements adequately alerted the shareholders to this critical position**. That is, the financial statements did not adequately disclose the issue and the auditor issued an unqualified opinion. The auditor was later held liable for the second dividend due to the shareholders (insufficient evidence was believed to exist to hold them liable for the first dividend) and Lindley L.J. described the auditor's duty as follows: "An auditor, however, is not bound to do more than **exercise reasonable care and skill in making inquiries and investigations**."

| | |
|---|---|
| **Negligence** | Negligence is conduct that fails to take proper care over something. In law this entails a breach of any contractual duty or duty of care in tort owed to another person or persons. If auditors have been negligent, the client may sue them for breach of an implicit term of contract to exercise reasonable care and skill in order to recover any consequential loss suffered. A judge will seek proof not only that the ultimate decision taken by an auditor where damage was suffered was incorrect, but also that the method in arriving at the decision was flawed (e.g. that the requirements of the auditing standards and company law were not followed). |

| **Privity of contract** | Privity of contract relates to the contractual relationship that exists between two or more contracting parties. Essentially, a contract confers rights and imposes liabilities only on its contracting parties. |
| --- | --- |
| | The company (client entity shareholders) has a contract in the form of an engagement letter with the auditor (see **Chapter 5**, Section 5.3) and hence can sue the auditor for breach of contract if the auditor is negligent in carrying out the terms of the contract. Note that only the company can sue the auditor under the law of contract – other third parties, such as banks, creditors and shareholders, etc., are not in a contractual relationship with the auditor. |
| | A duty may exist to a third party not named in the engagement letter/contract (i.e. one who does not have privity of contract) if a relationship was reasonably foreseeable and that third party can prove that a loss suffered was as a result of negligent conduct. Such foreseeable third party might be a bank that requires the company to be audited prior to lending it money. If the auditor was aware of this and failed to give reasonable care, an action may be brought against them by the bank if it suffers a loss as a result of relying on the audited financial statements. See *Foss v. Harbottle* (1843) for more on the rights of minority shareholders. |
| **Causal relationship** | The question of causal relationship considers the relationship between an event that is said to be negligent and the loss suffered by the plaintiff. For example, the auditor is believed to have not acted with a duty of care and issued an incorrect opinion on the financial statements that was subsequently relied upon. The court will seek to establish whether there is a link between the auditor's negligence and the damages suffered by the innocent party. |
| | In *Galoo Ltd v. Bright Grahame Murray* (1994), Galoo alleged that had the auditors audited its accounts properly, it would have been discovered that Galoo was insolvent, causing Galoo to cease trading. Galoo therefore claimed that the auditors' failure to highlight this caused Galoo to continue trading and to suffer further trading losses. |
| | It was held that there was no causal relationship between the alleged negligence and the losses incurred. The financial statements may have allowed the company to continue trading, but the company's existence was not the cause of its losses. Event A (the negligent audit) was necessary for Event B (the loss incurred during subsequent trading) to occur, but was not in itself the cause of Event B. |

**Is the auditor's legal position affected?** No, again it is simply clarifying to whom the auditor owes a duty, as established by the *Caparo* case – **it is not restricting their liability to the members of the company as a body**.

**Does it guarantee that the auditor will not owe any duty of care to third parties?** No, the auditor should remain vigilant to prevent a duty of care from arising. Unless there is an effective disclaimer, an auditor may owe a duty of care to a lender or other third party – the test is whether the auditor, in making statements in the audit report, has assumed a responsibility to a third party who may be provided with those statements. The test is an objective one in that it is asking if it is *reasonable* to assume that responsibility?

Whether a duty of care to a third party exists will depend on all the circumstances. The following factors, however, will be relevant:
* the precise relationship between the auditor and the third party;
* the precise circumstances in which the audit report came into existence;
* the precise circumstances in which the audit report was communicated to the third party and for what purpose, and whether the communication was made by the auditor or another party (such as the client entity);
* the present or absence of other advisors on whom the third party would, or could, rely;
* the opportunity, if any, given to the auditor to issue a disclaimer.

Accordingly, the auditor needs to be alert to the possibility that circumstances may be such that, unless care is taken to limit their exposure, they may, however inadvertently, have assumed responsibility and created a duty of care. For example, if during the audit the client entity is in discussion with a lender, a duty of care to the lender may have arisen. Similarly, events subsequent to the audit may cause a duty of care, e.g. the client entity receives a request for the most recently audited financial statements. To avoid such pitfalls, the auditor's relationship with lenders and other third parties needs to be managed carefully, using established risk management techniques, and clear statements defining the auditor's duties, if any.

CASE: *ROYAL BANK OF SCOTLAND V. BANNERMAN, JOHNSTONE, MACLAY* (2013)

Royal Bank of Scotland (RBS) provided overdraft facilities to APC Limited, which in turn was audited by Bannerman, Johnstone, Maclay. Included in the bank facility letter was the requirement for the company to provide audited accounts each year to the bank. It subsequently transpired that the auditors had failed to detect fraud that had occurred in the company. The bank claimed that they were owed a duty of care by the auditors, as they knew that the bank would be relying on the audited accounts. The auditor, knowing this, should have disclaimed liability to RBS, but did not do so. The ruling judge held that in the absence of the disclaimer, the auditors owed a duty of care to RBS and found in its favour.

CASE: *BARCLAYS BANK PLC V. GRANT THORNTON LLP (UK) (2015)*

The effectiveness of the Bannerman paragraph was tested in *Barclays Bank plc v. Grant Thornton LLP* (2015). Barclays and VEH Essen Hotel Group entered into a facility agreement and Grant Thornton subsequently took over as the auditor of VEH. While VEH was exempt from the requirement to prepare group accounts, as part of its agreement with Barclays it had committed to prepare non-statutory group accounts. Grant Thornton were hired directly by VEH to carry out this audit. The non-statutory audit report contained 'Bannerman clauses', which though largely following the standard Bannerman paragraph, included the phrase "responsibility to anyone other than the **company and the company's directors**" (the standard wording refers to the *"company's members as a body"* rather than the company's directors).

VEH subsequently went into administration and Barclays sued Grant Thornton, stating that they owed them a duty of care in relation to the non-statutory audit report and that this duty was breached by Grant Thornton's negligence in not detecting an alleged fraud of the finance director who manipulated the financial records in order to make it appear that they were meeting the covenants laid down by Barclays. The court dismissed the claim, stating that Barclays was a sophisticated commercial party and thereby capable of interpreting the disclaimer noted on the face of the reports. Grant Thornton had been engaged directly by the management of VEH and therefore the disclaimer meant they owed a duty of care only to VEH.

## 1.9 CONCLUSION

The need for audit grew from the increased separation of ownership and stewardship of companies. The owners of organisations (the shareholders/principals) need confidence that those charged with governance are acting in their best interests and providing them with accurate financial and other information. The auditor fulfills that need by issuing an independent opinion on the financial statements, increasing confidence in the information being produced by those charged with governance.

Increasing numbers of corporate failures have led to increased legislative and regulatory requirements for the auditor. Additionally, the growth of capital markets offering more opportunity for investing overseas has required more uniformity, not just in accounting standards but also in auditing standards. Within the RoI and the UK/NI, international bodies and standards are becoming increasingly recognised and are being adjusted to address key issues within these jurisdictions. The legal environment in the RoI saw significant change when the Companies Act 2014 came into effect in June 2015, consolidating previous Acts and reforming Irish company law. The Companies (Accounting) Act 2017 came into force on 9 June 2017 and applies to financial years commencing on or after 1 January 2017.

The audit regulatory environment is a dynamic landscape that continues to evolve to meet the requirements of all relevant stakeholders, by:
- issuing strong standards on auditing; and
- ensuring those eligible to audit are members of a RAB/RSB and that those bodies operate stringent entrance requirements, a strict code of ethics and continuing professional development for members in order to maintain a level of professionalism and competence among auditors.

The EU Audit Regulation Directive 2016 has had a transformative effect on the audit profession. It has focused on transparency, independence, improved regulatory supervision and coordination of audit supervision and enabled a more dynamic and competitive audit market in the EU.

## Summary of Learning Objectives

**Learning Objective 1** Understand what is meant by the term 'assurance engagements'.

**Assurance engagements** deliver statements that inspire confidence in a subject matter. The most common assurance engagement is that of the **external audit**. However, common to all assurance engagements, including financial statement audits, are a number of core elements:
- a subject matter;
- users of the subject matter;
- a set of criteria; and
- an examination leading to an opinion being expressed on the subject matter.

**Learning Objective 2** Understand the objective of an external audit of financial statements.

ISA 200 defines the objective of an audit as a process "to enhance the degree of confidence of intended users in the financial statements. This is achieved by the expression of an opinion by the auditor on whether the financial statements are prepared, in all material respects, in accordance with an applicable financial reporting framework."

The auditor issues only a "**reasonable assurance**" as to the "**truth and fairness**" of the financial statements due to the **inherent limitations** of an audit, including the:
- need for **judgement**;
- inherent limitations of **accounting and internal controls**;
- inherent limitations in the **audit report itself**;
- fact that **not all items in the financial statements are tested**;
- **timing of the audit report**; and
- fact that **audit evidence indicates what is probable, not fact**.

**Learning Objective 3** Be able to explain why and how the auditing profession has evolved.

The need for external audit assurance has increased over the years due to the increase in capital markets and, in turn, the separation of ownership and control of organisations. The auditor offers the shareholder an **unbiased (independent) opinion** that the financial statements are free from **material misstatement**.

**Learning Objective 4** Be able to demonstrate a detailed understanding of the legal and regulatory frameworks that govern external audits in the RoI and the UK/NI.

## The Legislative Environment

The Companies Acts in both the RoI (CA 2014) and the UK/NI (CA 2006) require companies to **appoint an auditor** and **have their annual accounts audited** unless they meet two out of three of the following criteria:

|  | UK/NI | RoI |
|---|---|---|
| Turnover | £10.2 million (or less) | €12 million (or less) |
| Balance Sheet Total | £5.1 million (or less) | €6 million (or less) |
| Average Number of Employees | 50 (or less) | 50 (or less) |

The auditing standards also require the inclusion of a **statement of directors' and auditors' responsibilities** to be included somewhere with the financial statements, and these responsibilities reflect those laid down in law.

## The Regulatory Environment

The regulatory environment is made up of the following:

**IAASB** – develops and promotes ISAs and other assurance standards and improves uniformity of auditing practices and related services globally.

**IAASA** – is the competent authority in the RoI, with overall responsibility for the regulation of auditing and accounting and the setting of auditing standards (ISAs (Ireland)).

**FRC** – is the competent authority in the UK, with overall responsibility for the regulation of auditing and accounting and the setting of auditing standards (ISAs (UK)).

**ISAs** – International Standards on Auditing, accepted as best practice by professional accountancy bodies (see Learning Objective 5 for more detail).

**RABs/RSBs** – monitor and enforce regulations as prescribed by the IAASA and the FRC, principally they require adequate education and experience, eligibility and supervision and monitoring of their members (i.e. auditor practitioners).

**Appointment, Removal and Resignation of Auditors**

Auditors are appointed by shareholders at the AGM and may be removed only by shareholders at an EGM. The auditor, should they wish to resign, has a duty to report to the shareholders the reasons for doing so by providing a Statement of Circumstances. The auditor has the right to address the shareholders at a general meeting, giving reasons for their resignation.

**Learning Objective 5** Be able to demonstrate an understanding of the setting and use of ISAs in the RoI and the UK/NI.

The IAASB develops and promotes ISAs for use worldwide; in the UK/NI they are issued by the FRC, with the necessary amendments to reflect the local legislative and business environments (ISAs (UK)). In the RoI, the IAASA have licensed the ISAs as issued by the FRC, with amendments to reflect the Irish legal and business environments (ISAs (Ireland)). An auditor who does not apply these standards to an audit engagement is left open to regulatory action. Auditing standards include objectives for and requirements of the auditor, including application and other explanatory material.

**Learning Objective 6** Be able to demonstrate an understanding of the case law that has shaped the legal liability of auditors.

Duties are laid down in company law and breach of these duties due to negligence toward a person to whom the auditor owed a duty of care, and who suffered loss as a result of that negligence, may be subject to liability.

## QUESTIONS

### Self-test Questions

1.1   What is an audit and why are they required?

1.2   What is meant by the term 'reasonable assurance'?

1.3   Name and explain four limitations of an audit.

1.4   What is meant by 'agency theory'?

1.5   What conditions must be met for a company to be eligible for audit exemption (in either the RoI or UK/NI)?

1.6   Distinguish between the auditor's and the directors' responsibilities.

1.7   What is the role of the IAASA/FRC?

1.8   What is the role of the IAASB?

1.9   Outline your understanding of the 'Three Es' required by an auditor.

1.10  In what circumstances might an individual be ineligible to act as an auditor?

1.11  Who is responsible for the appointment and removal of the auditor?

1.12  What duties and rights does the auditor have when they choose to resign or withdraw from the engagement?

1.13  What is meant by the term 'duty of care'? Who does the auditor owe a duty of care to?

1.14  What is meant by the term 'negligence'?

1.15  What are the key questions a judge will ask when considering a legal claim against an auditor?

1.16  What is professional indemnity insurance?

## Review Questions

(See Suggested Solutions to Review Questions in **Appendix C**.)

### Question 1.1

Hanley & Burn is an audit partnership that has been in practice since 1950. Over this time it has built up a large client base offering both audit and non-audit services. For the year ended 31 December 2013, Hanley & Burn issued an unqualified audit opinion in relation to a long-standing Irish client, Preston Ltd. During 2015 it was revealed that Preston Ltd had delayed the recording of expenses between 2010 and 2013 in an effort to smooth profits and ultimately to hide the losses being made. The amounts in question were material and resulted in the collapse of the company during 2014. Hanley & Burn are currently facing legal proceedings brought by the shareholders who claim that Hanley & Burn was negligent in its role as auditor.

**Requirement**  Outline for Hanley & Burn the decision process of the presiding judge in the case of *Preston Ltd Shareholders v. Hanley & Burn*.

### Question 1.2

John Brown is the CFO of a large investment company. He is meeting with the board of directors in the coming weeks and has recently received the agenda for the meeting. One of the points on the agenda is for Mr Brown to explain "how some of the companies in the portfolio have proven to have material misstatements in their financial statements despite being supported by an independent audit report".

**Requirement**  Prepare a response for Mr Brown to use at the meeting. The response should include **four** specific reasons why material misstatements may exist in a set of financial statements following the issue of a clean audit opinion.

## APPENDIX 1.1: SCHEDULE OF LANDMARK LEGAL CASES SHAPING AUDIT LEGAL LIABILITY

| Year | Case Name and Key Findings |
|---|---|
| 1896 | *Re Kingston Cotton Mill Co.* (UK)<br>Auditor must use reasonable skill and care.<br>Auditor is a "watchdog, not a bloodhound". |
| 1931 | *Ultramares Corporation v. Touche* (USA)<br>Accountant only has a liability to those in contractual relationship – not to third parties. |
| 1932 | *Donoghue v. Stevenson* (UK)<br>A duty of care is owed to a third party where it is reasonably foreseeable that one's acts or omissions could result in injury to that third party. |
| 1951 | *Candler v. Crane, Christmas & Co.* (UK)<br>If no contractual relationship exists, auditors are not liable for losses suffered by a third party. |
| 1963 | *Hedley Byrne & Co v. Heller & Partners* (UK)<br>A duty of care is owed to third parties where the third party is known to the auditor, or ought to have been known to the auditor, as having the intent to rely on the audited financial statement for a particular reason. (E.g. if the client entity made the auditor aware that the bank was waiting on the signed financial statements in order to make a final decision on a large loan, then the auditor would know of the intent to rely on the financial statements for the purpose of the provision of a loan.) |
| 1977 | *Anns v. Merton London Borough Council* (UK)<br>Special relationship is replaced by the proximity principle and loss must have been reasonably foreseeable. The duty of care for financial loss is significantly extended. |
| 1981 | *Jeb Fastner Ltd v. Marks Bloom & Co.* (UK)<br>Duty of care extended to those who may use accounts for investment decisions. |
| 1983 | *Twomax Ltd v. Dickinson McFarlane & Robinson* (UK)<br>Duty of care extended to virtually anyone who can prove that they relied on negligently prepared financial statements to make an investment decision. |

**1990**   *Caparo Industries plc v. Dickman and Others* **(UK)**
Auditors usually only owe a duty of care to the client entity and its
shareholders. Duty of care owed to third parties only when there is:
- forseeability of damage;
- proximity of relationship; and
- the fairness of imposing a duty of care.

**1990**   *James McNaughton Paper Group Ltd v. Hicks Anderson & Co.* **(UK)**
When deciding if a special relationship exists, one needs to consider six steps
(see details of this case below).

**1991**   *Morgan Crucible Co. plc v. Hill Samuel Bank Ltd* **(UK)**
By making specific representations after a known bidder was identified,
a relationship of proximity exists and a duty of care is owed to the
bidder.

**1994**   *Galoo Limited v. Bright Grahame Murray* **(UK)**
A plaintiff can only claim for loss when breach is the cause of the loss, not
where it provides an opportunity for the loss.

**1996**   *ADT Ltd v. BDO Binder Hamlyn* **(UK)**
A partner of Binder Hamlyn that made specific negligent representations
during a takeover discussion was held to owe a duty of care to a third party
as it knew the information would be relied upon.

**2003**   *Royal Bank of Scotland v. Bannerman, Johnstone, Maclay* **(UK)**
A duty of care, in the absence of a disclaimer, may be held to have been
owed when information is passed on to a third party for a specific purpose
and the third party will rely on the information.

**2015**   *Barclays Bank plc v. Grant Thornton* **(UK)** *LLP*
A duty of care was not owed to Barclays due to the inclusion of a disclaimer
similar to the 'Bannerman paragraph' stating that Grant Thornton would not
accept "responsibility to anyone other than the company and the company's
directors". The court held that Barclays were sufficiently sophisticated to
understand the implications of the disclaimer included on the face of the
reports (see **Section 1.8**).

## APPENDIX 1.2: LANDMARK LEGAL CASES

### Donoghue v. Stevenson (1932) – 'Duty of Care'

The facts of this case were as follows: a woman was drinking ginger beer. When she went to pour some more out of the bottle, she discovered the remains of a snail in the bottle. She brought an action against Stevenson, the producer of the drink, claiming damages for her injuries. Although there was no contract between the two, the manufacturer was found to have owed a duty of care to Donoghue and was ordered to pay damages. This case established the '**neighbour principle**', whereby a person will owe a duty of care not to injure those whom it can be reasonably foreseen would be affected by their acts or omissions. The importance of this case is that it is now shown that a duty of care may be owed to people who may not be in a contractual relationship with the company.

### Candler v. Crane, Christmas & Co. (1951)

In this case, a set of accounts had been negligently prepared for a client. A third-party plaintiff used these accounts for the purpose of making an investment. The investment failed and the third party sued the accountants. The court ruled, by majority, that as there was no contractual relationship between the parties, the action for negligence failed.

The dissenting judge, Lord Justice Denning stated:
> "They owe a duty to their client and also, I think, to any third party to whom they themselves show the accounts, or to whom they know their employer is going to show the accounts so as to induce him to take some action on them. I do not think, however, the duty can be extended further so as to include strangers of whom they have heard nothing and to whom their employer without their knowledge may choose to show their accounts. Once the accountants have handed the accounts to their client, they are not, as a rule, responsible for what he does with them without their knowledge or consent."

### Hedley Byrne & Co. v. Heller & Partners (1963)

In this case a certificate of creditworthiness was negligently given by a firm of merchant bankers to an advertising agency in relation to a client of Heller's. Heller had said that the company was good for normal business arrangements and for the proposed advertising contract about which they were being approached. The bank claimed that they owed no duty of care to the plaintiff in the absence of any contractual or fiduciary relationship with the advertising agency. The courts held that the duty of care was owed, and applied the findings of Lord Justice Denning, the dissenting judgment in the *Candler v. Crane* case (see above).

Heller & Partners, however, did not have to pay any damages as they had a clause in the contract disclaiming any liability if their advice was relied upon.

Lord Denning stated:

"I can see no logical stopping place short of all those relationships where it is plain that the party seeking information or advice was trusting the other to exercise such a degree of care as the circumstances required, where it is reasonable for him to do that, and where the other gave the information or advice when he knew or ought to have known that the inquirer was relying on him. I say 'ought to have known' because in questions of negligence we now apply the objective standard of what the reasonable man would have done."

The decision by the House of Lords in *Hedley Byrne* indicated that actions for professional negligence may arise if financial loss is suffered by third parties through their reliance on the professional skill and judgement of persons with whom they were not in a contractual or fiduciary relationship.

The effect of the *Hedley Byrne* decision is that someone possessed of a special skill, quite irrespective of contract, may be considered to have undertaken to apply that skill for the assistance of another person and thereby to have accepted a duty of care to that person. A negligent though honest misrepresentation that causes financial loss to another may thus, in certain circumstances, give rise to an action for damages at the suit of a person with whom no contract exists.

Legal counsel in the case drew attention to the US case of *Ultramares Corporation v. Touche*, where the court decided that auditors were not liable for negligence to a plaintiff who lent money on the strength of accounts on which the auditor had reported, but which they did not know were required for the purpose of obtaining financial assistance or would be shown to the plaintiff. In so deciding, the court recognised that it would be quite wrong to expose the auditors to a potential liability "in an indeterminate amount for an indefinite time to an indeterminate class".

**Conclusion** The *Hedley Byrne* decision modified the liability of accountants for professional negligence in an important but limited respect. It did not introduce a new concept of negligence. Negligence must first be shown. Auditors may owe a duty of care to those not having a contractual or fiduciary relationship and may be negligent if, and only if, they know, or ought to have known, that a financial report, account or statement prepared by them has been prepared for a special purpose or transaction, will be shown to a particular person or class of persons and may be relied upon by that person or class of persons in that particular connection.

The *Hedley Byrne* decision underlines the importance of observing best practice, and legal counsel has further advised that, where an accountant specifically restricts the scope of his report or expresses appropriate reservations in a note attached to and referred to in the financial statements he has prepared or the report to which he has made thereon, this can constitute a disclaimer, which will be effective against any action for negligence brought against him by the third parties.

### Anns v. Merton London Borough Council (1977)

In this case, a local authority did not adequately inspect a building (block of flats), which was later found to have inadequate foundation, causing the flats to suffer from structural defects. The court held that the local authority owed a duty of care to the residents. This introduced the principle of proximity and the concept of reasonable foreseeability (in that the council would have been expected to reasonably foresee that an inadequate inspection of the building could have led to later structural defects impacting on the residents).

This was recognised in the Irish case of *Siney v. Dublin Corporation* (1980), where the Supreme Court ruled that the local authority providing housing was under a duty of care to a tenant to ensure that the housing was fit for human habitation.

These cases, although not involving auditors, led to a wider definition of third-party liability than that given in the *Candler v. Crane* case (see above). The courts will consider the relationship between the person suffering the injury and the alleged wrongdoer, and whether there is any factor that can reduce or limit the duty of care owed.

### Jeb Fastners v. Marks Blooms & Co. (1981)

In this case, the defendant was the auditor of a company that was aware it was in need of refinancing. The company's accounts contained assets that were significantly overvalued and the auditors failed to detect this misstatement. The court said that the auditor owed a duty of care to any person or any class of persons whom they do not know but should be able to reasonably foresee might use the audited financial statements of the company for their investment decision.

It was held that the auditor should have foreseen that the audited financial statements would have been used for a purpose of valuing the company in a takeover and that by doing so would suffer a financial loss.

No damages were awarded, however, as the main reason for the takeover was to obtain the services of two of the directors of the company being acquired. It was held that the plaintiff would not have acted any differently had they known that the assets were overvalued and therefore it was not shown that they had suffered economic losses due to the auditor's negligence.

### *James McNaughton Paper Group v. Hicks Anderson & Co. (1991)*

James McNaughton was considering the takeover of a group of companies. Draft accounts were prepared by a firm of accountants, Hicks Anderson & Co., and they held meetings with the claimant where they made representations that the target company was breaking even. Following the takeover, this was found to be inaccurate and the target takeover group was, in fact, insolvent. James McNaughton Paper Group took an action against Hicks Anderson, claiming that they would not have proceeded with the takeover had they known the true financial position and they had relied on the representations in making their decision. The court decided that no duty of care was owed to the plaintiff because:

- the accounts were prepared for the target company and not for McNaughton;
- the accounts were in draft form;
- the accountants were not involved in negotiations;
- the accounts showed a loss, so it was clear that the company was in a poor state;
- it was expected McNaughton would consult with their own financial experts; and
- the representations made were general and did not change the figures in the accounts.

This case would seem to put more obstacles in front of third parties in attempting to take an action following on from the *Caparo* decision (see above).

### *Morgan Crucible v. Hill Samuel & Co. (1991)*

Morgan Crucible made a takeover bid for First Castle Electronics plc. The chairman of the target company recommended to the shareholders that the bid be rejected in a circularisation sent. More circulars, which were also issued by the merchant bank Hill Samuel, referring to the audited financial statements and the unaudited interim statements, were sent. They also circularised a profit forecast showing an expected increase in profits of 38%. This forecast contained a letter from the company's auditors stating that the forecast had been prepared in accordance with the company's stated accounting policies and was made after due and careful inquiry.

Morgan Crucible had an increased offer accepted. They subsequently found that the company they had acquired was worthless and sued the merchant bank, the auditors and the directors as they felt it was foreseeable that they would rely on the circularisations that were issued and the profit forecast. They claimed that the accounting policies were flawed and statements negligently prepared, with the profit being overstated. They argued that all these factors had led them to their bid price.

The court, relying on the *Caparo* decision, initially dismissed the claim. Morgan Crucible appealed. The Court of Appeal found that, as they were an identified bidder, it was reasonable that they would rely on the representations. It was held that there was, in fact, a relationship of proximity between each of the defendants and the plaintiffs, thus giving rise to a duty of care. The case was sent forward for trial.

### ADT Ltd v. BDO Binder Hamlyn (1996)

Binder Hamlyn issued an unqualified audit report on the financial statements of Britannia Securities Group, which ADT was considering taking over. A partner of Binder Hamlyn attended a meeting with ADT, where he confirmed that the financial statements showed a true and fair view of the target company's state of affairs. ADT, relying on this representation, completed the takeover, only to find that the company was worth £40 million and not the £105 million purchase price paid.

The judge held that Binder Hamlyn owed a duty of care to ADT based on the representations made at the meeting, as Binder Hamlyn knew the purpose for which the information was to be used. The judge awarded ADT £65 million, the difference between the price paid and subsequent value found to be correct. Binder Hamlyn stated that it intended to appeal and the case was subsequently settled out of court.

**2**

# ETHICS AND CORPORATE GOVERNANCE

## LEARNING OBJECTIVES

Having studied this chapter on ethics and corporate governance you should:

1. understand the overarching principles and supporting ethical provisions of the relevant ethical standards in either the Republic of Ireland or the UK/NI;
2. know the threats to integrity, objectivity and independence as outlined in the relevant ethical standards;
3. be able to demonstrate your understanding of the relevant ethical standard by being able to identify examples of threats and their respective safeguards;
4. know what is expected of the firm with regard to the internal system of quality control as laid down by ISQC 1; and
5. understand the relevance of the *UK Corporate Governance Code* and the *Irish Corporate Governance Annex* to the external auditor.

## CHECKLIST OF RELEVANT STANDARDS

The relevant standards, in both the RoI and the UK/NI, covered in this chapter are:

- In the RoI only: *Ethical Standard for Auditors (Ireland)* April 2017
- In the UK/NI only: *Ethical Standard (2016) – Integrity, Objectivity and Independence*
- International Standard on Quality Control 1 *Quality Control for Firms that Perform Audits and Reviews of Financial Statements, and other Assurance and Related Services Engagements* (ISQC 1)

Note, in general when referring to ISAs, it should be understood as referring to the UK and Ireland versions, unless otherwise specified as either ISA (UK) or ISA (Ireland). See the Introduction for an extant list of auditing standards for the RoI and the UK/NI.

## KEY TERMS AND DEFINITIONS IN THIS CHAPTER

**Audit Assurance Engagement**  The objective of an audit is to gain reasonable assurance about whether the financial statements as a whole are free from material misstatement, whether due to fraud or error, and to issue an auditor's report that includes an opinion.

**Corporate Governance**  Is "the system by which companies are directed and controlled" (Cadbury Report 1992).

**Covered Person**  Includes partners, principals, shareholders and employees of the audit firm who form part of the engagement team or the chain of command of the engagement, or are involved in non-audit services provided to the client entity.

**Engagement Partner**  The partner, or other person, in the firm responsible for the engagement and its performance, and for the report that is issued on behalf of the firm.

**Ethics Partner**  A partner in the firm "possessing the necessary seniority, relevant experience, authority and leadership levels … as having the responsibility for ensuring the firm's compliance with supporting ethical provision 1.1." (Ethical Standard (RoI and UK versions), paragraph 1.12)

**Independence**  Defined as "freedom from conditions and relationships which, in the context of an engagement, would compromise the integrity or objectivity of the firm or covered persons." (Ethical Standard for Auditors (Ireland), paragraph 120; Ethical Standard (2016), paragraph 123)

**Integrity**  Defined as "being trustworthy, straightforward, honest, fair and candid; complying with the spirit as well as the letter of applicable ethical principles, laws and regulations; behaving so as to maintain the public's trust in the auditing profession; and respecting confidentiality except where disclosure is in the public interest or is required to adhere to legal and professional responsibilities." (Ethical Standard for Auditors (Ireland), paragraph 120; Ethical Standard (2016), paragraph 123)

**Objectivity**   Defined as "acting and making decisions and judgments impartially, fairly and on merit (having regard to all considerations relevant to the task in hand but no other), without discrimination, bias, or compromise because of commercial or personal self-interest, conflicts of interest or the undue influence of others, and having given due consideration to the best available evidence." (Ethical Standard for Auditors (Ireland), paragraph I20; Ethical Standard (2016), paragraph I23)

**Persons Closely Associated**   Defined as: (a) a spouse (or equivalent); (b) a dependent child; (c) a relative who, during the engagement, has lived in the same household as the associated person for at least one year; (d) a firm whose managerial responsibilities are discharged by, or which is directly or indirectly controlled by, the firm / person with whom they are associated, or by any person mentioned in (a), (b) or (c) or in which the firm or any such person has a beneficial or other substantially equivalent economic interest; (e) A trust whose managerial responsibilities are discharged by, or which is directly or indirectly controlled by, or which is set up for the benefit of, or whose economic interests are substantially equivalent to, the firm / person with whom they are associated or any person mentioned in (a), (b) or (c).

**Third Party Test**   Consideration of whether the ethical outcomes required by the overarching principles and supporting ethical provisions have been met should be evaluated by reference to the perspective of an objective, reasonable and informed third party.

## 2.1 INTRODUCTION

In **Chapter 1**, Section 1.5, we noted that following the enactment of the legislation brought in to implement the EU Audit Regulation and Directive (ARD), the IAASA and the FRC were appointed the RoI's and UK's competent authorities, respectively. As such, they are responsible for the oversight of the audit market in their respective jurisdictions. As we have seen, this responsibility includes the setting of auditing and **ethical standards**.

To comply with the ARD, in June 2016 the FRC issued a revised ethical standard – *Ethical Standard (2016) – Integrity, Objectivity and Independence* (ES 2016) – for audits in the UK/NI. The IAASA, as it did for its ISAs, licensed this revised standard and reissued it with the necessary amendments reflecting Irish legislative differences as the *Ethical Standard for Auditors (Ireland) April 2017* (ESA 2017). In conjunction with ES 2016/ESA 2017, when considering ethical issues the *International Standard on Quality Control 1* (ISQC 1) should also be consulted.

In terms of corporate governance, the framework in both the RoI and UK/NI comprises the FRC's *UK Corporate Governance Code*, company legislation, and regulations such as the listing rules for listed companies. The implementation of the ARD also required the FRC to update the *UK Corporate Governance Code*, which it did in April 2016.

In the first part of this chapter we will broadly follow the structure of the ES 2016/ESA 2017, so in **Section 2.2** we examine the "overarching principles and supporting ethical provisions", which introduces the concept of professional ethics and the importance of integrity, objectivity and independence; in **Section 2.3**, the "general requirements and guidance", which includes the areas of compliance and assessment and identification of threats; and in **Sections 2.4–2.7**, specific circumstances that give rise to threats are addressed along with the guidance on how to safeguard against such threats.

**Section 2.8** discusses ISQC 1, which focuses on the **internal quality control system of the audit firm**. In studying this section you should understand the requirements of the audit firm with regard to implementing a sound system of quality control, as well as examples of policies and procedures that audit firms are expected to put in place.

Finally, in **Section 2.9** we introduce the topic of **corporate governance**. While corporate governance may seem apparently unrelated to the role of the external auditor, it has a number of impacts on the audit profession. At the close of this section you should have an appreciation of the similarities between the *UK Corporate Governance Code* (the 'Code'), the Irish Corporate Governance Annex (the 'Irish Annex') and the ES 2016/ESA 2017, and the impact of the Code on the performance of individual audits and on the auditing profession in general.

## 2.2  OVERARCHING PRINCIPLES AND SUPPORTING ETHICAL PROVISIONS

The primary objective of the audit of the financial statements of an entity is for the auditor to provide independent assurance to the shareholders/members that the directors have prepared the financial statements in a true and fair manner. There are a number of ethical issues which are of great importance to the client entity–auditor relationship because of the need for the auditor to be *seen* to be impartial and independent of the client entity, creating greater confidence in the auditor's opinion. It is not enough for the auditor to know that they are independent of the client entity, they need to demonstrate this independence to the outside world.

ES 2016 and ESA 2017 identify the overarching principles of integrity, objectivity and independence, along with related supporting ethical provisions. These are intended to ensure that the users of the financial statements can trust and be confident that the audit opinion is professionally sound and objective.

Part A of the ES 2016/ESA 2017, paragraphs 1 and 2, outlines the two overarching principles.
1. "The firm, its partners and all staff shall behave with integrity and objectivity in all professional and business activities and relationships."
2. "In relation to each engagement, the firm, and each covered person, shall ensure (in the case of a covered person, insofar as they are able to do so) that the firm and each covered person is free from conditions and relationships which would make it probable that an objective, reasonable and informed third party would conclude the independence of the firm or any covered person is compromised."

**Figure 2.1** helps to illustrate the relationship between integrity, objectivity and independence.

FIGURE 2.1: OVERARCHING PRINCIPLES

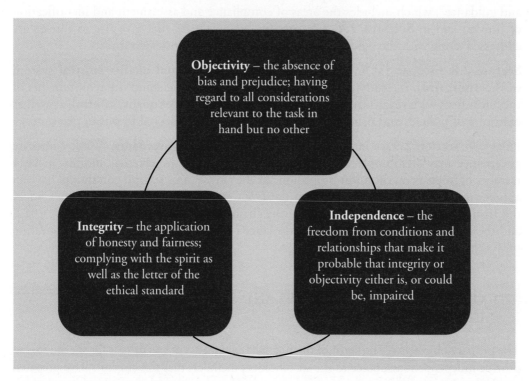

In respect of 'independence', Part A, paragraphs 2.1D–2.13, specify the **supporting ethical provisions** that require policies and procedures to be in place to ensure (insofar as is possible) that:

- The firm and each covered person is not compromised with respect to a client entity, including that they are not "involved in the decision-taking of any such entity".
- No existing or potential conflicts of interest between the audit firm and the client entity arise from direct or indirect relationships.
- The firm does not accept or continue any engagements if there is "any threat of self-review, self-interest, advocacy, familiarity or intimidation created by financial, personal, business, employment or other relationships" between the firm and the client entity.
- The "firm's independence is not compromised as a result of conditions or relationships that would compromise the independence of a network firm … or a third party firm".
- Conditions or relationships that do exist, notwithstanding the need for safeguards, do not compromise the independence of the firm or any covered person.
- Auditors "remain alert to conditions or relationships which could compromise the independence".
- Audit firm employees or **covered persons** "who become aware of any condition or relationship which could impair independence" should alert the **engagement partner** or **ethics partner**.
- Policies and procedures are in place to ensure prompt action of any items reported in the above item, including identification and implementation of safeguards or withdrawal as appropriate.

- That fee-setting policy precludes the practice of determining fees or partner and staff remuneration and evaluation in a manner that would compromise independence.
- No gifts or hospitality should be accepted unless the "value thereof [is] trivial or inconsequential".
- There is no acceptance or continuance of an engagement with a client entity with whom the firm is in litigation.
- The firm shall not provide non-audit services to a client entity where doing so would introduce a threat to independence.

Before we move on to look at the ES 2016/ESA 2017 in greater detail, it is useful to understand the overall structure of the standard – recognising that Part A is the primary objectives, while Part B is the achieving of these objectives (see **Figure 2.2**).

FIGURE 2.2: OVERVIEW OF THE ETHICAL STANDARD

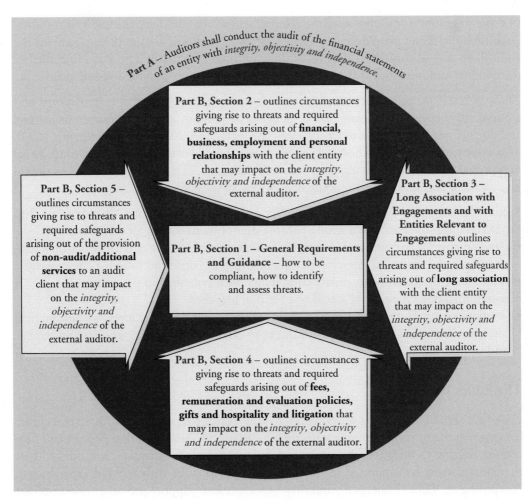

Part A – Auditors shall conduct the audit of the financial statements of an entity with *integrity, objectivity and independence.*

**Part B, Section 2** – outlines circumstances giving rise to threats and required safeguards arising out of **financial, business, employment and personal relationships** with the client entity that may impact on the *integrity, objectivity and independence* of the external auditor.

**Part B, Section 5** – outlines circumstances giving rise to threats and required safeguards arising out of the provision of **non-audit/additional services** to an audit client that may impact on the *integrity, objectivity and independence* of the external auditor.

**Part B, Section 1 – General Requirements and Guidance** – how to be compliant, how to identify and assess threats.

**Part B, Section 3 – Long Association with Engagements and with Entities Relevant to Engagements** outlines circumstances giving rise to threats and required safeguards arising out of **long association** with the client entity that may impact on the *integrity, objectivity and independence* of the external auditor.

**Part B, Section 4** – outlines circumstances giving rise to threats and required safeguards arising out of **fees, remuneration and evaluation policies, gifts and hospitality and litigation** that may impact on the *integrity, objectivity and independence* of the external auditor.

## 2.3 GENERAL REQUIREMENTS AND GUIDANCE

### Introduction

Having set out the overarching principles and their supporting ethical provisions, Part B, Section 1 of the ES 2016/ESA 2017 sets out general requirements and guidance on compliance, threats and safeguards. It highlights: the role of the ethics partner; identifying and assessing breaches and threats (potential or actual); identifying safeguards to protect against threats; the consideration of third parties who may be involved in audit engagements; at the end of the audit process, confirmation that any threats have been addressed; and that "those charged with governance" have been kept informed of any ethical issues and that any significant threats have been documented.

### Establishing Policies and Procedures

In order to ensure it complies with the requirement of the standard, the audit firm should establish policies and procedures to ensure that for all audits or assurance engagements the audit firm, and all connected to it (including all those who are in a position to influence the conduct and outcome of the audit), act with integrity, objectivity and independence.

These policies and procedures should be conducted within an effective organisational and administrative environment, one that is "designed to prevent, identify, eliminate or manage and disclose any threats to its independence" (ES 2016/ESA 2017 Part B, paragraph 1.2D). This organisational and administrative environment should have a system of recording actual or potential incidents threatening the integrity of the audit. All policies and procedures should give regard to the "scale and complexity of activities "of the auditor (paragraph 1.4D).

Section 1, paragraph 1.11 outlines some key policies and procedures that an audit firm should establish to "promote a strong control environment", some of which include:
- requirements for partners and staff to report instances of "family and other personal relationships" and "financial interests" in a client entity, or "decisions to join a client entity";
- monitoring mechanisms to ensure compliance with policies and procedures;
- communication channels of actual or potential breaches;
- "empowerment of its staff to communicate without fear to senior levels within the firm any concerns about the firm's commitment to quality work and professional judgment and values".

### The Ethics Partner

Each firm should designate a senior partner – the **ethics partner** – with the responsibility for ensuring the firm's compliance with the ES 2016/ESA 2017, and that policies and procedures relating to integrity, objectivity and independence are adequate. It is advised that the ethics partner be supported in this role by "other persons with relevant experience ... comprising an 'Ethics Function'", and that "sufficient staff support and other resources" are made available (paragraphs 1.12 and 1.21).

The role of the ethics partner includes:
- providing guidance to individual partners and staff to achieve a consistent approach to the application of the ethical standard;
- reporting any significant facts to those charged with governance (see below); and
- the provision of training, from induction to continuous professional development.

### Breaches

Where an actual or potential breach is identified, the **engagement partner**, in the first instance, or the ethics partner where appropriate, should assess the implications of such a breach. In doing so they should determine if safeguards can be put in place or if there is a need to withdraw from the audit engagement.

Unintentional breaches may arise and do not always call into question the firm's ability to provide an audit opinion. So long as adequate reporting mechanisms were in place that allowed prompt action by the ethics partner to address the breach and to identify the necessary safeguards, there is no threat to the integrity, objectivity or independence of the audit. All breaches, potential and actual, and their resulting safeguards/actions should be fully documented, including the rationale of the decision making.

### Identification and Assessment of Threats

An auditor needs to be aware of the conditions and relationships that could give rise to threats to integrity, objectivity or independence. **Table 2.1** outlines the categories of threats identified in ES 2016/ESA 2017, Part B, Section 1, paragraph 1.29. Specific examples of circumstances giving rise to each type of threat are discussed throughout the rest of this chapter.

TABLE 2.1: THREATS TO INTEGRITY, OBJECTIVITY AND INDEPENDENCE

| | |
|---|---|
| **Self-interest threat** | Arises where an auditor/audit firm has a financial or other interest in the client entity that might cause them to be reluctant to take actions that would adversely impact on their/its own interests (e.g. ownership of shares in the client entity). |
| **Self-review threat** | Arises when the results of a non-audit service performed by the auditor, or by others within the audit firm, are reflected in the financial statements. The auditor is likely to be reluctant to highlight errors if they themselves, or their audit firm, performed and were paid for the work. |
| **Management threat** | Arise when partners or employees of the audit firm take decisions on behalf of the **management** of the client entity. They can also arise where the results of non-audit services are used to make judgements and decisions. In such instances the auditor is not sufficiently objective when assessing the outcome of any such decisions that are subsequently reflected in the financial statements. |

| Advocacy threat | Arises when the auditor/audit firm act as an advocate on behalf of the client entity (e.g. as a legal advocate). To do so requires the auditor to adopt a position closely aligned to that of management, which creates an actual and perceived threat. |
|---|---|
| Familiarity (or trust) threat | Arises when the auditor/audit firm accept, or insufficiently question, the client entity's point of view due to the close relationship held, usually as a result of long association. |
| Intimidation threat | Arises when the auditor's conduct is influenced by fear or threats due to aggressive or dominating characters within the client entity's management team. |

The auditor should at all times consider the significance of threats to integrity, objectivity and independence when:
- accepting or retaining engagements;
- planning engagements;
- forming an opinion and signing the audit report for an engagement;
- accepting or continuing non-audit services; and
- when potential threats are reported.

Where threats are identified the engagement partner should "assess the effectiveness of the available safeguards and apply such safeguards as are sufficient to eliminate the threats or reduce them to a level where independence would not be compromised." (ES 2016, Part B, Section 1, paragraph 1.45; ESA 2017, Part B, Section 1, paragraph 1.39)

### Other Firms Involved in Engagements

The lead firm for any engagement is responsible for ensuring that any other involved firm is independent of the client entity. This is the specific responsibility of the engagement partner, who does so by obtaining **sufficient appropriate audit evidence** (see **Chapter 6**) to support that independence.

In an audit of **public interest entities (PIEs)**, ES 2016/ESA 2017 also requires that the client entity communicate its policy on the engagement of external auditors and non-audit services to others involved in an engagement – **and that the audit firm's engagement partner has verified this.**[1]

### Communication with Those Charged with Governance

Should any instances or matters arise that may impact upon the integrity, objectivity or independence of the firm or its covered persons, it is the responsibility of the **ethics partner** to inform those charged with governance, which includes the audit committee where relevant.

---

[1] ES 2016, Part B, Section 1, paragraph 1.55; ESA 2017, Part B, Section 1, paragraph 1.49.

The purpose of the communication is to "ensure full and fair disclosure", and will include information about the audit firm's ethical policies and processes, the potential threats and the safeguards in place.

In an audit of a PIE, ES 2016/ESA 2017 again requires additional communication to the audit committee, to include items such as:
- written disclosure of relationships;
- details of non-audit services, including related fees;
- written confirmation as to the independence of the firm and its covered persons;
- inconsistencies between the relevant ethical standard and the firm's policies for the provision of non-audit services as well as any apparent breach of that policy; and
- any independence issues.[2]

## Documentation

For each engagement the **audit working papers** should include documentation on any significant threats to objectivity, integrity and independence, including the safeguards applied to mitigate identified threats.

Specifically, before accepting or continuing any engagement, the firm should assess and document:
1. "whether it meets the ethical outcomes of the overarching principles and supporting ethical provisions", and that it complies with the requirements of the relevant ethical standard; and
2. whether there are any threats to its integrity, objectivity or independence, and the safeguards in place.

## Provisions Available for Audits of Small Entities

Section 6 of ES 2016/ESA 2017 provides exemptions to the rules for small company audits, which specifically excludes **public interest entities (PIEs)**. The definitions of small companies are laid down in the respective jurisdictional legislation. Section 6 takes into account the difficulties faced by small firms in applying Sections 1–5 when auditing small entities. Where an audit firm applies the exemptions allowed under Section 6, it must ensure it fully takes the steps outlined within it and that it discloses in the audit report that it has applied the Ethical Standard – Provisions Available for Audits of Small Entities (ES – PASE) (see ES 2016/ESA 2017, paragraphs 6.15–6.17).

These reduced rules include alternative provisions around the economic dependence rule and the self-review threat associated with the non-audit service rule (paragraphs 6.5–6.10). It also allows for exemption from: the management and advocacy threats associated with the provision of non-audit services (paragraphs 6.11 and 6.12); and the rules surrounding partners and other persons approved as a statutory auditor joining an audited entity (subject to provisions listed at paragraphs 6.13 and 6.14).

---

[2] ES 2016, Part B, Section 1, paragraph 1.66; ESA 2017, Part B, Section 1, paragraph 1.59.

## 2.4 FINANCIAL, BUSINESS, EMPLOYMENT AND PERSONAL RELATIONSHIPS

Part B, Section 2 of the ES 2016/ESA 2017 addresses threats to integrity, objectivity and independence from specific circumstances in connection with financial, business, employment and personal relationships with the client entity. It also gives examples of safeguards that can, in some circumstances, eliminate the threat, or at least reduce it to an acceptable level.

When assessing these relationships and the potential threat that they pose, the role or position of the person in the relationship must be considered. A person who has the ability to influence, i.e. an "**influential individual**", such as a senior partner, will generally be subject to greater scrutiny and restriction than a more junior member of the audit team. This extends to "**persons closely associated**" with the influential individual, including family members. It should be noted that the identified threat should be material in the context of the entity and the individual.

**Table 2.2** outlines the principal threats of such relationships, and the safeguards that can be adopted to mitigate them.

TABLE 2.2: FINANCIAL, BUSINESS, EMPLOYMENT AND PERSONAL RELATIONSHIPS –
THREATS AND POSSIBLE SAFEGUARDS

| Examples of Specific Threats | Type of Threat(s) | Possible Safeguards |
|---|---|---|
| Auditor/ audit firm hold a direct or indirect financial interest in the client entity | Self-interest | • First, it is important to note that the ethics partner should be made aware of any direct or indirect financial interests of partners, staff or covered persons.<br>• An influential individual (i.e. someone in a position of responsibility or managerial employee participating in the audit) who has a financial interest in the client entity:<br>  ♦ should not be permitted to work on the audit engagement or non-audit services and, where possible, in any department servicing the client; or<br>  ♦ should dispose of the interest (including those of a **person closely associated** with the influential individual).<br>• A policy should exist permitting a minimum shareholding that is not material to the client entity, or the individual (or covered persons). |

| | | |
|---|---|---|
| | | • If the engagement partner (or a person closely associated with them, which could include immediate family members, e.g. spouse or dependant) holds a direct or indirect interest in the client entity, they should either:<br>  ◆ dispose of the interest; or<br>  ◆ the audit firm should decline (or withdraw from) the engagement where disposal of the shares is not an option. |
| Acceptance or provision of loans or guarantees **or** Existence of a business relationship | Self-interest Intimidation | • The audit firm, its partners, influential individuals and covered persons to the audit of a client entity should not be permitted to accept or provide loans or guarantees to clients other than in the normal course of business under normal business terms (arm's-length transactions).<br>• If influential individuals engage in such activities, they should not be permitted to work on the audit engagement or non-audit services and, where possible, in any department servicing the client entity. Alternatively, the influential individual (or their covered persons) should cease the activity. |
| | | • If the firm or a partner (or connected person to that partner) has engaged in such activities and cannot withdraw from the activity, then the firm should decline (or withdraw from) the engagement. |
| Secondment of audit firm staff to client entity | Self-review Management | • The secondment of partners should not be permitted.<br>• Other audit firm staff can be seconded but only for a short period and should not perform non-audit services that would not be permitted under Part B, Section 5 of the relevant ethical standard.<br>• Individuals seconded should have no future involvement in the audit until the specified period of time has passed.<br>• Audit firm staff should not make decisions or judgements that are the responsibility of management, e.g. authorising transactions, preparation of financial statements. |
| Audit firm staff taking direct employment with client entity | Familiarity | • The audit firm should take swift action to ensure that no further work is performed by the individual on that client entity and that no significant connections remain between the firm and the individual after their departure.<br>• Furthermore, the auditor should be aware of company legislation that prohibits partners from taking up key positions in client entities for a specified period of time. |

| Family members employed by a client entity in a financial role or a role deemed to influence financial decisions | Self-interest Familiarity | • In this situation, the individual employed by the audit firm shall not be permitted to work on or have any influence on the respective audit.<br>• If it is a person closely associated with a partner of the audit firm, then the audit firm should decline or withdraw from the engagement. |

## 2.5  LONG ASSOCIATION WITH ENGAGEMENTS AND WITH ENTITIES RELEVANT TO ENGAGEMENTS

Long association between the auditor/audit firm and the client entity can, naturally, develop into a close business relationship. When one becomes overly familiar with an individual it can create a sense of obligation towards that individual, which may be in conflict with one's duty to report on their responsibilities with respect to the financial statements.

The ES 2016/ESA 2017, Part B, Section 3, paragraph 3.1, states:

"The firm shall establish policies and procedures to monitor the length of time and extent of involvement that partners and staff in senior positions, including those from other disciplines, serve as members of the engagement team(s) for recurring engagements for particular entities."

**Table 2.3** below outlines specific threats of long association with the client entity and the possible safeguards.

TABLE 2.3: LONG ASSOCIATION – THREATS AND POSSIBLE SAFEGUARDS

| Examples of Specific Threats | Type of Threat(s) | Possible Safeguards |
|---|---|---|
| Long association with the audit engagement | Self-interest Self-review Familiarity | • Rotation of partners and senior members of the engagement team after a predetermined number of years. (***Note:*** with respect to listed entities and PIEs, there is a more prescriptive ruling that requires, for example, the audit engagement partner to rotate every five years.)<br>• Introduction of a review partner with no prior involvement.<br>• Commission an independent engagement quality control review. |

With regard to PIEs, more onerous rules prescribe that "the key audit partners responsible for carrying out a statutory audit of a public interest entity shall cease their participation in the statutory audit of the audited entity not later than **five years** from the date of their appointment. They shall not participate again in the statutory audit of the audited entity before five years have elapsed following that cessation" (ES 2016, paragraph 3.10R; ESA 2017, paragraph 3.9R). The same provision applies in respect of listed entities. Specific audit firm rotation rules also exist with respect to PIEs as laid down in Article 17 of the EU Audit Regulation 2014, whereby the audit firm should ensure that it does not accept or continue an audit engagement that would cause those requirements not to be complied with.

## 2.6  FEES, REMUNERATION AND EVALUATION POLICIES, GIFTS AND HOSPITALITY, LITIGATION

Part B, Section 4 of the ES 2016/ESA 2017 provides guidance on fees, remuneration and evaluation policies, gifts and hospitality and litigation. As such, it addresses some critical issues that have led to concerns and significant frauds over the years. For example, the issue of high proportional fees is considered to be a main factor in the failure of Arthur Andersen to report Enron's accounting irregularities. Naturally, a business will strive to maintain its most significant customers. When it comes to audit firms, however, clients who represent a significant percentage of the overall fees of a firm can cause it to behave in a manner that protects the relationship at the cost of the firm's integrity. Put simply, the auditor does not want to risk losing a large-fee client and for this reason may be reluctant to issue a qualified audit opinion.

To avoid actual or perceived threats to the audit firm's integrity, objectivity and independence, the auditor should be able to freely question and, if necessary, disagree with the client entity's management, regardless of consequences to their own position. Section 4 lays out guidelines for the auditor to mitigate against the threats in each of the areas given.

### Fees

The majority of Section 4 is concerned with the area of fees. The key requirements and safeguards are:
- the audit should be assigned "sufficient partners and staff with appropriate time and skill to perform the engagement in accordance with all applicable Engagement and Ethical Standards, irrespective of the engagement fee to be charged" (paragraph 4.1);
- fees for engagements "shall not be influenced or determined by the provision of non-audit/additional services" (paragraph 4.3D);
- an engagement shall not be undertaken on a contingent fee basis, i.e. where the fee is calculated on a predetermined basis relating to the outcome of the engagement (paragraph 4.6R); and
- where overdue fees owed by the client entity "cannot be regarded as trivial", the engagement partner and ethics partner should consider whether it can continue the engagement – overdue fees, if substantial, may influence decisions (ES 2016, paragraph 4.29; ESA 2017, paragraph 4.25).

Where combined audit and non-audit fees of a public interest entity or other listed entity regularly exceed 10% of the annual fee income of the firm, the firm/auditor shall not act as auditor, or shall resign as auditor or not stand for reappointment, as appropriate, or alternatively relinquish non-audit services to reduce the fees earned from the entity. The size of the fee relative to the total fees of the firm may influence the decision-making of the auditor if they feel that the decision will jeopardise the future of the engagement (i.e. the firm will lose a large client that is influential to its profitability). One should note that where profits are not shared on a firm-wide basis, the 10% is calculated by reference to the engagement partner's share of profit.

The auditor should follow the same rules and procedures where the total fees receivable from a non-listed entity that is not a public interest entity will regularly exceed 15% of the annual fee income of the firm.

Compliance with these key requirements will protect the audit firm's integrity, objectivity and independence – and its reputation.

## Remuneration and Evaluation Policies

Section 4 requires an audit firm to ensure that the remuneration packages and performance reviews of audit team members are not based on the selling of non-audit services to the client entity. If the audit engagement team is focused on winning non-audit services with audit clients in order to boost their remuneration, they may place the importance of this above their responsibility to adequately and fairly audit the financial statements. In other words, there is a risk that in trying to win new business, the auditor may not want to upset the client and so might ignore or downplay issues to maintain a good relationship.

## Gifts and Hospitality

Section 4 further provides that the audit firm, its partners and 'influential individuals' (including persons closely associated with them – see **Section 2.4**) are not permitted to accept gifts or hospitality from an audit client, unless the gift is insignificant. Although not specified in any standards, cash of all values is deemed significant. The auditor should use their own judgement in assessing gifts and hospitality offered by the client and if in any doubt, should consult with the ethics partner.

## Threatened and Actual Litigation

Litigation instances can arise where the client entity sues the audit firm for damages. For example, while testing the client entity's computer system the auditor might inadvertently cause it to crash, resulting in a financial loss to the client entity in down-time and lost revenue – for which it may commence a law suit against the audit firm.

With respect to threatened and actual litigation against the auditor by the client entity, the guidance from Section 4 is straightforward: if it is anything other than insignificant, the audit firm shall either not continue with or not accept the audit engagement.

Examples of specific threats and their safeguards that are associated with fees, remuneration and evaluation, gifts and hospitality and litigation are given in **Table 2.4** below.

TABLE 2.4: FEES, REMUNERATION AND EVALUATION, GIFTS AND
HOSPITALITY AND LITIGATION – THREATS AND POSSIBLE SAFEGUARDS

| Examples of Specific Threats | Type of Threat | Possible Safeguards |
|---|---|---|
| Excessive fees | Self-interest Intimidation | • Reduce non-audit services to audit clients.<br>• Withdraw from or decline the engagement where non-audit services cannot be reduced.<br>• Withdraw from or decline audits that will represent >15% (10% plcs) of overall annual fee income of the firm.<br>• Introduce early warning policies and procedures whereby fees approaching 5%–10% for listed companies, or 10%–15% for non-listed companies are flagged for monitoring by the ethics partner. |
| Threatened/actual litigation by client entity | Self-interest Advocacy Intimidation | Decline or withdraw from the engagement. |
| Gifts and hospitality | Self-interest Familiarity | Determine policies and procedures outlining what is reasonable in terms of frequency, nature and value of hospitality and gifts. |
| Remuneration and evaluation of audit personnel | Self-interest | A policy should exist prohibiting any element of remuneration or performance reviews from being connected to the winning of non-audit services from audit clients. |

## 2.7 NON-AUDIT/ADDITIONAL SERVICES

The provision of non-audit services to an audit client gives rise to a multitude of threats and so for many it is the most significant section of the ES 2016/ESA 2017. Part B, Section 5 describes non-audit services as "professional services" provided to not only the client entity, but to any affiliates of the client entity or to another entity in respect of the client entity.[3] Professional services can include tax consultancy, IT consultancy, performance of due diligence for proposed acquisitions, payroll services or assistance with investment appraisals.

**Table 2.5** outlines the types of threat that the provision of non-audit services can give rise to and the possible safeguards.

---

[3] ES 2016, Part B, Section 5, paragraph 5.8; ESA 2017, Part B, Section 5, paragraph 5.7.

TABLE 2.5: NON-AUDIT SERVICES – THREATS AND POSSIBLE SAFEGUARDS

| Examples of Specific Threats | Type of Threat | Possible Safeguards |
|---|---|---|
| Provision of non-audit services | Self-interest<br>Self-review<br>Management<br>Advocacy<br>Intimidation | • Policies and procedures to communicate the intended provision of non-audit services to the audit engagement partner for their consideration.<br>• Consideration of the concept of "informed management" (see below).<br>• Avoidance of decisions or judgements that are the responsibility of management, e.g. authorising transactions. preparation of financial statements.<br>• If considered to be inconsistent with the objectives of the audit of the financial statements, the audit firm should either:<br>  ♦ not undertake the non-audit service; or<br>  ♦ not accept/withdraw from the audit engagement. |

The most common non-audit service provided to audit clients is accounting services. It is specifically noted that unless there is "**informed management**", the provision of accounting services can pose a management threat (ES 2016, paragraph 5.154; ESA 2017, paragraph 5.144). The concept of informed management is recognised in paragraph 1.29 and exists when a member of the client entity's management, who has the "capability to make independent management judgments" and who is authorised to do so, is designated to receive the results of the non-audit/additional service. The results of non-audit/additional services should be supported by "objective analysis" and reasonable alternatives given. Paragraph 1.29 further states that: "In the absence of such informed management it is unlikely that any other safeguards can eliminate a management threat or reduce it to a level where independence is not compromised".

Before accepting an engagement for the provision of non-audit services, the audit engagement partner should be notified. It is for them to consider:

• the relevance and impact of the subject matter (of the non-audit service) on the financial statements of the entity;
• how much professional judgement will be required by the non-audit service;
• the size of the engagement and its associated fee;
• the basis on which fees are to be calculated; and
• finally, the staff who would work on or be involved in the non-audit service.

As one can see from **Table 2.5**, the provision of non-audit services to an audit client gives rise to a larger number of threats than any other matter discussed. A pertinent example is Arthur Andersen, whose non-audit services to Enron represented 52% of its fee income. The Enron scandal illustrates the importance of safeguarding against threats to the independence (and integrity and objectivity) of the auditor. A summary of the relevant facts is given below.

THE ENRON SCANDAL[4]

The Enron scandal came to light in 2001 and led to the bankruptcy of the Enron corporation. Arthur Andersen, having audited Enron's accounts for 16 years, was initially found guilty of obstruction of justice in relation to the reported shredding of documents relating to Enron. The United States District Court later overturned this ruling, but Arthur Andersen had already closed its doors due to the mass of audit engagements brought to an end by its other clients.

Enron's downfall was caused by a series of issues concerning revenue recognition, marked-to-market accounting (accounting for the fair value of an asset or liability by reference to the current market price) and the use of special-purpose entities to manage risks associated with poorly performing assets. Fuelling this was a series of corporate governance failures relating to excessive executive remuneration (which was, ultimately, the driver of a dysfunctional corporate culture), and a lack of financial risk-management (hedging of risk through special-purpose entities owned by Enron itself).

Arthur Andersen is alleged to have engaged in the reckless application of auditing standards, driven by a conflict of interests. This cannot be fully determined due to the shredding of thousands of documents in connection with its audit of Enron. The Houston firm of Arthur Andersen, the office responsible for the Enron engagement, obtained fees representing approximately 27% of its public fee income. It is believed that Andersen's audit was either:
(a) influenced by the size of annual fee; or
(b) carried out incompetently.

The magnitude of the effects felt by Enron's collapse led to the introduction of the Sarbanes–Oxley Act of 2002 (SOX), the main provisions of which include:
• the restriction of public accounting companies providing non-audit services to audit clients;
• the introduction of the Public Company Accounting Oversight Board;
• the requirement that directors sign off on the annual reports and, in particular, on their confidence with respect to internal controls;
• the increased disclosure of company relationships with unconsolidated entities;
• the requirement for the audit committee of the client entity to be independent; and
• the renunciation of certain director emoluments.

SOX is a US federal law and as such relates only to those companies (and their subsidiaries) listed on the New York Stock Exchange (NYSE). While SOX is not enforced in the RoI or the UK/NI, local auditors are often exposed to companies that are required to comply with SOX due to their connection with a company listed on the NYSE.

## 2.8 INTERNATIONAL STANDARD ON QUALITY CONTROL 1

Having established the **need** for auditors to safeguard against threats to their integrity, objectivity and independence by acting within the relevant ethical standard, we can now consider how they actually go about doing this. The answer is by the implementation of

---

[4] To follow the events that led to the collapse of Enron, two documentary films have been made: *Enron: The Smartest Guys in the Room* and *The Crooked E: The Unshredded Truth about Enron*.

a **system of internal control** within the audit firm. Without detailed policies, procedures and guidance around ethical issues, staff may knowingly or inadvertently engage in activities that could be damaging to the audit firm. When we refer to **quality control**, we must consider it at two levels: at a 'macro' level that considers the ethical quality control of the organisation as a whole; and at an 'engagement' level, which considers the ethical quality control of a specific engagement being carried out.

The International Standard on Quality Control 1 *Quality Control for Firms that Perform Audits and Reviews of Financial Statements, and other Assurance and Related Services Engagements* (ISQC 1) outlines an audit firm's responsibility with respect to a system of quality control for audits of financial statements, and for reviews of the performance of that audit. ISQC 1 is closely linked to the ethical standard (ES 2016 or ESA 2017) and states in its opening paragraph that it should be read in conjunction with the ethical requirements.

ISQC 1, paragraph 3, describes the audit firm's system of control as consisting of "policies designed to achieve the objective set out in paragraph 11 and the procedures necessary to implement and monitor compliance with those policies". Paragraph 11 reads:

"The objective of the firm is to establish and maintain a system of quality control to provide it with reasonable assurance that:
(a) The firm and its personnel comply with professional standards and applicable legal and regulatory requirements; and
(b) Reports issued by the firm or engagement partners are appropriate in the circumstances."

The standard prescribes guidelines on the elements that should be included in an audit firm's internal quality control environment by outlining the areas where a set of policies and procedures should exist to support the ethical behaviour of the auditor. These are:
1. **Leadership responsibilities for quality** within the audit firm should be assigned and should clearly set out the responsibilities to promote an internal culture that recognises the importance of quality.
2. Relevant **ethical requirements policies and procedures**, which allow the firm to monitor its compliance with ethical requirements.
3. **Policies and procedures for acceptance and continuance** of client relationships.
4. **Human resource policies and procedures** that help to ensure sufficient, competent and capable personnel are available to carry out audits.
5. **Engagement performance policies and procedures** promoting consistency, supervision and review of responsibilities with respect to the performance of each engagement carried out by the firm.
6. **Monitoring of quality control** procedures and evaluation, communication and remedy of deficiencies.

ISQC 1, paragraph 16D-2, also requires the auditor/audit firm to ensure it has "sound administrative and accounting procedures"; embedded "internal quality control mechanisms" that help with decisions and procedures at all levels throughout the firm; "effective procedures for risk assessment"; and "effective control and safeguard arrangements for information processing systems".

The above demonstrates the expectations of how an auditor/audit firm ensures compliance with the ES 2016/ESA 2017. It is not sufficient for an audit firm to rely on the ethics of its individual staff members; rather, it should introduce a system that prevents, detects and safeguards against threats to independence.

Following the myriad corporate scandals that have occurred over the last decade, the issue of professional ethics is an increasingly important topic for discussion, both globally and locally. Considering the importance of independence not only to the individual firm but to the auditing profession as a whole, it is paramount that the auditor repairs the negative perception held by the public. This can be achieved by ensuring strict adherence to the ethical and quality control standards.

The importance of business and professional ethics is not just one associated with the auditing profession, it is a topic that has received dedicated attention following a wave of corporate governance failings in the UK and the RoI. Corporate governance encourages directors to conduct business with integrity and fairness. In **Section 2.9**, the concept of corporate governance and how it relates to the external auditor is discussed.

## 2.9 CORPORATE GOVERNANCE

The framework for corporate governance in the RoI and the UK/NI comprises the *UK Corporate Governance Code* ('the Code'), company legislation, and regulations such as the listing rules for listed companies. As noted in **Chapter 1**, as part of its implementation of the EU Audit Regulation and Directive (ARD), in June 2016 the FRC completed updates to the Code, its auditing standards and its guidance on audit committees. The changes to the Code were primarily associated with a new provision requiring the audit committee as a whole to have competence relevant to the sector in which the entity operates; and the removal of the provision relating to the tender of audit services every 10 years, which is superceded by the Competition and Markets Authority (CMA) and EU requirements for mandatory tendering and rotation of audit firms.

**Figure 2.3** summarises the evolution of corporate governance in the UK and the RoI.

### What is Corporate Governance?

**Corporate governance** can be simply defined as "the system by which companies are directed and controlled" (*Report on the Committee on the Financial Aspects of Corporate Governance,* commonly known as 'The Cadbury Report', 1992). The *UK Corporate*

## FIGURE 2.3: THE EVOLUTION OF CORPORATE GOVERNANCE IN THE UK AND RoI

Failures in corporate governance in the UK in the early 1990s, such as Maxwell Communications and the Bank of Credit & Commerce International (BCCI), led the Financial Reporting Council (FRC), the London Stock Exchange and the accounting profession to set up a committee to investigate the growth in numbers of such failures. This committee, headed by Sir Adrian Cadbury, produced the Cadbury Report in 1992.

The Greenbury Report was issued in 1995. In 1998, a review of the Cadbury and Greenbury reports by the Hampel Committee resulted in the *Combined Code.*

In 1999 the Turnbull Report provided direction on the internal control requirements of the *Combined Code,* including how to carry out risk management. In the wake of the Enron scandal in the US and the collapse of Arthur Andersen, the Smith Report on the independence of external auditors was issued to the UK Government in 2003. Additionally, Derek Higgs carried out a review of the role and effectiveness of non-executive directors and of audit committees, fuelled by unrest resulting from the Enron, WorldCom and Tyco collapses in the US. In 2002 the US introduced new legislation, under the Sarbanes–Oxley Act, designed to protect investors by improving accuracy and reliability of corporate disclosures. Instead of introducing new legislation, the UK opted to review the internal control provisions within the *Combined Code.*

Essentially a consolidation and refinement of all reports and codes issued to date relating to good corporate governance, the *UK Corporate Governance Code* was published in 2010 by the FRC. It requires listed companies to disclose how they have complied with the Code and to explain where they have not complied with it (the 'comply or explain' approach).

The crisis in the banking sector in the RoI, causing some banks to be nationalised, led the Central Bank of Ireland to issue a new corporate governance code dedicated to the reform of the financial services sector – the *Corporate Governance Code for Credit Institutions and Insurance Undertakings.* The *UK Corporate Governance Code* is still in use with respect to non-financial listed companies. The 'Irish Annex' (2010) implemented the nine recommendations arising from a report commissioned by the ISE and IAIM in early 2010.

*UK Corporate Governance Code* 2010 was updated in 2012, 2014 and again in 2016 (applicable to accounting periods beginning on or after 17 June 2016) to take account of the views of stakeholders, including listed companies, investors and audit firms. The 2016 Code reflected the changes needed to implement the EU Audit Regulation and Directive.

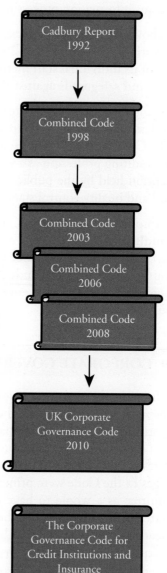

*Governance Code* sets out standards of good practice, or 'principles', in relation to board leadership and effectiveness, remuneration, accountability and relations with shareholders (see **Figure 2.4** below).

FIGURE 2.4: MAIN PRINCIPLES OF THE *UK Corporate Governance Code*

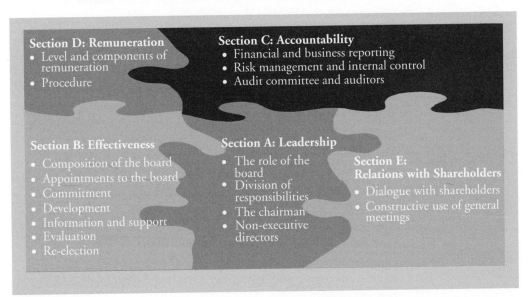

The Code consists of main principles – Leadership, Effectiveness, Accountability and so on – each of which has a more expansive 'supporting principle', and a number of provisions. However, the Code itself states that "[it] is not a rigid set of rules" and that "the way in which they [the principles] are applied should be the central question for a board". The Code notes that the "foundation of its flexibility" is its "**comply or explain**" approach – basically, companies are required to either state their compliance with the provisions or, if they have not complied, explain why.

The 'comply or explain' approach is intended to encourage companies to "provide a clear rationale for the action it is taking", and for shareholders or investors to "challenge companies' explanations if they are unconvincing". In this way it can be considered a self-regulating approach – shareholders will choose to divest and investors will decide not to invest if they are not satisfied with the corporate governance compliance. To better help companies and investors understand 'comply or explain', the FRC issued What Constitutes an Explanation under *'Comply or Explain'?: Report of Discussions between Companies and Investors.*[5] **Table 2.6** below outlines the key elements of the Code.

---

[5] See www.frc.org.uk/Our-Work/Publications/Corporate-Governance/What-constitutes-an-explanation-under-comply-or-ex.pdf (accessed April 2018).

TABLE 2.6: KEY ELEMENTS OF THE *UK Corporate Governance Code*

| Leadership | • "Every company should be headed by an **effective board**".<br>• "There should be a **clear division of responsibilities** ... between the running of the board and ... the running of the company".<br>• "The **chairman** is responsible for leadership of **the board**" – and is a separate role to the chief executive officer (CEO).<br>• "The board should **meet sufficiently regularly** to discharge its duties effectively".<br>• Non-executive directors should comprise at least half the board and "should constructively challenge and help develop proposals on strategy". |
|---|---|
| **Effectiveness** | • "The board and its committees should have the appropriate balance of skills, experience, independence and knowledge ... to discharge their respective duties".<br>• There should be "a formal, rigorous and transparent procedure" for the appointment, re-election, induction, training and evaluation of directors.<br>• "All directors should be able to allocate sufficient time to the company to discharge their responsibilities effectively".<br>• Information "should be supplied in a timely manner ... in a form and of a quality appropriate to enable it to discharge its duties". |
| **Accountability** | • "The board should present a fair, balanced and understandable assessment of the company's position and prospects" – including financial and business reporting.<br>• The board is responsible for risk management and internal control.<br>• The audit committee holds responsibility for internal audit.<br>• The board should be mindful of its responsibilities with respect to external auditors. |
| **Remuneration** | • "Executive directors' remuneration should be designed to promote the long-term success of the company".<br>• "Performance-related elements should be transparent, stretching and rigorously applied" – no director should be involved in deciding their own remuneration. |
| **Relations with shareholders** | • The board should ensure "a dialogue with shareholders based on the mutual understanding of objectives".<br>• "The board should use general meetings to communicate with investors and to encourage their participation". |

## The Irish Corporate Governance Annex

As noted previously, the *UK Corporate Governance Code* is recognised in the RoI as the framework for corporate governance. The Irish Stock Exchange (ISE (trading as Euronext Dublin since 27 March 2018)) in its *Listing Rules* includes Appendix 4 – The Irish Corporate

Governance Annex (the 'Irish Annex'), which declares that it recognises the Code as "the standard for corporate governance internationally" and regards it "as being the pre-eminent corporate governance code and is widely emulated".

As explained in the Irish Annex, the ISE's *Listing Rules* require all companies listed on the Main Securities Market to apply the Code, and to give details in their annual report of their compliance. It affirms the 'comply or explain' approach of the Code, requiring a company to "set out the nature, extent and reasons for non-compliance".

## Audit Committees

Section C: Accountability of the Code contains sub-section 'C.3: Audit Committee and Auditors', a provision of which is that the board should establish an audit committee of at least three or, in the case of smaller companies, two independent non-executive directors. At least one member of the committee should have "recent and relevant financial experience"; and as a whole it should have "competence relevant to the sector in which the company operates".

The main role and responsibilities of the audit committee should be set out in written terms of reference. The principal aspects include:
- monitoring the integrity of financial statements and related announcements;
- reviewing the company's internal financial controls and risk management systems;
- monitoring and reviewing the effectiveness of the company's internal audit function;
- making recommendations regarding appointments, re-appointment and removal of the external auditor, remuneration and terms of engagement;
- development and implementation of policy regarding engagement of the external auditor to supply non-audit services; and
- reviewing and monitoring the external auditor's independence and objectivity.

## Corporate Governance – the External Auditor and the Audit Committee

Set out below are some provisions of the 2016 *UK Corporate Governance Code* that have specific relevance to the external auditor or audit committee.
- Provision C1.1: "The directors should explain in the annual report their responsibility for preparing the annual report and accounts, and state that they consider the annual report and accounts, taken as a whole, is fair, balanced and understandable and provides the information necessary for shareholders to assess the company's position and performance, business model and strategy. There should be a statement [in the financial report or in the audit report] by the auditor about their reporting responsibilities."
- Provision C3.4: "Where requested by the board, the audit committee should provide advice on whether the annual report and accounts, taken as a whole, is fair, balanced and understandable and provides the information necessary for shareholders to assess the company's position and performance, business model and strategy."

- Provision C.3.7: "The audit committee should have primary responsibility for making a recommendation on the appointment, reappointment and removal of the external auditors. If the board does not accept the audit committee's recommendation, it should include in the annual report, and in any papers recommending appointment or re-appointment, a statement from the audit committee explaining the recommendation and should set out reasons why the board has taken a different position."

  *Note:* the 2016 update saw the removal of the requirement for companies to put the external audit contract out to tender at least every 10 years as this was superseded by the Competition and Markets Authority (CMA) and EU requirements for mandatory tendering and rotation of audit firms.

- Provision C.3.8: "A separate section of the annual report should describe the work of the [audit] committee in discharging its responsibilities. The report should include:
  - the significant issues that the committee considered in relation to the financial statements, and how these issues were addressed;
  - an explanation of how it has assessed the effectiveness of the external audit process and the approach taken to the appointment or reappointment of the external auditor, information on the length of tenure of the current audit firm when a tender was last conducted and advance notice of any retendering plans; and
  - if the external auditor provides non-audit services, an explanation of how auditor objectivity and independence are safeguarded."

### Developments in Corporate Governance

**Figure 2.3** above illustrated the evolution of corporate governance and the various reports that have been issued. It also highlights the changing face of corporate governance, with revisions and updates to the Code now occurring more frequently. In this section we will consider how the corporate governance landscape has changed in recent years.

The 2014 revisions of the Code focused on the importance of risk management and the enhancement of the quality of information available to investors. A statement with regard to **going concern** has always been a feature of the financial statements; however, the Code now requires the entity to state whether or not it believes it will be able to continue in operation, specifying the period covered by this statement and why it considers it appropriate. It is expected that the period assessed will be significantly longer than 12 months.

The Code also requires a more robust explanation of the principal risks faced by the entity and how these are being managed. Remuneration also features heavily in the changes and requires that companies design and implement remuneration policies and procedures promoting the long-term success of the entity. The changes also call for provisions enabling variable pay elements to be held for vesting periods so that performance can be validated in advance of payment. The subsequent revision in 2016 focused on the competence of the audit committee and the removal of a reference to 10-year rotation, making way for the EU Directive with respect to same.

While the Code only relates directly to listed companies (i.e. those listed on the London Stock Exchange and the Irish Stock Exchange), some larger private (unlisted) companies have embraced its principles and provisions. This is particularly so in the wake of the financial crisis and at a time when good corporate governance is more important than ever. For this reason, in early 2010 the European Confederation of Directors' Associations (ecoDa) published *Corporate Governance Guidance and Principles for Unlisted Companies in Europe*, a document intended to serve as a practical tool for unlisted companies seeking to improve their governance structures and policies.

Additionally, in the RoI in 2010, the Central Bank of Ireland issued the *Corporate Governance Code for Credit Institutions and Insurance Undertakings*, recognising the increased requirement for good corporate governance in financial institutions considering their impact on the wider economy. This was revised in 2015 and the impact of those revisions came into effect in January 2016.

The alleged corporate governance failures in the banking sector have raised concerns for external auditors, some of which face the risk of being sued for losses allegedly resulting from their failure to uncover the transactions involved. The auditing profession will, therefore, welcome further reform of corporate governance in the UK and the RoI, which can only serve to reduce the level of audit risk to which external auditing firms are exposed.

Governance compliance is showing signs of improvement, albeit at a slow rate, and there is much debate around the adequacy of the 'comply or explain' method of regulation. In its *Corporate Governance Review 2017*, Grant Thornton UK reported that 66% of FTSE 350 companies reviewed achieved full compliance with all provisions of the Code.[6] While this may seem a low percentage, it has seen a steady increase in the last five years – in 2012 it was only 51%. In the period covered by the review, 36 companies moved from non-compliance to compliance. The most common area of non-compliance relates to the provision requiring at least half the board to be independent non-executive directors.

The matter of remuneration has been a contentious issue for many years and continues to be a concern. In 2014, Grant Thornton UK's review reported that executives' "average remuneration over and above base salary represents 319% of basic pay" (the average basic salary of executives in the UK in 2014 was £427,540). The September 2014 revision of the Code attempted to address this by requiring boards to ensure that executive remuneration be "designed to promote the long-term success of the company", and to clearly show shareholders how this was being achieved. Despite this, the 2017 report highlights that although "61% of companies connect strategic priorities and KPIs [key performance indicators] ... only 20% go one step further and include clear linkage to executive remuneration".

Similarly, while it is encouraging that 62% of FTSE 350 companies comply with the strategic report requirements, only 14% were found to provide "high quality, informative insights". Also worrying is that only 22% of companies provided "insightful disclosures on

---

[6] Grant Thornton, *Corporate Governance Review 2017*. Available at www.grantthornton.co.uk/globalassets/1.-member-firms/united-kingdom/pdf/publication/corporate-governance-review-2017.pdf (accessed February 2018). The review covers the annual reports of 305 of the UK's FTSE 350 companies with years ending between April 2016 and April 2017. It assesses compliance with: the disclosure requirements of the *UK Corporate Governance Code* (2016 and 2014) and the requirements for narrative reporting as set out in section 414C CA 2006, as amended.

the review of effectiveness of internal controls". **Figure 2.5** gives some further highlights from Grant Thornton's *Corporate Governance Review 2017.*

FIGURE 2.5: HIGHLIGHTS FROM GRANT THORNTON'S *CORPORATE GOVERNANCE REVIEW 2017*

| | | | |
|---|---|---|---|
| Full compliance with the *UK Corporate Governance Code* reaches a new high of 66% (up from 62% in 2016).<br><br>95% comply with all but one or two of the 55 provisions of the Code. | 33% (27% in 2016) of companies now provide detailed accounts of their principal risks – an improvement due largely to greater disclosure of how principal risks are connected to strategy, why they are significant and how exposure to them has changed during the year. | 28 FTSE 350 companies were non-compliant with the 10-year tender requirement, which became effective for organisations with financial periods beginning on or after 17 June 2016. | Non-audit fees were £1.2 million (£1.6 million in 2016).<br><br>23% of the FTSE 350 had non-audit fees of more than 70% of their audit fee – the cap set in the EU audit reform. |

## 2.10 CONCLUSION

An auditor relies on their independence, therefore protecting it is central to their success. The ethical standards (as issued by the IAASA or the FRC) exist not only to protect the shareholders and other stakeholders but also to protect the auditor by giving them the tools to ensure that at all times high standards of integrity, objectivity and independence are maintained. The Ethical Standard provides practical examples of threats to independence, or perceived independence, and gives examples of how these can be safeguarded against.

The ISQC outlines the policies and procedures that should be in place in all audit firms to control the quality of work and compliance with ethical requirements. With respect to corporate governance, the *UK Corporate Governance Code* provides the basic principles of good corporate governance – the provisions of which have a **direct** link with the auditor, addressing areas such as the appointment of external auditors and the conduct expected of directors and the audit committee when engaging with external auditors.

The auditor is likely to encounter fewer risks in an organisation that has strong corporate governance.

## SUMMARY OF LEARNING OBJECTIVES

**Learning Objective 1** Understand the overarching principles and supporting ethical provisions of the relevant Ethical Standard in either the Republic of Ireland or the UK/NI.

Part A of the ES 2016/ESA 2017 requires an auditor to carry out the audit of financial statements with integrity, objectivity and independence and identifies a number of threats to these values, namely: self-interest threat; self-review threat; management threat; advocacy threat; familiarity threat; and intimidation threat. Independence is considered the cornerstone of auditing as it provides the freedom from situations and relationships that make it probable that a reasonable and informed third party would conclude that objectivity is either actually impaired or perceived to be impaired. It is the independence of the auditor that supports the credibility of the audit opinion issued by the auditor.

**Learning Objective 2** Know the threats to integrity, objectivity and independence as outlined in Part B, Sections 2–5 of the ES 2016/ESA 2017.

The auditor faces myriad threats to their integrity, objectivity and independence. They must ensure that they are alert to these threats and put in place solid systems and procedures to minimise the risk of any breaches.

Specific circumstances addressed by Part B of ES 2016/ESA 2017 are: Financial, Business, Employment and Personal Relationships (Section 2); Long Association with Engagements and with Entities Relevant to Engagements (Section 3); Fees, Remuneration and Evaluation Policies, Gifts and Hospitality, Litigation (Section 4); and Non-audit/Additional Services (Section 5) give rise to the threats noted in Part A above.

**Learning Objective 3** Be able to demonstrate your understanding of the relevant ethical standard by being able to identify examples of threats and their respective safeguards.

The audit firm should appoint an ethics partner to deal with the specific threats outlined in Part B, Sections 2–5, by implementing safeguards that protect against their impact on the independence (and integrity and objectivity) of the auditor.

The most significant threat being around the provision of non-audit services, due to the number of threats it gives rise to. The firm should have strong policies and procedures to manage the provision of non-audit services.

ISQC 1 clearly sets out the key elements of an appropriate system of quality control.

**Learning Objective 4** Know what is expected of the firm with regard to the internal system of quality control as laid down by ISQC 1.

ISQC 1, paragraph 3 describes the audit firm's system of control as consisting of "policies designed to achieve the objective set out in paragraph 11 and the procedures necessary to implement and monitor compliance with those policies." Paragraph 11 of ISQC 1 states that "the objective of the firm is to establish and maintain a system of quality control to provide it with reasonable assurance that:

(a) The firm and its personnel comply with professional standards and applicable legal and regulatory requirements; and

(b) Reports issued by the firm or engagement partners are appropriate in the circumstances."

**Learning Objective 5** Understand the relevance of the *UK Corporate Governance Code* and the *Irish Corporate Governance Annex* to the external auditor.

Corporate governance has evolved over the years and is codified in the RoI and the UK in the form of the *UK Corporate Governance Code* (issued by the FRC), which sets main principles with respect to board leadership, effectiveness, remuneration, accountability and relations with shareholders. The Code impacts the auditor directly, in that its provisions make specific reference, for example, to the external auditor's appointment. It also indirectly affects the audit by reducing risk in organisations and hence reducing **audit risk** for the auditor.

## QUESTIONS

### Self-test Questions

2.1   What is the primary objective of an audit of financial statements?

2.2   What is meant by the term 'integrity, objectivity and independence' in the relevant ethical standard?

2.3   Name and explain five threats to integrity, objectivity and independence.

2.4   What type of threat would exist if a director held shares in an audit client?

2.5   What type of threat would exist if an audit manager moved to an audit client?

2.6   What type of threat would exist if an audit firm guaranteed a loan to an audit client?

2.7   What type of safeguards would you expect to be in place to protect against the self-interest threat of a family member of an audit partner working as CFO in an audit client?

2.8   What type of safeguards would you expect to be in place to deal with the numerous threats caused by long association with an audit client?

2.9   Besides the relevant ethical standards, what other standards/codes exist to deal with the threat of long association?

2.10  Besides the direct provisions relating to the auditor in the *UK Corporate Governance Code*, why else would the auditor be interested in a company adopting its provisions?

## Review Questions

(See Suggested Solutions to Review Questions in **Appendix C.**)

### Question 2.1

Your firm has been the auditor of Trafford Ltd since the company's formation 10 years ago. The company's owner and managing director, Arnold Ferguson, is an old school friend of an audit partner in your firm, who has also acted as the partner on the audit of Trafford Ltd throughout the client's relationship with your firm. Arnold Ferguson has a reputation for being a very hands-on managing director, and is involved in many aspects of the business. He does not suffer fools gladly; indeed, he has been known on occasion to be vocal in his castigation of underperforming staff. In the past he has been quite curt in his replies to questions from members of the audit team; he does not respond well to his judgements being questioned. This approach has, however, served him well over the years, and under his leadership Trafford Ltd has grown to be one of the largest manufacturers of fertiliser in Ireland. As a result of this growth, the scope of the Trafford Ltd audit has grown significantly, with the audit fee increasing over the years. The fee for last year's audit was €/£65,000. Your firm's total fee income from audits last year was approximately €/£250,000. As a result of Trafford Ltd's growth, Arnold Ferguson is keen to keep a close watch on internal controls. He has recently contacted your audit partner to enquire about the possibility of your firm providing internal audit services to Trafford Ltd.

**Requirement** From the information provided, identify four threats to your firm's integrity, objectivity and independence and suggest what action your firm should take prior to commencing the next annual financial statement audit for this client, quoting relevant guidance.

### Question 2.2

An audit client of your firm, Istanbul Ltd, has informed you that they are considering raising funds through a stock market flotation. You have had a meeting with Istanbul Ltd's finance director, Rick Parry, who explained that he is aware that it will have to look closely at improving its corporate governance arrangements prior to listing. Rick has asked you for some advice on the type of structure and arrangements he needs to introduce to Istanbul Ltd.

**Requirement** Draft a memo to Rick explaining the types of corporate governance arrangement required of a listed company, including relevant guidance.

### Question 2.3

The managing partner of XL Audit & Co. is planning a training programme to help ensure the firm is fully compliant with the requirements of the International Standard on Quality Control 1. You have been asked to assist in compiling relevant material for the training presentation.

**Requirement** Set out the six elements of a system of quality control as set out in ISQC 1 and summarise the key features of each element that should be highlighted by the course presenter.

# 3

# FRAUD AND COMPLIANCE WITH LAWS & REGULATIONS

LEARNING OBJECTIVES

Having studied this chapter on fraud and compliance with laws and regulations you should:

1. understand fraud in the context of audit;
2. understand the types of fraud that can occur and the forms it can take;
3. be able to demonstrate your understanding of the 'fraud triangle' by identifying conditions that give rise to fraud;
4. be able to explain the respective responsibilities of the management of the entity and the auditor with regard to fraud;

5. be able to identify the necessary audit procedures to detect fraud;
6. know the duty and right of auditors to report to third parties;
7. understand what is meant by the term 'aggressive earnings management';
8. be able to identify ways in which computer-assisted audit techniques (CAATs) can assist the auditor in detecting fraud; and
9. know the auditor's responsibilities with respect to the client entity's compliance with laws and regulations.

## Checklist of Relevant Standards and Guidance

The relevant standards, both in the RoI and the UK/NI, covered in this chapter are:
- ISA 200 *Overall Objectives of the Independent Auditor and the Conduct of an Audit in Accordance with International Standards on Auditing*
- ISA 210 *Agreeing the Terms of Audit Engagements*
- ISA 240 *The Auditor's Responsibilities Relating to Fraud in an Audit of Financial Statements*
- ISA 250 Section A—*Consideration of Laws and Regulations in an Audit of Financial Statements*
- ISA 315 *Identifying and Assessing the Risks of Material Misstatement through Understanding the Entity and its Environment*
- ISA 330 *The Auditor's Responses to Assessed Risks*

Note, in general when referring to ISAs, it should be understood as referring to the UK and Ireland versions, unless otherwise specified as either ISA (UK) or ISA (Ireland). See the Introduction for an extant list of auditing standards for the RoI and the UK/NI.

## Key Terms and Definitions in this Chapter

**Analytical Review**    Comprises the analysis of movements and relationships between items of data. It involves the comparison of recorded values with expectations developed by the auditor.

**Auditor's Expert**    If expertise in a field other than accounting or auditing is necessary to obtain sufficient and appropriate audit evidence, the auditor shall determine whether to use the work of an auditor's expert.

**Forensic Audit**    A forensic audit involves the examination or investigation of an entity's (or individual's) financial information in order for it to be used as evidence in court. A forensic audit usually occurs as a result of allegations of fraud and its outcome forms part of the evidence for the prosecution.

**Fraud Risk Factors**   Events or conditions indicating an incentive or pressure to commit fraud or that provide an opportunity to commit fraud.

**Management Representations**   A written statement by management provided to the auditor to confirm certain matters or to support other audit evidence.

**Professional Scepticism**   Refers to a particular state of mind that an auditor must maintain to conduct audit engagements appropriately. The 'scepticism approach' enables the auditor to recognise that circumstances may exist that cause the financial statements to be materially misstated. The auditor should, therefore, be alert and remain cautious about information and events that indicate the existence of material misstatement.

**Segregation of Duties**   The division of key tasks in a transaction to ensure that no one individual can perform a transaction from beginning to end.

**Those Charged With Governance**   The person(s) with responsibility for overseeing the strategic direction of the entity and obligations related to the accountability of the entity, including overseeing the financial reporting process.

## 3.1 INTRODUCTION

There is a 'perception gap' between the public and the auditing profession in relation to the auditor's duty in respect of the detection of fraud and error. Auditors place their emphasis on ensuring that, subsequent to their independent examination, the financial statements show a **true and fair view** of the state of the entity's affairs at the reporting date, and of its profit or loss for the period then ended. In order to do this, they must determine, with reasonable certainty, whether or not the financial statements are materially misstated as a result of fraud, error or non-compliance with laws and regulations. The public believes, however, that it is the duty of the auditor to detect and prevent fraud and error. In fact, it is the responsibility of **management**, not the auditor, to ensure that the operation of the entity is conducted in accordance with relevant laws and regulations and that steps are taken to prevent and detect the occurrence of fraud.

When planning and performing the audit (see **Chapter 5**), to reduce audit risk to an acceptably low level the auditor must consider the risks of material misstatements in the financial statements due to fraud or error. The auditor is concerned with both fraud and error, since either may cause a material misstatement in the financial statements.

The impact of fraud can have extreme effects on many stakeholders. Where there is fraud, the shareholders, without doubt, suffer a loss, but so too do lenders, employees and suppliers.

The existence of the following factors increases the risk of fraud or error occurring:
- lack of **segregation of duties** between various functions;
- unnecessarily complex corporate structures;
- understaffed accounting departments;
- inadequate working capital;
- significant transactions with related parties; and
- volatile business environments.

Based on a risk assessment, the auditor should design audit procedures so as to have a reasonable expectation of detecting misstatements arising from fraud or error that are material to the financial statements. The auditor must gather **sufficient appropriate audit evidence** to determine whether the financial statements give a true and fair view of the state of the entity's affairs at the reporting date, and of its profit or loss for the period then ended. Therefore, the auditor should aim to identify all material fraud or error as these directly affect the audit opinion on the true and fair presentation of the financial statements. The auditor should, however, be mindful that there are various factors that hamper the detection of fraud.

It is important to note at this point that IAS 8 *Accounting Policies, Changes in Accounting Estimates and Errors*, at paragraph 41, states that:
> "Financial statements do not comply with IFRSs if they contain either material errors or immaterial errors made intentionally to achieve a particular presentation of an entity's financial position, financial performance or cash flows."

This chapter considers the nature of fraud and the impact it has had on the auditing profession. **Section 3.2** first outlines the difference between fraud and error; **Section 3.3** then discusses the primary types of fraud surrounding the audit of financial statements, and looks at some large-scale frauds, starting with the infamous collapse of Enron.

In **Section 3.4** we explore the conditions that are said to be present to cause people to commit fraud. This is known as the 'fraud triangle'. Having set the scene of fraud, these sections lead to a discussion on who is responsible for the prevention and detection of fraud, which we consider in **Section 3.5**.

**Section 3.6** discusses ISA 240 *The Auditor's Responsibilities Relating to Fraud in an Audit of Financial Statements*. In this key section of the chapter, we outline the audit procedures the auditor is required to carry out with respect to detecting fraud impacting on the financial statements of an entity. This section also discusses the auditor's responsibilities with regard to reporting actual or suspected fraud.

In **Section 3.7** we briefly discuss the concept of 'aggressive earnings management' before moving on, in **Section 3.8**, to consider the limitations of audit procedures with regard to their ability to detect fraud and error. The use of computer-assisted audit techniques (CAATs), although discussed more fully in **Chapter 9**, is also considered in **Section 3.9**, specifically in relation to the detection of fraud.

**Section 3.10** gives the reader an insight into the world of fraud today, discussing some key statistics on fraud in the RoI and the UK/NI.

Finally, in **Section 3.11** we examine the auditor's responsibilities, and the related audit procedures, surrounding the client entity's compliance with laws and regulations.

## 3.2  ERROR VERSUS FRAUD

An error, in auditing terms, is a simple, unintentional mathematical or clerical mistake in the financial statements. Examples include:

- the unintentional misapplication of an accounting policy;
- an incorrect accounting estimate arising from oversight;
- a misinterpretation of facts; or
- a mistake in the gathering of the initial data.

ISA 240, paragraph 11(a), defines fraud as "an intentional act by one or more individuals among management, those charged with governance, employees, or third parties, involving the use of deception to obtain an unjust or illegal advantage". The standard also explains that the auditor is required to be concerned with fraud that causes a material misstatement in the financial statements.

To be able to detect fraud the auditor must first understand more about the types of fraud and how they can manifest themselves in the financial statements – this is the focus of **Section 3.3**.

## 3.3  TYPES OF FRAUD

Fraudulent material misstatements may arise from **fraudulent financial reporting** or from the **misappropriation of assets**. The Association of Certified Fraud Examiners (ACFE), in a survey published in 2016, reported total losses of $6.3 billion as a result of fraud, with an average loss per case of $2.7 million. While misappropriation of assets represents approximately 83% of fraud schemes, it is not the most expensive type of fraud. The average fraud associated with misappropriation of assets is believed to be in the region of $125,000 (approximately €100,000/£88,000). In contrast, fraudulent financial reporting (also known as financial statement fraud), although occurring less frequently, is believed to cost companies on average $975 million (approximately €784 million/£690 million) per case.[1]

---

[1] Association of Certified Fraud Examiners, *Report to the Nations on Occupational Fraud and Abuse: 2016 Global Fraud Study*. See www.acfe.com/rttn2016/docs/2016-report-to-the-nations.pdf

## Misappropriation of Assets

Misappropriation of assets involves the theft of an entity's assets and is often perpetrated by **employees** in relatively small and immaterial amounts. It may also involve management, who are usually better able to disguise or conceal misappropriations in ways that are difficult to detect. Often, false or misleading records are created in order to conceal the fact that assets are missing or have been pledged without authorisation. Unlike fraudulent financial reporting, **misappropriation of assets** usually occurs **solely** for personal gain. Methods employed include:

"• Embezzling receipts (for example, misappropriating collections on accounts receivable or diverting receipts in respect of written-off accounts to personal bank accounts).

• Stealing physical assets or intellectual property (for example, stealing inventory for personal use or for sale, stealing scrap for resale, colluding with a competitor by disclosing technological data in return for payment).

• Causing an entity to pay for goods and services not received (for example, payments to fictitious vendors …).

• Using an entity's assets for personal use (for example, using the entity's assets as collateral for a personal loan or a loan to a related party)." (ISA 240, paragraph A5)

**Table 3.1** below gives further examples of misappropriation of assets perpetrated by employees.

TABLE 3.1: EXAMPLES OF MISAPPROPRIATION OF ASSETS PERPETRATED BY EMPLOYEES

| 'Skimming' | Fraudulent Expenses |
|---|---|
| 'Skimming' involves taking funds before they are entered into the accounting records. This can include individuals operating a till who pocket the cash and do not ring up the sale into the till. The cash reconciliation (actual cash received versus the sum of the till receipts) does not reveal any variances and so the fraud goes undetected unless other mitigating controls are introduced by the entity. | Fraudulent expense claims is probably the most accepted type of fraud – it is seen to be so petty that it is more of a white lie than an actual fraud. The reality is that fraudulent expense claims (monies claimed for out-of-pocket expenses not actually incurred or not incurred for a valid business purpose) cost companies thousands every year. |
| **Payroll Fraud** | **Purchasing Fraud** |
| The payroll clerk is very well positioned to steal thousands from a company without ever being caught if the right segregation of duties is not in place. Common payroll frauds include:<br>• creation of fictitious employees with the perpetrator's bank account being the beneficiary of the salary; | Accounts payable clerks are also well positioned to commit fraud in a number of ways if sufficient segregation of duties is not in place. These can include:<br>• creation of fictitious suppliers being paid fictitious invoices, the beneficiary of payments being the perpetrator; |

| | |
|---|---|
| • rounding of amounts paid on high-volume payrolls with the rounding difference being paid to the perpetrator's bank account. | • payment for purchases that do not relate to valid business expenses;<br>• altering supplier bank account details temporarily so the perpetrator is in receipt of funds instead of the actual supplier. |

Below are some cases that were brought to court in recent years relating to the misappropriation of company assets.

In the RoI in 2012, a youth centre manager was jailed for six months when she stole over €100,000 from a community youth centre. The individual in question was said to have a gambling addiction that drove her to steal from her employer. The money was taken simply by writing cheques to cash and then cashing them at the local supermarket. The individual was responsible for the bank reconciliations, which allowed her to conceal the fraud by forging bank statements to show a higher balance in the bank. This allowed the fraud to be concealed for a long period before eventually it came to light when the bank wrote to the board of management indicating that the bank accounts were overdrawn.

In 2014, a woman received a two-year suspended sentence after stealing €132,000 from her employer in order to repay a previous employer €90,000 that she had also stolen. The woman in question, who was employed as a credit controller, perpetrated the fraud by emailing one of her employer's customers, giving them her personal bank account details and indicating that the company had changed its bank account. Once she received the money into her own account she emailed the customer to advise them to revert to the previous bank details. The reason cited for the original theft was to assist her parents, whose business had gone into liquidation. Not able to deal with what she had done, the individual confessed to her father, who met with the CEO of the company to explain what had taken place.

Both cases show the clear need for segregation of duties and independent review. It is wholly the responsibility of an entity to protect itself from fraud rather than rely on the morals of employees, which can sometimes be rocked by events in their personal lives. Most events involving employee misappropriation of assets are carried out by individuals who have no previous offences and are led astray either by personal circumstances or the ease with which the fraud can be carried out. The value of the fraud often starts off quite small and increases when the perpetrator realises that they have not been found out. Once the act of fraud takes place it becomes difficult to stop because the original fraud usually requires a degree of cover-up that leads to further acts of fraud.

Not all misappropriation of assets is carried out by employees – third parties, unrelated to the entity, can also misappropriate the assets of an organisation. Table 3.2 highlights some frauds carried out by third parties.

TABLE 3.2: MISAPPROPRIATION OF ASSETS PERPETRATED BY THIRD PARTIES

| Supplier Payment Fraud | 'Shell Company' |
|---|---|
| A common type of fraud involves a third party impersonating a supplier and instructing an entity that its bank account details have changed. Often the instruction will be received on the supplier's headed paper (likely stolen or fraudulently created) and providing the entity with the third-party's bank account details. The entity, in changing the details, then makes a number of payments to the third party before the fraud eventually comes to light when the real supplier complains of non-payment. | 'Shell companies' are often set up to obtain goods without payment. In these instances the perpetrator sets up a fake company and attempts to purchase large volumes of goods on credit. When the entity seeks payment for the goods supplied they cannot get in contact with the customer – who never actually existed. In the absence of a credit control function to vet customers in advance of the supply of goods this type of fraud has caught out many organisations. The situation is compounded when salespersons, eager to reach sales targets and earn bonuses, make the sale without considering whether payment will be received. |

| Supplier Payment Fraud (continued) | Physical Asset Theft |
|---|---|
| Some fraudsters are more sophisticated and go to the trouble of setting up fake email domains that are almost identical to either:<br>(a) the supplier – making it appear as though the request is coming from the supplier organisation; or<br>(b) the entity itself – making it appear as though a senior member of the entity has given an instruction for a transfer of funds to be made to a bank account in accordance with details provided in the email.<br><br>If strong controls do not exist around the editing of master data and the approval for payment of funds, then these types of fraud easily pass through the organisation resulting in substantial losses before the fraud is detected. | Basic physical controls are often lacking in entities resulting in the common theft of physical assets, such as inventory or property, plant and equipment. An entity needs to be mindful that assets of a certain nature and size are more susceptible to theft than others. A very common example is cigarettes: small in size and expensive, a small quantity can be quite profitable to the common thief. In more recent times, phone credit is no longer sold in cards and is instead generated electronically at the point of sale to avoid the high-volume theft that the phone companies experienced. |

More damaging than those given in **Table 3.2** are the increasing numbers of cyber-attacks. Cyber-attacks take many forms, including 'phishing' or Trojans hiding destructive malware, and can be for different reasons, from sheer destructiveness to attempts to steal funds or data for financial gain. Many organisations are ill-equipped to deal with the extremely large volume of customer data they hold – vulnerable data that requires a high degree of IT monitoring and defending. From the auditor's point of view, cyber-attacks can:

1. bring a company to the point where it can no longer operate, rendering it insolvent;
2. result in financial losses that may or may not go undetected and may or may not be recoverable; or
3. result in significant financial loss resulting from liabilities imposed under a breach of data protection.

The whole area of computing, including cybercrime, is considered in more detail in **Chapter 9**.

## Fraudulent Financial Reporting

Fraudulent financial reporting involves intentional misstatements. The fraudulent acts centre on the creation of financial opportunities for an individual or entity, e.g. through the manipulation of stock prices or performance-related bonuses. The intention is to present financial statements that give a misleading impression of the financial affairs of the entity. These may include omissions of amounts or disclosures in financial statements to deceive the users of the financial statements. **Generally, management are the perpetrators of this type of fraud**, motivated by what they consider to be their own best interests in terms of reporting on the financial position and performance of the entity. Methods employed include:

"• Manipulation, falsification (including forgery), or alteration of accounting records or supporting documentation from which the financial statements are prepared.
• Misrepresentation in, or intentional omission from, the financial statements of events, transactions or other significant information.
• Intentional misapplication of accounting principles relating to amounts, classification, manner of presentation, or disclosure." (ISA 240, paragraph A3)

There is no direct gain from fraudulent financial reporting; instead the gain comes indirectly in the form of bonuses or salary increases that are fuelled by the fraudulent financial reporting activities. For example, if directors are paid a bonus based on maintaining or improving profit, then they could either delay the recording of expenses or else recognise revenue before the activities associated with that revenue have been completed, hence maintaining/increasing profit and receiving their bonus. In some instances there may be no financial gain at all: the incentive is instead the maintenance of shareholder confidence by misleading the shareholders' view of the financial statements and thereby maintaining the entity's reputation and position.

Management are in a better position to perpetrate this type of fraud due to their ability to override controls. The ACFE's 2016 Global Fraud Study indicates that the higher the level of the perpetrator's authority, the greater the loss tends to be. According to the study, on average the cost of frauds committed by owners/executives is four times higher than those committed by managers, and nearly 11 times higher than those committed by employees. The number of people involved in the fraud also has a significant impact: a sole perpetrator, on average, defrauds $85,000; two people $150,000; but five or more conspirators and the average loss is $633,000. **Table 3.3** below outlines some of the fraudulent financial reporting that can happen as a result of management overriding controls.

TABLE 3.3: EXAMPLES OF FRAUDS INVOLVING MANAGEMENT OVERRIDING CONTROLS

| Fraudulent Act | Description | Sample Auditor Response |
|---|---|---|
| Fictitious journal entries | The recording of fictitious journal entries generally tends to occur close to the year end, when final results are becoming clearer and are not the results desired by management, causing them to reverse or alter valid journal entries and to create fictitious ones. | Review all journal entries around the year end and obtain back-up as to their validity. Give particular attention to: 1. high-value journal entries; and 2. reversed journal entries. |
| The deliberate application of inappropriate judgement or assumptions | Involves management altering its judgements or assumptions to achieve a desired result. For example, making light of significant uncertainties surrounding the going concern assumption, or changing position on the collectability of receivables in order to justify a lower provision. | Ensure an appropriately qualified and experienced member of the audit team is assigned to the audit of balances that require the application of judgement and assumptions. |
| Concealing or non-disclosing of facts | The concealment or non-disclosure of facts that could impact amounts recorded in the financial statements is quite common and includes such things as omitting to share details of legal claims, or product quality issues. | Review: • board meeting minutes; • interim accounts (issued after the date of the financial statements); and • legal invoices and correspondence to identify any undisclosed matters. Inquire of management and obtain **management representations** for any oral disclosures. |
| Omission, advancement or delaying of recognition of financial statement items | Involves the 'smoothing' of profits by knowingly moving transactions from one period to another (inappropriate application of cut-off) to achieve a desired result. | Perform cut-off testing, be mindful of incentives (such as bonus targets) and assign appropriately qualified and experienced audit staff to perform searches for unrecorded liabilities (missing liabilities). Adequately qualified and experienced audit personnel should also be assigned the review of complex revenue recognition transactions due to the high degree of fraud in this area. At all times the auditor should apply professional scepticism. |

| Complex transactions | Often complex transactions can be structured in a manner to misrepresent the financial position or performance of the entity. | Assign the audit of complex transactions to an appropriately qualified and experienced member of the audit team and obtain the advice of an auditor's expert, where necessary. |
|---|---|---|

## Maintaining Professional Scepticism

The auditor needs to take an approach of "ongoing questioning" when performing an audit – continually asking whether the "information and audit evidence obtained in any way suggests that a material misstatement due to fraud may exist" (ISA 240, paragraph A7). This **professional scepticism** should be applied not only to audit evidence being obtained, but also to the behaviour of individuals in the organisation. Perpetrators of fraud are often those who come to auditors for explanations and assurance of information. For example, an individual who has committed fraud may be unusually interested in how the audit is going to be conducted – either to settle concerns that the fraud might be discovered or to better understand how to hide it. Other general characteristics of behaviour or factors that may be indicative of fraud that the auditor should be aware of include:
- unusual behaviour, e.g. defensiveness or failure to reassign work when overloaded;
- stale items in the bank reconciliation, missing lodgements or missing cheques – with each reconciliation performed, the reconciling items may be on the increase;
- excessive journal entries posted or credit notes issued;
- missing documents and lack of explanations and procedures to locate the documents;
- absence of original invoices, which are substituted by copies;
- common names, addresses, etc. that relate to an employee or family and friends of employees;
- excessive purchases relative to the nature of the entity;
- duplication of payments;
- fictitious employees noted on wages records;
- inventory levels relative to the nature of the entity, e.g. inventory levels held inconsistent with expectations;
- large and often round-sum payments made with little or no back-up documentation;
- post-office boxes used as shipping addresses; and
- undue pressure from the client to complete the audit.

## Accounting Frauds and Irregularities

As noted previously, of the two types of fraud – misappropriation of assets and fraudulent financial reporting – it is fraudulent financial reporting that has the potential for a larger impact. **Table 3.4** below gives a brief outline of some high-profile accounting frauds and irregularities since the turn of the century. This gives a 'flavour' of the financial irregularities in which a company and/or its employees might engage, and highlights the resounding impact of such actions.

TABLE 3.4: EXAMPLES OF ACCOUNTING FRAUD AND IRREGULARITIES

| Who | When | Fraud/Irregularity | Impact | How Uncovered |
|---|---|---|---|---|
| **Tesco** | 2014 | Overstatement of incomes and understatement of costs – long-term agreements with customers front-loaded (revenue recognised up-front rather than over the life of the deal). | Tesco fined £129 million; a further £85 million (plus interest) was paid to investors who purchased shares in the period 29 August to 19 September 2014 (the period when misleading valuation of shares and bonds took place). | Internal review of figures when preparing interim financial results – profit warning issued. |
| **Mobily** (Saudi telecoms) | 2013 | Revenue recognition – early recognition of a promotional program. | $5 billion reduction in share value. | Senior management alerted audit committee, which carried out an investigation. |
| **Caterpillar and ERA Mining Machinery Limited** | 2012/ 2013 | **Alleged** – improperly recognised revenues and inventories. **Alleged** – engagement by senior management in "deliberate misconduct beginning several years prior to Caterpillar's acquisition". | $580 million write-down of $734 million investment. | Discovered by Caterpillar in January 2013 following its investment made in 2012. |
| **Barclays** | 2012 | Libor rate-fixing and concealment of toxic assets through 'off balance sheet' accounting. | Immeasurable market impact. £7.47 billion sale of toxic assets. £290 million fine to Barclays. Allegations of other banks' involvement led to Deutsche Bank advising it had set aside €1 billion to deal with potential litigation around Libor fixing. | At the onset of the financial crisis, liquidity concerns drew public scrutiny towards Libor. |

| | | | | |
|---|---|---|---|---|
| **Hewlett-Packard and Autonomy** | 2012 | **Alleged** – Autonomy improperly recognised revenue (upfront booking of long-term sales commitments and of sales made on a sale-or-return basis). **Alleged** – Autonomy's then-management made misrepresentations and failed to make required disclosures. HP believe this was done to mislead investors and potential buyers. | $8.8 million write-down by HP of its investment in Autonomy ($5 million of which is alleged by HP to be resulting from improprieties). | Actual margins of 20% rather than the expected 40% on acquisition led to investigations by HP, revealing alleged fraud. |
| **Olympus** | 2012 | Concealment of investment losses, which were secretly liquidated. | $1.7 billion | Internal whistleblower (who was fired for questioning dubious deals). |
| **Saytam** | 2009 | Falsification of revenues, margins and cash balances. Improperly recognised revenue. | INR1.5 billion | Perpetrator wrote to the board about his involvement. |
| **Lehman Brothers** | 2008 | **Alleged** – removal of 'toxic assets' from the balance sheet by selling them to Cayman Island banks on a promise that they would buy them back. | $50 billion | The company went bankrupt. |
| **American Insurance Group** | 2005 | **Alleged** – told traders to inflate stock prices as well as booked loans as revenue and encouraged its clients to go to insurers from which they obtained a payoff. | $3.9 billion | Believed to be a whistleblower tip-off that led to SEC-regulator investigations. |

| | | | | |
|---|---|---|---|---|
| **Healthsouth** | 2003 | **Alleged** – instructed subordinates to falsify transactions to inflate revenue to meet shareholder expectations. | $1.4 billion | Posted a massive trading loss following the sale by its CEO of $75 million worth of stock – led to SEC suspicions. |
| **Tyco** | 2002 | Set aside cash through unapproved loans and fraudulent stock sales and then extracted this cash from the company disguised as executive remuneration payments. | $500 million inflation of revenue (financial reporting fraud). $150 million misappropriation of funds. | Investigations by SEC and Manhattan DA revealed questionable accounting practices. |
| **WorldCom** | 2002 | Capitalised expenses and falsified revenue to inflate profits. | $11 billion inflation of assets. $180 billion losses for investors. Loss of 30,000 jobs. Led to introduction of Sarbanes–Oxley (see **Section 2.7**). | Internal audit uncovered part of the fraud, leading to further investigations. |
| **Enron** | 2001 | Inappropriate revenue recognition. Inappropriate use of special-purpose entities. Marked-to-market accounting (method of valuing assets at their current price). Capitalisation of expense items. | $74 billion in losses for shareholders; loss of thousands of employee and investor pensions. Also a factor in the introduction of Sarbanes–Oxley and the reason Arthur Andersen no longer operates within the auditing arena. | Internal whistleblower. |

## 3.4 THE 'FRAUD TRIANGLE' – WHY PEOPLE COMMIT FRAUD

The 'fraud triangle' presents the theory that three conditions – incentive/pressure, opportunity and rationalisation – must be present for fraud to take place (see **Figure 3.1**). It explains fraudulent behaviour as a three-stage process that can be applied at both an individual and a company level.

The first stage is the incentive/pressure to commit fraud, i.e. there must be a reason. Incentives/pressures are numerous. It could be simply personal gain, including the collection of performance-related bonuses (an incentive), or it could be pressure from parent companies, shareholders, lenders, etc. to meet financial performance targets. The second stage is opportunity – the chance to commit the fraud and for it to remain undetected. As we have noted, **management** has the ability to override controls and so have a greater opportunity to commit fraud. The third stage is rationalisation, the justification of fraudulent behaviour. We will look at each of these in more detail below.

FIGURE 3.1: THE FRAUD TRIANGLE

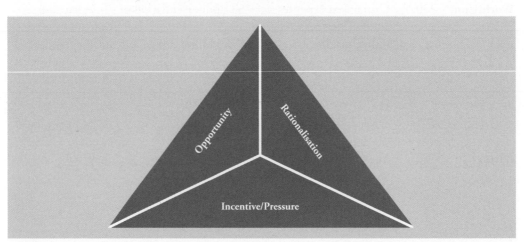

Before we look in more detail at the three stages of the fraud triangle, we need to consider the role that the economic climate has in the process. The first thing to note is that fraudulent activity occurs in 'booms' and in recessions, the difference is only in the driving forces. In a boom, the motivating incentive/pressure may be to maximise financial gain (whether the individual's or the entity's) while it is possible, and a healthy financial performance may provide the opportunity by making it easier to hide the fraud. Healthy financial performances also allow companies to pay bonuses to staff, particularly management, which come to be relied upon as a regular source of income and an entitlement. In a downturn or recession, bonuses are often curtailed, suspended or unachievable, leaving staff (especially management) 'out of pocket'. The incentive/pressure then may be to maintain an income they have become accustomed to. The opportunity may also be more accessible as companies can become complacent in the boom and fail to prioritise their risk management and internal controls, making it easier to commit fraud. The fraud is easily rationalised by the individual by thinking that it is only what they are entitled to, or by the company by thinking it is the only way to maintain the company, keep jobs alive and so on.

## The Fraud Triangle – Risk Factors

Fraudulent behaviour, in general, is a complex matter involving the interrelationship between the individual (as a person and as an employee) and the company/management. It can be explained by many examples of incentives/pressures, opportunities and rationalisations. **Table 3.5** below highlights some common examples of risk factors relating to fraudulent financial reporting in terms of the fraud triangle.

TABLE 3.5: THE FRAUD TRIANGLE – FRAUDULENT FINANCIAL
REPORTING: COMMON RISK FACTORS

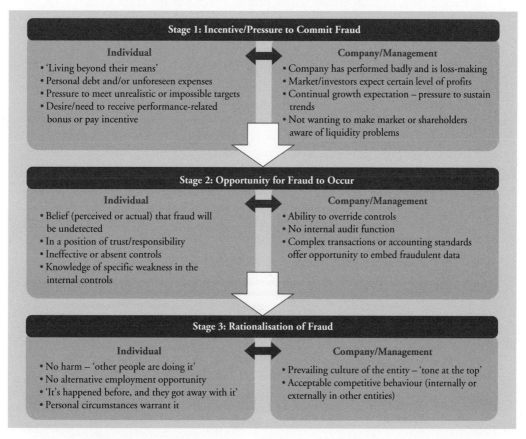

**Stage 1: Incentive/Pressure to Commit Fraud**

| Individual | Company/Management |
|---|---|
| • 'Living beyond their means' <br> • Personal debt and/or unforeseen expenses <br> • Pressure to meet unrealistic or impossible targets <br> • Desire/need to receive performance-related bonus or pay incentive | • Company has performed badly and is loss-making <br> • Market/investors expect certain level of profits <br> • Continual growth expectation – pressure to sustain trends <br> • Not wanting to make market or shareholders aware of liquidity problems |

**Stage 2: Opportunity for Fraud to Occur**

| Individual | Company/Management |
|---|---|
| • Belief (perceived or actual) that fraud will be undetected <br> • In a position of trust/responsibility <br> • Ineffective or absent controls <br> • Knowledge of specific weakness in the internal controls | • Ability to override controls <br> • No internal audit function <br> • Complex transactions or accounting standards offer opportunity to embed fraudulent data |

**Stage 3: Rationalisation of Fraud**

| Individual | Company/Management |
|---|---|
| • No harm – 'other people are doing it' <br> • No alternative employment opportunity <br> • 'It's happened before, and they got away with it' <br> • Personal circumstances warrant it | • Prevailing culture of the entity – 'tone at the top' <br> • Acceptable competitive behaviour (internally or externally in other entities) |

Further examples of fraud risk factors are given in ISA 240, Appendix 1, for both mis-statements arising from fraudulent financial reporting and from the misappropriation of assets. Appendix 2 provides examples of possible audit procedures to address the assessed risks of material misstatement due to fraud; while Appendix 3 offers examples of circumstances that might indicate the possibility of fraud.

A high-profile case, the concealment of Barclays Bank's 'toxic assets' and the rigging of interest rates (Libor), provides a good illustration of the fraud triangle (see **Example 3.1**).

EXAMPLE 3.1: THE FRAUD TRIANGLE IN PRACTICE – BARCLAYS AND LIBOR

"A network of traders working on both sides of the Atlantic conspired to influence both the Libor and Euribor interest rates – the rates at which the banks lend to each other. It was, in effect, a worldwide conspiracy against the free functioning of the market."

*The Observer*, 30 June 2012

The Libor scandal cost Barclays £290 million in fines. 'Libor' is the term used to describe the average interest rate that banks pay to borrow money, and can represent the health of a bank. If the Libor is healthy, then the bank is deemed healthy and therefore gets offered lower interest rates. Derivative traders took bets on which way the Libor would go and subsequently fixed the rate (by colluding with fellow bankers) to support their preference. In reality Barclays was in trouble, suffering losses from toxic structured products, which were concealed through an offshore company, Protium. (This questionable accounting practice is the same as that operated by Lehman Brothers.)

The substance of the transaction was not that of a sale of the assets to Protium but a temporary transfer, funded by Barclays themselves through loans to Protium. Essentially, Barclays sold the toxic assets to themselves, but through this 'off balance sheet' approach they remained out of view of the shareholders. Bankers at Barclays were rewarded well for the generation of large profits, creating an aggressive bonus culture. Additionally, ex-employees of Barclays were said to be paid substantial fees for arranging the sale through Protium.

Barlcays' employees told the Financial Conduct Authority and various other authorities that all the banks that comprise the Libor panel "were contributing rates that were too low". Misconduct was said to be "widespread, involving staff in New York, London and Tokyo as well as external traders".

Let us consider the details with reference to the fraud triangle.

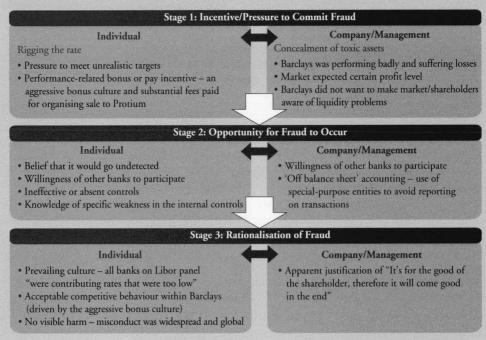

To summarise the theory of the fraud triangle: if an individual cannot see a reason (i.e. an incentive/pressure) to commit fraud, then they will not proceed; if they cannot perceive a way (opportunity), then they cannot proceed; finally, if they cannot justify or rationalise the wrong to themselves, even if the first two conditions exist, then they are unlikely to proceed.

## 3.5  RESPONSIBILITY FOR THE PREVENTION OR DETECTION OF FRAUD AND ERROR

The primary responsibility for the prevention and detection of fraud rests with the client entity's directors (particularly the finance director), **management** and **those charged with governance**. This is highlighted in ISA 210 *Agreeing the Terms of Audit Engagements,* paragraph 6, where it indicates that it is the responsibility of directors to maintain adequate internal controls and to safeguard the assets of the company. The auditor is not required to assist in this function, but they should inform directors and relevant management of their responsibilities through the **engagement letter** issued at the start of the audit, and through other relevant communications, which could include the **planning meeting**. The fact that an audit is carried out may, however, act as a deterrent to potential fraudsters.

### Responsibilities of Management

Management must set the '**tone at the top**' for the running of their business. Management can do this through:

- Developing an accepted **code of conduct** for all employees. For example, Barclays issued a code of conduct to be signed by all staff following the Libor rate-fixing scandal. Staff are now mandatorily required to sign the document, which centres on five key values: respect, integrity, service, excellence and stewardship.
- Promoting a **culture of honesty and integrity** within a positive working environment. This is often demonstrated in a tone-at-the-top document but, more importantly, should be embodied in the actions of senior management, encouraging employees to follow their example.
- Implementing an **ethics programme** based on a strong set of core values to be communicated to the entire organisation.
- Establishing penalties and procedures for dealing with **disciplinary matters** – usually implemented through HR disciplinary procedures.
- Establishing an **appropriate control environment** and maintaining strong internal controls that provide reasonable assurance with regard to reliability of financial reporting, effectiveness and the efficiency of operations and compliance with applicable laws and regulations.
- Establishing an **internal audit function**, an **audit committee** and an **independent compliance function** to which the auditor can report any incidence of suspected fraud.
- Taking appropriate action in response to actual, suspected and alleged fraud.
- Developing an employee '**whistleblower**' charter. Some of the largest fraudulent financial reporting cases were revealed by whistleblowers (see **Table 3.4** above), organisations should therefore create a safe environment that encourages whistleblowing.

## Responsibilities of the Auditor

The auditor is required to provide reasonable assurance that the financial statements are free from material misstatement, whether caused by fraud or error. There is the unavoidable risk that some material misstatements may, however, go undetected. The auditor's responsibility is to obtain **sufficient appropriate audit evidence** to support their opinion on the true and fair presentation of the financial statements. More specific requirements of the auditor are dealt with in **Section 3.6**.

## 3.6  AUDIT PROCEDURES AND FRAUD

In Parts II and III of this textbook we discuss the audit and assurance process and procedures in greater detail. The discussion here is specific to the context of fraud, but by necessity mentions terms and phrases that are more properly introduced in later chapters. Key terms are denoted as purple bold (in the first instance) and a brief explanation can be found at the start of the relevant chapter.

ISA 240 *The Auditor's Responsibilities Relating to Fraud in an Audit of Financial Statements* outlines the following key requirements for the auditor when discharging their responsibility with respect to the detection of fraud:
- application of **professional scepticism**;
- ensuring adequate discussion among the engagement team;
- application of appropriate risk procedures and related activities;
- identification and assessment of the risks of material misstatement due to fraud;
- adequate response to the assessed risks of material misstatement due to fraud;
- evaluation of audit evidence;
- obtaining written representations;
- communicating suspicions of fraud; and
- documentation.

## Professional Scepticism

ISA 200 *Overall Objectives of the Independent Auditor and the Conduct of an Audit in Accordance with International Standards on Auditing*, paragraph 15, prescribes the auditor to "plan and perform an audit with professional skepticism recognizing that circumstances may exist that cause the financial statements to be materially misstated". The essence of scepticism is doubt, and doubt stimulates informed challenge and enquiry. The auditor should be alert to **inconsistencies** in audit evidence collected, and challenge those that may pose a risk of fraud. While the auditor is not asked to put aside their experience with regard to the honesty and integrity of the client entity's management, they must accept that circumstances may have shifted the moral high ground of individuals and the conditions of the fraud triangle may come into play.

The **ethical standards** (as issued by either the IAASA or the FRC – see **Chapter 2**) reflect a fear that auditors will develop close ties with the management teams of client entities that will develop into trust (familiarity) and lead to a lack, or reduced levels, of professional scepticism. The rigorous assessment of when, and the degree to which, professional scepticism is required is fundamental to an effective audit. The importance of the application of professional scepticism is never more relevant than when recognising the possibility that a material misstatement due to fraud could exist.

## Discussion among the Audit Engagement Team

ISA 240, paragraphs A10–A11, requires the members of the **audit engagement team** to discuss the "susceptibility of the entity's financial statements to material misstatement due to fraud" and how it might occur. This discussion should occur with a questioning mind and professional scepticism. Items to be discussed would include:

- How and where the financial statements may be susceptible to **material misstatement** due to fraud; how **management** could perpetrate and conceal fraudulent financial reporting; and how assets of the entity could be misappropriated.
- Circumstances that might indicate aggressive earnings management and any practices that management might follow that could lead to fraudulent financial reporting.
- How external and internal factors affecting the entity could: create an incentive/pressure for management or others to commit fraud; provide the opportunity for fraud to be perpetrated; indicate a culture or environment that enables management or others to rationalise committing fraud.
- Management's involvement in overseeing employees with access to cash or other assets susceptible to misappropriation.
- Any unusual or unexplained changes in behaviour or lifestyle of management or employees that have come to the attention of the engagement team.
- The importance of maintaining professional scepticism and a proper state of mind throughout the entire audit process regarding the potential for material misstatement due to fraud.
- Circumstances that might indicate: the possibility of fraud; the risk of management override of controls; how an element of unpredictability must be incorporated into the **nature, timing and extent** of procedures performed; and how the audit procedures are selected relative to the likelihood of material misstatement.
- Allegations of fraud that have already come to light.

## Risk-assessment Procedures and Related Activities

There are some specific procedures that the auditor must carry out when trying to establish if any risk of fraud exists within the client entity. Throughout ISA 240 the auditor is guided with regard to the types of procedure relating to a risk assessment of the client entity, including:

- The auditor must discuss with management and those charged with governance the procedures they follow when fulfilling their responsibilities for detecting fraud. Discussions should include management's assessment of fraud occurring, procedures to minimise fraud occurring and the ethical attitudes communicated to the organisation.
- The auditor should ascertain if management and **those charged with governance** are aware of any fraud that has occurred or is occurring.

- The auditor should determine the procedures implemented by the internal audit team aimed at detecting fraud and the conclusions reached.
- Those charged with governance should be approached to determine what processes and procedures have been used by management to identify the risks of fraud occurring and how management responded to these risks.
- The auditor should consider what fraud risk factors, if any, already exist.
- **Analytical review** techniques should be used by the auditor to identify any unexpected relationships that might suggest the possibility of material misstatement due to fraud. For example, a review of trends in stock prices or PE ratios. In the case of the Tesco accounting scandal, a review of the share price over time could have indicated that there was a risk of fraud.

### Identification and Assessment of the Risks of Material Misstatement Due to Fraud

The auditor must identify situations where there is a higher than usual risk of fraud or error occurring. They should also identify what types of transaction and assertion they believe could be impacted.

"There is no special recipe, checklist or manual for detecting fraud, no such thing exists and no such thing is truly capable of being developed to address all forms of fraud."[2]

While the above statement is true, fraud investigations over the years have revealed that fraudulent behaviour tends to exist where:
- there are no **internal controls** or the controls in place are weak or inadequate;
- there is inadequate **segregation of duties**;
- there is inadequate management of staff;
- there are **inherent risks** of fraud existing in the industry;
- the entity has financial difficulties;
- the entity is suffering a loss of market share;
- there are aggressive bonus structures;
- there is unusual behaviour; or
- there are unusual circumstances/transactions or swings in business.

You will be familiar with some of these features from the discussion on the 'fraud triangle' in **Section 3.4**.

ISA 240, paragraph 26, emphasises the high risk of fraud around revenue recognition, stating that "based on a presumption that there are risks of fraud in revenue recognition, [the auditor] shall evaluate which types of revenue, revenue transactions or assertions give rise to such risks". Such risks often result in over- or under-statement of revenues and Appendix 2 to ISA 240 outlines specific responses to fraudulent financial reporting.

### Responses to the Assessed Risks of Material Misstatement Due to Fraud

Once the auditor identifies risks, they must then decide how to address these risks. Audit procedures must be planned to ensure that they assign appropriate levels of staff and audit techniques to minimise the risk of not detecting a **material misstatement**. As will be discussed

---

[2] Corné Mouton, "Fraud Prevention", *Accountancy Ireland*, April 2013, Vol. 45, No. 2, 37–38.

further in **Chapter 4**, errors (and therefore risks) can exist at the **financial statement level** (i.e. the entire set of financial statements are affected by the risk) *or* at the **assertion level** (e.g. when an individual account balance is affected by the risk). The auditor needs to determine the level of risk and apply appropriate procedures to address that risk. Risks at the financial statement level are naturally more concerning as their impact is far greater.

### Responses at the Financial Statement and Assertion Levels

ISA 240 requires that the auditor responds to risk, both at the financial statement level (risk that impacts on the entire set of financial statements) and at the assertion level (risks that impact on, say, the completeness of revenue – see **Chapter 4**). ISA 240, paragraph 29, advises that to assess risk at the overall financial statement level it is essential to assign and supervise audit personnel appropriately. Additionally, it notes the need for "unpredictability in the selection of the nature, timing and extent of audit procedures".

### Audit Procedures to Address Risks of Management Override of Controls

**Section 3.3** outlined the susceptibility of financial statements to fraud through management override of controls. ISA 240, paragraph 31, stresses that "Due to the unpredictable way in which such override could occur, it is a risk of material misstatement due to fraud and thus a **significant risk**". **Table 3.1** above also identified various types of fraud resulting from management's override of controls and the audit procedures that can address these risks. In particular, ISA 240, paragraphs A44 and A45, state the need for testing the appropriateness of journal entries and for reviewing accounting estimates for bias. The standard advises the auditor to perform audit procedures that respond to the identified risks in the particular situation(s) in the client entity. In other words, the auditor needs to draw upon their experience and expertise to assess what procedures are required within each unique situation.

### Evaluation of Audit Evidence

At the conclusion stage of the audit, the auditor performs a **final analytical review**, which is designed to analyse movements and relationships between figures in the financial statements and consider these against expectations. The auditor, at this conclusion stage of the audit, should have gained sufficient understanding of the financial statements to appreciate the movements and relationships and be able to justify them with **corroborating evidence**. During this review, if the auditor identifies a movement or relationship that is not corroborated by previous audit procedures, it might indicate an unidentified risk and as such the auditor needs to perform further audit procedures that are appropriate to deal with the newly identified risk.

ISA 240, paragraph 32, outlines a number of procedures that the auditor should carry out irrespective of the auditor's assessment of the risks of management override of controls. These include: testing "the appropriateness of journal entries"; reviewing and evaluating accounting estimates for bias; evaluating significant transactions as to "whether the business rationale (or the lack thereof) of the transactions suggest that they may have been entered into to engage in fraudulent financial reporting or to conceal misappropriation of assets".

## Written Representations

Throughout the audit, **management** will make statements to the auditor that are often verbal and therefore cannot be put onto the auditor's audit working file. As such, the auditor, in order to solidify this information, will present management with a list of statements made by them (implicitly or explicitly) in order to obtain confirmation that the auditor's understanding is correct and that the directors stand over any **representations** they have made.

A detailed discussion on written representations (commonly known as 'management representations') is included in **Chapter 18**, Section 18.6.

## Communicating Suspected or Actual Instances of Fraud

Having identified all risks, responded to those risks and obtained written representations from management, the auditor may be faced with an actual or suspected fraud. The auditor now needs to consider how to communicate knowledge of this fraud both to management and, potentially, to third parties.

If the auditor suspects fraud or discovers a material error, having obtained all the necessary evidence, they should report their findings in a timely manner to an appropriate level of management, the directors or those charged with governance. The auditor must make sure they are fully informed of the nature of the fraud and the magnitude of the situation. The situation must be fully documented in the **audit working papers**.

ISA 240, paragraph 41R-1, emphasises the auditor's responsibility to communicate suspected fraud in the audit of PIEs. Further, it requires the auditor to follow-up with the entity as to the action taken by it to address the suspected fraud. Where no action has been taken by the entity the auditor is required to inform the authorities responsible for investigating such irregularities.

### *Discussion with Directors and/or those Charged with Governance*

If a material fraud is discovered that affects the financial statements, directors and/or those charged with governance should be asked to consider amending the financial statements to reflect the impact of the fraud. The impact on other audit work must also be considered. Management can be asked to carry out additional procedures to determine if the auditor has uncovered the full extent of the fraud. If management, other than the directors, are suspected of committing a fraud, the directors should be informed.

Even if fraud, or suspected fraud, has not been encountered, the auditor should discuss with the directors the concerns they have relating to fraud. For example:
- concerns about the nature, extent and frequency of management's assessments of the controls in place to prevent and detect fraud;
- a failure of management to appropriately address identified material weaknesses in internal control, or to appropriately respond to an identified fraud;

- the auditor's evaluation of the entity's control environment, including questions regarding the competence and integrity of management;
- actions by management that may be indicative of fraudulent financial reporting; and
- concerns about the adequacy and completeness of the authorisation of transactions that appear to be outside the normal course of business.

### Indifference of Management to Reported Fraud Suspicions

Once the auditor reports their suspicions, it is expected that those charged with governance will take action. If management and directors are indifferent to investigating the fraud, the auditor will need to reassess their integrity and the control environment. They will also need to consider the impact on the **audit report**.

If the auditor believes that the financial statements are materially affected by fraud or error, an explanatory paragraph should be added to the audit report to qualify it, depending on the circumstances (audit reports are discussed in detail in **Chapter 19**). Additionally, the auditor should seek legal advice about reporting to a third-party authority.

### Audit Continuance

If the auditor suspects that fraud exists at the management level, this calls into question the integrity of the client entity and, as such, the auditor may feel that they cannot continue the engagement. If a misstatement resulting from fraud, or suspected fraud, is discovered and it brings into question the auditor's ability to continue performing the audit, the auditor should, in line with ISA 240, paragraph 38:

- consider the professional and legal responsibilities applicable in the circumstances, including whether there is a requirement for the auditor to report to the person(s) who made the audit appointment or, in some cases, to regulatory authorities;
- consider the possibility of withdrawing from the engagement; and
- if the auditor withdraws from the engagement, they must discuss with the appropriate level of management and those charged with governance the reason for the withdrawal. The auditor must also consider whether there is a professional or legal requirement to report their withdrawal and the reasons for it to the person(s) who made the audit appointment or, in some cases (e.g. in the case of money laundering, discussed in **Section 3.11**, or any reason in the public interest), to regulatory authorities.

**Table 3.6** below outlines the process the auditor must follow when considering to whom actual and suspected instances of fraud should be communicated. The table identifies the various parties to whom the auditor may communicate and the obligations they hold to each of those parties.

TABLE 3.6: AUDITOR'S OBLIGATION TO REPORT FRAUD OR ERROR

| When | To Who | Obligation |
|---|---|---|
| Auditor concludes:<br>• financial statements do not give 'true and fair' view<br>• do not comply with applicable accounting framework<br>• proper books/records have not been kept | 1. Shareholders<br>2. Members<br><br>via audit report | Disclose within the audit report |
| Auditor discovers or suspects fraudulent activity by **non- or low-level management employees or parties external to the entity** | Senior management/ audit committee (where not suspected of involvement) | Make them aware and allow them the opportunity to investigate and disclose to the relevant authority* |
| Auditor discovers or suspects fraudulent activity at **senior management** level | Audit committee (where not suspected of involvement) | Make them aware and allow them the opportunity to investigate and disclose to the relevant authority* |
| Auditor discovers **exceptional** fraudulent activity | Those charged with governance (where not suspected of involvement) | Auditor's ability to continue the audit is called into question, should consider withdrawing from the audit, implications for the audit report and/or informing the relevant authority* |
| Breaches of law in the public interest, e.g. money laundering | Relevant authority | Public duty to disclose to the relevant authority |
| Breaches of law not in the public interest, e.g. Volkswagen emissions scandal | Senior management/ audit committee (where not suspected of involvement) | Make them aware and allow them the opportunity to investigate and disclose to the relevant authority* |

\* Where those charged with governance, i.e. management/audit committee, do not satisfactorily investigate and disclose as necessary, the auditor should consider disclosing directly to the relevant authority after obtaining legal advice.

## Documentation

Having identified all risks, responded to those risks, obtained representations from management and reported actual and suspected instances of fraud, the auditor now needs to ensure that the audit file reflects the process followed. In order to be able to demonstrate that they have carried out their duties in accordance with auditing standards, the auditor must be able to demonstrate all the steps taken and the evidence gathered. The auditor does this by documenting the details surrounding each risk identified and concluding upon each.

There has been an increase in regulatory requirements relating to the documentation of audit procedures performed to detect fraud, and the steps taken to report detected and/or suspected fraud. ISA 240, paragraphs 44–47, list the matters that must be documented, and include:

- discussions with management regarding fraud and attempted fraud (see **Appendix 3.1** of this chapter for a sample client fraud questionnaire);
- "significant decisions" reached during the audit engagement team discussions regarding the susceptibility of the entity's financial statements to material misstatements due to fraud;
- "identified and assessed risks of material misstatements due to fraud at financial statement and at the assertion level";
- "overall responses to the assessed risks of material misstatements due to fraud at the financial statement level and the nature, timing and extent of audit procedures ... with the assessed risks of material misstatement due to fraud at the assertion level";
- the "results of audit procedures, including those designed to address the risk of management override of controls";
- "communications about fraud made to management, those charged with governance, regulators and others"; and
- if the auditor has concluded that improper revenue recognition does not present a risk of material misstatement due to fraud, the reasons supporting that conclusion.

## 3.7 AGGRESSIVE EARNINGS MANAGEMENT

A discussion of the topic of fraud cannot adequately be concluded upon without reference to the practice of **aggressive earnings management**. Aggressive earnings management is the use of methods by management to create an unrealistic, positive picture of company results. It is a form of fraudulent financial reporting and usually takes the form of inappropriate revenue recognition or delaying of expense recognition. These practices are also known as 'profit smoothing' or 'window dressing'.

In 2001, the then Auditing Practices Board issued a Consultation Paper entitled *Aggressive Earnings Management*, which defined aggressive earnings management as:

> "accounting practices including the selection of inappropriate accounting policies and/or unduly stretching judgements as to what is acceptable when forming accounting estimates.
>
> These practices, while presenting the financial performance of the companies in a favourable light, did not necessarily reflect the underlying reality."[3]

Auditors should be alert and responsive to the existence of aggressive earnings management. The practice is more prominent in entities where there are risks around management override

---

[3] Auditing Practices Board, Consultation Paper: *Aggressive Earnings Management* (CCAB Ltd, 2001). See www.frc.org.uk/getattachment/fa2e4c67-cbaa-48ab-a8e9-46b93bfa881e/Aggressive-Earnings-Management-June-2001.pdf.

of controls, a fact the auditor should be conscious of when considering the existence of aggressive earnings management. The auditor should:

- recognise the pressures on directors or management to report a specific level of earnings;
- act with greater professional scepticism when alerted to circumstances indicative of aggressive earnings management;
- take a strong stance with directors when requesting adjustments for misstatements identified during the audit; and
- communicate openly and frankly with the entity, in particular management/those charged with governance and the audit committee.

## 3.8 LIMITATIONS OF AUDIT PROCEDURES IN DETECTING FRAUD OR ERROR

There are unavoidable limitations where, even though the audit may be properly planned and performed, fraud or error may not be detected. ISA 200 *Overall Objectives of the Independent Auditor and the Conduct of an Audit in Accordance with International Standards on Auditing*, at paragraph 3, states that:

> "the purpose of an audit is to enhance the degree of confidence of intended users in the financial statements. This is achieved by the expression of an opinion by the auditor on whether the financial statements are prepared, in all material respects, in accordance with an applicable financial reporting framework."

Thus, the auditor's primary responsibility is not to detect fraud. In addition, the auditor is only required to give an opinion on the financial statements, not a guarantee. Therefore, the evidence gathered, in terms of its persuasiveness, is limited to that required to arrive at their opinion.

Due to the volume of transactions going through an entity's general ledger and bank accounts, including all journal entries and other adjustments, the auditor uses **sampling methods** when performing audit tests. It is inevitable that not every error or misstatement will be detected. Management could also have concealed fraud from the auditors, deliberately manipulated the books and records of the entity, made intentional misrepresentations or deliberately not recorded transactions. Where judgement has been exercised by management (e.g. when determining whether or not a receivable needs to be provided against), it may be difficult to ascertain whether misrepresentations were caused by fraud or error. Additionally, unless 100% of transactions are tested, the auditor must accept the possibility that the fraud may simply go undetected in the financial statements. This is referred to as **sampling risk**, i.e. the fraudulent item may not have been selected in the sample tested by the auditor and hence go undetected. Sampling risk is discussed in more detail in **Chapter 6**, Section 6.8.

Fraud often involves collusion (two or more people working together) which overrides **segregation of duty** controls implemented by the client entity. By collaborating, fraudsters can create an apparent existence of corroborating evidence. This makes the fraud more difficult to detect.

## 3.9  FRAUD AND CAATs

Computer-assisted audit techniques (CAATs) are discussed in detail in **Chapter 9** and are a very important tool for auditors in the detection of fraud. In order to work effectively, CAATs must be strategically adapted to the situation and the various audit objectives and procedures of the entity under review. There are many benefits to utilising CAATs when searching for indications of fraudulent activity.

Advancements in technology have created the opportunity to better prevent and detect fraud. However, with technology there are also greater opportunities to *commit* fraud. No longer is the concentration on information systems, instead the discussion now focuses on **data management**. Technology continues to offer organisations more ways to do business – e-commerce, cloud computing and EDI technologies, for example – and it also changes the environment in which the auditor collects evidence. E-commerce allows organisations to sell to multiple buyers at the same time, any time of the day or night and from any part of the globe. Naturally this has increased the number and size of global/international organisations and the volume and velocity of transactions generated by them. The modern auditor must be familiar and competent with regard to data management, and an ability to 'mine big data' is as important as knowledge of accounting and auditing standards.

When we consider 'big data' we need to take into account the capture, storage and transfer of the data. That is:
1. how reliable is the data entry process?;
2. where is the data stored?; and
3. is there a possibility that the data may be intercepted or manipulated once entered?

We will consider the answers to these questions in greater detail in **Chapter 9**.

**Data analytics** offers the ability to analyse data and draw meaningful conclusions. In general, computers have greatly improved the effectiveness and efficiency of audits, allowing auditors to carry out mundane tasks significantly faster and with greater accuracy, which leaves more time to concentrate on risk and to formulate questions to be posed to management based on the results of their findings. Data analytics is taking that effectiveness and efficiency to the next level and is transforming how the auditor conducts reviews and collects audit evidence. The auditor now has the opportunity to leave behind the concept of sample testing and instead perform analysis on the entire population. This analysis allows the auditor to identify irregularities and inconsistencies in the data that may indicate fraud or operational risks, and so adjust the audit approach to be taken.

Such 'big data' analysis can be particularly effective in countering 'auditor fatigue', which arises

> "when an individual is looking for anomalies or mistakes in a population but the vast majority of the population does not contain any anomalies. The risk is that the auditor gets so used to seeing acceptable transactions that they fail to identify the anomalies or mistakes when they do come across them."[4]

---

[4] Andrew Brown, *Corporate Fraud* (Chartered Accountants Ireland, 2010), p. 101.

The process surrounding data analysis using CAATs involves 'cleaning' the data to ensure it is adequate for auditor review, preparing the test, sample testing to ensure it is correctly set up and then reviewing highlighted transactions. Andrew Brown, as noted above, further outlines the specific requirements and application of 'Proactive Fraud Prevention Using Data Analysis'.

Data analytics allow the auditor to search large volumes of data for certain characteristics. Common analytics performed by the auditor include:
- search for duplicate payments (same vendor/amount/date);
- match vendor details (address, bank details) to employee details;
- analyse overridden transactions;
- identify large round-sum payments; or
- identify scrapped inventory followed by re-orders.

In selecting data analysis tools the auditor is interested in one that can handle large volumes of data efficiently and that offers a large array of analytical and statistical functions (ideally it should allow the auditor the ability to write further queries). The most commonly used data analysis tool is spreadsheets/Excel; other tools include desktop software, such as Microsoft Access, or server-based software, such as SQL or Oracle. There is also more specialised audit software available, such as the ACL Analytics software, which can deal with very large datasets and allow the data to be 'locked down', enabling the auditor to write queries to extract data with certain criteria. The queries or scripting can then be easily repeated.

Embedded audit software allows the auditor to carry out 'continuous auditing'. The software is embedded in the client entity's computer system and continuously reads client data to identify anomalies (usually in controls).

While it is true that technology is enabling a new wave of fraud in the form of cyber-crime, technological trends such as **cryptocurrencies** (e.g. bitcoin) offer more secure methods of transacting, circumventing the concerns associated with traditional currencies. Bitcoin is by far the most used cryptocurrency. Its supply, which is controlled by an underlying algorithm, is capped at 21 million – so when 21 million bitcoin have been purchased no more will be released. Therefore the demand for bitcoin increases and, as there is a limited supply, the individual value of bitcoin will increase.

Individuals purchase bitcoin in order to trade online without the use of financial institutions. The personal identity of the individual using bitcoin is not known to the buyer or seller, albeit law enforcement authorities have found ways to identify individuals behind transactions by following the transactions, each of which has an encryption that extracts the origin of the transaction. It is this compounding of transactions that provides each subsequent transaction with its authenticity.

Bitcoin is built on **blockchain technology**, which is essentially a continually growing list of data where each transaction (a 'block') contains a cryptographic hash of the previous transaction, including a date stamp. This makes it inherently resistant to modification. Once a transaction is recorded the data therein cannot be amended without amending all subsequent transactions – so providing a method for firms to securely collect information.

While the science behind the technology may be lost on the typical auditor, it is essential that they understand how it can benefit their processes, as well as the wider profession. These technologies offer the auditor the opportunity to spend more time asking what the anomaly is related to: fraud, error or just an unusual factor of the client entity's business.

## 3.10 THE BUSINESS ENVIRONMENT AND FRAUD

In times of recession and financial difficulty, the occurrence of fraud becomes more and more prevalent as incentive and opportunity increase. In such times, where individuals and companies suffer financially, behaviour can change and the line of morality (and legality) can be crossed, resulting in activities undertaken in order to maintain the lifestyles, financial performance, etc. to which individuals and businesses have become accustomed. This is not to say that fraud does not take place during 'boom' years. Significant fraud can go undetected during boom years precisely because the indicators of fraud are less evident.

In the UK in 2010, the National Fraud Authority, which closed in March 2014, commenced the Annual Fraud Indicator (AFI). The AFI 2017 report (conducted by Crowe Clark Whitehill) indicated that the cost of fraud in the private sector is estimated to be £140 billion (compared with £21.2 billion reported in 2013), and £40.4 billion in the public sector. The primary fraud areas noted with regard to the private sector included: procurement fraud among large enterprises (estimated losses of £69.1 million); payroll fraud, including frauds associated with fictitious employees, diversion of payments into fraudulent accounts, inflated salary master-data and false overtime claims; financial sector sales fraud, which amounted to £5.2 billion (compared to £3.2 billion for the 2016 report); and non-financial sales sector fraud, down to just under £1.3 billion from £1.4 billion in 2016.[5]

While Ireland does not have detailed statistics relating to fraud, figures from the Central Statistics Office (CSO) show that recorded fraud, deception and related offences were down, from 5,579 in 2015 to 4,902 in 2016 (a drop of 12.1%). While the statistics give an indication of the number of frauds reported, they do not give any indication of their gravity. The actual number of frauds committed is likely to be well in excess of the number reported by the CSO – as many frauds go undetected and those that are detected do not always get reported (the defrauded entity choosing to resolve the matter internally rather than risking damage to its reputation).

---

[5] See www.croweclarkwhitehill.co.uk/wp-content/uploads/sites/2/2017/11/Annual-fraud-indicator-2017.pdf

The Prevention of Corruption (Amendment) Act 2010 was signed into law on 15 December 2010 and is intended to improve the strength of anti-corruption legislation while providing specific **protection to the whistleblower**. The Act, while welcomed, is somewhat piecemeal in its application in that it refers to corruption offences against a public office/department only (not private sector companies). In the UK, the Bribery Act 2010 establishes company liability for corrupt acts committed by a person(s) acting on behalf of the company. The Act prohibits bribery of public officials and business-to-business bribery.

As we have seen from **Table 3.4** above, whistleblowers play an important role in the detection of fraud and as such can be seen to be truly fighting corruption. In the RoI, the Protected Disclosures Act 2014, commonly known as the 'whistleblower's act', came into operation in July 2014. Its aim is to protect workers in both the public and private sectors against reprisal if they disclose information relating to wrongdoing in their workplace. In the UK, the equivalent protection is provided through the Public Interest Disclosure Act 1998.

The area of **forensic audit** is becoming an increasingly popular area of the profession due to the rise in corporate fraud. The primary objective of a fraud audit (a special investigation a forensic auditor might be asked to perform) is to either prove or disprove the occurrence of fraudulent behaviour for use as evidence in court. More recently, the role or skill set of the forensic accountant is being increasingly called upon to assist entities in their anti-fraud efforts.

## 3.11 CONSIDERATION OF LAWS AND REGULATIONS IN AN AUDIT OF FINANCIAL STATEMENTS

### Introduction

A topic closely connected to that of fraud is the area of the client entity's compliance with laws and regulations. When a company does not act within the constraints of the law, it is said to be **non-compliant** with laws and regulations. During the course of an audit, the auditor may become aware of instances of non-compliance and they must consider if there is a duty to report the matter. The auditor needs to be familiar with their responsibilities in detecting non-compliance of the client entity with laws and regulations. ISA 250 Section A – *Consideration of Laws and Regulations in an Audit of Financial Statements* addresses this issue.

**Table 3.7** below outlines the respective responsibilities of directors and auditors with respect to adherence to laws and regulations. The types of law and regulation are considered later in this section.

The responsibilities outlined in **Table 3.7** are not dissimilar to those with respect to fraud. There are essentially two categories of laws and regulations that the auditor must consider:
- those that relate directly to the financial statements (Type 1); and
- those that support the legal framework in which the client entity's business is conducted (Type 2).

TABLE 3.7: RESPECTIVE RESPONSIBILITIES OF DIRECTORS AND
AUDITORS WITH RESPECT TO LAWS AND REGULATIONS

| Directors | Auditors |
|---|---|
| Have an **active role** with respect to adherence to laws and regulations – i.e. they must actively put measures in place to ensure compliance with laws and regulations. | Have **no preventative role** – i.e. they are not responsible for preventing client non-compliance with laws and regulations. |
| Have a **preventative role** in ensuring no instances of non-compliance with laws and regulations can occur. | Frequently the auditor plays a **deterrent role**, in that the client entity is less likely to knowingly engage in non-compliance if it feels there is a chance the auditor will detect it. |
| Have a **detective role** in ensuring that instances of non-compliance with laws and regulations are identified and rectified. | Have a **detection role**, which is based on **'reasonable expectation'**, similar to their responsibility to detect **material misstatements**. |

Laws and regulations that relate directly to financial statements include company law disclosure requirements, distribution rules, requirements in relation to accounting records and taxation laws. The legal framework in which the company operates can be more far-reaching and the auditor should gain a general understanding of this through inspection of correspondence and inquiry of directors. Adherence to legal and regulatory requirements will always form part of the **written representations** (as discussed above in **Section 3.6**).

The auditor should remain alert to instances of non-compliance. In relation to Type 1 (those impacting directly on the financial statements), the auditor must obtain **sufficient appropriate audit evidence**. For Type 2, the auditor is only required to carry out procedures to identify instances of non-compliance that may have a material effect on the financial statements. An example of a Type 2 non-compliance is Volkswagen's emission scandal. The extent and gravity of the actions had a serious financial impact, which would have caused a significant audit risk.

EXAMPLE 3.2: TYPE 2 NON-COMPLIANCE – VOLKSWAGEN

In 2015, the EU's anti-fraud agency launched an investigation into Volkswagen's use of software to cheat on EU carbon dioxide emissions tests. Compliance with emissions regulations is mandatory and non-compliant vehicles cannot be sold in the EU. Volkswagen's actions were in breach of an EU Directive relating to the availability of consumer information. It had therefore committed a Type 2 offence in the purposeful act of cheating on emissions tests.

While it is not the responsibility of the auditor to design and perform audit procedures to detect such a fraud, if the auditor becomes aware of fraud in the course of performing the audit procedures (e.g. if they had come across unusual payments made to a software provider to assist them in the fraudulent act), then they must consider if they have a duty to report it to the appropriate authority.

No such abnormalities appear to have crossed the auditor's path, and as such it may be reasonably determined that they could not have known of the fraud. The fraud resulted in a swift reduction in share price of 23% after Volkswagen admitted to the cheat. It's September three-quarter results, despite boasting a 5.3% increase in revenue, showed a loss of €1,731 million compared to a profit of €2,928 million for the same period in 2014. The auditor will, no doubt, be applying stringent going concern reviews as well as considerable assessment of contingent liabilities and provisions in their review of the year end December 2015 accounts. 'Special items' (e.g. one-off exceptional costs) in the September results were valued at €6,685 million and the auditor will be eager to know if this is the full extent of the potential cost of the fraud.

This case highlights, first, the auditor's obligation with regard to detecting non-compliance with Type 2 laws, but it also emphasises the auditor's responsibilities in assessing the impact of fraud.

To date, the US authorities have extracted $25 billion in fines, penalties and restitution from Volkswagen in respect of 580,000 tainted diesel vehicles sold in the US. In Europe, where the company sold 8 million tainted diesel vehicles, Volkswagen has not paid any fines.

## Audit Procedures when Non-compliance is Identified or Suspected

Where the auditor becomes aware of actual or suspected non-compliance, according to ISA 250A, paragraph 18, they should "obtain:
(a) An understanding of the nature of the act and the circumstances in which it has occurred; and
(b) Further information to evaluate the possible effect on the financial statements."

Similar to the fraud requirements noted above, the auditor should discuss suspected instances of non-compliance with management/those charged with governance and allow them the opportunity to rectify it. If the non-compliance is not rectified, legal advice should be sought by the auditor. This may have an impact on the **audit report** and may give indications of risk (e.g. management integrity). **Table 3.8** below considers the steps that should be taken by the auditor in reporting non-compliance.

TABLE 3.8: AUDITOR'S REPORTING OF NON-COMPLIANCE

| | |
|---|---|
| Step 1 | Obtain all information to support suspicions. |
| Step 2 | Where those charged with governance/management are not suspected, then the auditor should disclose suspicions to them and give them time to investigate and report the matter to the necessary authorities (where required). Failure to do so by management should lead the auditor to seek legal advice regarding the next course of action. |

Step 3    Where most of the entity's senior management are believed to be associated with non-compliance, the auditor should obtain legal advice before proceeding to inform the relevant authority.

Step 4    Where the auditor concludes that the non-compliance has a material impact on the financial statements, they should consider the implications for the audit report (see **Chapter 19**).

Step 5    The auditor must determine if there is a responsibility to report the identified or suspected non-compliance to parties outside the entity.

The June 2016 revisions to ISA 250A are predominantly connected to guidance for auditors on their responsibility to report non-compliance to the relevant authorities when related to **public interest entities (PIEs)** or when deemed to be in the "public interest". The term 'public interest', however, is not straightforward. ISA 250A, paragraph A19-9, states that "'Public interest' is a concept that is not capable of general definition. Each situation must be considered individually." The important point for the auditor to remember is that a disclosure in the public interest is limited to a disclosure to an appropriate authority.

Auditors should further be aware that certain sectors, such as the financial services sectors in the RoI and the UK, have detailed laws and regulations that require directors to have in place systems to ensure compliance with these laws and regulations. Breaches of these laws and regulations could have a material effect on the financial statements. Furthermore, under the Companies Act 2014 (RoI) and Companies Act 2006 (UK), it is a criminal offence to give an auditor information or explanations that are misleading, false or deceptive.

When considering reporting actual or suspected instances of non-compliance, the auditor should consider if it is connected with a law or regulation that stipulates periods for reporting (albeit, when necessary, the auditor should always report to the authorities as soon as is practicable).

Although in practice the auditor will seek legal advice when considering reporting any known or suspected instance of non-compliance, ISA 250A does provide some comfort regarding concerns around the auditor's risk of liability for breach of confidence.

ISA 250A also prescribes that if, during an audit of a **regulated entity**, the auditor becomes aware of information believed relevant or of material significance to the regulator's functions, then the auditor should bring such information to the appropriate regulator as soon as is practicable. To be competent in this regard the auditor will need to ensure all audit staff involved in such regulated entity audits have a reasonable understanding of the provisions of any applicable legislation, any rules and guidance issued by the regulator and any specific requirements that may apply to the particular regulated entity under audit. If the auditor finds an apparent breach, it is essential the information is assessed as to whether: it falls under their reporting responsibilities; is of material significance to the regulator; or is considered criminal conduct.

## Money Laundering

Money laundering can be defined as:

> "the process by which the proceeds of crime, either money or other property, are converted into assets that appear to have a legitimate rather than an illegal origin. The aim of the process is to disguise the criminal source of the money/property in order to allow the holder to enjoy it free from suspicion as to its source."[6]

Legislation is in place to deter, detect and disrupt money laundering and terrorist financing. This requires an auditor who knows, suspects or has reasonable grounds to suspect money laundering, on the basis of information obtained in the carrying out of an audit, to report it to the relevant authorities. Anti-money laundering legislation would be considered 'Type 2'. The legislation applicable to the RoI is the Criminal Justice (Money Laundering and Terrorist Financing) Act 2010 as amended by the Criminal Justice Act 2013. For the UK/NI, the Money Laundering Regulations 2007 apply.

## Concluding on and Documenting Non-compliance

All identification and conclusions drawn with regard to a client entity's non-compliance with laws and regulations should be fully documented in the audit file. The auditor needs to demonstrate that they have adequately carried out their responsibilities with respect to the detection of non-compliance. The auditor does this by ensuring adequate documentation is included on the audit file, which shows the process followed by the auditor and the conclusions reached, all of which should be supported by audit evidence. This evidence may take the form of copies of records, documents and minutes of discussions held with management, those charged with governance or parties outside the entity.

## 3.12 CONCLUSION

Fraud is being committed in all parts of the world and has been committed throughout time. Many or most entities have been victims of fraud to some extent, even though they may not know it. As shown in **Table 3.4**, the cost of fraud can be immeasurable, far exceeding just the financial cost. The 'fraud triangle' explains what all frauds have in common: there must be an **incentive/pressure** to commit it; there must be an **opportunity** that reveals itself, giving rise to its occurrence; and the perpetrator must be able to **rationalise** or justify it to themselves.

---

[6] Vaeni Mac Donnell, *An Introduction to Business Law* (2nd Edition, Chartered Accountants Ireland, 2015).

While it is true that fraud is unavoidable, companies must still seek to prevent it insofar as is possible by strengthening their fraud prevention and detection controls and increasing internal reviews to identify control deficiencies. All the while the auditor must remain vigilant and apply professional scepticism with respect to the existence of fraud, watching out for warning signs that fraud could occur.

ISA 240, paragraphs 17–24, detail specific procedures to be undertaken by the auditor when considering the possibility of fraud, and are summarised in **Table 3.9** below.

TABLE 3.9: SUMMARY OF AUDIT PROCEDURES PERFORMED
BY THE AUDITOR RELATING TO FRAUD

| Procedures to be performed by the auditor | Expansion on procedure |
|---|---|
| Make inquiries of management | The auditor should engage in discussions with those charged with governance and others, as appropriate, to obtain an understanding of how management exercise control of the processes in place for identifying and responding to the risks of fraud. Additionally, the auditor should discuss with management the internal controls that have been established to mitigate these risks. |
| Perform audit procedures to identify the risk of material misstatements due to fraud | Includes evaluating management's integrity and the inherent risks relating to the client's business Evaluate any unusual or unexpected relationships. |
| Perform walkthrough tests | Walkthrough tests should be performed to confirm the adequacy of the system and related documentation and whether or not the control objectives are met. |
| Identify and assess risk at both the individual transaction level and for the financial statements as a whole | The auditor should identify and assess the risk of fraud occurring at both levels. This will include evaluating the efficiency of the internal control procedures relevant to the assessed risks. |
| Use audit software (CAATs) to test controls | For example, searching for journal entries over a certain limit. |
| Determine audit responses to the assessed risks | Includes the assignment and supervision of personnel, the accounting policies used and the unpredictability when selecting the audit procedures. |
| Design and perform audit procedures responsive to management override of controls | See examples included at **Table 3.1** and further examples in **Appendix 3.2** of this chapter. |
| Consider whether any identified misstatements or errors indicate the possibility of fraud occurring | The auditor must consider for each misstatement or error found whether or not they believe it to be intentional or unintentional (i.e. caused by fraud or error). |

## SUMMARY OF LEARNING OBJECTIVES

**Learning Objective 1** Understand fraud in the context of audit.

Error is considered a simple, unintentional mathematical or clerical mistake in the financial statements. Fraud, on the other hand, is an intentional act using deception to obtain an unjust or illegal advantage.

**Learning Objective 2** Understand the types of fraud that can occur and the forms it can take.

Fraud can be classified into two categories:
- **Fraudulent financial reporting** The intention is to present the financial statements to give a misleading impression of the performance or position of the entity for personal gain. This is usually perpetrated by management due to their ability to override controls.
- **Misappropriation of assets** Involves the theft of an entity's assets and is often perpetrated by employees (as opposed to senior management), generally for immaterial amounts.

**Table 3.4** supports an understanding of the different types of fraud.

**Learning Objective 3** Be able to demonstrate your understanding of the 'fraud triangle' by identifying conditions that give rise to fraud.

Generally, there are three conditions present when fraud occurs:
- incentive/pressure to commit fraud;
- opportunity for fraud to occur; and
- rationalisation (by the individual or company).

To summarise the theory of the fraud triangle: if an individual cannot see a reason to commit fraud (i.e. incentive/pressure), then they will not proceed; if they cannot perceive a way (opportunity), then they cannot proceed; finally, if they cannot justify or rationalise the wrong to themselves, even if the first two exist, then they are unlikely to proceed.

**Learning Objective 4** Be able to explain the respective responsibilities of the management of the entity and the auditor with regard to fraud.

Management have an active role to both prevent and detect fraud. While they may act as a deterrent, auditors have no obligation with respect to prevention. The auditor's detection responsibility is limited to "reasonable expectation" and is concerned with fraud causing material misstatement in the financial statements.

**Learning Objective 5** Be able to identify the necessary audit procedures to detect fraud.

ISA 240 advises the following audit procedures to assist the auditor in the detection of material misstatements in the financial statements resulting from fraud:

- Maintain **professional scepticism** when considering the possibility of fraud.
- Ensure adequate discussion occurs among the engagement team regarding the possibility of fraud.
- Apply appropriate procedures and related activities to identify and assess the risk of material misstatement due to fraud and adequately respond to those assessed risks.
- Evaluate and conclude on audit evidence through appropriately designed audit procedures.
- Obtain written representations from management and those charged with governance with regard to fraud.
- Ensure adequate documentation exists to support risks identified and conclusions thereon.

**Learning Objective 6** Know the duty and rights of auditors to report to third parties.

Reporting to third parties is a delicate matter for the auditor and so must ensure that they follow a systematic approach before reporting any suspected frauds (or breaches in laws and regulations) to regulatory authorities. The auditor should always maintain a state of professional scepticism when considering the possibility of fraud. The auditor should always ensure they have sufficient audit evidence before making any accusations and they should consider the suspected involvement of management (at various levels) when deciding to whom in the organisation to report the actual or suspected fraud or breach. Finally, before ever reporting to a third party, the auditor should always seek legal advice.

**Learning Objective 7** Understand what is meant by the term 'aggressive earnings management'.

Aggressive earnings management is the use of methods by management to paint an unrealistically positive picture of an entity's results.

**Learning Objective 8** Be able to identify ways in which computer-assisted audit techniques (CAATs) can assist the auditor in detecting fraud.

CAATs are a very important tool for the auditor in the detection of fraud. They involve the use of computer techniques in the form of audit software programmes or the interrogation of the client entity's computer systems and reports. Data analytics tools are the most common form of CAATs adopted by the auditor when detecting fraud.

**Learning Objective 9** Know the auditor's responsibilities with respect to the client entity's compliance with laws and regulations.

When a client entity does not act within the constraints of the law, they are said to be non-compliant with laws and regulations. The auditor's duty with respect to the detection of non-compliance is limited to two categories:
- Type 1 – laws and regulations that relate directly to the financial statements; and
- Type 2 – laws and regulations that support the legal framework in which the client entity's business is conducted.

The auditor has an active role to play in detecting Type 1 non-compliance, whereas with regard to Type 2 the responsibility arises only once they become aware of non-compliance during the course of other audit procedures. The reporting of non-compliance should be given the same consideration as that discussed above, in **Learning Objective 6**.

## QUESTIONS

### Self-test Questions

3.1   What is the difference between fraud and error?
3.2   Material misstatements can arise from which two types of fraud? What is the difference between them?
3.3   Why are management in a better position to perpetrate fraudulent financial reporting?
3.4   What types of fraudulent acts might a manager engage in when committing fraudulent financial reporting?
3.5   What are the three conditions that are said to be present when fraud occurs?
3.6   What types of incentive/pressure might be in place that could contribute to fraud?
3.7   Who is responsible for preventing and detecting fraud?
3.8   What types of audit procedure might the auditor use to identify fraud?
3.9   What is meant by the term 'professional scepticism'?
3.10  In what type of control environment might fraud be more likely to occur?
3.11  What responsibility has the auditor to report fraudulent activity to third parties?
3.12  What matters relating to fraud must be documented by the auditor?
3.13  What is aggressive earnings management?
3.14  Why is it more difficult for the auditor to detect fraud than error?

### Review Questions

(See Suggested Solutions to Review Questions in **Appendix C**.)

### Question 3.1

Qualitax Limited, a manufacturer of electrical goods, is a large company with good growth prospects. There is always the possibility that it could become a takeover target. You have been appointed audit senior in respect of the audit for the year ending 31 December 2018. The audit partner is concerned about the risk of fraud at Qualitax Limited and is planning a meeting of the audit team in advance of the interim audit visit to brief them about his concerns.

**Requirement** As part of the briefing meeting, prepare a memo outlining the key requirements of ISA 240 *The Auditor's Responsibilities Relating to Fraud in an Audit of Financial Statements*.

### Question 3.2

(a) Briefly discuss the auditor's responsibility for detecting fraud.
(b) Discuss whether fraud is more easily perpetrated by management or by employees not in management positions.

## CHALLENGING QUESTIONS FOR PART I

(Suggested Solutions to Challenging Questions are available through your lecturer.)

This challenging question aims to test your knowledge of **Chapters 1–3**. It is intended to test your practical application of what you have learned in these chapters and so you are presented with a case study on which you are asked to deliver on a number of requirements.

### Question I.1

You are an audit manager for Smith & Reilly, a long-established accountancy practice. Generally, Smith & Reilly deal with smaller entities, however a strategic decision has been made to try to secure larger company audits. Recently a partner of Smith & Reilly met the directors of Décor Company Limited at a conference and gave them his business card. The partner has been a believer in Décor's long-term success for quite some time and bought shares in Décor two years ago. Recently the partner received a call from the directors of Décor, due to the sudden departure of the previous auditors. The partners advise you that James Collins will actually perform the audit (in the role of audit manager) if Smith & Reilly decide to proceed, but he is currently out on stress leave due to the bankruptcy of a family business that he has been a part of for many years. The partners of Smith & Reilly are really keen to get business like this, as Décor alone would increase its fee income by 21%. This type of business, along with the expected new business won due to the new bonus structure introduced by Smith & Reilly, which weights performance of its employees based on their ability to win new business with existing audit clients, will really help to put the firm on the map.

### Requirement

(a) The audit engagement partner for Décor has asked you, in the absence of James Collins:
   (i)  to identify any ethical, regulatory or legislative reasons why they should not accept this audit;
   (ii) to advise the partner of Smith & Reilly of any issues you have identified, as well as methods of overcoming any potential acceptance risks.
(b) The directors of Décor have specifically requested that the audit report state that the auditors guarantee the accuracy of the financial statements, as there is a possibility of

a takeover by a potential buyer and they want the buyer to use the audited financial statements as part of its due diligence. The directors have indicated that they will pay extra for such a guarantee. You have been asked to outline a response to the directors specifically addressing this request.

(c) During your review of Décor you come across a newspaper report in relation to one of their non-executive directors (see Appendix 1) alleging his involvement in a fraud in a US company, where he also serves as director. A partner of Smith & Reilly comments on the increase of fraud and is concerned that the staff members of the firm are not sufficiently knowledgeable about the presence of conditions that can lead to fraud. You are asked to draft a memo outlining the conditions that can lead to large-scale fraud in businesses of different types and size.

(d) Comment on the internal quality control systems that Smith & Reilly should implement to ensure it complies with its ethical responsibilities.

## APPENDIX 1: NEWSPAPER REPORT

### ADG Accounting Scandal

Reports emerging today reveal that the directors (Fred Alter and John Roche) of Handy Store Limited allegedly used improper revenue recognition in order to boost revenue and therefore the profit on which their bonus was based. The company was allegedly suffering due to the economic downturn, resulting in a reduction in salary of many top executives. Additionally, with bonuses being tied to waning profits, the directors had taken a hard knock to the comfortable lifestyles to which they had become accustomed. The internal audit department, which now operates with just two staff members following cost-cutting exercises, is alleged to have defended itself from not having found the error sooner due to a lack of resources.

## APPENDIX 3.1:  EXAMPLE OF A CLIENT FRAUD QUESTIONNAIRE[7]

**Large Company Limited**
**31 December 2017**

|  | Initials | Date |
|---|---|---|
| Prepared by: |  |  |
| Reviewed by: |  |  |

**Client Fraud Questionnaire**

Meet with those charged with corporate governance (board of directors or a director representing the board) and a member of management/senior staff (separate to the board) to discuss Fraud. Use the Checklist below as a template to record the discussion. Copy and paste the template for each person you speak to:

|  |  | Yes | No |
|---|---|---|---|
| 1 | Attendees:<br>**Thomas Hogan (Chairperson)**<br>**John Kelly**<br>Do you have any knowledge of any fraud, attempted fraud or suspected fraud that could result in a material misstatement of the financial statements?<br>*If Yes, please give particulars:* | ☐ | ☐ |
| 2 | Have there been any allegations of fraud within or against the company during the financial period?<br><br>*If Yes, please give particulars:* | ☐ | ☐ |
| 3 | Have any types of fraud ever occurred within the company?<br>*If Yes, please state what types of fraud have occured:* | ☐ | ☐ |
| 4 | Do you know of any unusual activity relating to making journal entries and other adjustments in the accounts?<br>*If Yes, please give particulars:* | ☐ | ☐ |
| 5 | Where do you believe the greatest risk of fraud is likely to occur in the company?<br>*Record response here:* | | |
| 6 | How do you monitor operations and procedures in order to prevent or detect fraud?<br>*Record response here:* | | |
| 7 | What controls has management established to manage fraud risks that have been identified, or that prevent, deter and detect fraud?<br>*Record response here:* | | |

---

[7]  Source: based on *Procedures for Quality Audit* (© Chartered Accountants Ireland, 2010), Appendix 2 and updated by the authors December 2017.

## APPENDIX 3.2: EXAMPLES OF FRAUD

### Exploitation of Systems Flaws

If employees become aware of system flaws, they can be used to commit fraud. One such fraud involved an accounts payable clerk who discovered that the cancelling of a purchase invoice resulted in the system placing it for payment. The clerk, using dormant supplier accounts, changed the associated bank account details and cancelled invoices, resulting in him receiving payment directly to his bank account. This cost the company approximately €260,000.

To identify such a fraud the auditor can use data analysis tools to match employee's and supplier's bank account details. Additionally, they can review changes to supplier masterdata (i.e. bank account details) and agree to supporting documentation that backs up the change. For example, a request from the supplier to change its bank details should be validated by contacting the supplier to confirm that the letter is authentic. From a management perspective, adequate segregation of duties, such as separating the roles of masterdata editing and accounts payable functions, would have prevented this fraud.

### Pyramid Schemes

A number of frauds involving pyramid schemes have occurred over the years where, for example, an individual posing as an investment advisor convinces unsuspecting investors that they could make above-average returns. A 'return' is paid to investors with their own money, and then as new funds are secured from new investors, this new money is used to pay further returns, encouraging more investment. One such scheme eventually collapsed, and this 'borrowing from Peter to pay Paul' exercise resulted in a loss of €4 million to investors.

### The Fictitious Firm

Here, the fraudster sets up a fictitious supplier, which may even be registered with the CRO, or equivalent. Invoices are submitted and payments are made to this company. The key to concealing this type of fraud is keeping the payments small. The auditor should review any new suppliers detected. The company address should be checked to ensure the company is not assigned to a PO box number. The address of the individual authorising the payments to such a company should also be investigated.

### Inventory Theft

Inventory is the balance sheet item most susceptible to theft. It may be written off as a loss, stolen to sell as scrap or simply not entered onto the balance sheet. The auditor should investigate inventory shortfalls relative to the nature of the entity, investigate journal entries relating to write-offs and stock write-downs, and perform variance analysis procedures.

## Tampering with Employee Records

This is especially prevalent in large companies where not everyone knows everyone else's names. When an employee leaves the firm, the fraudster, who generally is associated with the payroll department, instead of removing the employee from the records alters their bank account details to those of the fraudster's own bank account. The auditor should identify employees who have ceased employment with the client entity and ascertain whether payments were made to those individuals or their bank accounts after their leaving dates.

Additionally, it is common for fictitious employees to be added to the payroll with the bank details matching those of the fraudster. The auditor can catch such instances by first reviewing changes to masterdata and matching these to requested back-up and, secondly, using data analysis tools to identify duplicate bank accounts. Once again the company protects itself from this type of fraud by implementing adequate segregation of duties between masterdata editing and payroll functions.

## Identity Theft

Identity theft is the misuse of personal information to impersonate someone for financial gain. It can take the form of identity cloning (assuming someone else's identity), financial theft (from existing accounts or the setting up of new accounts used to misappropriate assets) and benefit theft (impersonating an individual to obtain benefits). The most common method of stealing personal information is by way of a 'phishing attack', where an individual receives an email requesting personal information from a trusted individual or organisation. This information is then used to steal the individual's identity. The auditor and, indeed, management have a duty to protect their clients and employees. The auditor has a legal duty to protect a client's personal and financial information, thus audit clients must be protected from the risk of identity theft. The auditor must ensure that the client's management are alert to the occurrence of identity theft and that management protect their staff from this crime. Personal records should be safeguarded, passwords changed regularly, memory keys encrypted, anti-virus and anti-spyware programmes installed, only reputable suppliers dealt with and clear policies and procedures implemented and reviewed regularly.

# PART II

# THE AUDIT AND ASSURANCE PROCESS: PLANNING AND CONTROLS

## THE AUDIT AND ASSURANCE PROCESS

The figure below outlines the stages involved in the completion of an audit engagement. This is a detailed overview and the coming chapters will deal with each of these areas in turn. As each new area of this figure is introduced, you will see this diagram repeated, with the respective area to be discussed highlighted.

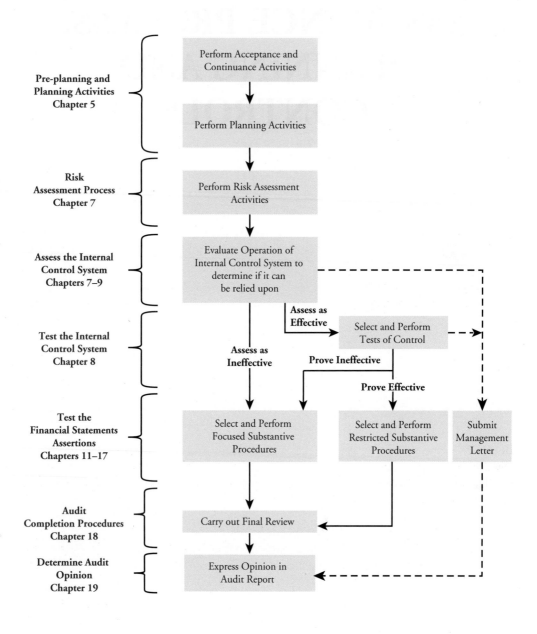

# 4

# THE AUDIT PROCESS

## LEARNING OBJECTIVES

Having studied this chapter on the audit process you should:
1. understand the key terms used in the external auditing environment;
2. understand the main stages of the external audit process;
3. gain an initial understanding of the terms 'management assertions' and 'audit objectives';
4. understand the difference, and relationship, between controls testing and substantive testing.

## KEY TERMS AND DEFINITIONS FOR THIS CHAPTER

Before we move into more specific audit discussions, it is important to understand some key auditing terms used in this chapter, and indeed in this textbook. It is important to familiarise yourself with these terms and their meaning in order to understand the context of further discussions.

**Analytical Procedures**   These comprise the analysis of movements and relationships between figures in the financial statements. They involve the comparison of recorded values with expectations developed by the auditor.

**Audit Engagement**    When a company has to go through the audit process, an auditor may use the term 'audit engagement'.

**Audit Programme**    Records the specific details of controls testing and substantive testing. It becomes a guide to the audit engagement team as to the work to be performed in a particular area.

**Controls Activities**    Policies and procedures adopted by management of the entity to assist in ensuring the orderly and efficient conduct of its business, including adherence to internal policies, the safeguarding of assets, the prevention and detection of fraud or error, the accuracy and completeness of the accounting records and the timely preparation of reliable financial information.

**Emphasis of Matter**    A paragraph in an **unqualified audit report** that draws the reader's attention to a particular matter disclosed in the financial statements that the auditor believes to be of significance.

**Going Concern**    A going concern is a business that operates without the threat of liquidation in the near future, evaluated for at least the next 12 months from date of signing of the financial statements. The directors of a client entity must perform an assessment on going concern to be satisfied that it is appropriate to prepare the financial statements on that basis. If a client entity is not a going concern, the financial statements are prepared on a **break-up basis**.

**Management Assertions**    Explicit or implicit representations made by management in presenting a set of financial statements to the auditor. Management are saying, "We believe that these financial statements represent: transactions that occurred and balances that exist; are complete transactions and balances; accurately recorded transactions and correctly valued balances; transactions and balances that pertain to the entity; transactions that are recorded in the correct financial period; and are fairly classified, presented and disclosed." The objective of the auditor is to prove or disprove these assertions by obtaining evidence, and so they are also referred to as **audit objectives**.

**Materiality**    The magnitude of an omission or misstatement of accounting information that, in light of surrounding circumstances, makes it probable that the judgement of a reasonable person relying on the information would have been changed or influenced by the omission or misstatement. Essentially, it is the concept of significance to the users of financial statements.

**Misstatement**    An instance where a financial statement assertion is not in accordance with the criteria against which it is audited (e.g. IFRS or FRS). Misstatements may be classified as fraud (intentional); as other illegal acts, such as non-compliance with laws and regulations (intentional or unintentional); or as errors (unintentional).

**Modified Opinion**    A modified opinion suggests that the information provided to the auditor was limited in scope and/or that the company being audited has not maintained the accounting principles of the particular financial reporting framework under which the accounts were prepared. That is, the financial statements do not give a true and fair view, or that the truth and fairness of the financial statements cannot be determined.

**Policies and Procedures**    Policies outline the principles or rules that guide decisions (e.g. it is company policy to only accept return of goods within 28 days of sale). Procedures outline what action is to be taken or what steps are to be followed when performing a particular task (e.g. when a customer presents a return: request a receipt or invoice and check that the date on the receipt of invoice is within 28 days of sale; for returns over €100 contact a supervisor to approve the return).

**Professional Scepticism**    Professional scepticism refers to the state of mind which an auditor must maintain when conducting the audit engagement appropriately. The 'scepticism approach' enables the auditor to recognise that circumstances may exist that could cause the financial statements to be materially misstated; therefore they should be alert and remain cautious about such information and events that indicate the possible existence of material misstatement in the financial statements.

**Unqualified Audit Opinion**    A 'clean' audit opinion, indicating the auditor's opinion that a client entity's financial statements are truly and fairly presented in accordance with agreed criteria (e.g. IFRS or FRS). This is the desired auditor's opinion of an audited entity.

## 4.1 INTRODUCTION

This chapter provides an overview of the external audit process from beginning to end. The individual topics are not dealt with in any depth here; rather they are introduced *in outline* to allow the reader to appreciate the overall complexity of the audit process from the outset. Topics introduced within this chapter include a reference to the chapter in which they are then discussed in more detail.

Two specific topics are critical to an understanding of the audit process: management assertions (audit objectives); and controls testing and substantive testing. **Management assertions** (also known as **audit objectives**) is a core concept, one that it is important to understand clearly as it features throughout the audit process, and is introduced in **Section 4.3**.

The second topic relates to the distinction between **controls testing** and **substantive testing**. Essentially these are two distinct types of audit **procedure**. **Section 4.4** explains the difference, but also the relationship, between the two. The area of controls testing is dealt with in detail in **Chapter 8**; substantive testing is fully examined in **Chapters 11–17**.

## 4.2 AUDIT PROCESS OVERVIEW

### Introduction

The audit process is comprised of a number of stages and it is important to have an appreciation of the broad process involved in an audit engagement. **Figure 4.1** below provides an overview of the stages for which the auditor must gather evidence in order to enable them to form an opinion on the financial statements of the client entity. It may come as a surprise that the auditor does not commence direct testing on the financial statements until later in the process, following a number of other key stages, i.e. an extensive **planning stage**.

FIGURE 4.1: AUDIT PROCESS OVERVIEW

| AUDIT STAGE | RELATED CHAPTERS |
|---|---|
| Audit Acceptance | Chapter 5 |
| Audit Planning | Chapters 5, 6, 7 and 10 |
| Assessment of Controls | Chapters 7 and 8 |
| Controls Testing | Chapters 8 and 9 |
| Substantive Testing | Chapters 11–17 |
| Audit Completion | Chapter 18 |
| Auditor's Report | Chapter 19 |

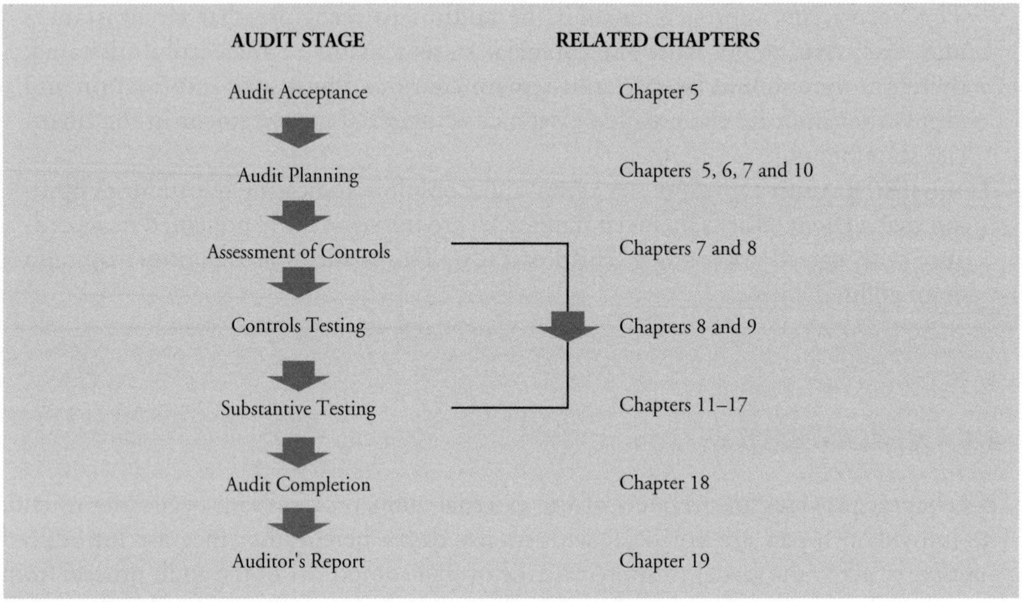

### Audit Acceptance

As we have seen in **Chapter 2**, the auditor is bound by the Ethical Standard as issued by either the IAASA or the FRC, which prescribes the manner in which auditors should behave. For this reason, the auditor cannot simply accept an engagement without first considering, in line with International Standard on Quality Control 1 *Quality Control for Firms that Perform Audits and Reviews of Financial Statements, and other Assurance and Related Services Engagements*:

1. if they can act without infringing any **Ethical Standards**;
2. the **competency, capabilities and resources** within the audit firm;
3. the **integrity of the client entity**.

**Audit acceptance** is discussed in full in **Chapter 5**, Sections 5.2 and 5.3 – at this stage you just need to be aware of the basic considerations the auditor must undertake before accepting or continuing an engagement with a client entity.

## Audit Planning

ISA 300 *Planning an Audit of Financial Statements,* paragraph 4, states the "objective of the auditor is to plan the audit so that it will be performed in an effective manner". In order to plan the engagement, the auditor needs to gain an understanding of the client's business and perform a risk assessment to allow them to develop an audit strategy, defining the nature, timing and extent of testing in response to identified risks. It is at the audit planning stage that the auditor will set the **materiality level** against which audit activities and findings will be measured. (The concept of **materiality** was introduced in **Chapter 1** and a full discussion on the topic is contained in **Chapter 5**, Section 5.4.)

## Assessment of Controls

Controls and controls testing are discussed in detail in **Chapter 8**, however it is important to have an early understanding of their relationship to substantive testing. It is the assessment of controls that determines the next stage of the audit, i.e. the controls testing; an incorrect assessment can lead to an inefficient and costly audit process. If the auditor initially assesses that the controls are operating effectively and consistently throughout the period being audited, the controls can be tested to prove this initial judgement and so **reduce the volume of substantive testing to be performed** later. If the initial assessment is proved, through testing, to be incorrect, then the auditor will have wasted valuable time testing the controls and will still need to perform a focused level of substantive testing. A more detailed discussion of this is contained in **Chapter 8**.

## Controls Testing

**Controls testing** are audit procedures performed to test the operating effectiveness of controls in preventing, detecting and correcting material misstatements at the relevant assertion level. The specific details of the testing to be performed are outlined in the **audit programme**. A fuller discussion on assertions and controls testing is given at **Sections 4.3** and **4.4**. An auditor might use inspection of documents, observation of specific controls, reperformance of the control, or other audit procedures to gather evidence about controls. **Chapter 8** discusses controls and controls testing in greater detail.

## Substantive Procedures

Substantive procedures (also referred to as **substantive testing**) are audit procedures performed to test material misstatements (monetary errors) in an account balance, transaction class or disclosure (notes to the financial statements). There are two categories of substantive procedures:

1. **substantive analytical procedures**; and
2. **tests of details**.

The specific details of the substantive testing to be performed are outlined in the **audit programme**. **Chapters 11–17** discuss substantive procedures in detail.

## Audit Completion

As an audit reaches the completion stage, the auditor will perform procedures to obtain further audit evidence in order to draw a conclusion and finalise the audit process. The auditor will perform the following when concluding on a client entity's financial statements:

1. final analytical procedures;
2. evaluation of misstatements identified during the audit;
3. a subsequent events review (any events occurring after the reporting period);
4. evaluation of the going concern assumption;
5. management representations (letter of representation);
6. review of provisions, contingent liabilities and contingent assets;
7. final review of working papers;
8. communicating with those charged with governance; and
9. concluding on related parties.

These topics are discussed in detail in **Chapter 18**.

## Auditor's Report

The **auditor's report** is the end product of the audit process. It contains the auditor's opinion on the financial statements and is presented alongside the financial statements of the client entity. As discussed in **Chapter 1**, the auditor's report is intended to add credibility to the financial statements.

ISA 700 *Forming an Opinion and Reporting on Financial Statements*, paragraph 6, states that the auditor should "express clearly that opinion through a written report".

It is at this stage that the auditor makes a final decision on the truth and fairness of the financial statements after considering all errors and misstatements found during the audit.

## 4.3  MANAGEMENT ASSERTIONS/AUDIT OBJECTIVES

Now that we have established an understanding of the stages involved in an audit engagement, we can consider the two specific topics that were highlighted in the introduction to this chapter as being of critical importance. The first of these is the concept of **management assertions**.

Throughout this textbook the phrase 'management assertions' (or just 'assertions') is used regularly. Management assertions are also frequently referred to as audit objectives; the terms are used interchangeably – *assertions* made by management are also the *objectives* of the auditor. **Chapter 6**, Section 6.2. considers management assertions in the context of audit evidence, but at this point we will consider what the auditing standards have to say about assertions.

ISA 315 *Identifying and Assessing the Risks of Material Misstatement through Understanding the Entity and its Environment*, paragraph A123, states that:

"In representing that the financial statements are in accordance with the applicable financial reporting framework, management implicitly or explicitly makes assertions regarding the recognition, measurement, presentation of classes of transactions and events, account balances and disclosures."

Essentially this means that, in providing an auditor with a set of financial statements, the directors or those charged with governance are asserting that:

- the **transactions** represent events that **occurred** in the period and the **balances exist** at the date of the statement of financial position;
- all events that occurred are included in the **transactions; balances** that exist at the date of the statement of financial position are **completely** recorded;
- all **transactions** and **balances** belong to the entity; they have the **rights and obligations** to them;
- all transactions are **accurately recorded**, and all **balances** in the statement of financial position are accurately **valued** under the applicable financial reporting framework;
- all transactions are correctly 'cut off', i.e. **recorded** in the correct accounting period; and
- all **transactions** and **balances** are correctly **classified** and **presented** in the financial statements and are supported by the **disclosures** required under the applicable financial reporting framework under which the financial statements are prepared.

The audit objective is to validate these assertions with respect to all transaction classes and account balances by considering the types of potential misstatement that may occur. In achieving this objective, the auditor gains comfort over the truth and fairness of the financial statements (and the assertions made by the directors).

**Table 4.1** below lists the assertions that are relevant to:

(a)  financial statement transactions (e.g. in the area of revenue and receivables, revenue is a transaction, each sale representing an individual transaction); and

(b)  financial statement balances (e.g. in the area of revenue and receivables, receivables is a balance representing the money owed by customers).

The assertions alter slightly, depending on whether the auditor is auditing a transaction class or balance in the financial statements. **Table 4.1** outlines the question the auditor needs to ask in order to meet the audit objective. The significance of **Table 4.1** cannot be underestimated – it is key to understanding the auditor's approach to designing audit procedures. You will see this table adapted for each financial cycle as we walk through the audit process. For now you need to familiarise yourself with the objective of each type of assertion. (Assertions by financial cycle will be discussed in **Chapter 8** and again when discussing substantive procedures in **Chapters 11–17**.)

TABLE 4.1: THE APPLICATION OF MANAGEMENT ASSERTIONS/
AUDIT OBJECTIVES TO TRANSACTIONS AND BALANCES

| TRANSACTIONS (e.g. revenue, expenses, bank transactions, fixed asset additions, etc.) | BALANCES (e.g. asset, liability and equity balances in the statement of financial position) |
|---|---|
| **Occurrence** Did an event occur that supports the recording of the transaction in the general ledger? | **Existence** Are the balances recorded in the statement of financial position made up of items that actually exist at the year end? |
| **Completeness** Have all events that occurred been completely recorded in the general ledger? | **Completeness** Have all balances that exist been completely recorded in the statement of financial position? |
| **Classification/Recording (Accuracy)** Has the transaction been accurately recorded in terms of nominal value? | **Valuation** Are all balances that have been included in the statement of financial position a fair reflection of their value (in line with the applicable financial reporting framework)? |
| **Rights and Obligations** Does the entity have the rights and obligations to the transactions? Is the entity named the buying/selling / paying/receiving party? | **Rights and Obligations** Does the entity have the rights and obligations to the balances? Have they the right to the inflow of economic benefits or the obligation to honour the outflow of economic benefits? |
| **Cut-off** Have the transactions been recorded in the correct period? | |
| **Presentation/Classification and Disclosure** Are all transactions and balances classified and presented in line with the applicable financial reporting framework? Do the financial statements include all disclosures necessary to present the financial statements in a true and fair light in line with the applicable financial reporting framework? | |

## 4.4  CONTROLS TESTING VERSUS SUBSTANTIVE TESTING

In this section we will discuss the second key topic of this chapter: controls testing versus substantive testing. Both will be discussed and explained extensively in later chapters, but it is important to understand at this point the differences between them. The discussion here, including the two examples, is not intended to be a full discussion on the subject of controls and substantive testing; rather it is intended to allow you to appreciate the fundamental difference and relationship between these two audit procedures.

### Controls Testing and the Control Environment

**Figure 4.2** below demonstrates the **control environment** that exists in a client entity where the financial statements are central. A weak control environment will produce a poor quality set of financial statements, whereas a strong control environment is more likely to produce a set of financial statements free from material misstatement. The figure also demonstrates

FIGURE 4.2: THE CONTROL ENVIRONMENT IN WHICH
FINANCIAL STATEMENTS ARE PRODUCED

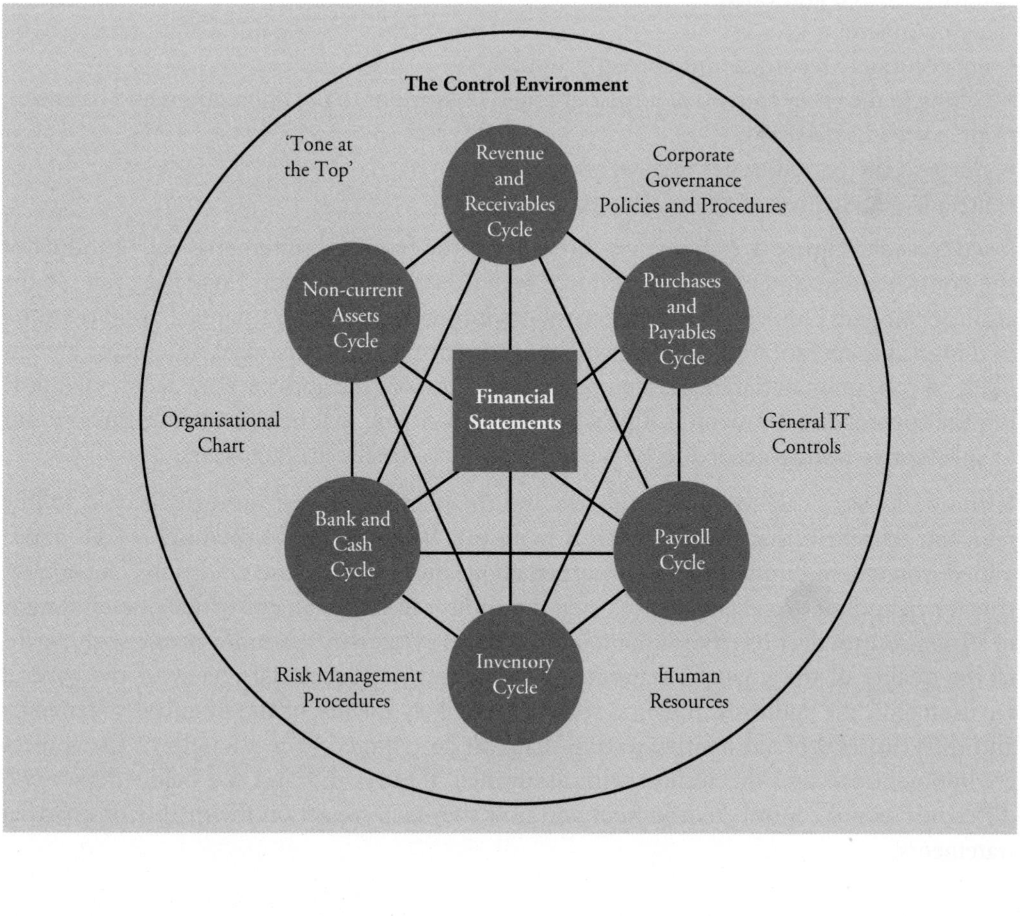

that controls can exist at a macro level (i.e. they serve the client entity as a *whole*) or at a transaction and account balance level (i.e. they are specific to a *particular* financial cycle). The controls noted on the outer ring of the figure are referred to as **organisational controls** (e.g. the existence of a '**tone-at-the-top**' document), whereas those within the inner ring are financial cycle-specific, such as revenue and receivables.

Controls are concerned with the operating effectiveness of internal controls. The auditor's assessment of controls aims to answer all of the following:
- Is the design of the control environment and the specific control activities related to the various financial cycles strong?
- Did the controls operate according to the control design?
- Did the controls operate for the entire period under review?

**Chapter 8** deals with controls and the control environment in greater detail; thus, at this point, you need to understand only that the control environment and the control activities within the client entity have the ability to impact on the quality of a set of financial statements, and for that reason they are of great interest to the auditor.

**Substantive testing** is concerned with testing the truth and fairness of a set of financial statements by considering the specific figures within the financial statements. The audit objective is to ensure that all transactions and balances:
- have occurred and exist;
- are complete;
- are accurately recorded and correctly valued;
- belong to the client entity (i.e. it has rights and obligations to the transactions and balances);
- are correctly classified;
- relate to the period under review; and
- are adequately presented and disclosed.

If we consider **Figure 4.2** above, we can see that the financial statements are a product of the control environment and the control activities related to each financial cycle. If the auditor can gain comfort that the control environment and each financial cycle is strong in design and operation, then there is some assurance that the financial statements are less likely to contain material misstatements. For this reason, the auditor may decide that testing the control environment and proving that it is strong will help to reduce the amount of substantive testing needed to be performed on the financial statements.

If you walk into a café to buy a sandwich and the premises appear unhygienic, you will be reluctant to believe that the sandwich is fit to eat. If, however, the premises is well maintained, you will instantly feel less concerned about the quality of the sandwich. The same is true for an auditor in a client entity: when the auditor feels that an entity demonstrates signs of strong control over its environment and financial cycle, they are more at ease with regard to the quality of the financial statements. By performing an initial review of the control environment, the auditor can gain a sense of the likely quality of the financial statements, and thus the level of substantive testing that will be required. The strength of the control environment provides the auditor with **assurance**. **Figures 4.3** and **4.4** below depict two different types of control environment and how they can impact on the quality of financial statements.

FIGURE 4.3: IMPACT OF A STRONG CONTROL ENVIRONMENT ON THE AUDITOR'S CONFIDENCE IN THE FINANCIAL STATEMENTS

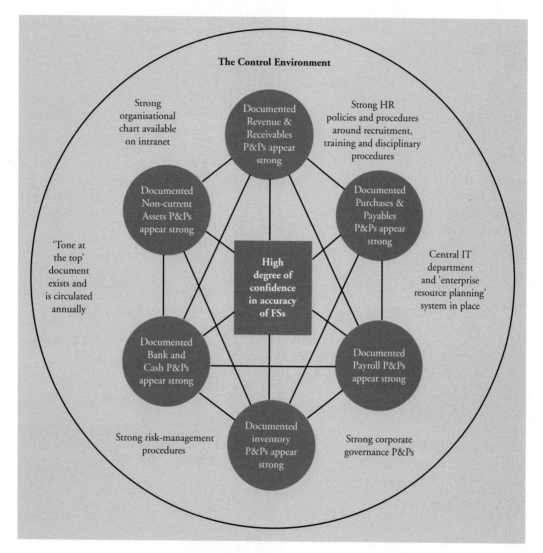

In **Figure 4.3**, the control environment is strong – organisational controls exist, and within the financial cycle **policies and procedures** (P&Ps) are documented. In this instance then, the auditor may assume that there is a **low probability** that the financial statements contain errors and that it is, therefore, worthwhile to test the control environment. **If the auditor can prove that the control environment is strong, the level of substantive testing needed later can be reduced.** This reduced testing comes in the form of: performing an increased level of audit procedures prior to the year end; reducing sample sizes; and the use of substantive analytical procedures over **tests of details**, which are more time-consuming.

FIGURE 4.4: IMPACT OF A WEAK CONTROL ENVIRONMENT ON THE
AUDITOR'S CONFIDENCE IN THE FINANCIAL STATEMENTS

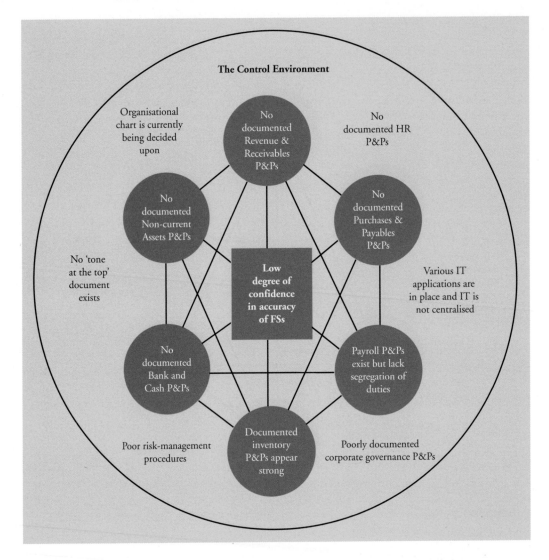

**Figure 4.4**, in contrast, depicts a weak control environment – a lack of organisational controls and no documented policies and procedures – which would lead the auditor to believe that there is a **high probability** that the financial statements contain errors. As such, there is no benefit to testing the control environment: it would provide no assurance and, essentially, would have been an inefficient use of time.

The above topics are discussed in considerable detail in the coming chapters; again, at this point the purpose is to appreciate some key auditing terminology and activities in order to better understand the audit process.

## 4.5 CONCLUSION

The **audit opinion** is intended to provide reasonable assurance that the financial statements are presented fairly, in all material respects, and give a true and fair view in accordance with the applicable financial reporting framework. The single biggest risk to the auditor is in issuing an incorrect audit opinion. Similar to many organisations, the audit firm aims to make a profit and as such the auditor needs to strike a balance between **minimising audit risk and maximising audit efficiency**. The auditor must take on clients with acceptable risk, plan the audit to deal with risk areas in the most efficient and effective way and issue an appropriate audit opinion, while at the same time make an acceptable profit from the engagement. All of the stages of the audit are designed to address these two priorities.

## SUMMARY OF LEARNING OBJECTIVES

**Learning Objective 1** Understand the key terms used in the external auditing environment.

The key terms and definitions provided at the outset of this chapter should be fully read and understood by the student before progressing on to further chapters.

**Learning Objective 2** Understand the main stages of the external audit process.

The audit process is comprised of a number of stages and it is important to have an early appreciation of the broad process involved in an audit engagement. The broad stages include: audit acceptance; audit planning; assessment of controls; controls testing; substantive tests; audit completion; and the audit report. The actual financial statements are only considered in detail at the **substantive** stage and much of the procedure prior to this is centred on planning. These various planning activities are aimed at ensuring that the nature, timing and extent of substantive audit procedures are adequate to address the risks and assertions that exist in the financial statements so as to ensure that the auditor detects material misstatements.

**Learning Objective 3** Gain an initial understanding of the terms 'management assertions' and 'audit objectives'.

In providing the auditor with a set of financial statements, the directors explicitly or implicitly represent that the financial statements are complete, accurate, relate to transactions and balances that actually occurred or exist, contain only transactions that relate to the period under review, are appropriately classified and include adequate and complete disclosures. These are referred to as 'management assertions' or just 'assertions'. The audit *objective* is to validate these assertions with respect to all transaction classes and account balances by considering the types of potential misstatement that may occur. In achieving this objective, the auditor gains comfort over the truth and fairness of the financial statements. As such, the terms 'management assertions' and 'audit objectives' are often used interchangeably.

**Learning Objective 4** Understand the difference, and relationship, between controls testing and substantive testing.

Controls testing is concerned with the operating effectiveness of the client entity's internal controls, i.e. the control environment. The auditor should perform an initial review of the control environment and, if the suggestion is that it is a strong environment, then the auditor may choose to undertake controls testing. If the auditor can prove (through testing) that the financial statements were prepared within a strong control environment, then there is some assurance over the assertions of the transaction classes and balances in the financial statements. This assurance allows the auditor to perform a reduced level of substantive testing (i.e. testing of actual figures and disclosures in the financial statements) and hence perform a more efficient audit. This reduced testing is reflected by an increased level of audit procedures prior to the year end; reducing sample sizes; and the use of substantive analytical procedures over tests of details.

## QUESTIONS

### Self-test Questions

4.1 What are the main stages of an external audit?
4.2 What is the significance of the acceptance stage of an audit?
4.3 What is meant by the term audit assertions?
4.4 List five audit assertions.
4.5 Why would an auditor not test the control environment in every instance?
4.6 What is the difference between controls testing and substantive testing?

### Review Questions

No review questions are included in this chapter as each topic is dealt with and examined in detail in later chapters. At this point you should have a basic appreciation for the broad stages involved in an audit, what is meant by the term audit assertions, and the difference and relationship between controls testing and substantive testing.

# THE AUDIT AND ASSURANCE PROCESS

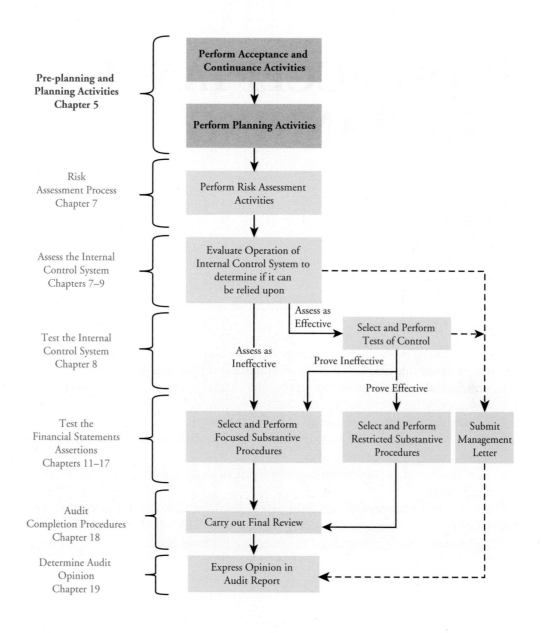

# AUDIT ACCEPTANCE AND PLANNING

LEARNING OBJECTIVES

Having studied this chapter on audit acceptance and planning you should:
1. understand and be able to apply the audit acceptance and continuance considerations;
2. know the role and contents of an engagement letter;
3. know the stages of audit planning and be able to distinguish between the overall audit strategy and the audit plan;
4. have developed an understanding of the role of analytical procedures at the planning stage;
5. appreciate the concept of materiality, including how and why it is calculated; and
6. be able to discuss the options available to the auditor with regard to the nature, timing and extent of audit procedures when designing the audit plan.

## CHECKLIST OF RELEVANT STANDARDS

The relevant standards, in both the RoI and the UK/NI, covered in this chapter are:
- ISA 210 *Agreeing the Terms of Audit Engagements*
- ISA 220 *Quality Control for an Audit of Financial Statements*
- ISA 300 *Planning an Audit of Financial Statements*
- ISA 320 *Materiality in Planning and Performing an Audit*
- ISA 330 *The Auditor's Responses to Assessed Risks*
- ISA 520 *Analytical Procedures*
- ISA 570 *Going Concern*
- ISA 600 *Special Considerations – Audits of Group Financial Statements (Including the Work of Component Auditors)*
- ISA 610 *Using the Work of Internal Auditors*
- ISA 620 *Using the Work of an Auditor's Expert*
- ISQC 1 *Quality Control for Firms that Perform Audits and Reviews of Financial Statements, and other Assurance and Related Services Engagements*

Note, in general when referring to ISAs, it should be understood as referring to the UK and Ireland versions, unless otherwise specified as either ISA (UK) or ISA (Ireland). See the Introduction for an extant list of auditing standards for the RoI and the UK/NI.

## KEY TERMS AND DEFINITIONS FOR THIS CHAPTER

**Analytical Procedures**   Analytical procedures comprise the analysis of movements and relationships between figures in the financial statements. They involve the comparison of recorded values with expectations developed by the auditor.

**Audit Plan**   The audit plan is more detailed than the overall audit strategy. It includes the nature, timing and extent of audit procedures to be performed.

**Audit Strategy**   The audit strategy includes the more general audit requirements, such as the resources required, the budget, the timing and the management of how the audit is to be carried out.

**Auditor's Expert**   If expertise in a field other than accounting or auditing is necessary to obtain **sufficient appropriate audit evidence**, the auditor shall determine whether to use the work of an auditor's expert. For example, if the entity has revalued property in the period, the auditor will require the use of an expert in the form of a property valuer as the auditor is not an expert in this field.

**Engagement Letter**   A written contract, signed by the client and the audit firm, confirming the auditor's acceptance of the appointment and including a summary of the responsibilities of those charged with governance and of the auditor, the scope of the engagement and the form of any reports to be issued by the auditor.

**Random Sampling**   The process of applying auditing procedures to less than 100% of a population, such that each unit has an equal chance of being selected.

**Recurring Audit**   Long-standing audit client.

> **Sample Population**   All of the items that make up the balance or transaction being tested by the auditor, e.g. the receivables balance population is made up of all the customers' individual balances.

## 5.1 INTRODUCTION

This chapter deals with the issues and activities facing the auditor prior to commencement of the fieldwork of an audit. These are referred to as the audit acceptance and planning stages. Collectively, these stages allow the auditor to identify key areas of risk and concern, which will help them to make decisions such as:

- whether to accept or continue an audit engagement;
- what level of audit staff will be required to carry out the audit;
- whether outside experts will be needed; and
- the nature, timing and extent of the work to be done.

**Section 5.2** outlines the considerations that the auditor must take into account when deciding whether or not to accept or continue an audit engagement. Once the engagement is accepted, the auditor issues an audit engagement letter, which is discussed in **Section 5.3**.

In **Section 5.4** we consider the requirements of ISA 300 *Planning an Audit of Financial Statements*. Within this section we discuss the overall **audit strategy** and the **audit plan**. This section deals with some specific procedures that the auditor needs to carry out at the planning stage. Two topics are of particular importance as they are regularly referred to in later chapters: the concept of **materiality** and the use of **analytical procedures**. The audit plan is introduced later in this section. The audit plan is more detailed than the overall audit strategy and determines the **nature**, **timing** and **extent** of further audit procedures. Finally, within this section we address the importance of documenting the audit plan and audit strategy. It should be noted that there are specific planning considerations for the auditor of a group and these are considered separately in **Chapter 20**.

## 5.2 AUDIT ACCEPTANCE

### Introduction

When approached by a new client who wishes to engage an audit firm for performance of an external audit of its financial statements, the auditor is required to consider whether or not they should accept the engagement. Similarly, each year in relation to existing audit clients, the auditor must consider whether or not to continue the engagement with the client. This process for new and existing clients is known as **acceptance and continuance**.

### Acceptance and Continuance

As stated in ISQC 1 *Quality Control for Firms that Perform Audits and Reviews of Financial Statements, and other Assurance and Related Services Engagements*, paragraph 26:

"The firm shall establish policies and procedures for the acceptance and continuance of client relationships and specific engagements, designed to provide the audit firm with reasonable assurance that it will only undertake or continue relationships and engagements where the firm:

(a) Is competent to perform the engagement and has the capabilities, including time and resources, to do so;
(b) Can comply with relevant ethical requirements; and
(c) Has considered the integrity of the client, and does not have information that would lead it to conclude that the client lacks integrity."

ISA 220 *Quality Control for an Audit of Financial Statements*, paragraph 12 states that:

"The engagement partner shall be satisfied that appropriate procedures regarding the acceptance and continuance of client relationships and audit engagements have been followed, and shall determine that conclusions reached in this regard are appropriate."

There may be instances where there is an outgoing auditor (predecessor auditor) that the potential engagement is replacing. Under ISA 300 *Planning an Audit of Financial Statements*, the auditor should communicate with the " ... predecessor auditor, where there has been a change of auditors, in compliance with relevant ethical requirements" (paragraph 13(b)).

The overriding theme is that an audit firm will want to avoid engaging with a client entity that brings with it unacceptable levels of risk. It is therefore essential that a thorough assessment is made of the prospective engagement prior to the audit firm commencing or continuing engagement with the client entity.

**Table 5.1** summarises the auditor's considerations when deciding to engage with a new client entity or to continue an engagement with an existing client. The final decision on acceptance or continuance of an engagement is the responsibility of the audit engagement partner. Where the engagement partner determines that the audit firm can engage successfully with the client entity, the next stage in the initial phase of the audit process is the issuance of an **engagement letter** (see below, **Section 5.3**).

While the considerations above are essential for new client entities, they are equally as important when considering whether or not to continue engagement with existing client entities. When it comes to continuing audits, the auditor should reconsider each of the points noted above with respect to continued management integrity, audit firm competence and ethical compliance to ensure there is no change to the initial assessment of these areas. ISA 220, paragraph 13, states:

"If the engagement partner obtains information that would have caused the firm to decline the audit engagement had that information been available earlier, the engagement partner shall communicate that information promptly to the firm, so that the firm and the engagement partner can take the necessary action."

TABLE 5.1: QUESTIONS AN AUDITOR MUST CONSIDER BEFORE
ACCEPTING OR CONTINUING AN AUDIT ENGAGEMENT

**1. Can I act? Is there any reason why I should not or cannot accept this engagement?**

**(a) Competence and Resources**

Does the audit firm have the competency and resources to perform this engagement?

- Do the personnel have the knowledge of the relevant industry or subject matters?
- Do the personnel have experience with relevant regulatory or reporting requirements, or the ability to gain the necessary skills and knowledge effectively?
- Does the audit firm have sufficient personnel with the necessary capabilities and competences?
- Will the use of outside experts be required?
- Does the audit firm have individuals who meet the criteria and eligibility requirements to perform 'engagement quality control review' in place, where applicable?
- Will the audit firm be able to complete the engagement within the reporting deadline?

**(b) Ethics**

Will this engagement contravene any ethical requirements?

- Is my audit firm sufficiently independent of the client?
- Will acceptance of the audit create an actual, or perceived, conflict of interest with an existing audit client?

**(c) Predecessor Auditors**

Have I contacted the predecessor auditors?

- Do the predecessor auditors indicate any unusual circumstances surrounding their removal or resignation from their position of auditor? The incoming auditor should request a copy of the statement of circumstances from the predecessor auditor.

**2. Should I act? Is it wise to accept this engagement?**

**(d) Client Integrity**

Are there any questions over the potential client that will create unacceptable risk?

- What is the identity and business reputation of the client entity's principal owners, key management, related parties and those charged with its governance?
- What is the nature of the client entity's operations, including its business practices?
- What are the attitudes of the client entity's key players towards such matters as aggressive interpretation of accounting standards and the internal control environment?
- Is the client entity aggressively concerned with maintaining the audit firm's fees as low as possible?
- Are there indications of an inappropriate limitation on the scope of audit work?
- Are there indications that the client entity might be involved in money laundering or other criminal activities?
- What are the reasons for the proposed appointment of the firm and non-reappointment of the predecessor auditor?

EXAMPLE 5.1: THE ACCEPTANCE DECISION

You are an audit manager in the audit firm Baxter & Hynes. The firm has been approached by Minder Ltd, which has decided to change its auditors as the directors are not happy with the efficiency and professionalism of the exiting audit firm. Minder Ltd received a qualified opinion from its auditors in the prior year with which it continues to disagree. Minder Ltd is the parent of two subsidiaries, Black Ltd and Red Ltd. You recall something in the newspaper with respect to the alleged fraud of a director within Black Ltd. Red Ltd is the direct competitor of one of your largest clients. From a query with the entity's accounts department, you note that the payroll function for Black Ltd and Red Ltd is carried out by your firm. The client's year end is 30 June 2018 and the entity is requesting that the audit be completed by the end of August 2018. July and August is a busy period for Baxter & Hynes.

Should Baxter & Hynes engage with this client entity?

Baxter & Hynes would be advised not to accept the engagement after considering the following:
- **Integrity of the Client** (1) A senior member of the client entity is alleged to have committed fraud, which calls into question the integrity of the client entity. (2) There may be reasons, other than those stated, behind its intention to remove the exiting auditors. The exiting auditors should be contacted to enquire if there are any reasons why they feel Baxter & Hynes should not accept the engagement. This may be driven by the qualification in the prior year rather than the efficiency and professionalism of the exiting auditors. The existence of that qualification brings with it a risk that most audit firms would prefer to avoid. (3) Finally, the client entity appears to be putting undue pressure on the audit firm to complete the audit within an eight-week period.
- **Ethical Considerations** (1) Acceptance of this audit would create an actual or perceived conflict of interest with an existing audit client of Baxter & Hynes, due to the fact that Red Ltd is the direct competitor of an existing client. (2) Additionally, a self-review, self-interest, advocacy, familiarity or management threat can arise due to the fact that Baxter & Hynes carry out other services for the client entity in the form of payroll.
- **Competence to Perform** Baxter & Hynes may not have the resources to complete this audit in the time period requested.

## 5.3 AUDIT ENGAGEMENT LETTERS

### Introduction

When an audit engagement is accepted, an **engagement letter** must be issued by the audit firm to the client entity. As stated in ISA 210 *Agreeing the Terms of Audit Engagements*, the auditor and the client entity should agree on the terms of the engagement and the terms should be recorded in writing. Issuance of an engagement letter is in the interest of both the audit firm and the client entity as it helps avoid any misunderstandings with respect to the engagement. The client entity and the auditor should agree on all the terms of the engagement and this agreement should be recognised through the signing of the engagement letter by both parties.

## Engagement Letter Contents

As outlined in ISA 210, the auditor should ensure that the engagement letter documents and confirms the scope and objective of the appointment.

The following are the main points to be included in an engagement letter:
* the objective of the audit of the financial statements;
* management's responsibility for the financial statements;
* the scope of the audit, including reference to applicable legislation, financial reporting framework, regulations, or pronouncements of professional bodies to which the auditor adheres;
* the form of any reports or other communications resulting from the engagement;
* the fact that, because of the test nature and other inherent limitations of an audit, together with the inherent limitations of internal control, there is an unavoidable risk that even some material misstatement may remain undiscovered;
* a request for unrestricted access to whatever records, documentation and other information are required in connection with the audit; and
* the basis of the audit fee calculation.

An example of an audit engagement letter can be found in Appendix 1 of ISA 210.

## Recurring Audits

A new engagement letter may not be required each year of a continuing engagement (**recurring audit**). However, each year the auditor should "… assess whether circumstances require the terms of the audit engagement to be revised and whether there is a need to remind the entity of the existing terms of the audit engagement" (ISA 210, paragraph 13).

Factors that could trigger the need for a new engagement letter may include the following:
* any indication that the client misunderstands the objective and scope of the audit;
* any revised or special terms of the engagement;
* a recent change of senior management or those charged with governance;
* a significant change in ownership;
* a change/rotation of an audit partner in an audit firm;
* a significant change in the nature or size of the client entity's business; or
* legal or regulatory requirements.

In some cases the client entity may request a change to the terms of the engagement. Should this arise, the auditor and the client entity should agree on the new terms, as outlined in ISA 210, paragraphs 14–17, provided that the auditor feels there is reasonable justification for changing the terms. Where the auditor is unable to agree to a change of the engagement and is not permitted to continue the original engagement, the auditor should withdraw and consider whether there is any obligation, either contractual or otherwise, to report to other parties, such as those charged with governance or shareholders, the circumstances necessitating the withdrawal.

Once the auditor has accepted the new engagement, or agreed to continue an existing engagement, the audit planning stage can commence.

## 5.4 AUDIT PLANNING

### Introduction

ISA 300 states that the auditor should plan an audit so that the engagement will be "performed in an effective manner" (paragraph 4) and reduce audit risk to an acceptably low level. In order to achieve this, planning an audit at two levels is necessary, with ISA 300 requiring the auditor to:
1. establish an "overall audit strategy" (paragraphs 7–8); and
2. "develop an audit plan" (paragraph 9).

It is important at this point to understand what is meant by overall audit strategy and audit plan. An **audit strategy** essentially describes the general terms of how an audit is to be carried out; an **audit plan** details the specific procedures to be carried out to implement the strategy and complete the audit.

Audit engagement partners and key audit team members should be involved in the planning phase of the audit in order to share knowledge and experience with junior team members and to alert the team to areas where the assessed risk of misstatement could be high. It also helps to ensure that audit work is assigned to team members with the appropriate level of skill and experience. The nature and extent of planning activities will not be the same on all engagements and will depend on the size and complexity of the client, the auditor's previous involvement with the client and changes in circumstances that occur during the audit engagement.

It is important for the audit team to realise that planning is not a discrete activity; while it initially takes place at the commencement of the audit, planning does not cease at this point. Planning is a dynamic process that should continue during the entire audit cycle, being amended and adapted as new information becomes available or issues arise during the course of audit testing.

### The Overall Audit Strategy

The audit strategy helps to define the overall approach that the auditor will take in carrying out the audit. The detailed audit plan outlines the testing that the audit team must perform in order to gain **sufficient appropriate audit evidence** about the transactions, balances and disclosures contained in the financial statements. However, before the auditor can develop a detailed audit plan they must first consider a number of key factors to enable them to ensure that the audit plan is the most effective and efficient in achieving the audit objectives and minimising audit risk. The audit strategy therefore guides the audit plan.

Outlined below are the key areas the auditor must consider when developing the overall audit strategy:

1. characteristics of the engagement;
2. **nature, timing and extent** of resources
3. the need for experts;
4. determining **materiality**;
5. understanding the client entity (risk and internal control assessment);
6. preliminary **analytical procedures**;
7. going concern. and
8. significant factors

### Characteristics of the Engagement

It is important for the auditor to gain an understanding of the broad characteristics of the client they are dealing with. In doing so, the auditor should consider:

- the **characteristics of the engagement that define its scope**, such as the financial reporting framework used, industry-specific reporting requirements or the locations of divisions within the entity;
- the **reporting obligations** for the entity, in order to determine the timing of the audit (i.e. to ensure filing dates are met);
- key dates and format for **communication with management**;
- identification of **material transactions, classes of transactions and balances within the financial statements**;
- consideration of **prior years' issues and errors**;
- consideration of **experience gained** during other engagements performed for the client entity or during the acceptance and continuance phase;
- consideration of **laws and regulations** that apply to the client entity (including tax laws); and
- identification of **related parties** and transactions with related parties requiring disclosure.

### Nature, Timing and Extent of Resources

As part of the planning stages of the audit, the resourcing of the engagement must be considered. ISA 300, paragraph 11, states:

"The auditor shall plan the nature, timing and extent of direction and supervision of engagement team members and the review of their work."

An audit team usually consists of a partner, manager, audit senior and junior (see **Table 5.2** below). The following are factors to be considered when selecting the audit team:

- Does the proposed audit team have the necessary skills and resources?
- Does the proposed audit team have the correct level of staff for the job?
- Are all staff members independent of the client?
- Is continuity of staff required?
- Has an engagement quality control reviewer been assigned?
- Is each member of the team aware of their role and responsibility within the audit team?

- Have dates for audit team meetings been set?
- Have dates been agreed with the client for the audit planning meeting and commencement of the audit, attendance at stocktakes, etc.?
- If the work of experts or other auditors is to be relied upon, have these parties been contacted and dates agreed by which their fieldwork is to be completed?
- Has a budget been set for the audit engagement and does it reflect the level and amount of time each audit team member will work on the client entity audit?

Continuity of team members from year to year can introduce efficiency into the audit as those team members will have gained knowledge and experience from working with the client previously. Too much continuity, however, may represent a **familiarity threat** to the auditor's integrity, objectivity and independence (see **Chapter 2**).

TABLE 5.2: ROLES AND RESPONSIBILITIES OF AN AUDIT TEAM

| | Audit Partner | Audit Manager | Audit Senior | Audit Junior |
|---|---|---|---|---|
| **Roles and Responsibilities** | • Acceptance and continuance procedures.<br>• Review of planning and completion stages.<br>• Review critical areas of the audit file.<br>• Review financial statements prior to being issued.<br>• Signing of audit report on financial statements. | • Review of audit file.<br>• Responsible for planning the audit in conjunction with the audit senior.<br>• Review of financial statements prior to audit partner's review.<br>• Review of critical matters prior to audit partner's review.<br>• Review of audit file prepared by audit senior. | • Liaise with manager with regard to audit planning.<br>• Review audit junior's work.<br>• Notify manager of contentious issues.<br>• Perform audit work.<br>• Provide on-the-job training for audit junior.<br>• Prepare client audit working file and/or reports to other auditors. | • Perform assigned audit work.<br>• Notify audit senior of any issues. |

## The Need for Experts

ISA 620 *Using the Work of an Auditor's Expert,* paragraph 7, states:
"If expertise in a field other than accounting or auditing is necessary to obtain sufficient appropriate audit evidence, the auditor shall determine whether to use the work of an auditor's expert."

Instances where experts may be required include areas such as: valuation of complex financial instruments, property, jewellery, works of art, biological assets, etc.; actuarial calculation of liabilities associated with insurance contracts or employee benefit plans; or estimation of oil and gas reserves.

ISA 620 does not, however, diminish the fact that the auditor has "sole responsibility for the audit opinion expressed". The auditor must take steps, as necessary, to determine that "the work of that expert is adequate for the auditor's purposes" and only then may they "accept that expert's findings or conclusions in the expert's field as appropriate audit evidence" (paragraph 3).

Before engaging the work of the expert, the auditor is responsible for evaluating the necessary qualifications, competence, capabilities and objectivity of the expert.

In evaluating the *work* of the expert, the auditor must evaluate its adequacy, including:
- "the relevance and reasonableness of that expert's findings or conclusions, and their consistency with other audit evidence" obtained;
- the "relevance and reasonableness" of any assumptions or methods used by the expert;
- the "relevance, completeness, and accuracy of that source data" used by the expert to draw their conclusion. (ISA 620, paragraph 12)

Under ISA 620, paragraph 9R-1, for audits of public interest entities (PIEs), the auditor is required to obtain confirmation from the external expert as to their independence from the client entity. Furthermore, the auditor is required to state this in the additional report to the audit committee (paragraph A20-1).

The need for experts is considered in more detail in **Chapter 10** and again throughout the chapters on substantive procedures (**Chapters 11–17**).

At this point of the audit, the auditor will also consider whether or not to use the work of the client's internal audit. The directions of ISA 610 *Using the Work of Internal Auditors* are considered in detail in **Chapter 10**.

## Determining Materiality

In **Chapter 1** it was established that the auditor expresses an opinion with **reasonable assurance**. The auditor's overall objective is "To obtain reasonable assurance about whether the financial statements as a whole are free from **material misstatement**, whether due to fraud or error ..." (ISA 200, paragraph 11). Reasonable assurance is measured by reference to materiality.

### What is Materiality?
Let us remind ourselves of these key terms, introduced in **Chapter 1**:

---

**Misstatement** ISA 450 *Evaluation of Misstatements Identified During the Audit*, paragraph 4: "A difference between the reported amount, classification, presentation or disclosure of a financial statement item and the amount, classification, presentation or disclosure that is required for the item to be in accordance with the applicable financial reporting framework. Misstatements can arise from error or fraud."

**Materiality** "Misstatements, including omissions, are considered to be material if they individually or in the aggregate, could reasonably be expected to influence the economic decisions of users taken on the basis of the financial statements" (ISA 320, paragraph 2).

---

In short, when a misstatement (or the aggregate of all misstatements) is significant enough that it could change or influence the decision of an informed person, a material misstatement has occurred.

**Example 5.2** below outlines simply the concept of materiality.

EXAMPLE 5.2: UNDERSTANDING MATERIALITY

**Scenario 1**

The inventory balance included in the financial statements is the highest balance on the SOFP at €10,000,000. The auditor has discovered during the performance of audit testing that inventory has been **understated** by €2,500,000 (i.e. 25%).

If the error identified is not adjusted, then the financial statements will be materially misstated due to the size of the error in relation to the financial statements taken as a whole.

**Scenario 2**

The inventory balance included in the financial statements is the highest balance on the SOFP at €10,000,000. The auditor has discovered during the performance of audit testing that inventory has been **understated** by €2,500 (i.e. 0.025%).

If the error is not adjusted, the financial statements will not be materially misstated due to the size of the error in relation to the financial statements as a whole.

### How do I Calculate Materiality?

There is no prescribed mathematical formula that will generate **materiality** for every client. ISA 320 *Materiality in Planning and Performing an Audit*, paragraph 4, advises:

> "The auditor's determination of materiality is a matter of **professional judgment**, and is affected by the auditor's perception of the financial information needs of users of the financial statements."

The standard does, however, offer guidance on how to approach the calculation of materiality:

1. identification of a benchmark (critical balance); and
2. application of a percentage against that benchmark.

A benchmark, or critical balance, is the key figure in the financial statements. ISA 320, paragraph A3, indicates areas that can assist the auditor in identifying what the benchmark may be for a particular client's accounts and includes:

- **Financial Statement Elements** What makes up the financial statements, e.g. assets, liabilities, equity, revenue, expenses, etc.?
- **Items of User Focus** Is the user focused on financial performance and therefore more interested in revenue and profit?
- **Nature of the Entity** Its life cycle, the industry it operates in and the economic environment. For example, if the client entity is in property development, revenue could be nil in some years and so instead the benchmark may be assets held for resale.
- **Ownership Structure** If the company is financed primarily by debt rather than equity, the user may be more interested in assets, and the claims on those assets, than on the equity earnings.

ISA 320 avoids giving quantitative guidelines on what percentages to apply to the benchmark. However, common methods have developed in practice that can be used to quantify overall materiality, as set out in **Table 5.3**.

TABLE 5.3: MATERIALITY BENCHMARK PERCENTAGES

| Benchmark | % |
|-----------|------|
| Earnings before Tax | 5–10% |
| Total Revenues | ½–5% |
| Total Assets | ½–2% |
| Equity | 1–2% |
| Net Assets | ½–1% |

In summary, materiality reflects the maximum error(s) that the financial statements could contain before it would impact the auditor's opinion on those financial statements. Remember, the auditor cannot certify that the financial statements are *absolutely accurate* – they are providing "reasonable assurance" so, by definition, some errors may remain.

## What is Performance Materiality?

The context of performance materiality is set out in ISA 320, paragraph 9, where it is defined as:

> "the amount or amounts set by the auditor at less than materiality for the financial statements as a whole to reduce to an appropriately low level the probability that the aggregate of uncorrected and undetected misstatements exceeds materiality for the financial statements as a whole."

Put simply, performance materiality can be classified as working materiality. Performance materiality ensures the auditor performs the right level of audit procedures relative to the nominal amount and risk associated with each transaction, class of transaction or account balance. Essentially, it provides the auditor with a margin of error, or a 'safety net', against the risk of material misstatements going undetected. Furthermore, it allows the auditor to reduce, to an acceptably low level, the **aggregation** risk (i.e. the risk that the aggregate of undetected or uncorrected misstatements, which are individually below overall materiality but when taken together exceed overall materiality).

In essence, if the auditor tests more (as a result of applying performance materiality), then less is untested, which in turn reduces the risk of undetected material errors in the untested population.

Performance materiality is always set lower than overall materiality. The consideration when setting performance materiality is risk – which is the auditor's subjective assessment. It is therefore a matter of judgement at what value below overall materiality should performance materiality be set. The risk assessment process is considered in **Chapter 7**.

EXAMPLE 5.3: DETERMINING AND SETTING MATERIALITY
AND ASSESSMENT OF MISSTATEMENTS

(Refer to **Appendix B** at the end of this textbook, Large Company Limited (Directors' Report and Financial Statements).)

**Step 1 – Determine overall materiality level for the financial statements as a whole**

From the directors' report in the accounts of Large Company Ltd, we note that it is involved in the manufacture of furniture and that revenue has increased by 41% to

€280,250,000. We also note that it is believed that revenue will continue to grow due to a push into the luxury market. It is fair to say that any shareholder would be interested in revenue growth and how it drives the profitability of the company (i.e. taking into account the effect on margins of the purchasing of higher value products). We conclude that the benchmark (critical balance in the financial statements) is profit before tax. Profit before tax in the statement of profit or loss and other comprehensive income is €72,850,000. If we were to apply common methods (**Table 5.3**), we would take 5–10% of this profit before tax as materiality. As prudent auditors we will set materiality at the lower end of this percentage range, i.e. 5% (the choice is a matter of judgement and is based on the auditor's experience and (sometimes) on the internal guidance and practice of the audit firm). Applying the 5% would derive a materiality level for the financial statements as a whole to be €3,642,500.

### Step 2 – Set performance materiality

The auditor will still need to consider materiality levels for particular classes of transactions, account balances or disclosures, where appropriate. This is achieved by setting a performance materiality level, which acts as a 'safety net'. The performance materiality takes account of undetected errors by testing more transactions, balances, etc. than would otherwise have been tested if a higher materiality level had been applied. In other words, the application of lower performance materiality means more items get tested. If we set performance materiality level at, say, 75%, the performance materiality is €2,731,875 (€3,642,500 × 75%), and we create a safety net of €910,675, reducing the risk of the auditor issuing an incorrect opinion.

### Step 3 – Using materiality in assessing misstatements

If during testing the auditor was to find a misstatement with respect to investment revenue that resulted in it being overstated by a50,000, would the auditor consider this to be a material misstatement? No, a50,000 is well below materiality and does not pose a concern for the auditor. It will, however, be recorded on a **schedule of unadjusted misstatements/ differences** ('errors schedule') to ensure that when added to other misstatements the aggregate amount is considered.

Now consider that the auditor, during testing, finds that property, plant and equipment is overstated by €3,200,000. Is this material? Yes, if we consider performance materiality, then the overstatement is material as it exceeds €2,731,875. Individually this may not be material to the financial statements as a whole (although it is close and would depend on the relationship between the values or the percentage to the carrying value), but by its nature it might be material.

### Understanding the Client Entity (Risk and Internal Control Assessment)

ISA 315 *Identifying and Assessing the Risks of Material Misstatement through Understanding the Entity and its Environment* outlines the auditor's responsibilities with respect to:
1. risk assessment procedures and related activities;
2. the required understanding of the entity and its environment, including the entity's internal control systems;
3. identifying and assessing the risks of material misstatement; and
4. documentation.

A full discussion of the requirements of ISA 315 is given in **Chapter 7** and **Chapter 8**.

## *Preliminary Analytical Procedures*

ISA 520 *Analytical Procedures,* paragraph 4, defines **analytical procedures** as:
"evaluations of financial information through analysis of plausible relationships among both financial and non-financial data. Analytical procedures also encompass such investigation as is necessary of identified **fluctuations or relationships that are inconsistent** with other relevant information or that differ from expected values by a significant amount." (emphasis added)

The following outlines the stages where analytical procedures are used:
* **Planning Stage** – as part of understanding the client and assisting the risk-identification process. Often referred to as preliminary analytical procedures.
* **Substantive Testing Stage** – as an efficient method of testing.
* **Final Stage** – as a method of ensuring (prior to the signing of the audit report) that the auditor now understands all fluctuations or unusual relationships identified at the planning stage and during the audit.

Essentially, preliminary analytical procedures assist the auditor in understanding the entity, allowing them to better plan the nature, timing and extent of audit procedures. The main objective at this stage is to understand the client entity's business and transactions, but also to identify financial statement account balances and transactions that are likely to contain misstatements (the role of preliminary analytical procedures in the risk assessment process is dealt with in **Chapter 7**). It is important to note that preliminary analytical procedures do not aim to prove why there are unusual variances to prior year or why unusual relationships exist, but rather to highlight the fact that something unusual exists that warrants further investigation.

## *Going Concern*

ISA 570 *Going Concern* deals with the auditor's responsibilities relating to management's use of the going concern assumption in the preparation of the financial statements. The bulk of the **going concern** review is generally left to the completion stage of the audit. However, some consideration should be given to it at the planning stage where risks identified may indicate that the company cannot continue as a going concern. If a serious risk with respect to going concern exists, the entire basis of the financial statements would be incorrect as the going concern assumption is one of the fundamental assumptions on which financial statements are prepared. If the auditor proceeds without initial consideration of going concern, the entire audit may prove to be inefficient as the financial statements would look very different if they needed to be prepared on a break-up basis.

It is the responsibility of **management** and **those charged with governance** to determine whether the going concern assumption is appropriate in the preparation of financial statements. If, however, the going concern assumption is invalid, the financial statements would need to be prepared on a 'break-up basis'.

Indications of going concern problems can include:
* deteriorating liquidity position not backed by sufficient financing arrangements;
* aggressive growth strategy not backed by sufficient finance, which ultimately leads to overtrading;

- bankruptcy of a major customer of the company; or
- continuous losses.

Going concern is considered in more detail in **Chapter 18**.

### Significant Factors

The consideration of significant factors is an important part of developing an effective overall audit strategy. Identifying any significant factors can better inform the planning of the audit procedures. The Appendix to ISA 300 provides examples of matters that could be considered, including:

"• Significant business developments affecting the entity, including changes in information technology and business processes, changes in key management, and acquisitions, mergers and divestments;
- Significant industry developments such as changes in industry regulations and new reporting requirements.
- Other significant relevant developments. such as changes in the legal environment affecting the entity."

### The Audit Plan

The **audit plan** is more detailed than the overall audit strategy and determines the nature, timing and extent of audit procedures to be performed by the audit team in order to gain sufficient appropriate audit evidence over account balances and transactions and allow the audit firm to issue an opinion on the financial statements.

The audit plan includes the following elements, which are defined in ISA 330 *The Auditor's Responses to Assessed Risks,* paragraphs A5–A7:
- **Nature** of audit procedures "… refers to its purpose (i.e. test of controls or substantive procedure) and its type (that is, inspection, observation, inquiry, confirmation, recalculation, reperformance, or analytical procedure). The nature of audit procedures is of most importance in responding to the assessed risks."
- **Timing** of audit procedures "… refers to when it is performed, or the period or date to which the audit evidence applies."
- **Extent** of audit procedures "… refers to the quantity to be performed, for example, a sample size or the number of observations of a control activity".

### Nature of Audit Procedures

The two types of audit procedure used are **controls testing** and **substantive testing**. The auditor should consider which type of testing will address the assessed risk in the most efficient and effective manner and reduce the risk of material misstatements to an acceptably low level. An appropriate approach might be to include a combination of both controls testing and substantive testing. In deciding the combination the auditor should give consideration to a number of factors, including:
1. how the controls were applied at relevant times during the period under audit;
2. the consistency with which they were applied; and
3. by whom, or by what means, they were applied.

The relationship between controls testing and substantive testing was introduced in **Section 4.4** and is expanded upon in **Chapter 8**, Section 8.4.

### Timing of Audit Procedures

When the auditor has decided upon the nature of the audit procedures to be performed, consideration must then be given to the timing of the procedures, i.e. when the audit team will carry out the testing.

Audit procedures can be performed at an interim date, at year end or after year end.

**An interim audit occurs a few months before year end** and generally covers the planning activities, including controls testing. Some substantive testing may also be performed at this stage; however, roll-forward procedures must then be performed to audit the transactions from the interim testing date to the year end date. The most common substantive procedure carried out is on the receivables balance, whereby the auditor will audit the receivables balance at, say, the end of November and then, after the year end, they will only have to audit the transactions that occurred from 1 December to 31 December, hence reducing the amount of time needed on the audit after the SOFP date.

Other areas normally tested at an interim stage include non-current assets and their related additions and disposals. The auditor needs to be careful to ensure that an interim audit does not take place too early – a long period between the interim audit and the SOFP date creates unnecessary risk. An interim audit can assist in balancing the workload of the audit team, as well as help to identify issues at an early stage and give the audit team time to respond to those issues. In deciding whether or not to perform interim testing, the auditor should consider the following:

- How strong is the overall control environment? Performing a roll-forward between an interim date and the period-end is unlikely to be effective if the general control environment is poor.
- How strong are the specific controls over the account balance or class of transactions being considered?
- Is the required evidence available to perform the test?
- Would a procedure before the period-end address the nature and substance of the risk involved?
- Would the interim procedure address the period or date to which the audit evidence relates?
- How much additional evidence will be required for the remaining unaudited period between the date of the interim audit and the period-end?

Activities such as attendance at the physical inventory count usually occur at the reporting date, although occasionally they can take place before or after that date (see **Chapter 12**, Section 12.8).

Substantive testing is generally left until the **final audit (after the SOFP date)**, after the books and records have been completed and a draft set of financial statements has been prepared. Where the controls of the client entity are deemed weak, the auditor will perform the majority of the audit procedures after the year end date.

## *Extent of Audit Procedures*

Finally, the audit plan requires consideration of the extent of audit procedures. Extent of testing refers to the quantity of transactions (sample size) upon which specific audit testing is to be performed. As a general rule, where the assessed risk is deemed to be high, the extent of testing to be performed will be greater. The objective of the audit team is to obtain audit evidence that is sufficient and appropriate to gain comfort over the assertions surrounding the transactions, balances or disclosures being tested.

Sufficient appropriate audit evidence can be obtained by:
- **Selecting all items** (100% of the population)  This is appropriate when:
  - the population constitutes a small number of high-value items;
  - there is a significant risk and other means do not provide sufficient appropriate audit evidence; or
  - where computer-assisted audit techniques (CAATs) can be used in a larger population to electronically test a repetitive calculation or other process.
- **Selecting specific items**  This is appropriate for:
  - high-value or key items;
  - all items over a certain amount;
  - items to obtain information about matters such as the nature of the entity, the nature of transactions, and internal control; and
  - items to test control activities.
- **Selecting a representative sample** of items from the population. This can be performed using judgemental or statistical sampling methods.

Audit evidence and **sampling** are dealt with in more detail in **Chapter 6**.

## Documentation of Audit Plan and Strategy

Audit documentation supports the auditor's audit conclusions and, ultimately, the audit opinion; therefore the collection of audit documentation is an integral part of any audit procedure. This is discussed further in **Chapter 6**, Section 6.7.

It is important for the audit team to document each step involved in developing the overall **audit strategy** and the detailed **audit plan**. This is specified in ISA 300, paragraph 12:

"The auditor shall include in the audit documentation:
  (a) The overall audit strategy;
  (b) The audit plan; and
  (c) Any significant changes made during the audit engagement to the overall audit strategy or the audit plan, and the reasons for such changes."

The auditor should document the details of the audit strategy and audit plan as evidence that they were completed and to record the key decisions considered necessary to appropriately plan the audit and communicate significant matters to the audit team.

The usual means of documenting the detailed audit plan is to outline the:
- nature of testing to be performed;
- extent of testing to be performed;
- assertions that each test is intended to address (see **Chapter 6**);
- details of who is to perform the testing; and
- timing of various auditing activities.

### Communication of the Audit Plan

The audit plan should be made available to all members of the audit team. It may also be helpful for the audit team to communicate elements of the detailed audit plan to the client entity's management or those charged with governance. Doing so will allow them to gain a greater insight into the audit process and to identify the information that the audit team will request from the client entity's personnel.

## 5.5 CONCLUSION

A considerable amount of audit work is performed well before the client entity provides the final set of financial statements on which the auditor is required to provide an opinion.

The audit firm wishes to make a profit from the performance of the audit, but without taking any unnecessary risks on its reputation Therefore, the auditor:
- should not take on or continue engagements with client entities that bring with them undue risk;
- clearly outline the term of the engagement in the form of an **engagement letter** to avoid any misunderstandings with respect to the audit; and
- plan the audit to ensure it is efficient (achieves maximum productivity) without compromising its effectiveness in identifying material misstatements.

It is important for the audit team to realise that audit planning is a continuous process that does not cease when the overall strategy and the detailed audit plan are developed. Both should be updated and changed as necessary throughout the audit cycle in response to risks identified and as the results of audit testing become available. Reasons for significant changes should be documented along with the auditor's response to the events, and conditions or results of audit procedures that resulted in such changes.

### SUMMARY OF LEARNING OBJECTIVES

**Learning Objective 1** Understand and be able to apply the audit acceptance and continuance considerations.

When considering accepting or continuing an audit, the auditor will assess the client entity's integrity, the audit firm's competence to perform the audit and the ethical requirements. They will also contact the predecessor auditor in the case of a new engagement, to ensure there is no reason why they should not accept the engagement.

**Learning Objective 2** Know the role and contents of an engagement letter.

An engagement letter should be drawn up and signed by both parties to avoid any misunderstandings with respect to the engagement. In the case of a recurring audit, there may be instances when the engagement letter will need to be updated, e.g. due to changes in scope or legislation. There are many points that may be included in an engagement letter, such as the objective of the financial statement audit, management's responsibility for the financial statements, the scope of the audit, etc.

**Learning Objective 3** Know the stages of audit planning and be able to distinguish between the overall audit strategy and the audit plan.

The audit strategy essentially describes the general terms of how an audit is to be carried out. The audit plan details the specific procedures to be carried out to implement the strategy and complete the audit.

**Overall Audit Strategy** Where the auditor considers, for example:
- characteristics of the engagement;
- roles and responsibilities within the audit team;
- the need for experts;
- the determination of materiality;
- understanding the client entity (risk and internal control assessment);
- preliminary analytical procedures; and
- going concern.

**Audit Plan** Once the audit strategy is determined, the auditor should refine this to formulate a detailed plan that dictates the nature, timing and extent of audit procedures.

**Learning Objective 4** Develop an understanding of the role of analytical procedures at the planning stage.

The main objective of applying analytical procedures at this stage in the audit is to understand the client entity's business and transactions and to identify financial statement account balances and transactions that are likely to contain misstatements. Performing preliminary analytical procedures helps the auditor to better plan the nature, timing and extent of the audit procedures.

**Learning Objective 5** Appreciate the concept of materiality, including how and why it is calculated.

When a misstatement (or the aggregate impact of all misstatements) is significant enough that it could change or influence the decision of an informed person, a material misstatement is said to have occurred. In order to assess if an item is material, the auditor sets a monetary amount that represents a benchmark by which to measure the significance of misstatements as well as plan which transactions, balances, etc. will be tested and to what degree. The auditor must use their judgement when setting materiality by first identifying the benchmark (a key figure in the financial statements) and then applying a percentage to that benchmark (see **Table 5.3**).

**Learning Objective 6** Be able to discuss the options available to the auditor with regard to the nature, timing and extent of audit procedures when designing the audit plan.

The nature of the audit procedures refers to the purpose (what the specific procedure is trying to achieve) and type (what specific procedure will be used to achieve this). The auditor can adopt more substantive analytical procedures if the client entity's control environment is considered to be strong. The timing of audit procedures refers to when the auditor carries out testing. If the client entity's control environment is considered to be strong, more testing can be performed prior to the reporting date. Finally, extent refers to the quantity of the testing to be performed. For example, smaller sample sizes can be taken if the auditor has assessed the client entity control environment to be strong.

## QUESTIONS

### Self-test Questions

5.1   What four key areas would you, as auditor, consider before accepting an audit engagement?

5.2   What factors is the auditor interested in when assessing client integrity?

5.3   What factors is the auditor interested in when assessing their competence to perform an audit?

5.4   Name three ethical considerations the auditor should take into account when assessing whether or not to accept a new audit client or to continue an existing audit engagement.

5.5   What is an engagement letter and what does it contain?

5.6   Distinguish between the terms 'audit strategy' and 'audit plan'.

5.7   What are the key stages involved in developing the overall audit strategy?

5.8   What is meant by the term 'materiality'?

5.9   What is meant by the term 'analytical procedures'?

5.10  At what stage during the audit does the auditor use analytical procedures?

5.11  Why is it necessary for the auditor to consider going concern early on in the audit?

5.12  What is meant by the terms 'nature', 'timing' and 'extent' with regard to audit procedures?

5.13  Why is it important to document the audit plan and the audit strategy?

**Review Questions**

(See Suggested Solutions to Review Questions in **Appendix C.**)

## Question 5.1

Your audit firm has been asked to accept the position of auditor to CAT Ltd as the incumbent auditor is retiring. CAT Ltd is a long-established and successful large company that manufactures medicines. Your audit firm's first audit of the company will be for the year ended 31 December 2018. You have been asked by the audit partner to draft an engagement letter for the audit and to begin initial planning.

**Requirement**
(a) Explain the procedures that an auditor should adopt before accepting an appointment.
(b) Identify the matters that should be included in a letter of engagement.

## Question 5.2

You are employed by an audit firm, one of whose client entities is Leoville Ltd, a family-owned company in the textile industry. It has recently reached agreement with a rival company, Poyferre Ltd, to jointly develop and manufacture a new range of children's clothing for sale through multiple retailers. A new company, Las Cases Ltd, will be formed for this purpose, with Leoville and Poyferre each owning 50% of the share capital.

Several days ago, you accompanied the audit partner to a meeting with Leoville's shareholders and management at which they explained that the company would need to raise €4 million to fund its investment in Las Cases Ltd. It is proposed that this be funded entirely from debt and a preliminary meeting with its bankers has already been held.

Leoville has agreed with its bankers that it will make a formal presentation to them in four weeks' time in relation to this application for finance. The principal elements of the presentation will be:
• a business plan for the new venture; and
• Leoville's management accounts for the six months ended 30 June 2018.

At your meeting with Leoville's management, they indicated that they require assistance from your firm in relation to both of these matters. This assistance is to include the drafting of the business plan and preparation of trading projections for the new venture for the period from 1 January 2019 to 31 December 2019. It is apparent that management from both Leoville and Poyferre will have significant input into drafting the plan and, in addition, you are aware that they intend to retain specialist textile industry consultants to advise on particular aspects of the venture. In essence, it seems that your firm will be involved in 'project managing' the preparation of the business plan.

As Leoville's bankers have requested that the management accounts for the six months to 30 June 2018 be reviewed by Leoville's auditors, your audit firm has been requested to undertake such a review as soon as possible. You understand that the bank merely wishes your audit firm to confirm that the management accounts have been 'properly prepared'.

Your audit firm's operating procedures require that an engagement letter be issued for all assignments it is asked to undertake. The audit partner has asked that you prepare a draft of this letter for his review at a meeting to be held in two days' time.

**Requirement** Prepare a draft engagement letter for the work that Leoville Ltd has asked your audit firm to undertake.

## Question 5.3

You are an audit senior working for a firm of Chartered Accountants. The partner responsible for staff training has asked you to prepare some training material on the firm's audit approach for new trainees. The partner has specifically asked that the material addresses the firm's approach to planning, controlling and documentation of an audit in order to ensure that the trainees are aware of the high standards expected of an auditor in this area.

**Requirement** Prepare a memorandum to new trainees, highlighting the key points specified by the partner.

# GATHERING AUDIT EVIDENCE

## LEARNING OBJECTIVES

Having studied this chapter on gathering audit evidence you should:

1. understand what is meant by sufficient appropriate audit evidence;
2. be able to identify whether audit evidence is sufficient and appropriate with respect to specific assertions;
3. have an understanding of the methods of obtaining audit evidence;
4. have an appreciation of the types of testing carried out for controls testing and substantive testing (to support further learning in later chapters);
5. understand the concept of substantive analytical procedures and the essential considerations when deciding whether or not to use them;
6. understand how to carry out external confirmations;
7. understand the importance of audit documentation/audit working papers as well as their format;
8. obtain a strong insight into sampling, its risks, methods and projection techniques;
9. understand the auditor's responsibility with regard to opening balances; and
10. understand the auditing procedures applied to accounting estimates.

## CHECKLIST OF RELEVANT STANDARDS

The relevant standards, in both the RoI and the UK/NI, covered in this chapter are:
- ISA 230 *Audit Documentation*
- ISA 500 *Audit Evidence*
- ISA 501 *Audit Evidence – Specific Considerations for Selected Items*
- ISA 505 *External Confirmations*
- ISA 510 *Initial Audit Engagements – Opening Balances*
- ISA 520 *Analytical Procedures*
- ISA 530 *Audit Sampling*
- ISA 540 *Auditing Accounting Estimates, Including Fair Value Accounting Estimates, and Related Disclosures*

Note, in general when referring to ISAs, it should be understood as referring to the UK and Ireland versions, unless otherwise specified as either ISA (UK) or ISA (Ireland). See the Introduction for an extant list of auditing standards for the RoI and the UK/NI.

## KEY TERMS AND DEFINITIONS FOR THIS CHAPTER

**Audit Evidence**  All information used by the auditor in arriving at the conclusions on which the audit opinion is based, including the information contained in the accounting records underlying the financial statements and other information.

**Audit Trail**  The electronic or 'paper trail' that provides the auditor with audit evidence regarding the step-by-step documented history of a transaction.

**Control Risk**  The risk that a material misstatement could occur in an assertion. Controls should be put in place to address risks and should prevent, detect or correct fraud or errors that may occur. Absence of these types of control increases control risk. For example, where cash reconciliations are not performed daily, this poses a control risk.

**Corroborative Evidence**  Evidence or information that strengthens or supports other evidence or information received.

**Detection Risk**  The risk that the auditor will not detect a material misstatement that exists in an assertion.

**Directional Testing**  Refers to the direction in which the auditor performs a test. For example, to test for completeness the auditor performs tests from source documents to the general ledger; whereas to test for occurrence, the auditor performs tests in the opposite direction, i.e. from the general ledger to source documents.

**Dual Test**  A test that can be used to support both controls testing and substantive testing procedures.

**Inherent Risk**  The susceptibility of an assertion to a misstatement that could be material. Inherent risks exist due to the nature of the industry in which the client entity operates, product type or transaction types. For example, an entity that deals predominantly in cash is inherently risky.

**Significant Risk**   An identified and assessed risk of material misstatement that, in the auditor's judgement, requires special audit consideration.

**Substantive Analytical Procedures**   Refer to the calculation of an expected value based on data relationships to validate audit assertions. This can include the simple expectation that revenue in the current year will be the same as the prior year because there are no perceived factors indicating a change, or it can use the prior year as a base and then project to the current year based on perceived events that are deemed to have impacted on the revenue figure.

**Sufficient Appropriate Audit Evidence**   'Appropriate' refers to the requirement for evidence to be of a high quality and to be relevant to the objective of the audit procedure; 'sufficient' refers to the quantity of evidence obtained.

**Tests of Detail**   A type of substantive procedure that refers to the selection of a sample and the tracing of each item selected to evidence that supports the assertion being tested.

## 6.1 INTRODUCTION

This chapter is concerned with audit evidence, both in general and as it relates to specific auditable classes of transactions and balances in the financial statements.

The most appropriate place to start is with the definition of **sufficient appropriate audit evidence**. This is discussed in **Section 6.2**, which outlines the various layers of interpretation surrounding this term. Essentially, the term defines what is expected of the audit evidence gathered by the auditor. It is important to understand that within this term lies the requirement for audit evidence to be sufficient in quantity, reliable in source and relevant to the management assertions (audit objectives) being tested.

Having established the standard of evidence required, in **Section 6.3** we explore the various **methods of obtaining evidence** that are open to the auditor. A significant discussion is dedicated to one particular method of gathering evidence: **analytical procedures**. This method warrants particular attention due to the fact that it is used at three key stages of the audit process: the planning stage; the substantive testing stage; and the audit completion stage.

Having gained an appreciation of how audit evidence is collected and the standard of audit evidence required, in **Section 6.4** we explain how the auditor evaluates the evidence gathered. In **Section 6.5** we consider the types of testing procedure used by the auditor at the controls testing stage (**tests of detail**) and at the substantive testing stage (tests of details or **substantive analytical procedures**).

**Section 6.6** deals with the specific audit technique of **external confirmations** – one of the most reliable forms of audit evidence as it is independent, obtained directly by the auditor and exists in documentary form.

Audit documentation and the requirements of ISA 230 *Audit Documentation* are the subject of **Section 6.7**, which outlines the importance of audit documentation.

Auditing would not be possible without the use of **audit sampling**, and **Section 6.8** takes us through the various sampling methods, sample design considerations, the risks associated with sampling and the factors that influence sample size.

The final two sections of this chapter deal with two specific types of balances that exist in the financial statements. **Section 6.9** addresses how the auditor approaches the opening balances (comparatives figures) in the financial statements. **Section 6.10** outlines the audit procedures used when auditing accounting estimates.

The chapters that follow this chapter require you to have a full understanding of what is denoted by audit evidence and how the auditor collects and evaluates audit evidence.

## 6.2 SUFFICIENT APPROPRIATE AUDIT EVIDENCE

### Introduction

The primary purpose of an audit is for the auditor to issue an audit opinion on the financial statements. In order to do this, the auditor must gain evidence that supports the balances, transactions and disclosures in the financial statements. An **audit opinion** cannot be issued where **sufficient appropriate audit evidence** has not been obtained.

ISA 500 *Audit Evidence*, paragraph 5, defines **audit evidence** as:

> "Information used by the auditor in arriving at the conclusions on which the auditor's opinion is based ... [and] includes both information contained in the accounting records underlying the financial statements and information obtained from other sources".

Basically, audit evidence is information the auditor requires in order to support and conclude whether or not the financial statements give a **true and fair view**. Examples of audit evidence include:
- sales/purchase/sundry invoices;
- supplier statements;
- contracts for work to be performed;
- client entity's spreadsheets, e.g. budgets;
- client entity's control manuals;
- valuation reports, e.g. from surveyors or inventory valuation experts;
- minutes from shareholders'/directors' meetings;
- third-party confirmations, e.g. bank confirmations, legal confirmations or debtor confirmations; and
- audit working papers, e.g. those papers containing recalculations of depreciation, or workings and results of analytical procedures.

ISA 500, paragraph 6, requires the auditor to "design and perform audit procedures that are appropriate in the circumstances for the purpose of obtaining sufficient appropriate audit evidence". The meaning of the term sufficient appropriate audit evidence has many layers, as depicted in **Figure 6.1** below. Sufficiency refers to the quantity of evidence, whereas appropriateness refers to quality. Quality in this regard is a twofold term, referring to both the reliability and the relevance of the evidence.

FIGURE 6.1: SUFFICIENT APPROPRIATE AUDIT EVIDENCE

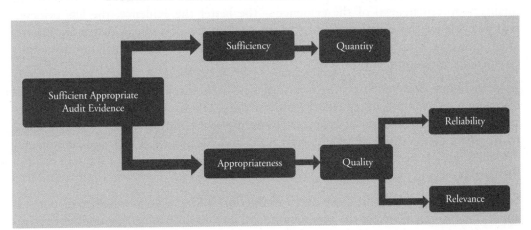

The auditor will seek sufficient appropriate audit evidence to satisfy all of the audit objectives (**management assertions**). In **Chapter 4**, Section 4.3 the assertions for transactions and account balances were introduced, a summary of which is given in **Table 6.1** below. Familiarity with these different assertions is critical to understanding what is sufficient and what is appropriate audit evidence.

TABLE 6.1: MANAGEMENT ASSERTIONS/AUDIT OBJECTIVES

| **Transactions**<br>**(e.g. revenue, expenses, bank transactions, fixed asset additions, etc.)** | **Balances**<br>**(e.g. asset, liability and equity balances in the statement of financial position)** |
| --- | --- |
| Occurrence | Existence |
| Completeness | Completeness |
| Classification/Recording | Valuation |
| Rights and Obligations | Rights and Obligations |
| Cut-off | |
| Presentation/Classification and Disclosure | |

## What is Sufficient Evidence?

ISA 500 states that the auditor must obtain evidence that is sufficient and appropriate. As we have seen, sufficiency refers to the quantity of evidence.

The quantity of audit evidence is directly linked to the risk of material misstatement identified at the assertion level. For example, if the auditor believes there is a risk that not all expenses are recorded, they will perform a greater degree of testing to search for unrecorded expenses. As a general rule, the higher the assessed level of risk, the more audit evidence is required. The quantity of audit evidence is also directly linked to the quality (appropriateness) of the evidence – the better the evidence, the less evidence required. Hence the sufficiency and the appropriateness of audit evidence are interrelated. However, simply obtaining a greater quantity of audit evidence will not necessarily compensate for poor quality.

In determining how much evidence is sufficient, in addition to the materiality of the transaction or balance being tested, the auditor will take into consideration any risks associated with that transaction or balance. For example, if controls testing indicated a risk with respect to the existence of property, plant and equipment (PPE), the auditor may decide to test a larger sample size to prove that PPE exists at the date of the statement of financial position.

Sample size is considered in more detail in **Section 6.8**, as well as whether or not it is appropriate to test 100% of the population, and how to determine the number of items in a population that should be selected for sampling purposes.

### What is Appropriate Audit Evidence?

Appropriate evidence is a measure of its quality and refers to both the **reliability** and **relevance** of the evidence.

#### *Reliability*

The reliability of audit evidence can vary and often the auditor needs to use **professional judgement** in deciding whether the audit evidence obtained can be relied upon. ISA 500, paragraph A31, states that audit evidence is more reliable when:
- it is obtained from an independent source, e.g. a bank confirmation letter;
- if generated internally, the entity's controls are effective; however, if the controls are not deemed to be effective, then the quality of the evidence produced by the entity will most likely not be reliable (for example, reports generated from an accounting system that has been found to be unreliable and susceptible to errors should not be assessed as reliable);
- it is obtained directly by the auditor, e.g. debtors' confirmation letters where responses are sent directly to the audit firm, removing the opportunity for the client entity's management to manipulate responses;
- it is in documentary rather than verbal form (verbal evidence can often be denied, whereas documentary evidence will be held on record by the auditor); and
- it is provided from original documents (for example, copies of sales contracts may have been manipulated to present the contract in a different light).

In general, the reliability of evidence depends on the circumstances surrounding its origin and source. Consider the following practical examples in **Table 6.2**, which highlight how the degree of reliability may vary depending on the nature of the audit evidence obtained.

In all instances the auditor should endeavour to gain the most reliable evidence available.

TABLE 6.2: RELIABILITY OF EVIDENCE – EXAMPLES

| Reliable audit evidence | Less reliable audit evidence |
|---|---|
| Confirmation of receivables balance received directly from the client entity's customer – it is completely independent of the client entity. | Receivables balance per year-end ledger provided by the client entity – not as independent as direct third-party confirmation. |
| Year-end receivables aged listing (showing all customers' balances by reference to the amount of time they have been outstanding), if controls testing has concluded that the system can be relied upon – strong control environment equates to more confidence over information produced in that environment. | Year-end receivables aged listing, if tests of controls have concluded that the system has material weaknesses and cannot be relied upon – weak control environment equates to less confidence over information produced in that environment. |
| Observation of the application of a control by the auditor, e.g. the need for two people to authorise an electronic payment through the bank by entry of passwords on the computer system – seeing is believing. | Documentation, such as written policies and procedures or workflow diagrams prepared by the client entity and provided to the auditor – better to witness the event than be told it happens. |
| Letter from solicitor confirming that there are no claims against the entity at the period end. | Oral representation from client entity stating that there are no claims against it at the period end. |
| Original bank statement – authenticity. | Copy of period-end bank statement from client. |
| Attendance by auditor at period-end inventory count. | Inspection of period-end inventory listing supplied by the client entity. |

### Relevance

The relevance of audit evidence refers to the "logical connection" (ISA 500, paragraph A27) of the evidence or test with the management assertion/audit objective that the auditor is trying to address. For example, if the auditor was testing the valuation assertion with respect to receivables and obtained confirmations from the client entity's customers regarding their account balances, this evidence would not be appropriate because it is not **relevant** to the assertion. The circularisation has merely proved that the customer acknowledges that they owe the money, but not that they have the ability to pay. **Table 6.3** outlines some further examples in assessing the relevance of audit evidence.

TABLE 6.3: ASSESSING THE RELEVANCE OF AUDIT EVIDENCE

| Transaction Class/ Account Balance | Management Assertion/ Audit Objective | Suggested Test | Is the suggested test relevant to address the assertion/ objective? | Why? |
|---|---|---|---|---|
| Non-current Assets | Existence | Obtain original invoice to support the purchase of the asset. | No | Obtaining original invoice only proves that the asset was purchased but not that it exists at year end. A more appropriate test would be to inspect the physical asset and confirm it is in use at the year end. |
| Receivables | Valuation | Obtain confirmation from the client entity's customer that the balance is correct. | No | Obtaining confirmation from the customer that it owes the amount does not provide comfort that the customer has the ability or inclination to pay. A more appropriate test to cover the valuation of a receivable would be to review receipts dated after the reporting date to see whether the balance has been paid. |
| Inventory | Completeness | Review of sales order book for the new year to see if inventory is saleable. | No | Reviewing the sales order book for new year helps to prove the valuation assertion (i.e. the inventory is saleable), but is not appropriate to prove completeness of inventory. A more appropriate test would be to observe the physical inventory count, make a selection of inventory items and compare them to the physical inventory count sheet to ensure they are correctly recorded. |
| Revenue | Completeness | Select invoice from general ledger and trace it to the invoice, the signed dispatch note and the original sales order. | No | When testing for completeness, the auditor should not start with the general ledger – tracing from general ledger to source tests for occurrence, not completeness. A more appropriate test would be to start from the source and trace back to the general ledger. |

The last example in **Table 6.3** illustrates the importance of the **direction** of the test (i.e. from source data to general ledger, or from general ledger source). This is referred to as **directional testing**. The direction of the test is important when considering the relevance of the test. In order to appreciate the concept of directional testing, consider **Example 6.1** below.

EXAMPLE 6.1: DIRECTIONAL TESTING

You are provided with a computer-system listing of customer orders raised during the period under review. You are also provided with the list of all the invoices that support the €3,000,000 revenue balance in the draft financial statements. You are testing the completeness assertion.

From the invoice listing that supports the €3,000,000 revenue figure in the financial statements, you select 20 invoices and trace them back to related signed customer POD (purchase order delivery) notes. You successfully trace all of the invoices back to a valid signed POD note. Have you satisfied your objective to test the completeness assertion?

**No**, you have not satisfied your objective to test the completeness assertion. You have proved the occurrence assertion (i.e. that the transactions recorded in the general ledger are supported by valid events, in this case, the delivery of the goods). However, you have not yet proved that all orders placed by customers and delivered to them are included in the general ledger. In order to prove completeness, you must start with the source data and trace the transactions recorded there to the general ledger. The correct test would be to select 20 customer orders, trace them to signed customer POD notes and sales invoices **and** ensure that these were recorded in the general ledger.

A single test may well provide evidence with respect to more than one assertion. For example, in **Table 6.3** above we refer to inspecting receipts from customers after the SOFP date. This test provides evidence with respect to not only the valuation assertion but also the existence assertion, as customers would not have paid the balance if it did not exist.

Different types of testing will be necessary in order to address each assertion at the financial statement level. In some instances a combination of tests will be used. The detailed audit testing plan will have been developed during the planning phase and will be updated as necessary throughout the audit process.

The term sufficient appropriate audit evidence should now be fully understood. Remember, the auditor will seek sufficient appropriate audit evidence to satisfy all of the audit objectives (management assertions). **Table 6.4** below illustrates the application of specific audit tests to address the different assertions (objectives).

TABLE 6.4: DEVELOPMENT OF AUDIT TESTS TO COVER ASSERTIONS

| Financial Statement Area | Audit Test | Nature of Audit Test | Assertions Addressed |
|---|---|---|---|
| Revenue | Select random months and request to see the completed bank reconciliations. Review the bank reconciliations to ensure they are signed by the reviewer. | Controls testing (tests of details) | ✓ Occurrence ✓ Existence ✓ Completeness ✓ Classification/ Recording ✓ Rights and Obligations |
| Property, Plant and Equipment (PPE) | Agreeing PPE additions (per the PPE note in the financial statements) to supporting documentation. | Substantive testing (tests of details) | ✓ Occurrence ✓ Classification/ Recording ✓ Rights and Obligations |
| Revenue | Calculate expected revenue by taking prior-year revenue and adjusting in line with sales price increases applied during the period. Compare this expected sales figure with the actual revenue recorded in the draft financial statements ensuring the difference is within a threshold range. | Substantive testing (substantive analytical procedures) | ✓ Occurrence ✓ Completeness ✓ Classification/ Recording |
| Accounts Payable | Reconcile balance per payables ledger to supplier statements. | Substantive testing (tests of details) | ✓ Completeness ✓ Classification/ Recording ✓ Existence ✓ Rights and Obligations |
| Inventory | Attend the physical inventory count and select random inventory items from the inventory count sheet and agree them to the physical inventory items in the warehouse. | Substantive testing (tests of details) | ✓ Completeness ✓ Classification/ Recording |

As we can see from **Table 6.4**, some tests will provide the auditor with evidence to both substantive test of details and controls test of details. These types of test are referred to as **dual tests** and are best described by way of example (**Example 6.2** below).

EXAMPLE 6.2: DUAL TESTING

An auditor undertaking controls testing uses statistical sampling methods and selects 50 purchase orders (POs) to perform the following test:
- ensure each PO was approved;
- trace each PO to a goods received note (GRN);
- compare the details on each PO to the details on the corresponding GRN to ensure they match;
- trace each transaction to its entry on the system to ensure it was accrued;
- trace each GRN to a matching purchase invoice; and
- compare the details per each GRN to the matching purchase invoice.

The above test, being a control test, is referred to as 'attribute sampling'; therefore there are two possible answers – 'Yes' or 'No' – to each part of the test itemised in the bulleted list above. If the auditor establishes that in each case the answer is 'Yes', they can conclude that controls with respect to the completeness and classification assertions are strong/effective.

Although the auditor still needs to carry out substantive procedures to validate the purchases figure in the financial statements with respect to all other assertions (i.e. occurrence, cut-off and classification), with respect to the completeness and classification assertions, the above test is sufficient. That is, the test has acted as a dual-purpose test in providing evidence to support both controls testing and substantive testing.

We now know what type of audit evidence is acceptable, in that it must be sufficient appropriate audit evidence and it must support all assertions for all transactions, balances and disclosures in the financial statements. The question we must address next is, "What methods can the auditor adopt to obtain this audit evidence?"

## 6.3  METHODS OF OBTAINING AUDIT EVIDENCE

There are a number of methods by which an auditor can obtain audit evidence. The method used will depend on the nature of the testing being performed. Some of the key methods are discussed below.

The auditor obtains evidence using one or more of the following procedures (see ISA 500, paragraphs A14–A25):
- inspection,
- observation,
- external confirmation,
- recalculation,
- reperformance,
- analytical procedures, and
- inquiry.

## Inspection

Inspection involves examining, reviewing, vouching, tracing or verifying records or other documents, processes, conditions or transactions. In general, inspection means physically checking, for example, physically inspecting an invoice or physically inspecting an asset.

Inspection of documents provides auditors with varying degrees of reliability depending on:
1. Whether the documents were generated internally or externally. Externally generated documentation is naturally more reliable due to its independence of the client entity.
2. Whether they were received directly by the auditors. If the auditor receives something directly from a third party, it is more reliable than if it is sent via the client entity. The possibility that the client might tamper with the document is avoided.
3. Whether its source is reliable. The auditor will have to consider the connection of the source to the client entity to ensure there is no conflict of interest.

EXAMPLE 6.3: USES OF INSPECTION

Examples of the use of inspection when gathering audit evidence include:
- The auditor inspects the bank statement to prove the existence of the bank balance (reliable third-party confirmation).
- The auditor vouches a receivable's confirmation letter to that receivable's balance per the receivables listing (reliable third-party confirmation).
- The auditor vouches the value of an investment to the price on the stock exchange (reliable third-party source).

## Observation

Observation consists of looking at a process or procedure being performed by others. It allows the auditor to obtain audit evidence on how adequately the process or procedure is performed. Observation will seldom gain adequate audit evidence on its own, but may identify areas where further audit evidence is required.

Observation is more effective when performed unannounced. If the parties performing the procedure are aware they are being observed, they are more likely to behave as prescribed by the policies and procedures rather than the way in which they would ordinarily carry out the activity. Arriving unannounced, however, can be difficult for the auditor to achieve.

EXAMPLE 6.4: USES OF OBSERVATION

Examples of the uses of observation when gathering audit evidence include:
- Observation of inventory count to confirm the inventory exists at the date of the statement of financial position.

- Observation of processes surrounding the sales system – inquiry of management would have indicated that there are processes; observation would then be used to verify that the systems are in place. If the observation concludes that the systems are strong, substantive testing on the debtors listing would be reduced. However, if observation indicated weak controls, increased substantive tests would need to be designed around the existence and completeness of the receivables listing.

## External Confirmation

External confirmation is the process of receiving direct representation from a third party to verify information included in the financial statements. The auditor contacts the third party either directly or through the client entity to request the confirmation be sent directly to them.

Since confirmations are written representations from independent third parties received directly by the auditor, they are highly persuasive evidence. ISA 505 *External Confirmations* deals with this topic and is discussed in more detail in **Section 6.6**.

EXAMPLE 6.5: USES OF EXTERNAL CONFIRMATION

Examples of the uses of external confirmation when gathering audit evidence include:
- period-end balances from banks;
- period-end receivables balances from customers;
- inventory counts from third-party warehouses holding inventory for the client; and
- terms of agreement or transactions from suppliers.

## Recalculation

As a method of obtaining audit evidence, recalculation consists of verifying the mathematical accuracy of documents and accounting records and re-computing financial statement amounts or supporting details, including client schedules.

EXAMPLE 6.6: USES OF RECALCULATION

Examples of the uses of recalculation when gathering audit evidence include:
- re-checking totals in inventory, payables and receivables listings (discussed in more detail in **Chapters 11–17**);
- extending inventory values by quantities and checking calculations (discussed in more detail in **Chapter 12**);
- recalculating balances denominated in a foreign currency to ensure they are carried in the financial statements at the correct amount (using a suitable exchange rate obtained from a suitable third party);
- recalculating the depreciation charge for the period under review, comparing this to the charge per the client and assessing for reasonableness (discussed in more detail in **Chapter 11**).

## Reperformance

Reperformance is the auditor's independent execution of procedures or controls (those originally performed as part of the entity's internal control system) either manually or through the use of computer-assisted audit techniques (CAATs) (see **Chapter 9**).

### EXAMPLE 6.7: USE OF REPERFORMANCE

Reperforming the bank reconciliation by obtaining a copy of the bank statement, general ledger balance and confirming cheques and receipts listed on the reconciliation as outstanding.

## Analytical Procedures

As a method of obtaining audit evidence, analytical procedures involve evaluating financial and non-financial information and comparing actual results to expectations. They also involve identifying significant fluctuations and relationships that deviate from expectations. Expectations should be developed based on the auditor's knowledge of the operations of the entity during the period under review and information obtained through performance of other audit tests.

Where deviations from expectations are significant, the auditor will inquire of management the reasons for the deviations. Management's explanations should be corroborated through inspection of documentation. This approach is outlined in ISA 520 *Analytical Procedures*, paragraph 7:

"If analytical procedures performed in accordance with this ISA ... identify fluctuations or relationships that are inconsistent with other relevant information or that differ from expected values by a significant amount, the auditor shall investigate such differences by:
(a) Inquiring of management and obtaining appropriate audit evidence relevant to management's responses; and
(b) Performing other audit procedures as necessary in the circumstances."

### EXAMPLE 6.8: USES OF ANALYTICAL PROCEDURES

Examples of the use of analytical procedures when gathering audit evidence include:
- comparing profit and loss expenses year-on-year to identify any unexpected fluctuations (preliminary analytical procedures are performed at the planning stage to identify possible risks);
- comparing period-end accruals and prepayments to prior-period balances and investigating any unexpected fluctuations (substantive analytical procedure);
- comparing income statements year-on-year to see if unexpected fluctuations have been explained and corroborated throughout the audit (final analytical procedures).

It is important to note that analytical procedures occur within three stages of the audit process: the planning stage; the substantive testing stage; and the audit completion stage. This is illustrated, with examples, in **Figure 6.2**.

Preliminary analytical procedures are addressed in greater detail in **Chapter 7**; substantive analytical procedures are addressed in **Chapters 11–17**; and more detail on final analytical procedures can be found in **Chapter 18**.

FIGURE 6.2: USES OF ANALYTICAL PROCEDURES IN THE AUDIT PROCESS

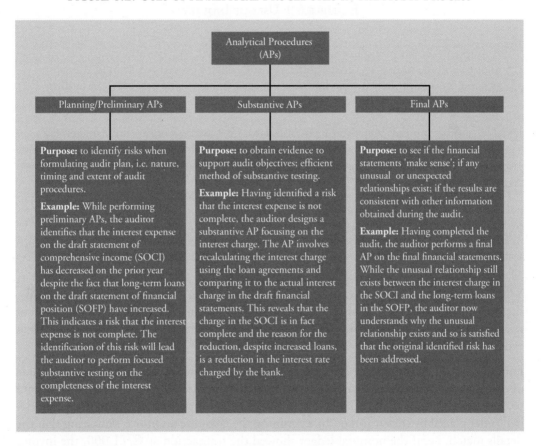

All of the audit procedures discussed above, or combinations thereof, may be used as risk assessment procedures, tests of controls or substantive procedures, depending on the context in which they are applied by the auditor.

## Inquiry

Inquiry is the most utilised technique for gathering audit evidence. It consists of "seeking information from knowledgeable persons, both financial and non-financial, within the entity or outside the entity" (ISA 500, paragraph A22). It is never used alone to provide sufficient audit evidence, but rather is used in conjunction with other corroborating evidence.

Inquiries may consist of oral or written requests for information from persons inside the entity or from third-party sources. The response to these inquiries will necessitate the auditor to either:

- obtain **corroborative evidence** to substantiate the response to the inquiry; or
- if the information received differs significantly from other information received, to modify or perform additional audit procedures.

In instances where no corroborative evidence can be obtained the auditor may consider it necessary to obtain written representations from management.

EXAMPLE 6.9: USES OF INQUIRY

Examples of the uses of inquiry when gathering audit evidence include:

- Inquiries made to management concerning the control procedures around the sales process. In order to rely on the information that management provides, the auditor must reinforce it with further corroborative evidence, for example, by observing the process.
- The auditor inquires why motor expenses have increased significantly. Management may state that this is because of rising fuel prices throughout the year. In order to rely on this information, the auditor must corroborate this information by reviewing invoices or looking at industry trends.
- The auditor inquires as to the valuation of receivables in the statement of financial position. The auditor must obtain sufficient audit evidence to substantiate the valuation and corroborate management's explanation – inquiry alone does not satisfy the valuation assertion.

When collecting evidence, the auditor is interested in tracing and vouching the **audit trail** – the step-by-step documented history of a transaction. Tracing refers to the identification of related documents for a specific transaction; vouching is the comparison of the details at each stage of the transaction.

For example, when the auditor reviews the nominal ledger for revenue and selects a sample of revenue transactions, they would seek to **trace** these transactions first to the invoice sent to the customer; then to the related signed customer delivery docket; and then to the original order placed by the customer. In examining the data, the auditor is **vouching** that the details match, i.e. if the nominal ledger showed the transaction as €/£1,000, the invoice should be for €/£1,000 (excluding VAT); and if the invoice for €/£1,000 referred to an order for 1,000 pens, the auditor would expect that the signed customer delivery docket showed that 1,000 pens were delivered and that the customer order showed that each pen was to be billed at €/£1. The auditor is using the audit trail to trace and vouch the details of the transaction. The audit trail is an important aspect of an audit and is looked at in detail for each cycle in **Chapters 11–17**.

Thus far we have established what is acceptable audit evidence (**Section 6.2**) and how to collect it (**Section 6.3**). This leads us to **Section 6.4**, where we discuss how to evaluate the audit evidence.

## 6.4 EVALUATING AUDIT EVIDENCE

The goals in evaluating audit evidence are to decide, after considering all relevant audit evidence obtained, whether:
- the assessment of the risks of material misstatement at the assertion level are appropriate; and
- sufficient evidence has been obtained to reduce the risks of material misstatement in the financial statements to an acceptably low level.

When misstatements or deviations are found in the course of performing audit testing, consideration should be given to the following.
- The reason for the misstatement or deviation:
  - ◆ are there indicators or warning signals of possible fraud?
- Do the misstatements/deviations:
  - ◆ indicate a previously unidentified risk or weakness in an internal control that could be material?;
  - ◆ impact on risk assessments and other planned procedures?; or
  - ◆ point to the need to modify or perform further audit procedures?

Remember, an audit is a cumulative process of gathering and evaluating audit evidence. All evidence obtained should be evaluated together and the auditor should ensure that evidence is corroborative and not contradictory.

## 6.5 TYPES OF TESTING

### Introduction

The auditor will carry out a number of different audit activities to support the audit procedures, as outlined in **Table 6.5** below.

TABLE 6.5: AUDIT PROCEDURES AND ACTIVITIES

| Audit Procedure | Tests/activities performed | Discussed in detail in: |
|---|---|---|
| Risk Assessment | Inherent risk<br>Control risk<br>Detection risk | **Chapter 7**, 'The Risk Assessment Process' |
| Controls Testing | Tests of details | **Chapter 8**, 'Controls and Controls Testing' |
| Substantive Testing | Tests of details; or substantive analytical procedures | **Chapters 11–17**, on substantive procedures |

### Controls Testing

In **Chapter 4** we introduced controls testing and discussed the fact that a client entity's internal control system can reduce the likelihood of an error occurring in the financial statements. If the risk of error in the financial statements is reduced, the auditor can reduce the level of substantive testing required on the financial statements. The auditor must first assess the effectiveness of the internal control environment by performing controls testing (e.g. trace samples, review performance of reconciliations, etc.) in order to ensure the control activity documented operates effectively throughout the period under review. If it is felt that the design is strong and that the control activities are consistently performed by the client entity, then audit evidence should be obtained to support this view. The tests carried out to prove the effectiveness of the client entity's internal control environment are known as **controls testing**.

There are a number of factors for the auditor to consider when designing controls testing. As a general rule, it is not worth testing controls that are believed to be unreliable, i.e. controls where there is a strong likelihood that exceptions will be found (see **Chapter 4**, Section 4.4).

For most tests of control, sample sizes selected are based on the expectation that no exceptions will be found. For example, the auditor wishes to determine whether the client entity performs bank reconciliations every month. They randomly select three months and request to see the bank reconciliations performed for those months. In doing so they do not expect there to be any instances where the bank statement is not reconciled. Even one exception will lead them to conclude that bank reconciliations are not prepared every month.

Other controls testing, however, may tolerate a deviation. For example, the auditor wishes to determine whether the client entity raises invoices to customers only when a signed customer purchase order delivery (POD) has been received. The auditor selects 200 invoices posted to the sales ledger and then traces them to the signed POD; one instance is found where there is no signed POD. Due to the fact that there is a 1% tolerable deviation rate, two missing PODs can be found (i.e. 200 × 1%) and the auditor can still conclude that the client only raises invoices to customers when supported by a signed customer POD.

Where no deviations are expected to be found, the auditor can take a smaller sample size than in instances where a deviation can be tolerated.

In considering the controls of an organisation, a four-step approach is usually involved:

**Step 1**    Identify risks and objectives for the financial cycle being considered (e.g. the revenue and receivables cycle).

**Step 2**    Gain an understanding of the internal controls surrounding the financial cycle being tested (e.g. the specific controls in place to prevent, detect and correct possible errors with regard to revenue and receivables).

**Step 3**    Assess the information obtained at Steps 1 and 2 and decide whether it is worthwhile to test the controls (e.g. does the auditor believe that the controls surrounding revenue and receivables are strong in design and consistently applied through the period under review and, as such, likely to prevent, detect and correct errors within the revenue and receivables cycle).

**Step 4**    Controls testing (e.g. apply controls testing procedures (tests of details) in order to gather evidence to support the controls in place for revenue and receivables).

Once the auditor has determined that they will test the controls, detailed tests using what is referred to as **'attribute sampling'** will be performed. Attribute sampling has two possible outcomes (usually 'yes' or 'no'). If we consider the example of bank reconciliation above, the client either did or did not perform a bank reconciliation in July.

The assessment of the control environment and its impact on substantive testing is discussed at length in **Chapter 7**; a full discussion on the controls testing can be found in **Chapter 8**.

## Substantive Testing

While, as explained above, it is possible to reduce the level of substantive testing where the control environment is identified as strong, ISA 330 *The Auditor's Responses to Assessed Risks*, paragraph 20, states that the following substantive procedures should be performed at a minimum for each material class of transactions, account balance and disclosure, irrespective of the assessed risk of material misstatement:

"(a) Agreeing or reconciling information in the financial statements with the underlying accounting records ... ; and

(b) Examining material journal entries and other adjustments made during the course of preparing the financial statements."

Substantive testing should be performed on:
- areas that have been identified as significant risk areas; and
- material classes of transactions, account balances and disclosures.

The purpose of substantive testing is to obtain evidence to support the financial statement assertions. Two procedures can be used: **substantive analytical procedures** or **tests of details**. The nature, timing and extent of substantive procedures will depend on the assessed levels of inherent and control risks.

### *Substantive Analytical Procedures*

Substantive analytical procedures involve a comparison of amounts or relationships in the financial statements, with a precise expectation developed from information obtained from understanding the entity and other audit evidence gained during the engagement. **Table 6.6** identifies the stages involved in building an expectation and the considerations (required by ISA 520 *Analytical Procedures*), along with a worked example by way of explanation.

The performance of substantive analytical procedures can be broken down into four steps:
1. Calculate a 'threshold level', based on performance materiality, which represents the maximum monetary value the auditor is willing to accept when comparing the expected result to the actual figures, i.e. those in the financial statements.
2. Calculate an 'expectation' of the current-year balance, explaining the basis of the calculation and an assessment of the reliability of the data used. The auditor should consider the practicality of calculating the expected value – if there are too many variables making up the value that the auditor is trying to prove, it may not be possible or practicable.
3. Calculate the deviation between the actual figures and the 'expectation'. If the deviation is below the threshold level, no additional substantive testing is required.
4. If the deviation is above the threshold level, perform further substantive testing to provide sufficient appropriate audit evidence around the unexpected deviation.

The degree of reliability of the data (or information) used to develop expectations needs to be consistent with levels of assurance and precision intended to be derived from the

TABLE 6.6: STEPS, CONSIDERATIONS AND WORKED EXAMPLE OF A SUBSTANTIVE ANALYTICAL PROCEDURE

| Step | Auditor's Considerations | Worked Example |
|---|---|---|
| 1. Identify balance, transaction or assertion(s) to be addressed. | Consider the suitability of the substantive analytical procedure given the assertion(s) being addressed (i.e. ensure the test is relevant to cover the assertion(s)). | Payroll – Assertions: completeness, occurrence, classification/recording, rights and obligations.<br><br>Payroll figure in the statement of comprehensive income is €1,000,000. |
| 2. Calculate the tolerable misstatement value. | The tolerable misstatement value is the maximum difference between the calculated expectation and the actual value of the transaction/ balance in the financial statements. The size of the tolerable misstatement is influenced by materiality and risk. | The tolerable misstatement value will be influenced by the materiality of the payroll figure and the identified risks associated with the payroll.<br><br>Tolerable misstatement is set at 5%, i.e. €50,000. |
| 3. Assess the practicality of calculating a precise expectation within the tolerable misstatement (i.e. are there too many variables making up the value that the auditor is trying to prove?). | How practical is it to be able to build a precise expectation of the payroll value in the statement of comprehensive income to be within the tolerable misstatement? If there are not too many variables influencing the base number (i.e. the environment is stable), then it is more likely to be possible to build a precise expectation. | The audited payroll figure for the prior year was €1,100,000. Three staff were let go at the beginning of the year with combined salaries of €110,000.<br><br>No pay increases were granted during the year. There is no overtime or bonuses.<br><br>Using the above information it seems that it is practical to build a precise expectation to be within the tolerable misstatement calculated. |

| Step | Auditor's Considerations | Worked Example |
|---|---|---|
| 4. Assess the reliability of the source information being used to build the expectation. | All source information will need to be subject to audit procedures to confirm it is complete, accurate, valid, etc. As a result, it may prove to be inefficient to perform the substantive analytical procedure if the source information needed to build the expectation requires extensive tests of details. | Information needed: Prior-year payroll figure – reliable? – yes, audited last year. Salaries of the three members of staff let go – reliable? – easily validated by checking their employment contracts, P45s/termination letters. No expectation that anything else has changed, so the information to be used to build the expectation is reliable/easily auditable (i.e. the environment is relatively stable). |
| 5. Calculate the expectation. | All calculations must be retained as audit evidence and each piece of source information must be cross-referenced to evidence supporting its validity, completeness, etc. | Prior-year payroll  €1,100,000<br>Less: Reduction in salaries  (€110,000)<br>Expected Payroll  €990,000 |
| 6. Compare the calculated expectation to the actual figure in the financial statements and compare the difference to the tolerable misstatement. | If the calculated difference between the figure in the financial statements and the calculated expectation is less than the tolerable misstatement, then no further testing is required. However, if it is greater than the tolerable misstatement, then the auditor must investigate the difference by inquiring of management and performing appropriate other audit procedures as necessary in the circumstances. | Figure per financial statements  €1,000,000<br>Calculated expectation  €990,000<br>Difference  €10,000<br>Tolerable misstatement  €50,000<br>Margin of safety  €40,000 |

analytical procedure. Other substantive procedures may also be required to determine whether the underlying data is sufficiently reliable. Controls testing may also be considered to address other assertions, such as the data's completeness, existence and classification.

In considering whether the source data is sufficiently reliable for achieving the audit objective, the following questions may be asked:
- Is the data from an internal source or a source external to the client entity?
- If it is internal data, was it obtained by persons not directly responsible for its accuracy?
- Was the data developed under a reliable system with adequate internal controls?
- If broad industry data was used in developing an expectation, is it comparable for use within the entity?
- How relevant is the data?
- Was the data subject to audit testing in the current or prior year?

**Table 6.7** below provides examples of common substantive analytical procedures the auditor might carry out on various classes of transactions and account balances.

TABLE 6.7: EXAMPLES OF SUBSTANTIVE ANALYTICAL PROCEDURES

| Financial Statement Area | Substantive Analytical Procedure |
|---|---|
| Revenue | Selling price applied to volume information about shipments (i.e. volume sold multiplied by price should equal revenue). This would have to be applied to an entity with a simple and stable pricing structure and where volume could easily be validated. |
| Depreciation expense | Depreciation rates applied to property, plant and equipment balances after allowing for the effect of additions and disposals. |
| Payroll expense | Pay rates applied to number of employees, taking into account staff joining or leaving and any other significant variables. |
| Commission expense | Commission rate applied to sales. |
| Interest charge | Interest rate for loan agreement applied to the reducing balance of the loan. |

## Tests of Details

Tests of details is an audit procedure used to obtain audit evidence to corroborate a financial statement amount. They are used to obtain audit evidence regarding assertions. As discussed earlier in this chapter, when designing a procedure the auditor needs to consider carefully the nature of the assertion for which evidence is required to ensure that the evidence collected is relevant to the objective of the test.

In **Table 6.8.** below, which outlines some practical examples of substantive tests of details, the procedure's relevance to the assertion/objective is illustrated. In the table, particular attention is brought to the two instances where the assertion addressed has the clarification "(partial)".

In the first instance, the completeness assertion for payables, although the test may reveal invoices on the selected supplier statement that are not recorded, it does not give comfort that some other supplier balances have been omitted altogether. And in the second instance, the valuation assertion of PPE, a physical inspection will discover if the vehicle is physically damaged, not in use, etc., but it would not uncover any non-physical causes of impairment.

TABLE 6.8: EXAMPLES OF SUBSTANTIVE TESTS OF DETAILS

| Financial Statement Area | Test of Detail | Assertion Addressed |
|---|---|---|
| Revenue | 1. Trace last goods dispatch notes (GDNs) (e.g. 10 GDNs raised prior to year end) to the signed PODs; check they are only recorded in the general ledger of the current period if signed for by the customer prior to the year end date.<br>2. Trace the last 10 revenue entries from the general ledger to ensure they were not recorded in the general ledger unless actually signed for by the customer prior to the year end date. | ✓ Cut-off |
| Receivables | Assess the adequacy of the bad debt provision by reviewing the aged receivables listing. | ✓ Valuation |
| Payables | Reconcile a sample of balances per the aged payables listing to the respective supplier statements. | ✓ Completeness (partial)<br>✓ Existence<br>✓ Valuation<br>✓ Rights and Obligations |
| Payables | Trace post-year-end payments to the underlying liability ensuring that if evidence suggests that the liability existed at the year end date, then liability is included within payables or accruals on the SOFP. | ✓ Completeness |
| Property, Plant and Equipment (PPE) | Review vehicle registration certificates for vehicles included within PPE to ensure they belong to the client entity. | ✓ Rights and Obligations |
| Property, Plant and Equipment (PPE) | Physically inspecting a sample of vehicles included within PPE to ensure they exist, are in use and are in good working condition. | ✓ Existence<br>✓ Valuation (partial) |
| Bank | Check bank reconciliations agree to bank statement and bank confirmation. | ✓ Existence<br>✓ Completeness<br>✓ Valuation<br>✓ Rights and Obligations |

| Prepayments | Recalculation of prepayments by agreeing to source support documentation. | ✓ Existence<br>✓ Valuation<br>✓ Rights and Obligations |
|---|---|---|
| Income Tax Charge | Recalculation of income tax charge | ✓ Classification/ Recording |

### Disclosures

In line with the IAASB's emphasis on the review and completeness of disclosures, the FRC's revision of ISA 330 in June 2016 (subsequently adopted by the IAASA) expands paragraph 20 to better emphasise the need for the auditor to consider disclosures in their substantive procedures. (The expanded meaning is shown in bold below.)

"The auditor's substantive procedures shall include the following audit procedures related to the financial statement closing process:

(a) Agreeing or reconciling **information in** the financial statements with the underlying accounting records, **including agreeing or reconciling information in disclosures, whether such information is obtained from within or outside of the general and subsidiary ledgers**; and

(b) Examining material journal entries and other adjustments made during the course of preparing the financial statements." (ISA 330, paragraph 20)

## 6.6 EXTERNAL CONFIRMATIONS

### Introduction

As outlined earlier in this chapter, **external confirmation** is the receiving of direct representation from a third party to verify information included in the financial statements, and is one of the prescribed methods of obtaining audit evidence. External confirmation can form a very reliable source of evidence, provided the process is controlled adequately. It ticks three essential boxes when it comes to reliability:

- its source is an independent third party;
- it is obtained directly by the auditor; and
- it exists in documentary form.

ISA 505 *External Confirmations* outlines some guidance with regard to the use of external confirmations to ensure its reliability is not compromised.

### Designing External Confirmation Requests

The design of the external confirmation request can affect the response rate and the reliability of the responses. Therefore it is important that the auditor carefully considers:

- the layout and presentation of the request;
- previous experience from similar audit engagements (e.g. if response rates for receivables confirmations in a particular industry tend to be low, it may be inefficient to use this method);

- the method of communication (i.e. hard or soft copy response); and
- authorisation by the client entity's management to comply with the request (i.e. permission to the third party to release requested information to the auditor) can encourage a higher response rate.

In general the request should be easy for the third party to understand and easy to respond to.

A **positive confirmation request** is generally the most effective and reliable type of requested response. It requests the confirming party to reply in all cases, whether they agree or disagree with the balance. It is used to obtain evidence over the existence, rights and obligations and, to some degree, the completeness and valuation assertions. Positive confirmation requests can take two forms: one where the information to be confirmed is included on the request; the other where the third party is asked to add the information themselves. Each has its advantages and disadvantages (see **Table 6.9**).

TABLE 6.9: ADVANTAGES AND DISADVANTAGES OF INCLUDING
CONFIRMABLE BALANCES ON CONFIRMATION REQUESTS

|  | Advantages | Disadvantages |
|---|---|---|
| **1. Information to be confirmed included on the request.** Example: requests sent to a sample of receivables to confirm the balance outstanding at year end. The balance is included on the request and the confirming party need only sign in agreement. | Less work required by the confirming party – might increase the response rate. | Not very reliable audit evidence, as the confirming party may reply to the request without actually checking that the information is correct. |
| **2. Information to be confirmed NOT included on the request.** The confirming party is required to add the information. Example: requests sent to a sample of receivables to confirm the balances outstanding at year end. The balance is not included on the request and the confirming party is asked to complete the request by inputting the balance they believe was outstanding at the stated year end. | More reliable audit evidence – confirming party cannot sign without checking the balance; balance must be included on their response. | Extra work involved for the confirming party – response rate may be reduced. |

ISA 505 also suggests that the auditor perform some testing on the addresses of the third parties to whom the confirmations are being sent, as supplied by the client entity, to ensure their validity prior to posting.

A **negative confirmation request** is one whereby the confirming party is asked to respond only if they disagree with the information provided on the request. This is not considered a reliable form of request as a non-response may simply indicate that the confirming party did not receive the request, or else chose to ignore it.

## Controlling Responses to External Confirmation Requests

It is essential that the auditor instruct the confirming party to respond directly to them rather than to the client entity. If the response goes directly to the client, it may be subject to manipulation and its reliability would be compromised. In order to encourage responses directly to the auditor and to improve the response rate, the auditor usually includes a self-addressed, stamped envelope. If the response is in the form of an e-mail or fax, the auditor should be confident of its source. If there is any doubt about the source, the auditor should modify or add procedures to resolve doubts over the reliability of the information to be used as audit evidence.

The auditor may need to send a reminder or follow up the confirmation request with a phone call or e-mail to encourage a response. A verbal response to a confirmation request is not deemed to be an external confirmation as it is not a written response (ISA 505, paragraph A15); it is therefore not sufficient audit evidence and alternative procedures will be required where such a confirmation is received.

## Evaluating Responses to External Confirmation Requests

ISA 505 indicates four possible results from external confirmation requests, as outlined in **Table 6.10** below.

Should an instance arise where those charged with governance refuse to permit the auditor to send the external confirmation, the auditor should try to ascertain why. If management will not remove this **limitation of scope** (a circumstance where the auditor is prevented from receiving all information and explanations they deem necessary to form an opinion), the auditor should seek to identify an alternative method of testing the assertion. If an alternative method cannot be identified, and the matter is material, the effect on the audit report should be considered (see **Chapter 19**).

TABLE 6.10: EXTERNAL CONFIRMATION RESPONSE TYPES AND AUDITOR ACTIONS

| Response Type | Auditor Actions Required |
|---|---|
| **Appropriate** – confirming party agrees with information provided or provides information requested without any exception. | No further procedures with respect to this test are required. |
| **Unreliable** | Modify or add procedures to resolve doubts over the reliability of the information to be used as audit evidence. |
| **Non-response** | Perform alternative procedures. |

| **Exception** – confirming party responds with information that differs from that requested for confirmation. | Identify reason for exception. The exception may or may not indicate a misstatement. For example, cash in transit/goods in transit may not render the client balance incorrect. Where the exception does relate to a misstatement made by the client, this misstatement should be recorded in the schedule of unadjusted misstatements ('errors schedule') – see **Chapter 18**). |
|---|---|

## 6.7 AUDIT DOCUMENTATION

ISA 220 *Quality Control for an Audit of Financial Statements,* paragraph 17:

> "On or before the date of the auditor's report, the engagement partner shall, through a review of the audit documentation and discussion with the engagement team, be satisfied that sufficient appropriate audit evidence has been obtained to support the conclusions reached and for the auditor's report to be issued".

Thus the auditor cannot establish if sufficient appropriate audit evidence has been obtained unless the audit documentation can be reviewed.

ISA 230 *Audit Documentation*, paragraph 2, outlines the main purpose of **audit documentation** as providing:

> "(a) Evidence of the auditor's basis for a conclusion about the achievement of the overall objectives of the auditor; and
> (b) Evidence that the audit was planned and performed in accordance with ISAs … and applicable legal and regulatory requirements."

Audit documentation also assists the audit team in planning and performing the audit, reviewing work and conclusions and in referring to prior-year work and conclusions; it can also be used as part of the audit's quality review.

Audit documentation is commonly referred to as '**audit working papers**'. Audit working papers should record all of the evidence gathered during the course of the audit and can take the form of copies of source files (e.g. invoices) viewed by the auditor as well as calculations performed (e.g. substantive analytical procedures).

ISA 230 outlines the required standard of audit documentation by referring to the documentation's intended purpose. Paragraph 8 of ISA 230 states that an experienced auditor with no previous connection to the audit should be able to pick up the audit file and understand clearly:

- the nature, timing and extent of the procedures performed to comply with ISAs;
- the results of such procedures;
- any significant matters that arose during the audit, and conclusions reached on those matters.

A sample audit working paper is provided below at **Example 6.10** and includes such basic information as:
- the name of the individual who prepared the audit working paper, the reviewer and partner, and the date;
- working paper reference number;
- name and year end of the client entity;
- nature of test and assertion being addressed;
- test objective; and
- test details and extent (i.e. what is being tested and the size of the sample being tested).

EXAMPLE 6.10: SAMPLE AUDIT WORKING PAPER

| | | Working Paper Reference | PC1 |
|---|---|---|---|
| **Client Name** | Woodco | **Prepared by** | Mary Foley |
| **Client's Year-end** | 31-Dec-18 | **Preparation Date** | 17-Jan-19 |
| **Testing Type** | Controls Testing | **Reviewer** | Brian Maher |
| **Cycle Under Testing** | Purchases | **Review Date** | 22-Jan-19 |
| **Assertion** | Completeness | **Partner** | Gerry Nolan |
| | | **Partner Review Date** | 21-Mar-19 |

| | |
|---|---|
| **Objective** | To ensure all purchases and corresponding goods/services received are recorded in a timely fashion, confirmation that open purchase orders (POs) are reviewed weekly by the finance reporting manager in accordance with company written policy; and POs more than one month old are followed up for investigation. |
| **Control Activity Identified to Cover Assertion** | Open PO report is reviewed weekly by the finance reporting manager and items greater than one month old are followed up. |
| **Test Details** | Randomly selected five weeks from 1 January 2018 to 31 December 2018 and requested a copy of the Open PO review. **(See sample size calculation @ Working Paper Reference PC1a)** <br> • Ensured review was signed off as being reviewed by the finance reporting manager. <br> • From each review, selected one item greater than one month old to ensure explanations were obtained for its age. |

| Week | PO Review Obtained | Working Paper Reference | PO Number Selected | PO Date | Explanation Available | Working Paper Reference |
|------|--------------------|-----------------------|--------------------|---------|----------------------|------------------------|
| 2 | Yes | PC2 | PO00012678 | 12-Dec-17 | Yes | PC7 |
| 14 | Yes | PC3 | PO00013787 | 01-Feb-18 | Yes | PC8 |
| 30 | Yes | PC4 | PO00036372 | 03-Mar-18 | Yes | PC9 |
| 41 | Yes | PC5 | PO00046529 | 19-Jun-18 | Yes | PC10 |
| 49 | Yes | PC6 | PO00026383 | 19-Jul-18 | Yes | PC11 |

| | |
|---|---|
| **Conclusion** | Open PO review is performed weekly – receipt of goods/services and accruals are recorded in a timely fashion. |
| **Is the Control Effective?** | Yes |

As can be seen in **Example 6.10**, as well as the basic elements, note that each characteristic of the test is recorded (i.e. which week was selected, which PO number was selected, etc.). These details are important to allow a reviewer to validate the conclusions reached. Note also that beside each week selected a working paper reference is given, which means that a copy of the open PO report review can be obtained in the audit file at that reference; the same is true of the explanation obtained. Finally, a conclusion is drawn on the test to determine if the objective was reached. All of this information helps to address the objective of a working paper audit document (i.e. it supports the decision drawn by the auditor).

Audit working papers can be a 'hard' or 'soft' copy document; the references to the reviews and the explanations contained within the working paper can also be either in print or electronic versions. Working papers can also take the form of audit programmes, analyses carried out in Excel, summaries of significant matters, receivables confirmations, as well as board meeting minutes or correspondence with respect to significant matters.

Once all matters are concluded upon and an opinion reached, the 'Final Audit File' should be reviewed to ensure it supports the audit opinion. This file, once completed, should not be amended without noting the specific reasons why the amendments were made, when and by whom.

## 6.8 AUDIT SAMPLING

### Introduction

ISA 530 *Audit Sampling*, paragraph 5(a), defines audit sampling as: "The application of audit procedures to less than 100% of items within a population of audit relevance such that all sampling units have a chance of selection".

The auditor's objective when using audit sampling is to provide an appropriate basis from which to draw conclusions about the population from which the sample is selected. Audit sampling can use either a statistical or non-statistical approach.

In general terms, sampling is the examination of a few items (the sample units) drawn from a defined mass of data (the population), with a view to inferring characteristics about the mass of data as a whole.

Sampling has been an accepted auditing technique since the early part of the 20th Century when it was introduced due to the growth of American companies. Prior to this the volume of transactions and balances was small enough to facilitate the auditor performing tests of 100% of the population. The American Association of Public Accountants (now the American Institute of Certified Public Accountants) was the first to make reference to sampling in its Federal Reserve Bulletin in 1917, by including a reference to the selecting of a few items of inventory within a programme of audit procedures on inventory. It is recognised today as an essential feature of most audits.

The three main reasons for the importance of sampling are:
1. In the modern business environment it is **not economically feasible** to examine the details of **every transaction** and account balance.
2. Testing a sample of transactions is **faster** and **less costly** than testing the whole population.
3. Auditors are required to form an opinion about the truth and fairness of the financial statements. They are **not required to reach a position of certainty** or to be concerned about the statements' absolute accuracy. The task can usually be accomplished by testing samples of evidence; there is no need to test the whole population.

Sampling, however, may not be appropriate in certain circumstances, primarily:
• when the auditor has already been advised of **a high level of errors or systems failures** or a **possible fraud**;
• where **populations are too small** (e.g. only 10 non-current fixed assets were purchased in the period) it may be more effective to check them all;
• where **all the transactions in a population are material** (e.g. a manufacturer of airplanes may only sell a few in a year, but each contract would be worth several million euro);
• where data is **required by law to be fully disclosed** in the financial statements, e.g. directors' emoluments;
• where the **population is not homogeneous** and therefore the sampling result (error rate) cannot be projected against the untested element of the population.

## Judgemental/Non-statistical Sampling versus Statistical Sampling

There are two key types of sampling: judgemental (or non-statistical) sampling; and statistical sampling. In an audit it is important to be able to distinguish between these two approaches.

### Judgemental Sampling

Judgemental sampling refers to the use of sampling techniques where the auditor relies on their own judgement to decide:
• how large the sample should be;

- which items from the population should be selected; and
- whether to accept or not accept the population as reliable, based on the results obtained from the sample units examined.

This sampling method has advantages over statistical sampling in that it is generally **faster**, and therefore **less costly** to apply. However, unlike statistical sampling, the method provides **no measure of sampling risk** and, should the auditor's judgement be challenged (particularly in a court of law), the conclusions reached with respect to the sample may be **difficult to defend**. Furthermore, when using judgemental sampling it is **difficult not to introduce sample bias** – whether it be in relation to sample size, the items selected or the conclusions reached with respect to the population.

### *Statistical Sampling*

Statistical sampling refers to the use of sampling techniques that rely on probability theory to help determine:
- how large the sample should be; and
- whether to accept or not accept the population as reliable based on the results obtained from the sample units examined.

ISA 530, paragraph 5(g), defines statistical sampling as "An approach to sampling that has the following characteristics:
  (i)  Random selection of sample items; and
  (ii) The use of probability theory to evaluate sample results, including measurement of sampling risk."

Statistical sampling has certain important advantages over judgemental sampling:
- it is **unbiased**;
- should aspects of the sampling be challenged, because it is based on probability theory and therefore considered to be objective (rather than based on the auditor's subjective judgement), it is **readily defensible**; and
- it **permits quantification of sampling risk**. For example, if a sample is selected on the basis of a 5% sampling risk, there is a 5% chance that the sample is not representative of the population and, as a result, a 5% chance that an inappropriate conclusion may be reached about the population.

However, statistical sampling can be more **complex and costly to apply** than judgemental sampling due to the time associated with setting it up and the associated skill.

### Designing the Sample

The design of a sample requires the auditor to give some consideration to the specific purpose to be achieved and the combination of audit procedures that are most likely to assist in the achievement of these objectives.

When designing the sample, auditors need to consider the following.
- **Population** The population (classes of transactions or account balances) is the data set from which the sample will be chosen. In order to draw valid conclusions about the whole population from a sample, the essential feature of the population is that it be homogeneous.

- **Level of confidence (level of desired assurance)**  Auditors work to levels of confidence that can be expressed precisely. For example, a 5% confidence level means that there are 19 chances out of 20 that the sample is representative of the population as a whole. Stated differently, there is one chance in 20 that the sample, on which the auditor draws conclusions, is non-representative of the population as a whole.
- **Precision**  From a sample it is not possible to say that the auditors are, say, 95% certain that the error rate in a population of inventory calculations is 5%, but only that the error rate is 5% ± y%, where ± y% is the precision interval. The level of confidence and the precision interval are related in that, for a given sample size, higher confidence can be expressed in a wider precision interval, and vice versa.
- **Tolerable rate of deviation**  "A rate of deviation from prescribed internal control procedures set by the auditor in respect of which the auditor seeks to obtain an appropriate level of assurance that the rate of deviation set by the auditor is not exceeded by the actual rate of deviation in the population" (ISA 530, paragraph 5(j)). Controls testing includes attribute sampling where there are only two possible outcomes to the test, usually 'yes' or 'no' ("Yes, the bank statement was reconciled in the month of July" or "No, it was not"). The tolerable rate of deviation answers the question: "How many 'no' responses will the auditor accept to still be able to conclude that the control is effective?".
- **Tolerable misstatement**  ISA 530, paragraph A3, defines tolerable misstatement as "the application of performance materiality…, to a particular sampling procedure. Tolerable misstatement may be the same amount or an amount lower than performance materiality." (Remember, performance materiality is an amount set by the auditor that is less than overall materiality to take account of risk associated with specific transactions, classes of transactions or balances.) The auditor seeks to obtain an appropriate level of assurance that the monetary amount set by the auditor (i.e. the tolerable misstatement) is not exceeded by the actual misstatement contained in the balance.

  The essential procedure is to set a tolerable misstatement, then to project the error rate implied by the sampling results onto the population and compare the two.
- **Materiality**  A subset of risk, materiality is fundamental to auditing and, with all populations being sampled, materiality should be considered when deciding the sample size. Populations that are material to the overall audit opinion (e.g. inventory, receivables, payables) must be sampled with smaller precision intervals and higher confidence levels. Similarly, the more risk the auditor believes is associated with a transaction or balance, the greater the confidence level (and smaller the precision interval) required. Risk in this regard refers to the risk of material misstatement.

## Sample Selection Methods

The methods used to select the sample are as important as the number of items tested. In order for the results of the sample to be used to calculate a projected misstatement, the sample should be:

- Random – a random sample is one where each item of the population has an equal (or specified) chance of being selected. Statistical inferences may not be valid unless the sample is truly random.

- Representative – the sample should be representative of the items in the whole population. For example, it should contain a similar proportion of high- and low-value items as that of the population.

The following are some examples of sample selection methods as outlined in ISA 530, Appendix 4.

**Random sampling** This is simply choosing items subjectively while trying to avoid bias. Bias might be a tendency to favour items in a particular location or in an accessible file or, conversely, in picking items because they appear unusual. Simple random sampling means that all items in the population have (or are given) a number. Numbers are selected by a means that gives every number an equal chance of being selected. This is done using random number tables or computer- or calculator-generated random numbers.

**Systematic selection** This method involves making a random start and then taking every nth item thereafter. The sampling interval is decided by dividing the population size by the sample size, e.g. if the population is 1,000 and the number to be sampled is 100, the sampling interval will be every tenth transaction. The starting point is determined randomly within the first 10 items.

**Block sampling** This method involves randomly choosing one block of items, e.g. all March invoices. This sampling method has none of the desired characteristics and is not recommended. Analogous to this is **cluster sampling**, where data is maintained in clusters (groups or bunches), such as wage records kept in weeks and purchase invoices in months. The idea is to select a cluster randomly and then to examine all the items in the chosen cluster. The problem with this method is that the sample may not be representative as the month or cluster chosen may have unique characteristics.

**Monetary Unit Sampling** (MUS) The application of value-weighted selection is appropriate for those populations within which there are large variances. Large-variance populations are those where the individual units of the population are of widely different values, e.g. receivables or inventory. The method is suited to populations where errors are not expected. It implicitly takes into account the auditor's concept of materiality.

Two further methods of sampling are:

**Attribute sampling** This provides results based on two possible attributes, e.g. correct/not-correct, and is used primarily in connection with controls testing and the testing of internal controls, e.g. non-monetary testing. It is generally used in compliance testing where the extent of application of a control is to be determined, i.e. the test "complies/does not comply". Each deviation from a control procedure is given an equal weight in the final evaluation of results.

**Multi-stage sampling** This method is appropriate when data is stored in two or more locations. For example, inventory in a chain of shops. The first stage is to randomly select a sample of shops and the second stage is to randomly select inventory items from the chosen shops.

## Sampling Risk versus Non-sampling Risk

Having considered the methods open to the auditor in selecting the sample, we now need to consider the risks that exist when performing testing using sampling. The methods of sampling discussed above should help to reduce sampling risk, but they can never entirely eliminate the risk associated with sampling.

Let us first consider the question "What is sampling risk?" ISA 530, paragraph 5(c), defines sampling risk as "The risk that the auditor's conclusion based on a sample may be different from the conclusion if the entire population were subjected to the same audit procedure". Naturally, if you extrapolate an error rate onto a total population, you will not predict the *actual* error contained in that population; rather it suggests the likely outcome of testing 100% of the population.

Non-sampling risk is the risk that the auditor reaches an erroneous conclusion for any reason not related to sampling risk. The use of inappropriate procedures to test noted assertions would be an example of a non-sampling risk (e.g. vouching invoices from the general ledger to the signed POD to test for completeness). The audit evidence yielded would be inappropriate whether 100% of the population were tested or just a sample.

## Calculation of Sample Size

As mentioned above, sample size can be determined by the application of a statistical formula or through the exercise of professional judgement. ISA 530 does not provide formulas, but it does provide factors that may impact on the auditor's determination of sample size.

**Table 6.11** below summarises the factors that influence the size of a sample for controls testing and substantive testing.

TABLE 6.11: FACTORS INFLUENCING SAMPLE SIZE

| Factor | Impact on Controls Testing Sample Size | Impact on Substantive Testing Sample Size |
|---|---|---|
| Risk (audit risk components) | The greater the reliance on the results of a control test using audit sampling, the lower the sampling risk the auditors are willing to accept and, consequently, the larger the sample size. That is, if inherent risks identified are high, the auditor will have gained no comfort with respect to inherent assurance and so cannot take too many risks. To avoid sampling risk, the auditor must test a larger proportion of the population. | The higher the assessment of inherent risk, the more audit evidence is required to support the auditor's conclusion – therefore the larger the sample size at the substantive stage (unless the control environment is strong enough to mitigate any inherent risk noted). Low inherent risks and low control risks mean that detection risk will be high and therefore sample sizes will be small (a full discussion on this can be found in **Chapter 7**). |

| Desired level of assurance | The greater the level of assurance the auditor wishes to achieve, the larger the sample size needed in order to more accurately predict the actual deviation in the population. | The greater the level of assurance the auditor wishes to achieve, the larger the sample size in order to more accurately predict the actual value of the misstatement in the population. |
|---|---|---|
| Tolerable rate of deviation/ Tolerable misstatement | The lower the tolerable rate of deviation, the larger the sample size, and vice versa. | The lower the tolerable misstatement, the larger the sample size required. |
| Expected deviation rate/Expected misstatement | The higher the expected rate of deviation, the larger the sample size required to allow the auditor to more accurately estimate the actual rate of deviation. | If errors are expected, a larger sample needs to be examined to confirm that the actual value of the misstatement is less than the tolerable misstatement. |
| Population value | N/A | The less material the monetary value of the population to the financial statements, the smaller the sample size that may be required. |
| Stratification | N/A | Should stratification be possible, then the auditor will be able to achieve lower sample sizes (see **Example 6.12** below). |
| Population size (number of units in the population) | The population size has virtually no effect on the sample size (unless population is small, in which case the auditor would likely decide that it is more efficient to test 100%). | Virtually no effect on the sample size unless population is small (in which case it may be more efficient to test 100%). |

## Projecting the Error into the Population

Now that we understand what is meant by the term 'sampling', and we know the various approaches used to select a sample and determine its size, we must consider how to use the results of the sample tested. For example, if the total population value is €1,000 and 20% of the population was tested, which is €200, and a €4 error was found, the error rate is 2% (4 ÷ 200). The sample tested is representative of the entire population and so we expect that errors will arise at the same rate throughout the population. This means there is likely a 2% error rate in the balance of the population not tested. The population not tested is €1,000 × 80% = €800 and 2% of this is €16. The total error in the population is deemed to be €20 (€4 + €16). We have 'projected' the error found in the population tested against the balance of the population not tested.

Once errors have been identified, they should be projected to the population after excluding any anomalies that may impact on the projection (ISA 530, paragraph A19). Projection of an error (or extrapolation of an error) is best described by way of example.

### EXAMPLE 6.11: PROJECTING ERRORS

An auditor is performing substantive tests of details on the revenue figure in the financial statements. The reported revenue is €8,560,000, from 4,710 invoices. The auditor decides that the most appropriate test is to select, using statistical methods, a sample of invoices from the sales (revenue) account in the general ledger and vouch the invoices back to signed customer proof of delivery (POD) documents. This will test occurrence, rights and obligations and recording and classification assertions. Using the sample size formula prescribed by the audit firm, the auditor calculates a sample size of 200.

The auditor obtains the general ledger listing and selects 200 invoices, which total €774,661. Three invoices are found where the signed POD cannot be obtained and inquiry of management has yielded no acceptable answers. The total value of the three invoices is €25,231. The auditor must now project the error to the population.

Materiality is €430,000.

**Projecting the Error**

|  | € |
|---|---|
| Value of balance tested | 774,661 |
| Value of total population | 8,560,000 |
| Value of balance not tested | 7,785,339 |
|  |  |
| Value of errors found (not noted as anomalies) | 25,231 |
|  |  |
| Error rate *(value of errors found/value tested)* | 3.3% |
| Projected *(error rate × value not tested)* | **253,572** |

The €25,231 is a known error (it is confirmed to be wrong). The €253,572 is likely to be wrong (projection based on error rate found). The amounts of the misstatements are not individually material (i.e. they are less than the materiality figure of €430,000), however both amounts (the known error and the projected/likely error) will be recorded on the schedule of unadjusted misstatements ('errors schedule') to be assessed at the end of the audit in aggregate with other errors found. If in aggregate a material error is found, the auditors will return to the projected error to see if they can more accurately quantify the error rate by testing more of the population to see if they get a more favourable error rate, hence reducing the known error value.

## Stratification

Let us now consider stratification and the benefits it may bring. At the beginning of the discussion on sampling, the advantages and disadvantages of judgemental and statistical sampling were discussed. Stratification combines these two methods so as not to reduce the reliability of the judgemental influence, i.e. it takes advantage of the best parts of both methods: judgement, which can help with efficiency; and statistics, which avoids bias.

Stratification, as noted above, divides the population into groups based on a characteristic. The use of stratification can help to reduce sample sizes, making the audit more efficient while also increasing the monetary value of the population being tested, but in a way that does not reduce reliability or introduce bias in a negative way. The information supplied in **Example 6.11** is now used in **Example 6.12** to illustrate how stratification can improve on efficiency and effectiveness of sample testing.

EXAMPLE 6.12: STRATIFICATION OF THE POPULATION

The details are the same as in **Example 6.11** but, on receiving the general ledger listing, the auditor uses CAATs (computer-assisted audit techniques) to divide the population (invoices) according to their value. The following is the result of the stratification.

|  | Block 1 | Block 2 | Block 3 | Total Population |
|---|---|---|---|---|
| Value in € | 3,240,000 | 3,220,000 | 2,100,000 | 8,560,000 |
| Number of units in stratum | 10 | 500 | 4,200 | 4,710 |
| Value of sample in € | 3,240,000 | 225,000 | 40,000 | 3,505,000 |
| Number of units in sample | 10 | 20 | 50 | 80 |
| % value tested (value tested / total value of population) | 100% | 7% | 2% | 41% |
| % units tested (volume tested / total volume in the population) | 100% | 4% | 1% | 2% |

Now that stratification has been applied, we can see that vouching just 10 of the invoices will cover €3.24 million of the total monetary value of the population – resulting in a lower sample size needed. By stratifying further we can ensure our sample covers a range of middle-value invoices by applying statistical sampling methods to the Block 2 invoices. This leaves the high-volume, low-value invoices, and again statistical sampling methods should be applied to determine an appropriate sample size.

Now let us compare the two approaches taken.

|  | Stratification Applied | No Stratification Applied |
|---|---|---|
| Value of total population | €8,560,000 | €8,560,000 |
| Number of units | 4,710 | 4,710 |
| Value of sample | €3,505,000 | €774,661 |
| Number of units in sample | 80 | 200 |
| % overall value tested | 41% | 9% |
| % overall units tested | 2% | 4.2% |

We can see from the above that the stratification approach has given us significantly more coverage of the total value, which is more important than the number of items tested. In **Example 6.11**, having sampled 200 units of the population the auditor has only tested €774,661 of the value (9%); whereas by applying stratification, with only 80 units sampled a value of €3,505,000 has been tested (41%). This means that there is less of a balance on which to project an error, resulting in a more accurate assessment of the value of the error.

From the auditor's perspective, stratification has saved time and so made the testing more **efficient**. In addition, it has offered a greater degree of confidence over the actual value of the error, making the audit more **effective**. It is important to remember, however, that statistical methods must be used in selecting the sample units for Block 2 and Block 3 to ensure that all units have an equal chance of being selected.

Finally, let us consider the effect of the existence of an anomaly, again using the details from **Example 6.11**.

### EXAMPLE 6.13: CONSIDERING ERRORS RELATING TO ISOLATED EVENTS

The details are the same as in **Example 6.11** except that three invoices were found where the signed POD cannot be obtained and inquiry of management has yielded no acceptable answers with respect to two of those invoices, valued at €15,340. With regard to the third invoice, management advised that the delivery driver crashed en route and the inventory was destroyed. The client entity's settlement clerk (who validates the delivery on receipt of the signed POD) misheard what had happened and thought the event had taken place after delivery of the goods. As such the delivery was recorded as completed and the invoice for €9,891 was issued and sent to the customer. This was the driver's only delivery that day. The auditor validated this story to the insurance claim and corroborated it with the settlement clerk.

**Projecting the Error**

The invoice error of €9,891 is considered an anomaly (an isolated incident) and it is not representative of the population. It should be excluded from the error rate calculation.

|                                                                                      | €         |
|--------------------------------------------------------------------------------------|-----------|
| Value of sample                                                                      | 774,661   |
| Value of total population                                                            | 8,560,000 |
| Value of population not tested                                                       | 7,785,339 |
| Value of sample tested, excluding anomaly (€774,661 – €9,891)                        | 764,770   |
| Value of errors found (not noted as anomalies)                                       | 15,340    |
| Error rate *(value of errors found ÷ value tested excluding anomaly)*                | 2.0%      |
| Projected *(error rate × value not tested)*                                          | **156,161** |

A known error of €25,231 still exists, but only €15,340 of this is considered as non-anomalous. Therefore, the projected error (likely total error in the population) is only €156,161.

## 6.9 OPENING BALANCES

When collecting audit evidence regarding the figures in the financial statements, the auditor should not forget that comparative figures are included in a set of financial statements. The auditor must therefore obtain audit evidence relating to those comparative figures.

IAS 1 *Presentation of Financial Statements* requires that comparative information shall be disclosed in respect of the previous period for all amounts reported in the financial statements, both on the face of financial statements and notes, unless another standard requires otherwise.

With respect to continuing audit engagements, the audit of opening balances is not so onerous. The auditor compares the draft financial statements of the current period with the signed financial statements of the prior period (which are supported by their own audit files). The auditor is simply ensuring that the prior period's closing balances have been correctly brought forward to the current period.

ISA 510 *Initial Audit Engagements – Opening Balances,* paragraph 3, states that the auditor's objective is to "obtain sufficient appropriate audit evidence about whether:
(a) Opening balances contain misstatements that materially affect the current period's financial statements; and
(b) Appropriate accounting policies reflected in the opening balances have been consistently applied in the current period's financial statements".

An issue arises, however, for initial audit engagements where either:
• the financial statements were not audited in the prior period (perhaps due to exemptions from the need to be audited, as discussed in **Chapter 1**); or
• the financial statements were audited by a predecessor auditor (i.e. you were not the auditor in the prior year).

In these circumstances, audit procedures regarding opening balances can include:

- review of predecessor auditor's working papers to obtain evidence in relation to opening balances. For audits of PIEs, the additional requirement to report to the audit committee, now requires the auditor to obtain "an understanding of the predecessor auditor's methodology used to carry out the audit, sufficient to enable the auditor to communicate with those charged with governance those matters required by paragraph 16R-2(g) of ISA [UK and Ireland] 260" (ISA 510, paragraph 8R-1);
- evaluation of whether audit procedures performed in the current period provide evidence relevant to the opening balances of the prior period;
- performance of specific audit procedures to obtain evidence regarding the opening balances.

If, through these procedures, the auditor identifies that misstatements do exist in the opening balances and that they could materially affect the current period's financial statements, then they must perform additional audit procedures to determine the effect on the current-period financial statements. Where that effect is material, the auditor must qualify their opinion if the necessary adjustments are not made.

It is important to note that opening balances encompass matters requiring disclosure that existed at the beginning of the period, such as contingencies and commitments (ISA 510, paragraph 4(b)).

If the auditor cannot obtain sufficient appropriate audit evidence with respect to opening balances, they must issue a **qualified audit opinion** or a **disclaimer opinion**. For example: "We do not know if these financial statements give a true and fair view because we cannot obtain the evidence needed to form an opinion." Audit opinions are discussed in more detail in **Chapter 19**.

## 6.10  AUDITING ACCOUNTING ESTIMATES

Where elements of financial statement items are estimated due to the fact that they cannot be measured precisely, the nature and reliability of source information to support the estimate can vary greatly. This is therefore a risky area for auditors as it can be difficult to obtain sufficient appropriate audit evidence to support the estimate.

Coupled with the possible lack of supporting evidence is the fact that accounting estimates can also be influenced by the different requirements of the various financial reporting frameworks relevant to the financial statement item being audited. ISA 540 *Auditing Accounting Estimates, Including Fair Value Accounting Estimates, and Related Disclosures*, paragraph 7, defines an accounting estimate as: "An approximation of a monetary amount in the absence of a precise means of measurement. This term is used for an amount measured at fair value where there is estimation uncertainty, as well as for other amounts that require estimation. Where this ISA [UK and Ireland] addresses only accounting estimates involving measurement at fair value, the term 'fair value accounting estimates' is used." Estimation uncertainty is the lack of precise measurement of an accounting estimate and can be difficult to ascertain in an audit.

To address these issues, ISA 540 provides the auditor with some guidance on how to approach the audit of estimates. ISA 540 advises that, before commencing an audit of estimates, it is essential that the auditor:

- familiarise themselves with the reporting framework relevant to the accounting estimate (including disclosure requirements);
- understand how management identifies transactions, events and conditions that may give rise to the need for accounting estimates to be recognised;
- understand how management make the accounting estimate, including an understanding of the data, the assumptions and the use of experts (if applicable) to build that estimate. The auditor will also seek to understand if there is a change in how the estimate was applied in prior periods, and how management has assessed estimation uncertainty. ISA 540, paragraph 7(c), defines estimation uncertainty as "The susceptibility of an accounting estimate and related disclosures to an inherent lack of precision in its measurement.";
- review the outcome or re-estimations of accounting estimates included in prior periods to assess the information used in those estimates and management's ability to measure estimates as precisely as is practical with information available at that time.

The degree of review will, of course, be impacted by the risk assessment procedures. In responding to the assessed risks of material misstatement, the auditor shall undertake one or more of the following activities (ISA 540, paragraph 13):

- determine whether **events occurring up to the date** of the auditor's report provide audit evidence regarding the accounting estimates;
- test management's **methods and assumptions** used in deriving the accounting estimate;
- test effectiveness of any **related controls** that support the estimate;
- calculate their own estimate or an estimate range in order to evaluate management's estimate;
- where **estimation uncertainty** exists, the auditor should, in addition, understand how management considered **alternative assumptions** and why they were rejected over assumptions used. Where management has not adequately considered alternative assumptions, the auditor shall assess such alternatives and their impact on the estimates compared to that of management's;
- assess management's **decision to recognise, disclose or exclude** accounting estimates;
- evaluate the **adequacy of disclosures with respect to estimation uncertainty**;
- apply professional scepticism with respect to the existence of **management bias**; and
- obtain **written representations** from management regarding whether those charged with governance believe significant assumptions used in making accounting estimates are reasonable.

ISA 540, paragraph A26-1, reminds the auditor of the requirements of the additional report to the audit committee (as further discussed in **Chapter 18**, Section 18.9 ) when auditing PIEs: "the auditor's obligations for auditing accounting estimates, including fair value accounting estimates, and related disclosures set out in this ISA [UK and Ireland] may inform the auditor's assessment and communication in the additional report to the audit committee of the valuation methods applied to the various items in the financial statements".

## 6.11 CONCLUSION

At the outset of the chapter we examined the term 'sufficient appropriate audit evidence' and learned that this refers to the quantity, reliability and relevance of the audit evidence collected. Then, having gained an understanding of the type of evidence that should be collected, we established the methods the auditor might use in order to collect the evidence.

According to ISA 220, paragraph 17: "On or before the date on the auditor's report, the engagement partner shall, through a review of the audit documentation and discussion with the engagement team, be satisfied that sufficient appropriate audit evidence has been obtained to support the conclusions reached and for the auditor's report to be issued." This quote tells us that we cannot establish if sufficient appropriate audit evidence has been obtained unless we have audit documentation that can be reviewed.

ISQC 1, paragraph 45, prescribes that "The firm shall establish policies and procedures for engagement teams to complete the assembly of the final engagement files on a timely basis after the engagement reports have been finalized." Again, this reiterates the importance of audit evidence and documentation. An engagement quality control reviewer must be able to pick up a final audit file and appreciate/agree with the audit conclusion reached.

It is not practical for the auditor to test 100% of transactions and balances that support the figures in the financial statements and, for this reason, sampling is an acceptable tool used to gather evidence and reach conclusions. This is only so, however, if the sample design is carried out in accordance with ISA 530. The auditor seeks to reduce audit risk to a minimum to avoid drawing the wrong conclusion and expressing an incorrect opinion, but they wish to do this at the lowest possible cost. Through planning, risk assessment and the use of sampling techniques, the auditor strives to perform an efficient audit that concentrates on risk and materiality.

## SUMMARY OF LEARNING OBJECTIVES

**Learning Objective 1** Understand what is meant by sufficient appropriate audit evidence.

ISA 500 explains what is, and is not, considered to be audit evidence. **Sufficient** refers to the **quantity** of evidence that must be obtained – which will have a direct link to the reliability of the audit evidence available, i.e. the more reliable the evidence, the less of it that is required.

**Appropriate** refers to the **reliability** and the **relevance** of the evidence obtained. The reliability will depend on factors such as source (independent of entity and received directly by the auditor), form (written or oral), effectiveness of controls and whether they are original documents. Relevance relates to the appropriateness of the test in addressing the noted assertions.

**Learning Objective 2** Be able to identify whether audit evidence is sufficient and appropriate with respect to specific assertions.

The requirement for audit evidence to be sufficient appropriate audit evidence requires the evidence to be relevant. Relevance specifically refers to the appropriateness of the test in addressing the noted assertions. Throughout the text examples are provided that demonstrate how the auditor considers the relevance of audit procedures with regard to the assertion being tested.

**Learning Objective 3** Have an understanding of the methods of obtaining audit evidence.

ISA 500 outlines the following methods of obtaining audit evidence: inquiry; inspection; observation; external confirmation; recalculation; reperformance; and analytical procedures.

**Learning Objective 4** Have an appreciation of the types of testing carried out for controls testing and substantive testing (to support further learning in later chapters).

**Controls testing** is generally concerned with tests of details, whereby attribute sampling is used to assess if the control is operating consistently as described by management ('yes' or 'no') and that the control is effective in addressing the financial statement assertions. Testing controls and proving their effective operation will assist in reducing the level of substantive procedures when testing the financial statements.

**Substantive testing** also uses tests of details where samples of the population of transactions and balances are used to determine an error rate that can be applied to the total population. Substantive analytical procedures can also be used as a form of substantive testing.

**Learning Objective 5** Understand the concept of substantive analytical procedures and the essential considerations when deciding whether or not to use them.

**Substantive analytical procedures** involve the building of an expectation (an estimate) of what the value of the balance or class of transactions should be and comparing it to the draft financial statements to see if it is within a tolerable misstatement. Substantive analytical procedures also encompass the comparison of comparative figures, ratios and relationships.

All of the above are designed in response to identified risks, ensuring that sufficient appropriate audit evidence is obtained to support all balances and classes of transactions at the assertion level.

**Learning Objective 6** Understand how to carry out external confirmations.

The auditor must give careful consideration to the **design of the external confirmation request** to ensure it provides a reliable source of evidence and to encourage a high response rate. This can be achieved by the use of **positive confirmations or negative confirmations**. Additionally, the auditor must consider carefully the responses to ensure the source is reliable and, where **questions over reliability of source** arise, perform additional audit procedures as necessary. Similarly, where **no response is obtained**, alternative procedures must be carried out to meet the assertions.

Where **management refuses to permit the use of external confirmations** and the reasons are not considered valid, then the auditor should consider the implications for the audit report (**limitation of scope**).

**Learning Objective 7** Understand the importance of audit documentation/audit working papers as well as their format.

**Audit documentation** forms the backbone of audit evidence – without it, review is impossible. Audit documentation supports the basis of the audit opinion and the planning activities carried out. Audit documentation can exist in hard copy or soft copy, or within an audit programme or application.

**Learning Objective 8** Obtain a strong insight into sampling, its risks, methods and projection techniques.

When using sampling in an audit, all samples should be **random** (no bias) and **representative** of the population (to support projection of sample results).

**Sampling risk** is introduced when sampling is used. It is the possibility that an alternative outcome would have been achieved if 100% of the population was tested.

**Non-sampling risk** is the risk that an erroneous conclusion is reached that is not related to sampling risk (i.e. it relates to auditor competency).

**Statistical sampling** has significant benefits over **judgemental (non-statistical) sampling** when it comes to reliability and defensibility if questioned. Judgemental sampling, however, does take into account experience and is usually easier to apply. **Stratification of a population** can help to combine the benefits of both statistical and judgemental sampling.

**Sample size** is influenced by a number of factors, predominantly related to **risk**, **materiality** and **tolerable misstatement**.

On completion of sampling, the errors found need to be projected to the population. When projecting the error to the population, the **error rate** should be adjusted for noted and supported **anomalies**.

**Learning Objective 9** Understand the auditor's responsibility with regard to opening balances.

When collecting audit evidence regarding the figures in the financial statements, the auditor must not forget that comparative figures are included in a set of financial statements and so audit evidence relating to those comparative figures must be obtained.

**Learning Objective 10** Understand the auditing procedures applied to accounting estimates.

When assessing estimates, the auditor needs to familiarise themselves with the applicable **financial reporting framework** and the **estimate type**, as well as gain a clear understanding of the **methods and assumptions** used by management to build the estimate. The auditor should also consider **estimation uncertainty** and how management has considered alternative outcomes and that these are adequately disclosed. The auditor should gain comfort that **adequate procedures** are in place for management to **identify the existence of transactions or events giving rise to accounting estimates**.

## QUESTIONS

### Self-test Questions

6.1   What are the advantages of statistical sampling over judgemental sampling?

6.2   What does sufficient appropriate audit evidence mean?

6.3   What is your understanding of relevant evidence?

6.4   Define your understanding of analytical procedures.

6.5   Name the methods of obtaining audit evidence.

6.6   What are the two types of substantive testing?

6.7   What should the auditor take into consideration when designing substantive analytical procedures?

6.8   What are the benefits of external confirmations?

6.9   What should the auditor take into consideration when designing an external confirmation?

6.10  Why is audit documentation so important?

6.11  Distinguish between sampling and non-sampling risk.

6.12  What is an anomaly with respect to sampling?

6.13  What factors influence the sample size for a substantive test of details?

6.14  What problem is the auditor faced with when auditing the opening balances of an initial engagement?

6.15  What should the auditor consider when auditing accounting estimates?

### Review Questions

(See Suggested Solutions to Review Questions in **Appendix C**.)

### Question 6.1

Fresh Food Ltd is a supplier of food and drink to supermarkets. As audit senior you have been asked to review the work performed by the audit junior on payables and purchases for the year end 31 December 2018 audit. Total purchases were €38 million in the last year and the company has 175 suppliers on its records.

You have received the following summary information on the work performed by the audit junior on supplier statement reconciliations:

| Supplier Name | Balance Per Aged Payables Listing €000 | Balance Per Supplier Statement €000 | Audit Junior's Comments |
|---|---|---|---|
| A | 34 | 80 | Appears to be cut-off issue as supplier has recorded €45,200 in invoices in December not recorded by client. |
| D | 89 | 55 | Credit note on statement but not on the client ledger. |

| | | | |
|---|---|---|---|
| R | 120 | 122 | Difference is not material for further work. |
| W | 61 | 70 | Difference is due to €3,000 cash payment from October not yet received by the supplier and claim by Fresh Food Ltd for discount of €4,000, which has not been granted on supplier statement. |

**Requirement**

(a)  Explain the purpose of the audit procedures carried out in respect of supplier statement reconciliations.

(b)  What follow-up work would you request of the audit junior?

## Question 6.2

In the table below, for each noted transaction class/account balance indicate whether the suggested test is relevant to cover the noted assertion, and why.

| Transaction Class/Account Balance | Management Assertion/ Audit Objective | Suggested Test |
|---|---|---|
| Property, plant and equipment (PPE) | Rights and obligations | Physically inspect the item of PPE. |
| Inventory | Valuation | Attend the physical inventory count and select a sample of items from the warehouse floor and compare them to the physical inventory count sheets to ensure they are included. |
| Payables | Completeness | Trace a sample of items from the payables ledger and compare them to the supplier statement. |
| Investments | Valuation | Review of investment certificates for each investment included on the statement of financial position. |
| Purchases | Occurrence | Trace a sample of items from the purchases ledger to the signed goods receipt note (GRN) and approved purchase order. |
| Revenue | Recording | Trace a sample of items from the sales (revenue) ledger to the invoice and the signed customer purchase order delivery and then to the sales order. Validate the quantities signed for by the customer, match the quantities invoiced and the price quoted on the sales order, match the values on the invoice. |
| Inventory | Completeness | Select a sample of items from the final inventory listing and trace the volumes of the inventory item to the physical inventory count sheets. |

# THE AUDIT AND ASSURANCE PROCESS

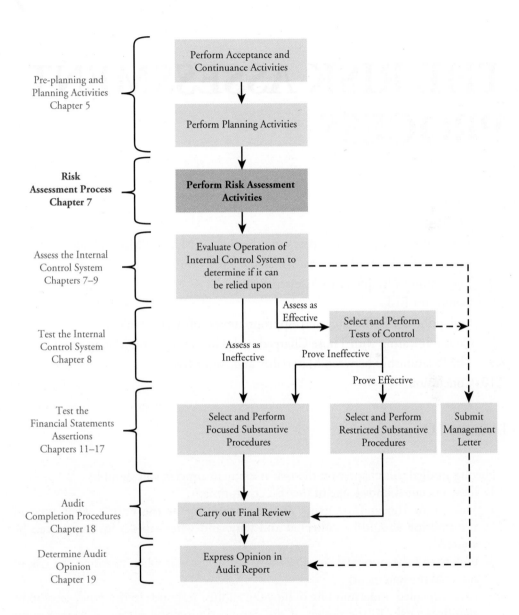

# 7

# THE RISK ASSESSMENT PROCESS

## LEARNING OBJECTIVES

Having studied this chapter on the risk assessment process you should:
1. have a detailed knowledge of the risk environment;
2. know how the auditor gains an understanding of the entity, what type of information should be collected and why, and where this information can be sourced;
3. understand the principal considerations of the auditor when assessing the risk of material misstatement;
4. have a detailed understanding of how the auditor responds to risk (and, separately, significant risk) in the design of the nature, timing and extent of further audit procedures;
5. have an appreciation of the assessment of the sufficiency and adequacy of evidence and the importance of documenting the risk process; and
6. have an appreciation of the relationship between materiality and audit risk.

## CHECKLIST OF RELEVANT STANDARDS

The relevant standards, in both the RoI and the UK/NI, covered in this chapter are:
- ISA 200 *Overall Objectives of the Independent Auditor and the Conduct of an Audit in Accordance with International Standards on Auditing*
- ISA 265 *Communicating Deficiencies in Internal Control to Those Charged with Governance and Management*
- ISA 315 *Identifying and Assessing the Risks of Material Misstatement through Understanding the Entity and its Environment*
- ISA 320 *Materiality in Planning and Performing an Audit*
- ISA 330 *The Auditor's Responses to Assessed Risks*
- ISA 500 *Audit Evidence*

Note, in general when referring to ISAs, it should be understood as referring to the UK and Ireland versions, unless otherwise specified as either ISA (UK) or ISA (Ireland). See the Introduction for an extant list of auditing standards for the RoI and the UK/NI.

## KEY TERMS AND DEFINITIONS FOR THIS CHAPTER

**Assertions**   "Representations by management, explicit or otherwise, that are embodied in the financial statements, as used by the auditor to consider the different types of potential misstatement that may occur." (ISA 315, paragraph 4(a))

**Audit Risk**   The risk that the auditor will fail to reach an appropriate conclusion about the entity and the accounting information on which they are reporting. In other words, an **unqualified audit opinion** may be issued when in fact a material misstatement exists in the financial statements; or the issuing of a **qualified opinion** when there is no material misstatement.

**Business Risk**   "A risk resulting from significant conditions, events, circumstances, actions or inactions that could adversely affect an entity's ability to achieve its objectives and execute its strategies, or from the setting of inappropriate objectives and strategies." (ISA 315, paragraph 4(b))

**Control Risk**   A risk that is directly linked to the design and implementation of the entity's internal control function (e.g. an entity that lacks segregation of duties may pose many control risks).

**Detection Risk**   The risk that audit procedures will fail to detect a material misstatement.

**Inherent Risk**   A risk that exists due to the nature of the client entity's industry, products or transactions (e.g. a company governed by management with a poor reputation is inherently risky).

> **Internal Control**   "The process designed, implemented and maintained by those charged with governance, management and other personnel to provide reasonable assurance about the achievement of an entity's objectives with regard to reliability of financial reporting, effectiveness and efficiency of operations, and compliance with applicable laws and regulations. The term 'controls' refers to any aspects of one or more of the components of internal control." (ISA 315, paragraph 4(c))

## 7.1 INTRODUCTION

As previously discussed, the objective of an audit of financial statements is to enable the auditor to express an opinion as to whether the financial statements give a **true and fair view**, in accordance with an applicable financial reporting framework, of the state of the entity's affairs at the reporting date. The auditor should plan and perform an audit with an attitude of **professional scepticism**, recognising that circumstances could exist that may cause the financial statements to be materially misstated (ISA 315 *Identifying and Assessing the Risks of Material Misstatement through Understanding the Entity and its Environment*). In order to mitigate against undetected **material misstatement**, the auditor must consider the risks of it arising at the **assertion level** and plan the audit in a manner that will reduce such risks to an acceptable level.

This chapter discusses the concepts of **business risk** and **audit risk** and the approach of the auditor with regard to identifying and responding to such risks.

We commence our discussion in **Section 7.2** with an overview of the **risk environment**, distinguishing between business risk and audit risk, before taking an in-depth look at the question: 'What is audit risk?' The answer to this question leads us into extensive discussions on the **components** of audit risk: **inherent risk**, **control risk** and **detection risk**.

In **Section 7.3** we first consider the risk assessment procedures used by an auditor to gain an understanding of the entity and its environment – answering the question, "**How** does the auditor gain this understanding?". Next we look at the types of information of interest to the auditor and why they can assist the auditor in assessing risk – answering the question, "**What** information should be collected and **Why**?". Lastly in this section, we consider the sources to which the auditor can look to obtain the required information – i.e. "**Where** does the auditor find the information they are looking for?".

Having established how, what, why and where the information is obtained, in **Section 7.4** we examine the issue of assessing the risk of material misstatement. This is discussed under three main headings:
• What risk has been identified?
• What is the potential magnitude of the potential misstatement?
• How likely is it to occur?

Once the risks have been assessed, the auditor must then design a **response** to those risks. The response is reflected in the **nature, timing and extent** of the audit procedures.

We discuss the auditor's approach to this in **Section 7.5**, and it is expanded upon in **Section 7.6** when we consider the specific response to significant risks, concentrating on non-routine transactions and matters of judgement.

In **Section 7.7** we discuss the auditor's considerations with regard to the collection of **sufficient appropriate audit evidence** and documentation. In **Section 7.8** the importance of communicating deficiencies in internal controls to those charged with governance is emphasised. Finally, in **Section 7.9** we remind ourselves of the relationship between materiality and audit risk.

> Remember: the risk assessment process commences at the planning stage of the audit and impacts on the nature, timing and extent of subsequent audit procedures, which should be designed to ensure audit procedures minimise the risk of material misstatement not being detected by the auditor.

## 7.2 THE RISK ENVIRONMENT

The risk environment can be a complicated subject to understand. The word 'risk' is generally used to indicate exposure to danger. In any business, exposure to risk may exist in the **macro environment** or in the **micro environment**. For example, in the **macro environment** the euro to Sterling conversion may be volatile, creating a risk driven by the national, regional or global economy. In the **micro environment** (i.e. a company's immediate area of operations), all transactions are in euro and so they have no exposure to this macro-environment risk.

The auditor recognises two types of risk: business risk and audit risk. **Business risk** is one that will impact on the client entity's goals and objectives. The auditor is only interested in business risk insofar as it might impact on audit risk. **Audit risk** is simply the risk that the auditor will issue the wrong opinion. So, for example, if a new competitor were to enter the client entity's market, this would threaten its profit margins and in turn its ability to continue as a going concern. This would clearly be a business risk of interest to the auditor – a failure to recognise and better understand this business risk may lead to the auditor issuing an unqualified (or clean) audit opinion when in actual fact the entity may not be a going concern and hence the basis on which the financial statements are prepared is incorrect. The auditor should also be mindful of **engagement risk**, which relates to the acceptance considerations discussed in **Chapter 5**, Section 5.2; and **independence risk**, relating to the ethical standards (see **Chapter 2**).

The auditor assesses audit risk on three levels: inherent risk; control risk; and detection risk. Each of these will be discussed in greater detail later in the chapter, but a basic understanding of what they are is required to appreciate the risk environment.

**Inherent risk** exists due to the nature or circumstances of the entity. In our foreign exchange example, an entity that transacts in foreign currencies is exposed to an inherent risk merely by this fact – foreign exchange is volatile by nature and is inherently risky. In reviewing inherent risk it is necessary for the auditor to review the business risks of the entity. A **control risk** is one associated with the internal control function of an entity. The entity that transacts in foreign currencies can 'hedge' the inherent risk and reduce its exposure if it has a strong internal control environment. If, however, its internal controls are deficient, then the inherent risk is compounded by this control risk. A **detection risk** is the risk that audit procedures will fail to detect a material misstatement. Foreign exchange transactions can be difficult to account for and are prone to error, increasing the potential of a detection risk.

## Business Risk

All entities are exposed to business risk – the risk that they may not meet their objectives. The types of business risk will depend on the nature of the entity's activities and the industry in which it operates, how it is regulated, its size and the complexity of its operations. It is the responsibility of management and those charged with governance to consider the business risks facing the entity and to respond appropriately.

An entity will have a number of business objectives set by management, such as profitability, corporate social responsibility (CSR), share price, etc. In order to achieve business objectives, management needs to be aware of the associated risks. **Figure 7.1** identifies some risks to management's ability to achieve their objectives.

Management is expected to identify risks faced by the entity, estimate the impact of those risks on the entity and put in place plans that mitigate each risk to an acceptable level. These risks are normally collated in a document referred to as the **risk register**. The risk register should include:
- a description of the risk;
- the consequences for the business if the risk were to occur;
- the probability of it occurring;
- the magnitude of its impact – while the risk probability may be small, its impact may be major;
- a risk rating (normally categorised as high, moderate or low) – a high rating requires immediate attention;
- the risk control identified to mitigate the risk; and
- the risk owner.

An example of a risk register is given in **Table 7.1**.

TABLE 7.1: EXAMPLE OF A RISK REGISTER

| Risk # | Description of Risk | Consequence of Risk | Probability of Occurrence | Magnitude of Impact | Risk Rating | Risk Control | Risk Owner |
|---|---|---|---|---|---|---|---|
| 0001 | | | Possible | Major | High | | |
| 0002 | | | Unlikely | Major | Moderate | | |
| 0003 | | | Likely | Minor | High | | |

FIGURE 7.1: EXAMPLES OF BUSINESS RISK

**Objective:**
Maintain strong
CSR and business
reputation

**Risk:**
• brand
  impairment

**Objective:**
Implement change
management

**Risk:**
• industrial action
  by workforce
• demotivated
  workforce

**Objective:**
Maintain or increase
share price

**Risk:**
• share price drop
  associated with a
  dividend decision

**Objective:**
Maintain desired
market share

**Risk:**
• technological
  obsolescence
  resulting in
  failing profits
  and market
  share

**Objective:**
Maintain
high standard
of corporate
governance

**Risk:**
• high-level fraud

**Objective:**
Maintain efficient
and effective
operations

**Risk:**
• health and safety
  breach
• fire, flood, etc.
• IT down-time

**Objective:**
Maintain strong IT
infrastructure

**Risk:**
• cyber attacks
• loss of data
• down-time
• data protection
  breaches

**Objective:**
Maintain customer
satisfaction

**Risk:**
• defective
  products (also a
  financial risk)

**Objective:**
Maintain strong
working capital

**Risk:**
• insolvency

**Objective:**
Increase
profitability

**Risk:**
• exchange rate
  fluctuations
• increased costs
• defective products

Auditors will expect to see not only that an entity keeps a risk register (indicating that management is aware of risks) but also that the risk register is frequently updated in response to new risks and to ensure that risk controls for previously identified risks are being undertaken in a timely manner.

> **Remember:** not all business risks will translate into risks associated with the preparation of the financial statements. Ultimately, the auditor is concerned only with those risks that could affect the financial statements and result in them being materially misstated.

## Engagement Risk

Engagement risk (see **Chapter 5**) relates to the risks considered by the auditor prior to commencement of an audit engagement. An example of engagement risk would be where a competitive tendering process has forced the auditor to accept an unreasonably low fee, thus restricting the time available to perform an effective audit (affecting audit quality) and/or increasing pressures on the auditor's **integrity**, **objectivity** and **independence** (see below).

A further example of engagement risk is that the auditor may accept a client whose inherent risk at the entity level is unduly high because of, for instance, management with low integrity.

## Independence Risk

Independence in fact is the risk that, even though the auditor's procedures have detected misstatements that cause the financial statements to not give a **true and fair view**, the auditor may fail to report the misstatement because of a lack of independence. (Independence is discussed in detail throughout **Chapter 2**.)

## Audit Risk

With every audit conducted, an audit opinion is expressed on the truth and fairness of the financial statements. This opinion is issued only after the auditor has obtained sufficient appropriate audit evidence over the account balances and classes of transactions in the financial statements, which provides **reasonable assurance** about the truth and fairness of the financial statements. The concept of reasonable assurance acknowledges that there is a risk that the audit opinion may not be appropriate. The risk that the auditor will fail to reach a proper conclusion about the company and the accounting information on which the auditor is reporting is known as **audit risk**.

The auditor should plan and perform the audit to reduce audit risk to an acceptably low level consistent with the audit objective. In order to do so, the auditor must design and carry out a detailed **audit plan** that will provide sufficient appropriate audit evidence to allow them to draw reasonable conclusions on which to base an audit opinion. When audit risk is reduced to a reasonably low level, reasonable assurance has been achieved.

**Figure 7.2** below depicts audit risk and its components. We have already established that audit risk is the risk that the auditor will issue an inappropriate audit opinion. If an inappropriate opinion is issued it is because a material misstatement existed in the financial statements that was not detected. As such, the auditor must first assess the risk of the financial statements containing a material misstatement. This is done by assessing inherent risk and control risk. Once the auditor understands the level of inherent and control risks they can better manage the chances of detecting any errors by applying a detection risk appropriate to the inherent and control risks. This is considered further as we proceed through this section and the remainder of the chapter.

Before we discuss the components of audit risk, we will first consider the levels of material misstatement that might exist in the financial statements. Remember, the auditor is only concerned with risk that could potentially lead to a material misstatement in the financial statements. Therefore, it is important to first understand the levels of material misstatement that can arise from risk before considering the components of risk.

FIGURE 7.2: THE COMPONENTS OF AUDIT RISK

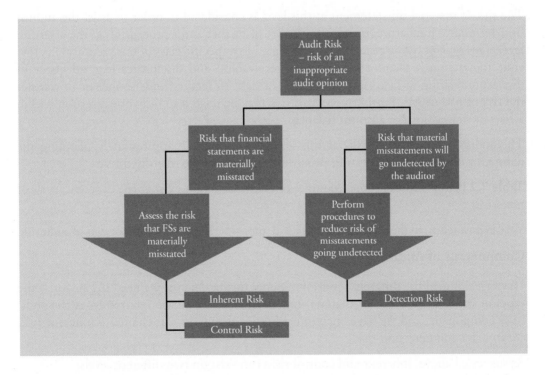

## Levels of Material Misstatement

The auditor's primary concern is detecting material misstatements in the financial statements. In order to assess whether there are misstatements that materially impact on the financial statements taken as a whole, the auditor must consider risk at two levels:
1.  the financial statement level (also known as **entity level**); and
2.  the classes of transactions, account balances, disclosures and the related assertions level.

## 1. The Financial Statement Level

At the financial statement level, the risk of material misstatement is deemed to be **pervasive**, i.e. it can impact the entire set of financial statements and, therefore, can impact on many transactions, balances and assertions. Risks of this nature are often related to an entity's control environment, fraud risk or the risk of management override of controls.

The auditor's response to risks at this level includes considering:
- the significance of these types of risk;
- ensuring that personnel assigned to the audit have sufficient knowledge, skill and ability to adequately assess and conclude on the risk, and at the same time ensure there is an appropriate level of supervision;
- the need for experts; and
- the existence of indicators that the company is not a **going concern**.

## 2. The Classes of Transactions, Account Balance and Disclosure and the Related Assertion Level

The risk of material misstatement at this level is considered in order to assist the auditor in determining the nature, timing and extent of further audit procedures at the assertion level. This type of risk is generally more isolated to a specific class of transactions (e.g. revenue transactions), account balance (e.g. receivables) and disclosures (e.g. adequacy of disclosure relating to factoring (the selling of debt to secure funds sooner or to transfer the risk of bad debt)). Furthermore, this risk may be related to only one assertion within a class of transactions or account balance.

The auditor's response to risks at this level would include appropriately planning the nature, timing and extent of audit procedures to address the identified risks.

**Table 7.2** below outlines some examples of risks that might exist at the different levels of materiality.

We can now return to the topic of audit risk and, more specifically, the components of audit risk.

### Components of Audit Risk

Having examined the different levels of material misstatements, we need to categorise the types of risk that can lead to material misstatements. These are referred to as the audit risk's components and we have encountered them already in this chapter – inherent risk, control risk and detection risk.

As suggested above, inherent and control risks can exist on two different levels:
- financial statement (entity) level; or
- account balance and class of transaction level (related specifically to a figure in the financial statements).

With regard to detection risk, two types of risk can arise:
- **sampling risk**; and
- **quality control risk** (also known as '**non-sampling risk**'),

both of which were introduced in **Chapter 6**, Section 6.8.

TABLE 7.2: EXAMPLES OF RISKS AT THE DIFFERENT LEVELS OF MATERIALITY

| Risk Type | At Financial Statement Level | At Classes of Transactions, Account Balance and Disclosure and the Related Assertion Level |
|---|---|---|
| **Control Risk** | Lack of existence of an organisational structure or **chart of authority** (a document detailing who has authority to perform which actions within the organisation). Without these there is a risk that there is insufficient hierarchy and control over approval of transactions in the entire organisation. This type of risk can therefore impact on the **entire set of financial statements**. | No credit checks are performed on new credit customers and no credit limits are applied. There is a risk that the **receivable** balance is not collectable, which therefore has an impact on the **valuation assertion**. Note how this risk is more focused than the one referred to with respect to the financial statement level. While this risk will require the auditor to adapt the nature, timing and extent of the audit procedures, it does not pose as significant a risk as the control risk noted for material misstatement at the financial statement level. |
| **Inherent Risk** | A new competitor product was launched on 1 January that rivals the entity's top-selling product and will likely require it to sell this inventory at a loss. The risk is that the entity may not be able to continue as a going concern if its top-selling product has been replaced. If the entity is not a going concern, the accounts will have to be prepared on a **break-up basis** and therefore the risk impacts on the **entire set of financial statements**. | A new competitor product was launched on 1 January that rivals one of the entity's lower-selling products and will likely require it to sell this inventory at a loss. The risk relates to the inventory balance and affects the valuation assertion – the **inventory balance** that existed at 31 December will need to be written down to the lower of cost and net realisable value (NRV). The risk is concentrated in one area, does not affect the entire set of financial statements and so is not as significant as the inherent risk noted at the financial statement level. |
| **Fraud** | There is a risk that management is engaged in 'profit-smoothing' to secure their bonuses, which are based on profitability. This fraudulent practice calls into question management's integrity and raises concerns over the **entire set of financial statements**. | There is a risk that individuals in the organisation are engaged in fraud of a specific kind. For example, the payroll clerk (due to a lack of segregation of duties) is adding fictitious employees and paying the related salary to her own bank account. The transaction impacted is the **salary expense account** and the assertion is **occurrence**. |

## Inherent Risk

ISA 200 *Overall Objectives of the Independent Auditor and the Conduct of an Audit in Accordance with International Standards on Auditing*, paragraph 13(n)(i), defines inherent risk as:

> "The susceptibility of an assertion … to a misstatement that could be material, either individually or when aggregated with other misstatements, before consideration of any related controls".

Some factors may pose inherent risks but be adequately controlled by the entity to mitigate or reduce the risk. Inherent risks tend to exist due to the nature of the client entity's industry, product or transaction types. Examples of inherent risks are outlined in **Table 7.3** below.

TABLE 7.3: EXAMPLES OF INHERENT RISK

| Inherent Risk | |
| --- | --- |
| **Financial Statement (Entity) Level** | **Account Balance and Class of Transactions Level** |
| Usually related to the environment in which the client entity operates and therefore have a pervasive impact on the financial statements. | Generally confined to a particular class of transactions or account balance, and in some cases to a particular assertion within the account balance or class of transactions. |
| <ul><li>Management integrity/reputation.</li><li>Profitability relative to the industry.</li><li>Management experience and competence.</li><li>High turnover of key personnel.</li><li>Unusual pressures on management.</li><li>Nature of entity's business (e.g. technological advancement often renders inventions quickly obsolete).</li><li>Nature of industry (e.g. building trade).</li><li>Complex IT systems.</li><li>Quality of IT systems.</li><li>Qualified opinion in previous years.</li></ul> | <ul><li>Susceptibility to misappropriation or loss (e.g. cash).</li><li>Complex transaction (e.g. pensions).</li><li>High degree of judgement (e.g. provisions are often quite subjective).</li><li>Quality of specific computer applications (e.g. the payroll package).</li><li>Non-routine transactions (e.g. property revaluation).</li><li>Existence of consignment stock.</li></ul> |

## Control Risk

Control risk is the risk that a material misstatement (or series of misstatements that is material) could occur relating to an assertion and will not be prevented, detected or corrected in a timely manner by the entity's internal controls. This risk is directly linked to the design and implementation of the entity's internal control function. The entity should put controls in place to address risks and these controls should prevent, detect or correct fraud or errors that may occur. Examples of control risks are provided in **Table 7.4**.

TABLE 7.4: EXAMPLES OF CONTROL RISK

| Control Risk | |
|---|---|
| **Financial Statement (Entity) Level** | **Account Balance and Class of Transactions Level** |
| Normally entity-level control related (i.e. the types of control that impact the entire organisation). | Derived from lack of controls related to a particular financial statements cycle, such as the revenue cycle, and so the risk is isolated to a specific balance in the financial statements or class of transactions (and assertion). |
| • Poor management attitude and lack of action regarding financial reporting.<br>• Culture of management overriding controls.<br>• Complex or poor-quality IT systems.<br>• Lack of existence of a chart of authority.<br>• Lack of written policies and procedures.<br>• Lack of business planning, budgeting and monitoring of performance.<br>• Lack of procedures around risk management.<br>• Lack of internal audit function. | • Non-routine transactions (e.g. the purchase of non-current fixed assets, because they occur ad hoc and in small volumes, generally do not have specific controls related to them).<br>• Changes in third parties carrying out controls, e.g. moving the outsourcing of payroll from one third party to another.<br>• Controls changing in line with changes in procedures/business.<br>• Lack of segregation of duties within a particular cycle.<br>• Lack of effective, competent personnel specific to a particular cycle. |

## Detection Risk

Detection risk is the risk that the auditor "will not detect a misstatement that exists … that could be material, either individually or when aggregated with other misstatements" (ISA 200, paragraph 13(e)). Detection risk is a function of an audit procedure and of its application by the auditor. Detection risk cannot be reduced to zero – there will always be a risk that the auditor has not detected a misstatement, predominantly due to the fact that the auditor tests on a sample basis.

Audit sampling, including sampling risk and non-sampling (or quality control) risk (the two types of risk associated with detection risk), has been sufficiently dealt with in **Chapter 6**, Section 6.8. In the context of risk assessment, the important point to note is that sampling risk cannot be avoided; non-sampling risk, on the other hand, can be mitigated against by ensuring an attitude of professional scepticism, the appointment of a quality audit team and appropriate planning that supports a strong audit programme (see **Chapter 5**).

We will now examine how the auditor assesses each of these components of audit risk in order to determine the audit approach. **Figure 7.3** below shows how the auditor considers each layer of the components of audit risk. First, they assess the existence of inherent risks that might impact on the client entity's financial statements. Secondly, they consider if the entity's control environment mitigates these inherent risks or presents any new risks. This combination of inherent and control risks assessment gives the auditor an indication of the volume and extent of errors that could flow into the financial statements, and hence gives an indication of how much testing needs to be performed to provide **reasonable assurance** that the financial statements are free from material misstatement.

FIGURE 7.3: INHERENT, CONTROL AND DETECTION RISK ASSESSMENT

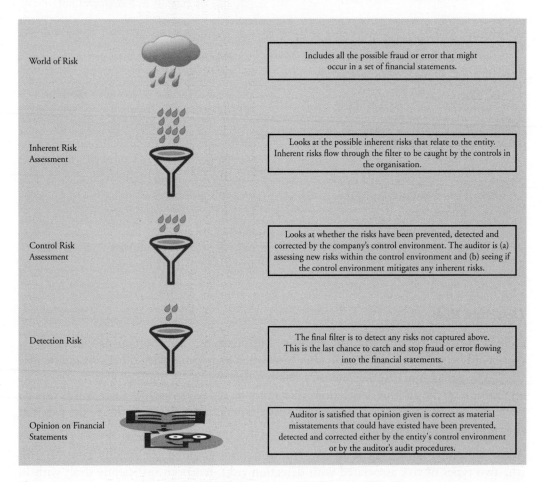

Using an earlier example where, in the risk environment ('the world of risk') there exists a volatile rate of exchange rate between euro and Sterling, if the client entity only transacts in euro then this risk does not flow to the financial statements. If, however, the client entity does engage in such transactions, then an inherent risk exists. If the client entity sufficiently controls foreign exchange transactions, then the risk of error relating to these transactions flowing into the financial statements is low; hence the level of testing required by the auditor would be lower than if the entity did not have sufficient controls in place to control the accuracy of foreign exchange transactions.

## Relationship between the Three Components of Audit Risk

The relationship between the three components of audit risk can be summarised as follows:

- The greater the risk of material misstatement (i.e. due to high inherent and control risks), the lower the level of detection risk that can be accepted. The auditor has obtained no assurance from the inherent and control risks assessments, and so must carry out focused **substantive procedures** in order to ensure that all possible misstatements that may have flowed into the financial statements as a result of the high-risk environment are captured.

  There is a higher chance of an error in the financial statements if they have been prepared in a high-risk environment. Therefore the auditor, in order to ensure they issue an appropriate opinion, must perform a high level of substantive testing (i.e. by taking a low detection risk approach).

- The lower the risk of material misstatement (i.e. due to low inherent and control risks), the higher the level of detection risk that can be accepted. Few risks have been present, so the auditor can carry out a reduced level of substantive testing on the basis that the expectation of fraud or error flowing into the financial statements is low due to the low-risk environment.

  If there are low inherent and control risks, not much risk has been taken by the entity, so the auditor can afford to take some risk at the detection stage by performing a reduced level of substantive testing.

**Table 7.5** below depicts the above in a summarised format.

TABLE 7.5: RELATIONSHIP BETWEEN INHERENT, CONTROL AND DETECTION RISKS

| Detection Risk | | Control Risk | | |
|---|---|---|---|---|
| | | High | Medium | Low |
| Inherent Risk | High | Low | Low | Medium |
| | Medium | Low | Medium | High |
| | Low | Medium | High | High |

Values within the dotted oval represent the level of substantive testing expected in each scenario.

## 7.3 THE AUDITOR'S APPROACH TO ASSESSING THE RISK OF MATERIAL MISSTATEMENT

### Introduction

Only after the risk of material misstatement is assessed can a meaningful audit plan be developed that will provide the auditor with sufficient appropriate audit evidence to express an opinion on the financial statements. In order to do this, the auditor needs to understand the entity and the environment within which it operates. ISA 315, as outlined in paragraph 1, "deals with the auditor's responsibility to identify and assess the risks of material misstatement in the financial statements, through understanding the entity and its environment, including the entity's internal control."

This understanding will allow the auditor to assess the risks of material misstatement and develop an audit plan in response to these risks. For example, the findings will be used when considering the following:
- setting an appropriate **materiality level** (the more risks associated with an entity, the lower the materiality level should be – see discussion in **Chapter 5**, Section 5.4);
- the ability of the entity to continue as a going concern;
- significant risk areas that need special audit consideration; and
- the appropriateness of management's oral and written representations.

The auditor should use professional judgement when assessing the level of understanding that is required of the entity and its environment, with the overriding consideration being whether the understanding that has been obtained is sufficient "to assess the risks of material misstatement at the assertion level and design further audit procedures responsive to assessed risks." (ISA 315, paragraph 20)

### Risk Assessment Procedures Used to Gain an Understanding of the Entity

Gaining an understanding of the entity is a continuous process during the audit. As introduced in **Chapter 6**, Section 6.3, there are a number of ways the auditor can obtain audit evidence. Below we consider how these methods can be specifically used to gain a sufficient understanding of the entity and its environment to identify risk. First, let us remind ourselves of the methods introduced in **Chapter 6**:
- inquiries of management and others within the entity;
- analytical procedures;
- observation and inspection;
- cumulative audit knowledge and experience; and
- discussion among the engagement team.

In addition to these, the auditor can decide to perform other auditing procedures to help in the identification of material misstatements, such as contacting external independent parties, e.g. the entity's legal representative or valuation experts used by the entity.

## Inquiries of Management and Others within the Entity

The audit team should carry out preliminary information-gathering at meetings with the entity's management and other employees in order to gain an understanding of, for example:

- the control processes in place within the entity, such as the revenue and receivables cycle, purchases and payables cycle, and treasury cycle, etc.;
- the management structure;
- instances of fraud taking place during the reporting period;
- changes in key personnel taking place during the reporting period;
- application of accounting policies within the entity; and
- related parties and related-party transactions taking place during the reporting period.

Inquiries of personnel other than management are important to corroborate information obtained from management and to provide the auditor with a different perspective in identifying risks of material misstatements. ISA 315, paragraph 6(a), requires the auditor's procedures to include:

> "Inquiries of management, of appropriate individuals within the internal audit function (if the function exists), and of others within the entity who in the auditor's judgment may have information that is likely to assist in identifying risks of material misstatement due to fraud or error."

ISA 315 recognises that the internal auditor is likely to have a strong understanding of the client entity, its control environment and risks and, as such, requires the external auditor to make inquiries of the internal audit function/department as part of the process of gaining an understanding of the client entity. The objective here is to enhance the overall performance of the external audit by extracting the knowledge and findings of the internal audit function, specifically in the area of risk. (A full discussion on the use of the internal auditor can be found in **Chapter 10**.) Internal auditors carry out regular reviews of an entity's controls and business risk strategy, along with devising reports containing recommendations on control deficiencies or risks, and so are best placed to provide the external auditor with valuable insight.

## Analytical Procedures

The performance of **analytical procedures** at the beginning, during and at the end of the audit may identify unusual transactions, incorrect treatment of transactions/balances and omissions from the financial statements. When using analytical procedures as a risk-assessment tool, the auditor develops expectations for classes of transactions and account balances based on factors such as the economic climate, changes in the entity's trading operations during the reporting period or information obtained from management. Where actual results differ significantly from expected results, this can alert the auditor at the early stages of the audit to areas where material misstatement might exist and where there is a need for further investigation during substantive testing.

It is important to note the distinction between the use of analytical procedures at the different stages of the audit process. At the planning and completion stages, the auditor is not collecting evidence but is instead using the technique to **identify** possible unexplained variances that require further investigation – which will then provide the audit evidence. At the fieldwork (substantive stage) the auditor is using analytical procedures to collect evidence to support the various **management assertions/audit objectives**.

Now that we understand the types of risk that the auditor is alert to (i.e. inherent and control risks) and we are more familiar with the methods used to identify risk, we can apply this understanding by way of **Example 7.1**.

EXAMPLE 7.1: IDENTIFICATION OF INHERENT AND CONTROL RISKS

You are the auditor of Large Company Limited, a company involved in the manufacture of furniture for sale in Ireland and abroad, and have been asked to carry out a risk assessment. The following information has been made available to you:
• a draft copy of the directors' report; and
• the draft statement of comprehensive income and statement of financial position.

These documents are included in **Appendix B**, which contains extracts of the financial statements of Large Company Limited. Typically financial statements contain a large amount of information in many different formats and layout – you will be expected to identify and find the relevant information to be able to perform analysis and testing.

**Using these documents:**
1. identify the possible inherent and control risks that exist in Large Company Limited;
2. identify if these risks are at the entity level (financial statement level), or account balance and class of transactions level.

To work through these requirements, we first compare the results of 2017 with those of 2018 (i.e. perform a **preliminary analytical review**) to identify any risks. The table below shows each line item in the statement of financial position and then in the statement of comprehensive income, and the changes in absolute terms and in percentage terms from 2017 to 2018. The auditor's aim is to identify any large, unexpected variances or relationships between the figures.

**Preliminary Analytical Review – Workings Example**

STATEMENT OF FINANCIAL POSITION

AS AT 31 DECEMBER 2018

| | 2018 | 2017 | Absolute Change | % Change |
|---|---|---|---|---|
| **Non-current assets** | **€000** | **€000** | **€000** | |
| Property, plant and equipment | 130,050 | 140,500 | (10,450) | –7% |
| Other intangible assets | 1,150 | 1,140 | 10 | 1% |

*continued overleaf*

| | 2018 | 2017 | Absolute Change | % Change |
|---|---|---|---|---|
| **Non-current assets** | €000 | €000 | €000 | |
| Derivative financial instruments | 1,900 | 1,460 | 440 | 30% |
| Financial assets | 112,200 | 110,200 | 2,000 | 2% |
| Pension assets | 1,200 | 1,000 | 200 | 20% |
| | **246,500** | **254,300** | **(7,800)** | |
| **Current assets** | | | | |
| Inventories | 49,774 | 35,020 | 14,754 | 42% |
| Receivables: | | | | |
| amounts falling due after one year | 8,700 | 10,250 | (1,550) | –15% |
| amounts falling due within one year | 6,500 | 7,250 | (750) | –10% |
| | **15,200** | **17,500** | **(2,300)** | **–13%** |
| Derivative financial instruments | 390 | 170 | 220 | 129% |
| Available-for-sale investments | 4,200 | 5,000 | (800) | –16% |
| Cash and other cash equivalents | 104,200 | 105,530 | (1,330) | –1% |
| | **173,764** | **163,220** | **10,544** | **6%** |
| **Payables:** | | | | |
| amounts falling due within one year | (135,680) | (142,600) | 6,920 | –5% |
| **Net current assets** | **38,084** | **20,620** | **17,464** | **85%** |
| **Total assets less current liabilities** | **283,384** | **273,920** | **9,464** | **3%** |
| **Payables:** | | | | |
| amounts falling due after more than one year | 109,940 | 116,630 | (6,690) | –6% |
| **Provision for liabilities** | 750 | 500 | 250 | 50% |
| | **(110,690)** | **(117,130)** | **6,440** | **–5%** |
| **Net assets excluding pension asset** | 172,694 | 156,790 | 15,904 | 10% |
| **Pension asset** | 1,200 | 1,000 | 200 | 20% |
| **Net assets including pension asset** | **173,894** | **157,790** | **16,104** | **10%** |
| **Capital and reserves** | | | | |
| Called-up share capital | 84,050 | 78,160 | 5,890 | 8% |
| Share premium account | 2,990 | 570 | 2,420 | 425% |
| Other reserves | 1,600 | 28,700 | (27,300) | –95% |
| Retained earnings | 85,254 | 50,360 | 35,094 | 70% |
| **Shareholders' funds** | **173,894** | **157,790** | **16,104** | **10%** |

*continued overleaf*

STATEMENT OF COMPREHENSIVE INCOME

FOR THE YEAR ENDED 31 DECEMBER 2018

| | 2018 | 2017 | Absolute Change | % Change |
|---|---|---|---|---|
| | €000 | €000 | €000 | |
| Revenue | 280,250 | 198,500 | 81,750 | 41% |
| Cost of sales | (140,250) | (120,800) | (19,450) | 16% |
| **Gross profit** | 140,000 | 77,700 | 62,300 | 80% |
| Distribution costs | (23,000) | (20,000) | (3,000) | 15% |
| Administration costs | (35,000) | (34,000) | (1,000) | 3% |
| | 82,000 | 23,700 | 58,300 | 246% |
| Other operating income | 750 | 700 | 50 | 7% |
| **Operating profit – continuing operations** | 82,750 | 24,400 | 58,350 | 239% |
| **Exceptional items** | | | | |
| Profit/(loss) on sale of tangible fixed assets | 420 | (120) | 540 | 450% |
| Impairment of investment property | (10,000) | – | (10,000) | 100% |
| Loss on disposal of available-for-sale investments | (120) | – | (120) | 100% |
| **Profit on ordinary activities before interest** | 73,050 | 24,280 | 48,770 | 201% |
| Investment income | 350 | 330 | 20 | 6% |
| Interest payable and similar charges | (550) | (550) | 0 | 0% |
| **Profit on ordinary activities before taxation** | 72,850 | 24,060 | 48,790 | 203% |
| Tax on profit on ordinary activities | (12,456) | (8,500) | (3,956) | 47% |
| **Profit on ordinary activities after taxation** | 60,394 | 15,560 | 44,834 | 288% |

**Below are some risk observations from the auditor's review of the directors' report, coupled with the preliminary analytical procedure above.**

*Inherent Risks:*
- A new line of furniture has broken into the luxury market; this is a dramatic change for the company considering the impact on revenue, and therefore imposes an entity-level risk.

*continued overleaf*

- According to the directors' report, foreign trade has increased by €42 million, which will add to the complexity of transactions and pose a risk at the account balance and class of transaction level. (Risk associated with complex transactions – foreign exchange.)
- A key member of staff is retiring (John Hogan). The auditor will seek to understand the operational involvement of the individual in order to assess the potential risk impact at either an entity or lower level.
- Considerable political donations were made during the year, which will require additional disclosure, posing a risk at the disclosure level.
- Complicated transactions exist in the form of derivatives (which are up 30% for long term and 129% for short term on the prior year's SOFP), which pose a risk at the class of transactions and account balance level.
- Provisions for liabilities are up 50% – provisions require a high degree of judgement and so pose an inherent risk at the account balance, class of transactions, assertion and disclosure level.

## Controls Risks:

- Revenue has increased by 41% in just one year, which may indicate a cut-off risk and, due to the impact this would have on revenue, cost of sales, inventory, receivables and payables, this is considered to be an entity-level risk (financial statement level).
- Revenue has increased by 41%, yet receivables have decreased by 13% overall. This may indicate some incorrect classification or netting of receivables and payables balance (account balance level risk).
- Cost of sales has risen by only 16%, compared to a 41% increase in sales. Additionally, inventory balances are up 42% on the prior year, which may indicate that closing inventory has been overvalued (account balance level risk), or that incorrect cut-off/counting procedures have been applied. This may be explained by the fact that some furniture lines have been classified in the luxury market and so are generating higher margins (gross margin is up 11%), but it will be highlighted as a risk until investigated further.
- Payables: amounts falling due within one year are down 5% despite all categories of expenses being up and inventory levels being up, which may indicate that accruals are not complete (account balance, class of transaction and assertion level risk).
- Distribution costs, which are normally a function of sales, are up only 15%, while sales have risen by 41%. This may indicate that accruals are not complete (account balance, class of transactions and assertion level risk).
- Pension assets are up despite the retirement of a long-standing employee during the year, which may indicate a control risk around non-routine transactions (account balance, class of transactions and assertion level risk).
- Interest has not changed; one would expect that interest charged to the income statement would decrease in line with the 6% decrease in long-term payables noted on the SOFP. The calculation of accruals will need to be validated (account balance level risk).

While the above are some examples of risks that an auditor may highlight as a result of their preliminary review, they do not form an exhaustive list. **Note**: though the details in the notes may explain some of the concerns around the risks identified, at the time of the risk review you only have access to the three documents provided: a draft of the directors' report and the

*continued overleaf*

draft statements of comprehensive income and financial position. The auditor would now request further information to gain a further understanding of the risks identified.

*For illustration purposes, note also some consistencies which exist with respect to relationships*:
- Fixed assets are down, and we note a large profit from the sale of fixed assets, which indicates fixed assets were disposed of during the period.
- Financial assets are up, as is investment income.

## Observation and Inspection

As tools of risk assessment, observation and inspection can be used to corroborate information obtained from management and other personnel. For example:
- observation of the entity's activities and operations;
- inspection of documents and entity records, e.g. business plans, internal control manuals, etc.;
- reading reports prepared by management and those charged with governance, e.g. quarterly management accounts, monthly/annual budgets, minutes of directors'/management meetings; and
- tracing transactions through the information system relevant to financial reporting – **walkthrough testing** (which is often used for the purpose of controls testing and is discussed in **Chapter 8**, Section 8.4).

## Cumulative Audit Knowledge and Experience

For continuing audit engagements, i.e. audits that are performed annually by the auditor, information obtained in prior years in relation to the entity and the environment in which it operates can be used, provided that the auditor determines whether changes have occurred during the reporting period that may affect the relevance of such information in the current-period audit.

## Discussion among the Audit Engagement Team

Prior to the commencement of the audit, it is worthwhile for the audit engagement team to discuss the potential for the entity's financial statements to be materially misstated. This will allow more experienced team members to share their knowledge of the entity, including significant risk areas and past instances of fraud or misstatement, with the rest of the team.

## Types of Information Considered when Gaining an Understanding of the Entity and its Environment

As stated in ISA 315, paragraphs 11–12, the auditor's understanding of the entity and its environment consists of familiarity with the following:
1. The entity and its environment, including:
    (a) industry, regulatory and other external factors, including the applicable financial reporting framework;

(b)  nature of the entity, including its operations, ownership and governance structures, types of investment and its structure;

(c)  the entity's selection and application of accounting policies;

(d)  the entity's objectives and strategies and related business risks; and

(e)  the measurement and review of the entity's financial performance.

2.  The entity's internal control environment (discussed in detail in **Chapter 8**).

Focusing on each of these components will provide the auditor with a detailed knowledge and understanding of the entity before assessing the risk of material misstatements and developing the audit plan. In order to gain a suitable understanding of these areas, there are certain factors that the auditor should consider. The application notes to ISA 315 provide examples of these, some of which are presented below, according to their categories.

## INDUSTRY, REGULATORY AND OTHER EXTERNAL FACTORS

**Industry** – ISA 315, paragraph A24: "Relevant industry factors include industry conditions such as the competitive environment, supplier and customer relationships, and technological developments."

**Regulatory** – ISA 315, paragraph A26: "The regulatory environment encompasses, among other matters the applicable financial reporting framework and the legal and political environment". For example, the applicable tax laws that govern the client entity form part of the regulatory environment. The applicable reporting framework might be IFRS or FRS.

**Considerations Specific to Public Sector Entities** – specific laws, regulations or other authority may affect the entity's operation (ISA 315, paragraph A28).

**Other External Factors** – other external factors may include general economic conditions, interest rates, credit availability or currency revaluation (ISA 315, paragraph A29).

## NATURE OF THE ENTITY

**Operations** – this is normally one of the first things the auditor will consider and may include: revenue sources and markets; involvement in e-commerce; whether the entity is involved in, for example, retail or manufacture; geographic dispersion and industry segmentation; warehouse and office locations; and key customers (ISA 315, paragraph A31).

**Ownership and Governance Structure** – ISA 315, paragraph A30: "This understanding assists in determining whether related party transactions have been appropriately identified, accounted for, and adequately disclosed in the financial statements."

**Existing and Potential Investment Types** – ISA 315, paragraph A31: "Planned or recently executed acquisitions or divestitures; investment and dispositions of securities and loans; capital investment activities; investments in non-consolidated entities, including partnerships, joint ventures and special-purpose entities." This understanding provides the auditor with an insight into possible complicated accounting transactions and valuations, as well as giving the auditor an insight to the direction of the client entity.

**Entity Structure and Financing** – ISA 315, paragraph A30: "Whether the entity has a complex structure, for example with subsidiaries or other components in multiple locations. Complex structures often introduce issues that may give rise to risks of material misstatement. Such issues may include whether goodwill, joint ventures, investments, or special-purpose entities are accounted for appropriately". The financing structure is also of interest to the auditor: What is the debt to equity ratio? Does the entity use derivative financial instruments? This type of information again gives the auditor an insight into the existence of complex accounting transactions and going concern (ISA 315, paragraph A31).

**Financial Reporting** – an understanding of accounting principles and industry-specific practices will give the auditor an insight into potential issues around areas such as: revenue recognition; valuation of long-term contracts; or accounting for fair values (ISA 315, paragraph A31).

## Selection and Application of Accounting Policies

ISA 315, paragraph A35 states that: "An understanding of the entity's selection and application of accounting policies may encompass such matters as: the methods the entity uses to account for significant and unusual transactions; the effect of significant accounting policies in controversial or emerging areas ... changes in the entity's accounting policies". It also refers to the adoption of new financial reporting standards, laws and regulations.

## Objectives and Strategies

As we have noted, an entity's objectives and strategies can be subject to business risk, which is broader than the risk of material misstatement of the financial statements. ISA 315, paragraph A38, explains that: "An understanding of the business risks facing the entity increases the likelihood of identifying risks of material misstatement, since most business risks will eventually have financial consequences and, therefore, an effect on the financial statements. However, the auditor does not have a responsibility to identify or assess all business risks because not all business risks give rise to risks of material misstatement."

Examples of business risks provided by ISA 315, paragraph A37, include: "development of new products or services that may fail; a market which ... is inadequate to support a product or service; or flaws in a product or service that may result in liabilities and reputational risk".

ISA 315, paragraph A39, provides examples of matters that the auditor should be alert to that may indicate business risk and in turn lead to a material misstatement. Some of these examples include: new products or services giving rise to product liability; expansion of the business without accurate estimation of demand; or the introduction of a new IT system where systems and processes are incompatible.

## MEASUREMENT AND REVIEW OF THE ENTITY'S FINANCIAL PERFORMANCE

ISA 315, paragraph A44: "The measurement and review of financial performance is not the same as the monitoring of controls … though their purpose may overlap:
- The measurement and review of performance is directed at whether business performance is meeting the objectives set by management (or third parties).
- Monitoring of controls is specifically concerned with the effective operation of internal control."

The entity might typically measure its financial performance using key performance indicators, period-on-period financial performance analysis or comparison of financial results with its competitors. (See ISA 315, paragraph A45, for further examples.)

## INTERNAL CONTROL

The auditor must gain an understanding of the entity's internal controls relevant to the audit in order to identify potential areas where misstatements could occur, consider factors that affect the risk of material misstatement and to design the nature, timing and extent of further audit procedures (ISA 315, paragraph 12).

As defined in ISA 315, paragraph A51:
"Internal control is designed, implemented and maintained to address identified business risks that threaten the achievement of any of the entity's objectives that concern:
- the reliability of the entity's financial reporting;
- the effectiveness and efficiency of its operations; and
- its compliance with applicable laws and regulations."

The components of an entity's internal controls are:
- the control environment;
- the entity's risk assessment process;
- the information system, including the related business processes relevant to financial reporting and communication;
- control activities; and
- monitoring of controls.

These are discussed in more detail in **Chapter 8**, Section 8.2.

At this stage of the risk assessment process, the auditor must consider how the design and implementation of the entity's system of internal control prevents material misstatements from occurring and, if they did occur, how the system would detect and correct them. Assessing the internal control system in this way can also identify weaknesses in the internal control function. Where weaknesses are detected, the risks of material misstatement will be increased (see **Chapter 8**).

### Internal Control Limitations

No matter how well internal controls are designed and implemented by the entity, they can only provide **reasonable assurance** over the achievement of financial reporting management assertions (audit objectives). Possible limitations to internal control include:
- human error/mistake;
- human decision-making – the correct decision is not always made;
- controls can be circumvented as a result of collusion by two or more people;
- controls can be circumvented as a result of management override of control; or
- segregation of duties is often not possible within smaller entities, resulting in internal control functions not operating in an ideal manner.

Again, a full discussion on the internal control environment is given in **Chapter 8**.

### Sources of Information

Having discussed the type of information that the auditor should obtain, we will now consider where the auditor can find the required information, i.e. the sources of this information.

Information can be financial or non-financial, and can be sourced from within the entity itself or externally (see **Table 7.6**).

TABLE 7.6: SOURCES OF INFORMATION

| Financial Information | |
|---|---|
| **Internal** | **External** |
| • Budgets | • Industry information |
| • Management accounts | • Competitive intelligence |
| • Financial reports | • Credit rating agencies |
| • Financial statements | • Creditors/suppliers |
| • Minutes of directors' meetings | • Government agencies |
| • Income tax returns | • Franchisors |
| • Decisions made on accounting policies | • Media and other external parties |
| • Judgements and estimates | |
| • Internal audit reports | |

## Non-financial Information

**Internal**

- Vision/mission statement
- Stated objectives and strategies
- Organisational structure
- Minutes of directors' meetings
- Job descriptions
- Operating performance
- Business drivers
- Capabilities
- Policy and procedure manuals
- Non-financial performance measures/metrics

**External**

- Trade association data
- Industry forecasts
- Government agency reports
- Newspaper/magazine articles
- Information on the internet
- Industry regulators

## 7.4 ASSESSING THE RISKS OF MATERIAL MISSTATEMENT

When the auditor has obtained an understanding of the entity and its environment, including the internal control function, an assessment of the risk of material misstatement occurring at the financial statement level and at the assertion level for classes of transactions, account balances and disclosures must be made. In order to make this assessment, the auditor shall, according to ISA 315, paragraph 26:

"(a)  Identify risks throughout the process of obtaining an understanding of the entity and its environment, including relevant controls that relate to the risks, and by considering the classes of transactions, account balances, and disclosures … in the financial statements;

(b)  Assess the identified risks, and evaluate whether they relate more pervasively to the financial statements as a whole and potentially affect many assertions;

(c)  Relate the identified risks to what can go wrong at the assertion level, taking account of relevant controls that the auditor intends to test; and

(d)  Consider the likelihood of misstatement, including the possibility of multiple misstatements, and whether the potential misstatement could result in a material misstatement."

This assessment will dictate the nature, timing and extent of further audit procedures to be performed, which will be designed and performed in response to the assessed risks.

The risk assessment process should be adequately documented by the audit team and include information such as:
- engagement team discussions on the entity's control environment;
- how the understanding has been gained;
- key points of the understanding gained;
- the identified and assessed risks of material misstatement;

- identification of significant risks that need to be specifically addressed; and
- risks for which substantive procedures alone will not provide sufficient appropriate audit evidence.

## Factors to Consider when Assessing Risk

The factors that the auditor should consider when making a risk assessment are dealt with under three key areas:

1. What risks have been identified – are they at the entity (financial statement) level or assertion level, and are there related internal control procedures that mitigate the risk?
2. What magnitude of misstatement could possibly occur and is it at the entity (financial statement) level or at the assertion level?
3. How likely is the event or risk to occur?

**Table 7.7** below provides examples of the specific types of risk that the auditor should consider with respect to these three key questions.

TABLE 7.7: RISK ASSESSMENT FACTORS

| **1. What risks have been identified?** | |
|---|---|
| **Financial statement (entity) level** | • Risks resulting from poor entity-level internal controls or general IT internal controls.<br>• Risk factors relating to management override of controls and fraud.<br>• Risks that management has chosen to accept, such as a lack of segregation of duties in an entity. |
| **Assertion level** | • Specific risks relating to the occurrence/existence, completeness, classification/recording and valuation, rights and obligations, cut-off and presentation and disclosure of:<br>  ♦ revenues, expenditures, and other transactions;<br>  ♦ account balances; and<br>  ♦ financial statement disclosures.<br>• Risks that could give rise to multiple misstatements. |
| **Related internal control procedures** | • Significant risks.<br>• The appropriately designed and implemented internal control procedures that help to prevent, detect or mitigate the risks identified.<br>• Risks that can only be addressed by performing tests of controls. |
| **2. What magnitude of misstatement could possibly occur?** | |
| **Financial statement (entity) level** | • What events, if they occurred, would result in a material misstatement in the financial statements? Consider:<br>  ♦ management override;<br>  ♦ fraud;<br>  ♦ unexpected events; and<br>  ♦ past experience. |

*continued overleaf*

| **Assertion level** | • Consider:<br>   ♦ the inherent nature of the transactions, account balance or disclosure;<br>   ♦ routine and non-routine events; and<br>   ♦ past experience. |
|---|---|

**3. How likely is the event (risk) to occur?**

| **Financial statement level** | • Consider:<br>   ♦ 'tone at the top';<br>   ♦ management's approach to risk management;<br>   ♦ policies and procedures in place; and<br>   ♦ past experience. |
|---|---|
| **Assertion level** | • Consider:<br>   ♦ relevant internal control activities; and<br>   ♦ past experience. |

## 7.5 THE AUDITOR'S RESPONSE TO ASSESSED RISKS

When the auditor has assessed the risks of material misstatement at the financial statement (entity) level, further audit procedures should be designed whose nature, timing and extent are in response to the assessed risks. There should be a clear link between the risks identified and the audit procedures performed to mitigate those risks. The overall aim of the auditor's response to assessed risks is to reduce audit risk to an acceptably low level.

ISA 330 *The Auditor's Responses to Assessed Risks*, paragraph 7, states that the auditor should consider the following when designing further audit procedures:

"(a) Consider the reasons for the assessment given to the risk of material misstatement at the assertion level for each class of transactions, account balance, and disclosure, including:

(i) The likelihood of material misstatement due to the particular characteristics of the relevant class of transactions, account balance, or disclosure (that is, the inherent risk); and

(ii) Whether the risk assessment takes account of relevant controls (that is, the control risk), thereby requiring the auditor to obtain audit evidence to determine whether the controls are operating effectively (that is, the auditor intends to rely on the operating effectiveness of controls in determining the nature, timing and extent of substantive procedures); and

(b) Obtain more persuasive audit evidence the higher the auditor's assessment of risk."

The nature of audit procedures used in response to assessed risks is critical in order to reduce audit risk to an acceptably low level.

## Nature, Timing and Extent of Further Audit Procedures in Response to Assessed Risks

### Nature

The 'nature' of audit procedures refers to their **purpose** and their **type**. The purpose of procedures is either **controls testing** or **substantive testing**. The type, or method, of the audit procedure are the **tests of details** (inspection, observation, inquiry, confirmation, recalculation and reperformance) and **substantive analytical procedures** (see **Chapter 6**, Section 6.3).

It is important to realise that certain forms of testing are more appropriate for some assertions than for others. For example:
- controls testing is not appropriate for gaining comfort over the cut-off assertion, whereas substantive testing would be;
- substantive testing is usually more appropriate than controls testing for gaining comfort over the completeness and classification assertions for accounting estimates, such as prepayments, accruals or provisions (e.g. provision for bad debt, provision for slow-moving inventory, etc.); and
- when it comes to revenue, controls testing is more suitable for addressing risks relating to the completeness assertion, whereas substantive procedures are better for addressing risk relating to the valuation assertion.

When considering the nature of the testing to be performed, the auditor must remain firmly focused on the risks identified and the related risk assessment, i.e. the higher the assessed risk, the more reliable and relevant must be the audit evidence obtained by substantive testing.

### Timing

Timing simply refers to when the audit procedures are performed. They can be performed at an interim date or at the period end, and after the year end. As a general guide, the higher the assessed risk the more likely it is that the auditor will consider it more effective to perform audit procedures nearer to and after the period end. In some circumstances, in order to introduce an element of unpredictability into audit testing, it is worthwhile to perform some audit procedures at an unpredictable or unannounced time. In other instances, performing audit procedures before the period end can alert the auditor to significant matters at an early stage of the audit. Key points to consider when deciding whether to perform audit procedures at an interim date (i.e. before year end) are:
- How long before the year end can the auditor start interim testing?
- How strong is the overall control environment? Performing a **'roll forward'** between an interim date and the period end is unlikely to be effective if the control environment is poor.
- How strong are the specific controls over the account balance or class of transactions being considered?

- Is the required supporting documentation/evidence available to perform the test? Electronic files could subsequently be overwritten, or procedures to be observed could occur only at certain times.
- Would a procedure before the period end address the nature and substance of the risk involved?
- Would the interim procedure address the period or date to which the audit evidence relates?
- How much additional evidence will be required for the remaining period between the date the procedure is performed and the period end?

It is important to remember that certain procedures can only be performed at or after the period end, such as cut-off testing, unrecorded liabilities testing and subsequent events testing.

### *Extent*

Extent relates to the quantity of a specific audit procedure to be performed. For example, the sample size to be used when testing client cut-off procedures, the number and value of receivables balances to be circularised or the number of observations of a control activity to be performed.

The extent of the testing to be performed is determined by the judgement of the auditor after considering the:
- materiality;
- assessed risk; and
- the degree of assurance necessary.

Where the assessed risk is greater, the extent of testing to be performed will be increased as appropriate. As a general rule:
- where risk is assessed as high, the greater the extent of testing to be performed; and
- where risk is assessed as low, the extent of testing to be performed will be less.

## 7.6  SIGNIFICANT RISKS

As discussed in **Section 7.5**, as part of the risk assessment process within an entity, the auditor must consider each risk individually and how pervasive it could be in the financial statements. Not all risks, however, will be of equal significance and therefore not all risks will have the potential to lead to a material misstatement in the financial statements. Risks that have the potential to impact significantly on the financial statements and which need special audit consideration in order to mitigate the risk are known as **significant risks** (ISA 315, paragraph 4(e)).

When determining significant risks (which will arise on most audits) the auditor must use professional judgement and assess:
- the nature of the risk;
- the likely magnitude of the potential misstatement; and
- the likelihood of the risk occurring.

ISA 315, paragraph 28, offers guidance to the auditor in deciding what risks are significant risks. This includes, amongst others, consideration as to whether the risk is fraud-related or if it involves significant transactions with related parties.

Significant risks that often arise on audit engagements include:
- fraud risk;
- management override of controls;
- revenue recognition;
- personal expenditure of directors being included in the expenses of the company; and
- undisclosed related party transactions.

Significant risks, particularly in smaller entities, often relate to:
- significant non-routine transactions, i.e. unusual transactions for the entity – involve a risk of incorrect processing, classification and disclosure in the financial statements; or
- matters that require significant judgement – are inherently risky given that they are often very subjective in nature, represent the views of a small number of individuals, e.g. the directors, and cannot be substantiated by third-party evidence.

TABLE 7.8: RISKS RELATING TO NON-ROUTINE
TRANSACTIONS AND MATTERS OF JUDGEMENT

|  | Characteristics |
|---|---|
| **Significant non-routine transactions** | • High inherent risk (likelihood and impact).<br>• Occur infrequently.<br>• Not subject to systematic processing.<br>• Unusual due to their size or nature (e.g. the acquisition of another entity).<br>• Require management intervention:<br>  ♦ to specify accounting treatment; or<br>  ♦ for data collection and processing.<br><br>• Involve complex calculations or accounting principles.<br>• Nature of transactions makes it difficult for the entity to implement effective internal controls over the risks. |
| **Significant matters of judgement** | • High inherent risk.<br>• Involve significant measurement uncertainty (such as the development of accounting estimates).<br>• Accounting principles involved may be subject to differing interpretation (such as preparation of accounting estimates or application of revenue recognition).<br>• Required judgement may be subjective, complex, or require assumptions about the effects of future events (such as judgements about fair value; valuation of inventory subject to rapid change). |
| (**Source**: *Guide to Using ISAs in the Audits of Small- and Medium-Sized Entities* (IFAC).) | |

## The Auditor's Response to Significant Risks

The auditor must gain an understanding of the internal controls designed and implemented around any significant risks identified.

Assessment of the robustness of the internal controls surrounding significant risks is necessary in order for the auditor to have all the information needed to develop an appropriate audit approach. As a general rule:
- where the controls identified around significant risk areas are weak or where no controls exist, the auditor must perform appropriate substantive testing in order to mitigate the risk of a material misstatement going undetected; or
- where the controls identified around significant risk areas are strong, the level of substantive testing performed can be reduced as deemed appropriate by the auditor.

If the client entity's internal controls are assessed as weak (or non-existent) and the auditor does not believe that substantive procedures alone can reduce the risk of material misstatement to an acceptably low level, then the impact on the audit opinion must be considered.

Where it is concluded by the auditor that management has not responded appropriately to a significant risk through the design and implementation of appropriate controls, this is noted as an **internal control weakness** and should be communicated to those charged with governance (see **Section 7.8**).

It is important to note also that where controls exist around significant risks, these controls must be tested during each audit engagement by the audit team. Reliance on evidence attained in previous audits is not permitted without some key considerations, outlined in ISA 330, paragraph 13.

ISA 315, paragraph 30, refers to those risks for which "it is not be possible or practicable to obtain sufficient appropriate audit evidence only from substantive procedures". It explains that such risks may "relate to the inaccurate or incomplete recording of routine and significant classes of transactions or account balances, the characteristics of which often permit highly automated processing with little or no manual intervention. In such cases, the entity's controls over such risks are relevant to the audit and the auditor shall obtain an understanding of them".

For all significant risks identified, it is essential that the auditor documents the:
- nature of the significant risk identified;
- management's response to the significant risk; and
- the audit response to the significant risk, i.e. testing to be performed to mitigate the audit risk (i.e. the risk that the auditor expresses an inappropriate opinion.

## 7.7 EVALUATING THE SUFFICIENCY AND APPROPRIATENESS OF AUDIT EVIDENCE

Once audit procedures have been performed and audit evidence obtained, the auditor should consider the initial risk assessment at the assertion level and conclude if the risks identified still remain appropriate. Overall, the auditor should then make an assessment as to whether the audit evidence obtained is sufficient and appropriate to reduce the **audit risk** (i.e. the risk that the auditor expresses an inappropriate opinion is reduced to an acceptably low level (ISA 330, paragraph 25). Whether audit evidence is sufficient and appropriate is a matter of the auditor's professional judgement.

Where the auditor concludes that sufficient appropriate audit evidence has **not** been obtained, attempts should be made to obtain such evidence. Where it is not possible to obtain such evidence, the auditor must consider the impact on the audit opinion to be issued.

As discussed in detail in **Chapter 6**, it is essential that the auditor document the nature, timing and extent of audit procedures that have been performed in response to assessed risks of material misstatement at the assertion level. Equally, the auditor must document the results of the testing performed.

## 7.8 COMMUNICATING WITH THOSE CHARGED WITH GOVERNANCE AND MANAGEMENT

ISA 265 *Communicating Deficiencies in Internal Control to Those Charged with Governance and Management*, paragraph 9, states: "The auditor shall communicate in writing significant deficiencies in internal control identified during the audit to those charged with governance on a timely basis." This written communication is referred to as a **management letter** and is dealt with in more detail in **Chapter 8**, Section 8.10. At this point it is sufficient to be aware that the communication should include:
- the deficiency identified;
- the level of risk associated with the deficiency, i.e. low, moderate or high; and
- suggestions as to how the control environment can be improved in order to remove the deficiency.

The risk assessment process does not end after the initial assessment is made and communication of control deficiencies is made to those charged with governance/ management. Rather, the auditor must remain alert throughout the audit for additional risk areas that are identified and for evidence of internal controls not operating as intended. When this occurs, the original risk assessment must be updated to reflect the new information. The audit plan should also be amended, if necessary, in response to new risks identified.

## 7.9 THE RELATIONSHIP BETWEEN MATERIALITY AND AUDIT RISK

When planning the audit, the auditor considers what might cause the financial statements to be materially misstated. The auditor's understanding of the entity and its environment establishes a frame of reference within which they plan the audit and exercise professional judgement in assessing the risk of material misstatement in the financial statements, Throughout the audit this understanding informs the auditor's response to the identified risks and helps in establishing the level of materiality and, as the audit progresses, if it remains valid.

For instance, where significant risks of material misstatement are identified, audit materiality should be adjusted to reflect the new information obtained. Where this is the case, the auditor must consider the impact on the audit approach and may consider it necessary to alter the nature, timing and extent of the audit plan.

> **Remember**: the key point is that there is an inverse relationship between audit risk and materiality:
> * the greater the audit risk, the lower the level of materiality; and
> * the lower the audit risk, the greater the level of materiality.

## 7.10 CONCLUSION

Assessing the risk of material misstatements occurring in the financial statements is critical for the auditor in order to determine an appropriate audit plan that will reduce the **audit risk** (i.e. the risk that the auditor issues an inappropriate opinion is reduced to an acceptably low level). This is a complex process and the auditor must develop the skills necessary in order to:
* understand the business and related business risks;
* gain an understanding of the internal control system (including evaluating the design of controls and determining whether they have been implemented);
* assess the risks of material misstatement;
* develop overall responses to risks; and
* develop responses to risks at the assertion level.

A suitable risk assessment process should be carried out by the auditor and should include appropriate audit procedures to respond to the identified risks. Failure to carry out an adequate assessment of risks exposes the auditor to a high level of audit risk, which may result in the issuing of an incorrect audit opinion.

## SUMMARY OF LEARNING OBJECTIVES

**Learning Objective 1**  Have a detailed knowledge of the risk environment.

**The risk environment is made up of:**
- Business risk – the auditor is only concerned with business risks that could impact on the financial statements and lead to material misstatements;
- Audit risk – the risk of the auditor issuing an inappropriate audit decision.

**Audit risk comprises:**
- Engagement risk (see **Chapter 5**)
- Independence risk (see **Chapter 2**).

The components of audit risk are:

1. inherent risk – driven by the environment in which the company operates;
2. control risk – driven by the organisational controls introduced by management;
3. detection risk – driven by the strength of the auditor's substantive testing.

The auditor will assess inherent and control risks that exist in the client entity and plan substantive testing at an appropriate level to respond to the risks identified. Detection risk is the only risk component within the control of the auditor.

**Risk can exist at two levels of material misstatement:**
- the financial statement level (also referred to as the entity level);
- the class of transaction, account balance and disclosure, and related assertions level.

Risks that occur at the financial statement level are more significant for the auditor, so staff with relevant expertise and experience to deal with the risks at hand should be assigned.

**Learning Objective 2**  Know how the auditor gains an understanding of the entity, what type of information should be collected and why, and where this information can be sourced.

ISA 315 offers guidance on **what** type of information the auditor should try to obtain. Broadly, the auditor should seek to understand: the entity and its environment; and the entity's internal controls. Focusing on each of these areas will provide the auditor with a detailed knowledge and understanding of the entity before assessing the risk of material misstatements and developing the audit plan.

In order to gain an understanding of the entity and its environment, the auditor can use a number of methods, including: inquiries of management; analytical procedures; observation and inspection; cumulative audit knowledge and experience; and discussion among the audit engagement team.

The auditor should look for both financial and non-financial information to support their understanding, which can be obtained from both internal and external sources.

**Learning Objective 3** Understand the principal considerations of the auditor when assessing the risk of material misstatement.

When assessing the risk of material misstatement, the auditor will consider:
1. What risk has been identified and whether it is at the entity (financial statement) level or the assertion level?
2. What is the potential magnitude of the risk identified?
3. How likely is the risk to occur?

Asking these questions will allow the auditor to better **plan** a response to the risks identified.

**Learning Objective 4** Have a detailed understanding of how the auditor responds to risk (and, separately, significant risk) in the design of the nature, timing and extent of further audit procedures.

Low detection risk – Nature: perform tests of details (as opposed to substantive analytical procedures).

Timing: perform audit procedures after or very close to year end.

Extent: large sample sizes.

High detection risk – Nature: perform more substantive analytical procedures, less tests of details.

Timing: perform more audit procedures at interim stage.

Extent: sample sizes will be smaller.

Not all risks will be of equal significance and, therefore, not all risks have the potential to lead to a material misstatement in the financial statements. Risks that have the potential to impact significantly on the financial statements and which need special audit consideration in order to mitigate the risk are known as **significant risks**.

**Learning Objective 5** Have an appreciation of the assessment of the sufficiency and adequacy of evidence and the importance of documenting the risk process.

Whether audit evidence is sufficient and appropriate is a matter of professional judgement for the auditor. Where the auditor concludes that sufficient appropriate audit evidence has not been obtained, attempts should be made to obtain such evidence. Where it is not possible to obtain such evidence, the auditor must consider the impact on the audit opinion to be issued.

**Learning Objective 6** Have an appreciation of the relationship between materiality and audit risk.

Factors may be identified during the course of the audit that impact on the preliminary assessment of materiality. This may result in the auditor exercising judgement and reducing materiality due to risk assessments performed. Earlier audit procedures may need to be revisited, to see if the change in materiality impacts on the required nature, timing and extent of audit procedures performed.

## QUESTIONS

### Self-test Questions

7.1    Explain the relationship between materiality, audit risk and audit planning.
7.2    Distinguish between inherent risk, control risk and detection risk.
7.3    What is the overall aim of the auditor's response to assessed risks?
7.4    Distinguish between business risk and audit risk.
7.5    Identify three key ways the auditor can obtain an understanding of the entity.
7.6    Identify and give details of two sources of external and internal information from which the auditor can gain an understanding of the entity.
7.7    Identify five internal control limitations.
7.8    How should the auditor communicate material weaknesses in the entity's internal control environment to those charged with governance?
7.9    Outline the auditor's considerations when designing further audit procedures.
7.10   What are the two types of audit procedure an auditor can use to assist in reducing the assessed risk of misstatement to an acceptably low level?

### Review Questions

(See Suggested Solutions to Review Questions in **Appendix C**.)

### *Question 7.1*

You are the audit senior on the audit of Oh So Chic Ltd, a retailer of cutting-edge designer clothing. The audit is scheduled to commence in two weeks. The audit partner has drawn the following information to your attention and would like to know your thoughts.

**Significant Risk** The client's financial director explained, during a recent meeting with the audit partner, that sales have slowed down during the year under review. Normally the company experiences a very quick turnaround time for inventory, given that its lines have been very much in demand in the past. As fashion trends are moving away from designer to high street, the financial director is concerned about the appropriateness of the year-end inventory valuation. The value of inventory held at the year end is €2.75 million, which is material to the financial statements.

**Internal Control** The financial director also revealed at the meeting that a key member of the accounts team had been absent from work through sickness for the final five months of the accounting period under review. His responsibility included preparation of the following key reconciliations:
• daily till reconciliations; and
• monthly supplier statement reconciliations.

In his absence, the above reconciliations were not prepared.

**Other Information** The company is considering commencing a contract to supply goods to Gorgeous Shoes Ltd, a company owned by a director of Oh So Chic Ltd, in an attempt to improve company sales.

**Requirement**
(a) Outline the approach you would adopt to address the significant risk identified in relation to inventory.
(b) Discuss the impact of the absence of the key member of the accounts team on the audit plan and approach, including a discussion of the financial statement areas and assertions that may be affected.
(c) Document, briefly, the audit considerations if a contract is to be agreed between Gorgeous Shoes Ltd and Oh So Chic Ltd.

## Question 7.2

You are an audit manager for Brian & Co. working on the audit plan for TechMad Ltd. TechMad is a software development company that makes bespoke software solutions for blue-chip companies. TechMad commenced trading in 2014 and has grown rapidly over the past four years with 2018 revenue hitting €9,500,000. The company was formed by two friends, both of whom have strong software programming experience. Considering their lack of business and accounting knowledge they invited another friend, Mary, to look after the accounts. Although she is not a qualified accountant, Mary has had a lot of experience in bookkeeping over the years.

At 31 December 2018, TechMad had five new software applications in progress. Two of these applications were almost complete and were due to be launched in January 2019. The other three applications were two months into a six-month build. Mary has indicated that she has recognised the revenue in relation to the two applications that will be ready for launch in January, but she has not recognised anything at all in relation to the other three applications, which are only a third complete.

In 2018 TechMad broke into international markets, selling into China, the United States and the UK. Much of the revenue growth in 2018 was due to this breakthrough. Prior to 2018 TechMad had been self-funded, but due to the sharp increase in sales the software development team needed to grow quickly and 70 new software developers were employed during 2018. This large increase in wages was funded by a loan issued in June 2018.

When questioned about the control environment, Mary indicated that the company is so small that there is no need for specific controls as she keeps a tight control of the finances.

**Requirement**
(a) Outline six potential audit risks in the audit of TechMad Ltd, noting the specific audit risk component and whether the risk exists at the financial statements level or at the classes of transactions/account balance level.
(b) Considering the level of risks and the control environment, what audit approach do you think will be most effective and efficient for Brian & Co. to take?
(c) Distinguish between audit risk and business risk.

## Question 7.3

Parallel Ltd is a long-established FMCG company owned by an Australian holding company. Its biggest customer sector is Irish supermarkets, accounting for 80% of its sales. Parallel Ltd has been audited by Brett & Co. for the past four years. You are the audit manager for the year ended 31 December 2018 and through your conversations with management, have learned the following:

- The parent company was disappointed with the fall in profits in 2017 and warned management that they needed to take more control of costs considering that up to October of 2017 they had been on track to meet profit targets.
- A number of staff members were on strike during 2018 due to disputes over pay decreases. The striking staff members were mainly in finance support (accounts receivable and accounts payable and related functions) and distribution.
- Due to the striking of distribution staff, some invoices needed to be marked as delivered without signed purchase order delivery dockets.
- Marketing costs have been cut by approximately 60% as part of the cost-saving exercise.
- All service contracts (outsourced activities) were sent out for tender during 2018 to ensure the best price was being achieved. As a result, payroll is now under a new service provider.
- The financial controller has recently been replaced (management did not go into details regarding her departure). There was a one-month gap between the departure of the previous financial controller and the arrival of the new.

You have prepared an analytical review based on a comparison of 2018 actual versus budgeted figures, as follows:

|  | 2018 Actual Figures | Budget | Variance | Variance |
|---|---|---|---|---|
|  | €000 | €000 | €000 | % |
| **Sales** | 4,900 | 4,812.00 | (88.00) | 2% |
| **Production Costs** | | | | |
| Material A | 1,180 | 1,000.00 | 180.00 | 18% |
| Material B | 1,150 | 1,200.00 | (50.00) | -4% |
| Material C | 500 | 520.00 | (20.00) | -4% |
| Material D | 152 | 150.00 | 2.00 | 1% |
| Factory electricity | 170 | 160.00 | 10.00 | 6% |
| Labour 133 | 111.00 | 22.00 | 20% | |
| Factory rent | 8 | 8.00 | 0.30 | 4% |
| Machinery depreciation | 20 | 20.00 | 0.00 | 0% |
| **Total production costs** | 3,313 | 3,169 | 144.30 | 5% |
| **Gross profit** | 1,587 | 1,643 | (56.30) | -3% |

**Overheads**

| | | | | |
|---|---|---|---|---|
| Office rent | 40.00 | 83.00 | (43.00) | -52% |
| Sales salaries | 235 | 240.00 | (5.00) | -2% |
| Distribution salaries | 295 | 300.00 | (5.00) | -2% |
| Marketing | 180 | 300.00 | (120.00) | -40% |
| Finance salaries | 325 | 330.00 | (5.00) | -2% |
| Depreciation office equipment | 100 | 58.00 | 42.00 | 72% |
| Debtors write off | 25 | 100.00 | (75.00) | -75% |
| | 1,200 | 1,411 | (211.00) | -15% |
| **Net profit** | **2,400** | **2,822** | **(422.00)** | **7%** |

**Requirement**

(a) Your audit partner has asked you to write a memo outlining the inherent and control risks identified during your discussion with management.

(b) List five questions you would raise with management based on your analytical review (you should take your earlier discussion into account).

# THE AUDIT AND ASSURANCE PROCESS

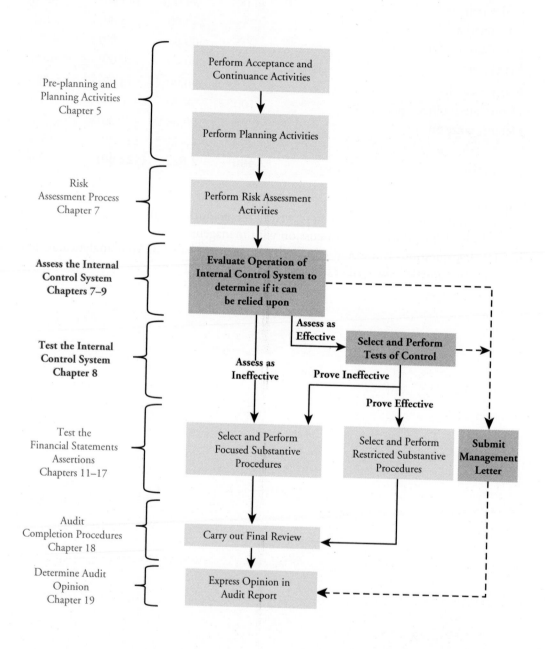

# 8

# CONTROLS AND CONTROLS TESTING

## LEARNING OBJECTIVES

Having studied this chapter on controls and controls testing you should:
1. have a detailed knowledge of what makes up the internal control system;
2. appreciate the importance of client entity internal controls to the auditor;
3. demonstrate a detailed knowledge of the stages involved in the review of the internal control system of the client entity by the external auditor;
4. gain an understanding of the management assertions (audit objectives) relative to each financial cycle;
5. appreciate the control activities that should exist relative to each financial cycle;
6. gain an appreciation of when it is most efficient to test controls;
7. be able to select and apply appropriate control tests to typical financial cycles, which address the management assertions (audit objectives); and
8. be able to explain how the auditor communicates control deficiencies to the client entity.

## CHECKLIST OF RELEVANT STANDARDS

The relevant standards, in both the RoI and the UK/NI, covered in this chapter are:
- ISA 265 *Communicating Deficiencies in Internal Control to Those Charged with Governance and Management*
- ISA 315 *Identifying and Assessing the Risks of Material Misstatement through Understanding the Entity and its Environment*
- ISA 330 *The Auditor's Responses to Assessed Risks*

Note, in general when referring to ISAs, it should be understood as referring to the UK and Ireland versions, unless otherwise specified as either ISA (UK) or ISA (Ireland). See the Introduction for an extant list of auditing standards for the RoI and the UK/NI.

## KEY TERMS AND DEFINITIONS FOR THIS CHAPTER

**Computer-assisted Audit Techniques (CAATs)**    CAATs involve the use of IT systems by an auditor to support their testing of financial statements.

**Control Deviations**    Situations where actual events differ from those expected. For example, an auditor selects 200 invoices and traces them to customer-signed proof of delivery notes (PODs), but finds five deviations in that five of the customer PODs are not signed.

**Exception Report**    A report run from the client entity's computer system highlighting unusual activity. For example, within payroll, an exception report might be run for overtime in excess of 10 hours.

**Knowledge-based Systems**    A knowledge-based system allows an auditor to design a questionnaire containing the most common questions related to a particular procedure and to support this with troubleshooting information that can help to guide them with respect to best practice.

**Master Data**    Also known as 'standing data', master data relates to the information held by an entity that supports transactions. Customers' names and their bank account details are examples of master data. The integrity of master data is of utmost importance to any entity.

**Misappropriation**    The dishonest use of the assets of the client entity, such as stealing inventory or abuse of a company phone.

**Organisational Structure**    The hierarchical arrangement of authority and rights and duties within an organisation.

**Policies and Procedures**    Policies outline the principles or rules that guide decisions within an organisation (e.g. it might be a company's policy to only accept return of goods within 28 days of sale). Procedures outline what action is to be taken or what steps are to be followed when performing a particular task (e.g. when a customer presents a return, the procedure might be to request a receipt or invoice and check that the date on the receipt or invoice is within 28 days; for returns over €100, contact a supervisor to approve the return).

**Segregation of Duties**    The division of key tasks in a transaction to ensure that no one individual can influence a transaction from beginning to end.

**System Control**    A system control is one that is embedded into an entity's IT system. For example, the system can ensure the segregation of duty control requirement is met by ensuring that only those individuals with credit control rights can approve the opening of a new customer account on credit.

**Tests of Controls**    Audit procedure to test the effectiveness of a control used by the client entity to prevent or detect material misstatement.

**'Tone at the Top'**    The words and actions of the directors and senior management of an organisation, in this case relating to internal controls and ethical values.

**Walkthrough Test**    The tracing of a single transaction from beginning to end to establish if it operates as described in the policies and procedures of the client entity.

## 8.1  INTRODUCTION

After the auditor has identified an entity's risk environment (see **Chapter 7**), the next step is to gain an understanding of the internal controls for each financial cycle. ISA 315 *Identifying and Assessing the Risks of Material Misstatement through Understanding the Entity and its Environment*, paragraph 12, states that: "The auditor shall obtain an understanding of internal control relevant to the audit."

The auditor uses their understanding of internal controls to:
• identify types of potential misstatement;
• consider factors that may affect the risks of material misstatement; and
• design the nature, timing and extent of further audit procedures.

**The purpose of the above is to identify the existence of internal controls that mitigate the risk factors identified within each cycle relevant to the specific risk identified at the assertion level.**

In **Section 8.2** we will introduce the internal control system and discuss its components as laid down by the Committee of Sponsoring Organizations of the Treadway Commission (COSO). In this section we will also discuss the objectives of internal controls and their importance to the client entity. **Section 8.3** discusses the importance of the internal control system to the external auditor, addressing the question, "Why is the auditor interested in the controls of the entity?".

The auditor does not test the controls of an entity in every instance. First, before testing, the auditor must determine whether or not they believe the control environment (or the specific financial cycle controls) to be strong. The stages involved in reviewing the internal controls of the client entity are the subject of discussion in **Section 8.4**, which sets the scene for **Sections 8.5–8.9**. **Section 8.4** explains the four-stage approach used to review controls. In **Sections 8.5–8.9** we apply this approach to specific financial cycles, namely: the revenue and receivables cycle; the purchases and payables and payroll cycles; the inventory cycle; the bank and cash cycle; and the investments cycle. It is essential to understand the generic application described within **Section 8.4** but, more importantly, to be able to apply this process to individual financial cycles. Typical financial cycle processes are described in order to demonstrate the key control activities expected within each cycle, but the reader should be mindful that these can vary from company to company. There are a number of different methods used to describe the processes (for example, narratives and flowcharts), which are intended to give the reader an insight into the types of methods used by companies to describe their internal control environment.

Finally, in **Section 8.10** we discuss how the auditor communicates any deficiencies in the control environment to the client entity.

## 8.2  THE INTERNAL CONTROL SYSTEM

Before exploring the importance of the internal control system to the work of the auditor, it is important to first understand its importance to the entity.

The *UK Corporate Governance Code* recommends that "The board should maintain sound risk management and internal control systems."[1] Detailed advice on the application of a strong internal control system is provided by the Committee of Sponsoring Organizations of the Treadway Commission (COSO). Formed in 1985 to sponsor the national commission on fraudulent reporting, COSO issued *Internal Control – Integrated Framework*, a document designed to provide detailed advice to companies on the application of a strong internal control system. It defines internal control as:

> "a process, effected by an entity's board of directors, management, and other personnel, designed to provide reasonable assurance regarding the achievement of objectives relating to operations, reporting and compliance."[2]

### Internal Control Objectives

The internal control system is not simply a fraud or error prevention activity, but rather a system that helps the orderly running of the business. The objectives of internal

---

[1] The *UK Corporate Governance Code* (April 2016), p.5 (Financial Reporting Council).
[2] *Internal Control – Integrated Framework: Executive Summary* (Committee of Sponsoring Organizations of the Treadway Commission, 2013) p.3. See www.coso.org/documents/990025p_executive_summary_final_may20_e.pdf (accessed July 2016).

control, endorsed both by the FRC in its pronouncements and by the COSO guidelines, include:

- safeguarding of the company's assets;
- ensuring the correct classification and completeness of the accounting records;
- the timely preparation of financial information;
- the efficient conduct of the entity's business (including adherence to internal policies); and
- the prevention and detection of fraud.

### Responsibilities for Internal Control

COSO states that "Everyone in an organization has responsibility for internal control". While the chief executive officer (CEO) holds ultimate responsibility for internal controls, there are a number of other groups in an entity that will also impact on the effectiveness of any internal control system. **Management** is responsible for communicating, enabling and evaluating adherence to requirements defined by external laws, regulations, standards, internal policies and standards of conduct. All employees are responsible for performing their roles in compliance with set policies and procedures. Internal auditors are responsible for evaluating the system of internal controls, reporting on weaknesses and recommending courses of action to remedy these. While external auditors hold no direct responsibilities with regard to the entity's internal control system, "they provide another independent view on the reliability of the entity's external reporting".

### Components of Internal Control

Internal controls may be incorporated within computerised accounting systems. However, the internal control system extends beyond those matters relating directly to the accounting system. COSO outlines five components of internal control, which are outlined in **Figure 8.1** below.

The COSO components of internal control are recognised within the ISAs in the form of Appendix 1 of ISA 315, which further explains the components as they relate to an audit of financial statements. These requirements are considered throughout this chapter.

### Types of Internal Control

The auditor is required to consider how the design and implementation of internal controls **prevent** material misstatements from occurring and, if material misstatements did occur, how the system would **detect** and correct them. The auditor will assess the quality of these controls, which are usually broken down into **manual** and **automated** controls.

FIGURE 8.1: FIVE COMPONENTS OF INTERNAL CONTROL

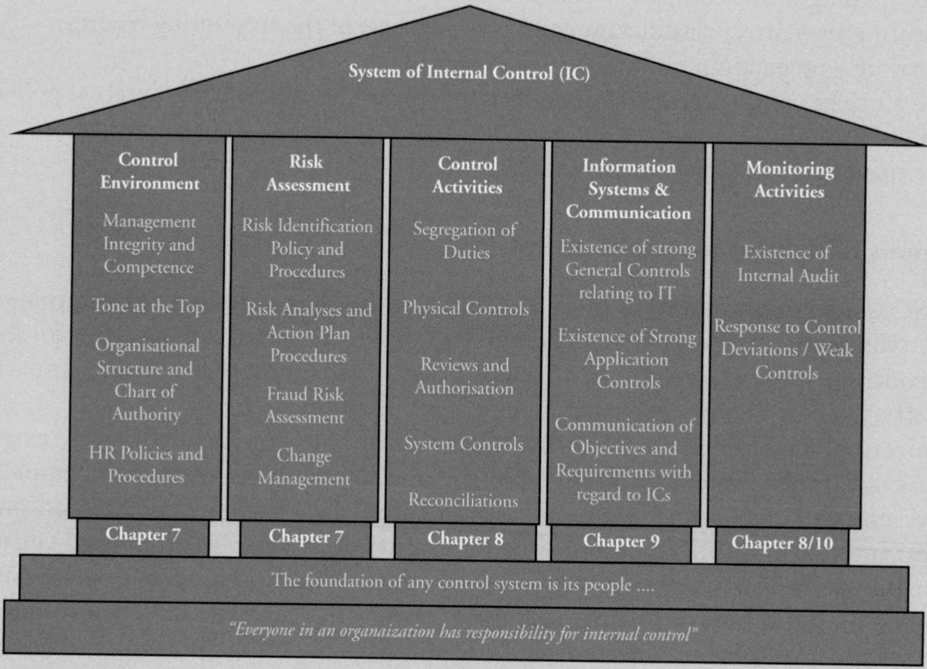

**Source:** *Internal Control – Integrated Framework* (COSO, 2013).

## Manual Controls

Manual controls are carried out by the entity's employees and, therefore, are subject to **human error**. Examples of manual controls include:
- performance of bank reconciliations; and
- credit checks performed by the credit controller.

Such controls require that the assigned individual:
1. performs the control periodically (i.e. daily, monthly, weekly, etc.); and
2. performs the control as described within the relevant policy and procedure.

Human error can be minimised by the introduction of higher level (management) reviews to ensure timely and accurate performance.

## Automated Controls

Automated controls are controls embedded within the client entity's computerised accounting system. Once the system is configured to deal with the control, it should occur automatically. That is, once it is set up correctly to perform a certain control, it will behave in the same way every time. Examples of automated controls include:
- systematic prevention of orders where the order will result in the customer exceeding their credit limit; or
- inability to input an order for an out-of-stock item.

Such controls work seamlessly, once they are properly set up in the system.

### Detective Controls

Detective controls detect errors that have already occurred in the system, providing an opportunity for them to be corrected. An example would be the performance of a bank reconciliation, which should highlight any errors in posting, missing postings, etc.

### Preventative Controls

Preventative controls prevent an error occurring in the first place. For example, the inability to enter an order for a customer where the order will cause the customer to exceed their credit limit or where the customer account is overdue (this demonstrates an automated preventative control). It is important, however, to consider the ability to override the control. For example, as discussed in **Chapter 3**, Section 3.5, management are best positioned to override controls by either giving instruction to employees to enter transactions that are not valid, knowing staff are unlikely to question them, or by creating journal entries to 'smooth profits'.

Automated controls are preferred over manual controls as they are not subject to human error (once they have been properly configured in the system). Preventative controls are preferred over detective controls as they are intended to avoid an occurrence of the error in the first place. However, it is never possible to eliminate manual and detective controls due to the complexity of business and the limitations of systems within each entity. Therefore, an auditor will always encounter a combination of the above controls.

## 8.3  WHY THE INTERNAL CONTROL SYSTEM IS IMPORTANT TO THE EXTERNAL AUDITOR

### Introduction

Understanding and testing controls addresses the requirements of two key auditing standards:
- ISA 315 *Identifying and Assessing the Risks of Material Misstatement through Understanding the Entity and its Environment*; and
- ISA 330 *The Auditor's Response to Assessed Risks*.

Meeting the requirements of ISA 315 (discussed throughout **Chapter 7**) will allow the auditor to gain a greater understanding of the client entity's operations and, ultimately, empower them to perform a more robust audit. With respect to ISA 330, the auditor's aim is to ensure that they appropriately address risks. When designing the nature, timing and extent of audit procedures, the auditor will often search for control activities that mitigate risks and therefore reduce the level of substantive audit procedures. An understanding of the client entity's controls therefore allows the auditor to perform a more effective and efficient audit.

### Nature, Timing and Extent of Audit Procedures at the Assertion Level

ISA 330, paragraph 6, states:

"The auditor shall design and perform further audit procedures whose **nature, timing, and extent** are based on and are responsive to the assessed risks of material misstatement at the **assertion level**." (emphasis added)

### Nature, Timing and Extent of Substantive Audit Procedures

The auditor is concerned with ensuring that they design appropriate procedures with respect to nature, timing and extent in order to ensure that all risks are addressed. However, they also need to ensure that they do so in the most **efficient and effective** manner. Efficiency in this context means the time the auditor spends on the audit – the more time that is spent, the more costs incurred. Effectiveness refers to the quality of the work performed. The auditor should never jeopardise quality and increase audit risk for the sake of efficiency, i.e. perform a more time-efficient test that does not meet the definition of **sufficient appropriate audit evidence** (see **Chapter 6**, Section 6.2).

A systems-based (or controls-approach) audit means that the auditor understands and tests the system of controls operating within the client entity sufficiently to be satisfied that these controls:

1. mitigate risks;
2. address the audit objectives; and
3. worked effectively throughout the entire period under review.

In doing so, the auditor can rely on those systems of internal controls to reduce the nature, timing and extent of audit procedures and improve the overall efficiency of the audit, without negatively impacting on its quality. This is demonstrated in **Figure 8.2** below.

FIGURE 8.2: HOW EFFECTIVE CONTROLS INFLUENCE THE NATURE, TIMING AND EXTENT OF SUBSTANTIVE AUDIT PROCEDURES

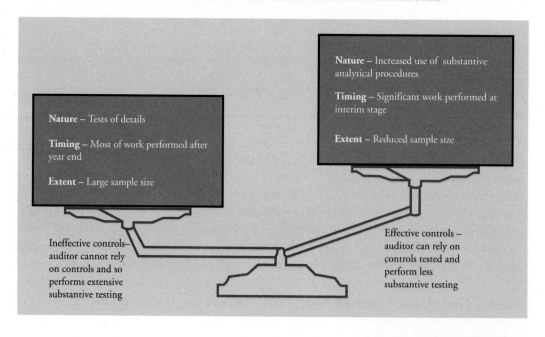

## *Tying Controls to Assertions*

ISA 315, paragraph A129, states:

"In making risk assessments, the auditor may identify the controls that are likely to prevent, or detect and correct, material misstatements in specific assertions ... Often, only multiple control activities, together with other components of internal control, will be sufficient to address a risk."

Additionally, paragraph A131 reminds the auditor that controls "can be either directly or indirectly related to an assertion". We can consider this by way of **Example 8.1** below.

### EXAMPLE 8.1: INDIRECT, DIRECT AND MULTIPLE CONTROL ACTIVITIES

For example, the existence of an organisational chart and a chart of authority act as **indirect control activities** to the purchases cycle. These documents are controlled by senior management. The organisation chart dictates hierarchy within an entity; the chart of authority dictates who in the entity can perform certain transactions and activities and to what value (e.g. who can place a purchase order and to what value, and who can approve purchase orders).

A **direct control activity** would include, for example, the inability of an employee to approve a purchase order in the system for which they are not authorised (which addresses the rights and obligations assertion). This control activity, however, cannot be effective without the organisational chart and chart of authority (the indirect control activities). Therefore, **multiple control activities** are required to cover one assertion.

Additionally, because control activities are parts of a system of controls, control activities can be further supported by the control component of the information systems.

## Understanding and Testing the Entity's Entire Internal Control System

Due to the fact that control activities are often supported by other control components (see **Example 8.1** above), it is essential that the auditor gains assurance over the entire control system. The control environment was discussed in detail in **Chapter 7**; now, in **Example 8.2**, let's see how the auditor would conclude on the effectiveness of the client entity's internal control system. This type of **audit working paper** is used to record the accounting systems in a way that is sufficient for the purposes of complying with the auditing standards and relevant legislation. Note also that for each item, the auditor references where the supporting documents are stored in the audit file.

EXAMPLE 8.2: AUDIT WORKING PAPER – INTERNAL CONTROL SYSTEM

| Dairy Fresh Limited<br>31 December 2018<br>Audit Programme – Internal Control System | | Working Paper Reference: P1 | |
|---|---|---|---|
| **Objective:** | To ascertain if the control environment is adequate to support the other control components. | | |
| | Initials | Date | Date |
| Prepared by: | | | |
| Reviewed by: | | | |

## INTERNAL CONTROL SYSTEM

The following aspects of the entity's operations give an overview of its internal control system.

**Main factors of client's control system, for example:**

- Management are experienced and have been with the entity for an average of 10 years and hold qualifications in each of their respective disciplines (see working paper reference **P1A**).
- Finance staff/bookkeeper has been with the entity seven years (a copy of his qualifications can be found at working paper reference **P1B**).
- The organisational chart can be found at **P1C**. It is not complex and management and directors are involved in the daily operations of the business.
- A chart of authority exists (see working paper reference **P1D**) and adequately addresses all types of transaction/activity and the individual(s) responsible for approval.
- Human resources (HR) policies and procedures are in place and adequately address employee recruitment, retention, training and disciplinary procedures. Full testing of same can be found at working paper reference **P1E**.

**Management attitude to internal control is positive, demonstrated by:**

1. Ensuring adequate investment in information systems.
2. Imposing systematic controls (automated through the client's IT system) to ensure the adherence to the chart of authority. Tested at working paper reference **P1I**.
3. Ensuring multiple authorisations are required for transactions that are more susceptible to misappropriation/fraud (e.g. two signatures for bank transfers).
4. Setting of objectives for all employees related to their achievement of key business indicators (KBIs), which measure the application of internal controls (see copies of five employees' objectives at working paper reference **P1F**).
5. Actively communicate a tone-at-the-top document to all employees (see employee survey at working paper reference **P1G**).
6. Follow through on disciplinary procedures with regard to non-adherence to internal control standards/instances of fraud (see review of such procedures applied to issues occurring in the period at **P1H**).

**Conclusion:** based on results of testing performed above as at 1 March 2019, we will rely on all of the controls above. Any control deficiencies have been discussed with management and any significant deficiencies have been communicated in writing to the directors.

## 8.4 STAGES INVOLVED IN REVIEWING INTERNAL CONTROLS

### Introduction

Up to this point we have discussed what an internal control system is and why it is so important to the client entity as well as to the auditor. Now we must consider how the auditor goes about using the client entity's system of internal control when carrying out an audit. There are a number of stages involved in reviewing a client entity's system of controls. We have already established that if the auditor tests the control system and finds it to be operating efficiently, it can be relied upon to reduce the level of substantive testing needed to be performed on the financial statements (this is known as the **controls approach**). However, testing the controls within a client entity may not always be the most efficient approach. The auditor will only test the controls if they believe that:

1. it will help to reduce substantive testing; and
2. the result of controls testing will show the controls to be effective.

In assessing the operating effectiveness of specific controls, the auditor may consider using audit evidence from a previous audit (ISA 330, paragraph 13). In planning to use previous audit evidence, the auditor should establish its "continuing relevance ... by obtaining audit evidence about whether significant changes in those controls have occurred subsequent to the previous audit" (paragraph 14). If there have been no significant changes, rotational controls testing may be performed, whereby the auditor tests the controls at least once in every third audit.

It is important that the auditor follows a process to determine whether or not testing controls will make the overall audit more efficient. **Figure 8.3** below sets out the steps the auditor will take before commencing testing.

FIGURE 8.3: STAGES INVOLVED IN SYSTEM-BASED (CONTROLS-APPROACH) AUDIT

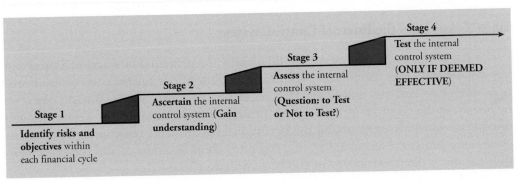

## Stage 1: Identify Risks and Objectives within each Financial Cycle

### Identifying Risks

As discussed in **Chapter 7**, the risks will have been identified during the planning stage and will be both specific to the client entity's current operating environment as well as to some unavoidable inherent risks.

Remember, the auditor is predominantly concerned with the risk of material misstatement and so will start with the risks previously identified, and look to potential controls in the client entity's internal control system that might mitigate these risks, thereby reducing the overall audit risk. Having identified the inherent risks and the controls that might mitigate inherent risks, the auditor can focus on weak controls that pose further previously unidentified risks.

### Identifying Financial Statement Assertions (Objectives)

When designing tests of controls, substantive analytical reviews and tests of details, the auditor must ensure that sufficient comfort has been obtained over **all** financial statement management assertions (audit objectives). It is therefore essential that the financial statement assertions or objectives are considered for **each transaction class and each account balance**.

In reviewing the client entity's controls, the auditor will focus on those controls that will help to reduce risk at a an assertion level. For example, businesses that experience seasonal cash flows, such as agriculture, will have an inherent risk in the revenue and receivables cycle. If the auditor is concerned with the collection of receivables, i.e. the valuation of receivables, they will want to identify controls that address the valuation assertion associated with the receivables. Controls could include the application of credit limits based on references, background checks by the credit controller and weekly analysis of the aged receivables listings with documented follow-up by the credit controller. If the auditor can obtain evidence to show that these controls are working there will be less of a concern around the valuation of receivables.

> **Note**: it is important to be familiar with the concept of financial statement assertions. A discussion on the assertions can be found in **Chapter 4**, Section 4.3.

## Stage 2: Ascertain the Internal Control System

For each financial cycle, the auditor should identify the **principal business activities** and **key documents**. They should then determine the flow of documents and extent of controls relative to each risk and financial statement management assertion/audit objective by reviewing the client entity's policy and procedure documentation, as well as through discussions with management and the operational departments relevant to the financial cycle being assessed. The possibility of using previous audit evidence and rotational controls testing, as discussed above can also be considered.

## *Obtaining Information on Controls*

The auditor can seek to gain an understanding of the client entity's systems of internal control in a number of ways:

- **Inquiry** – the auditor can inquire of management or the individuals responsible for operating the system.
- **Questionnaires** – in many cases, the audit firm will have developed a predetermined set of questions (usually in the form of **knowledge-based systems**) relevant to each financial cycle, which, when answered, help the auditor to form an understanding of the process from beginning to end.
- **Flowcharts** – flowcharts are diagrammatic representations of the sequences of movements or actions in a particular transaction cycle. They depict certain aspects of processes. **Figure 8.5** in **Section 8.6**, later in this chapter, is an example of a flowchart within the purchases and payables cycle.

  Using flowcharts has a number of advantages:
  - aids the understanding of the accounting and internal control system;
  - when drawn up by the auditor, they allow a better understanding of the organisation;
  - can help to highlight strengths and weaknesses, as well as unnecessary steps, in a process; and
  - the drawing of flowcharts can be simplified through the use of **CAATs**.

  There are disadvantages too:
  - developing a flowchart can be time-consuming;
  - when dealing with more simple systems, narratives may be more appropriate;
  - preparing them requires experience; and
  - symbols tend to mean different things to different people/organisations.

- **Narratives** – narratives are written documents that describe the connected events of a transaction in chronological order. **Example 8.4**, in **Section 8.5**, provides an example of a narrative within the revenue and receivables cycle.

  Advantages of narratives:
  - simple to prepare and do not require too much expertise; and
  - describe the process in detail.

  Disadvantages of narratives:
  - do not highlight strengths and weaknesses as clearly as flowcharts do; and
  - can be lengthy to prepare and read.

Once the auditor has ascertained how the internal control system is intended to operate, they should perform a **walkthrough** test (i.e. trace one transaction of each type through the system), observing the operation of the controls as described in the client entity's policy and procedure documentation and reported by management and staff. The purpose of the walkthrough is to determine if the systems observed by the auditor match those recorded in the client entity's policy and procedure documentation (i.e. staff members may tell the auditor what they should be doing rather than what they are actually doing).

EXAMPLE 8.3: A WALKTHROUGH TEST

A walkthrough is a **test of a single transaction from beginning to end (cradle to grave) to prove or disprove the existence of the controls as documented by the client entity.**

The following is an example of a walkthrough that might be performed with respect to the receivables cycle.

**Documented Control Activities** Sales orders are entered into the computer system by an employee. Orders cannot be entered for customers where:
1. the order will result in the customer exceeding their credit limit;
2. the customer's account has been placed on hold; or
3. the goods are not in stock.

Pricing is predetermined in **master data** and cannot be amended by the employee. Orders are marked as dispatched only when the driver signs the goods dispatch note (GDN). Orders are marked as invoiced only when the driver returns a signed proof of delivery (POD).

**Performance of a Walkthrough** The auditor would observe an order being taken by the employee, ensuring that no adjustments can be made to price (e.g. by requesting them to try to amend the price to see if it is possible). Record the name of the customer and order value. On completion of the observation, review the customer account to ensure that the order does not exceed the assigned customer credit limit and confirm with the credit controller that the customer account was not on hold. Trace the transaction through to dispatch and confirm that the date of the driver signature on the GDN matches the date it is marked as dispatched on the system. Trace the transaction through to invoicing, ensuring that the date the order was invoiced matches the date on the signed POD. Ensure all other details of all documents match.

The tracing of one transaction proves that the process operates as described. It does not, however, prove that it operates consistently in this manner throughout the entire period, which is why the auditor performs further **tests of controls** using sampling procedures.

## Categories of Control Activities

Control activities can be categorised as follows:
- **Organisational Controls** (OC) – encompass written policies and procedures, the hiring and retaining of appropriately qualified personnel, and the existence of a **chart of authority**. A chart of authority outlines who in the organisation can approve which transactions and to what value. Similarly, an **organisational chart** indicates hierarchy within the organisation.
- **Segregation of Duties** (SOD) – controls that involve restricting staff responsibilities to certain tasks within a process. For example, in the revenue cycle (see **Example 8.4** below) the individuals responsible for taking orders should not be able to approve new customers or grant credit limits.
- **Physical Controls** (PC) – include safeguarding of items such as documentation and inventory, or imposing restricted access to physical locations and computer systems. This can be in the form of access cards for entry to different locations.

- **Reviews and Authorising** (R&A) – refers to double-checking tasks performed and approval for transactions. For example, inventory picked in the warehouse based on an order should be checked prior to dispatch by someone independent of the picker to ensure that no errors have been made and that the order picked equals the order taken. Authorisation should be given for certain transactions, such as returned stock or bad debt write-offs.
- **System Controls** (SC) – involve the configuration of systems to prevent invalid recordings. For example, during order entry the system should prevent the employee from taking an order that will result in a customer exceeding their credit limit or ordering items that are currently out of stock.
- **Reconciliations** (R) – as a form of control, the checking that two sources of data record the same amount, e.g. reconciling of bank statement to bank balance per general ledger.

As we have seen, the most efficient way to get an overview of the controls in place in a client entity is to perform a walkthrough of the process. The extent of documentation required will vary depending on the size, nature and complexity of the client entity and is a matter of the auditor's professional judgement.

## Stage 3: Assess the Internal Control System

We have now reached stage three of a system-based (controls-approach) audit: the auditor's assessment of the client entity's controls. Having identified the risks and objectives relating to the cycle and gained an understanding of how the controls relating to that cycle should operate, the auditor now needs to assess the information that has been gathered in order to decide whether it would be efficient to go ahead and test the controls.

The purpose of evaluating the internal control system is to establish its reliability and formulate a basis for testing its effectiveness in practice. Having completed stages 1 and 2 as outlined above, the auditor is now armed with knowledge of:
- related risks;
- related financial statement assertions; and
- documented internal control systems,

all of which will allow an informed decision to be made as to whether or not to test the related controls. **To controls test, or not to controls test – this is the question the auditor must now answer**.

If controls testing concludes that the controls are effective, then the auditor need only carry out a reduced level of substantive procedures; if concluded as ineffective, then more extensive substantive procedures are required.

While **substantive** testing must be performed regardless of the results of the controls testing, an internal control system that has been confirmed, i.e. tested, to be effective can reduce the level of substantive testing by reducing sample sizes or by the use of **substantive analytical procedures** rather than **tests of details**, which can be more time-consuming. **Figure 8.4** below illustrates the auditor's decision-making process when deciding whether or not to test the internal controls – in particular, it highlights how much the decision is influenced by the auditor's judgement.

FIGURE 8.4: WEIGHING UP THE DECISION TO TEST CONTROLS

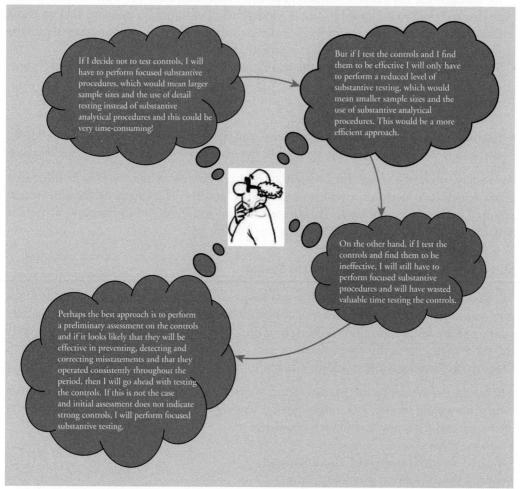

It is essential that the auditor is confident that controls testing will confirm that the controls are effective – if the auditor were to proceed to the controls testing stage and the controls proved to be ineffective, the audit would be less efficient as time would have been wasted in testing the controls and focused substantive testing would still have to be performed.

## Stage 4: Test the Internal Control System

Having reached the final stage of a system-based (controls-approach) audit, we are now going to test the controls, but only if the auditor confidently expects the controls to be effective and has decided that it is an efficient audit approach.

The audit objective is to select and perform tests designed to establish whether or not there is compliance with the internal control system as documented by the client entity. The controls must be effective in practice and on paper.

**Tests of controls** are:
1. concerned only with those areas subject to effective controls;
2. concerned only with those controls mitigating risks and supporting management assertions/audit objectives (financial statement assertions);
3. a representative sample of transactions throughout the period; and
4. likely to cover a larger number of items than a walkthrough test.

In designing tests of controls, the auditor must ask:
- What tests of the operating effectiveness of controls (if any) will reduce the nature, timing and extent of substantive testing?
- What controls require testing because they cannot be tested substantively?

Typical tests of controls will involve:
- tracing samples;
- checking for authorisation;
- testing for sequential numbering;
- observing control activities taking place; and
- confirming performance of reconciliations.

## 8.5  INTERNAL CONTROLS AND THE REVENUE AND RECEIVABLES CYCLE

In **Section 8.4** we discussed the four stages involved in a system-based (controls-approach) audit. We will now apply this approach to each of the key financial cycles, starting with the revenue and receivables cycle.

### Stage 1: Identify Risks and Objectives within the Revenue and Receivables Cycle

#### Risks

Specific risks associated with the revenue and receivables cycle include:
- **Previous experience with the client**   For example, where a **significant risk** existed in the past in relation to the recoverability of aged receivables balances (an example of an aged receivables listing can be found in **Chapter 13**, Example 13.1), the auditor should be alert to this in the current audit and may choose to perform focused substantive testing in this area.
- **Reliability of estimates**   Estimates made by the client in the past may have been unreliable, e.g. the basis of the bad debt provision determined by the client in the past was deemed unreliable, resulting in adjustments by the auditor being necessary to fairly state the provision. The auditor will be alert for this in the current audit when performing tests in this area and again may perform focused substantive testing in this area.
- **Complexity of business**   The more complex the transaction, the greater the risk. For example, where recognition of a sale occurs only after a number of key stages have been completed or actions taken, then the auditor will remain alert to the possibility that revenue may have been recognised in the period that is not true revenue, i.e. revenue has been accounted for in the period but all the necessary stages resulting in revenue recognition have not been completed before the period end. In such an instance, the auditor may feel gaining a better understanding of how this is managed and testing its related controls will help to reduce substantive testing later.

- **Scope for fraudulent activity**   In relation to revenue and receivables, this could include:
  - ◆ creation of false customer accounts, resulting in overstated revenue figures and receivables balances; or
  - ◆ misappropriation of cash receipts where the business is cash-based.

## Control Objectives

As introduced in **Chapter 4** (and discussed continually throughout this textbook), each transaction class and account balance tested by the auditor must address all the audit assertions (audit objectives). The specific audit objectives relevant for the revenue and receivables cycle are shown in **Table 8.1**.

TABLE 8.1: CONTROL OBJECTIVES – REVENUE AND RECEIVABLES

| Management Assertion/ Audit Objective | Control Objective for Transaction Class | Control Objective for Account Balance |
|---|---|---|
| | **Revenue** | **Receivables** |
| **Existence or occurrence** | • Recorded revenue transactions represent goods shipped.<br>• Recorded cash receipts transactions represent cash received.<br>• Recorded revenue adjustment transactions represent authorised discounts, returns, allowances and bad debts. | • Receivables balances represent amounts owed by customers at the date of the SOFP. |
| **Completeness** | All revenue, cash receipts and revenue adjustment transactions that occurred have been recorded. | Receivables include all claims on customers at the date of the SOFP. |
| **Rights and obligations** | The entity has rights to the receivables balance and cash resulting from recorded revenue transactions. | Receivables at the date of the SOFP represent legal claims of the entity on customers for payment. |
| **Classification/ Recording (accuracy) or valuation** | All revenue, cash receipts and revenue adjustment transactions are accurately journalised, summarised and posted to the correct accounts. | • Receivables represent gross claims on customers at the date of the SOFP and agree with the sum of the aged receivables ledger.<br>• The provision for bad debts represents a reasonable estimate of the difference between gross receivables and their net realisable value (NRV). |
| **Cut-off** | All revenue, cash receipts and revenue adjustment transactions are recorded in the correct accounting period. | |

| **Presentation and disclosure** | The details of revenue, cash receipts and revenue adjustment transactions support their presentation in financial statements, including their classification and related disclosures. | • Receivables are properly identified and classified at the date of the SOFP.<br>• Appropriate disclosures have been made concerning debts that have been factored or otherwise assigned. |
|---|---|---|

## Stage 2: Ascertain the Internal Control System within the Revenue and Receivables Cycle

In **Section 8.4** we determined that at stage two of a system-based (controls-approach) audit, for each financial cycle, the auditor should identify the **principal business activities** and **key documents**. The auditor should then determine the flow of documents and extent of controls relative to each risk and management assertion/audit objective by reviewing the client policy and procedure documentation, as well as through discussions with management and the operational departments relevant to the financial cycle being assessed. We will now consider this in relation to the revenue and receivables cycle.

Each step within the revenue and receivables cycle should feature a number of key controls in order to ensure the objectives at **Table 8.1** above are achieved. These controls also act to minimise the possibility of material misstatement due to fraud or error.

The components of a client entity's revenue cycle should comprise a number of key steps. **Example 8.4** demonstrates the types of control and the control activities that exist in a typical revenue and receivables cycle within an automated environment.

EXAMPLE 8.4: NARRATIVE OF REVENUE AND RECEIVABLES CYCLE
(IN AN AUTOMATED ENVIRONMENT)

COMPANY PROFILE AND REVENUE POLICIES

**Company:** Dairy Fresh Ltd
**Products:** Dairy
**Industry:** Fast Moving Consumer Goods (FMCG)
**Customer Profile:** 70% large wholesale and supermarket players, 20% convenience (smaller convenience stores), 10% restaurants
**Revenue Recognition:** Revenue is recognised on delivery (within the industry the signed POD is largely recognised as proof of delivery).
**Computer Environment:** The company has an enterprise resource planning (ERP) system that is fully integrated, with the exception of the payroll package.
**Customer Credit Terms:** 30 days from last day of the month in which invoice was issued.

**Ordering and Granting of Credit:** All customers order directly online using a user name and password (**system control**) assigned to them on approval of their credit application form.

All new customers must complete a credit application form and sign:
1. the company's terms and conditions (T&Cs), and
2. a direct debit (DD) mandate.

The sales representative enters the details from the credit application form onto the company's internal system. All fields must be populated for the details to be saved (**system control**). Once inputted, the application is reviewed by the credit controller (**segregation of duties**). The application form must include: (a) who the credit controller should contact to assess the prospective customer's creditworthiness; and (b) the appropriate credit limit identified (**review and authorisation**). When satisfied that the prospective customer is:
1. creditworthy,
2. has signed the T&Cs, and
3. has signed the DD mandate,

the credit controller approves the customer, assigning a credit limit (**review and authorisation**). The account is only activated after a credit limit has been assigned (**system control**). Only the credit controller has the ability to enter a credit limit (**segregation of duties** and **system control**). The system automatically generates a customer number, username and password, which are e-mailed directly to the customer, notifying them of their assigned credit limit. The customer is now able to place orders online.

Each customer is automatically assigned to the approved price list, which is signed off by the head of revenue and finance. The revenue teams are notified of all new customers being set up and can propose discounts from the agreed price list based on the proposed volume that the customer will generate. This proposal is completed via the ERP system and must be approved electronically by the head of finance before it becomes active on the customer account (**segregation of duties** and **review and authorisation**).

When the customer enters an online order, the system first checks:
1. that the customer is not entering an order that will result in them exceeding their credit limit (if so, the order is referred to a credit controller for approval) (**system control**);
2. that the customer is not on hold (customers whose accounts are overdue are automatically placed on hold by the system (**system control**)); and
3. that the goods are in stock. The order is automatically valued based on the price list assigned to that customer (**system control**).

The order is automatically assigned a sequential order number (**system control**). In the system the order is assigned a status of '**awaiting dispatch**'.

**Dispatch and Invoicing:** All orders processed become visible to the warehouse the following morning. The warehouse 'picker' prints a manual copy of a goods dispatch note (GDN) from the system in duplicate form. The picker picks each order according to the printed sheets and stages them ready for collection by the driver, attaching the duplicate GDN signed by him.

The driver physically counts the goods to be delivered and compares the results to the GDN. Once satisfied that the two agree, the duplicate GDN is signed (**physical control**). The driver only has access to the staging area and not to the warehouse (**physical control**). The driver returns one copy to the office and retains the other copy (**segregation of duties, physical control, reviews and authorisation**). On receipt of the GDN signed by the driver, the 'settlement clerk' marks the order as '**dispatched**' in the system. The system generates and prints a duplicate proof of delivery note (POD) for the driver. The stock now shows as in transit rather than in warehouse.

On delivery of the goods the driver has the customer count the goods delivered and sign a copy of the POD as proof of delivery and acceptance of the goods in good condition. Any discrepancies with respect to volume/condition are marked on the POD and signed in duplicate by the driver and the customer. The driver returns to the office and gives a copy of the signed POD to the settlement clerk. The settlement clerk inspects the documentation (**reviews and authorisation** and **physical control**) and marks the order as delivered in the system (**segregation of duties**). The system now assigns a status of '**delivered not yet invoiced**' to the order. Each evening, before finishing, the settlement clerk runs a system activity (automated client computer **system control**) that bills all orders with a status of *delivered not yet invoiced*. This causes the invoices to be generated and automatically e-mailed to the customer, and creates the necessary entries in the books of first entry: DR Cost of Sales, CR Inventory; and DR Receivables (Customer), CR Revenue. The order now has a status of '**complete**'.

**Accounting:** In order to ensure that revenue is complete, the accounting department runs three exception reports (reports from the client entity's computer system highlighting unusual transactions):

1. Orders with a status of '**awaiting dispatch**' for more than 24 hours. This report is sent to the warehouse to investigate why/if orders have not been dispatched. This helps to highlight issues where goods were dispatched but not marked in the system as such.
2. Orders with a status of '**dispatched**' for more than 24 hours. This report is sent to the settlement department to investigate why/if a POD has not yet been returned by the driver. This helps to highlight issues where a POD was returned but not marked in the system as such and ensures timely follow-up of the driver.
3. Orders with a status of '**delivered not yet invoiced**' for more than 24 hours. This report is sent to the settlement department to investigate why/if the system activity was run to trigger invoicing.

These exception reports are signed off as reviewed by the financial controller and filed.

Most customers pay by DD. The accounts receivable team run a computer program on the last working day of each month that highlights the amounts due from customers (based on predefined credit terms). The instruction for direct debits is approved by the credit controller prior to sending it to the bank (**segregation of duties**).

A few customers pay by cheque. All post is opened by two individuals, and a summary is made of all cheques received and signed by both individuals (**physical control**). The cheques are sent directly to the cash office (persons charged with lodging receipts who are independent from the accounts receivable department to avoid 'teeming and lading' (a process of stealing a customer's cheque and delaying the posting of the receipt onto their GL account until a cheque comes in from another customer, which is used to post to the account of the customer from whom the cheque was stolen and so on) (**segregation of duties**). The summary of cheques along with remittance advices are sent to the accounts receivable department, which allocates the cheques to the related transactions as outlined in the remittance advice. The accounting department reconciles the bank daily, ensuring that the amount banked equals the amount posted to customer accounts (**reconciliation** and **segregation of duties**).

As part of the accounting end-of-period procedures, the following **reconciliations** are performed by the accounts assistant and reviewed and signed off by the financial controller (**reviews and authorisation** and **segregation of duties**):
- reconciliation of the aged list of receivables to the general (nominal) ledger; and
- bank reconciliation.

On notification from the accounting department that all activities have been processed for month end, the accounts receivable department activate a computer program that automatically e-mails customer statements to all customers (**system control**). The system generates a report highlighting any exceptions/errors that occurred during the activity, which is signed off by a member of the accounting department (**system control** and **review and authorisation**).

All credit note requests are entered into the system by the credit claims department. Once entered they must be approved as follows:
- if price related – system (automated computer-approval process) approval by the sales and accounting departments (**segregation of duties** and **review and authorisation**); or
- if quality/quantity related – system approval by settlement department following physical inspection of POD (**physical control**, **segregation of duties** and **review and authorisation**).

Every month the credit controller reviews the aged receivables listing and follows up on accounts that are overdue. The financial controller follows up on overdue accounts with the credit controller, signs off and files the review (**physical control**). Bad debts are proposed by the credit controller through the system, but only come off the customer account after system (automated computer) approval by the accounting and sales departments (**system control** and **segregation of duties**).

## Stage 3: Assess the Internal Control System within the Revenue and Receivables Cycle

We have now reached stage three in the system-based (controls-approach) audit of revenue and receivables. Having identified the risks and objectives relating to the audit of the revenue and receivables cycle and gained an understanding of how the controls relating to that cycle should operate, the auditor now needs to assess what has been learnt so far in order to decide whether it is efficient to go ahead and test the controls.

Where the revenue figure and receivables balance are not material to the financial statements, limited tests of controls and substantive testing will be performed. It is worth noting, however, that revenue and receivables are normally material figures in the financial statements for most companies.

Where a significant audit risk has been identified in relation to the revenue and receivables cycle, the level of substantive testing to be performed will need to be increased and the tests of controls may become more important to help reduce the level of substantive testing. **Example 8.5** below demonstrates the type of working paper the auditor might use to assess the risks within the revenue and receivables cycle.

A key consideration in deciding whether or not to test controls will be the risk assessment made by the auditor **and** their initial assessment of the control environment.

EXAMPLE 8.5: AUDIT WORKING PAPER – RISK ASSESSMENT FOR
REVENUE AND RECEIVABLES

| Dairy Fresh Limited<br>31 December 2018<br>Audit Programme – Revenue and Receivables Risk Assessment | | Working Paper Reference: R1 | |
|---|---|---|---|
| **Objective:** | To summarise the risk assessment for the revenue and receivables cycle. | | |
| | Initials | Date | Date |
| **Prepared by:** | | | |
| **Reviewed by:** | | | |

**Risk Assessment:** a list of the risks identified relating to revenue and receivables and the planned approach to address these risks.

| Risk Identified | Level of Risk | Controls Testing | Response to Risk | Ref. |
|---|---|---|---|---|
| **Receivables** may not be recoverable. Preliminary analytical review indicates that receivables have increased significantly. | High | No | Review management's provision for bad debts.<br>Challenge the assumptions made and consider the outturn of last year's provision.<br>Ensure sufficient provision for specific large receivables, including Z Limited and Y Limited. | R11 |
| All **revenue** may not be recorded | Medium | Yes | Take a controls approach in relation to the completeness assertion by ensuring regular reviews are carried out by the client entity on goods ordered not yet delivered and goods delivered not yet invoiced. If these reports are reviewed regularly, controls relating to the completeness assertion can be relied upon and therefore reduced level of substantive testing performed. | R10 |

## Stage 4: Test the Internal Control System within the Revenue and Receivables Cycle

Having reached the final stage of the system-based (controls-approach) audit of revenue and receivables, we are now going to test the internal controls relating to revenue and receivables (but only if the auditor has deemed the controls to be effective and decided that it is an efficient audit approach).

The audit objective is to select and perform tests designed to establish compliance with the system controls as documented by the client entity.

Once an understanding is obtained in relation to the revenue and receivables cycle, a testing plan can be designed based on the key controls that are in operation.

*Note:* the auditor will only proceed with testing the controls if it is believed that the controls are strong and if walkthrough tests show that the client entity's procedures are operating exactly as documented by management. When designing such tests it is essential that the auditor remembers the assertions that must be addressed by the controls tests. It should be further kept in mind that the objective of tests of controls is to obtain sufficient appropriate audit evidence that the control operated effectively throughout the entire period under review (thus, the samples should cover the entire period).

Specific tests connected to the revenue and receivables cycle are shown in **Example 8.6** below.

EXAMPLE 8.6: AUDIT WORKING PAPER – REVENUE AND
RECEIVABLES CONTROLS

| Dairy Fresh Limited 31 December 2018 | | | Working Paper Reference: D1 | |
|---|---|---|---|---|
| **Revenue and Receivables Controls Audit Programme** | | | | |
| **Objective:** | To ascertain if the revenue and receivables cycle is adequately controlled by the entity with respect to all assertions. | | | |
| | **Initials** | **Date** | **Date** | |
| **Prepared by:** | | | | |
| **Reviewed by:** | | | | |

Ensure the audit plan is reflected in the following tests. The following steps are suggestions only and should be removed or added to as necessary to address the risks of material misstatement identified at the risk assessment stage.

| Risk Identified | Assertion | Test | Ref. |
|---|---|---|---|
| **Organisational and IT controls** | | | |
| 1. Lack of policies and procedures surrounding revenue and receivables that may result in inconsistent application of policies and lack of adherence to desired procedures. | Valuation Occurrence Recording (accuracy) Completeness Rights and obligations Cut-off | Assess the appropriateness of the accounting policy and procedure documentation and the accounting estimates method for revenue and receivables. Ensure the accounting policy is in accordance with accounting standards and applicable law. | |

| | | | |
|---|---|---|---|
| 2. Inappropriate access may result in a lack of segregation of duties (SOD). | Valuation Occurrence Recording (accuracy) Completeness Rights and obligations | Obtain a report from the system outlining who in the organisation has access to which step in the revenue and receivables function. Review the report to ensure that no SOD issues exist (e.g. that order entry personnel do not have access to credit control). | |

**Ordering and Granting of Credit**

| | | | |
|---|---|---|---|
| 1. Customers with poor credit ratings may get deliveries of inventory, increasing risk of bad debts. | Valuation | Inspect a sample of customers set up in the period and confirm they were approved by the credit controller, that a credit check was performed and a credit limit assigned and authorised. | |
| | Valuation | Run a report from the system and ensure no customers exist without a credit limit. | |
| 2. Customers exceeding their credit limits or with overdue amounts may get deliveries of inventory, increasing the risk of bad debts. | Valuation | * **System check (test of one)** Attempt to enter an order that will result in the customer exceeding their credit limit. Ensure the system does not permit you to enter the order. | |
| | Valuation | * **System check (test of one)** Attempt to enter an order for a blocked customer. Ensure the system does not permit you to enter the order. | |
| | Valuation | Obtain in Excel format: 1. a sample of aged receivables listing for a random number of months; and 2. a copy of each customer's credit limit. Using VLOOKUP, compare the customer balances to the credit limits. For customers exceeding credit limit, ensure that it was approved by the credit controller. | |
| 3. Invalid prices are entered at order entry stage. | Classification/ recording (accuracy) | Observe the order entry clerk entering an order and ensure they cannot amend pricing. | |

| Dispatch and Invoicing | | | |
|---|---|---|---|
| 1. Not all goods delivered are invoiced. | Completeness | Randomly select 30 working days and obtain the signed review of the three **exception reports:** 1. Orders awaiting dispatch >24hrs; 2. orders dispatched >24 hrs; 3. orders delivered not yet invoiced >24hrs. Inspect the document for evidence of review.<br>** **Alternative test** Trace a sample of 100 customer orders to GDN, signed POD and invoice. | |
| 2. Invoices are raised for goods not delivered or the invoice does not match the goods delivered. | Occurrence (existence) Classification/ recording (accuracy) Rights and obligations | *** Trace a sample of invoices to customer-signed PODs and sales orders. Ensure GDN is signed by a driver. Match the details from the invoice to the signed customer POD/GDN and sales order. | |
| 3. Prices are incorrectly applied to the invoice or discounts may not be approved. | Occurrence Classification/ recording (accuracy) | * **System check (test of one)** Using test data, attempt to change the customer invoice price and ensure the system does not permit you to make the change. With assistance from IT department, inspect who has access to pricing master data (ensure no SOD issues).<br>** **Alternative test** Select a sample of 100 invoices and compare the prices charged to the approved customer price list at that time. | |

| Accounting | | | |
|---|---|---|---|
| 1. Credit notes are issued for invalid reasons. | Occurrence Classification/ recording (accuracy) | Trace a sample of credit notes to ensure they were approved. For 'quantity' credit notes, trace the credit note back to the signed POD to ensure quantity marked on the POD. | |
| 2. Invoices may be recorded in the incorrect period. | Completeness | Obtain a copy of the review of the three exception reports at 31 Dec 2018. Inspect the document for evidence of review. | |
| | Cut-off | Select the last 30 invoices posted to the general ledger and trace them to signed PODs, ensuring that the date on the POD matches the invoice and posting date in the system. | |
| 3. Customer balances may be written off without proper authorisation. | Occurrence Classification/ recording (accuracy) Rights and obligations | * **System check (test of one)** Observe the credit controller inputting a bad debt proposal. Ensure it is not activated onto the customer account until approved by the sales and finance functions. ** **Alternative test** Select a sample of 50 bad debts written off in the period and trace to approval by the finance and sales functions. | |
| 4. Trade receivables may be old and go uncollected. | Valuation | Obtain a copy of the review of the aged receivables listing balance for five random months. Ensure there is evidence of review. | |

| 5. Not all remittances are entered onto the customer's account. | Valuation | Select 100 random days and obtain a copy of the dual-signed cheque receipts listing. Trace the amounts to the customers' accounts. Obtain a copy of the reconciliation of the bank statement for five random months to ensure that the amount lodged to the bank matched the amount entered onto customer accounts. | |
|---|---|---|---|

\* System check (test of one) – when a system test is carried out to determine the existence of a control, generally the auditor will only need to perform the test once, as once set up correctly the system should behave in the same way every time. The auditor need then only test for changes in configuration.

\*\* Alternative testing method – although tests requiring lower sample sizes (because they cover a greater volume) or that are a system check (test of one) are considered more efficient and effective.

\*\*\* Note a change in the direction of this test would be required if testing for completeness (i.e. general ledger to source for completeness and source to general ledger for occurrence (existence)).

**Conclusion**
Subject to the matters noted for the reviewer, in my opinion the revenue and receivables are adequately controlled with respect to all assertions.

## 8.6 INTERNAL CONTROLS AND THE PURCHASES AND PAYABLES AND PAYROLL CYCLES

In **Section 8.4** we discussed the four stages of a system-based (controls-approach) audit. We have completed the four stages for revenue and receivables and will now discuss the four stages with reference to the purchases and payables cycle and the payroll cycle.

### Stage 1: Identify Risks and Objectives within the Purchases and Payables and Payroll Cycles

The specific audit objectives relevant to the purchases and payables and payroll cycles are outlined in **Table 8.2** below.

TABLE 8.2: CONTROL OBJECTIVES – PURCHASES AND PAYABLES (INCLUDING PAYROLL)

| Management Assertion/Audit Objective | Control Objective for Transaction Class | Control Objective for Account Balance |
|---|---|---|
| | **Purchases and Payroll Expenses** | **Payables and Payroll Accruals** |
| **Existence or Occurrence** | • Recorded purchases transactions represent goods and services received.<br>• Recorded payment transactions represent payments made to suppliers and payables.<br>• Recorded payroll expenses relate to employee services received. | • Recorded trade payables represent amounts owed by the entity at the date of the SOFP.<br>• Accrued payroll liability balances represent amounts owed at the date of the SOFP. |
| **Completeness** | • All purchases/payment transactions that occurred have been recorded.<br>• Payroll expenses include all such expenses incurred. | • Trade payables include all amounts owed by the entity to suppliers of goods and services at the date of the SOFP.<br>• Accrued payroll liabilities include all amounts in respect of payroll and payroll deductions at the date of the SOFP. |
| **Rights and Obligations** | Recorded purchases and payroll transactions represent the liabilities of the entity. | Trade payables and accrued payroll liabilities are liabilities of the entity at the date of the SOFP. |
| **Classification / Recording (accuracy) or Valuation** | Purchases/payment transactions and payroll transactions are correctly recorded in the accounting systems. | • Trade payables and accrued payroll liabilities are stated at the correct amount owed.<br>• Related expense balances conform with applicable accounting standards. |
| **Cut-off** | All purchases/payment and payroll transactions are recorded in the correct accounting period. | |
| **Presentation and Disclosure** | The details of purchases/payments and payroll transactions support their presentation in the financial statements, including their classification and disclosure. | • Trade payables, accrued payroll liabilities and related expenses are properly identified and classified in the financial statements.<br>• Disclosures pertaining to commitments, contingent liabilities and related party payables are adequate. |

## Stage 2: Ascertain the Internal Control System within the Purchases and Payables Cycle

In **Section 8.4** we determined that at stage two of a system-based (controls-approach) audit, for each financial cycle the auditor should identify the **principal business activities** and **key documents**. The auditor should then determine the flow of documents and the extent of controls relative to each audit risk and management assertion/audit objective by reviewing the client entity's policy and procedure documentation, as well as through discussions with management and the operational departments relevant to the financial cycle being assessed. We will consider this first in relation to the purchases and payables cycle, and then to the payroll cycle.

When we looked at the four stages involved in a system-based (controls-approach) audit of revenue and receivables in the previous section, we did so by way of a narrative description of the process (see **Example 8.4**). Below, at **Figure 8.5**, we use a flowchart to similarly explain and understand the purchases and payables system.

The key internal controls over the purchases and payables cycle are:
- Segregation of duties;
- Authorisation of purchase orders (POs) and payments to suppliers;
- Chart of authority;
- Matching (purchase order to goods received note to supplier invoice);
- Review of supplier statement reconciliations; and
- Review of exception reports.

### Segregation of Duties

In order to reduce the risk of fraudulent or erroneous purchases, it is common for an enforced segregation of duties to be built into the purchasing procedures, whereby different members of staff are responsible for:
- raising purchase orders and accepting goods from suppliers;
- receiving goods from suppliers and recording purchase invoices on the purchase ledger; and
- raising purchase orders and processing payment.

We can see from **Figure 8.5** below that none of these tasks are carried out by the same person (department). Generally, the ability to perform tasks is restricted in the system (i.e. an individual's access rights are determined centrally, restricting individuals to transactions related to their assigned function in the organisation), which allows the auditor to more easily test the control by testing the configuration of the system.

### Authorisation of Purchase Orders and Supplier Payments

In order to mitigate the risk of unnecessary or fraudulent purchases, it is common for only a small number of experienced staff to have the authority to raise purchase orders (POs). For example, in **Figure 8.5** we can see that there is a purchasing department,

FIGURE 8.5: FLOWCHART OF PURCHASES AND PAYABLES
CYCLE (IN AN AUTOMATED ENVIRONMENT)

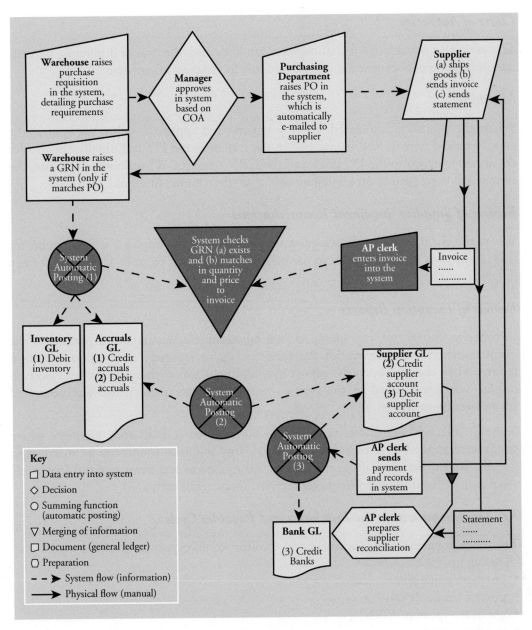

which is separate from the requester, the approver and the accounts payable (AP) department.

Similarly, authorisation of payments to suppliers is often restricted to senior employees. In a computerised environment, two separate automated approvals are commonly required.

In addition, prior to approving payment, the approver should sign-off on back-up documentation (usually a supplier statement reconciliation).

### Chart of Authority

The value of purchases that a staff member can authorise often varies depending on their seniority and level of experience. This is outlined in the chart of authority.

### Matching

Where the process is automated, a PO is entered and approved within the system, the goods received note (GRN) is matched in the system to the PO and, finally, the invoice details are matched to the PO price and the GRN quantity. Where differences arise, the system will reject further processing outside a pre-determined threshold.

### Review of Supplier Statement Reconciliations

Where the client entity receives regular statements from its suppliers, it is common for these statements to be reconciled to the balance per the trade payables ledger and for any differences to be investigated.

### Review of Exception Reports

In order to ensure that expenses occurred are complete, accurate and pertain to the client entity, it is important for the client entity to regularly review two exception reports. First, the aged open PO report may highlight issues where goods were received but no GRN was raised in the system, meaning no accrual/expense was generated (completeness assertion).

Secondly, the aged goods received invoices not received (GRIR) may highlight where goods were accrued in error as being received. Any instances found can be matched to supplier statements to see if: (a) the invoice was mislaid or was never received (recording assertion); or (b) the goods were never received (occurrence assertion).

### Key Documents within the Purchases and Payables Cycle

The following are the key documents the auditor would expect to find in a typical purchases and payables cycle:
- purchase requisition;
- purchase order (PO);
- goods receipt note (GRN);
- purchase invoices;
- debit notes;
- aged payables listing; and
- payment summary/payment proposal.

## Stage 2: Ascertain the Internal Control System within the Payroll Cycle

We will now consider the key internal controls associated with a typical payroll cycle within a computerised environment. The headings in this section denote the principal business activities, with a brief explanation and followed by the principal internal control activities an auditor would expect to find.

### Recruitment of Employees

An 'employee authorisation' form should be completed for all new employees (signed by human resources (HR) and the hiring manager). This form includes employee **master data**, such as name, title, contracted hours, starting salary (rate per hour), Personal Public Service number (PPS number, in the RoI) or National Insurance number (in the UK/NI), start date, etc.

The HR department is responsible for entering the employee's master data. No other department should have access to add new employees or to edit employee master data.

Prior to the processing of payroll, whether weekly or monthly, a person independent of the individual who inputs the master data should run an edit report from the system (showing all changes made to employee master data) and compare it to the employees' authorisation forms.

**Key control**: segregation of duties between the HR department and the payroll function with respect to employee master data and independent review of data entry.

### Recording Hours Worked

Most large companies record hours worked using a clock-in system. A clock-in system allows the employee to record start and finish times. This information is stored and interfaced with the payroll program.

Salaried employees receive the same amount every month and as such salaried employees usually do not clock in (a clock-in system for salaried staff can, however, be helpful to record days worked, sick days, holidays, etc. to maintain control).

**Key control**: the computerised transfer from the clock-in system provides a strong control of the occurrence assertion (i.e. the event took place, the employee worked the hours). This is an example of a system (automated) control.

### Recording Other Payroll Variables

Other payroll variables can include commission, bonuses, holidays, sick days, expenses, etc. and should be requested directly from the payroll clerk's manager. The payroll clerk should never enter any variables onto the system without authorisation forms being completed.

**Key control:** exception reports (see below under 'Accounting') allow the manager to validate the information entered by the payroll clerk, giving assurance over occurrence, classification/recording and rights and obligations.

## Calculating Payroll

The payroll department is responsible for calculating the payroll once all information regarding each employee has been collected. To calculate their payroll most companies use special payroll software that integrates information from different sources. Thus it will take:
- employee master data (which only HR has access to);
- the employees' hours worked, as verified by the employee; and
- other payroll variables, such as bonuses, commission, etc. (which are entered directly by the payroll clerk).

**Key control:** automating the segregation of duties (SOD) protects the integrity of the master data and so reduces the possibility of misstatements occurring.

## Payroll Reports

Once the payroll calculations have been posted, a number of reports may be generated, all of which should be reviewed by appropriate personnel. These reports include:
- **Gross to net reports** Reports the gross amount owed to employees and all deductions necessary to determine the figure paid to the employee. These should be reviewed and signed off by HR.
- **Exception reports** Can include: number of bonus hours paid, number of holidays, number of sick days, value of bonuses paid, number of overtime hours paid, wages exceeding a certain value, employees with no recorded hours (which may indicate a termination of employment that has not been activated in the system), etc. They should be reviewed and signed off by HR.
- **Departmental summary reports** Reports the total number of employees and hours charged to a department, including overtime hours, bonuses, etc. They should be reviewed and signed off by department directors/managers; the payroll employee should only process details that have been authorised.
- **Payroll control summary total** Used by the finance department to reconcile amounts paid out of the bank to the journal entries posted to the accounting system.

## Accounting

The finance department needs to be satisfied that payroll-related postings are correct. The following common controls exist relating to the accounting (finance) department review of payroll postings:
- Most payroll packages interface directly with the client entity's accounting package and post the payroll transactions automatically.

- Payroll postings should be reviewed by a member of the finance department and reconciled with the payroll control summary total report (a report that summarises all related payroll totals for accounting).
- The finance department should also reconcile the net payment according to the payroll control summary total report to the amount paid out of the bank account.

**Key control:** the review and sign-off of exception reports, summary reports and reconciliations are all essential controls and give assurance over occurrence, completeness, recording and rights and obligations.

### Termination of Employment

- Managers should notify the HR department and the payroll function when an employee leaves the organisation.
- HR should be the only department that has the system access to terminate employment and should do so in a timely fashion to avoid the payment of employees after they cease to be employed by the entity.
- The payroll function should ensure that the employee is no longer active on the payroll system.

### Stage 3: Assess the Internal Control System within the Purchases and Payables Cycle

Stage three of a system-based (controls-approach) audit of the purchases and payables cycle is to assess what has been learned in the earlier stages and to decide whether it is efficient to go ahead and test the controls.

In most companies, purchases and payables represent both a material value and a high volume. It is therefore normally more efficient for the auditor to test controls around the purchasing and payables cycle to assist in reducing substantive testing. As we have seen in our discussion of audit sampling (**Chapter 6,** Section 6.8), the value of transactions/balances and the risk assessment will influence the sample size. Therefore, the material values and inherent risks associated with purchases and payables mean that the sample sizes for substantive testing may be substantial – making it extremely time-consuming and costly. However, if preliminary assessments of the purchases and payables cycle indicate that controls are not strong, or have not been effective throughout the entire period, a purely substantive approach may be the most efficient in the long run.

In considering whether or not to test controls, the auditor will also take into account whether or not any changes to procedures or systems have occurred in the period. If they have, the auditor will need to test the old as well as the new procedures/system – which may not warrant the time saved on substantive testing.

## Stage 3: Assess the Internal Control System within the Payroll Cycle

In the payroll cycle, the decision on whether to test the controls or if substantive analytical procedures would be more efficient will depend on the number of people employed by the entity. As payroll normally has a limited number of changing variables, the charge for the year can usually be calculated to within a threshold of the actual figure. For example, by obtaining from HR a list of all employees' salaries and multiplying by 12, the auditor should get close to the annual salary figure in the financial statements, albeit they may need to take into consideration new starters and leavers in the period and time apportion. For this reason, it can be more efficient to avoid testing controls and instead perform focused substantive tests. The decision to move straight to focused substantive tests will include consideration of:

- the number of employees (and the number of new hires and terminations in the year);
- the number of changes in salary during the period, and whether they were applied across the organisation or ad hoc to some employees only;
- the predictability of overtime; and
- the availability of information on headcount and changes from HR.

## Stage 4: Test the Internal Control System within the Purchases and Payables Cycle

Having reached the final stage in a system-based (controls-approach) audit of the purchases and payables cycle, we are now going to test the internal controls relating to purchases and payables (if the auditor has deemed the controls to be effective and decided that it is an efficient audit approach).

The audit objective is to select and perform tests designed to establish compliance with the internal system controls as documented by the client entity.

The tests of controls will include testing the operation of controls over a sample of transactions from the period, and obtaining documentary evidence of the controls in operation. **Example 8.7** shows what an audit working paper might look like for the purchases and payables cycle.

EXAMPLE 8.7: AUDIT WORKING PAPER – PURCHASES
AND PAYABLES CONTROLS

| Dairy Fresh Limited<br>31 December 2018<br>Purchases and Payables Controls Audit Programme | | Working Paper Reference: P1 | |
|---|---|---|---|
| Objective: | To ascertain if the purchases and payables cycle is adequately controlled by the entity with respect to all assertions. | | |
| | Initials | Date | Date |
| Prepared by: | | | |
| Reviewed by: | | | |

**The following steps are suggestions only and should be removed or added to as necessary to address the risks of material misstatement identified at the risk assessment stage.**

| Risk Identified | Assertion | Test | Ref. |
|---|---|---|---|
| **Organisational and IT Controls** | | | |
| 1. Lack of policies and procedures surrounding purchases and payables functions may result in inconsistent application of policies and lack of adherence to desired procedures. | Valuation Occurrence Recording (accuracy) Completeness Rights and obligations Cut-off | Assess the appropriateness of the accounting policy and procedure documentation and the accounting estimates method for purchases and payables. Ensure the accounting policy is in accordance with accounting standards and applicable law. | |
| 2. Inappropriate system access may result in a lack of segregation of duties (SOD). | Valuation Occurrence Recording (accuracy) Completeness Rights and obligations | Obtain a report from the system outlining who in the organisation has access to which steps in the system for purchasing and payable functions. Review the report to ensure that no SOD issues exist (e.g. those individuals with access to supplier master data do not have access to AP functionality). | |
| 3. Purchases may be approved at an inappropriate level/ payments may be approved at an inappropriate level. | Valuation Occurrence Completeness Rights and obligations | Obtain a copy of the entity's chart of authority (COA) and review to ensure authorisation levels are reasonable. | |
| **Raising the PO** | | | |
| 1. Goods and services ordered are not properly authorised, increasing the risk of non-business purchases. | Rights and obligations Occurrence | *System check (test of one) Observe the entry of a purchase requisition and ensure that a workflow approval is triggered in accordance with the chart of authority. ** Alternative test Randomly select 200 POs raised and ensure they were approved in accordance with the COA. | |

| | | | |
|---|---|---|---|
| 2. Unauthorised suppliers are used, increasing the risk of losing bulk discounts. | Rights and obligations Occurrence | Obtain a report showing suppliers added to the system. Obtain tendering documents and approval of supplier set-up from the procurement department. | |
| | | *System check (test of one) Observe the PO entry process and ensure that the purchasing department cannot raise a PO with a supplier that is not contained within the approved supplier listing. | |
| | | ** Alternative test/ † Dual test Select 200 supplier invoices posted to the system and ensure that: (a) there is a related GRN and the quantity and price match (to within predefined tolerance); (b) there is a related PO and the quantity and price match (to within predefined tolerance); (c) there is a purchase requisition and the quantity and price match (to within predefined tolerance). | |
| **Receiving the Goods** | | | |
| 1. Goods or services are physically received and accrued but were not ordered. | Occurrence Recording (accuracy) Rights and obligations | * System check (test of one) Observe the goods-in process and request the warehouse operative to attempt to enter a GRN for which there is no PO. | |
| | | ** Alternative test/ † Dual test See dual test at Raising the PO, 2(c). | |

| | | | |
|---|---|---|---|
| 2. GRNs are raised in the system for goods that were not received. | Occurrence | Obtain a copy of the review of the open aged GRIR reports for a randomly selected five-month period and ensure there is evidence of review and follow-up. <br> ** **Alternative test/ † Dual test** See dual test at Raising the PO, 2(c). | |
| 3. GRNs are not raised in the system for goods received, resulting in incomplete accruals. | Completeness | Obtain a copy of the review of the aged open PO report for a randomly selected five months and ensure that there is evidence of review and follow-up. <br> ****Alternative test** <br> Randomly select 50 supplier reconciliations from throughout the period and ensure there is evidence of review and follow-up. | |
| 4. Invoices are received for goods not received or for goods in poor condition. | Occurrence <br> Recording (accuracy) <br> Rights and obligations | Observe the goods check-in area to ensure goods are being counted and physically inspected (see Raising the PO, 2(c)). | |
| **Accounting** | | | |
| 1. Payments are made to incorrect bank accounts. | Occurrence <br> Classification/ Recording (accuracy) <br> Rights and obligations | Randomly select 200 supplier payments from throughout the period and ensure they were approved and that there is evidence that the back-up was reviewed prior to payment. | |

| | | Ensure only the purchasing department can make changes to supplier bank account details and that personnel in the procurement department are: (a) not cheque signatories; and (b) not part of the AP function. | |
| --- | --- | --- | --- |
| 2. Payments may be made for goods or services not received. | Occurrence Classification/ Recording (accuracy) Rights and obligations | See test at Accounting, 1(a). Obtain five randomly selected months' bank reconciliations and ensure there is evidence of review and follow-up. | |

\* System check (test of one) – when a system test is carried out, there is only ever one test (as, once set up correctly, the system should behave in the same way every time). The auditor need then only test for changes in configuration of the computer system.

\*\* Alternative testing method – although those tests requiring the testing of a lower sample size (because they cover a greater volume of the population) or that are a system test of one are considered more efficient and effective (i.e. those requiring lower sample sizes are performed more quickly and those that are system checks require a test of one item only and therefore are more efficient).

† Dual test – the same test can be used to cover: (a) multiple assertions; (b) multiple risk; and/or (c) control and substantive testing.

**Conclusion**
Subject to the matters noted for the reviewer, in my opinion the purchases and payables are adequately controlled with respect to all assertions.

## Stage 4: Test the Internal Control System within the Payroll Cycle

Having reached the final stage of a system-based (controls-approach) audit of the payroll cycle, we are now going to test the internal controls relating to the payroll cycle (if the auditor has deemed the controls to be effective and decided that it is an efficient audit approach).

The audit objective is to select and perform tests designed to establish compliance with the system controls as documented by the client entity. The tests of controls will include the testing of the operation of controls over a sample of transactions from the period, obtaining documentary evidence of the controls in operation. A typical working paper relating to controls testing over the payroll cycle can be found at **Example 8.8** below.

EXAMPLE 8.8: AUDIT WORKING PAPER – PAYROLL CONTROLS

| Dairy Fresh Limited<br>31 December 2018 | | Working Paper Reference: P1 | |
| --- | --- | --- | --- |
| **Payroll Controls Audit Programme** | | | |
| Objective: | To ascertain if the payroll cycle is adequately controlled by the entity with respect to all assertions. | | |
| | Initials | Date | Date |
| Prepared by: | | | |
| Reviewed by: | | | |

The following steps are suggestions only and should be removed or added to as necessary to address the risks of material misstatement identified at the risk assessment stage.

| Risk Identified | Assertion | Test | Ref. |
| --- | --- | --- | --- |
| **Organisational and IT Controls** | | | |
| 1. Lack of policies and procedures surrounding payroll area may result in inconsistent application of policies and lack of adherence to desired procedures. | Valuation<br>Occurrence<br>Recording (accuracy)<br>Completeness<br>Rights and obligations | Assess the appropriateness of the accounting policy and the accounting estimates method for payroll. Ensure that the accounting policy is in accordance with accounting standards and applicable law. | |
| 2. Inappropriate system access may result in a lack of segregation of duties (SOD). | Valuation<br>Occurrence<br>Recording (accuracy)<br>Completeness<br>Rights and obligations | Obtain a report from the system outlining who in the organisation has access to which functions in the payroll system. Review the report to ensure that no SOD issues exist (e.g. those individuals with access to employee master data do not have access to payroll application). | |

**Hiring Employees/Amending Employee Master Data**

| | | | |
|---|---|---|---|
| 1. Fictitious employees may be added or incorrect master data may be input (employees may not exist). | Occurrence Recording (accuracy) Rights and obligations | Ensure only HR has access to add/edit employee master data. | |
| | | Obtain four random copies of the reviewed edit reports. Ensure: (a) there is evidence of review by someone who does not have access to employee master data; and (b) select three changes from each report and compare to employee authorisation forms. | |

**Recording Payroll Variables and Calculating Payroll**

| | | | |
|---|---|---|---|
| 1. People may be paid for hours they did not work or bonuses, commission, etc. that was not approved. | Occurrence Recording (accuracy) Rights and obligations Completeness | For five months' payroll, randomly selected, reconcile the recorded hours worked to the hours paid per the payroll system. Ensure an authorisation form exists for any changes made to information. | |
| | | Randomly select five months' department summary report reviews and confirm evidence of review. | |
| 2. Payroll may be calculated incorrectly. | Recording (accuracy) | * **System check (test of one)** Check the mathematical accuracy of one payslip. | |

**Accounting**

| | | | |
|---|---|---|---|
| 1. The amount paid to employees from the bank may not equal the amount calculated according to the payroll system. | Recording (accuracy) Completeness Occurrence | Randomly select five months and ensure that the amount paid from the bank account was reconciled to the amount per the payroll control summary report. | |
| 2. The amounts entered into the finance system may not equal the amounts calculated according to the payroll system. | Recording (accuracy) Completeness Occurrence | Randomly select five months and ensure that the journals posted to the accounting system were reconciled to the amount per the payroll control summary report. | |

| **Termination of Employment** | | |
|---|---|---|
| Individuals may be paid after their employment has been terminated. | Occurrence | Randomly select five months of department summary report reviews and confirm evidence of review. |
| | | For five months' payroll, reconcile the recorded hours worked to the hours paid per the payroll system. Ensure an authorisation form exists for any changes made to information. |

\* System check (test of one) – when a system test is carried out, there is only ever one test (as, once set up correctly, the system should behave in the same way every time). The auditor need then only test for changes in configuration.

**Conclusion**
Subject to the matters noted for the reviewer, in my opinion the payroll system is adequately controlled with respect to all assertions.

## 8.7  INTERNAL CONTROLS AND THE INVENTORY CYCLE

In previous sections we have discussed the four stages in a system-based (controls-approach) audit to review the internal controls of different cycles (revenue and receivables; purchases and payables; and payroll). We will now apply the same approach to the inventory cycle.

### Stage 1: Identify Risks and Objectives within the Inventory Cycle

Adopting the same approach as for the previous cycles, the first stage is to identify the risks and objectives. Inventory is associated with the following risks:
• inventory obsolescence;
• risk associated with the completeness and existence assertions, particularly with regard to consignment stock, etc.;
• cut-off (it can be difficult to determine or apply cut-off for year-end movements of inventory;
• theft;
• risk of inventory NRV being less than cost.

TABLE 8.3: INTERNAL CONTROL OBJECTIVES – INVENTORY

| Management Assertion/ Audit Objective | Control Objective for Transaction Class | Control Objective for Account Balance |
|---|---|---|
| | **Inventory Movements** | **Inventory Balances** |
| **Existence or Occurrence** | • Recorded purchase transactions represent inventory acquired. <br> • Recorded transfers represent inventory transferred between locations or categories. <br> • Recorded revenue transactions represent inventory sold. | Inventory included in the SOFP physically exists at the year end date. |
| **Completeness** | All purchases, transfers and sales of inventory that occurred have been recorded. | Inventory includes all materials, products and supplies on hand at the date of the SOFP. |
| **Rights and obligations** | The entity has rights and obligations associated with the inventory recorded during the period. | The entity has rights to the inventory included at the date of the SOFP. |
| **Classification/ Recording (accuracy) or Valuation** | The costs of materials purchased and of labour and overheads applied have been accurately determined and are in accordance with applicable accounting standards. | Inventory is properly stated at the lower of cost or NRV, in accordance with applicable accounting standards. |
| **Cut-off** | All purchases, transfers and sales of inventory are recorded in the correct account period. | |
| **Presentation and Disclosure** | Transactions relating to inventory have been properly identified and classified in the financial statements. | Inventory is properly identified and classified in the financial statements. Disclosures referring to the classification, basis of valuation and the pledging of inventory is adequate. |

## Stage 2: Ascertain the Internal Control System within the Inventory Cycle

The second stage is the point when the auditor identifies the principal business activities and the key documents to gain a better understanding of the client entity's policies and procedures in the context of the risks identified and the management assertions/audit objectives. In terms of inventory, generally the auditor would attend the year-end physical inventory count as part of the substantive procedures. A more detailed discussion of what is expected of the client entity when conducting a physical inventory count is given in **Chapter 12**.

The key documents the auditor would expect to find in a typical inventory cycle include:
* inventory requisitions forms;
* goods receipt notes (GRNs);    *purchase.*
* goods dispatch notes (GDNs);    *Sales*
* inventory cards;
* inventory write-off forms;
* aged stock listing; and
* status stock listing.

## Stage 3: Assess the Internal Control System within the Inventory Cycle

Having identified the risks and objectives relating to the inventory cycle and gained an understanding of how the controls should operate, the auditor now needs to assess what has been learned so far in order to decide whether it is efficient to go ahead and test the controls.

In a non-manufacturing environment, the movement of inventory is normally tested within the purchases and payables cycle and the revenue and receivables cycle and is not dealt with separately under inventory cycle control documentation. Therefore, the likelihood is that it will be more efficient to perform focused substantive tests on the inventory balance – because stock movements will have already been assessed/tested in those cycles and, regardless of the results of any controls testing, the auditor is likely to attend the year-end physical count anyway. In a manufacturing environment, a more in-depth understanding of inventory movement controls does need to be gained by the auditor (see **Chapter 12**).

Typical inventory tests of control include:
* inventory status;
* inventory counts;
* inventory write-offs;
* standard costing review;
* inventory safeguarding; and
* inventory reconciliations.

Many of these are **dual-purpose tests**, in that they will also support substantive testing.

### Inventory Status

Typical controls around inventory status management might include:
* Status of inventory should be known at all times, especially if consignment inventory is held or inventory is subject to retention of title, e.g. obsolete, damaged, third party, held on consignment (review and authorisation control).

- Reviews of damaged, obsolete and slow-moving inventories should be carried out periodically throughout the year (review and authorisation control).
- Obsolete, damaged and short-dated inventory should be segregated from good inventory and the status of same recorded against the perpetual records, where possible (physical control).

### Inventory Counts

Physical inventory counts should be carried out periodically (at least once a year). Internal controls might include

- The count should be carried out by personnel who are independent of the stores function (segregation of duties control).
- The count should be carried out in accordance with documented and predetermined inventory count procedures and instructions (organisational control).
- The count should be a 'blind count' (i.e. the expected results of the count should not be known to counters), performed by two individuals who compare results and investigate differences (review and authorisation and reconciliation controls).
- The final count results should be compared to perpetual records (reconciliation control).
- All differences between physical and perpetual records should be investigated (review and authorisation control).
- Unresolved differences between the physical count and perpetual records should be written off following authorisation from management (review and authorisation control).

### Inventory Write-offs

Typical controls as part of inventory write-off might include:
- Inventories identified for write-off should be appropriately authorised by relevant management personnel prior to being recorded in the system (review and authorisation control).
- Disposal of inventory should be based on informed decisions that are evidenced in writing (review and authorisation control).

### Standard Costing Review

Typical controls around the standard costing of inventory might include:
- Standard costs should be reviewed by management to ensure they relate to actual costs being incurred. Standard costs should be reviewed by management to ensure they are reliable and that costing is made on a consistent basis year on year (review and authorisation control).
- Standard cost variances should be reviewed by management periodically and differences investigated (review and authorisation and reconciliation controls).

### Inventory Safeguarding

Typical controls as part of the safeguarding of inventory might include:
- Inventory should be held in an environment that prevents deterioration (physical control).
- Access to stores should be restricted, e.g. access cards (physical control).

### Inventory Reconciliations

The following reconciliations and reviews should be carried out by the finance department in order to ensure sub-ledgers are in line with the general ledger balances and that adequate provisions are in place:
- Inventory sub-ledgers should be reconciled to the general ledger periodically (reconciliation control).
- Provisions for obsolete, damaged and short-dated inventory should be reviewed regularly by management (review and authorisation control).

## Stage 4: Test the Internal Control System within the Inventory Cycle

Having reached the final stage of a system-based (controls-approach) audit of the inventory cycle, we are now going to test the internal controls relating to the inventory cycle (if the auditor has deemed the controls to be effective and decided that it is an efficient audit approach).

Remember, the audit objective is to select and perform tests designed to establish compliance with the system controls as documented by the client entity.

**Example 8.9** describes the audit programme that the auditor can carry out to ensure that the control activities are operating effectively and efficiently throughout the period. The management assertion (audit objective) of the test is shown to ensure that the relevant member of the audit team understands that each test must cover an objective in order to support the reduction in substantive testing. ***Note:*** within this audit programme only the following are considered: inventory counts, inventory safeguarding, inventory write-offs and inventory reconciliations. The receipt and issue of inventory is considered within the purchases and payables cycle and the revenue and receivables cycle.

EXAMPLE 8.9: AUDIT WORKING PAPER – INVENTORY CONTROLS

| Dairy Fresh Limited<br>31 December 2018<br>Inventory Controls Audit Programme | | Working Paper Reference: I1 | |
|---|---|---|---|
| **Objective:** | **To ascertain if the inventory cycle is adequately controlled by the entity with respect to all assertions.** | | |
| | Initials | Date | Date |
| **Prepared by:** | | | |
| **Reviewed by:** | | | |

**Ensure the audit plan is reflected in the following tests. The following steps are suggestions only and should be removed or added to as necessary to address the risks of material misstatement identified at the risk assessment stage.**

| Risk Identified | Assertion | Test | Ref. |
|---|---|---|---|
| **Organisational and IT Controls** | | | |
| 1. Lack of policies and procedures surrounding the area of inventory may result in inconsistent application of policies and lack of adherence to desired procedures. | Valuation Occurrence Recording (accuracy) Completeness Rights and obligations Cut-off | Assess the appropriateness of the accounting policy and procedure documentation and the accounting estimates method for inventories. Ensure that the accounting policy is in accordance with accounting standards and applicable law. | |
| 2 Inappropriate access may result in a lack of segregation of duties (SOD). | Valuation Occurrence Recording (accuracy) Completeness Rights and obligations | Obtain a report from the system outlining who in the organisation has access to which functions in the inventory system. Review the report to ensure that no SOD issues exist (e.g. individuals with access to physical inventory should not have access to perform inventory write-offs). | |
| **Inventory Status** | | | |
| 1. Inventory held may not belong to the client or may be obsolete or out of date. | Occurrence Valuation Rights and obligations | During attendance at the physical inventory count, identify damaged, obsolete and short-dated inventory; obtain a status inventory report and compare a sample to ensure appropriate status is recorded. Additionally, ensure that any inventory held for third parties are segregated from the client entity's inventories. | |

| | Valuation | During attendance at a physical inventory count, observe the segregation of damaged, obsolete and short-dated inventory. | |
|---|---|---|---|
| **Inventory Counts** | | | |
| 1. Not all goods delivered are invoiced. | Existence Valuation | Ensure stocktake instructions exist and are documented and attend physical inventory count to ensure they are adhered to. | |
| | | Select a random sample of five months and request physical inventory count records to confirm physical inventory counts are taking place as prescribed and inspect reconciliations between count records and perpetual inventory records. | |
| **Inventory Write-offs** | | | |
| 1. Stock may be written off without authorisation. | Occurrence Recording (accuracy) | Select a sample of write-offs of inventory to ensure they were adequately approved. Ensure disposal records exist for the selected inventory. | |
| **Standard Costing** | | | |
| 1. Standard costing applied to inventory may not be reasonable. | Valuation | Request a sample of standard cost variance reviews to ensure they are taking place periodically and to ensure there is evidence of management's investigation of differences. | |
| **Inventory Safeguarding** | | | |
| 1. Inventory may be subject to misappropriation. | Existence | Observe physical security of warehouse. | |
| **Inventory Reconciliations** | | | |
| 1. Inventory balances may be written off without proper authorisation. | Completeness Existence Valuation | Request and inspect a sample of five months' randomly selected reconciliations between the inventory sub-ledger and the general ledger. | |

## 8.8  INTERNAL CONTROLS AND THE BANK AND CASH CYCLE

We will now look at the bank and cash cycle and its four stages in a system-based (controls-approach) audit.

### Stage 1: Identify Risks and Objectives within the Bank and Cash Cycle

When auditing the bank and cash cycle the auditor should be mindful of risks, which may include:
- existence of bank accounts not disclosed;
- fraudulent outstanding lodgements included in bank reconciliation;
- 'window dressing', i.e. transactions around the year end date; and
- money laundering.

**Table 8.4** identifies the specific audit objectives associated with the bank and cash cycle.

TABLE 8.4: INTERNAL CONTROL OBJECTIVES – BANK AND CASH

| Management Assertion/ Audit Objective | Control Objective for Account Balance |
|---|---|
| **Existence** | To ensure that recorded bank and cash balances exist at the date of the SOFP. |
| **Completeness** | To ensure that all bank and cash balances that exist are fully recorded at the date of the SOFP. |
| **Rights and Obligations** | To ensure the entity has the rights and any related obligations to all bank and cash balances shown in the SOFP. |
| **Valuation** | To ensure bank and cash balances are properly valued and a provision has been made for any balances that may not be recoverable. |
| **Cut-off** | All transactions have been accounted for in the correct accounting period. |
| **Presentation and Disclosure** | To ensure cash balances are properly classified and disclosed in the SOFP and that lines of credit, loan guarantees and other restrictions on bank and cash balances are appropriately disclosed. |

### Stage 2: Ascertain the Internal Control System within the Bank and Cash Cycle

Stage 2 identifies the principal business activities and key documents to allow the auditor to gain a better understanding of the entity's policies and procedures and how they relate to the associated risks and objectives. The key control areas relevant to the bank and cash cycle should include:

- payments,
- receipts, and
- bank account.

## Payments

Typical controls that would be expected to be in place as part of the management of payments might include:

- Payments should be properly authorised, usually by two individuals (organisational and review and authorisation controls). Only authorised staff can make payments, which is ensured through the establishment of mandates with the bank. Where signatories on the account changed during the year, review the bank mandate form (a document indicating who can sign off on cheques or credit transfers) to ensure that this has been updated correctly.
- Payments should only be made in respect of legitimate liabilities; supporting documentation should be reviewed by management prior to authorisation of payments (review and authorisation control).
- Every payment run should be reviewed by management and matched to appropriate invoices (review and authorisation control).
- Reconciliations should be performed between the amounts appearing on bank statements and the amounts posted to the payables sub-ledger (reconciliation control). The reconciliation should be performed by someone independent of the individuals who do the postings to the payables accounts (segregation of duties control).
- There should be segregation of duties between the personnel dealing with receipts and payments, those dealing with revenue transactions, those dealing with purchases transactions and the individuals authorising payments (segregation of duties control).
- Cheque books should be stored securely in a safe and only authorised personnel should have access to them (physical control).

## Receipts

Typical controls that would be expected to be in place as part of the management of receipts might include:

- Receipts should be collected and banked intact. If receipts are received by post, post should be opened by two individuals and cheques sent directly to the cash office and remittances to the receivables department or accounting, depending on the purpose of the receipt, in order for the receipt to be reflected on the accounting system for later reconciliation to the bank statement (physical control and segregation of duties control).
- Reconciliations of amounts banked to amounts posted should be performed by someone independent of the cash custodians and the individuals posting cash to the ledgers (reconciliation and segregation of duties controls).
- A cash to revenue reconciliation should be performed and reviewed by management (review and authorisation control).

## *Bank Accounts*

Typical controls that would be expected to be in place as part of the management of bank accounts might include:
- Bank reconciliations should be performed and reviewed by management on a regular basis (reconciliation and review and authorisation controls).
- There should be restrictions on the opening and closing of accounts – only authorised staff should be able to open bank accounts (organisational control).

Key documents within the bank and cash cycle are:
- remittance advices (for cash received);
- payment run summaries (if paid by BACS);
- bank statements;
- bank reconciliations;
- cheque books;
- lodgement books; and
- bank mandates.

The most efficient way to get an overview of the controls in place is to perform a walk-through test.

## Stage 3: Assess the Internal Control System within the Bank and Cash Cycle

Having identified the risks and objectives and gained an understanding of how the controls should operate, the auditor now needs to assess whether it is efficient to go ahead and test the controls.

Controls testing is normally carried out on bank and cash transactions to reduce substantive testing in the purchases and revenue cycles (as they interlink due to the payment of suppliers and receipt of cash from customers). However, cash and bank balances at year end are normally tested using focused substantive testing, which is usually the most efficient method.

## Stage 4: Test the Internal Control System within the Bank and Cash Cycle

Having reached the final stage of the system-based (controls-approach) audit of the bank and cash cycle, we are now going to test the internal controls relating to the bank and cash cycle (if the auditor has deemed the controls to be effective and decided that it is an efficient audit approach). The audit objective is to select and perform tests designed to establish compliance with the system controls as documented by the client entity.

Tests of controls for bank and cash include:
- inspection of the reconciliations between the bank balances per bank statements and the bank balances per the general ledger, ensuring that they have been prepared and regularly reviewed for all bank accounts;

- check the signatories on all the bank accounts (i.e. obtain copies of bank mandates currently in force for each account and ensure that they are up to date and only include current staff). Obtain a copy of the bank mandate, which contains sample signatures of the authorised signatories;
- test the authorisation of the opening and closing of bank accounts; and
- check that all bank accounts exist.

## 8.9 INTERNAL CONTROLS AND THE INVESTMENTS CYCLE

We will now apply the four stages of a system-based (controls-approach) audit to the investments cycle.

### Stage 1: Identify Risks and Objectives within the Investments Cycle

When auditing the investments cycle the auditor should consider risks such as:
- investments not registered in the company name (rights and obligations);
- valuations associated with investments;
- classification of investments; and
- income cut-off associated with investments.

**Table 8.5** shows the specific objectives associated with the investments cycle.

TABLE 8.5: INTERNAL CONTROL OBJECTIVES – INVESTMENTS

| Management Assertion/Audit Objective | Control Objective for Transaction Class | Control Objective for Account Balance |
|---|---|---|
| **Existence or Occurrence** | Recorded investment revenues, gains and losses are the result of transactions and events that occurred during the period. | Recorded investment balances represent investments that exist at the date of the SOFP. |
| **Completeness** | All investment transactions and events are included in the statement of comprehensive income. | All investments that exist at the date of the SOFP are recorded in the SOFP. |
| **Rights and Obligations** | The entity has rights and obligations associated with the investment income, profits and losses recorded during the period. | All recorded investments are owned by the client entity, which hold the risks and rewards associated with them. |
| **Classification/ Recording (accuracy) or Valuation** | Investment revenues, gains and losses are accurately recorded. | Investments are stated at valuation as appropriate for the particular types of investment held. |

| | | |
|---|---|---|
| **Cut-off** | Investment revenues, gains and losses are recorded in the correct period (particularly those around the year end date). | |
| **Presentation and Disclosure** | Appropriate disclosures in the financial statements are made concerning:<br>1. related party investments;<br>2. the bases for valuing investments; and<br>3. the pledging of investments as collateral and any other disclosures as required under the applicable reporting standards. | Investment balances are properly identified, presented and disclosed in the financial statements in line with the applicable financial reporting standards. |

## Stage 2: Ascertain the Internal Control System within the Investments Cycle

In this stage, the auditor should identify the principal business activities and key documents to gain a better understanding of the entity's policies and procedures relevant to the risks and objectives identified. Ideally, the following should be present in the control environment of the investments cycle:

- Authority and responsibility for investing activities should be given to an individual deemed to be a person of integrity and with sufficient knowledge and experience in dealing with investments.
- The information system in place should reliably and accurately record the data required for accounting for the various categories of investments.
- Internal audit should closely monitor the effectiveness of controls over investing activities.
- Title to the investments (ownership documents), usually in the form of a share or debenture certificate, should be held in a secure location.

The auditor would expect to find the following key documents in a typical investments cycle (although investment ownership documents can take many forms):

- debenture certificates,
- shareholding certificates,
- investment contracts, and
- dividend vouchers.

## Stage 3: Assess the Internal Control System within the Investments Cycle

Having identified the risks and objectives relating to the investments cycle and gained an understanding of how the controls should operate, the auditor now needs to assess whether it is efficient to test the controls. Depending on the number of investments, it may be more appropriate for the auditor to test the balance substantively. If this is the case, there is no need to continue with the tests of controls.

### Stage 4: Test the Internal Control System within the Investments Cycle

Having reached the final stage of a system-based (controls-approach) audit of the investments cycle, we are now going to test the internal controls relating to the investments cycle (if the auditor has deemed the controls to be effective and decided that it is an efficient audit approach). The audit objective is to select and perform tests designed to establish compliance with the system controls as documented by the client entity.

Tests of controls for the investments cycle include:
- inspection of controls over the custody of investments and obtaining a confirmation of investments from all custodians of investments;
- checking the authorised signatures;
- testing authorisation of additions and disposals of investments;
- checking existence of all investments;
- checking completeness of all investments.

## 8.10 MANAGEMENT LETTERS

Throughout this chapter we have described how an auditor might go about gaining an understanding of the client entity's system of internal controls, and in the process discover weaknesses in its design, operation or consistent application. The auditor has a responsibility to inform those charged with governance of the client entity of their findings. This is done by a **management letter**.

ISA 265 *Communicating Deficiencies in Internal Control to Those Charged With Governance and Management*, paragraph 9, states:
> "The auditor shall communicate in writing significant deficiencies in internal control identified during the audit to those charged with governance on a timely basis."

When communicating to management, the auditor must consider if there are any reasons why it would be inappropriate to communicate certain deficiencies directly to those charged with governance. For example, instances of suspected fraud where those charged with governance are suspected to be connected. Additionally, the auditor may be alerted by third parties to matters of importance, which in the auditor's professional judgement should be brought to the attention of management.

The management letter is a by-product of the audit and it is important that the auditor highlights to those charged with governance that the purpose of the audit was not to identify deficiencies in the audited entity's controls but to express an opinion on the financial statements. Therefore, the auditor should note that any deficiencies identified relate only to those controls reviewed as part of the audit procedures used to express an opinion on the financial statements and are not intended to be an exhaustive list of all possible control deficiencies within the entity.

When preparing the management letter, the structure should be such that it clearly outlines for management a description of each deficiency, an explanation of its *potential* effects on the client entity's financial statements and a recommendation to address the deficiency.

ISA 265, paragraph A6, outlines examples of matters that the auditor may consider for inclusion in a management letter, some of which are listed below:

- deficiencies that may lead to material misstatement in the financial statements;
- weaknesses that increase the susceptibility of the related asset or liability to loss or fraud; and
- weaknesses that are considered important to the financial reporting process (e.g. key organisational controls, or controls connected to the prevention and detection of fraud).

An example of a management letter is given at **Example 8.10** below. You can see from Appendix 1 in the example that for each control deficiency and its related risk, a remedial recommendation is included.

EXAMPLE 8.10: SAMPLE MANAGEMENT LETTER

**Morris & Co.**
**Chartered Accountants**
**Andy Place**
**Cork**

**Client reference: 56767**

**Management Letter**

**The Board of Directors**
**Dairy Fresh Ltd**
**Heath Road**
**Cork**

Under international standards on auditing, auditors are encouraged to report on 'significant deficiencies' in internal control identified during the audit that, in the auditor's professional judgement, could adversely affect the entity's ability to record, process and generate financial statements that are consistent with the management assertions.

In performing the audit of the financial statements of Dairy Fresh Ltd for the year ended 31 December 2018, we considered Dairy Fresh's internal control system in order to determine the nature, timing and extent of our audit procedures. Our consideration of internal control did not entail an in-depth study and evaluation of any of its components and was not intended for the purpose of making detailed recommendations or evaluating the adequacy of internal controls to prevent or detect all errors and irregularities.

We remind you that management is responsible for establishing and maintaining internal control. In fulfilling this responsibility, estimates and judgements by management are required to assess the expected benefits and related costs of internal control policies and procedures.

Although the purpose of our consideration of internal control was not to provide assurances thereon, matters came to our attention that in our professional opinion are of importance. These matters are noted in Appendix 1, which includes a column for your considered response.

We would be pleased to discuss the above noted matters with you and, if you have any queries or concerns, please do not hesitate to contact us.

Kind regards,

Morris & Co.

**Appendix 1**

| Control Deficiency | Risk | Recommendation | Management's Response |
|---|---|---|---|
| No authorisation required for the credit controller to perform write-offs on a customer's account. | Monies that may be collectable may be written off. | The credit controller should only be permitted to perform write-offs of insignificant amounts (these amounts should be formalised). Any significant amounts should only be written off after a member of the finance department and a member of the sales department have authorised the write-offs. Another member of the finance department should review all write-offs to ensure adequate approval was obtained. | |

## 8.11 CONCLUSION

We must remember that audit firms are profit-making organisations and, as such, wish to make a maximum return on an audit engagement, but this should never be at the expense of increasing audit risk. This means that the auditor needs to perform the audit in the most efficient and effective manner possible. The most efficient way to audit can be to take a controls approach (system-based approach). In this approach the auditor gains an understanding of the client entity's internal controls and tests those internal controls to prove that they worked consistently throughout the year and that they address the control objectives. By doing this, the auditor gains assurance over the management assertions (audit objectives) of the figures in the financial statements. This assurance allows the auditor to take a more relaxed approach with respect to substantive testing. While the auditor has increased the efficiency of the audit, the quality of the audit is in no way jeopardised.

An essential consideration for the auditor, however, is whether or not they believe the internal controls are effective. Prior to commencing controls testing, the auditor will gain sufficient understanding of the internal control environment to be able to decide if the controls documented as being in place adequately address the risks; if they are not deemed adequate, it will not be worthwhile testing them – proceeding with testing if the controls are not effective would be a waste of time and no assurance would be gained to allow reduced substantive testing.

## Summary of Learning Objectives

**Learning Objective 1** Have a detailed knowledge of what makes up the internal control system.

The *UK Corporate Governance Code* recommends that "The board should maintain sound risk management and internal control systems". COSO provides advice on the application of a strong internal control system. The internal control system comprises five components: the control environment; risk assessment; control activities; information systems; and communication and monitoring activities. Although ultimate responsibility for internal control lies with the directors, **everyone in the organisation has responsibility**.

Controls can be referred to as manual or automated, and preventative or detective. Automated and preventative controls are preferred, although the auditor recognises that, due to the complexity of business, a combination of all four will be found.

**Learning Objective 2** Appreciate the importance of the client entity's internal controls to the auditor.

The auditor is required, under ISA 330 *The Auditor's Responses to Assessed Risks*, to design and perform procedures whose nature, timing and extent are responsive to address the risk of material misstatement at the assertion level. Reviewing control systems (a) gives the auditor greater insight into the client entity's organisation and ultimately provides better knowledge on which to audit the entity; and (b) allows the auditor to perform a more efficient audit, as testing and relying on the control system will allow a reduced level of substantive testing to be performed.

**Learning Objective 3** Demonstrate a detailed knowledge of the stages involved in the review of the internal control system of the client entity by the external auditor.

There are four key stages involved in the review of controls by the auditor:
1. Identify risks and objectives within each financial cycle.
2. Ascertain the internal control system (generally by use of narratives and flowcharts).
3. Assess the internal control system – the auditor, at this stage, must decide whether it is an efficient approach to test the controls.
4. Test the controls (only if the stage 3 assessment determines it is an efficient approach; if not, the auditor will proceed to focused substantive testing).

**Learning Objective 4** Gain an understanding of the financial statement assertions (audit objectives) relative to each financial cycle.

The auditor's consideration of internal controls is intended to provide assurance over the assertions for each account balance, transaction class and disclosures in the financial statements sufficient to reduce the level of substantive testing to be performed. As such, the auditor must first understand the assertions relative to each financial cycle and ensure that controls testing addresses these assertions (audit objectives), i.e. occurrence/existence, completeness, rights and obligations, classification/recording and valuation, cut-off and presentation and disclosure.

**Learning Objective 5** Appreciate the control activities that should exist relative to each financial cycle.

Control activities generally fall into one or more of a number of categories:
- organisation controls (**OC**);
- segregation of duties (**SOD**);
- physical controls (**PC**);
- reviews and authorising (**R&A**);
- system controls (**SC**); and
- reconciliations (**R**).

While the specific control activities vary from cycle to cycle, they generally fall into one or more of the above.

**Learning Objective 6** Gain an appreciation of when it is most efficient to test controls.

The auditor should only test controls that have been assessed to be strong, either by initial review of those controls or through the performance of a walkthrough test. Testing controls that are likely to fail is an inefficient use of the auditor's time.

**Learning Objective 7** Be able to select and apply appropriate control tests to typical financial cycles, which address the management assertions (audit objectives).

The audit objective is to select and perform tests designed to establish compliance with the system controls as documented by the entity. The controls must be effective in practice and on paper. Tests of control are:
1. concerned only with those areas subject to effective controls;
2. concerned only with those controls mitigating risks and supporting audit objectives (management assertions);
3. a representative sample of transactions throughout the period; and
4. likely to cover a larger number of items than a walkthrough test.

Typical tests of controls will involve: tracing samples; checking for authorisation; testing for sequential numbering; observing control activities taking place; and confirming performance of reconciliations.

**Learning Objective 8** Explain how the auditor communicates control deficiencies to the client entity.

A management letter is sent by the auditor to those charged with governance, outlining to them significant deficiencies in internal controls that were noted while performing the audit. In the management letter the auditor will clearly outline that the purpose of the audit was to express an opinion on the financial statements and not to perform an extensive review of controls. The letter will describe each deficiency and its associated risk and recommend remedial action.

## QUESTIONS

### Self-test Questions

8.1    What is COSO?

8.2    According to COSO, who in the organisation is responsible for internal controls?

8.3    According to COSO, what are the five components of internal control?

8.4    Distinguish between detective and preventative controls.

8.5    How do controls impact on the nature, timing and extent of substantive audit procedures?

8.6    What are the stages involved in reviewing and testing controls?

8.7    Why is the decision whether or not to test controls important to the auditor?

8.8    Name six categories of control activities.

8.9    Explain the purpose of flowcharts and narratives in documenting internal control systems.

8.10   What is 'segregation of duties' and why is it important to the control of an entity?

8.11   What types of control activity should exist around completeness of revenue?

8.12   What types of control activity should exist around valuation with respect to revenue?

8.13   What is a walkthrough test?

8.14   How might the auditor test the controls around valuation of revenue?

8.15   What control activities should exist to ensure the completeness of purchases?

8.16   What key activities should be segregated in the payroll cycle?

8.17   What is the significance of an organisational chart and chart of authority with respect to the purchases function?

8.18   How might the auditor test the occurrence assertion with respect to new employees?

8.19   Name five key controls that should exist around physical inventory counts.

8.20   How might the auditor test the occurrence assertion with respect to inventory write-offs?

8.21   Name four key tests the auditor should perform when testing the bank and cash cycle.

## Review Questions

(See Suggested Solutions to Review Questions in **Appendix C.**)

### *Question 8.1*

You are the audit senior for Hart & Ryan Chartered Accountants and are currently reviewing the audit working papers for Express Ltd, which employs in excess of 1,000 staff based in sites throughout Ireland and the UK. Due to the large number of employees, the volume of leavers and joiners is generally high. You receive the following process document with respect to payroll:

**Joiners** Individual managers, on hiring a new employee, forward a 'starter form' to HR. The starter form includes the employee's name, address, PPS/NI number, phone number, bank details, department, position and salary/wage rate. On receipt, HR notes in an Excel spreadsheet the details from the form. On a weekly basis HR then forwards the list of starters to Terry, the payroll supervisor, who enters the new employees onto the payroll package. Only Terry has access to add employees.

**Leavers** Individual managers complete a 'leaver form', which includes the employee's name, date of exit and holidays outstanding, and forward it to the HR department. HR marks on its employee spreadsheet the date that the employee exited, the number of days holidays due and then forwards the form to payroll. Only Terry has access to remove employees from payroll.

### Hours worked

*Salary* – salaried employees do not have timesheets and are automatically paid the same amount each week.

*Wages* – wages are paid at an hourly rate. The individual managers record on a predefined Excel spreadsheet the following pieces of information:
- number of basic hours worked;
- number of overtime hours worked;
- commission due; and
- number of leave days taken.

James, the payroll assistant, enters all the details received by the managers into the payroll system.

Once all details are entered, Terry runs a 'gross to net report' and reviews this for anything that looks unusual. Once he is satisfied, he generates the payslips and sends the file to the bank for payment into employees' bank accounts.

Terry sends the summary payroll report to the accounts department, which uses it to reconcile to the bank and make the necessary entries into the accounting system.

The payroll system can print the following exception reports:
- new starters added that week;
- leavers exiting that week;
- number of basic hours per department (individual manager); and
- number of overtime hours per department (individual manager).

Each week Terry reviews these, signs and files them in the payroll department.

**Requirement**

(a) Identify for your assistant five weaknesses of the payroll process described above. For each of the weaknesses identified you should note the risk connected to that weakness.

(b) List the controls you believe Express Ltd should introduce to mitigate each risk identified in (a) above.

(c) For each cycle listed below, identify one test you would perform to address the noted assertion:
   (i) Revenue cycle, occurrence assertion.
  (ii) Receivables cycle, valuation assertion.
 (iii) Fixed assets cycle, existence assertion.
 (iv) Purchases cycle, completeness assertion.

## Question 8.2

You are a newly appointed Audit Senior for Auditors R Us Chartered Accountants to a long-standing client Pearl Ltd. Pearl is a well-established manufacturer and distributor of bathroom furnishings operating from one central location, which houses the head office, production and the warehouse operations.

In preparation for the interim audit, you are reviewing the minutes from the audit planning meeting. Based on your initial assessment you believe the inventory cycle to be high-risk. At the planning meeting you requested the policies and procedures around the inventory functions, including inventory count procedures and related accounting policies. Despite numerous follow-up calls, however, these are yet to be received.

From meeting with the staff you have obtained the following information:
- Pearl imports 60% of the materials required for production from China. Purchases are made four months in advance as materials may be in transit for up to three months. Inventory is accounted for on receipt.
- Pearl sells the majority of its bathroom furnishings to Bathrooms Unlimited, a large chain of home furnishings in Ireland, and recently secured a two-year contract with them to be its sole supplier of bathroom accessories. This contract was secured by offering a four-month credit period instead of the standard one month.
- Pearl operates a perpetual stock system, whereby each warehouse is divided into 15 sections and at least one section is counted at the monthly inventory count. The section to be counted is determined at random on the day of the count. By the year end, at least 12 sections will have been counted.

- The inventory count is performed by one team, comprising the warehouse supervisor and one other employee from the warehouse.
- To assist the count team, inventory descriptions and quantities as per the ERP system are noted on the count sheets.
- When a difference is noted between the physical count and the ERP system, this is noted on the count sheet for update in the ERP.
- Damaged and obsolete materials are stored in the warehouse beside useable materials and are recorded on the inventory count sheet as 'in stock and available for use'. Pearl also hold inventory for a local DIY store, and these goods are stored with the bathroom accessories.
- The warehouse is not closed for stocktaking, deliveries are made to customers and goods are accepted in the normal manner.
- The first Monday following the count, the warehouse supervisor inputs the results of the inventory count into the ERP system, taking account only of the differences previously noted on the count sheets.
- All employees have access to the warehouse at all times of the day.
- The audit senior has noted that in previous years, the auditor has not been allowed attend the year-end count.
- As a consequence of the perpetual counts, Pearl does not perform a complete physical count at the year end and, instead, uses the book stock balances to calculate the value of stock for the financial statements.

**Requirement**
(a) Identify and explain six weaknesses in Pearl's inventory cycle and provide a recommendation to address each of these weaknesses.
(b) For three of the control activities recommended in (a), identify a specific controls test that could be performed to gain assurance over the operation of those control activities, and identify one assertion the test would address.
(c) ISA 315 *Identifying and Assessing the Risks of Material Misstatement Through Understanding the Entity and its Environment* states that the auditor should use professional judgement to assess the risk of material misstatement. List two risk factors relating to inventory.

# 9

# AUDITING IN A COMPUTERISED ENVIRONMENT AND E-COMMERCE

LEARNING OBJECTIVES

Having studied this chapter on auditing in a computerised environment and e-commerce you should:

1. understand the IT audit process, and the steps that should be taken when key controls are automated;
2. understand what is meant by computer-assisted audit techniques (CAATs);
3. be able to consider the cost–benefit relationship of applying CAATs; and
4. understand the impact e-commerce and other computer technologies have on businesses and on the audit process.

KEY TERMS AND DEFINITIONS FOR THIS CHAPTER

---

**Application Controls**  An 'application' is a specific computer program, such as the payroll programme used to calculate wages and salaries. Application controls are the specific controls embedded in the application to ensure the integrity of input data, data processing and the output data. (Also known as IT application controls.)

**Enterprise Resource Planning (ERP)**  A system used by organisations to manage multiple aspects of the business.

**General IT Controls**  Those controls that support the entire IT system. If an entity's general IT controls are weak, this will impact on its **application controls.**

**Interface Controls**  Controls designed to control the transfer of data from one system to another.

**IT Controls**  The terms 'IT controls' and 'computer controls' are used interchangeably to describe controls operated by computers.

**Logical Security Controls**  Protection of computer software through the introduction of safeguards such as user identification (user name) and passwords or other authentication, firewalls or routers.

**Real Time**  Transactions that occur in 'real time' are those that are completed without any delay or requirement for manual intervention (i.e. systems that respond to inputs immediately).

**Server Room**  A room that houses mainly computer servers. Climate is one of the factors that affects the energy consumption and environmental impact of a server room and so access to this area should be restricted to maintain required levels of control.

---

## 9.1 INTRODUCTION

Discussions on audit procedures thus far have been relevant for both manual and computer-controlled environments. This chapter considers the specific advantages and disadvantages, as well as the challenges, faced by the auditor when the client entity relies on IT systems.

Whether auditing a small company or a large multinational, computers will have been used by the client entity in processing financial information (input transactions and accounting records). Small companies tend to use 'off the shelf' general accounting software to meet their requirements, while larger companies will often have bespoke (tailor-made) software to suit their needs. In many cases, these software solutions are full **enterprise resource planning (ERP)** systems, designed to cover all, or the majority of, the core functions of an enterprise.

The auditor will have to consider the role of the entity's computer/IT systems and design the audit plan to assess the relevant IT controls. Regardless of the computer systems used, the three key areas of an audit – the audit objective, audit approach and internal controls assessment – will remain largely unchanged than if the audit was being carried out in a non-computerised environment. That is:

- the **audit objective** is unchanged as the auditor must still obtain **sufficient appropriate audit evidence** to draw reasonable conclusions on which to base the **audit opinion**;
- the audit approach is unchanged as the auditor must continue to plan, assess, record and evaluate;
- the internal controls assessment is unchanged as the IT controls also need to be assessed and tested.

The normal elements of internal control discussed throughout **Chapter 8**, such as personnel, authorisation, monitoring, physical controls and appropriate segregation of duties, are just as important in a computer-controlled system as they are in a manual system.

**Section 9.2** discusses the audit approach when the client entity operates in a computerised environment, and **Section 9.3** then explains the types of control the auditor would expect to see in this environment, concentrating on general IT controls and IT application controls.

The topic of **computer-assisted audit techniques (CAATs)** is introduced in **Section 9.4** and is a key learning point of this chapter. This section describes what CAATs are and how they might be used by the auditor to perform a more efficient and effective audit. The section also discusses the key considerations of the auditor prior to adopting procedures that involve the use of CAATs.

Finally, in **Sections 9.5** and **9.6** we discuss how emerging technologies impact on the complexity of an audit and the auditor's response.

## 9.2 THE AUDIT APPROACH IN A COMPUTERISED ENVIRONMENT

Traditionally, auditors were focused on verifying that data was correctly inputted into a computer system and that the output matched the input. Often what happened **in** the computer itself was not fully assessed. This approach was called '**auditing around the computer**'. Audit activity was primarily focused on ensuring that the source documentation was processed correctly, which the auditor would verify by checking source documentation to the output documentation.

This approach is no longer relevant in many cases, where more sophisticated IT systems operate in **real time** and process a huge amount of transactions and information. In 'real time' there is less, if any, input documentation – there is no 'paper trail'. The auditor's approach now is described more as '**auditing through the computer system**'. This involves the auditor performing tests on the **IT controls** to evaluate if they are effective.

After performing these tests, if the IT controls are found to be effective then, as with the assessment of the internal control system, a reduced level of **substantive procedures testing** will be required. In evaluating the IT controls however, the complexity and the level of skill and experience required will often involve the use of IT audit specialists. With this caveat, the auditor will need to decide if reliance should be placed on IT controls. In making this decision, a first step is to assess the client entity's use of computer systems. There are three key aspects to consider:

- the extent of use of IT systems;
- the importance of the IT system to the business; and
- the complexity of the IT system.

In general, the greater the extent of the IT system used, its importance to the business and its complexity, the greater the need to assess IT controls. Furthermore, a computer system can become more complicated if there is a high degree of customisation or if it is not managed centrally.

When the auditor decides that there is a need to assess IT controls, the key focus will be to identify and evaluate the controls in place that ensure the **integrity**, **accessibility** and **confidentiality** of the data processed and stored by the computer systems. Typically, the auditor will ask:

- what controls are in place to prevent unauthorised changes to the data? (integrity);
- how accessible is the data? (accessibility); and
- what controls are available to ensure that only authorised personnel can access the data? (confidentiality).

The auditor will also need to consider some other key factors that will influence the effective application of controls within the IT system, including:

- Whether processing is **centralised** or **decentralised**:
    - in centralised systems, where several processes, such as wages, sales and purchases, etc. are processed in the same computerised environment in one location, the auditor may opt to identify a small number of controls that will provide assurance over several areas of the entity's accounting system;
    - in a decentralised environment there is often an increased level of effort required to identify and evaluate the controls in place.
- The **complexity** and **level of customisation** of the IT system – in less complex systems the auditor may find that identifying and evaluating key controls requires fewer resources.
- The availability of skilled and experienced audit staff – testing IT controls requires members of the audit team to be appropriately trained and technically competent.

All of the above considerations will help the auditor to decide whether or not it is efficient to test the IT system controls. If the initial assessment is that the IT system is an integral part of the controls in the client entity, and that the auditor has sufficiently skilled audit staff to handle the complexities of the IT system in place, then they may decide to rely on those IT system controls to reduce the level of substantive testing to be performed on the financial statements.

## 9.3  CONTROLS IN A COMPUTERISED ENVIRONMENT

### Introduction

When discussing IT controls it is important to remember that they are a sub-set of the entity's overall internal control system, as discussed in **Chapter 8**. The need for the auditor to understand the client entity's controls, and specifically how it responds to risks arising from IT, is expressed in ISA 315, paragraph 21, and the relevant application paragraphs.

FIGURE 9.1: INTERNAL CONTROL SYSTEM AND IT SYSTEM COMPONENTS

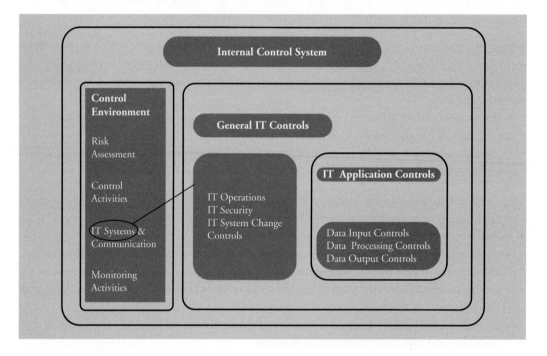

**Figure 9.1** below shows the internal control system and the supporting role of the IT system within it.

There are two categories of IT controls:

1. **General IT controls** are controls over the environment in which the computer system operates. Broadly speaking, these types of controls include organisational controls, systems development controls, maintenance controls, access controls and other general controls.
2. **Application controls** are in place to ensure the accuracy and completeness of data input controls, data processing controls and data output controls. They are designed to detect errors before, during and after the processing of specific types of transaction.

Once it has been decided that it is worthwhile to assess the IT controls, the auditor will first evaluate the general IT controls. If the auditor considers the general controls to be weak, there is little to be gained from assessing the application controls – the IT system is already found to be compromised – and a wholly substantive approach would be considered. Strong general IT controls will provide some assurance that it is worthwhile to continue to assess the application controls.

Before we move on to discuss general and application controls in more detail, we must consider the types of control within the context of the computerised environment. We have noted that IT controls are a part of the overall internal control system, and in **Chapter 8** we discussed controls as being **preventative**, **detective** or **corrective**. IT controls can be classified in the same way (see **Example 9.1**).

Preventative controls are considered to be the strongest type of control as they avoid errors from occurring in the first place.

EXAMPLE 9.1: PREVENTION, DETECTION AND CORRECTION CONTROLS

- **Preventative control** – when a new employee joins the entity, access is not granted to the IT system without authorisation from the line manager.
- **Detective control** – once a month, the IT manager should review the list of individuals with IT access and compare it to an active employee report.
- **Corrective control** – unnecessary IT access is regularly reviewed and removed.

## General IT Controls

As set out above, the key audit objective when reviewing general client entity's IT controls is to ensure that the integrity, accessibility and confidentiality of the data are appropriately controlled. In order to meet this objective, the auditor will look to identify and test relevant control activities under each of the general IT control categories as follows:
- IT operations;
- IT security; and
- IT system change controls.

### IT Operations

IT operations refers to the processes associated with management of the client entity's IT service, which should aim to deliver an IT system that has the right fit for the entity and operates effectively. IT service management activities can include the introduction of:
- **Interface Controls** As part of this control, measures should be in place to monitor data flows between systems to ensure that interfaces operate as intended. The auditor should also look to review any procedures that the client entity has in place to identify and remediate data flows that fail to operate correctly.
- **Operator Controls** Under this category, responsibility for scheduling and monitoring operational tasks should be divided between employees (always giving consideration to segregation of duty requirements). Additionally, the client entity should ensure that adequate operators are in place to sufficiently meet the required workload.

- **Standby Facilities** In case of unforeseen or catastrophic events that cause the normal place of business or business processes to become unworkable, the entity should make appropriate arrangements to ensure business continuity and security. This may involve arrangements with third parties, such as specialist service providers, and flexible working arrangements.

## IT Security

IT security is a level of security applied to computers and networks. It incorporates any level of security applied to the protection of:
- the computer equipment,
- information contained within the IT systems, or
- services associated with the IT system,

from unauthorised access, unauthorised change or destruction. IT security can include:
- **Logical Access Controls** Computer systems should be secured with the use of passwords and other suitable security parameters. These measures should be regularly reviewed to ensure that they remain effective.
- **User Access Management** Organisations should ensure that appropriate controls are in place to govern access to their computer systems. In particular, a process should be established to ensure that sufficient user access management controls are in place, i.e. that the granting of user access is appropriately approved and that accounts are removed when staff leave employment or change roles. Furthermore, access levels should reflect the role of the user, with the necessary segregation of duty rules in mind. Fore example, an accounts receivable clerk should only have access to view and edit customer account transactions.
- **System Security** This control deals with making sure that antivirus software is up-to-date, and that there is adequate protection for the system through use of firewalls, etc. Entities should ensure that all employees who use the systems are provided with guidance and policies in relation to the use of e-mails, internet access and other business tools. System security also encompasses the management of the **server room** (see **Section 9.6**).
- **Physical Security** In addition to good logical security settings, entities should also ensure that physical access to their computer systems is appropriately restricted, particularly with respect to the server room, where even the climate is of key importance to the operational effectiveness of the computer systems; therefore strict physical access controls are essential.
- **Data Centres** The use of external contractors to store and manage an organisation's data is a feature of cloud computing (see **Section 9.6**).

## IT System Change Controls

IT system changes can include items such as software acquisition, regular maintenance and replacement and program changes. It is essential that changes to the IT environment are regulated to ensure that they do not compromise existing computerised controls or, in themselves, prove inadequate in controlling the entity's data. As such, the following should be considered when making any changes to the IT system controls.
- **Systems Development Controls** These controls relate to the development of the IT system. There should be controls to ensure that users' needs are addressed and that

all system changes are approved. Typically, this will involve co-ordination between users and management, and experts who will be implementing and developing the computer system. All changes to the IT system should be authorised by management.

- **System Change Documentation** There should be adequate documentation of the system, which usually consists of either flowcharts or narrative descriptions, or a combination of both. For all system changes, there should also exist examples of input documentation and output documentation. Details on organisation charts, job descriptions for personnel, details of the system hardware and the location of equipment on the premises should also be included to ensure that a clear understanding of the change is communicated.

- **System Change Testing and Training** There should also be adequate testing and training. Individual programs should be tested to ensure that they are working properly, typically involving the use of test data. This also involves the testing of the actual hardware in the system to ensure that it is functioning properly. All staff should have adequate system training to perform their role satisfactorily. Additionally, there should be a process for user acceptance (i.e. a process whereby the employee acknowledges receipt of training and accepts that the applications being implemented are sufficient for them to carry out their tasks).

  Both during and following the initial development of the system, responsible employees in a department should be identified as 'superusers' (experts in the system's operations as it affects their department) and given in-depth training. Superusers are responsible for ensuring user requirements are fully met by the system implementation and provide ongoing support and advice to other users on the processes and best practice of the new system.

- **Segregation of Duties** This is a very basic internal control to ensure that there is adequate segregation between systems maintenance, operators, data preparation and the end users' department. Segregation of duties is particularly important in ensuring that those who are responsible for making changes to IT systems and developing IT systems do not have access to the production or live systems.

- **File Controls** These controls will ensure that only correct files are taken for processing, that files are maintained in a library and only given to authorised persons. Electronic files should also be properly labelled, and logged in and out from the library.

## Application Controls

Application controls comprise three groups of controls, namely:
- data input controls;
- data processing controls; and
- data output controls.

These controls support the general IT controls and, in turn, contribute to a strong system of internal control. They provide the auditor with assurance that the recording, processing and reports generated by the computer system are performed properly. Unlike general controls, application controls are specific to particular IT applications and generally operate differently for each application. For example, the application controls within the payroll software will differ from those in the purchasing system or the revenue system.

Set out below in **Figure 9.2** is a summary of the type of controls expected at each stage in the data processing cycle.

FIGURE 9.2: COMPUTERISED ENVIRONMENT CONTROLS

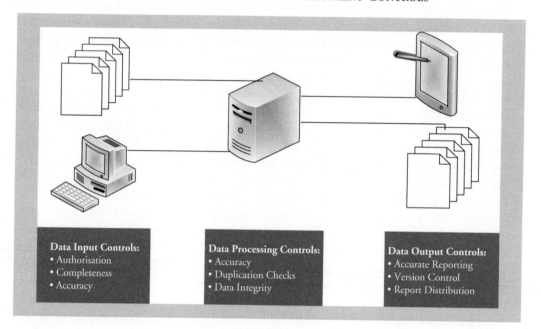

**Data Input Controls:**
- Authorisation
- Completeness
- Accuracy

**Data Processing Controls:**
- Accuracy
- Duplication Checks
- Data Integrity

**Data Output Controls:**
- Accurate Reporting
- Version Control
- Report Distribution

### Data Input Controls

Input controls are extremely important as it is at the input stage that many errors occur. The controls are designed to ensure that the input data has been authorised correctly, is complete, and is accurate. If input errors are detected by the IT system, these need to be reviewed, corrected and resubmitted for inputting.

Approval workflows are often embedded into the computer environment, whereby a request for approval is raised in the system and the system, using preconfigured approval criteria, routes the document to the individual in the organisation permitted to approve this type of transaction.

### Authorisation

Each transaction should be properly authorised in accordance with management's instructions and general rules. Authorisation can occur, and be evidenced, in a number of ways. Automated (system) authorisation is often based on passwords and restricted access to perform certain tasks. **Example 9.2** compares automated authorisation to manual approval.

EXAMPLE 9.2: MANUAL VERSUS AUTOMATED AUTHORISATION

The credit controller has put an outstanding customer balance out to a debt-collection agency, which advises that the customer has gone into liquidation and no money is available to ordinary creditors. According to company policy, all bad debt write-offs should be approved by the head of sales and the CFO.

**Manual Approval** – the credit controller completes a manual bad debt write-off form, which is presented to the head of sales and CFO for physical sign-off. The credit controller then presents the approved form to the designated accounts receivable clerk, who applies the write-off to the customer's account on the system. Monthly, the credit controller compares the actual bad debts written off in the system to the approvals authorised by her, to ensure each write-off is complete, accurate and valid.

**Automated Approval** – the credit controller raises a bad debt request directly in the system. The system is configured to route the document to the head of sales and the CFO for approval. On log-in to the computer system, the head of sales and CFO are advised of a pending approval. Once both IT automated computerised approvals have been obtained, the bad debt write-off is automatically applied to the customer's account.

Clearly, the IT automated computerised approval: (a) reduces the number of steps involved in the process and so is more efficient; and (b) operates using all automated preventative controls, making it overall a more reliable process.

## Data Accuracy and Completeness

Some specific controls to ensure that the data being inputted is complete and correct are shown below in **Table 9.1**.

TABLE 9.1: DATA INPUT CONTROLS – ACCURACY AND COMPLETENESS

| Control Name | Explanation | Example |
|---|---|---|
| **Control Totals** | Also known as 'batch check' totals, they are the number of documents or records to be processed. | A payroll clerk counts the number of overtime records to be entered and compares this to the actual number of overtime records inputted to the system. |
| **Hash Totals** | Computed by adding together values that would not typically be added together, e.g. employee numbers, inventory code numbers, etc. Hash totals are only used for the purpose of control. | Employee numbers are totalled before and after a payroll run in order to confirm that no employee records are missing or incorrectly added. |

| | | |
|---|---|---|
| **Editing Checks** | Controls intended to detect incorrect, unreasonable or incomplete data. They include:<br>• **Key verification** – fields are restricted to certain data types. | **Key verification** Dates must be entered in a specified format to avoid any incorrect data.<br>When processing invoices, complete customer account codes, stock quotes, quantities, etc. are required. |
| | • **Missing data check** – ensures all data is inputted and that no fields are missing. | **Missing data check** If any fields are empty the input will be rejected for further review and follow-up. For example, you cannot complete an order without entering in the quantity of inventory. |
| | • **Check digit verification** Account numbers are verified using a predetermined mathematical calculation and matched to a check digit contained within the number. If it matches the check digit, the account number will be accepted as being a valid entry. | **Check digit verification** Examples include credit card numbers, which include a check digit in order to recognise valid credit card numbers. |
| **Sequence Checks** | Checks sequentially numbered documents to ensure that there are no missing or duplicate sequence numbers. | Credit notes are processed in sequence and missing and duplicate sequence numbers are investigated. |

## Data Processing Controls

Processing controls are designed to provide **reasonable assurance** that the computer processes have been performed as intended. They ensure that the transactions are not duplicated or lost or improperly changed in any way and that errors are identified and corrected on a timely basis.

These controls include the following.
• **Reasonableness checks** A reasonableness check will ensure that the item is reasonable, e.g. if customers usually order no more than six to eight items of a typical inventory item, and if the processed order is for more than eight items, the computer will flag the order for follow-up to ensure it is genuine and for a valid quantity.
• **Naming conventions** All files should follow a standard naming convention so that only the correctly named files are used in processing. For example, the file name may be matched to the operator's instructions before processing can start.
• **Before and after report** This report will show the number of accounts that should be updated and the actual number of accounts that were updated. For example, if deliveries

were made to 100 different customers, the report will also show that 100 customer accounts were updated with invoices.

- **Control totals**   The computer checks that the sum of the totals of the input documents for each run matches the total processed amount in that run.

### Data Output Controls

Data output (reporting) controls are designed to ensure that the processing has been correctly carried out, and the output reports are then distributed to authorised personnel only. These controls include:

- **Visual scanning** – this involves reading and scanning to see if the output looks reasonable, and could involve comparing actual results with estimated results and/or source documents being matched to output reports on a sample basis.
- **Reconciliation** – this involves the output totals being matched to input totals and processing totals by the various relevant departments within the organisation, for example, the user department and the computer department.

## 9.4 COMPUTER-ASSISTED AUDIT TECHNIQUES (CAATs)

### Introduction

The use of computers and computer software, referred to as computer-assisted audit techniques (CAATs), is now commonplace in an audit of financial statements. In fact, it would be impractical to consider performing an audit without using CAATs to some degree. The information to be audited will be held by the client entity in electronic format and the sheer volume of transactions make CAATs an essential tool for the auditor to achieve the audit objective in the most effective and efficient manner.

Regardless of whether or not the auditor decides to test relevant IT controls, the client entity's IT systems can be used to support the testing of other areas of the audit. CAATs can impact on the audit procedures in two ways:

1. the auditor may wish to test the IT system controls to reduce the level of substantive testing; and
2. even if the IT system controls are not relied upon, the IT applications (whether the client entity's internal applications or the use of external audit software) will be used in performing focused substantive procedures. **Figure 9.3** below depicts this concept.

CAATs can be used to support the audit in a wide range of areas. For example, if there is a large volume of data CAATs provide a more comprehensive audit than the traditional methods of sampling or analytical review. Without CAATs, the auditor would have to select a sample of transactions for review; however, CAATs will allow for much greater coverage and, in many cases, even 100% coverage. CAATs can even support the sample selection process by assisting with statistical sampling methods. The auditor, however, must consider the cost–benefit of using CAATs.

FIGURE 9.3: AUDIT TESTING IN A COMPUTERISED ENVIRONMENT

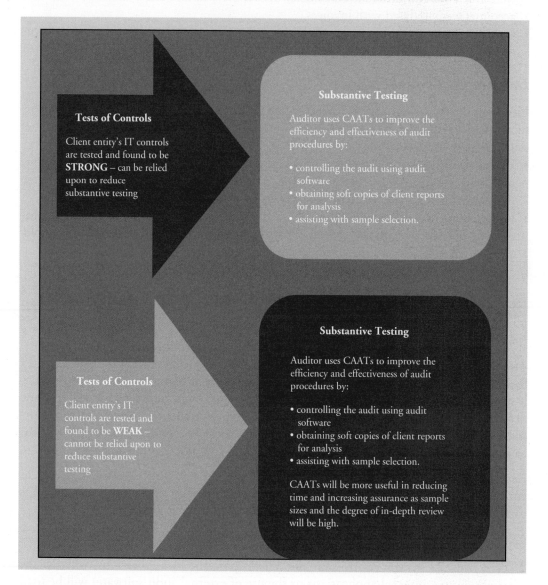

## Types of CAATs

CAATs can be categorised into four broad categories:
1. network security evaluation software/utilities;
2. operating system (OS) and database management systems (DBMS) security evaluation software/utilities;
3. software and code-testing tools; and
4. data analysis software – software used to analyse 'big data' reports to identify trends, errors, fraud, etc.

**Network security evaluation software** allows the auditor to detect network performance issues. When assessing an entity's security controls, the auditor is interested in:
- scanning the client entity's 'firewalls' to identify open ports;
- penetration testing (identifying and reporting on noted vulnerabilities found in the client entity's operating systems).

**OS and DBMS evaluation software** – all laptops, desktops, etc. run operating system software, e.g. Microsoft Office, and DBMS refers to software that handles the storage, retrieval and updating of data in a computer system. DBMS evaluation software is usually embedded software, whereby the database operation produces an audit trail of information (e.g. who performed an operation, what database object was impacted and when).

**Software and code-testing tools** are run to identify software bugs. They validate and verify that a software product meets the business and technical requirements that guided its development and design.

**Data analysis software** is the most commonly used CAAT as it allows the auditor to extract data from commonly used file formats and the tables of most database systems and therefore can be used during the audits of almost any application on any technology platform. The data software allows the auditor to perform a variety of queries and analysis on the imported data. ACL is a commonly used data extraction and analysis software system. The analysis allows the auditor to quickly identify irregularities or patterns in transactions that could be an indicator of fraud or error, or of a control deficiency.

Some features of data analysis software include:
- data queries;
- data stratification;
- sample extractions;
- missing sequence identification;
- combining/joining files and tables for further analysis;
- comparison of data from two different sources;
- statistical analysis and calculations.

EXAMPLE 9.3: USE OF DATA ANALYSIS SOFTWARE

The auditor has extracted the client entity's trade receivables listing and uploaded it to an audit software package, such as ACL. In the software, the contents of each column heading are defined as:

| [Column 1] | [Column 2] | [Column 3] | [Column 4] |
|---|---|---|---|
| Customer name | Invoice date | Invoice number | Invoice value |

The audit software reads the file and applies a number of predefined tests, generating reports highlighting key risk areas. This might include:

- the total value of the file, i.e. trade receivables;
- customers with negative balances (credit balances);
- customers with significantly aged invoices;
- those customers owing the most;
- those customers owing significantly less than in the prior year (if prior year's report was also uploaded).

The auditor, rather than manually totting the file and preparing these reports, can instead use their time for analysis and focus on risk – which is a much more effective use of their time.

## Cost versus Benefit

Typically, interrogative software, audit-specific software or bespoke CAATs are expensive to set up in the first year of the audit, but are far more cost-effective and efficient in the long run as they can be used on future audits (usually with only minor modifications). A key consideration for the auditor is the level of planning and preparation required, as it is critical that the use of CAATs is fully planned so that the software application used is correctly configured to conduct the necessary tests.

The **benefits** associated with CAATs generally far outweigh any cost and include:

- Can be used in the **assessment of the client entity's IT environment**. Audit software tools can be run to find various parameter settings that influence a client's security, which can then be compared against the entity's predefined security policy.
- Can **test the entire population**, or a much greater part of the population than would be feasible using a manual sampling approach.
- Common tests can be designed and programmed so that they can be **repeated within the same audit entity or across the audits of different entities** and thus increase audit efficiency.
- The use of data analysis tools allows **scrutiny of transactions** and concentrated attention on erroneous and exceptional transactions, even when data volumes are very large. This can be done in a fraction of the time required for manual methods.
- Audit software can offer the auditor a **uniform**, **user-friendly interface** for performing audit testing, regardless of the data formats presented by the client entity's applications.
- The audit software can **record exceptions existing in the audit process**, such as unreviewed work, missing tests, etc. Additionally, advanced features of audit software can allow for certain routines (macros) to be programmed and therefore further improve audit effectiveness and efficiency.
- **Attack and penetration testing** can be performed by the auditor (particularly in an e-commerce environment) to detect vulnerabilities in networks.

## Other Considerations in Using CAATs

In addition to carrying out a cost–benefit analysis, the auditor should also consider the following before using CAATs.

### 1. Maintaining Necessary Expertise

The auditor must consider the level of expertise needed within the audit team to perform the audit. While audit software offers many features, it cannot perform the audit on its own and relies on the inputs of the auditor in the same way that any computer system does. The designing of tests requires strong audit skills along with strong knowledge of the client entity, as well as expertise with the audit software.

### 2. Availability of the Necessary Information in a Useable Format

The auditor will need to inquire as to the downloadable formats available from the client entity to ensure that they can be used by the audit software or other application being used by the auditor. However, it should be noted that most audit software packages can handle data in multiple formats and in most circumstances the software can be configured to handle available data.

### 3. Maintaining Sound Audit Software

Like any system implementation, the introduction of audit software is not without its complications. The client entity's IT staff may be reluctant to allow the auditor permission to access the source data, being concerned that the audit software may interfere with the IT system. This is a valid concern for any IT department and the auditor needs to be confident that they have carried out the necessary testing and training on the audit software to minimise the risk of contaminating the client entity's IT system.

One common solution is for the auditor to work on a copy of the data instead of working in the 'live' system, which greatly reduces the risk that data is contaminated and the risk of inadvertent changes to the client entity's IT system and/or data. Once implemented and operational, audit software, similar to any IT environment, will require maintenance and will change management procedures to ensure it can be used year after year.

## Substantive Testing

If the auditor determines:
- that the benefit of using CAATs outweighs the cost;
- that the audit team has the necessary up-to-date expertise to use CAATs;
- that the client's environment and reports are suitable for CAATs; and
- if applicable, that they maintain sound audit software,

then significant efficiencies can be achieved by using CAATs to assist with substantive testing.

In **substantive testing**, the auditor is trying to verify the truth and fairness of transactions and balances (completeness, accuracy, etc.) in the financial statements (see **Chapter 4**).

The amount of substantive testing that the auditor will perform will depend upon the results of the **tests of controls**. Where controls have been found to be ineffective or have not been tested, a greater level of substantive testing will be necessary.

There is a variety of ways in which CAATs can be used to support the audit approach and in this section we will discuss various types of substantive procedures that an auditor can perform using CAATs. For instance, in the audit of receivables, the auditor can extract a sample to be circularised and configure the program to print out the confirmation letters with the addresses and balances to be confirmed (e.g. mail merge). The use of appropriate software provides the auditor with the ability to select a sample using an appropriate statistical approach, such as **monetary unit sampling** (MUS). (See also **Chapter 6**, Section 6.8.)

The CAATs software can also be configured to search for unusual items, such as large and unusual balances or credit balances in the receivables balances. Other tests might include totalling the accounts receivable ledger and comparing it to the balance on the receivables account in the general ledger. In the review of receivables, the auditors may also use the audit software to *age* the receivables listing in order to help identify possible bad debts.

In the audit of payroll, the program could be used to recalculate the payroll cost for the year, which could then be agreed to the general ledger. It could identify employees who might have worked excessive hours for further follow-up by the auditor.

Some further examples of specific uses of CAATs in various financial cycles are provided below in **Figure 9.4**.

FIGURE 9.4: SPECIFIC USES OF CAATS – FURTHER EXAMPLES

| Inventory | Non-current Fixed Assets | Purchases and Payroll |
|---|---|---|
| • Testing overhead allocations.<br><br>• Checking the mathematical accuracy of the inventory records by multiplying the cost by the quantity.<br><br>• Adding the total values of inventory items to come up with a total value of inventory included in the financial statements.<br><br>• Identifying slow-moving items by comparing to sales records. | • Analysing assets by different classes.<br><br>• Reperforming depreciation calculations to ensure that they have been correctly calculated.<br><br>• Verifying the mathematical accuracy of different asset classes and agreeing to the financial statements.<br><br>• Selecting a sample of additions during the year for further testing.<br><br>• Selecting a sample from the repairs and maintenance account for further testing to ensure that those items should not have been capitalised. | • Comparison of goods received with purchases orders as part of cut-off testing.<br><br>• Identify any large or unusual purchases.<br><br>• Identify any employees who are also suppliers.<br><br>• Stratify purchases by month to detect unusual patterns.<br><br>• Comparison of employees' bank account details to suppliers' bank account details.<br><br>• Interrogate purchases nominal to identify potential duplicate payments (e.g. same supplier, same amount, same invoice date). |

## 9.5 E-COMMERCE

### Introduction

Electronic commerce, or 'e-commerce', is the use of information systems and networks (such as the internet) to conduct buying or selling activities. It has been one of the most significant business growth areas in recent years and it continues to expand and be an important source of business for many organisations.

A company selling products on its website is a commonly observed example of e-commerce. Other 'business-to-consumer' (B2C) examples of e-commerce include online banking, online booking systems and online advertising. In recent years, mobile technology is increasingly being used for e-commerce.

Many organisations also engage in 'business-to-business' (B2B) e-commerce. In addition to the examples given above, B2B e-commerce activities can also include electronic supply-chain management and electronic invoicing. For example, businesses may electronically submit orders to a supplier for goods, track fulfilment of their order and check the goods into inventory when they are delivered.

Key technology components of e-commerce are:
- websites or web applications;
- infrastructure (databases and servers) hosting web applications;
- browsers;
- networks (World Wide Web, wide-area networks and virtual private networks); and
- electronic funds transfer (EFT).

### Considerations

When auditing a client entity that is involved in e-commerce, there are a number of important factors that the auditor should consider.
- **Complexity**  In an online environment it is very likely that transactions will be much more complex than in a business that only engages in traditional trading techniques. The auditor will need to ensure they are fully aware of the transaction flows in order to identify relevant risks and controls. They will also need to consider the existence of mobile technology-enabled trading. An overview of the complexity of the network environment can usually be depicted as a 'network topology', which shows the layout of connected devices in a network.
- **Volume**  For many e-commerce-enabled businesses, the volume of transactions is higher than traditional business channels. This can pose several difficulties for the auditor and may demand the use of CAATs or some such automated techniques in order to ensure appropriate coverage of the population.
- **Transaction Speed**  In addition to the high volume of transactions, in the online environment transactions tend to be fully automated and completed in real time or at high speed. This usually means that the opportunity for manual intervention is limited, and controls must be fully automated. The auditor must rely on automated controls in order to obtain sufficient assurance.

- **Security** In an online environment, the need for appropriate security is vitally important. An e-commerce-enabled website is equivalent to a shop and should be secured appropriately. Businesses will typically be responsible for collecting sensitive information, such as credit card numbers and personal details, and will need to ensure that these are not lost or accessed by intruders. The internet is fundamentally insecure and, in addition to its responsibilities to its customers, the auditor will also need to ensure that the client entity has protected its own information assets.
- **Third Parties** In the e-commerce environment, there is increased use of third parties as outsourced partners to support the business. For example, many organisations rely on third parties to process payments on their behalf. In addition to considering the controls and practices at the client entity, the auditor may also need to understand and review the controls in place at relevant third-party organisations.
- **Systems Resilience** For many e-commerce organisations, the online channels of selling and purchasing are core to their business activities. A website being offline for a period of time is equivalent to a traditional organisation being forced to close a shop. Where systems stability issues exist, auditors should consider the impact that this will have on the client entity. Client entities that are reliant on technology must have appropriate disaster recovery and business continuity plans in place.

### Auditing in an e-commerce Environment

The approach taken to performing an audit of an entity that uses e-commerce is very similar to a standard IT audit approach. The primary difference is that the elements of the client entity's IT environment are accessed by external parties (customers, suppliers and other business partners). Rather than just facilitating and supporting the entity's business processes, these elements are core components.

When conducting the audit of an entity that uses e-commerce, the steps outlined below should be considered by the auditor.

- **Map Flow of Transactions and Data** E-commerce can increase the complexity of processes, so in order to identify key risks and controls, auditors should consider using process or data flow diagrams to map the flow of transactions.
- **General IT Controls** Testing of general IT controls, as described above, should be completed for applications and infrastructures. Interfaces from externally facing websites and internal systems should be tested to obtain assurance that all data transferred is complete and accurate and cannot be intercepted.
- **Application Controls** Data input controls (described above) are typical of the application controls that should be tested as part of an e-commerce audit.
- **Network Controls** With e-commerce, as key elements of the IT environment are externally facing, the auditor should consider engaging the services of information security technical specialists to perform a penetration test of websites and mobile applications. A penetration test is where the actions of a computer hacker are simulated in order to identify security vulnerabilities or weaknesses. Firewalls are used by organisations to separate external internet traffic from internal network traffic. The firewalls in place between externally facing technology and other internal systems are key controls. The processes in place for managing firewall rules should be tested as part of an e-commerce audit.

### Electronic Data Interchange (EDI)

Electronic data interchange (EDI) is a system often used to support B2B e-commerce by facilitating the transmission of data between partner organisations. Data files (such as orders or invoices) are exported from the business applications systems used by the organisation, translated into a pre-agreed standardised format and uploaded to a value-added network (VAN) used by the group of business partners. A number of checks can be performed on the files being transmitted, including: field validation (to confirm, for example, that alphabetic characters are not included in a numeric field, such as a phone number); order number sequence checks; duplication checks; and delivery checks.

When auditing a company that is involved in EDI, there are some important factors that the auditor should consider.

- **Lack of a 'paper trail'** Electronic data exchange results in the reduction of a paper trail, or 'hard copy' documentation, which means the auditor must test the controls of the system to gain sufficient appropriate audit evidence. It is unlikely, due to the large volume of transactions, that every transaction can be audited; thus, the auditor tests the internal controls to identify the possibility of instigating unauthorised transactions.
- **Uncontrolled changes** Uncontrolled changes could be ruinous to any system using electronic data exchange because of the absence of an adequate paper trail and, therefore, no physical document examination by management. The very characteristics that make EDI appealing because of improved efficiencies cause the auditor concern if the audited entity has not established effective controls over the whole EDI system. Auditors may seek to establish whether all changes have been authorised by management and that there is a paper trail of all changes, which has been inspected by management. If the auditor detects any evidence that uncontrolled changes have taken place, it might warrant a letter to management to advise them that any uncontrolled changes can impact on the financial information.

## 9.6  RECENT AND EMERGING COMPUTING TECHNOLOGIES

### Introduction

The use of computers has grown exponentially over the last two decades and the auditor is constantly facing new challenges with regard to its evolution, but also constantly finding more ways of managing risk as a result of the benefits it brings. Below we will take a look at some of the more recent and emerging technologies that offer the client entity and the auditor a host of new ways of doing business and managing risk – as well as posing new risks, which must be controlled in a new way.

### Cloud Computing

Cloud computing enables distribution of computing tasks to a shared pool of resources, which can be accessed quickly with a minimal amount of effort for management. Cloud computing provides easy access to information systems services by combining information systems infrastructure and applications that can be retrieved through the internet. This avoids the need for an entity to operate a **server room**. The server room houses the IT system's physical servers, which are usually stored on racks, and the power source to operate the servers. The servers are the operational hub that the IT system runs on, and they contain all of an entity's data. Specialised IT expertise is required to manage the server room, from ensuring an uninterrupted power supply, appropriate fire-suppression systems and air conditioning, to the consideration of back-up data and cybersecurity to prevent unauthorised access to sensitive data. The server room requires various controls (e.g. physical to restrict access) and also presents risks, such as loss of data, data breaches (cybercrime) or business continuity if there is a system failure. For these reasons, more organisations are opting for cloud computing.

Cloud computing requires **data centres**, specialist businesses that store and manage data on behalf of their clients and make it available to them via 'the cloud'. They are experts in data management, as opposed to an entity that manages its own data as part of its day-to-day operations. There are five essential characteristics of cloud computing, as shown in **Figure 9.5** below and discussed in detail thereafter.

FIGURE 9.5: FIVE CHARACTERISTICS OF CLOUD COMPUTING

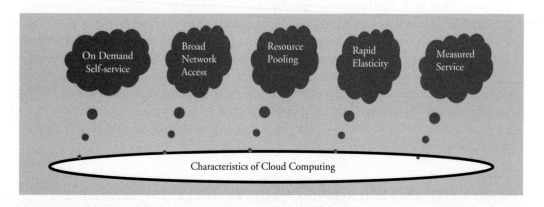

**On Demand Self-service** This is the availability of cloud services on demand. The users can individually access services at times convenient to them. In such an environment, the user accesses the cloud services in question via an online control panel.

**Broad Network Access** Services are accessible via the internet through a range of platforms, such as laptops, smartphones and personal digital assistants (PDAs (tablets)).

**Resource Pooling** The provider pools resources to serve multiple clients, which are configured to meet clients' individual needs.

**Rapid Elasticity** The provider can swiftly scale up and rapidly release services and resources.

**Measured Service** The use of resources by clients can be monitored, controlled and reported on by the provider.

## *Audit Considerations*

When auditing an entity that uses cloud computing there are three important factors that the auditor should consider.

1. **Access** The auditor should test the controls used by the entity to restrict access to authorised individuals only, and consider how management uses authentication and authorisation methods to control access (e.g. if management uses passwords, the auditor must consider who controls the issuing of the passwords, how often they are reset and how strong the passwords are).

2. **Data Protection** The auditor must consider if a breach in data protection has occurred, and whether that breach affected the client entity's financial performance, its reputation and whether the breach impacted on regulatory requirements. The auditor will examine the policies and procedures developed by the client to protect data stored by a third party.

3. **Technology Risks** Due to technologies constantly evolving, with a lack of standardised rules in how they should integrate, the auditor must consider if the client entity's technology has become obsolete or if it requires substantial investment to be updated. The auditor must also consider management's use of monitoring tools and the use of period back-ups. There is no right or wrong decision when it comes to cloud computing, there are 'pros and cons' to managing data through a self-managed server room or through the cloud.

## Blockchain Technology

Blockchain is probably the most talked about technology in the world of accounting and audit right now. It is a continuously growing list of data where each transaction (a 'block') contains a cryptographic hash of the previous transaction, including a date stamp, thereby making it inherently resistant to modification. Once a transaction is recorded, the data cannot be amended without amending all subsequent transactions. This provides a method for firms to securely collect information. Considering the level of corporate fraud over the last few decades, blockchain offers a new technology on which to base accounting software, making it more resilient against unauthorised changes. This in turn reduces the risk of material misstatement and therefore reduces audit risk. It has been argued that such technology may, in the future, reduce the need for the auditor at all. In the short-term at least, it will allow for more automation of audits, with the auditor less likely to need to spend weeks on site at a client entity's premises.

Blockchain offers an automated audit of all transactions, and all transactions are authenticated, or 'notarised', as one company transacts with another. While the science behind the technology may be lost on the typical auditor, it is essential that they understand how it can benefit their processes as well as the wider profession. These technologies will allow the auditor spend less time finding anomalies and more time asking what the anomaly is related to: fraud, error, or just an unusual factor of the client entity's business. Blockchain provides standardisation, which in turn permits the auditor to test a larger percentage of the population automatically – improving the effectiveness and efficiency of the audit.

The technology is still in its infancy and its potential is far-reaching, offering benefits in the form of reduced risk and increased efficiencies to the auditor, but also increased threats to the accounting and auditing profession as the world of technology continues to replace many tasks traditionally performed by the accountant and auditor.

### Artificial Intelligence

Artificial intelligence (AI) is also seen as a threat to the accounting and auditing profession as it advances evermore into the routine tasks of the accountant. Blockchain and AI are seen by some as the greatest advancements in accounting since Luca Pacioli invented double-entry bookkeeping nearly 525 years ago.

When it comes to AI, Google believes that robots will achieve human intelligence levels by 2029. However, in reality the majority of the tasks performed (or to be performed) by AI will surround the more repetitive or tedious tasks and, although this would remove some profitable revenue streams from accounting firms, it should leave them in a better position to move towards a more advisory and value-adding role.

AI operates based on predefined rules, examples and circumstances to which it is exposed, however it cannot always provide context to a situation. It is fair to say that the traditional roles of trainee accountants or accounting technicians in industry are likely to be taken over by AI. Functions such as accounts receivable and payable transactions and processes could be adequately performed by AI. However, this only makes it all the more important that the 'basics' of accounting are not forgotten and that the accountants and auditors of the future understand the route of transactions and do not become complacent or reliant on the power of technology to get it perfect every time. Doing so would eliminate what sets them aside from AI, which is their ability to apply **professional scepticism** – the human sense that something doesn't add up, which isn't always a tangible factor.

## 9.7 CONCLUSION

In this chapter we have seen that auditing in a computerised environment is very similar to auditing in a manual environment in that the auditor still needs to obtain sufficient and appropriate audit evidence to support his opinion.

Though the basic approach is very similar, the auditor will have to ensure that staff are properly trained and have the knowledge to be able to audit in a computerised environment.

The nature of the tests, i.e. **tests of controls** and **substantive tests**, is also similar to performing an audit in a non-computerised environment. The major difference is that the auditor uses CAATs in performing tests, in both tests of controls and substantive tests.

The world of computer technology has resulted in the auditor having to constantly adapt their audit procedures to take into account: new risks posed by the client entity's use of emerging technologies (such as EDI or cloud computing); improved control environments within the client entity as a result of emerging technologies (such as blockchain); new audit-enhancing software that is improving the effective and efficient approach to audit and therefore improving the quality and profitability of audit engagements.

As with many industries, technology (and artificial intelligence in particular) is changing the face of accounting and auditing. This offers enhancements to the profession as well as threats to its profitable revenue streams. The auditor will have to embrace all it has to offer and at the same time find ways to add value to a client entity that AI will struggle to replicate.

## SUMMARY OF LEARNING OBJECTIVES

**Learning Objective 1** Understand the IT audit process, and the steps that should be taken when key controls are automated.

Organisations are reliant on IT systems. Systems can vary in size and complexity, from 'off-the-shelf' accounting systems to customised **ERP** systems. The auditor will be required to consider the extent, importance and complexity of the client entity's IT system and design the audit plan in order to evaluate the relevant controls.

The IT audit approach is **risk-based** in nature. Auditors should review processes to identify risks and key control activities. Due to the lack of a paper trail, the auditor needs to **audit through the computer instead of around it**, which means they will require a greater understanding of IT controls.

**General IT controls** areas include: IT security; user access; IT operations; and change control. They relate to the IT computerised systems in their entirety and not just to a specific IT application. **Application controls** are specific aspects of functionality of process steps. If the auditor believes that general controls in the IT computerised system are weak, he is unlikely to test application controls and instead will take a wholly substantive approach.

**Learning Objective 2** Understand what is meant by computer-assisted audit techniques (CAATs).

While CAATs can be used to improve the coverage and efficiency as well as the effectiveness of audits, there is a cost incurred when implementing them. The use of CAATs at the substantive stage becomes more important to the auditor when the IT controls are considered to be weak – more substantive testing will need to be performed, which will increase the size of the samples.

**Learning Objective 3** Be able to consider the cost–benefit relationship of applying CAATs.

Typically, CAATs are expensive to set up in the first year of the audit, but are far more cost-effective and efficient in the longer term as they can be used in future years (usually with only minor modifications). The main benefits to be derived from the use of CAATs is that they can save time and produce more accurate testing results, and thus support the auditor's aim to perform efficient and effective audits.

**Learning Objective 4** Understand the impact e-commerce and other computer technologies have on businesses and on the audit process.

The IT audit approach can be used when assessing controls in an e-commerce environment. Elements of the IT environment will be externally facing and accessible from the internet (or other networks), and this increases the risk profile of those systems. Businesses involved in e-commerce cause specific difficulties for the auditor due, primarily, to the lack of a paper trail and reduced security when doing business on the Internet. The area of e-commerce has expanded further with the increased use of electronic data interchange (EDI), mobile phone technology and cloud computing. Emerging and expanding technologies, such as blockchain and artificial intelligence (AI), offer the auditor a reduced risk environment – but at the same time pose a threat to the future of the accounting and auditing profession.

## QUESTIONS

### Self-test Questions

9.1   Distinguish between general IT controls and application controls.

9.2   What are the benefits associated with using CAATs?

9.3   What important factors does the auditor need to consider when auditing a company that is involved in e-commerce?

9.4   When classifying the extent of the client entity's use of computer systems, what three areas might you consider?

9.5   What are the main objectives that should be considered in relation to the audit of a data processing environment?

9.6   List the three computer control categories.

9.7   List three controls that might be used to confirm the accurate conversion of data from one system to another.

9.8   List some relevant tests where CAATs might be used in the testing of inventory.

### Review Questions

(See Suggested Solutions to Review Questions in **Appendix C**.)

#### Question 9.1

(a)   CAATs have become an integral part of any audit. Discuss the crucial role they play for the auditor.

(b)   Specialised audit software is becoming increasingly popular due to its ability to assist the auditor in making their testing more effective and efficient.

With specific reference to the revenue and receivables cycle, explain the function and use of six specialised software procedures that can be used by the auditor.

(c)  An entity's IT system is integral to the operation of its business, and as such it is important for the auditor to consider a client entity's IT security controls.

Outline, with examples, three IT security measures that the auditor would expect to be in place in a client entity.

## Question 9.2

*Accountancy Ireland*, Volume 49, Number 1, February 2017 posed the question:

"In a very short space of time, we have gone from book ledgers to big data and data analytics. The rate of change is accelerating, so is there a risk that accountants could be surplus to requirements in a world of robotics and AI [artificial intelligence]?"

Brian Jackson
Audit Innovation Leader, Deloitte Ireland

Discuss this idea, outlining your view on how technology has changed the role of the accountant/auditor and how it may do so in the future.

## Question 9.3

Pal Pay Ltd (Pal Pay) has been a client of your firm since its establishment two years ago. Pal Pay sells a range of products online and offers all of its products in an e-commerce environment.

### Requirement
(a)  The audit partner has asked if you could provide an outline of the key areas that should be considered as part of the audit in this e-commerce environment.
(b)  You have also been asked to provide the finance director with an overview of the key control considerations that should be implemented when selling products online. In particular, the finance director has asked about security considerations.

# 10

# USING THE WORK OF OTHERS

## LEARNING OBJECTIVES

Having studied this chapter on the auditor's use of the work of others you should:
1. understand the external auditor's responsibility when using the work of others;
2. understand the options open to the auditor to gain an understanding of controls in place at service organisations that impact on the client entity's financial statement transactions;
3. understand the difference between internal and external audit;
4. understand the work of the internal auditor;
5. be able to identify independence issues connected to the internal auditor; and
6. understand the audit procedures that the external auditor must carry out with respect to the work of others.

## CHECKLIST OF RELEVANT STANDARDS

The relevant standards, in both the RoI and the UK/NI, covered in this chapter are:
- ISA 315 *Identifying and Assessing the Risks of Material Misstatement through Understanding the Entity and its Environment*
- ISA 330 *The Auditor's Responses to Assessed Risks*
- ISA 402 *Audit Considerations Relating to an Entity Using a Service Organisation*
- ISA 500 *Audit Evidence*
- ISA 610 *Using the Work of Internal Auditors*
- ISA 620 *Using the Work of an Auditor's Expert*

Note, in general when referring to ISAs, it should be understood as referring to the UK and Ireland versions, unless otherwise specified as either ISA (UK) or ISA (Ireland). See the Introduction for an extant list of auditing standards for the RoI and the UK/NI.

## KEY TERMS AND DEFINITIONS FOR THIS CHAPTER

**Auditor's Expert**  If expertise in a field other than accounting or auditing is necessary to obtain sufficient appropriate audit evidence, the auditor shall determine whether to use the work of an auditor's expert.

**Complementary User Entity Controls**  Controls that the service organisation assumes, in the design of its service, will be implemented by user entities.

**Governance**  The combination of processes and structures implemented by the board to inform, direct, manage and monitor the activities of the entity towards the achievement of its objectives.

**Internal Audit**  The process designed, implemented and maintained by those charged with governance, management and other personnel to provide **reasonable assurance** about the achievement of an entity's objectives with regard to reliability of financial reporting, effectiveness and efficiency of operations and compliance with applicable laws and regulations.

**Internal Audit Activity**  "A department, division, team of consultants or other practitioner(s) that provides independent, objective assurance and consulting services designed to add value and improve an organizations' operations. The internal audit activity helps an organization accomplish its objectives by bringing a systematic, disciplined approach to evaluate and improve the effectiveness of governance, risk management and control processes."[1]

**Internal Audit Independence**  "... the freedom from conditions that threaten the ability of the internal audit activity to carry out internal audit responsibilities in an unbiased manner."[2]

**Management's Expert**  "An individual or organization possessing expertise in a field other than accounting or auditing, whose work in that field is used by the entity to assist the entity in preparing the financial statements." (ISA 500, paragraph 5)

**Service Auditor**  An auditor who, at the request of the **service organisation**, provides an assurance report on the controls of that organisation.

**Service Organisation**  A third-party organisation (or element of a third-party organisation) that provides services to user entities that are part of those entities' information systems relevant to financial reporting.

**User Auditor**  An auditor who audits and reports on the financial statements of a **user entity**.

**User Entity**  A client entity is referred to as a user entity when it outsources a key function impacting on the financial statements (for example, when a client entity outsources its payroll function it is known as a user entity).

---

[1] The Institute of Internal Auditors, *International Standards for the Professional Practice of Internal Auditing (Standards)*, October 2017.
[2] Ibid., Attribute Standards 1100.

## 10.1  INTRODUCTION

The auditor cannot be expected to be an expert in all matters related to the financial statements and in some instances, due to proximity or time, they may need to call on 'the work of others'. For example:

- When reviewing the inventory of an art gallery, the auditor cannot be expected to competently value the associated works of art and, as such, may call on an expert's help.
- When faced with a **service organisation** providing services to the client entity, and that service represents controls that have the ability to impact on the client entity's financial statements, the auditor will need to look to the service organisation to obtain the information needed to support the audit procedures. This may involve using a third party to confirm the sound operation of those controls.
- When auditing the financial statements of a client entity that has an internal audit function, the auditor may find that they can use the work of the internal auditor to reduce their own work or, alternatively, use the services of one of the internal audit members to assist them with their work.

Before considering the auditor's use of the work of others, it is important to remember that the auditor has sole responsibility for the audit opinion expressed and that this responsibility is not reduced by the auditor's use of another's work. The standards dealt with in this chapter outline the degree to which the auditor can rely on the use of the work of others, but in no way diminish the responsibility of the auditor in the expression of an opinion.

**Section 10.2** discusses the auditor's approach when the entity uses a service organisation for a key task that impacts on the financial statements. Guidance on this topic is covered by ISA 402 *Audit Considerations Relating to an Entity Using a Service Organisation*.

In **Section 10.3** we will consider how the external auditor might use the client entity's **internal audit** department, and the requirements of the external auditor when considering to do so. Guidance on this topic is provided by ISA 610 *Using the Work of Internal Auditors*.

Finally, in **Section 10.4** we will discuss the provisions of ISA 620 *Using the Work of an Auditor's Expert*, which provides guidance on the use of an **auditor's expert**.

## 10.2  ENTITY'S USE OF SERVICE ORGANISATIONS

### Introduction

ISA 315 *Identifying and Assessing the Risks of Material Misstatement through Understanding the Entity and its Environment* (paragraph 12) and ISA 330 *The Auditor's Responses to Assessed Risks* (paragraph 8) both address the need for the auditor to obtain an understanding of the entity, including its internal controls, sufficiently to identify and assess the risks of material misstatement and for designing and performing further audit procedures responsive to those risks.

An issue arises for the auditor, however, **where certain procedures are not carried out by the client entity but instead by a service organisation employed by the client entity**. ISA 402 *Audit Considerations Relating to an Entity Using a Service Organisation*, paragraph 1, "deals with the user auditor's responsibility to obtain sufficient appropriate audit evidence when a user entity uses the services of one or more service organizations".

## Understanding Services Provided by a Service Organisation

ISA 402, paragraph 9, outlines the requirements of the auditor when gaining an understanding of a service organisation used by the entity, which include:
(a) the "nature" and "significance" of services provided, including their effect on the user entity's internal control;
(b) the "nature and materiality of the transactions processed … affected by the service organization";
(c) the "degree of interaction between the activities of the service organization and those of the user entity";
(d) the "nature of the relationship" between the two parties and "the relevant contractual terms for the activities undertaken by the service organization";
(e) the impact on the auditor's working arrangements where the client entity's accounting records are maintained by the service organisation.

The management of the entity that is using the service organisation, i.e. the **user entity**, must satisfy itself as to the effectiveness of the design and implementation of the service organisation's controls that are relevant to its operations, in the same way in which it satisfies itself with respect to its own internal controls. The auditor should then assess the user entity's documented procedures with respect to the service organisation. If the auditor is unable to obtain this understanding from the user entity, ISA 402, paragraph 12, advises the following activities:
"(a) Obtaining a type 1 or type 2 report, if available [see below];
(b) Contacting the service organization, through the user entity, to obtain specific information;
(c) Visiting the service organization and performing procedures that will provide the necessary information about the relevant controls at the service organization; or
(d) Using another auditor to perform procedures to provide the necessary information".

## Type 1 and Type 2 Reports

If the auditor is to rely on the controls in place at the service organisation, and which support transactions and balances in the client entity's financial statements, then they will: (a) need to obtain an understanding of those controls; and (b) should they wish to test them, need a method of doing so.

The type 1 and type 2 reports referred to in ISA 402, paragraph 12, assist the user auditor in understanding the service organisation's controls. Essentially they are **assurance** reports provided by a **service auditor**, i.e. an auditor requested by the service organisation to provide the reports. **Figure 10.1** highlights the difference between the two types of report.

FIGURE 10.1: THE DIFFERENCES BETWEEN TYPE 1 AND TYPE 2 REPORTS

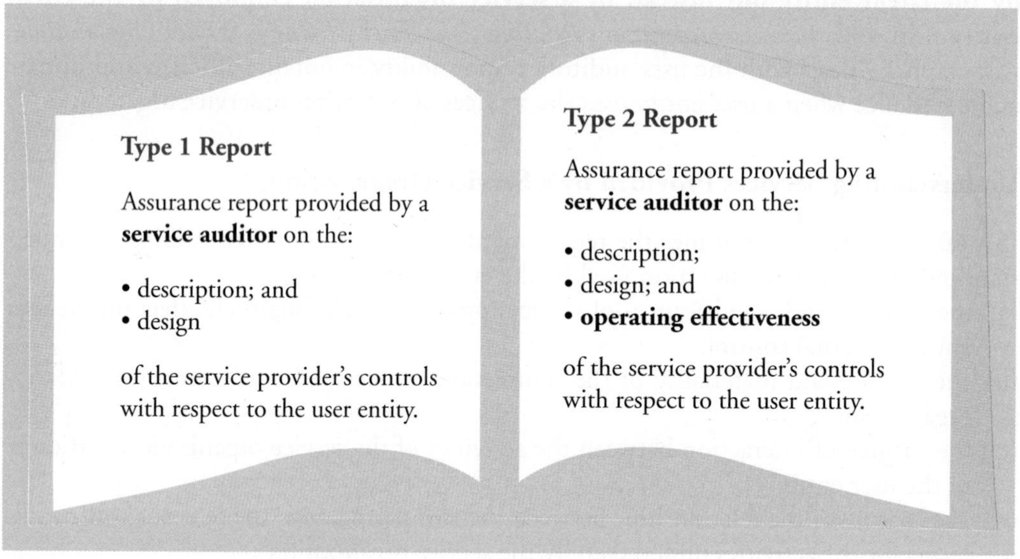

**Type 1 Report**

Assurance report provided by a **service auditor** on the:

• description; and
• design

of the service provider's controls with respect to the user entity.

**Type 2 Report**

Assurance report provided by a **service auditor** on the:

• description;
• design; and
• **operating effectiveness**

of the service provider's controls with respect to the user entity.

Clearly, a type 2 report will offer a greater degree of assurance to the user auditor because it includes reference to the **operating effectiveness** of the controls in place at the service organisation.

Before relying upon a type 1 or type 2 report, the auditor must be satisfied as to the **service auditor's professional competence and independence from the service organisation**. In addition, the user auditor must give consideration to the adequacy of the standards under which the type 1 or type 2 report was issued.

### Responding to the Assessed Risks of Material Misstatement

Should the auditor be unable to obtain **sufficient appropriate audit evidence** in the records held at the client's premises to support the relevant financial statement assertions, they should review the records of the service organisation or have another auditor perform those procedures on their behalf.

Where the testing of controls is necessary, and records are held at the service organisation, and the auditor cannot carry out that testing himself, then the auditor will require a **type 2 report**. The principal auditor remains responsible for the opinion provided on the financial statements and for this reason they **must be satisfied that the type 2 report constitutes sufficient appropriate audit evidence with respect to the competence and professionalism of its preparer and its form and content**.

With regard to tests of control, ISA 402, paragraph 16, advises that **one or more** of three procedures are followed:
"(a)  Obtaining a type 2 report, if available;
 (b)  Performing appropriate tests of controls at the service organization; or

(c) Using another auditor to perform tests of controls at the service organization on behalf of the user auditor."

The additional procedures are necessary when a type 2 report is not available.

Should the auditor be unable to obtain sufficient appropriate audit evidence with regard to service organisations, the audit report shall be modified as appropriate in accordance with ISA 705 *Modifications to the Opinion in the Independent Auditor's Report* (see **Chapter 19**).

## 10.3 USING THE WORK OF INTERNAL AUDITORS

### Introduction

The *UK Corporate Governance Code* ('the Code') emphasises the need for an **audit committee**, stating:
> "The board should establish an audit committee of at least three, or in the case of smaller companies two, independent non-executive directors".[3]

Provision C.3.2 of the Code outlines a number of key responsibilities with respect to audit committees, two of which are relevant to our discussion on internal audit:
> "• to review the company's internal financial controls and, unless expressly addressed by a separate board risk committee composed of independent directors, or by the board itself, to review the company's internal control and risk management systems;
> • to monitor and review the effectiveness of the company's internal audit function."

The audit committee is therefore responsible for the activities of the **internal audit** function. Provision C.3.6 of the Code advises that:
> "The audit committee should monitor and review the effectiveness of the internal audit activities. Where there is no internal audit function, the audit committee should consider annually whether there is a need for an internal audit function and make a recommendation to the board, and the reasons for the absence of such a function should be explained in the relevant section of the annual report."

Those acting within the internal audit function are not required to obtain qualifications in internal audit, and often are appointed due to their expertise in a particular area. Individuals can, however, seek to obtain a qualification in internal audit through The Institute of Internal Auditors (IIA), the internationally recognised authority and the principal educator with respect to internal audit.

Before proceeding, consider **Table 10.1** below, which highlights the roles and responsibilities of the internal auditor and the external auditor.

---

[3] Financial Reporting Council, *The UK Corporate Governance Code*, April 2016, Provision C.3.1.

TABLE 10.1: KEY DIFFERENCES BETWEEN INTERNAL AUDITORS AND EXTERNAL AUDITORS

|  | Internal Auditors | External Auditors |
|---|---|---|
| Report to: | Management (audit committee). | Shareholders/Members. |
| Objective: | Varies, depending on type of assignment, which can include:<br>• value-for-money assignments (3Es – economy, efficiency and effectiveness);<br>• audit of IT systems;<br>• financial audit;<br>• Sarbanes–Oxley (SOX) audit;<br>• operational assignments;<br>• due diligence. | To issue an opinion on the truth and fairness of the financial statements in accordance with an applicable financial reporting framework. |
| Report format: | Varies, depending on assignment type. | Independent auditor's report. |
| Status: | Usually an employee of the entity (although could be an outsourced function). | Independent of the client entity. |
| Governed by: | The Institute of Internal Auditors (although an internal auditor may operate without any qualifications). | Irish Auditing and Accounting Supervisory Authority (IAASA) in the RoI and the Financial Reporting Council (FRC) in the UK/NI.<br>Companies Acts (in order to act as auditor, the individual must have prescribed qualifications and be a member of an approved recognised accounting/supervisory body, e.g. ICAI). |

## Activities Undertaken by Internal Auditors

As more fully discussed in **Chapter 8**, advice on the application of a strong internal control system is provided by the Committee of Sponsoring Organizations of the Treadway Commission (COSO), which has outlined five key components of internal control. The importance of the internal audit department is evident throughout all of the components. As a recap, the five components are:
• the control environment;
• the risk assessment process;
• the control activities;
• IT systems and communication; and
• monitoring activities.

Typical activities in which an internal auditor engages include:
- observation and reporting on risk assessment exercises;
- participation in, and the planning of, internal audit engagements;
- formulating recommendations on improvements to weaknesses within the entity;
- participating in the implementation of recommended procedures;
- involvement in the identification and monitoring of key performance indicators (KPIs);
- participation in the annual internal audit planning process; and
- preparation of materials for, and attendance at, audit committee meetings.

## The Importance of Internal Audit

As defined by the European Confederation of Institutes of Internal Auditing (ECIIA):
"Internal auditing is an independent, objective assurance and consulting activity designed to add value and improve an organisation's operations. It helps an organisation accomplish its objectives by bringing a systematic, disciplined approach to evaluate and improve the effectiveness of risk management, control and governance processes."[4]

The Institute of Internal Auditors in its *IIA Position Paper: The Three Lines of Defense in Effective Risk Management and Control* (January 2013) describes how internal audit is regarded as the last line of defence in effective risk and management control. The first line of defence, naturally, is that of operational management, which has ownership, responsibility and accountability for directly assessing, controlling and mitigating risk. The second line of defence consists of the activities covered by the components of the control environment (see **Chapter 8**, Section 8.2) and essentially oversees the activities of the first line of defence. Internal audit is then considered the third line of defence. The independence and risk-based approach provided by the internal audit department provide comfort to the board of directors with respect to the entity's management of risk and the effectiveness of the first and second lines of defence. In addition, the internal audit activity adds value to the organisation by providing objective and relevant **assurance**. The internal audit department also contributes to effective and efficient governance, risk management and control processes.

From our discussion of fraud in **Chapter 3**, and specifically the fraud cases over the last decade included at **Table 3.4**, one can see that fraud is on the rise. Internal audit is in a unique position with respect to its access to, and in-depth knowledge of, the organisation, including its financial information. As illustrated by the WorldCom scandal of 2002, which was uncovered by an internal auditor, internal audit can play an instrumental role in the detection of fraud.

## The Independence of Internal Audit

**Chapter 2** outlined the importance of integrity, objectivity and independence to the external auditor; this is equally as important for the internal auditor.

---

[4] European Confederation of Institutes of Internal Auditing (ECIIA). See http://www.eciia.eu/what-we-do/what-is-internal-auditing/

The IIA's Code of Ethics provides principles relevant to the profession and practice of internal auditing, and its Rules of Conduct describe behaviour expected of internal auditors. The Code of Ethics applies to both individuals and entities that provide internal audit services, the purpose being to promote an ethical culture in the global profession of internal auditing.

Being independent, however, is somewhat more difficult for the internal auditor due to their direct employment by the client entity. If we consider **Chapter 2**, where we identified the threats to the external auditor's independence, we can also apply these to the internal auditor. This is considered in **Table 10.2** below.

TABLE 10.2: THREATS TO THE INTERNAL AUDITOR'S INDEPENDENCE

| **Self-interest threat** | The internal auditor's remuneration package is agreed within the client entity. Often the individual to whom the internal auditor reports will influence, if not dominate, the performance reviews of the internal auditor. For this reason it is essential that the head of internal audit reports directly to the audit committee. Consider a situation where the internal auditor reports directly to, say, the CFO and identifies a control failing or even fraud with respect to the CFO or their department. A **self-interest threat** arises due to the internal auditor's concern for their remuneration, or possibly their job, should they report failings with respect to their superior. Two key considerations need to be addressed: 1. the internal audit department's line of reporting; and 2. the bonus targets imposed (which should not be based on a reduced number of findings, as this could encourage the wrong behaviour). |
|---|---|
| **Self-review threat** (usually brought on through longevity of association) | A **self-review threat** can arise in two key instances with respect to the internal audit function. 1. The internal auditor has worked in the client entity for a number of years and finds an error or fraud that has existed for many years that has gone undetected by the internal audit department. The internal auditor may be reluctant to highlight the issue due to fear of being reprimanded for not identifying it earlier; or 2. the internal auditor has contributed to the recommendation and implementation of controls and, on occasion, has offered advice to various departments on the execution of their duties. If a control deficiency is discovered in a process they have designed and implemented, will they report it, considering they are partially to blame for its existence? |

| Familiarity threat | It is difficult to work in any organisation and not become familiar and even friendly with one's colleagues. On identification of an error or fraud connected to a close colleague, will the internal auditor disclose it? |
| | It is important either to rotate the heads of internal audit around the client entity group or, alternatively, impose internal independent audit reviews of the work performed by the local internal audit department. |
| Intimidation threat | The head of internal audit will often sit on the line of authority below that of senior management and there exists the threat of intimidation from superiors to not report instances of fraud or error. |
| | The audit committee should ensure the client entity enforces whistleblowing procedures to permit the anonymous reporting of concerns over fraud or error. |

## Other Considerations Affecting Internal Audit

### The Sarbanes–Oxley Act (SOX)

The Enron and WorldCom scandals in the USA (both companies were listed on the New York Stock Exchange) resulted in the introduction of the Sarbanes–Oxley Act (commonly referred to as SOX) in 2002, and specifically section 404. SOX required **those charged with governance** to formally declare (in an annual report) that they believe adequate accounting controls are in place in the organisation and to declare any material deficiencies in the company's internal controls. In order to gain this assurance, they needed to perform **'SOX' audits** (which involve the documentation, evaluation, testing and monitoring of their internal controls over financial reporting). In order to carry out these audits, many organisations have turned to their internal audit departments (or introduced one to tackle the issue where no internal audit department existed). The attestation made by the directors must be audited by an independent external auditor. This requirement only exists for companies listed on the New York Stock Exchange or subsidiaries of such listings.

### UK Corporate Governance Code

With a close eye on **corporate governance**, general public interest in this area has been heightened by a loss of confidence in corporate entities and those who run them to operate with integrity. The various scandals and high-profile company collapses focus public opinion, and the effectiveness of an internal (and external) audit is questioned. In this context, the role of the internal audit department is becoming increasingly important. While the internal audit department already features in the *UK Corporate Governance Code*, there is no doubt we will see increased provisions directly associated with the internal audit function.

## ECIIA Findings

The European Confederation of Institutes of Internal Auditing (ECIIA) has carried out a review of corporate governance codes in its member bodies and identified the following key issues for internal auditors.

- **Presence** – to date, 90% of EU Member States now either require or recommend the presence of an internal audit function in listed companies, with it being compulsory within the financial institutions sector.
- **Regulation** – continues to be loose with regard to the effectiveness of the audit function and also with regard to essential requisites, such as independence and scope.
- **Slashed resources** – cost-cutting is a priority for many organisations; unfortunately, too often management sees internal audit as a non-value-adding function and as such has slashed resources in this area.

In April 2015, the ECIIA published guidance entitled *Non-Financial Reporting: Building trust with internal audit,* which discusses the role internal audit can play to assist organisations when implementing the new European Directive on Non-Financial Reporting. The guidance notes that, "Internal audit is in a unique position to take a 'helicopter' view of an organization" and can help develop forward-thinking strategies on these issues. Internal audit will therefore have a crucial role to play in the new Directive. The document focuses on how internal audit can help to build trust with stakeholders by providing some assurance on the quality of the new non-financial reports.

In September 2015, the ECIIA promoted the idea that the internal audit function could also play a key role in the European Commission's attempts to achieve improvements in tax transparency by reviewing the disclosures made to tax authorities. The ECIIA believes that internal auditors are ideally placed to give assurance over this type of disclosure and, as such, continues to promote the increased use of internal audit in a more formal manner.

## Protection for the Whistleblower

In the RoI, the Prevention of Corruption (Amendment) Act 2010 aims to improve the strength of anti-corruption legislation while providing specific '**protection for the whistleblower**'. Throughout the world, people are generally afraid of being penalised by their employers if they 'blow the whistle'. Generally speaking, those who are most aware, or likely to be aware, of fraud are those in the internal audit department, therefore such protection will be welcomed by them. The Act, however, currently only covers whistleblowing relating to public sector offices/departments; thus, for now at least, the internal audit departments of private or listed companies will have to comply with the IIA's Code of Ethics, trusting that no retribution is sought by aggrieved management.

Further legal protection is now provided by the Protected Disclosures Act 2014. Its purpose being to protect individuals who make certain disclosures that are seen to be in the public interest, providing a means of redress if they are subsequently dismissed.

## External Auditor Considerations with Respect to the Internal Audit Function

ISA 315 requires the external auditor to make inquiries of the internal audit function as part of their risk assessment. In addition to the use of the internal audit function as part of the external audit's planning, often the activities of the internal audit department can be used by the external auditors to form part of their substantive audit evidence. ISA 610 *Using the Work of Internal Auditors* provides guidance to the external auditor should they wish to use the work of the internal auditor.

The external auditor can make use of the client entity's internal audit function in two ways:

1. Should the internal audit function be deemed to hold sufficient objectivity, be of a sufficient competency and carry out internal audit activities that are systematically planned using a disciplined approach, then the external auditor may choose **to rely on the work of the internal audit function as a means of providing audit evidence** on which to base their audit opinion.

2. The external auditor may also engage internal audit team members to **provide direct assistance** in gathering audit evidence on behalf of the external auditor. Should the external auditor wish to use the internal audit team in this way, similar to 1. above, they will need to assess the competency and objectivity of the internal audit function. However, ISA 610, paragraph 5-1, **specifically prohibits** the use of internal auditors to provide "direct assistance ... in an audit conducted in accordance with ISAs".

The prevention of the direct assistance of the members of the internal audit function, regardless of their competency and objectivity, was taken by the FRC contrary to some opposing debate from the profession. The FRC's decision is in response to the lack of independence offered by the internal audit function due to the array of threats to their independence (see **Table 10.2** above). As such, the external auditor never gets to assess the specific objectivity and competency of the internal auditor with regard to direct assistance because they are not permitted to engage in the activity anyway. It is worth mentioning at this point that external auditors in the UK/NI and the RoI only used the direct assistance of the internal audit function in limited instances prior to the prohibition and, as such, this change to the standard is not expected to have had a huge impact on the efficiency of audits.

ISA 610 continues to permit the use of the work carried out by the internal audit department as a means to modify the nature or timing of, or to reduce the extent of, audit procedures performed directly by the external auditor. Examples of work performed by the internal auditor that can be used by the external auditor include:

"• Testing of the operating effectiveness of controls.
• Substantive procedures involving limited judgment.
• Observations of inventory counts.
• Tracing transactions through the information system relevant to financial reporting.
• Testing of compliance with regulatory requirements.

- In some circumstances, audits or reviews of the financial information of subsidiaries that are not significant components to the group (where this does not conflict with the requirements of ISA 600 [UK and Ireland]." (ISA 610, paragraph A16)

**Table 10.3** below outlines the activities that the external auditor should undertake prior to using the work of the internal audit department to modify its external audit procedures. As we have seen, the external auditor's review of the internal audit function should focus on objectivity and competence, as well as on a disciplined approach to planning, performance, supervision, review and documentation of its activities.

TABLE 10.3: EXTERNAL AUDITOR REVIEW OF INTERNAL AUDIT FUNCTION

| Objectivity (see ISA 610, paragraph A7) | • **Organisational status** – does the organisational status of the internal audit function support the objectivity of the function? Ideally it should report directly to the audit committee and not those charged with governance.<br>• **Conflicting responsibilities** – managerial or operational duties assigned to internal auditors may lead to a self-review threat.<br>• **Employment/remuneration control** – should not be overseen by those charged with governance.<br>• **Restrictions imposed by those charged with governance**.<br>• **Membership of relevant professional body** – obligation to comply with ethical standards. |
|---|---|
| Competence (see ISA 610 paragraph A8) | • **Adequate and appropriate resourcing** relative to the size of the client entity.<br>• **Established policies for hiring and training** of internal auditors.<br>• **Adequate technical training and proficiency** in the field of auditing and the applicable financial reporting framework.<br>• **Necessary skills relevant to the client entity industry**.<br>• **Membership of a relevant professional body** – obligation to comply with continual professional development requirements. |
| Disciplined approach | • **Existence of proper planning** of internal audit engagements.<br>• **Evidence of supervision and review of work** carried out by the function.<br>• **Formal documentation** of work carried out – should include a clear distinction between the activities of the internal audit function and the other monitoring control activities performed by the client entity's normal operational controls.<br>• **Existence of appropriate quality control policies and procedures** – similar to those outlined for external auditors in ISQC 1.<br>• **Established policies for hiring and training** of internal auditors.<br>• **Adequate technical training and proficiency** in the field of auditing and the applicable financial reporting framework.<br>• **Necessary skills relevant to the client entity industry**.<br>• **Membership of relevant professional body** – obligation to comply with continual professional development requirements. |

After considering the objectivity, competency and quality of the internal audit department, the auditor still has a number of considerations before it modifies its procedures to incorporate the work of the internal audit department. ISA 610, paragraph 18, explains how in the following instances the use of the work of the internal auditor is not advised: where there is a significant use of judgement required; where the assessed level of risk of material misstatement is high; where the internal audit department is inadequately positioned in the organisational chart; or where the competence of the internal audit team is called into question.

The stipulation that "significant judgments" should not be delegated to an internal auditor and must *only* be made by the external auditor is expanded upon in paragraph A19, where it provides examples of what a significant judgement would be. This includes: assessing the risks of material misstatement; evaluating tests performed; evaluating the going concern assumption; evaluating significant accounting estimates; and evaluating the adequacy of disclosures.

ISA 610, paragraph 23, further reiterates the external auditor's sole responsibility for the audit opinion expressed and, as such, requires the external auditor to "perform sufficient audit procedures on the body of work of the internal audit function as a whole that the external auditor plans to use to determine its adequacy for purposes of the audit…". These procedures may include reperformamce of some of the work (paragraph 24).

## 10.4 USING THE WORK OF AN AUDITOR'S EXPERT

### Introduction

ISA 620 *Using the Work of an Auditor's Expert*, paragraph 7, states:
"If expertise in a field other than accounting or auditing is necessary to obtain sufficient appropriate audit evidence, the auditor shall determine whether to use the work of an auditor's expert."

As noted at the start of this chapter, the auditor must remember that they hold sole responsibility for the audit opinion expressed and that while it might be deemed necessary to obtain expert advice, it is done so knowing that **sufficient appropriate audit evidence** must be obtained with respect not only to the subject matter but also to the calibre of the expert.

The client entity's use of a **management's expert** in preparing the financial statements may have a bearing on the auditor's decision to use an **auditor's expert**. Factors that the auditor might consider include the management's expert's competence and expertise, their remit and the client entity's controls over their work.

### Nature, Timing and Extent of Audit Procedures

When designing the nature, timing and extent of the audit procedures, the auditor will take into consideration the **materiality** of the matter requiring expert advice, the risk of material misstatement of the matter and the significance of the expert's work to the overall audit.

Additionally, before engaging the work of the expert, the auditor is responsible for evaluating the necessary qualifications, competence, capabilities and objectivity of the expert.

The nature, scope and objectives of the audit engagement (in which the expert is to be involved), the respective roles and responsibilities, as well as the nature, timing and extent of communication, should be documented and agreed in writing between the expert and the auditor. This document should also require the expert to observe confidentiality requirements regarding any information disclosed.

### Evaluating the Adequacy of the Work of the Auditor's Expert

Once the expert has concluded on the matter at hand, the auditor needs to ensure that the conclusion appears relevant, reasonable and consistent with other audit evidence. Additionally, should the use of assumptions have been required by the expert, the auditor should assess the relevance and reasonableness of these assumptions in the given circumstances. Should source data have been required in concluding on the work assigned, the auditor should validate its completeness and accuracy.

In assessing the expert's work, the auditor should ensure that the substance of the expert's findings are properly reflected in the financial statement assertions. The auditor must also consider:

- the source of the data used (was it generated by the client entity or by some other external source?);
- the assumptions and methods used;
- when the work was carried out;
- reasons for any changes in assumptions and methods; and
- the result of the expert's work in light of the auditor's knowledge of the business and the results of other audit procedures.

The auditor is not the expert and therefore cannot judge all assumptions and methods used; however, they should seek to obtain an understanding of these to consider their reasonableness. This will involve discussions with the expert as well as with the client to ensure that explanations, assumptions and methods are not contradictory to other evidence obtained.

### Expert's Scope of Work

The scope of the expert's work will vary depending on the particular assignment. The scope of the expert's work should be documented in the form of written instructions, maintained on the audit working papers and should include:

- the objectives and scope of the expert's work;
- a general outline of specific matters the report is to cover;
- the intended use;
- the extent of the expert's access to records and files;
- clarification of the expert's relationship to the client entity (to ensure independence);
- requirements regarding the confidentiality of client information; and
- the assumptions and methods to be used by the expert.

In an audit of a **public interest entity (PIE)** that has involved the use of an auditor's expert, the auditor must obtain confirmation from the external expert regarding their independence. Furthermore, they must document the request, the advice received and confirmation of the expert's independence in the additional report provided to the audit committee.

## 10.5 CONCLUSION

While the auditor may call on various sources when concluding their opinion, the auditor holds **sole responsibility for that opinion**. For that reason, no reference should be made to the use of the work of auditors of service organisations, internal auditors or auditor's experts in the audit report, as doing so would be perceived as an attempt to diminish their own responsibility with respect to the conclusion drawn.

Therefore, when using the work of others, the auditor must be satisfied as to the adequacy of the qualifications, expertise and competence of individuals involved, as well as the reasonableness, accuracy, relevance and completeness of the conclusions drawn by others.

### Summary of Learning Objectives

**Learning Objective 1**   Understand the external auditor's responsibility when using the work of others.

The auditor has sole responsibility for the **audit opinion** expressed and that responsibility is not reduced by the auditor's use of another's work. The auditor must be satisfied with regard to the expert's qualifications and competency to carry out the task in question, as well as review the work and the conclusions drawn by that expert.

**Learning Objective 2**   Understand the options open to the auditor to gain an understanding of controls in place at service organisations that impact on the client entity's financial statement transactions.

**Entity's Use of Service Organisations – ISA 402** When an entity uses a service organisation that may impact on material transactions in the financial statements, the auditor, in line with ISA 315 and ISA 330, is required to obtain an understanding of the service organisation's internal controls relevant to the audit, sufficient to identify and assess risks of material misstatement.

This can be done in two ways:
- obtaining the information **directly** from the service provider; or
- obtaining a type 1 report from the **service auditor**, being a report on the description and design of the service provider's controls with respect to the entity.

If the service organisation's controls need to be tested, the auditor can conduct the testing, if permitted and practicable. Alternatively, a type 2 report can be requested, which provides information on the description and design of the internal controls relevant to the entity, as well as reporting on their **operating effectiveness**.

**Learning Objective 3**  Understand the difference between internal and external audit.

The external auditor's objective is to issue an independent opinion on the truth and fairness of the financial statements. This opinion is included in the independent auditor's report, which is addressed to the shareholders of the client entity. The external auditor must be independent of the client entity and must be a member of a RAB/RSB (e.g. ICAI). Strict rules exist around who can act as an external auditor.

An internal auditor, on the other hand, is employed directly by the client entity (often as an employee, though the function can be outsourced) and is responsible for the recommendation and review of the systems of control within the client entity. The scope and report format of their work can vary and is driven by the directors of the organisation (usually the **audit committee**). Professional internal auditors are usually members of the IIA, but can operate without any qualifications.

**Learning Objective 4**  Understand the work of the internal auditor.

Viewed as an independent and objective assurance provider around the areas of risk and control, the internal audit function should report directly to the audit committee of the organisation. The internal audit department is also value-adding, making the control environment as efficient and effective as possible. An IIA paper from 2013 asserts that internal audits are regarded as 'the last line of defence' in effective risk and management control.

ISA 610 prohibits the external auditor from obtaining direct assistance from the internal audit function in carrying out external audit procedures. This is due to the perceived lack of independence pertaining to the internal audit function. The standard does, however, permit the use of the work of the internal audit function provided the external auditor is satisfied that the internal auditors are: sufficiently competent and objective in carrying out that work; and apply a systematic and disciplined approach to their work.

**Learning Objective 5**  Be able to identify independence issues connected to the internal auditor.

While internal auditors can be subject to the same types of independence threats as those faced by external auditors, these threats can present themselves in a different way. Members of the IIA are subject to a code of ethics similar to that of external auditors. The ability of the internal auditor to be truly objective, however, is difficult due to their direct employment by the client entity.

**Learning Objective 6**  Understand the audit procedures that the external auditor must carry out with respect to the work of others.

"If expertise in a field other than accounting or auditing is necessary to obtain sufficient appropriate audit evidence, the auditor shall determine whether to use the work of an auditor's expert." (ISA 620, paragraph 7)

Before engaging the work of the expert, the auditor is responsible for evaluating the necessary qualifications, competence, capabilities and objectivity of the expert. Any conclusions reached by the auditor's expert require audit procedures as to their reasonableness and consistency with other audit evidence.

## QUESTIONS

### Self-test Questions

10.1 Can the auditor refer to the work of an auditor's expert in the audit report?

10.2 How might the auditor gain an understanding of the controls in place in a service organisation?

10.3 What options does the auditor have if they wish to rely on the controls in place in a service organisation where those controls impact on transactions of the client entity?

10.4 What are the key differences between external and internal auditors?

10.5 What are the benefits to the organisation of the internal audit department?

10.6 What current issues face the internal auditing profession?

10.7 How might the external auditor use the internal audit function to assist with the audit procedures?

10.8 What must the auditor check in relation to an auditor's expert whose work they intend to use for the purpose of an audit?

### Review Questions

(See Suggested Solutions to Review Questions in **Appendix C.**)

### Question 10.1

Your audit client, Elite Ltd, has recently added an internal audit function. It has indicated that it believes the presence of this internal audit team will dramatically reduce the work your audit firm will need to perform and it expects to see the impact of this on the audit fee.

**Requirement** The audit engagement partner is concerned about this request and asks you to draft him an e-mail indicating, with bullet points, where (if at all) you will be able to reduce your audit testing due to the existence of an internal auditor. The audit engagement partner has indicated that your report should include the audit requirements imposed by ISA 610 *Using the Work of Internal Auditors*.

### Question 10.2

You and your colleague have recently become managers of the audit firm in which you both trained. You have both been assigned to your first engagements as audit managers. As part of the training for new managers, you are reminded of your responsibility to control the timing of audits: "they must be efficient notwithstanding the need for effectiveness". There has been concern that many audits have been running over their budgeted times and reducing the margins being achieved. Your colleague is determined not to run over his allotted time and discusses with you his plans to perform the audit in the budgeted time or less.

First, your colleague knows that the audit client has an internal audit department and plans to obtain a copy of their audit work on internal controls and to use this to support a reduced level of substantive testing.

Secondly, the audit client uses a service organisation to perform a significant amount of work that impacts directly on the financial statements. Your colleague intends to request a type 1 report (third-party confirmation) from the service auditors to reduce the need for work on this area.

Finally, the property has been revalued and to avoid having to do any work on the valuation they intend to obtain an independent valuer to review the valuation received by the audit client.

**Requirement** You are concerned about your colleague's plans to reduce the hours spent on this audit. Prepare an informal e-mail outlining your concerns.

## Question 10.3

A paper by The Institute of Internal Auditors (IIA) from January 2013 asserts that internal audits are regarded as the last 'line of defence' in effective risk and management control.

**Requirement** The above being true, how important is the independence of the internal auditor? Your answer should make reference to at least **two** independence threats to which an internal auditor may be subject.

## CHALLENGING QUESTIONS FOR PART II

(Suggested Solutions to Challenging Questions are available through your lecturer.)

These challenging questions aim to test your knowledge of **Chapters 4–10**. For each question, you are presented with a case study on which you are asked to deliver on a number of requirements intended to test practical application of what you have learned in Part II: The Audit and Assurance Process: Planning and Controls.

### Question II.1

You are an audit manager for Smith & Reilly, a long-established accounting practice. Smith & Reilly has been approached by Jupiter Ltd to conduct its audit. The previous auditors have resigned due to the size of the fee charged to Jupiter Ltd relative to the firm's total fee income. Jupiter Ltd has shared the Statement of Circumstances from the previous auditors, which corroborates this. It is June 2018 and the year end is 31 December.

Smith & Reilly currently provide other services to Jupiter Ltd in the form of payroll and tax advice. They have given you a list of directors, and the non-executive director's name rings a bell with you. You remember reading an article about him in the newspaper some months back. Jupiter Ltd believes that the audit has taken up a huge amount of time in the past and so has requested that the audit commence at the end of January and be finished by mid-February. This concerns you as it is the largest company Smith & Reilly has ever audited and you are unlikely to have enough resources to complete the engagement in this timeframe. The directors of Jupiter Ltd have offered €200 vouchers for each member of the engagement team should this request be met. The partners of Smith & Reilly have recently promoted a new partner who will take responsibility with regard to the role of ethics partner.

The directors have also provided you with the following information. Jupiter Ltd is a successful hi-tech start-up formed in 2013. It expanded rapidly in 2015 and 2016, and in 2017 revenue plateaued. The company has now developed a strategy of launching new products to enhance its attraction to customers, but this will require significant investment in product development. In 2013, the company borrowed €/£5,000,000, which is due for repayment in September 2019. The company's bank and cash balances at the end of December 2018 is €/£500,000. As part of the audit, the directors would like Smith & Reilly to assist in the preparation of documentation required to secure further financing.

### Requirements
(a) You are asked to prepare a recommendation for the new partner on whether or not to proceed with the engagement for Jupiter Ltd.
(b) In preparation for the potential acceptance of this client, the partners have asked you to draft a letter to the directors regarding the requirement for them to sign an engagement letter, outlining the purpose of the engagement letter and some of the contents therein.

## Question II.2

The audit engagement for Large Company Limited has been accepted, with all recommendations laid down by you having been followed. You are the assigned audit manager on the engagement and have recently conducted the planning meeting with the directors. The minutes of that meeting are included below.

---

### LARGE COMPANY LIMITED
### PLANNING MEETING

21 October 2018

In attendance:   John Doe – Audit Manager, Smith & Reilly
James McCarthy – Audit Partner, Smith & Reilly
Thomas Hogan – Chairperson, Large Company Limited
Mark Hogan – Managing Director, Large Company Limited
Kevin Byrne – Finance Director, Large Company Limited
Kate Louis – CFO, Large Company Limited

#### Company Background

The company's principal activity is the manufacture of furniture. The directors expect revenue to increase in excess of 30% (from €198.5 million in 2017). The directors believe that this trend will continue for the foreseeable future as a new line of furniture has effectively broken into the luxury market. Demand for this range has also introduced sales in foreign countries, with an expected €40 million increase in revenue being attributable to exports. All other ranges are selling successfully and are expected to do so for the balance of the year and into the future. This demand has resulted in the opening of a branch in the UK and a branch in Northern Ireland, which means they are dealing with the consolidation of branch accounts and foreign exchange for the first time.

10% of the company's revenue is made up of contracts, which involve the design, production and fitting of ergonomically designed furniture. These contracts occasionally span the year end. See other intangible assets below.

The company employs 1,000 employees throughout the company, most of whom are employed in production. The head of production, credited with the recent development of the luxury products, left the company last month.

The company had just five people employed in finance, but this has increased due to the increased workload around consolidation and foreign exchange and the need to analyse revenue by geographical area and product to produce better management accounts. While the increase in staffing has helped, the systems need to be updated to cope with the increased volume of transactions and the added complexity with the introduction of the branches. An accountant is employed in each branch and they have implemented their own controls within each branch.

Due to the training of the new accounts staff, the company is behind on the reconciliation of account balances, but hopes to catch up on this before the year end.

Kate Louis outlines the following with regard to specific balances:

## Non-current Assets

The value of non-current assets has reduced in the period due to a deficit on revaluation of freehold land and buildings.

## Inventory

- Inventory includes raw materials, WIP and finished goods.
- An inventory count has not taken place since June, and Kate is worried that the physical inventory held will be different from that in the perpetual records.

## Trade Receivables

Kate has always been an advocate of ensuring receivables balances are regularly followed up and believes controls in this area to be strong. For this reason she spends time with the credit controller each month, understanding the ageing of receivables (although with the recent increase in business overseas, she has not had as much time for this).

## Other Intangible Assets

The other intangibles are made up of design patents, which are due to expire on 30 September 2019.

## Available-for-sale Investments

The directors have concerns over the value of investments.

## Payables and Accruals

The purchases and payables system is probably the most closely controlled, with this function being overseen by a very strong manager who has implemented excellent controls. The branches do not purchase anything directly themselves; all purchasing and payables are managed centrally.

## Requirements

(a) The audit partner requests that you send her a copy of the minutes and outline your opinion on:
   (i)   the inherent and controls risks identified by you at this meeting, along with the proposed audit approach to deal with these risks (i.e. detection risk);
   (ii)  whether or not you believe a controls approach should be taken; and
   (iii) how you believe you should deal with the more risky areas identified.

(b) Considering the size of the new client and the risks identified, the audit partner asks you to prepare a memo to the engagement staff outlining their requirement to collect sufficient appropriate audit evidence, as well as an explanation on what is sufficient appropriate audit evidence.

(c) The audit senior assigned to this engagement has never worked on an initial engagement and asks you to outline Smith & Reilly's responsibility with regard to the opening balances of Large Company Limited.

# PART III

# THE AUDIT AND ASSURANCE PROCESS: SUBSTANTIVE PROCEDURES

# THE AUDIT AND ASSURANCE PROCESS

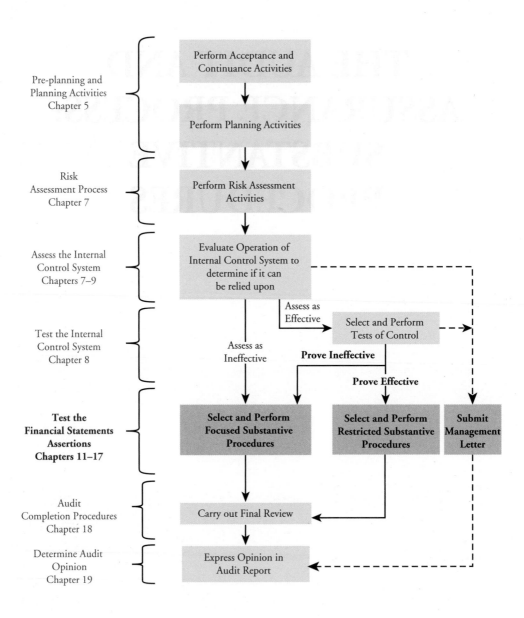

# 11

# THE AUDIT OF PROPERTY, PLANT AND EQUIPMENT

## LEARNING OBJECTIVES

Having studied this chapter on the audit of property, plant and equipment you should:
1. understand what is included in the audit of property, plant and equipment (PPE);
2. be able to identify the risks and audit objectives applicable to PPE;
3. be able to determine an appropriate audit strategy for PPE, taking into consideration the specific risks and audit objectives (assertions);
4. be able to develop an audit programme that addresses all the audit objectives (assertions) for PPE;
5. be able to describe and apply specific substantive testing procedures relating to the audit of PPE;
6. understand the role CAATs can play when auditing PPE; and
7. understand the auditor's approach relating to the disclosures of PPE.

## CHECKLIST OF RELEVANT STANDARDS

The relevant standards, both in the RoI and the UK/NI, covered in this chapter are:
- ISA 315 *Identifying and Assessing the Risks of Material Misstatement through Understanding the Entity and its Environment*
- ISA 330 *The Auditor's Responses to Assessed Risks*
- ISA 500 *Audit Evidence*
- ISA 510 *Initial Audit Engagements – Opening Balances*
- ISA 520 *Analytical Procedures*
- ISA 530 *Audit Sampling*
- ISA 540 *Auditing Accounting Estimates, Including Fair Value Accounting Estimates, and Related Disclosures*
- ISA 620 *Using the Work of an Auditor's Expert*
- IFRS 16 *Leases*
- IAS 16 *Property, Plant and Equipment*
- IAS 23 *Borrowing Costs*
- IAS 36 *Impairment of Assets*

Note, in general when referring to ISAs, it should be understood as referring to the UK and Ireland versions, unless otherwise specified as either ISA (UK) or ISA (Ireland). See the Introduction for an extant list of auditing standards for the RoI and the UK/NI.

## KEY TERMS AND DEFINITIONS FOR THIS CHAPTER

**Audit Trail**   The electronic or paper trail that provides the auditor with audit evidence regarding the step-by-step documented history of a transaction.

**Fixed Asset Register (FAR)**   A asset-by-asset listing of all fixed assets owned by the client entity, setting out purchase details (cost, purchase date, description, etc.), asset category, applicable depreciation rates and charges, and net book values (NBVs).

**Lead Schedule**   Acts as a summary of the balances and transactions to be audited that relate to a particular class of transactions and balances. It allows the auditor to control the audit procedures by referencing each balance or transaction to the location in the audit file where the related testing can be found.

**Substantive Analytical Procedure**   Also known as a '**proof in total**', a substantive analytical procedure is an audit procedure that is generally more efficient than **tests of details** and is permitted where a low level of inherent and control risks exist. It involves the auditor developing an independent calculation (expectation) of the balance being audited and comparing it with the actual balance as per the financial statements. If the auditor's independent expectation is within a threshold from the actual figure, then no further testing is required by the auditor in relation to the balance. (Other assertions, however, such as valuation, may still need to be considered.)

## 11.1  INTRODUCTION

The objective of substantive testing is to validate the transactions, balances and disclosures at the assertion level in response to identified risks (inherent, control and detection risks as discussed in **Chapters 7** and **8**). The auditor commences substantive testing by focusing on the risk of material misstatement within the transactions and balances being tested, and then identifying the assertions impacted by these risks and then identifying substantive audit procedures that will best test the existence of material misstatement driven by the identified risks.

**Sections 11.2–11.8** outline the requirements of IAS 16 *Property, Plant and Equipment* and consider how the auditor:
- identifies audit risks and audit objectives (management assertions) for property, plant and equipment (PPE);
- develops an audit plan for PPE and refines it into an audit programme;
- designs specific tests associated with PPE; and
- ensures adequate presentation and disclosure in the financial statements relating to PPE.

Throughout the chapter we consider how computer-assisted audit techniques (CAATs) can assist the auditor in carrying out audit procedures in the most effective and efficient way. In **Section 11.9** we consider the auditor's approach when auditing the reasonableness of disclosures relating to PPE.

## 11.2  WHAT IS PROPERTY, PLANT AND EQUIPMENT?

Property, plant and equipment (PPE), also commonly referred to as fixed assets, are those assets that are retained for use in an entity's operations and not consumed in the year of purchase or held for resale.

IAS 16, paragraph 7, states:
"The cost of an item of property, plant and equipment shall be recognised as an asset if, and only if:
(a) it is probable that future economic benefits associated with the item will flow to the entity; and
(b) the cost of the item can be measured reliably."

If you refer to Appendix B, Large Company Limited, Note 13, you will see that property, plant and equipment can include assets such as freehold land and buildings, plant and machinery or motor vehicles. On the face of the statement of financial position, the **net book value** (NBV) (cost less accumulated depreciation and impairments) is disclosed and expanded upon in a note to the financial statements.

The PPE note should also include details such as security held on assets, details of revaluation, assets held under finance lease or hire purchase, and details of capitalised interest costs.

With respect to the statement of comprehensive income, when it comes to PPE the auditor is concerned with the charge for depreciation and impairments in the year and any profits or losses arising from the sale of PPE in the period.

## 11.3 RISKS ASSOCIATED WITH PROPERTY, PLANT AND EQUIPMENT

In **Chapter 7** we discussed the topic of risk and considered how the auditor should go about detecting risks. We also discussed how the auditor should consider these risks when designing the nature, timing and extent of further audit procedures relative to each financial cycle. Accordingly, before developing the audit plan, the auditor needs to consider a number of risks that may be associated with PPE. Risks associated with PPE can include:

- **Rights and obligations** The client entity may not actually **own** the PPE included in the financial statements.
- **Existence** The PPE included in the financial statements might not actually **exist**. Proof of purchase at a point in time does not prove that the asset is *still* the property of the client entity and still in use.
- **Valuation (impairment)** The valuation of PPE may be overstated in the financial statements, e.g. the value of the tangible assets may have fallen to less than their current NBV.
- **Valuation (depreciation rate)** The depreciation rate, or useful economic life (UEL), applied to PPE may not be appropriate.
- **Obsolescence** PPE may have become obsolete (e.g. due to technological advancement).
- **Overstatement** The client entity may have failed to record disposals of PPE. This is extremely common in that entities continue to record new assets but do not consider that older assets have been disposed of and so they remain on the **fixed asset register (FAR)**. Although the assets disposed of often have a nil NBV, their inclusion results in cost and depreciation being overstated.
- **Overstatement (repairs and maintenance)** Revenue items may have been recorded in error as capital expenditure on PPE.
- **Data integrity** Control over PPE may be poor and the FAR may not have been kept up to date.
- **Revaluation** If the client has chosen to revalue assets, the auditor should be mindful that all assets in that class should be revalued. An auditor's expert may be needed to ensure that the valuation being applied is reasonable.
- **Idle assets** The FAR may include physical assets that are not in use. For an asset to be recorded as a capital asset under IAS 16 it must be in use; if it is not in use, it is likely to be impaired.
- **Incorrect classification** The note to the financial statements detailing fixed assets may classify assets incorrectly. For example, a new production line in the course of construction may be included within PPE.

## 11.4 AUDIT OBJECTIVES/MANAGEMENT ASSERTIONS FOR PROPERTY, PLANT AND EQUIPMENT

As discussed in **Chapter 6**, it is necessary for the auditor to seek **sufficient appropriate audit evidence** to satisfy all of the audit objectives and to eliminate the possibility of any of the risks outlined above going undetected. The auditor must design tests to address these assertions and thereby address the identified risks. In **Chapter 4** we introduced audit objectives (management assertions) and explained their generic meanings, while in **Chapter 8** we considered the management assertions specific to each financial cycle. **Table 11.1** below recaps the audit objectives/assertions for transactions and account balances as they relate to PPE.

TABLE 11.1: PROPERTY, PLANT AND EQUIPMENT – AUDIT OBJECTIVES

| Management Assertion/ Audit Objective | Control Objective for Transaction Class **PPE Movements** | Control Objective for Account Balance **PPE Balances** |
|---|---|---|
| **Occurrence/ Existence** | • Ensure recorded additions represent PPE acquired during the period under review.<br>• Ensure recorded disposals represent PPE sold, transferred or scrapped during the period under review.<br>• Ensure recorded depreciation represents depreciation on assets that exist. | Ensure that recorded PPE represent productive assets that are in use at the reporting date. |
| **Completeness** | Ensure that all additions and disposals that occurred during the period under review have been recorded. | Ensure that all PPE that exists and is owned by the entity at the year end is recorded in the PPE balance (i.e. the balance is complete and no assets are omitted). |
| **Rights and obligations** | Ensure the entity holds the rights to all PPE resulting from recorded purchase transactions. | Ensure the entity holds the rights and obligations (risks and rewards) to all recorded PPE at the reporting date. |
| **Classification/ Recording (accuracy) and Valuation** | • Ensure that all additions and disposals have been correctly recorded.<br>• Ensure all additions to, and disposals of, PPE have been recorded in the correct ledger accounts and adequately support their classification in the financial statements. | Ensure that PPE included in the financial statements are appropriately valued at cost, or valuation less accumulated depreciation and impairments, at the reporting date. |
| **Cut-off** | Ensure all additions and disposals have been recorded in the correct period (particularly transactions surrounding the year end date). | |
| **Presentation and Disclosure** | Appropriate disclosures in the financial statements are in line with applicable financial reporting standards. | Ensure PPE are correctly disclosed in the financial statements at the reporting date in accordance with IAS 16. |

Now that we understand the objectives of the auditor with regard to PPE, in the following sections we will consider how the auditor addresses these objectives through substantive testing.

## 11.5 DEVELOPING AN AUDIT PLAN FOR PROPERTY, PLANT AND EQUIPMENT

Before the audit of PPE is undertaken, an assessment of the audit risk must be completed. As discussed in detail in **Chapter 7**, audit risk is made up of three components: inherent risk, control risk and detection risk. We will examine these components specifically as they relate to PPE.

### Inherent Risk

Inherent risk can vary, depending on the types of PPE in question. A number of factors can include:

- the general economic environment – e.g. during a recessionary period a decline in a specific industry may result in the assets related to certain activities becoming impaired;
- the type of industry or sector that the client entity operates in – e.g. in a manufacturing company, scrapped or old machinery may not be taken off the fixed asset register (FAR), or small tools or equipment may be stolen;
- the specific types of asset being held by the client – e.g. assets of a technological nature can quickly become obsolete;
- susceptibility to theft, i.e. some assets are more susceptible to theft due to a combination of size (easily stolen), transferability (easily sold) and high value (significant gain) – e.g. a dentist's equipment is not likely to be vulnerable to theft because it is not easily resold and so the inherent risk is low;
- asset class – e.g. self-constructed assets require a considerable amount of review by the client entity's accountant to ensure each item capitalised is in line with IAS 16 recognition requirements. If this is not a regular occurrence, the accountant may not be familiar with the standard requirements.

### Control Risk and Detection Risk

Control risk can also vary, depending on the type of asset class. Fixtures and fittings may have a lower assessed level of control risk as these are sometimes processed as routine purchase transactions. On the other hand, land and buildings will have a higher control risk and will be subject to separate controls, such as capital budgeting and specific authorisation by the board of directors.

Fixed asset transactions are infrequent and high in monetary value, i.e. they are usually **material**, therefore a predominantly **substantive audit approach** (see **Chapter 8**) is normally adopted for PPE. As a result, the planned level of detection risk (see **Chapter 7**) is low. In other words, focused substantive procedures are required because no reliance is placed on controls. This approach is discussed in detail in **Section 11.7** below.

## 11.6  AUDIT TRAIL FOR PROPERTY, PLANT AND EQUIPMENT

To appreciate the role of the auditor in validating transactions, classes of transactions or balances at the assertion level it is important to first understand the audit trail associated with the relevant cycle. **Figure 11.1** outlines an audit trail that could be followed when validating the various management assertions associated with PPE.

FIGURE 11.1: PPE AUDIT TRAIL

| Financial Statements | Trial Balance | Nominal/ General Ledgers | Transactions |
|---|---|---|---|
| Summary of trial balances, presented in accordance with applicable financial reporting standards | Summary of totals of each nominal sub-ledger | Complete listing of all transactions<br><br>Sub-ledger is a subset of the nominal ledger | The recording of source documents into a journal entry (double-entry bookkeeping) |

| Statement of Comprehensive Income | € |
|---|---|
| Revenue | 15,000 |
| COS | 5,000 |
| Gross Profit | 10,000 |
| Expenses | 6,648 |
| Net Profit | 3,352 |

| Statement of Financial Position | € |
|---|---|
| Property, Plant & Equipment | 10,000 |
| Receivables | 2,000 |
| Payables | 1,500 |
| | 10,500 |
| Share Capital & Reserves | 3,352 |

| Nominal Ledger | Dr | Cr |
|---|---|---|
| Sales | | 15,000 |
| Expenses | 6,648 | |
| Purchases | 5,000 | |
| Land Cost | 7,000 | |
| Buildings Cost | 5,000 | |
| Buildings Depreciation | | 2,000 |
| Payables | | 500 |
| Receivables | 2,000 | |
| Share capital | | 5,000 |
| Reserves | | 2148 |
| | 25,648 | 25,648 |

| Trans # | Pure date | Asset Descrip' | Asset # | Cost |
|---|---|---|---|---|
| 362827 | 01.02.2001 | Highacre | 345 | 100 |
| 468488 | 09.04.2002 | Lowacre | 367 | 1,500 |
| 489505 | 02.09.2004 | Paddington Plot | 401 | 1,700 |
| 563837 | 03.08.2007 | Green Belt 1 | 407 | 400 |
| 578390 | 12.04.2018 | High Rise Plot 1 | 480 | 1,900 |
| 578396 | 14.04.2018 | High Rise Plot 2 | 481 | 1,400 |
| | | | | 7,000 |

| | Dr | Cr |
|---|---|---|
| Dr Land cost | 1,400 | |
| Cr Property DAC | | 1,400 |
| Being purchase of high-rise plot 2 | | |

The auditor is presented with the financial statements, which are supported by a trial balance (**SOFP for PPE**), which is made up of a summary of transactions in the form of a nominal ledger, which is made up of individual transactions, which are supported by source documents that validate the various assertions associated with the transaction or balance.

**Source Documents**

E.g. land purchase contract and property deeds

It is essential that the **direction** of the test is appropriate to the assertion being tested. So, when testing for occurrence/existence, the auditor will start with the financial statements and trace back through the trial balance, etc. to the source documents. However, when testing for completeness the auditor will always start with the source documents and trace upwards to the financial statements. Whatever the direction of the test, the source document data is used to validate whether the transaction has been appropriately recorded/valued and that it proves the entity's rights and obligations assertion over the transaction/balance. Sometimes a blend of source documents will be required to validate all assertions, while in other instances a single source document will validate a number of assertions.

Source documents associated with PPE include:
- asset purchase documents (e.g. invoices or purchase contracts);
- proof of title or ownership documents (e.g. vehicle registration certificates or property title deeds);
- lease agreements, which will assist in evaluating whether the lease is an operating lease or a finance lease and the cost, UEL, etc. associated with the asset; and
- insurance documents, which can be used to determine ownership (one would not insure an asset one did not own) and to some degree valuation.

While not mentioned in our audit trail, the main safeguard over PPE is the preparation of a **fixed asset register (FAR)**, which records all movements relating to PPE. The FAR should be maintained by the client entity, with the individual responsible for maintaining it independent of those who actually use the assets. In order for the FAR to be relied on, the auditor should perform a **walkthrough test** (see **Chapter 8**). These tests could include: randomly selecting an asset from the premises and confirming it is included on the FAR; randomly selecting an asset from the FAR and confirming its physical existence; tracing the cost of an asset from the FAR to its purchase invoice or contract; and agreeing UEL's noted on the FAR to the client entity's PPE policy. As with all documents supplied by the client, the auditor should check the mathematical accuracy of the document (which can be easily validated using tools such as Excel).

## 11.7  SUBSTANTIVE AUDIT PROGRAMME FOR PROPERTY, PLANT AND EQUIPMENT

An **audit programme** records the specific details of tests to be performed by the auditor. The audit programme becomes a guide to the **audit engagement team** as to the work to be performed in a particular area. As work is completed, a reference is included on the audit programme showing the location in the audit file where details of the tests performed are recorded. While the audit programme for any cycle will vary from entity to entity, in **Example 11.1** below we consider the typical tests the auditor would include in the audit programme for PPE. Students should note that in a real-life scenario, each test would be referenced to the location in the audit working file where the test is actually performed.

EXAMPLE 11.1: SUBSTANTIVE TESTING AUDIT PROGRAMME FOR
PROPERTY PLANT AND EQUIPMENT (LARGE COMPANY LIMITED)[1]

| Large Company Limited 31 December 2018 | Audit Materiality: | | €3,642,500 |
|---|---|---|---|
| | Performance Materiality: | | €2,731,875 |
| | | Initials | Date |
| | Prepared by: | | |
| | Reviewed by: | | |

**Property, Plant and Equipment Audit Programme**

Ensure that the audit plan is reflected in the following tests. The following tests are suggestions only and should be removed or added to as necessary to address the risks of material misstatement identified at the risk-assessment stage.

| **Accounting Policy** | |
|---|---|
| Assess the appropriateness of the accounting policy and the accounting estimates method for this area. Ensure that the accounting policy is in accordance with accounting standards and applicable law, and that the methods used for making the accounting estimates are appropriate. | Existence Completeness Rights and Obligations Recording, Valuation and Classification |
| **Initial Procedures** | |
| Obtain or prepare a lead schedule, agree to balance sheet and provide sufficient audit trail: (a) agree to nominal ledger; (b) agree opening balances to prior year's signed financial statements; and (c) prepare a commentary explaining the composition of the fixed asset balance, comparing the balance with prior-year comparatives and with expectations. | Existence/Occurrence Recording (accuracy) and Classification |
| **PPE Movements in the Period** | |
| Obtain or prepare separate schedules of: (a) additions within each category; and (b) disposals within each category. Vouch as appropriate a sample of the additions and disposals. | Occurrence Recording (accuracy) and Classification Rights and Obligations |
| Ensure additions meet the client's capitalisation policy. | Recording (accuracy) and Classification |
| Obtain a copy of the capital expenditure budget of the entity and vouch additions to it to confirm authority to purchase. | Occurrence Rights and Obligations |

---

[1] Source: based on *Procedures for Quality Audit 2010* (© Chartered Accountants Ireland, 2010), E1 and updated by the authors in December 2017.

| | |
|---|---|
| Consider the accounting treatment of any self-constructed assets. | Occurrence Recording (accuracy) Rights and Obligations |
| Consider possible unrecorded disposals (e.g. assets scrapped). | Completeness |
| Inquire if any fixed assets have been improved or constructed during the period and ensure capitalised or expensed as appropriate. | Completeness |
| Review nominal ledger accounts for repairs and renewals (or similar) for items that should have been capitalised. Review capital budgets and minutes to identify possible assets purchased but not capitalised. | Completeness |
| **Depreciation** | |
| (a) Consider reasonableness of provision of all depreciation with regard to: <br> (i) estimated useful lives; and <br> (ii) residual value. <br> (b) Test-check depreciation calculations (either via a sample or a substantive analytical procedure). <br> (c) Agree total to statement of comprehensive income charge. <br> (d) Challenge estimates made by management. | Recording (accuracy) and Classification Completeness Occurrence |
| **Asset Balances** | |
| Ascertain location of title deeds and inspect or confirm details with third party. If these are inspected on a rotational basis, check and note the last year they were inspected. | Existence Rights and Obligations |
| Inspect vehicle registration documents and agree details to company records and ensure that vehicles are registered in the company's name. | Existence Rights and Obligations |
| Select a sample of assets from the FAR and trace to the physical asset. <br><br> * Physical inspection may give indications of impairment/ obsolescence and therefore partially covers valuation. | Existence Valuation* |
| Select a sample of assets physically held by the entity and trace to the FAR. <br><br> * Physical inspection may give indications of impairment/ obsolescence and therefore partially covers valuation. | Completeness Valuation* |
| **Other Considerations** | |
| Revaluations – ensure that all revaluations are accounted for correctly. <br> Ensure that historical cost information is available for disclosure purposes. | Valuation Presentation and Disclosure |

| | |
|---|---|
| Impairment – inquire of management if they have considered carrying out an impairment review. Consider possible indications that assets are impaired in value and whether an impairment review is required. | Valuation |
| Finance leases – obtain or prepare a schedule of net book value and depreciation of assets held under hire-purchase contracts and finance leases. | Existence<br>Completeness<br>Recording (accuracy) and Classification<br>Rights and Obligations<br>Presentation and Disclosure |
| Operating leases – review lease costs expensed and consider whether the accounting treatment is correct. | Occurrence<br>Completeness<br>Recording (accuracy) and Classification<br>Rights and Obligations<br>Presentation and Disclosure |
| Capital commitments – review relevant documentation to ensure that any capital commitments have been identified (e.g. board minutes, after-date review and inquiries). | Presentation and Disclosure |
| Ensure financial statements disclosures comply with the appropriate legislation and applicable accounting standards. | Presentation and Disclosure |
| **Conclusion**<br>Subject to the matters noted for the reviewer, in my opinion sufficient audit assurance has been obtained to enable us to conclude that property, plant and equipment are not materially misstated. | |

## 11.8 SUBSTANTIVE TESTING PROCEDURES FOR PROPERTY, PLANT AND EQUIPMENT

The substantive testing audit programme in **Example 11.1** outlined the principal procedures involved in testing PPE. In this section we will look at each of these in more detail:
1. Initial procedures:
   (a) Opening balances
   (b) Accuracy of schedules provided by management
   (c) Lead schedule
   (d) Analytical reviews.

2. PPE movements in the period:
   (a) Additions
   (b) Disposals
   (c) Repairs and maintenance
   (d) Depreciation.
3. PPE balances
4. Other considerations
   (a) Impairment review
   (b) Revaluations
   (c) Leases
   (d) Unusual items.

## Initial Procedures

### *Opening Balances*

Initially, evidence must be obtained as to the accuracy of the opening balances and the ownership of the assets comprising the balances. The reason for this is twofold:
1. it confirms that the comparative figures in the financial statements (which must be included in the current year's financial statements) agree to the final accounts of the prior year; and
2. it highlights any final entries (last-minute adjusting journal entries) of the prior year not correctly carried forward, which may indicate an error in the current year's financial statement figures.

Auditing opening balances can be completed as follows:
- Agree the opening balances to the prior-year working papers and signed financial statements. This may highlight an opening balance in the current year's accounts that does not agree to the closing balance per the prior year's financial statements – in which case a change would be made to the opening balance of the current year, which would impact the closing balance of the current year. This usually arises due to final adjustments in the prior year that are not reflected in the actual accounts (nominal and general ledgers).
- Inspect the permanent audit file (file containing long-standing documents that do not change every year) for details of title deeds and registered charges, such as mortgages.
- If this is the first year of the audit engagement, the auditor will still need to establish that the opening balances are materially correct, which can pose a difficulty if either the client entity was exempt from audit in the prior year or a predecessor auditor carried out the audit. The audit of opening balances in such instances is discussed in detail in **Chapter 6**, Section 6.9, which addresses the requirements of ISA 510 *Initial Audit Engagements – Opening Balances*.

### *Accuracy of Schedules*

All schedules provided by the client entity (e.g. the **fixed asset register**; the additions and disposal listings and the depreciation charge for the period) should be totalled and cross-totalled to ensure their mathematical accuracy. Additionally, they should be agreed to the financial statements balances and transactions that they support. At least one item should be selected from the schedule and traced to its respective source data to validate the accuracy of the schedule before further testing is performed on it.

## *Prepare the Lead Schedule*

The **lead schedule** acts as a summary of the balances and transactions to be audited that relate to a particular class of transactions and balances. It allows the auditor to control the procedures by referencing each balance or transaction to the audit working paper, which records the audit tests that have been performed.

For PPE, the lead schedule is similar to the PPE note in the financial statements (see Note 13 in **Appendix B**). It contains a summary of the individual balances that make up the PPE balance, and acts as a checklist for the auditor to ensure that all aspects of the balance and the movements in the period leading to that balance are audited. As each item is tested, the lead schedule is updated with details of where it can be found in the audit file. An example of a lead schedule is shown below at **Example 11.2**. Note that the standard headings and information of any audit working paper are applied.

EXAMPLE II.2: LEAD SCHEDULE FOR PROPERTY, PLANT AND EQUIPMENT[2]

| Large Company Limited 31 December 2018 | Audit Materiality | | €3,642,500 |
| --- | --- | --- | --- |
| | Performance Materiality | | €2,731,875 |
| | | Initials | Date |
| | Prepared by: | | |
| | Reviewed by: | | |

**Property, Plant and Equipment Lead Schedule**

| | Freehold Land and Buildings €000 | Plant and Machinery €000 | Motor Vehicles €000 | Total €000 |
| --- | --- | --- | --- | --- |
| **Cost/Valuation:** | | | | |
| 1 January 2018 | 400,000 | 113,625 | 28,800 | 542,425 |
| Additions | 0 | 82,250 | 35,000 | 117,250 |
| Revaluation | (355,000) | 0 | 0 | (355,000) |
| Disposals | 0 | (49,000) | (14,655) | (63,655) |
| 31 December 2018 | 45,000 | 146,875 | 49,145 | 241,020 |
| | | | | |
| **Depreciation:** | | | | |
| 1 January 2018 | 319,800 | 61,725 | 20,400 | 401,925 |
| During 2018 | 18,000 | 48,705 | 14,500 | 81,205 |
| Revaluation | (337,800) | 0 | 0 | (337,800) |
| Disposals | 0 | (29,000) | (5,360) | (34,360) |
| 31 December 2018 | 0 | 81,430 | 29,540 | 110,970 |
| **Net book value:** | | | | |
| 31 December 2018 | 45,000 | 65,445 | 19,605 | 130,050 |
| 31 December 2017 | 80,200 | 51,900 | 8,400 | 140,500 |

---

[2] Source: Based on *Procedures for Quality Audit 2010* (© Chartered Accountants Ireland, 2010), and updated by the authors in December 2017.

### Analytical Review

An **analytical review** (see **Chapter 5**, Section 5.4) is usually performed at the start of each substantive procedure relating to each balance or class of transaction. Calculating ratios and analysing results against industry information, prior-year results, budgets, etc. allows the auditor to get a feel for the movements in the year and to make comparisons against norms. It therefore provides the auditor with additional insights into the client entity and the industry it operates in, and better prepares them for the audit programme.

At the close of the substantive procedures, the auditor's aim is to ensure that they can comment on all movements and key ratios (e.g. return on capital employed (ROCE); fixed asset turnover), with supporting explanations. If the auditor cannot explain any element, this will highlight the need to perform additional substantive procedures. The analytical review performed here differs from a substantive analytical procedure in that the auditor's aim is not to substantiate the balance (i.e. prove the assertions), but rather to ensure an understanding of the movements and relationships when performing substantive procedures.

An example of the type of analytical procedures carried out in relation to PPE is shown below in **Example 11.3**. Note the brief commentary that is included, which offers an explanation for the movement. While this does not constitute audit evidence, it does provide a summary of what makes up the movements, allowing the auditor to assess the completeness of the fieldwork to date.

## Property, Plant and Equipment Movements in the Period

Having performed the initial procedures, let us now consider the specific audit procedures the auditor should carry out in relation to the movements of PPE in the period. Essentially, these are:

- additions, i.e. purchase of new PPE;
- disposals;
- consideration of repairs and maintenance in the period; and
- depreciation.

### Additions

In order to audit the additions to PPE in the period, the auditor needs to establish: (a) what was purchased (which should be evident from the fixed asset register); (b) the cost of the asset purchased; (c) if the asset is permitted to be capitalised under IAS 16; and (d) that all additions have been recorded.

As stated in IAS 16, paragraph 16:
  "The cost of an item of property, plant and equipment comprises:
  (a) its purchase price, including import duties and non-refundable purchase taxes, after deducting trade discounts and rebates.

EXAMPLE 11.3: ANALYTICAL REVIEW ON PROPERTY, PLANT
AND EQUIPMENT (LARGE COMPANY LIMITED)

| Analysis | 2018 | 2017 | Movement | Commentary |
|---|---|---|---|---|
| **Return on PPE** (Revenue ÷ PPE) | = €280,250 ÷ €130,050 = 215% | = €198,500 ÷ €140,500 = 141% | **+74%** | This rise in return on PPE is partially driven by the deficit on revaluation that is masking some of the additions in the period. Additionally, revenue, due to a move into the luxury market, is significantly up on the prior year. |
| **PPE NBV year-on-year comparison** | €130,050 | €140,500 | **(€10,450)** | While the figure for fixed assets has decreased overall, additions of €117,250,000 occurred in the period, which are being masked by the high depreciation charge of €81,205,000 as well as the deficit on revaluation of freehold buildings and some small disposals. The new assets are helping to drive the revenue number. |

(b) any costs directly attributable to bringing the asset to the location and condition necessary for it to be capable of operating in the manner intended by management.

(c) the initial estimate of the costs of dismantling and removing the item and restoring the site on which it is located ...".

It should also be remembered that borrowing costs that are "directly attributable to the acquisition, construction or production of a qualifying asset form part of the cost of that asset" in line with IAS 23 *Borrowing* Costs, paragraph 1.

The following procedures should be performed in relation to additions to PPE:

- The auditor should obtain a copy of the client entity's fixed asset budget for the year under review. This document not only confirms authority to purchase but will also highlight any significant variances between actual and budgeted purchases. In addition, a review of budgeted expenditure not yet incurred will indicate if the entity has adequate funds and working capital to finance such additions. Budget approval should be verified through a review of the board minutes.
- An understanding of the client entity's capitalisation policy must be obtained. This gives an understanding of the client entity's policy in deciding whether a purchase is a capital item or whether it should be expensed to the statement of comprehensive income. Broadly speaking, most companies set a monetary value below which, regardless of their nature, purchases are expensed. The auditor must ensure that this policy is consistent year on year. The capitalisation policy is considered in **Example 11.4** below.

EXAMPLE 11.4: CAPITALISATION OF EXPENDITURES

A client entity's capitalisation policy is to capitalise all items greater than €1,000 that are of a capital nature.

Included in the fixed asset additions are a laptop at a cost of €1,200 and a keyboard at €400.

The client has correctly capitalised the laptop in line with its capitalisation policy, as the asset is of a capital nature and it cost more than €1,000. However, the client has incorrectly capitalised the keyboard in accordance with the capitalisation policy – although the assets are of a capital nature, the keyboard cost less than €1,000.

The cost of additions must be verified. If there are a large number of additions they can be completed on a sample basis (sampling is covered in **Chapter 6,** Section 6.8). This is done by tracing the amount capitalised as per the **additions schedule** (a list of assets purchased in the period) to the supporting purchase invoice/contract. A number of items on the invoice must be agreed:

1. The date of the invoice must be within the accounting period under review (**cut-off, occurrence**).
2. The invoice must be addressed to the client entity (**rights and obligations**).
3. The cost per the invoice must be agreed to the amount capitalised, as stated in the additions schedule (**recording/accuracy**).
4. VAT must have been properly accounted for. That is, if the client entity is registered for VAT, then the VAT is reclaimable and the assets must be capitalised at cost excluding the VAT element; if it is not VAT-registered the assets are capitalised at cost, including the VAT element (**classification, recording/accuracy**).
5. Ensure all costs capitalised are allowable under IAS 16 (as noted above):
   (a) For major additions, the assets should be physically inspected. It is important, on physical inspection, to ensure that details of the asset are agreed to the invoice and to the capitalised amount (e.g. serial number, description, etc.).

(b) When a client entity internally constructs its PPE, the auditor should verify that all costs have been properly classified, including costs of materials, labour, borrowing and overheads, if applicable. There is potential for **inherent risk** in this area and the auditor needs to evaluate company controls and perform substantive procedures, as necessary, to ensure costs are genuine, accurately recorded and complete.

## *Disposals*

The second key type of movement relating to PPE is the disposal of assets. The auditor should start by requesting a list of disposals during the period under review from the client (alternatively, these should be recorded in the fixed asset register). To ensure that all disposals have been accounted for, the auditor must confirm all such disposals with management, re-analyse any miscellaneous income that may relate to the sale of PPE and reconcile the results of a physical count of relevant PPE to the general ledger, as this may highlight any possible omissions (the completeness assertion).

Supporting documentation should be obtained and inspected for sales and trade-ins of PPE. This documentation should include cash remittance advices and/or sales agreements. These are examined to determine the accuracy of the accounting records, including the recognition of any related gain or loss. The gain or loss on disposal of a fixed asset is recalculated by the auditor to ensure its accuracy. Proceeds received should be traced to bank statements to confirm receipt and that the profit or loss on disposal was calculated correctly.

## *Repairs and Maintenance*

As stated in IAS 16, paragraph 12:
> "an entity does not recognise in the carrying amount of an item of property, plant and equipment the costs of the day-to-day servicing of the item. Rather, these costs are recognised in profit or loss as incurred."

Thus, repairs and maintenance costs are not capitalised but instead are expensed to the statement of comprehensive income as they are incurred. This is a classification issue and it is important to look out for it when auditing the costs capitalised. The auditor must also review the repairs and maintenance accounts for completeness to ensure that items of a capital nature have not been incorrectly expensed to the statement of comprehensive income.

## *Depreciation*

The client entity's depreciation methods must be reviewed to ensure that they are reasonable and consistent with the prior year. It is also important to ensure the depreciation policy used by the client entity is in agreement with the depreciation policy as outlined in the financial statements. The auditor will use one of two methods to verify the accurate recording of the depreciation charge:

1. **Test of Details** In this method, the auditor verifies the accuracy of the depreciation charge by recalculation. This can be completed on a sample basis. First, the auditor needs to obtain a schedule of depreciation charged by asset and agree this schedule to the charge in the financial statements. Then, selecting a sample of assets and recalculating the depreciation charge, the auditor reconciles the charge as calculated to the client entity's figure as per the lead schedule. The use of CAATs may mean that the auditor can easily test 100% of the population by repeating formulas in applications such as Excel (see **Chapter 9**).

2. **Substantive Analytical Procedure** (introduced in **Chapter 5**, Section 5.4) A substantive analytical procedure (also known as a '**proof in total**') is a widely used method for auditors to validate the depreciation charge in the financial statements. This involves computing the depreciation by class on an overall basis. **Example 11.5** below illustrates how to test depreciation on a reasonableness basis.

EXAMPLE 11.5: SUBSTANTIVE ANALYTICAL PROCEDURE ON DEPRECIATION

In the 'Depreciation' section of the Statement of Accounting Policies in **Appendix B**, relating to Large Company Limited, the company's policy with respect to expected useful lives is outlined. The auditor can use this to prepare a substantive analytical procedure (proof in total) on depreciation. It also states that the company charges a full year of depreciation in the year of purchase and a full year's depreciation in the year of disposal.

This information, along with elements of the PPE disclosure note and fixed asset register (which indicates that €60,000,000 of the plant and machinery is fully depreciated), allows the auditor to calculate an expected deprecation charge as follows:

**Freehold Land and Buildings** According to note 13, Property, Plant and Equipment, €15,000,000 of the €400,000,000 relates to freehold land, which means that €385,000,000 is depreciable (under IAS 16, land is not depreciable). Therefore, €385,000,000 charged as straight-line depreciation over 22 years would require an annual depreciation charge of €17,500,000.

**Plant and Machinery** According to the Disclosure Notes: Statement of Accounting Policies, 'Property, Plant and Equipment', plant and machinery has a useful life of three years, a full year's depreciation is charged on additions and on disposals, and the straight-line method is used to calculate depreciation. Furthermore, the fixed asset register indicates that €60,000,000 of plant and machinery is fully depreciated. The auditor's calculation would look something like this:

| | Cost €000 | NBV €000 | Useful Life (Years) | Expected Charge €000 |
|---|---|---|---|---|
| Balance at 1 January 2018 | 113,625 | N/A | 3 | 37,875 |
| Less: full depreciation | (60,000) | 0 | | (20,000) |
| Additions | 82,250 | N/A | 3 | 27,417 |
| | | | | 45,292 |

**Motor Vehicles** Also according to Large Company's Statement of Accounting Policies, motor vehicles have a useful life of four years, a full year's depreciation is charged on additions and disposals and the straight-line method is used to calculate depreciation. Thus, the auditor's calculation would be as follows:

| | Cost €000 | NBV €000 | Useful Life (Years) | Expected Charge €000 |
|---|---|---|---|---|
| Balance at 1 January 2018 | 28,800 | N/A | 4 | 7,200 |
| Additions | 35,000 | N/A | 4 | 8,750 |
| | | | | 15,950 |

| **Comparison of Expected Depreciation to Actual Depreciation** | **€000** |
|---|---|
| Total expected depreciation (17,500 + 45,292 + 15,950) | 78,742 |
| Actual depreciation charged | 81,205 |
| Difference | 2,463 |

This difference would be compared to a threshold (tolerable error) calculated by the auditor. If the difference was within the threshold, the depreciation charge would be accepted as not being materially misstated. If the difference was outside of the threshold, the auditor would have to perform further substantive procedures to be satisfied as to the accuracy of the depreciation figure. The tolerable error will take into account: materiality, risk and the value of the balance being tested.

Considering that the performance materiality for Large Company Limited is €2,731,875 (see **Example 11.2** above), it is likely that the difference would be above a calculated threshold and so further audit procedures would be performed.

Further audit procedures may include either performing tests of details or inquiring of management why they believe the expected depreciation charge based on your calculation differs from that of the actual charge in the financial statements.

**Assessing Reasonableness of Useful Lives** It is important that the auditor considers the reasonableness of the useful lives applied by the entity. It is not enough to compare the useful life in the depreciation calculation with that stated in the depreciation section of the statement of accounting policies detailed in the financial statements. The auditor must also consider if the estimate of useful life is appropriate. The three years' depreciation period for plant and machinery appears quite low, although it may be adequate for the type of equipment in this industry, and, considering that, as per **Example 11.2**, the PPE additions are 22% and disposals 11% of the opening balance, this may well be reasonable. Additionally, charging a full year's depreciation in the year of addition as well as the year of disposal seems excessive, and management should be queried in relation to this.

## Property, Plant and Equipment Balances

Having obtained evidence for the management assertions related to the movements of PPE, the auditor must then be satisfied as to the continued existence of the PPE balances. Existence can be determined in a number of ways, and three key methods of determining existence are discussed below:

1. **Physical inspection** The auditor should request to view (physically inspect) a sample of assets to confirm their existence. CAATs can be used to assist with the sample selection, ensuring the selection is unbiased. A physical inspection gives an opportunity to inspect the condition of the assets and to confirm that they are actually in use. Assets that appear unused (indicating obsolescence and impairment) should be queried with management to ensure that their valuation is recorded accurately in the financial statements. Tracing a sample of assets from the FAR to the physical asset will test for existence of the assets recorded, whereas selecting physical assets and tracing them to the FAR will test for the completeness of the FAR (i.e. it is not missing assets held and owned by the entity).

2. **Ownership documentation** The physical presence of an asset does not prove that it actually belongs to the client; thus, by inspecting ownership documents, such as property title deeds, vehicle registration certificates, etc., the auditor confirms the rights and obligations assertion.

3. **Insurance documentation** Reviewing insurance documentation will also provide evidence of existence and rights and obligations, as the client entity will only insure assets that it owns. The insurance value of assets will also give some indication of valuation.

## Other Considerations

Having performed the substantive procedures relating to PPE movements and PPE balances, there are some other matters that the auditor must consider before they have adequately completed their substantive procedures relating to PPE. These include:

- an **impairment** review;
- consideration of any **revaluations** of PPE; and
- substantive procedures for **leases** (where applicable to the entity).

### Impairment Review

The client entity is required to carry out an impairment review where there is any indication that an individual asset or class of assets may be impaired. The auditor's job in this context is twofold:

1. to ensure that the client has adequately considered the possibility of impairment; and
2. then, where impairment reviews have taken place, to ensure that these are in line with IAS 36 *Impairment of Assets*.

**1. The client entity's consideration of impairment** An **impairment review** is required by the client entity at the end of the first financial year following the purchase of an asset, and annually where an asset's useful life exceeds 20 years or is indefinite. IAS 36 recognises that an impairment review should be carried out when there is some indication that impairment has occurred. Impairments generally arise when there has been an event or change in circumstances, such as:

- something has happened to the asset (e.g. physical damage); or
- there has been a change in the economic environment in which the asset is used (e.g. taxes on assets with high emissions may render those assets uneconomical to use going forward and they may have become impaired); or
- there has been a change in the demand for the product that the asset is used to produce (e.g. a move away from carpets to laminate flooring, rendering carpet looms impaired).

**2. Ensuring client's impairment reviews are in line with IAS 36**  As required by IAS 36, the auditor must ensure that the **carrying value** of PPE does not exceed the greater of either its **net realisable value** (sales price less cost to sell) or its **value in use (net present value** (NPV)) of a cash flow or other benefits that an asset generates for a specific owner under a specific use. This can be tested by:

- reviewing the client entity's workings on the impairment (how have they calculated the impaired value?);
- reviewing the reasonableness of the assumptions used in the calculation of the impairment. (The auditor would inquire of management about any potentially overvalued assets. Obsolete and damaged assets should be physically inspected and compared to values included in the financial statements.);
- determining if any assets of the client entity are held that relate to discontinued activities.

The audit of estimates was discussed in **Chapter 6**, Section 6.10, which covers the requirements on the auditor when auditing estimates under ISA 540 *Auditing Accounting Estimates, Including Fair Value Accounting Estimates, and Related Disclosures.*

### Revaluation of Property, Plant and Equipment

The client entity may decide to revalue PPE to reflect a more accurate value in the statement of financial position. A revaluation of an asset should reflect the 'real' conditions and be based on actual market conditions. According to IAS 16, paragraph 36:

"If an item of property, plant and equipment is revalued, the entire class of property plant and equipment to which that asset belongs shall be revalued."

Thus, the auditor needs first to consider if the client entity has properly considered the entire class of PPE where one asset within that class has been revalued.

Also required by IAS 16, paragraph 31:

"Revaluations shall be made with sufficient regularity to ensure that the carrying amount does not differ materially from that which would be determined using fair value at the end of the reporting period."

This requires the auditor to ensure that if a policy of revaluation exists, then the client entity considers the revalued amount regularly to ensure that it is reflected at its fair value. The auditor can make inquiries of management as to their approach to these considerations and should review any exercises carried out by management that demonstrate their consideration of the fair value of revalued assets, even in years where no revaluation has taken place.

If assets have been revalued during the period under review, the auditor must obtain a copy of the valuer's report, as per ISA 620 *Using the Work of an Auditor's Expert* (see **Chapter 10**). Before considering the expert's report, the auditor should first consider the calibre of the expert by reviewing their experience in the subject area and their qualifications. The auditor should also consider the expert's relationship to the client entity to ensure that the report is not subject to bias.

In assessing the expert's work, the auditor should ensure that the substance of the expert's findings are properly reflected in the financial statement assertions. The auditor must also consider:

- the source of the data used (was it generated by the client entity or by some other external source?);
- the assumptions and methods used;
- when the work was carried out;
- the reasons for changes in assumptions and methods; and
- the result of the expert's work in light of the auditor's knowledge of the business and the results of other audit procedures (i.e. is the expert's work corroborated by other evidence found?).

As discussed in **Chapter 10**, Section 10.4, the auditor is not the expert and therefore cannot judge all assumptions and methods used. However, they should seek to obtain an understanding of these to consider their reasonableness. This will involve discussions with the expert as well as with the client entity to ensure that explanations, assumptions and methods are not contradictory to other evidence obtained.

### Leases

Leases may be classified as either **finance leases** (capitalised under PPE) or **operating leases** (charged to the statement of comprehensive income). For PPE held under lease agreements, it is important that the auditor obtains a copy of each lease agreement and ensures they are correctly classified in line with IFRS 16 *Leases*.

For assets held under finance leases, these assets should be included in the client entity's **fixed asset register**. The cost of assets held under finance leases should be verified by comparison with purchase invoices. This cost should also be agreed to the cost as stated in the finance lease agreement. Under IFRS 16:

"a lessee may elect to account for lease payments as an expense on a straight-line basis over the lease term or another systematic basis for the following two types of leases:

(i) leases with a lease term of 12 months or less and containing no purchase options – this election is made by class of underlying asset; and

(ii) leases where the underlying asset has a low value when new (such as personal computers or small items of office furniture) – this election can be made on a lease-by-lease basis."

The auditor needs to obtain a copy of the lease agreement and ensure that all conditions of the lease are recorded correctly and comply with the requirements of IFRS 16.

## Unusual Items

The auditor should use CAATs (such as Excel or specialised audit software) to review the PPE nominals or FAR to identify unusual transactions or balances, which may include interrogating the data to identify:
- negative NBV assets;
- assets held at a cost that is less than the minimum cost of capitalised assets as per the client entity's PPE policy;
- depreciation rates that are not in line with useful economic life (UEL) as per the client entity's policy;
- wording that might indicate inclusion of non-capital assets, e.g. 'repair' or 'training'.

## 11.9 DISCLOSURE REQUIREMENTS

Finally, the auditor will consider the adequacy of the disclosures. Disclosure requirements relating to PPE for most companies entail inclusion of the 'PPE Note'. However, the auditor needs to consider the requirements of IAS 16 and IFRS 16 to ensure that all disclosures are:
- complete, i.e. that no PPE-related disclosures are missing – the auditor can use IAS 16 as a checklist;
- accurate, i.e. they reflect the actual transactions and information relating to events surrounding PPE;
- related to events that actually occurred or assets (or charges against assets) that actually exist; and
- properly presented (i.e. in a manner expected by IAS 16).

The disclosure requirements in IAS 16, paragraphs 73–79, include requirements relating to:
- restrictions on title;
- contractual commitments;
- details of revaluations;
- details of finance leases; and
- details of borrowing costs capitalised.

The auditor must fully understand these requirements in order to review the adequacy of the client entity's disclosures.

## 11.10 CONCLUSION

While PPE can represent a material balance in the financial statements and, for some classes of assets, be inherently risky, the auditor frequently takes a focused substantive approach. The reason being that the volume of transactions relating to movements on fixed assets accounts is normally low and 100% (or at least a high percentage coverage) is normally possible. The auditor can therefore efficiently test PPE using a substantive approach.

When auditing the area of PPE, the auditor needs to pay special attention to the existence management assertion by physically inspecting the asset and ownership documents. Additionally, care must be taken when assets are revalued to assess not just the calculation presented by a valuer (auditor's expert), but also the expert's experience, qualifications and expertise.

Significant disclosure requirements exist in the area of PPE and the auditor should dedicate sufficient time to ensuring the completeness and accuracy of all PPE disclosures in the financial statements.

## SUMMARY OF LEARNING OBJECTIVES

**Learning Objective 1** Understand what is included in the audit of PPE.

IAS 16 governs the accounting treatment of PPE, which can include assets such as freehold land and buildings, plant and machinery, or motor vehicles. On the face of the statement of financial position, the net book value (cost less accumulated depreciation) is disclosed and this is expanded upon in a note to the financial statements. The auditor must audit the management assertions relating to the figures that appear on the face of the statement of financial position as well as the disclosure notes that support them.

**Learning Objective 2** Be able to identify the risks and audit objectives applicable to PPE.

The primary risks associated with PPE relate to the risks of:
- Existence – do the assets actually exist and are they in use?
- Valuation – are the assets worth the carrying value included in the financial statements (are they impaired due to obsolescence, damage, etc.)?;
- Have only items capitalisable under IAS 16 been capitalised?; and
- Are the recorded assets actually owned by the entity – does the client have the risks and rewards and are they in control of the asset?

All assertions are relevant for PPE on the transactions side (additions and disposals). The auditor will seek to ensure that the transactions occurred, are complete, properly classified (according to IAS 16) and pertain to the company. Additionally, the auditor will seek to ensure the accuracy of the depreciation figure included in the income statement.

With respect to the PPE balance, the auditor will seek to ensure that all PPE exists and is complete, that the entity has the rights to ownership and that all PPE is appropriately valued.

**Learning Objective 3** Be able to determine an appropriate audit strategy for PPE, taking into consideration the specific risks and audit objectives (assertions).

Generally, the volume of PPE purchased in the period is relatively low and so the auditor will normally take a substantive approach when testing PPE (i.e. no controls testing to reduce substantive testing).

**Learning Objective 4** Be able to develop an audit programme that addresses all the audit objectives (assertions) for PPE.

The key document of interest to the auditor when developing the audit programme is the fixed asset register (FAR). Other documents that may form audit evidence connected to PPE include:

- additions invoices;
- certificates of destruction;
- title deeds;
- vehicle registration certificates;
- accounting policy documents connected to PPE.

The key substantive testing procedures connected to PPE include:

- **Depreciation** The auditor normally conducts **substantive analytical procedures** when testing depreciation or, alternatively, will use CAATs to perform a 100% recalculation of the depreciation charge.
- **Valuation** The auditor will consider indications of impairment of assets; for assets revalued in the period the auditor will seek evidence not only on the valuation provided by the valuer (auditor's expert), but also on their expertise and competence.
- **Existence** The auditor will seek to prove existence by: (a) physical inspection of the asset; and (b) inspecting ownership documentation.
- **Completeness** The auditor will review capital commitments and minutes of board meetings to identify potentially unrecorded assets and pay particular attention to assets in the course of construction to ensure all costs incurred to date are recorded.
- **Additions and Disposals** The auditor will trace the transactions to source documentation to prove their occurrence.
- **Repairs and Maintenance** The auditor will review the repairs and maintenance general ledger account to ensure that no items included therein are of a capital nature (**completeness assertion**). Additionally, they will review the assets capitalised to ensure none is of a repairs and maintenance nature (**classification assertion**).

**Learning Objective 5** Be able to describe and apply specific substantive testing procedures relating to the audit of PPE.

Specific procedures relating to the audit of PPE (other than those relating to the standard audit of additions, disposals, depreciation and year-end balances) include the consideration of: impairment reviews; revaluations of PPE; leases; and a review of unusual items.

**Learning Objective 6** Understand the role CAATs can play when auditing PPE.

The auditor may use a combination of audit software, data analysis tools and other applications, such as Excel, when auditing the area of PPE. The primary use of CAATs when auditing PPE is the use of Excel in reperforming the depreciation calculation, or using interrogation software (such as ACL) to identify unusual items contained in the nominal ledger or FAR.

**Learning Objective 7** Understand the auditor's approach relating to the disclosures of PPE.

The auditor needs to consider the requirements of IAS 16 and IFRS 16 to ensure that all necessary PPE disclosures are: complete and in line with the relevant standards; accurate; relate to events that actually occurred; and are properly presented.

## QUESTIONS

### Self-test Questions

11.1  When should the cost of an item of PPE be recognised as required by IAS 16?

11.2  What is a fixed asset register and who should maintain it?

11.3  What are the benefits of performing an analytical review?

11.4  According to IAS 16, what should the costs of an item of PPE comprise?

11.5  Where should the costs of repairs and maintenance of PPE be recognised?

11.6  Describe the two methods an auditor uses to verify the accurate recording of the depreciation charge.

11.7  List three ways that the existence of PPE can be verified.

11.8  What circumstances may give rise to impairment of PPE?

11.9  When using the work of an auditor's expert, what should the auditor consider?

### Review Questions

(See Suggested Solutions to Review Questions in **Appendix C**.)

### *Question 11.1*

Builder Ltd, an engineering company, is a new client of your audit firm, in which you are the audit senior. The accounts clerk for Builder has provided you with the draft accounts showing the following property, plant and equipment (PPE) for the year ended 31 December 2018. Overall materiality is €67,000.

You are also provided with the following information.

1.  Summary PPE Movements

|  | Freehold Land and Buildings €000 | Plant and Machinery €000 | Motor Vehicles €000 | Total €000 |
|---|---|---|---|---|
| *Cost* | | | | |
| At 1 January 2018 | 1,231 | 679 | 423 | 2,333 |
| Additions | 122 | 242 | 147 | 511 |
| Disposals | – | (125) | (162) | (287) |
| Revaluation | 500 | 0 | 0 | 500 |
| **At 31 December 2018** | **1,853** | **796** | **408** | **3,557** |
| | | | | |
| *Depreciation* | | | | |
| At 1 January 2018 | 674 | 333 | 267 | 1,274 |
| Charge for year | 54 | 80 | 82 | 216 |
| Disposals | – | (99) | (138) | (237) |
| **At 31 December 2018** | **728** | **314** | **211** | **1,253** |

2. Extract from 'Fixed Asset Policy'
   Only capital items exceeding €3,000 are capitalised. A full year's depreciation is charged in the year of purchase and nil in the year of disposal. Useful economic lives are estimated as follows:

   | | |
   |---|---|
   | Freehold buildings | 30 years straight-line |
   | Plant and machinery | 10 years straight-line |
   | Motor vehicles | 8 years straight-line |

3. Extract from 'Nominal Listing' (sample of four items selected)

   | Date | Asset Category | Asset Description | Cost € |
   |---|---|---|---|
   | 02.04.2018 | Freehold Land and Buildings | Building 1 expansion | 15,000 |
   | 10.06.2018 | Plant and Machinery | Drilling machine | 8,500 |
   | 02.12.2018 | Motor Vehicles | Aldo Superior | 75,000 |
   | 20.08.2018 | Plant and Machinery | Drilling machinery | 1,500 |

Associated invoices:

**Track Ltd**

Builders Ltd
2 The Street
Louth

| Date | Description | Cost |
|---|---|---|
| 02.04.18 | Roof repairs | 15,000 |
| Net Invoice Value | | 15,000 |
| VAT | | 1,500 |
| Total | | 16,500 |

**Tooltastic Ltd**

Builders Ltd
2 The Street
Louth

| Date | Description | Cost |
|---|---|---|
| 10.06.18 | Industrial drilling machine | 7,500 |
| Net Invoice Value | | 7,500 |
| VAT | | 1,000 |
| Total | | 8,500 |

**Dino Cars Direct**

Builders Ltd
2 The Street
Louth

| Date | Description | Cost |
|---|---|---|
| 02.12.18 | Aldo Superior Registration 191D2346 | 75,000 |
| Net Invoice Value | | 75,000 |
| VAT | | 17,000 |
| Total | | 92,000 |

**Tooltastic Ltd**

Builders Ltd
2 The Street
Louth

| Date | Description | Cost |
|---|---|---|
| 20.08.18 | Drilling parts | 1,500 |
| Net Invoice Value | | 1,500 |
| VAT | | 300 |
| Total | | 1,800 |

**Requirement**
(a) Discuss your findings with regard to your testing on the PPE additions.
(b) Describe the audit procedure you should carry out to validate the revaluation of free-hold land and buildings.
(c) Describe the audit procedures you should use to validate the valuation assertion as it relates to the PPE balance.
(d) Discuss how you might use CAATs to audit the depreciation charge for the year.

## Question 11.2

You are a trainee accountant in a professional accountancy practice. It is your first audit and you have been assigned to the audit of PPE for the client entity, Floors & Floors Ltd, for the year ended 31 December 2018. Your audit senior has provided you with the following information:

1. Extract from 'PPE Policy'
   Only capital items exceeding €5,000 are capitalised. A full year's depreciation is charged in the year of purchase and nil in the year of disposal.

   **Useful lives:**

   | | |
   |---|---|
   | Freehold buildings | 50 years |
   | Plant and machinery | 10 years |
   | Motor vehicles | 5 years |

   Freehold land located in Dublin is revalued annually. All other freehold land and buildings are valued at cost. All other assets are held at cost.

2. Extracts from audit planning meeting notes dated 2 March 2019
   The production of carpets has been discontinued (manufacturing ceased in December 2018) – the market has been in decline for the last three years. The carpet looms are to be sold in 2019, and are currently included under plant and machinery as follows:

   | | |
   |---|---|
   | Cost | €300,000 |
   | Accumulated depreciation | €120,000 |

   Assets, which are fully depreciated, amount to:

   | | |
   |---|---|
   | Plant and machinery | €250,000 |
   | Motor vehicles | €100,000 |

   Buildings represent 40% of the value of freehold land and buildings at 1 January 2018. All of the additions in the period relate to the construction of buildings completed and in use by year end 31 December 2018.

3. Extracts from the PPE note

|  | Freehold Land and Buildings €000 | Plant and Machinery €000 | Motor Vehicles €000 | Total €000 |
|---|---|---|---|---|
| Cost | 1,500 | 1,233 | 500 | 3,233 |
| | | | | |
| Cost at 1 Jan 2018 | 1,500 | 1,233 | 500 | 3,233 |
| Additions in the period | 150 | 309 | 98 | 557 |
| Disposals in the period | – | (203) | (57) | (260) |
| Cost at 31 December 2018 | 1,650 | 1,339 | 541 | 3,530 |
| Acc. depreciation at 1 Jan 2018 | 300 | 540 | 245 | 1,085 |
| Charge | 15 | 134 | 91 | 240 |
| Disposals | | (203) | (57) | (260) |
| Acc. depreciation at 31 Dec 2018 | 315 | 471 | 279 | 1,065 |
| **NBV @ 31 Dec 2018** | **1,335** | **868** | **262** | **2,465** |

## Requirement

(a) Discuss any concerns you might have around the valuation of PPE.

(b) Test the depreciation charge for the year using substantive analytical procedures. Your audit senior has calculated the threshold to be used as €10,000. You should specify the source of the information used to calculate depreciation and the specific audit procedures you would perform on each set of numbers used in building your substantive analytical procedure.

# 12

# THE AUDIT OF INVENTORY

LEARNING OBJECTIVES

Having studied this chapter on the audit of inventory you should:
1. understand what is included in the audit of inventory;
2. be able to identify the risks and audit objectives applicable to inventory;
3. be able to determine an appropriate audit strategy for inventory, taking into consideration the specific risks and audit objectives (management assertions);
4. be able to develop an audit programme that addresses all the audit objectives (management assertions) for inventory;
5. be able to describe and apply specific substantive testing procedures relating to the audit of inventory;
6. understand the role CAATs can play when auditing inventory; and
7. understand the auditor's approach relating to disclosures of inventory.

## CHECKLIST OF RELEVANT STANDARDS

The relevant standards, both in the RoI and the UK/NI, covered in this chapter are:
- ISA 315 *Identifying and Assessing the Risks of Material Misstatement through Understanding the Entity and its Environment*
- ISA 330 *The Auditor's Responses to Assessed Risks*
- ISA 500 *Audit Evidence*
- ISA 501 *Audit Evidence – Specific Considerations for Selected Items*
- ISA 510 *Initial Audit Engagements – Opening Balances*
- ISA 520 *Analytical Procedures*
- ISA 530 *Audit Sampling*
- ISA 540 *Auditing Accounting Estimates, Including Fair Value Accounting Estimates, and Related Disclosures*
- ISA 620 *Using the Work of an Auditor's Expert*
- IAS 2 *Inventories*
- IFRS 15 *Revenue from Contracts with Customers*

Note, in general when referring to ISAs, it should be understood as referring to the UK and Ireland versions, unless otherwise specified as either ISA (UK) or ISA (Ireland). See the Introduction for an extant list of auditing standards for the RoI and the UK/NI.

## KEY TERMS AND DEFINITIONS FOR THIS CHAPTER

**Aged Inventory Listing**  Lists the total inventory balance broken down by the length of time the inventory has been on the entity's books.

**Bill of Material (BOM)**  A list of all components required to make a particular item of inventory, including quantities of each item needed to manufacture a finished product.

**Cycle Counts**  An entity's performance of ongoing counts of its inventory throughout the year instead of a full inventory count at the year end.

**Final Inventory Listing**  Breaks down the inventory balance in the financial statements by inventory item, along with the quantity and unit price per inventory item. Its total should represent the carrying value of inventory in the financial statements.

**Net Realisable Value (NRV)**  The value of inventory based on sales price less the cost to completion, less sales, marketing and distribution costs. It may also be defined as the value the inventory would achieve in the open market in its present condition.

**Physical Inventory Count Sheet**  A record of the physical assets held on the entity's premises, completed during a physical count of the assets.

**Roll-forward or Roll-back Procedures**  When the auditor is unable to attend the physical inventory count at year end, they may attend an earlier or later physical inventory count and, internal control procedures permitting, perform a roll-forward or roll-back to determine the existence of inventory at year end.

## 12.1  INTRODUCTION

The objective of substantive testing is to validate the transactions, balances and disclosures at the assertion level in response to identified risks (inherent, control and detection risks as discussed in **Chapters 7** and **8**). The auditor commences substantive testing by focusing on the risk of material misstatement within the transactions and balances being tested, and then identifying the assertions impacted by these risks and then identifying substantive audit procedures that will best test the existence of material misstatement driven by the identified risks.

**Sections 12.2–12.8** outline the requirements of IAS 2 *Inventories* and consider how the auditor:
- identifies audit risks and audit objectives (management assertions) for inventory;
- develops an audit plan for inventory and refines this into an audit programme;
- designs specific tests associated with inventory; and
- ensures adequate presentation and disclosure in the financial statements relating to inventory.

Throughout the chapter it is highlighted where CAATs can be used by the auditor in assisting with ensuring the effective and efficient audit of inventory.

In **Section 12.9** we consider the auditor's approach when auditing the reasonableness of disclosures relating to inventory.

## 12.2  WHAT IS INVENTORY?

Inventory is commonly referred to as 'stock'. In a manufacturing company, inventory consists of three elements: raw materials, work in progress (WIP) and finished goods. For example, in car manufacturing: one of the raw materials is steel; a component of WIP might be a chassis; and finished goods would be the finished car, which will be the final product for sale. However, in a retail company there will only be goods for sale.

IAS 2 is the standard governing the requirements for inventories and the auditor shall seek to ensure that inventories are recorded in compliance with this standard.

Inventory may be verified by a physical count (inventory count), most commonly at the year end or recorded on a continuous 'rolling' basis. In either case, extensive tests of control must be performed over both the recording of inventory and the maintenance of inventory records in order to "obtain sufficient appropriate audit evidence regarding the existence and condition of inventory" (ISA 501 *Audit Evidence – Specific Considerations for Selected Items*, paragraph 3). ISA 501, at paragraph 6, states that:
> "If the auditor is unable to attend the physical inventory counting due to unforeseen circumstances, the auditor shall make or observe some physical counts on an alternative date, and perform audit procedures on intervening transactions."

## 12.3 RISKS ASSOCIATED WITH INVENTORY

Throughout **Chapter 7** we discussed the topic of risk and considered how the auditor should go about detecting risks. We also discussed how the auditor should consider these risks when designing the nature, timing and extent of further audit procedures relative to each financial cycle. As such, before developing the audit plan, the auditor needs to consider a number of risks that may be associated with inventory. These may include:

- The reliability of the inventory recording system – see details of **cycle counting** below.
- The volume of transactions that have occurred during the year, i.e. sales, purchases and transfers. If this is high, then there is a greater chance of misstatements occurring.
- The saleability of products is constantly affected by demand and competition, and therefore valuation is always a risk (lower of cost and **net realisable value (NRV)**).
- Valuation allocations relating to materials, labour and overheads, accounting for scrap and obsolescence, joint product costs, etc.
- Timing of inventory counts and reliability of **roll-forward** and **roll-back procedures** in place if the inventory count is not held at the year end. Roll-forward procedures are required where the count is held and attended by the auditor in advance of the year end, and include tracking movements in and out of inventory between the count and the period end. Roll-back procedures are required where the physical count takes place and is attended by the auditor after the year end, and include tracking movements in and out of inventory between the period end and the date of the count. The assessment of controls surrounding the movements of inventory is critical in determining whether or not a count can be performed pre-year end.
- Location of inventory – often inventory may be stored in multiple locations or with a third party.
- Physical controls over inventory and its susceptibility to theft. Susceptibility to theft will take into consideration such factors as: (a) how easy it is to sell in a black market economy; (b) how moveable the product is; and (c) the value of the product. For example, cigarettes would be susceptible to theft as demand on the black market would be high (high retail value) and they are easy to transport. Mobile phones would be a similar example, although technological advances (built-in tracking devices) are making illegal re-sales increasingly difficult.
- The degree of fluctuation in inventory levels. The greater the fluctuation the more frequently one would expect the inventory item to be counted.
- The nature of the inventory and the requirement of specialist knowledge, e.g. valuing mining activities or works of art may require specialist knowledge (i.e. the use of an auditor's expert as covered in **Chapter 10**, Section 10.4).
- Susceptibility of the inventory to obsolescence. This is more prevalent in some industries than others. For example, the shelf-life in the grocery department of a store versus the clothing department, where inventory is not perishable (although changing fashions may have an effect).
- Risks associated with goods sold on a sale-or-return basis.
- Risks due to fraud, which include:
  - false sales;
  - movement of inventory between different locations with inventory counts on different days (entity might move inventory from one location to the other to increase inventory in both locations);

♦ application of inappropriate estimating techniques (e.g. inappropriate allocation of overheads);
♦ altered inventory count sheets; and
♦ additional inventory count records being added to those prepared during the count.

The auditor will focus less on those risk factors that they determine will not have a material impact on the financial statements, and will take into consideration the controls in place to mitigate any identified risks.

## 12.4 AUDIT OBJECTIVES/MANAGEMENT ASSERTIONS FOR INVENTORY

As discussed in **Chapter 6**, it is necessary for the auditor to obtain **sufficient appropriate audit evidence** to satisfy all of the audit objectives and to eliminate the possibility of any of the risks outlined above going undetected. The auditor must design tests to address these assertions and thereby address the identified risks. In **Chapter 4** we introduced audit objectives (management assertions) and explained their generic meanings before reintroducing the topic again throughout **Chapter 8**, making management assertions specific to each financial cycle. **Table 12.1** recaps the audit objectives/management assertions for transactions and account balances as they relate to inventory. As noted in Chapter 8, transactions associated with inventory are tested through the testing of purchases and payables cycle. The exception is cut-off, which is generally tested as part of the inventory cycle and the results used to validate the cut-off of revenue and receivables.

TABLE 12.1: INVENTORY – AUDIT OBJECTIVES

| Management Assertion/Audit Objective | Control Objective for Transaction Class<br>Inventory Movements | Control Objective for Account Balance<br>Inventory Balances |
|---|---|---|
| **Existence or Occurrence** | • Recorded purchase transactions represent inventory acquired.<br>• Recorded transfers represent inventory transferred between locations or categories.<br>• Recorded revenue transactions represent inventory sold. | Inventory included in the SOFP physically exist at the year end date. |
| **Completeness** | All purchases, transfers and sales of inventory that occurred have been recorded. | Inventory includes all materials, products and supplies on hand at the date of the SOFP. |
| **Rights and Obligations** | The entity has rights and obligations associated with the inventory recorded during the period. | The entity has rights to the inventory included at the date of the SOFP. |

| Classification/ Recording or Valuation | The costs of materials purchased and of labour and overheads applied have been accurately determined and are in accordance with applicable accounting standards. | Inventory is properly stated at the lower of cost or NRV, in accordance with applicable accounting standards. |
|---|---|---|
| Cut-off | All purchases, transfers and sales of inventory are recorded in the correct accounting period. | |
| Presentation and Disclosure | Transactions relating to inventory have been properly identified and classified in the financial statements. | Inventory is properly identified and classified in the financial statements. Disclosures referring to the classification, basis of valuation and the pledging of inventory is adequate. |

Now that we understand the objectives of the auditor with regard to inventory, in the following sections we will consider how the auditor addresses these objectives through substantive testing.

## 12.5 DEVELOPING AN AUDIT PLAN FOR INVENTORY

Before the audit of inventory is undertaken, an assessment of audit risk must be completed. As discussed in detail in **Chapter 7**, audit risk is made up of three components: inherent risk; control risk; and detection risks, which are determined by the auditor based on their assessment of inherent and control risks. We will consider these components specifically as they relate to inventory in order to determine the type of audit approach the auditor might take. Remember, the auditor's assessment of the required detection risk will determine the nature, timing and extent of further audit procedures.

An entity's inventory may or may not have a large number of inherent risks depending on the inventory type, industry and economic environment (see **Section 12.3**). With regard to the **control environment**, the auditor may have already tested a significant amount of controls for inventory while testing the purchases and revenue cycles (purchases will relate to inventory goods inward, and revenue will relate to goods outward).

Where inventory is material to the financial statements, the auditor is required to attend the physical inventory count of the client entity regardless of controls in place in the entity. As such, testing the controls cannot reduce this task to any large extent other than to reduce sample sizes reviewed during the observation of the inventory count. In a non-manufacturing environment, the auditor may decide that it is not efficient to test inventory controls and instead take some reliance (through controls testing) from revenue and purchases to support some inventory assertions and, for the balance, perform focused substantive testing.

In a manufacturing environment, however, the volume of testing using a wholly substantive (focused substantive) approach may be too onerous and the auditor may find it more efficient and effective to test only the controls surrounding inventory. When testing controls in a manufacturing environment, dual tests (those that support both controls testing and substantive testing objectives) are helpful, particularly in the area of standard costing. For example, during controls testing an understanding of the approach used to allocate overheads to individual items of inventory would need to be ascertained by the auditor, and this information will also assist the auditor when testing the cost of the inventory item at the substantive stage.

## 12.6 AUDIT TRAIL FOR INVENTORY

To appreciate the role of the auditor in validating transactions, classes of transactions or balances at the assertion level it is important to first understand the audit trail associated with the relevant cycle. **Figure 12.1** outlines an audit trail that would be followed when validating the various management assertions associated with inventory.

FIGURE 12.1: INVENTORY AUDIT TRAIL

| Financial Statements | Trial Balance | Nominal/General Ledgers | Transactions |
|---|---|---|---|
| Summary of trial balances, presented in accordance with applicable financial reporting standards | Summary of totals of each nominal sub-ledger | Complete listing of all transactions<br><br>Sub-ledger is a subset of the nominal ledger | The recording of source documents into a journal entry (double-entry bookkeeping) |

**Extract Statement of Financial Position**

| Non Current Assets | |
|---|---|
| Property, Plant & Equipment | 9,500 |
| | **9,500** |
| **Current Assets** | |
| Cash at Bank | 500 |
| Inventory | 2,110 |
| | **2,610** |

**TB-Extract**

| Nominal Ledger | Dr | Cr |
|---|---|---|
| Land Cost | 7,000 | |
| Buildings Cost | 5,000 | |
| Buildings Depreciation | | 2,500 |
| Cash at Bank | 500 | |
| Inventory-RM | 1,370 | |
| Inventory-WIP | 200 | |
| Inventory-FG | 500 | |

**Raw Materials Sub-Ledger**

| Transaction No | Purc Date | Description | Qty | Unit Cost | Inventory value |
|---|---|---|---|---|---|
| 12345 | 11.11.2018 | Wood Type A | 200 | 1 | 200 |
| 33445 | 12.11.2018 | Wood Type B | 150 | 2 | 300 |
| 65433 | 01.12.2018 | Wood Type C | 40 | 3 | 120 |
| 34566 | 12.12.2018 | Metal A | 100 | 2 | 200 |
| 44556 | 23.12.2018 | Metal B | 90 | 3 | 270 |
| 38363 | 31.12.2018 | Metal C | 80 | 3.5 | 280 |

| | Dr | Cr |
|---|---|---|
| Dr Inventory | 500 | |
| Cr Payables | | 500 |

The auditor is presented with the financial statements, which are supported by a trial balance (**SOFP for inventory**), which is made up of a summary of transactions in the form of a nominal ledger, which is made up of individual transactions, which is supported by source documents that validate the various assertions associated with the transaction.

**Source Documents**

E.g. inventory count sheets and purchase/sales invoices

It is essential that the **direction** of the test is appropriate to the assertion being tested. So, when testing for occurrence/existence, the auditor will start with the financial statements and trace back through the trial balance, etc. to the source documents. However, when testing for completeness the auditor will always start with the source documents and trace upwards to the financial statements. Whatever the direction of the test, the source document data is used to validate whether the transaction has been appropriately recorded/valued and that it proves the entity's rights and obligations assertion over the transaction/balance. Sometimes a blend of source documents will be required to validate all assertions, while in other instances a single source document will validate a number of assertions.

Source documents associated with inventory include:
- **aged inventory listing**;
- final inventory listing;
- **physical inventory count sheets**;
- **bill of materials (BOM)**;
- sales and purchase invoices;
- goods inwards and outwards documents: goods received notes (GRNs) and goods dispatch notes (GDNs).

### Aged Inventory Listing

The entity's aged inventory listing depicts the total inventory balance broken down by the length of time that it has been held (e.g. those purchased within the last 30 days, 60 days, 90 days or greater). The aged inventory listing allows the auditor to query items of inventory that have been held for long periods of time and are either: (a) not moving; or (b) have seen subsequent movement in later periods. An example of an aged inventory listing is given in **Example 12.1** below.

Examining Example 12.1, we see that the only finished goods listed for 'Chair C' have been held for more than 90 days. This may lead the auditor to believe that this inventory item is obsolete (no longer saleable). With regard to finished goods 'Table C', the entity appears to be building up large inventories of this item and the auditor might query why it continues to produce this item when a large inventory holding already exists. For raw material 'Wood Type C', the auditor might ask why new inventory items have been purchased in the last 60 days when there was €200,000 worth of inventory that was 90 days old. This inventory may be damaged and unusable, causing the entity to buy new batches. All of the above can be used to help with supporting the valuation assertion (i.e. answering the question: "Will the product sell for more than cost?").

EXAMPLE 12.1: AGED INVENTORY LISTING (LARGE COMPANY LIMITED)

| Inventory Description | Class | Total Value €000 | Current €000 | <30 days old €000 | 30–60 days old €000 | 60–90 days old €000 | >90 days old €000 |
|---|---|---|---|---|---|---|---|
| Table A | FG | 1,200 | 1,200 | | | | |
| Table B | FG | 5,200 | 4,000 | 1,000 | 200 | | |
| Table C | FG | 11,700 | 5,000 | 5,000 | 1,000 | 700 | |
| Chair A | FG | 1,164 | 1,164 | | | | |
| Chair B | FG | 900 | 800 | 100 | | | |
| Chair C | FG | 400 | | | | | 400 |
| Stool A | FG | 2,400 | 2,400 | | | | |
| Stool B | FG | 2,610 | 2,610 | | | | |
| Stool C | FG | 2,350 | 2,000 | 350 | | | |
| | | **27,924** | **19,174** | **6,450** | **1,200** | **700** | **400** |
| Batch of Table A | WIP | 5,130 | 5,130 | | | | |
| Batch of Chair A | WIP | 1,615 | 1,000 | 615 | | | |
| Batch of Stool C | WIP | 5,785 | 5,785 | | | | |
| | | **12,530** | **11,915** | **615** | **–** | **–** | **–** |
| Wood Type A | RM | 200 | 200 | | | | |
| Wood Type B | RM | 300 | 200 | 100 | | | |
| Wood Type C | RM | 1,500 | 1,000 | 300 | | | 200 |
| Metal A | RM | 1,600 | 1,600 | | | | |
| Metal B | RM | 2,400 | 2,000 | 400 | | | |
| Metal C | RM | 3,320 | 2,000 | 1,200 | | | 120 |
| | | **9,320** | **7,000** | **2,000** | **–** | **–** | **320** |
| Total | | **49,774** | **38,089** | **9,065** | **1,200** | **700** | **720** |
| | | **100%** | **76.5%** | **18.2%** | **2.4%** | **1.4%** | **1.5%** |

FG – Finished Goods
WIP – Work in Progress
RM – Raw Materials

## Final Inventory Listing

A **final inventory listing** breaks down the inventory balance in the financial statements by each inventory item, along with the quantity and unit price. It is used to compare (cross-reference) to **physical inventory count sheets** when confirming the completeness and existence of inventory items. It also supports the testing of cost, as the auditor can verify the unit price of raw materials to supporting purchase invoices or standard costing workings.

It is worth noting that the final inventory listing should be obtained from the client in soft copy. This will enable the auditor to interrogate the data and more easily facilitate comparison with the trial balance using Excel or an audit software package (e.g. ACL). The auditor could also then stratify the inventory balances to ensure that the most material balances are adequately considered, improving the efficiency and effectiveness of the testing. The auditor could also use simple sort functionality to identify negative inventory balances for further investigation. A detailed discussion of the uses of final inventory listings is given in **Section 12.8**, 'Inventory Balances'.

EXAMPLE 12.2: FINAL INVENTORY LISTING (LARGE COMPANY LIMITED)

| | | | Per Price (Cost) | |
| Inventory Description | Category | Quantity | Unit | Total Value |
| | | Units | € | € |
|---|---|---|---|---|
| Table A | Finished Goods | 4,000 | 300 | 1,200,000 |
| Table B | Finished Goods | 8,000 | 650 | 5,200,000 |
| Table C | Finished Goods | 12,000 | 975 | 11,700,000 |
| Chair A | Finished Goods | 12,000 | 97 | 1,164,000 |
| Chair B | Finished Goods | 9,000 | 100 | 900,000 |
| Chair C | Finished Goods | 2,000 | 200 | 400,000 |
| Stool A | Finished Goods | 8,000 | 300 | 2,400,000 |
| Stool B | Finished Goods | 8,700 | 300 | 2,610,000 |
| Stool C | Finished Goods | 4,700 | 500 | 2,350,000 |
| | | | | 27,924,000 |
| Batch of Table A | WIP | 19,000 | 270 | 5,130,000 |
| Batch of Chair A | WIP | 19,000 | 85 | 1,615,000 |
| Batch of Stool C | WIP | 12,856 | 450 | 5,785,200 |
| | | | | 12,530,200 |
| Wood Type A | Raw Materials | 2,000 | 100 | 200,000 |
| Wood Type B | Raw Materials | 3,000 | 100 | 300,000 |
| Wood Type C | Raw Materials | 5,000 | 300 | 1,500,000 |
| Metal A | Raw Materials | 8,000 | 200 | 1,600,000 |
| Metal B | Raw Materials | 8,000 | 300 | 2,400,000 |
| Metal C | Raw Materials | 8,300 | 400 | 3,320,000 |
| | | | | 9,320,000 |
| | | | Total | 49,774,200 |

## Physical Inventory Count Sheets

A physical inventory count sheet simply records the physical inventory counted. A client entity may have several different warehouses and within each warehouse there may be separate locations, in which case the client entity may have a physical inventory count sheet at a warehouse level, or individual sheets that relate to locations within the warehouse.

A physical inventory count should be performed independently by two individuals on separate count sheets. The count should be a 'blind count', i.e. the count sheets are not pre-populated with expected quantities (i.e. those recorded in the accounting records). When the independent counts have been completed, the two results are compared and any differences are investigated. Once the comparison is made and the counters are satisfied they have an accurate count, the auditor selects a sample from:

1. the inventory floor (i.e. physical location where inventory is held) to the physical inventory count sheet to test for completeness; and
2. the physical inventory count sheet to the inventory floor to test for existence.

Copies of the physical inventory count sheets are taken and **compared** to the **final inventory listings** at the audit fieldwork stage (i.e. the substantive part of audit work carried out after the year end date). The physical inventory count and the auditor's procedures are discussed in greater detail at 'Evidence on Quantity – Attending Entity Inventory Year-end Count' in **Section 12.8** below.

While still popular, the use of physical inventory count sheets is being replaced with barcode technology. Finished goods or raw materials that have barcodes can be scanned and the stock figure recorded. This eliminates the need to manually input the results from physical count sheets into the inventory system, reducing the risk of error and increasing the effectiveness and efficiency of the count. The barcode technology is either WiFi-enabled and updates the stock in real-time as scanned, or it is interfaced with the system on completion of the scan. In each case, the auditor's approach to validating the count should include a review of the technology to ensure that items have to be physically scanned to enter the system and that a manual override to add inventory items is not possible. If a manual override is possible, an exception report should be available to show all manual entries, so providing the auditor with an opportunity to investigate further. Barcode technology does not remove the need for the auditor to test for completeness – there is still a risk that inventory items may be missed and not scanned – and so the auditor must still select items from the physical inventory and trace them to ensure they have been recorded in the system.

EXAMPLE 12.3: PHYSICAL INVENTORY COUNT SHEETS
(LARGE COMPANY LIMITED)

**Location:** Stores 1
**Date:**
**Stores Type:** Raw Material
**Counter 1:** John Duffy

| | Count |
|---|---|
| Wood Type A | 200 |
| Wood Type B | 200 |
| Wood Type C | 1,000 |
| Metal A | 1,600 |
| Metal B | 2,000 |
| Metal C | 2,000 |

**Location:** Stores 1
**Date:**
**Stores Type:** Raw Material
**Counter 2:** Carl Ryan

| | Count | Agreed to Counter 1 |
|---|---|---|
| Wood Type A | 200 | Yes |
| Wood Type B | 200 | Yes |
| Wood Type C | 1,000 | Yes |
| Metal A | 1,600 | Yes |
| Metal B | 2,000 | Yes |
| Metal C | 1,800 | No* |

*Further investigation revealed an area missed by Counter 2. The confirmed quantity is 2,000.

Signed:          Counter 1    _____

                 Counter 2    _____

## Bill of Materials

The bill of materials (BOM) is a list of all components required to make a particular item of finished goods, including a description and quantity of each raw material required and the allocation of depreciation, labour and overheads required to manufacture the product.

## 12.7 SUBSTANTIVE AUDIT PROGRAMME FOR INVENTORY

An audit programme records the specific details of tests to be performed by the auditor. The audit programme becomes a guide to the audit engagement team on the work to be performed in a particular area. As work is completed, a reference is included on the audit programme showing the location in the audit file where details of the tests performed are included. The audit programme for any cycle will vary from entity to entity, and in **Example 12.4** below we consider the typical tests the auditor would include in the audit programme for inventory. Students should note that in a real-life scenario, each test would be referenced to the location in the audit working file where the test is actually performed.

### EXAMPLE 12.4: AUDIT PROGRAMME FOR INVENTORY[1]

| Large Company Limited 31 December 2018 | Audit Materiality | | €3,642,500 |
|---|---|---|---|
| | Performance Materiality | | €2,731,875 |
| | | Initials | Date |
| | Prepared by: | | |
| | Reviewed by: | | |

| **Inventory Audit Programme** | |
|---|---|
| Ensure the audit plan is reflected in the following tests. The following steps are suggestions only and should be removed or added to as necessary to address the risks of material misstatement identified at the risk assessment stage. | |
| **Accounting Policy** | |
| Assess the appropriateness of the accounting policy and the accounting estimates method for this area. Ensure that the accounting policy is in accordance with accounting standards (IAS 2 and IFRS 15) and applicable law, and that the methods used for making the accounting estimates are appropriate. | Existence Completeness Rights and Obligations Recording (accuracy), Valuation and Classification |
| **Initial Procedures** | |
| Agree opening balances to prior year's signed financial statements. | Presentation Completeness Valuation |
| Validate opening balances – obtain or prepare lead schedules and ensure totals are correct. 1. Distinguish between raw materials and consumables, work in progress, and finished goods and goods for resale. 2. Agree to sub-ledger (nominal listing) and trace to trial balance and onto SOFP. | Completeness Existence |
| Analytical review – prepare commentary explaining the composition of inventory balances and comparing them with prior periods and our expectations. Investigate significant changes in inventory levels and values. * To some degree. | Completeness Existence Valuation* |

---

[1] Source: based on *Procedures for Quality Audit 2010* (© Chartered Accountants Ireland, 2010), G1 and updated by the authors December 2017.

| Inventory Balances – Attendance at the Year-end Inventory Count | |
|---|---|
| Refer to full audit programme (see **Example 12.7** below) | Completeness<br>Existence<br>Valuation |
| **Inventory Balances – Valuation** | |
| Select a sample of inventory items from the final inventory listing and vouch against purchase invoices or standard costing records as appropriate. | Valuation |
| Ascertain and record basis of valuation of work in progress and finished goods.<br>Test check valuation of work in progress and ensure that:<br>1. material costs are correctly recorded;<br>2. the allocation of labour hours is correct;<br>3. the allocation of overheads is correct; and<br>4. the accounting for turnover and attribution of profit in long-term work in progress is appropriate. | Valuation |
| Using the aged inventory listing, identify and consider treatment of slow-moving and obsolete inventory. Ensure that provisions are adequate and consistent.<br>Challenge the estimation techniques used by management in the calculation of the provision.<br>Consider the outturn of the provision in previous years. | Valuation |
| Ensure that inventory and work in progress are valued at the lower of cost and net realisable value. In reviewing NRV, consider:<br>1. the saleability of inventory;<br>2. overall inventory levels and levels of key items;<br>3. post year-end sales of key inventory items;<br>4. use by/sell by dates of perishable goods;<br>5. indications of obsolescence. | Valuation |
| **Other Considerations** | |
| Where inventory is held by third parties on behalf of the company, obtain confirmations where amounts are material or attend physical inventory count at the third-party's premises. (ISA 501, para 8) | Existence |
| Where the company holds inventory on behalf of third parties, ensure such items are excluded from inventory. Where material, consider confirmation from the third party. | Rights and Obligations |
| **Cut-off** | |
| Review the documentation obtained at the period-end physical inventory counting relating to the last goods movements (in and out) in the period. | Cut-off |

| | |
|---|---|
| Agree this documentation to purchase and sales invoices recorded in the nominal ledger. Ensure these purchases and sales are recognised in the same period as the inventory movement to which they relate. | Cut-off |
| In addition, consider material purchases and sales invoices posted pre- and post-period end. Agree these invoices to goods receipts and dispatch documentation. Ensure that these sales and purchases are recorded in the correct periods. | Cut-off |
| **Contracts** | |
| Ascertain the nature of contracts, i.e. short term or long term, and ensure they are appropriately categorised. | |
| *Short-term Contracts* <br> Select a sample of contracts from the recorded inventory balances and trace to contracts; discuss the state of progress with the person in charge. <br> Vouch costs incurred to supporting documents, e.g. invoices, timesheets, etc. | Existence <br> Recording <br> (accuracy) and <br> Valuation |
| Review the allocation of overheads to contracts to ensure the basis is reasonable and consistent. | Valuation |
| Review the progress on these contracts post-period end and evaluate whether the contract is being valued at the lower of cost and NRV. | Existence <br> Completeness <br> Valuation |
| Review the level of provisions to ensure they are adequate. | Valuation |
| *Long-term Contracts* <br> Select a sample of contracts from the recorded inventory balances and trace to physical contract; discuss the state of progress with the person in charge. <br> Vouch amounts included in turnover to appropriate supporting documents, e.g. surveyors' certificates, as being the value of work done. | Completeness <br> Existence <br> Recording <br> (accuracy) and <br> Valuation |
| Vouch costs incurred to supporting documents, e.g. invoices, timesheets, etc., ensuring they are correctly allocated between current and future periods. | Valuation |
| Review the allocation of overheads to contracts to ensure the basis is reasonable and consistent. | Valuation |
| Vouch amounts invoiced on account to the revenue ledger and ensure the balance/excess on payments to account is correctly calculated and treated. | Recording <br> (accuracy) and <br> Valuation |

| Compare the costs to date against the estimated budgeted cost to the same stage of completion and consider the requirement for a provision. | Recording (accuracy) and Valuation |
|---|---|
| Ensure that any provisions/accruals for foreseeable losses are treated appropriately and consider the need for any further provision. | Recording (accuracy) and Valuation |
| **Disclosures** | |
| Consider the disclosure requirements of IAS 2 and IFRS 15 and ensure, if relevant to the client entity, that they adhere to the requirements of the standard. | Presentation and Disclosure |
| **Conclusion**<br>Subject to the matters noted for the reviewer, in my opinion sufficient audit assurance has been obtained to enable us to conclude that inventories are not materially misstated. | |

## 12.8 SUBSTANTIVE TESTING PROCEDURES FOR INVENTORY

The substantive testing audit programme in **Example 12.4** above outlined the principal procedures involved in testing inventory. In this section we will look at each of these in more detail:

1. Initial procedures:
   (a) Opening balances
   (b) Accuracy of schedules provided by management
   (c) Prepare the lead schedule
   (d) Analytical review.
2. Inventory balance:
   (a) Evidence on quantity – attending inventory year-end count
   (b) Cycle counts
   (c) Physical inventory count occurs before/after the year end
   (d) Evidence on price (value) – vouching cost and testing cost versus NRV
   (e) Validating cost by vouching to original purchase invoices or standard costing records
   (f) Ensuring inventory is valued at the lower of cost or NRV.
3. Other considerations:
   (a) Inventory provisions
   (b) Cut-off
   (c) Ownership.

## Initial Procedures

### Opening Balances

Before commencing further audit procedures, evidence must be obtained as to the accuracy of the opening balances of inventory. The reason for this is twofold:

1. it confirms that the comparative figures in the financial statements (which must be included in the current year's financial statements) agree to the final accounts of the prior year; and
2. it highlights any final entries (last-minute adjusting journal entries) of the prior year not correctly carried forward, which may indicate an error in the current year's financial statement figures.

The auditor tests opening balances as follows:

• Agree the opening balances to the prior-year working papers and signed financial statements. This may highlight an opening balance in the current year's accounts that does not agree to the closing balance of the prior year's financial statements – in which case a change would be made to the opening balance of the current year, which would impact the closing balance of the current year. This usually arises due to final adjustments in the prior year that are not reflected in the actual accounts (nominal and general ledgers).

• If this is the first year of the audit engagement, the auditor will still need to establish that the opening balances are materially correct, which can pose a difficulty if either the client entity was exempt from audit in the prior year or a predecessor auditor carried out the audit. The audit of opening balances in such instances is discussed in detail in **Chapter 6**, Section 6.9.

### Accuracy of Schedule

The auditor obtains the **final inventory listings** and **aged inventory listing** of the entity and tests their mathematical accuracy. The value of the aged inventory listing is agreed to the inventory balances in the trial balance and traced to the financial statements. At least one item should be selected from the schedule and traced to its respective source data to validate the accuracy of the schedule before further testing is performed on it.

### Prepare the Lead Schedule

The **lead schedule** acts as a summary of the balances and transactions to be audited that relate to a particular class of transactions and balances. For inventory it provides a summary of current- and prior-year inventory balances broken down into raw materials, work in progress and finished goods. It allows the auditor to control the procedures by referencing each balance or transaction to the audit working paper, which records the audit tests that have been performed.

The auditor prepares a lead schedule that agrees to the inventory note in the financial statements (see **Example 12.5** below).

EXAMPLE 12.5: INVENTORY LEAD SCHEDULE[2]

| Large Company Limited 31 December 2018 | Audit Materiality Performance Materiality | | €3,642,500 €2,731,875 |
|---|---|---|---|
| | | Initials | Date |
| | Prepared by: | | |
| | Reviewed by: | | |
| **Inventory Lead Schedule** | | | |
| | **2018** | **2017** | |
| | **€000** | **€000** | |
| Raw materials and consumables | 9,320 | 7,770 | |
| Work in progress | 12,530 | 10,750 | |
| Finished goods and goods for resale | 27,924 | 16,500 | |
| | 49,774 | 35,020 | |

## Analytical Review

An analytical review (covered in **Chapter 5**, Section 5.4) is usually performed at the start of each substantive procedure relating to each balance or class of transactions. Calculating ratios and analysing results against industry information, prior-year results, budgets, etc. allows the auditor 'to get a feel' for the movements in the year and to make comparisons against norms. It therefore provides the auditor with additional insights into the client entity and the industry it operates in, and better prepares them for the audit programme.

At the close of the substantive procedures, the auditor aims to ensure that they can comment on all movements and key ratios with supporting explanations. If the auditor cannot explain any element, this will highlight the need to perform additional substantive procedures. The analytical review performed here differs from a substantive analytical procedure in that the auditor's aim is not to substantiate the balance (i.e. prove the assertions), but rather to ensure an understanding of the movements and relationships when performing substantive procedures.

A standard analytical review for the audit of inventories would include:
• reconciling changes in inventory quantities from the beginning to the end of the year to purchases, sales and production records;
• comparing quantities and amounts of inventories in their various categories to those at the prior-year SOFP date and to the current period's sales and purchases;

---

[2] Source: based on *Procedures for Quality Audit 2010* (© Chartered Accountants Ireland, 2010), G and updated by the authors in December 2017.

- comparing gross profit and inventory turnover ratios year-on-year;
- obtaining industry comparisons and trends; and
- calculation of key ratios, such as inventory turnover, gross margin, etc.

An example of the type of analytical procedures carried out at the initial stages of substantive testing by the auditor is included at **Example 12.6** below.

### Example 12.6: Analytical Review of Inventory (Large Company Limited)

| | 31/12/2018 | 31/12/2017 | Movement |
|---|---|---|---|
| | € | € | € |
| Raw materials and consumables | 9,320 | 7,770 | 1,550 |
| Work in progress | 12,530 | 10,750 | 1,780 |
| Finished goods and goods for resale | 27,924 | 16,500 | 11,424 |
| | **49,774** | **35,020** | **14,754** |
| | | | |
| Increase in inventory | | | 42% |

Inventory turnover = Cost of sales ÷ Inventory

|  | 31/12/2018 | 31/12/2017 |
|---|---|---|
| | =140,250 ÷ | =120,800 ÷ |
| | 49,774 | 35,020 |
| | 2.82 times | 3.45 times |

While inventories have increased by 42%, inventory turnover has decreased by only 18%, indicating that the increase in inventory is supporting the increase in revenue.

### Inventory Balance

Having performed the initial procedures, now let us consider the specific audit procedures the auditor might carry out in relation to the inventory balance, which essentially includes the auditor obtaining evidence with regard to: the quantity of inventory at year end; and the price used to value inventory.

Inventory is essentially made up of two key variables: **quantity** and **price**. The final inventory listing (see **Example 12.2** above) records this information for all inventory items. The auditor's first task would be to recalculate the total value and ensure its mathematical accuracy before tracing this total value to the statement of financial position and the corresponding inventory note. Once satisfied that it agrees, the auditor must obtain **sufficient appropriate audit evidence** over the quantity and price that make up the total value. This is done by: (a) attending the entity's inventory count; and (b) vouching price (cost per unit) back to supporting purchase invoices or standard costing records, and assessing if there are any indicators that the **net realisable value** (NRV) may be less than cost.

Let us discuss this process in more detail, starting with how the auditor obtains evidence with regard to inventory quantities.

### Evidence on Quantity – Attending Entity Inventory Year-end Count

Attending the entity's year-end inventory count enables the auditor to inspect the inventory, observe compliance with management's procedures for recording and controlling the results of the count, and provides audit evidence as to the reliability of management's procedures. There are three steps involved: planning; attending; and completing the inventory count. The responsibilities of the auditor are detailed in the following audit programme in **Example 12.7.**

EXAMPLE 12.7: AUDIT PROGRAMME FOR ATTENDANCE AT
YEAR-END INVENTORY COUNT[3]

| Large Company Limited 31 December 2018 | Audit Materiality | | €3,642,500 |
|---|---|---|---|
| | Performance Materiality | | €2,731,875 |
| | | Initials | Date |
| | Prepared by: | | |
| | Reviewed by: | | |
| **Inventory Attendance Substantive Tests Audit Programme** | | | |
| **Planning the Inventory Count** | | | |
| Obtain and evaluate details of the client's planned inventory count procedures (ISA 501, para 4). Review and confirm that: <br> 1. client staff are properly briefed; <br> 2. proper controls have been set up to cover inventory movements and cut-off; and <br> 3. the overall procedures are adequate and will result in the accurate recording of inventory and work in progress. | Completeness Existence Rights and Obligations Valuation | | |
| Review the prior period's audit file and/or the audit planning memorandum for major inventory lines held, their location and any special knowledge required for identifying inventory, its condition, etc. | Existence Completeness Valuation | | |

---

[3] Source: based on *Procedures for Quality Audit 2010* (© Chartered Accountants Ireland, 2010), G2 and updated by the authors December 2017.

| Attending the Inventory Count | |
|---|---|
| Attend the client's physical inventory counting at sites where inventory held is material, unless impractical.<br>Note conclusions drawn from observing count, as to:<br>1. care taken by client staff;<br>2. accuracy of recording results;<br>3. execution of the count and the manner in which instructions were followed;<br>4. control of inventory movements;<br>5. control over issue of count sheets and their return, including ruling off of inventory sheets after last item and cancellation of issued but unused sheets;<br>6. recording of damaged, obsolete or slow-moving goods; and<br>7. control over counting to ensure that inventory is not double-counted or omitted, and note the manner in which problems were cleared. | Completeness<br>Existence<br>Valuation |
| Select a sample of items from the inventory on hand and:<br>1. count items and trace to the count sheets, note and reconcile any differences;<br>2. if an item looks obsolete or damaged, ensure a note is made to this effect; and<br>3. check that enough detail is recorded on the test schedule to ensure that the item can be traced to the final inventory listing. | Existence<br>Valuation |
| Select a sample of items from the count sheets and:<br>1. check to physical inventory, note and reconcile any differences;<br>2. if an item looks obsolete or damaged, ensure a note is made to this effect; and<br>3. check that enough detail is recorded on the test schedule to ensure that the item can be traced to the final inventory listing. | Completeness<br>Valuation |
| Review procedures taken to record the current stage of completion of work in progress and confirm that these are being followed. | Recording (accuracy) and Valuation |
| Inspect inventory area, and make enquiries of the staff to determine if there are slow-moving or obsolete items of inventory. In particular, enquire about and document items stored in relatively inaccessible areas, dirty or damaged items. | Valuation |
| Where the client uses numbered goods inward and outward dockets, note the last numbers used before the count commences. Where these are not in use, consider and document what other cut-off controls exist. (See cut-off items immediately below.) | Cut-off |

| | |
|---|---|
| Obtain a list of completed dispatch documents for goods not dispatched at the inventory count date and ascertain whether these were included in the inventory count. | Cut-off |
| Determine whether items in the goods inward area are included in the inventory count. | Cut-off |
| Note the numbers of the count sheets used to ensure that none is added or removed at a later date. | Completeness Existence |
| **Non-attendance at Year-end Inventory Count** | |
| If the physical counting is conducted at a date other than the date of the financial statements, perform additional audit procedures to obtain audit evidence about whether changes in inventory between the count date and the date of the financial statements are properly recorded. (ISA 501, para 5) | Completeness Existence |
| If unable to attend physical inventory counting, make or observe some physical counts on an alternative date and perform audit procedures on intervening transactions (roll-forward / roll-back). (ISA 501, para 6) | Completeness Existence |
| If attendance at the physical inventory counting is impracticable, perform alternative procedures to obtain sufficient appropriate audit evidence regarding the existence and condition of the inventory. (ISA 501, para 7) | Completeness Existence |
| **Agreeing Outcome of Inventory Count to Final Inventory Listing** | |
| Obtain final inventory listing and test-check additions and extensions. | Existence Completeness |
| Complete physical inventory audit programme and trace all items tested during the inventory count from physical inventory sheets (obtained during the inventory count) to the final inventory listing. | Completeness |
| Select a sample of items from the final inventory listing and trace back to the physical inventory sheets (obtained during inventory count). | Existence |
| Consider the extent and implication of goods in inventory subject to reservation of title. | Rights and Obligations |
| **Conclusion** Subject to the matters noted for the reviewer, in my opinion sufficient audit assurance has been obtained to enable us to conclude that the inventory count was adequately performed. | |

The audit programme shown in **Example 12.7** depicts an environment where physical counts take place. Where barcode technology (discussed above in **Section 12.6**) is used the count would take place using scanning technology.

The auditor's attendance at the inventory count provides evidence to support the existence and completeness assertions (audit objectives). This is straightforward enough when the inventory count occurs at the year end (as in Example 12.7), but difficulties arise where:
- the client entity performs **cycle counts**; and
- the physical inventory count **occurs either before or after the year end**.

### Cycle Counts

Some companies do not carry out a full inventory count at year end, instead they perform ongoing counts of inventory throughout the year, commonly known as cycle counts. Cycle counts prove less disruptive to the operations of a business, and ensure that any discrepancies in the inventory quantities can be identified and investigated on an ongoing basis; they also ensure that companies can meet tight year-end reporting deadlines.

When cycle counting is in place the auditor will not have a full inventory count report to rely on to test the existence assertion, and the 'book quantities' held at year end must be relied on. The auditor must, therefore, be confident that the inventory system is reliable (by testing the related controls). The following are factors that the auditor can assess in this regard:
1. Reliable internal controls over inventory.
2. Properly planned programme of cycle counting:
   (a) clear responsibility for the count;
   (b) detailed count plans to ensure all items are counted at least once, with high-value items counted on a more regular basis;
   (c) segregation of duties, i.e. counters are independent of those working within the warehouse where inventories are stored/managed.

### Physical Inventory Count occurs Before or After the Year End

If the physical inventory count takes place before or after the year end, the auditor needs to consider how to test the existence and completeness assertions for the volume of inventory included in the financial statements at year end. The counting of inventory may occur before or after the year end for various reasons. For audit purposes this is deemed acceptable, provided records of inventory movements in the intervening periods are maintained so that the movements can be examined and substantiated. A well-developed system of internal control and satisfactory inventory recording should lessen the difficulties in performing this calculation.

The physical count should ideally occur no more than three months before or after the year end. The auditor should still attend the count to validate the physical inventory counted (using the same audit programme noted above). Audit procedures thereafter, however, will involve reconciling the physical inventory at the time of the count to the physical inventory that existed at the year end. This is done by vouching the **inventory movements**, e.g. sales (inventory out) and purchases (inventory in) that support the reconciliation.

ISA 315 allows that tests of controls or substantive testing may be performed at an interim date, and that inventory counts are an example of such a procedure. Attending an inventory count before year end may facilitate an entity with tight reporting deadlines.

When considering whether to rely on inventory counts performed before or after the year end, the auditor should consider:
- the overall control environment;
- the risks over inventory;
- when relevant information is available, i.e. when the client entity's physical inventory count takes place;
- the reliability of the inventory control system;
- the length of period between the inventory count and the year end; and
- the materiality of inventory figures.

If the physical inventory count is performed **before the year end**, **roll-forward procedures** must be completed in order to agree the quantities counted to the inventory listing at year end; if the count takes place after year end, **roll-back procedures** are performed.

The following are examples of roll-forward procedures:
- Testing the completeness of raw material receipts between the physical inventory count and the year end. Method: test the sequence of goods received notes (GRNs) and trace a sample to the raw material sub-ledger.
- Testing the completeness of transfers from raw materials to work in progress, and from work in progress to finished goods. Method: test a sample of journal entries for the different transfers.
- Checking the completeness of dispatches of finished goods. Method: check the sequence of dispatch notes and trace a sample of items in sales reports to the finished goods sub-ledger.

Roll-back procedures would instead concentrate on the deduction of inventory inwards and the addition of inventory outwards, but would be validated in the same manner. (*Note*: sampling is covered in **Chapter 6**, Section 6.8.)

While some audit procedures relating to inventory can occur before or after the year end, other audit procedures relating to inventory can only be performed at the year end (for example, cut-off) as the risk only occurs at the year end.

Having addressed how the auditor obtains evidence relating to the existence and completeness assertions, we will now consider audit evidence relating to the valuation assertion. In simple terms, the auditor must obtain evidence relating to the cost of inventory and compare it to the likely net realisable value of the related inventory (i.e. comparison of cost versus NRV).

### Evidence on Price (Value) – Vouching Cost and Testing Cost versus NRV

There are two stages involved in validating the price used to value inventory:
1. validating cost by vouching to original purchase invoices/standard costing records; and then
2. ensuring that inventory is valued at the lower of cost or NRV.

IAS 2, paragraph 10, defines "cost of inventories" as "all costs of purchase, costs of conversion and other costs incurred in bringing the inventories to their present location and condition".

The cost of inventory may be stated at actual cost (**conventional costing** method) or at a standard cost (**standard costing** method). A standard costing system involves the company setting a budget/standard cost for inventory items at the beginning of the year, which is then used to price the inventory as it passes through the company's costing system. Any difference from the standard results in variances, i.e. when the cost of purchasing the goods is more/less than the standard. These purchase price variances are then allocated to cost of sales/inventory as appropriate.

Closing inventory should be valued on a FIFO (first in first out) basis using unit cost or weighted average. LIFO (last in first out) and replacement cost approaches are not acceptable. When examining the value at which inventory is recorded, the auditor should ascertain the prices at which finished goods have been sold post-year end as this will highlight any items that may need to be reduced to below cost. The auditor should ensure that the selling price takes into account any trade discounts allowed and whether such selling price has been reduced by disposal costs. This adjusted selling price should then be compared to the **carrying value** of the finished goods.

The auditor should also review post-year-end sales of inventory to establish whether or not the sales price (and therefore the NRV) is achievable. A provision may be required for slow-moving or obsolete inventory based on this review.

The auditor should determine the client entity's policy for the valuation of inventory and ensure that it is in line with IAS 2, i.e. that it must be valued at the lower of cost and **net realisable value** (NRV). (The NRV being the selling price less the cost to completion, less selling, marketing and distribution costs. It may also be defined as the value the inventory would achieve in the open market based on its present condition.) An example of how to test that the inventory is costed correctly would be to obtain a sample of invoices to support the cost of a sample of inventory, and obtain a copy of the most recent sales invoice to support the selling price. Compare the selling price to the cost to ensure it is valued at the lower of both.

Let us now consider in more detail the two stages of validating the value of inventory noted at the start of this section: 1. validating cost and 2. ensuring inventory is valued at the lower of cost or NRV.

### 1. Validating Cost by Vouching to Original Purchase Invoices or Standard Costing Records

**Validating Raw Material Cost Price**

As introduced above, when validating the original cost of inventories the auditor may be faced with two costing methods: conventional costing, which refers to 'goods bought for resale' (e.g. in the retail business the goods are sold as purchased with no alterations to the product); or standard costing, where inventory purchased represents raw materials that will be converted into finished goods. Along with raw materials, other costs will be incurred in turning raw materials into finished goods, such as: production wages and salaries; equipment depreciation; overheads such as light, heat and rent of the production area; and so on. The following considers the auditor's approach with regard to validating the 'cost' assigned to the client entity's inventory using both methods of costing.

**Conventional Costing**   The auditor needs to determine that the inventory is stated at the lower of cost and NRV. This can be tested by verifying the cost used by the client entity to value the inventory at the year end to a purchase invoice.

**Standard Costing**   The auditor must be satisfied that the standard cost approximates closely to the actual cost. This can be verified by agreeing the standard cost to a supporting purchase invoice for a sample of raw materials. Any purchase price variances that arise should be reviewed as they indicate the reasonableness of the standard (i.e. if large variances occur between the standard cost and the actual costs incurred for production, then the standard cost may not be an accurate reflection of the actual costs of making the finished good). Furthermore, in order for the auditor to adequately review the accuracy of the standard costs, they must first gain a good understanding of the client entity's standard costing system and how it determines standard costs. The auditor should also consider how often the standard costs are revised (e.g. annually/quarterly), who sets them, and how attainable are they? If standard costs are attainable, the level of variances should be low. The procedures for setting standard costs should also be reviewed by the auditor for reasonableness.

## Validating Work in Progress/Finished Goods (Short-term Contracts)

Work in progress and finished goods, by necessity, contain an element of labour and overheads to transform them from raw materials. The cost collection of these elements is usually captured on a **bill of material** (BOM) – a list of all components required to make a particular item of inventory, including quantities of each item needed to manufacture a finished product.

The following audit procedures should be carried out by the auditor in relation to the validation of work in progress and finished goods for short-term contracts:

- *Raw Material Element* Cost accounting records should be cross-checked to accounting records and vice versa. To test the materials component a BOM should be obtained and the raw materials indicated traced to their purchase invoices to validate the price paid (the cost).
- *Labour Element* The labour element of a BOM should be tested by comparing the labour content to job sheets/time sheets and comparing the labour rate to payroll records. The auditor should:
    - reconcile financial and cost accounting records;
    - ensure the wage rate indicated on the job sheet agrees to wage rates determined by social security documentation, etc. and that the total time indicated on the job sheet is the actual labour cost allocated to the job; and
    - ensure that idle time has not been charged to the job, and is instead charged to overhead expenses.

- *Overhead Element* An understanding should be gained of how overheads are allocated to inventory items, i.e. machine hours or labour hours. The basis for allocating overheads should be broadly in line with the prior year and based on normal production levels in the company. All overheads relating to abnormal activity levels should be written off to the income statement, e.g. idle time when machinery is being repaired. The overhead absorption calculation should then be reperformed by agreeing the relative factors to underlying documentation, e.g. machine hours to production schedule, labour hours to time sheets. All related supporting documentation should be examined.

## Validating Work in Progress/Finished Goods (IFRS 15 *Revenue from Contracts with Customers*)

Long-term work in progress, such as construction contracts, can cover many accounting periods and often prove to be a problematic area for auditors to review. The auditor may have to exercise judgement and involve an expert valuer. The auditor should:

- examine contracts to determine timescales and penalty clauses;
- ascertain which costing system was used and determine whether it can be relied on given the nature of the contract;
- ensure that costs incurred are accurate, genuine and complete;
- assess the stage of completion and ensure that costs are properly charged to the item based on the stage reached;
- inquire into the qualifications, etc. of the expert valuer certifying the completed work;
- ensure that all profits realised are eliminated from work in progress (IAS 2 does not allow elements of profit to be included in work in progress); and
- identify any losses on contracts as these have to be recognised in the valuation.

## Standard Costing – Treatment of Variances

As previously mentioned, the auditor should compare actual and standard costs of items included in the year-end valuation. Due to the nature of standard costing, differences will always arise between the standard and the actual cost of production. These variances may be as a result of differences relating to the price of raw materials, in the cost of labour or in the cost of overheads related to the product.

During the audit, the level of variances should be analysed to provide an indication of the reliability of the standard costs. Attainable standard costs will not give rise to large variances – the standard cost will approximate the actual cost. As a rule, variances resulting from inefficiencies (rather than from a poorly set standard cost) should be expensed to the statement of comprehensive income. However, if the standard costs are not set accurately, the variances that arise should be apportioned between cost of sales and inventory appropriately. The auditor should ascertain the last time the standard costs were reviewed and determine whether the current standard costs are still relevant in light of changes in general prices, production methods and product specification. Any changes in standard costs should be properly authorised.

**Example 12.8** illustrates the audit procedures that could be used to validate the components of a BOM.

EXAMPLE 12.8: AUDIT PROCEDURES FOR VALUATION
OF DIFFERENT CLASSES OF INVENTORY

If we look back at **Example 12.2** (final inventory listing), we can see that the unit cost price for inventory item 'Wood Type A' is priced at €100 per unit. Wood Type A is a raw material, so the auditor can validate this by simply obtaining a recent purchase invoice for Wood Type A and vouching that the €100 represents the price paid (net of VAT).

Inventory item Table A has a unit cost price of €300 and is a finished good. The auditor can validate this by reference to standard costing, which could be calculated from the BOM.

**Table A: BOM for batch of 100**

| | Units | Unit Cost €| Total €|
|---|---|---|---|
| Raw material – Wood type A | 99 | 100 | 9,900 |
| Raw material – Metal A | 99 | 200 | 19,800 |
| Labour (per hour) | 6.75 | 25 | 169 |
| Overhead (per labour hour) | 6.75 | 15 | 101 |
| Depreciation (Plant Item A) | 6.75 | 5 | 34 |
| Cost to produce batch of 100 | | | **30,004** |
| Cost to produce 1 unit | | | 300 |

For the raw material items, the auditor can perform the same test as that noted for raw materials above (vouch to purchase invoice). For the labour and overhead allocations, the auditor needs to test the standard costing assumptions for reasonableness by:
- Validating the total number of labour hours available in a year and the total cost of direct labour for a year (both of which could be obtained through testing payroll). The total cost divided by the total number of hours available should be close to €25. The total labour hours for the year should be that operating in the normal environment.
- Validating the total expected cost of direct overheads in the year (based on normal capacity) and the total number of labour hours in a period (as per above). The total direct overheads divided by the total number of labour hours should be close to €15.
- The auditor can validate the reasonableness of the depreciation by reference to the testing of non-current fixed assets.

The same type of exercise can be performed for work in progress by estimating its stage of completion to the above.

## 2. Ensuring Inventory is Valued at the Lower of Cost or NRV

The auditor must be alert to indications that the NRV may be lower than cost. Examples of when NRV is likely to be less than cost include when there has been:

- an increase in costs and a decrease in selling price – indicated in tests of details of samples selected above and sales invoices in the new period;
- physical deterioration of inventory or obsolescence – indicated by attendance at the physical inventory count;
- a marketing decision to sell below cost – indicated in management meeting minutes or through inquiry of management;
- errors in production or purchasing – indicated by high returns of customer product in the new period; or
- a fall-off in sales of the inventory item – indicated by zero/minimal orders of the inventory item in the order book in the new period.

CAATs can be used to assist with NRV testing by comparing inventory cost in the purchases listing to inventory sales price in the sales listing (depending on how the transactions are captured).

## Other Considerations

Having performed the substantive procedures relating to inventory movements and inventory balances, there are some other matters the auditor must consider before they have adequately completed the substantive procedures relating to inventory. These include: inventory provisions; cut-off; and ownership.

### Inventory Provisions

Inventory provisions are tested in two ways:

1. **Validating management provisions** The auditor should obtain a list of inventory items that make up the amount provided in the financial statements. This requires the auditor to review the accounting estimate (see **Chapter 6**, Section 6.10) for the inventory provision. Provisions can be made for a variety of reasons and the auditor should examine and validate these as follows:
    (a) Slow-moving stock – review the **aged inventory listing** to confirm that the inventory items provided for are in fact slow-moving and obtain explanations from management as to why the items are significantly aged.
    (b) Obsolete stock – while it may be significantly aged, obsolete stock could also relate to current stock that has been subject to a sudden change in market conditions (e.g. technological advancement that suddenly renders the product obsolete). The auditor should enquire into the reasons for obsolete inventory.
    (c) Damaged stock – the auditor should be able to validate damaged inventory using the **physical inventory count sheet**, which should have recorded all damaged inventory.

(d)  Stock that is out of date or close to sell by/use by date – out-of-date stock should be fully provided; stock that is close to its sell by/use by date should be written down to NRV. The auditor should be able to validate the existence of these items from the physical inventory count sheet.

In each instance the auditor is attempting to establish the reasonableness of the amount provided (i.e. 100% of the cost or part of the cost). Where part of the cost is provided, the auditor needs to consider if the NRV has been considered, i.e. that net cost (original cost less provision) is not greater than the NRV.

2.  **Assessing the completeness of the provision** The auditor must also consider whether management have considered all possible inventory items requiring a provision. With regard to damaged, out-of-date or short-dated inventory items, the auditor should have noted these when attending the physical inventory count (along with the client). The auditor should trace a sample of these inventory items to the provision listing prepared by management.

In relation to work in progress, the auditor should review the records for any items with no expenses charged in recent months. This may highlight inventory that has not been worked on recently, which could suggest that work in progress has been cancelled. Reviewing the aged inventory listing could also highlight such instances.

The auditor should also verify the aged inventory listing itself. This would be done by sampling the inventory, tracing them to their related GRNs and agreeing the date (age) of the inventory against the listing. CAATs can be used to prepare an aged inventory listing from the nominal listing (sub-ledger) should one not be provided by the client entity. Alternatively, the inventory listing can be interrogated to identify inventory balances beyond a certain date, which may indicate slow moving or obsolete stock.

## Cut-off

The cut-off assertion is concerned that all movements of inventory are recorded in the correct period. To test this assertion, the goods received notes (GRNs) and goods dispatch notes (GDNs) around the period end should be reviewed to ensure they are sequential; any missing numbers should be investigated. Further, a sample of goods in/out on either side of year end should be selected for testing to ensure they are recorded in the correct period. The last GRN and GDN numbers should have been obtained during the attendance at the year-end inventory count and these should be used as evidence of the last goods in and the first goods out.

In order to guarantee accurate cut-off, the auditor should ensure that:
- management allocate responsibility for ensuring cut-off details are accurate to one individual;
- there is no movement in or out of inventory while the inventory count is being performed;
- if movements are occurring, records are being kept of all movements and goods inward are being held in a separate location until the count has been completed.

The cut-off process, as it should work, is depicted below in **Figure 12.2**. You can see that GRN2374 is signed and dated 31 December 2018 and is therefore included in the 2018 transactions. If the auditor traced this GRN to the nominal listing and it was dated 2019, then there would be a cut-off error. Similarly, GRN2379 is signed and dated 1 January 2019 and is correctly recorded in the listing. The auditor will perform this test in both directions (from source document to nominal ledger and from nominal ledger to source document). The same method applies to GDNs.

FIGURE 12.2: TRACING GRNs TO TRANSACTIONS IN THE NOMINAL LEDGER

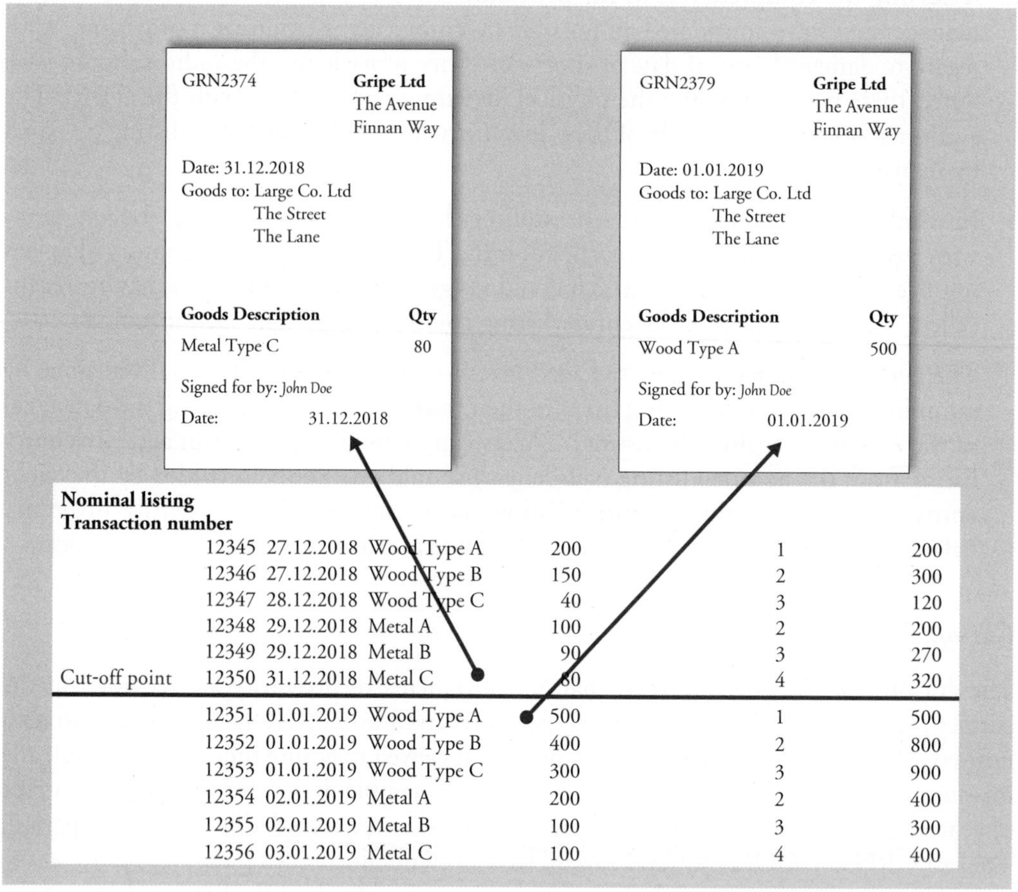

An alternative method of reviewing cut-off could include the auditor analytically reviewing inventory levels before and after the year end to identify unusual spikes or trends that may indicate a risk of material misstatement in cut-off.

## Ownership (Rights and Obligations)

Inventory items belonging to third parties should be identified and excluded from the final inventory listing. The auditor must also ensure that inventories that are awaiting dispatch and that have been included in sales are excluded from inventory figures.

The following situations often pose problems for auditors when reviewing inventory:

1. **The ownership of goods bought close to the year end** This relates to goods purchased but not yet delivered to the client entity at the date of the SOFP. The auditor must ascertain whether or not legal title has passed, based on the terms of the individual contract. The auditor must also determine whether the goods in question have been correctly or incorrectly included in the financial statements at the date of the SOFP. An adjustment may be required based on their findings.

2. **The ownership of goods sold close to the year end** This relates to goods sold but which are still on the client entity's premises at the date of the SOFP. The auditor must ensure that these goods are not included in inventory in the financial statements.

3. **Consignment inventory** This relates to goods that are not owned by the client but which are held on consignment or under a franchise agreement until a specified condition is met. These items should not form part of the inventory figure at the SOFP date. The auditor should also ensure that the opposite is the case – where inventory owned by the client, and held on consignment or under a franchise agreement by a third party, is included in the closing inventory figure at the date of the SOFP. In this case, the auditor should physically inspect the inventory where possible. If this is not permitted, either a confirmation from the third party as to the quantities and condition of items held should be requested, or the performance of other audit procedures that will provide sufficient appropriate audit evidence as to the existence and condition of the inventory.

4. **Goods sold on a sale-or-return basis** The auditor should pay close attention to goods sold on a sale-or-return basis and ensure that those inventory items, where the return period has not ended, are included within inventory or in line with IFRS 15.

## 12.9 DISCLOSURE REQUIREMENTS

Finally, with regard to inventory, the auditor will consider the adequacy of the disclosures, particularly with regard to the requirements of IAS 2. IAS 2, paragraph 36, requires that all disclosures:

- are complete, i.e. no inventory-related disclosures are missing. The auditor can use IAS 2 as a checklist;
- are accurate, i.e. reflect the actual transactions and information relating to the events surrounding inventory;
- relate to events that actually occurred or exist at the year end; and
- are properly presented, i.e. in a manner expected by IAS 2.

IAS 2, paragraphs 36–39, detail the disclosures required for inventory, which include:

- accounting policies used to value inventory, including the cost formula used;
- details of inventories valued at NRV;
- ensuring the correct classification of inventory between raw materials, work in progress and finished goods;
- ascertaining the value of inventory sold under 'retention of title' clauses and ensuring adequate disclosure. (Retention of title, otherwise known as reservation of title, relates to situations where the supplier retains title of the goods sold until payment is received.);

- ensuring correct disclosure of inventory pledged as security for liabilities of the client or third parties;
- details of the write-down of inventory expensed during the year;
- if a reversal of a write-down occurred, a description of the circumstances that caused this; and
- details of long-term contracts.

The auditor must fully understand these disclosure requirements in order to properly review the adequacy of the client entity's disclosures.

## 12.10 CONCLUSION

When testing the area of inventory, the auditor is most concerned with the completeness, existence and valuation assertions. Completeness and existence are addressed by attendance at the client entity's physical inventory count; the latter by remaining alert to indications of events that may give rise to cost being greater than NRV.

The auditor must consider the requirements of IAS 2 to ensure that all disclosures are complete, accurate, relate to events that actually occurred or exist at the year end and are properly presented.

The auditor must consider the impact of the audit of inventory on the audit opinion. This is achieved by considering whether any misstatements, found either individually or in aggregate (when combined with other misstatements detected throughout the audit), will result in the financial statements being materially misstated. As such, all misstatements found are taken to the auditor's errors schedule for consideration at the audit completion stage (discussed in detail in **Chapter 18**). The auditor's report on financial statements is considered in detail in **Chapter 19**.

SUMMARY OF LEARNING OBJECTIVES

**Learning Objective 1**   Understand what is included in the audit of inventory.

IAS 2 *Inventories* is the relevant standard governing inventories, and the auditor will seek to ensure that inventories are recorded in compliance with this standard.

Inventory is commonly referred to as stock. In a manufacturing company, inventory consists of three elements: raw materials, work in progress and finished goods.

**Learning Objective 2**   Be able to identify the risks and audit objectives applicable to inventory.

The primary risks associated with inventory relate to:
- the volume of transactions and the reliability of internal controls in tracking them;
- the risk of inventory items being worth less than cost;
- the complicated accounting associated with standard costing;
- the susceptibility of inventory to theft;

- the degree of fluctuations in inventory levels; and
- the susceptibility to obsolescence.

With respect to the movements of inventory in the period, the auditor is predominantly interested in the occurrence, accuracy and completeness of transactions.

**Learning Objective 3**    Be able to determine an appropriate audit strategy for inventory, taking into consideration the specific risks and audit objectives (management assertions).

When auditing the inventory balance, the auditor is seeking to ensure existence and completeness (that the inventory actually exists at the year end and all inventories that exist are included) and that the inventory is appropriately valued at the lower of cost or NRV (as per IAS 2).

**Learning Objective 4**    Be able to develop an audit programme that addresses all the audit objectives (management assertions) for inventory.

In general, in a non-manufacturing environment the auditor will not seek to test and rely on controls testing – because the majority of movements of inventory will have been tested within the revenue and receivables and purchases and payables cycles. Regardless of controls, where inventory is material to the financial statements the auditor must attend the physical inventory count at year end and, as such, the controls approach is rarely the efficient approach to take.

In a manufacturing environment the auditor may choose to test the controls around valuation (standard costing).

**Learning Objective 5**    Be able to describe and apply specific substantive testing procedures relating to the audit of inventory.

The aged inventory listing, final inventory listing and physical inventory count sheet are the key documents of interest to the auditor. Other documents that may form audit evidence connected to inventory include:
- bill of material (BOM);
- inventory purchase invoices.

With regard to the transactions, generally these will have been tested within the revenue and receivables and purchases and payables cycles. In a manufacturing environment the auditor will primarily be interested in the accuracy of the BOM.

For inventory balances the auditor will seek to:
- attend the **physical inventory count** to validate existence and completeness of inventory – sampling count sheets and comparing to the final inventory listing provided at the time of the audit fieldwork;
- ensure that inventory is **valued** at the **lower of cost or NRV** – by validating cost by reference to purchase invoices (or BOM) and considering any reasons why the sale value would be less than the validated cost; and
- with respect to rights and obligations, consider the existence of third-party inventory on the premises of the entity, or of entity inventory on the premises of a third party. Also consider inventory sold on a sale-or-return basis.

**Learning Objective 6**   Understand the role CAATs can play when auditing inventory.

The auditor may use a combination of audit software, data analysis tools and other applications, such as Excel, when auditing the area of inventory.

**Learning Objective 7**   Understand the auditor's approach relating to disclosures of inventory.

The auditor needs to consider the requirements of IAS 2 to ensure that all necessary inventory disclosures are: complete; accurate; relate to events that actually occurred; and are properly presented.

## QUESTIONS

### Self-test Questions

12.1   Define inventory.

12.2   List seven risks relating to inventory.

12.3   Outline the documents that support the auditor when validating the cost of inventory.

12.4   What is a 'blind count'?

12.5   List four standard analytical review procedures for the audit of inventories.

12.6   What conclusions should an auditor draw from observing an inventory count?

12.7   Which assertions are tested when a sample of items from the inventory count sheets is selected?

12.8   What procedures must an auditor perform if they are unable to attend the year-end inventory count?

12.9   How does IAS 2 state that inventory must be valued?

12.10   What circumstances might lead to NRV being lower than cost?

12.11   How is cut-off testing performed?

### Review Questions

(See Suggested Solutions to Review Questions in **Appendix C**.)

### *Question 12.1*

You are an audit senior completing a training contract with Hannon & Co. professional accounting practice. You have been assigned to the audit of Ryan's Ltd, which has prepared financial statements to 31 December 2018.

At the year end, Ryan's inventory levels had increased by 8% on the previous year. The increased levels of inventory held is primarily in the homeware section and is attributable, in part, to increased bulk purchasing and a decline in sales activity towards the end of the financial year. Ryan's inventory is recorded at cost as at 31 December 2018 and no inventory provision has been included in the 2018 financial statements.

Management decided that, in order to reduce homeware inventory, unit sales prices would be reduced across certain product lines at the beginning of January 2019, particularly on furniture products. In addition, a 2% discount on the reduced sales price will be offered to customers on these products. In 2018, homeware products were sold at a mark-up of 20% on cost.

Set out below are the products (with current sales prices) where sales prices will be reduced.

| Product | Current unit selling price | Units in stock | Total | Revised unit selling price |
|---|---|---|---|---|
| | £/€ | | £/€ | £/€ |
| Bedside locker | 150 | 900 | 135,000 | 125* |
| Double bed | 110 | 1,100 | 121,000 | 90* |
| Wardrobe | 210 | 6,000 | 1,260,000 | 175* |

* Before a further 2% discount.

All remaining furniture inventory products at the year end are new lines that are expected to sell well and consequently their prices will not be reduced.

**Requirement** Set out the substantive audit work you would perform in respect of the inventory items described above, together with any adjustments you deem necessary.

## Question 12.2

Your firm is the auditor of Tulla Licence Trade Wholesalers Limited. You are assigned to the audit of inventory and will be required to attend the physical inventory count and to perform the substantive audit procedures during the final field work after the year end. The inventory count is to take place on 28 December 2018 and the premises will be closed between then and 31 December 2018, with the exception of a small number of key customer orders that will be delivered during that time.

80% of the value of the inventory held by Tulla relates to its stock of matured whiskey, which represents just 10% of the volume of inventory items. Tulla purchases large volumes of Christmas-branded stock during November and December.

Tulla have a number of locations in the Republic of Ireland and Northern Ireland, all holding varying degrees of stock volumes.

## Requirement
(a) Detail the procedures you should perform to validate the existence and completeness of inventory before and during your attendance at the physical inventory count.
(b) Detail the checks you will perform over cut-off at the date of the physical inventory count and at the year end.
(c) Detail how you will verify that inventory quantities used in the valuation of inventory at year end are correct.
(d) Indicate how valuation of inventory can be considered during the physical inventory count.

# 13

# THE AUDIT OF REVENUE AND RECEIVABLES

LEARNING OBJECTIVES

Having studied this chapter on the audit of revenue and receivables you should:
1. understand what is included in the audit of revenue and receivables;
2. be able to identify the risks and audit objectives applicable to revenue and receivables;
3. be able to determine an appropriate audit strategy for revenue and receivables, taking into consideration the specific risks and audit objectives (management assertions);
4. be able to develop an audit programme that addresses all the audit objectives (management assertions) for revenue and receivables;
5. be able to describe and apply specific substantive testing procedures relating to the audit of revenue and receivables;
6. understand the role CAATs can play when auditing revenue and receivables; and
7. understand the auditor's approach relating to the disclosures of revenue and receivables.

## CHECKLIST OF RELEVANT STANDARDS

The relevant standards, in both the RoI and the UK/NI, covered in this chapter are:
- ISA 315 *Identifying and Assessing the risks of Material Misstatement through Understanding the Entity and its Environment*
- ISA 330 *The Auditor's Responses to Assessed Risks*
- ISA 500 *Audit Evidence*
- ISA 510 *Initial Audit Engagements – Opening Balances*
- ISA 505 *External Confirmations*
- ISA 520 *Analytical Procedures*
- ISA 530 *Audit Sampling*
- ISA 540 *Auditing Accounting Estimates, Including Fair Value Accounting Estimates, and Related Disclosures*
- IAS 1 *Presentation of Financial Statements*
- IFRS 15 *Revenue from Contracts with Customers*

Note, in general when referring to ISAs, it should be understood as referring to the UK and Ireland versions, unless otherwise specified as either ISA (UK) or ISA (Ireland). See the Introduction for an extant list of auditing standards for the RoI and the UK/NI.

## KEY TERMS AND DEFINITIONS FOR THIS CHAPTER

**Aged Receivables Listing**   A full list of individual customer balances that can be reconciled to the receivables figure in the financial statements. The balance for each customer is broken down by the length of time it has been outstanding (usually due within 30 days, 60 days, 90 days and greater than 90 days).

**Doubtful Debts Provision**   A credit balance set against receivables, representing the estimate of uncollectable amounts included in the trade receivables listing. The auditor will evaluate the adequacy of the doubtful debt provision when considering the valuation of receivables.

**Receivables Circularisation**   A letter sent to the client entity's customers by the auditor, the objective of which is to obtain independent evidence as to the existence and accuracy of the receivables balance in the financial statements. The auditor must receive permission from the client entity before circularising its customers.

## 13.1 INTRODUCTION

The objective of substantive testing is to validate the transactions, balances and disclosures at the assertion level in response to identified risks (inherent, control and detection risks as discussed in **Chapters 7** and **8**). The auditor commences substantive testing by focusing on the risk of material misstatement within the transactions and balances being tested, and then identifying the assertions impacted by these risks and then identifying substantive audit procedures that will best test the existence of material misstatement driven by the identified risks.

**Sections 13.2–13.8** outline the requirements of IFRS 15 *Revenue from Contracts with Customers* with respect to revenues and IAS 1 *Presentation of Financial Statements* with respect to classification of assets as 'current'. In doing so it considers how the auditor:

- identifies audit risks and audit objectives (management assertions) for revenue and receivables;
- develops an audit plan for revenue and receivables and refines this into an audit programme;
- designs specific tests associated with revenue and receivables; and
- ensures adequate presentation and disclosure in the financial statements relating to revenue and receivables.

Throughout the chapter it is highlighted where CAATs can be used by the auditor in assisting with ensuring the effective and efficient audit of revenue and receivables.

Finally, in **Section 13.9** we consider the auditor's approach when auditing the reasonableness of disclosures relating to revenue and receivables.

## 13.2 WHAT IS REVENUE AND RECEIVABLES?

In the financial statements of an entity, the **revenue figure represents the income earned by the business in return for the passing of title on goods or services**. The auditor needs to be sure that revenue is recognised in line with IFRS 15. The **receivables balance arises as a result of sales made and represents money due to the business from customers for those sales**. The auditor will consider the classification of 'current assets' in line with IAS 1.

The value of total sales generated (revenue) in the period under review and the value of period-end receivables is material to the financial statements in most businesses, which is why the testing performed on this area is so important.

As discussed in **Chapter 6**, ISA 500 *Audit Evidence* states the need for the auditor to obtain **sufficient appropriate audit evidence** over classes of transactions (revenue) and account balances (receivables).

We will now consider the steps the auditor takes when performing an audit on revenue and receivables.

## 13.3 RISKS ASSOCIATED WITH REVENUE AND RECEIVABLES

Throughout **Chapter 7** we discussed the topic of risk and considered how the auditor should go about detecting risks. We also discussed how the auditor should consider these risks when designing the nature, timing and extent of further audit procedures relative to each financial cycle. So, before developing the audit plan the auditor needs to consider a number of risks that may be associated with revenue and receivables. The auditor should consider and take into account the following with regard to identifying risks associated with revenue and receivables:

- previous experience with the client entity, e.g. where a significant risk existed in the past in relation to recoverability of receivables balances, the auditor should be alert to this in the current audit (this example would represent either an inherent risk if it is associated with the nature of the customers in the entity's industry, or a control risk if it is due to poor credit control procedures);

- reliability of estimates made by the client entity in the past, e.g. where the basis of the **doubtful debt provision** determined by the client in the past was deemed unreliable, resulting in the auditor having to make adjustments to fairly state the provision (an inherent risk exists around management's judgement), the auditor should be alert for this in the current audit;
- robustness of the client entity's accounting system, e.g. where cut-off errors were discovered in a prior audit as a result of sales invoices being posted to the system in the incorrect period (a control risk);
- complexity of the business, e.g. where recognition of a sale occurs only after a number of key stages have been completed or actions taken, the auditor should be alert to the possibility that sales may have been recognised in the period that are not true sales, i.e. sales have been accounted for in the period but all the necessary stages resulting in revenue recognition have not been completed before the period end (an inherent risk, which could be compounded by a control risk if poor controls are in place);
- scope for fraudulent activity, which in relation to revenue and receivables could include:
  - creation of false customer accounts, resulting in overstated revenue figures and receivables balances (a control risk); or
  - misappropriation of cash receipts where the business is cash-based (an inherent risk);
- indication of risks associated with certain revenue transactions, e.g. recognition of goods sold on a sale-or-return basis or recognition of revenue connected to work in progress (an inherent risk).

## 13.4 AUDIT OBJECTIVES/MANAGEMENT ASSERTIONS FOR REVENUE AND RECEIVABLES

As discussed in **Chapter 6**, it is necessary for the auditor to obtain sufficient appropriate audit evidence to satisfy all of the audit objectives and to eliminate the possibility of any of the risks outlined above going undetected. The auditor must design tests to address these assertions and thereby address the identified risks. In **Chapter 4**, we introduced **audit objectives** (**management assertions**) and explained their generic meanings, before reintroducing the topic throughout **Chapter 8**, making management assertions specific to each financial cycle. **Table 13.1** below recaps the audit objectives for transactions and account balances as they relate to revenue and receivables.

When designing **tests of controls**, **substantive analytical reviews** and **tests of details**, the auditor must ensure that sufficient assurance has been obtained over all of the assertions. This is usually achieved through designing an audit plan that includes all, or a combination of, the types of testing listed above.

Having discussed the objectives of the auditor with regard to revenue and receivables, we now consider how the auditor addresses these objectives through **substantive testing**.

TABLE 13.1: REVENUE AND RECEIVABLES – AUDIT OBJECTIVES

| Management Assertion/ Audit Objective | Control Objective for Transaction Class<br><br>Revenue | Control Objective for Account Balance<br><br>Receivables |
|---|---|---|
| Existence or occurrence | • Recorded revenue transactions represent goods shipped.<br>• Recorded cash receipts transactions represent cash received.<br>• Recorded revenue adjustment transactions represent authorised discounts, returns, allowances and bad debts. | • Receivables balances represent amounts owed by customers at the date of the SOFP. |
| Completeness | All revenue, cash receipts and revenue adjustment transactions that occurred have been recorded. | Receivables include all claims on customers at the date of the SOFP. |
| Rights and obligations | The entity has rights to the receivables balance and cash resulting from recorded revenue transactions. | Receivables at the date of the SOFP represent legal claims of the entity on customers for payment. |
| Classification/ Recording (accuracy) or valuation | All revenue, cash receipts and revenue adjustment transactions are correctly journalised, summarised and posted to the correct accounts. | • Receivables represent gross claims on customers at the date of the SOFP and agree with the sum of the aged receivables ledger.<br>• The provision for bad debts represents a reasonable estimate of the difference between gross receivables and their net realisable value (NRV). |
| Cut-off | All revenue, cash receipts and revenue adjustment transactions are recorded in the correct accounting period. | |
| Presentation and disclosure | The details of revenue, cash receipts and revenue adjustment transactions support their presentation in financial statements, including their classification and related disclosures. | • Receivables are properly identified and classified at the date of the SOFP.<br>• Appropriate disclosures have been made concerning debts that have been factored or otherwise assigned. |

## 13.5 DEVELOPING THE AUDIT PLAN FOR REVENUE AND RECEIVABLES

Before the audit of revenue and receivables is undertaken, an assessment of the audit risk must be completed. As discussed in detail in **Chapter 7**, audit risk is made up of three components: inherent risk; control risk; and detection risk. We will examine these components specifically as they relate to revenue and receivables.

The specific risks associated with revenue and receivables were given in **Section 13.3** (see also **Chapter 8**, Section 8.5 for a description of a typical revenue system, the specific controls the auditor would expect to find, and how to test those controls). In Chapter 8, one of the key points around revenue and receivables is whether or not controls should be tested. Remember: where the revenue and receivables balances are not **material** to the financial statements, limited controls and substantive testing will be performed. However, in most businesses revenue and receivables are material and transactions tend to be high in volume – therefore the auditor usually takes a **controls approach** when testing revenue and receivables in order to reduce the level of detailed **substantive testing** required.

The general rules the auditor should consider when deciding on the audit approach relating to revenue and receivables include:
- where the revenue figure and receivables balance are **not material** to the financial statements, limited controls and substantive testing will be performed;
- where a **significant risk** has been identified in relation to the revenue and receivables cycle, the level of substantive testing to be performed will be more rigorous;
- where a **strong control environment** has been identified, the extent of substantive testing to be performed will be much less than the level of substantive testing to be performed in an entity where a weak control environment has been identified.

Generally, a controls approach is the most productive (effective and efficient) approach when testing the area of revenue and receivables. Remember, however, that the auditor can decide to take a controls approach only in relation to certain assertions (audit objectives) and then perform focused substantive testing on the other assertions. With respect to **valuation**, quite often the auditor will choose to take a wholly substantive approach due to the risks associated with it.

## 13.6 AUDIT TRAIL FOR REVENUE AND RECEIVABLES

To appreciate the role of the auditor in validating transactions, classes of transactions or balances at the assertion level it is important to first understand the audit trail associated with the relevant cycle. **Figure 13.1** below outlines an audit trail that could be followed when validating the various management assertions associated with revenue and receivables.

In the figure, note that revenue in the financial statements is reported as €15,000, which agrees with the sales figure in the trial balance summary of the nominal ledger. If we take a single transaction from the nominal ledger, we can trace this to the journal entry and back

## FIGURE 13.1: REVENUE AND RECEIVABLES AUDIT TRAIL

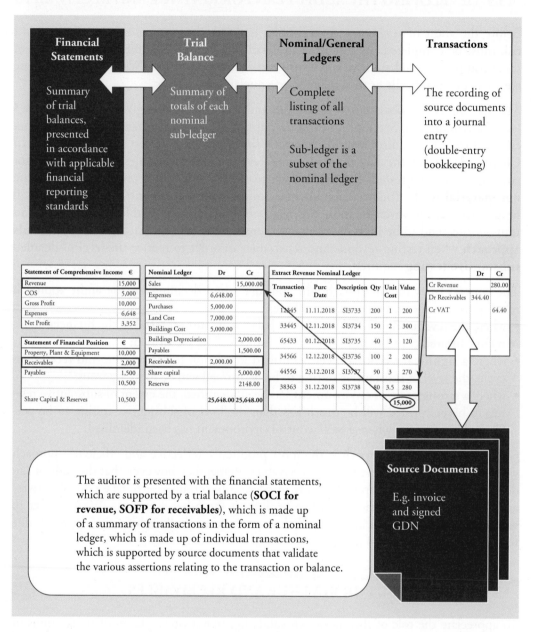

to the source documents (invoice and signed goods dispatch note (GDN)). By following this audit trail we can validate the following assertions: occurrence; rights and obligations (as the client entity will be named on the GDN); recording (the value and quantity will be included on the invoice, and the invoice quantity can be matched to the signed GDN); and cut-off (the date of delivery is noted on the signed GDN).

If we traced from the GDN to the financial statements we would be testing for completeness, but we could still validate rights and obligations, recording and cut-off at the same time, similar to above.

Whatever the **direction** of the test, the source document data is used to validate whether the transaction has been appropriately recorded/valued and that it proves the entity's rights and obligations assertion over the transaction/balance. Sometimes a blend of source documents will be required to validate all assertions, while in other instances a single source document will validate a number of assertions.

Key documents associated with revenue and receivables include:
- GDNs (summarises goods/services delivered to the customer and should be signed by the customer to evidence receipt of goods/services);
- sales invoices;
- bank statements (relevant to receivables insofar as it shows receipts from customers);
- customer statements (summary of all invoices owed by a customer at a point in time);
- customer remittances (summary of all invoices being paid in a single remittance, e.g. if the customer paid €10,000 they would send a remittance advising the invoices they are paying that equate to the €10,000);
- aged receivables listing.

## Aged Receivables Listing

The primary, and most important, document of interest to the auditor is the **aged receivables listing**, which is a full list of all the individual customer balances that exist at the date of the statement of financial position that can be reconciled to the receivables figure in the financial statements. Each customer's balance is 'aged', i.e. broken down by the length of time it has been outstanding (usually 30 days, 60 days, 90 days or greater than 90 days).

The aged receivables listing has a number of useful applications:
- a list from which to select a sample for details testing or to perform receivables circularisation (see **Section 13.8**);
- if received in Excel, it can be structured to show top-value customers' balances, credit balances, nil balances, etc. – helping to ascertain risk areas; and
- a list against which credit limits can be compared to assist with the valuation assertion.

An example of an aged receivables listing is shown in **Example 13.1** below. If you refer to **Appendix B**, Large Company Limited, Note 17, you will see that the totals in Example 13.1 agree to the note in the financial statements (i.e. total receivables: €3,750,000; current: €3,100,000; 30–60 days: €420,000; 60–90 days: €150,000; and greater than 90 days old: €80,000). The auditor must confirm this before commencing testing on the aged receivables listing.

EXAMPLE 13.1: AGED RECEIVABLES LISTING (LARGE COMPANY LIMITED)

| Customer Name | Credit Limit | Total Value €000 | Current €000 | 30–60 days old €000 | 60–90 days old €000 | Greater than 90 days old €000 |
|---|---|---|---|---|---|---|
| Customer A | 150 | 100 | 100 | | | |
| Customer B | 20 | 39 | 39 | | | |
| Customer C | 650 | 596 | 490 | | 55 | 51 |
| Customer D | 400 | 364 | 364 | | | |
| Customer E | 150 | 90 | 70 | 20 | | |
| Customer F | 10 | 4 | | | | 4 |
| Customer G | 25 | 18 | 18 | | | |
| Customer H | 20 | 14 | 10 | 4 | | |
| Customer I | 500 | 400 | 375 | 25 | | |
| Customer J | 800 | 650 | 650 | | | |
| Customer K | 200 | 15 | 15 | | | |
| Customer L | 900 | 785 | 810 | – | (25) | |
| Customer M | 15 | 20 | 20 | | | |
| Customer N | 40 | 30 | 20 | 10 | | |
| Customer O | 28 | 25 | 25 | | | |
| Customer P | 100 | 50 | 44 | 6 | | |
| Customer Q | 250 | 400 | – | 255 | 120 | 25 |
| Customer R | 200 | 150 | 50 | 100 | | |
| | | 3,750 | 3,100 | 420 | 150 | 80 |
| | | | 83% | 11% | 4% | 2% |

## The Use of CAATs

If the auditor obtains the client entity's sub-ledger showing all invoices outstanding from customers at year end, CAATs can be used to produce the aged receivables listing. For example, in Excel the auditor could assign an age category using a series of nested statements and use pivot tables to produce an aged report by customer and age. The report could be enhanced by obtaining the credit limit for each customer and using Excel's VLOOKUP function to bring the credit limits into the aged receivables listing. (The VLOOKUP function is a search tool that finds a value and displays the data in a cell that corresponds to the value.)

Excel, however, has its weaknesses. Its principal drawback is a lack of protection of the integrity of the original data, which can be unwittingly overwritten by the auditor. Using specialist audit software, such as ACL, allows the auditor to import the nominal listing and generates reports while maintaining read-only functionality on the imported data.

By obtaining a copy of the client entity's outstanding invoice listing (including customer name and invoice date) at year end, the auditor could also use CAATs as an analytical tool. For example to:

- categorise the invoices by customer;
- stratify the receivables listing by value;
- sort the listing in order of value to ensure adequate testing is given to larger balances;
- identify credit balances and round sum balances;
- total the ledger to facilitate comparison to the financial statements;
- merge the aged receivables listing with credit limit data to identify customers who are exceeding their credit limit, have old credit balances or nil credit balances.

## 13.7 SUBSTANTIVE AUDIT PROGRAMME FOR REVENUE AND RECEIVABLES

An audit programme records the specific details of tests to be performed by the auditor. The audit programme becomes a guide to the **audit engagement team** on the work to be performed in a particular area. As work is completed, a reference is included on the audit programme showing the location in the audit file where details of the tests performed are included. While the audit programme for any cycle will vary from entity to entity, in **Example 13.2** below we consider the typical tests the auditor might include in the audit programme for revenue and receivables. Students should note that in a real-life scenario, each test would be referenced to the location in the audit working file where the test is actually performed.

EXAMPLE 13.2: AUDIT PROGRAMME – REVENUE AND
RECEIVABLES (LARGE COMPANY LIMITED)[1]

| Large Company Limited | Audit Materiality | | €3,642,500 |
|---|---|---|---|
| 31 December 2018 | Performance Materiality | | €2,731,875 |
| | | Initials | Date |
| | Prepared by: | | |
| | Reviewed by: | | |
| Revenue and Receivables Audit Programme | | | |
| Ensure the audit plan is reflected in the following tests. The following steps are suggestions only and should be removed or added to as necessary to address the risks of material misstatement identified at the risk assessment stage. | | | |

---

[1] Source: based on *Procedures for Quality Audit 2010* (© Chartered Accountants Ireland, 2010), H1 and amended by the authors in December 2017.

| **Accounting Policy** | |
|---|---|
| Assess the appropriateness of the accounting policy and the accounting estimates method for this area. Ensure that the accounting policy is in accordance with accounting standards and applicable law, and that the methods used for making the accounting estimates are appropriate. | Existence Completeness Rights and Obligations Recording (accuracy)/ Valuation Classification |
| **Initial Procedures** | |
| Agree opening balances to prior-year working papers. | Presentation and Disclosure |
| Obtain the aged receivables and ensure its accuracy, agree totals to the figures in the trial balance and trace to the financial statements. | Completeness Existence |
| Obtain or prepare an aged analysis of trade receivables and test its reliability. | Valuation Classification |
| Obtain or prepare lead schedules and agree to financial statements | Occurrence/ Existence Completeness Recording (accuracy)/ Classification |
| Prepare commentary explaining the composition of receivables balances. Compare balances and receivables days with prior years and with expectations. Note any significant changes in the ratio of overdue accounts. Obtain explanations of any variations and consider implications for the doubtful debts provision. | Existence Completeness Recording (accuracy)/ Valuation |
| **Revenue Transactions** | |
| Obtain or prepare a schedule (nominal listing) of revenue: Check accuracy of the schedule, then select a sample and: 1. Trace the sample from the nominal ledger to the source document (signed customer delivery docket) confirming date, name, quantity and value matches the invoice and nominal ledger posting. | Occurrence Rights and Obligations Recording (accuracy)/ Classification |
| 2. Trace a sample of customer sales orders through to nominal ledger. | Completeness Recording Rights and Obligations Recording (accuracy)/ Classification |

| | |
|---|---|
| Repeat the above for deductions from revenue (i.e. trace from nominal ledger to source to test occurrence; and from source to nominal ledger to test completeness). | Occurrence<br>Rights and<br>Obligations<br>Recording (accuracy)<br>Completeness |

**Receivables Balance**

| | |
|---|---|
| Obtain or prepare a schedule of trade receivables:<br>Select a sample and:<br>1. circularise trade receivables, or explain why circularisation is not appropriate;<br>2. verify against post-year-end receipts and other evidence of the existence of the debtor;<br>3. examine correspondence about disputed balances;<br>4. enquire into all significant credit balances;<br>5. examine after-date sales credit notes;<br>6. re-analyse amounts due from parent, subsidiary and associated undertakings, directors and employees; and<br>7. identify credit balances and query with management as to how they arose.<br>In the case of each non-response to a receivables confirmation letter, perform alternative audit procedures to obtain relevant and reliable audit evidence (ISA 505, para 12).<br><br>If it is determined that a response to a receivables confirmation request is necessary to obtain sufficient appropriate audit evidence, and that, in this instance, alternative audit procedures will not provide the audit evidence required, the auditor must determine the implications for the audit and the auditor's opinion in accordance with ISA 505 (ISA 505, para 13).<br><br>* To some degree in that tests may confirm amounts owed but not the ability or intention to pay the amount. | Existence<br>Completeness<br>Rights and<br>Obligations<br>Valuation* |

**Collectability of Receivables Balance**

| | |
|---|---|
| Identify any outstanding receivables in breach of contract and/or late payment regulations. Ensure potential interest is quantified. | Valuation |
| Discuss bad and doubtful debts with management and review the entity's provisions. Discuss with the client any debts which are outside the terms of trade and unpaid. Evaluate explanations given for not providing against long-term outstanding balances. Examine correspondence where available and always corroborate management assertions. Challenge the estimation techniques used by management in the calculation of the provisions. Consider the outturn of the provision in previous years.<br>Identify and verify provisions made for reasons other than the age of debt. | |

| **Other Considerations** | |
|---|---|
| Test-check invoices immediately prior to and after year end:<br>1. to ensure they are entered in correct accounting period; and<br>2. to ensure inventory movement is in correct period. | Cut-off |
| Inquire into and verify correct treatment of inventories dispatched on sale or return. | Valuation<br>Cut-off |
| Inquire into any material receivable balances cleared by journal entry after the period end. | Cut-off |
| Obtain or prepare a schedule of **prepaid expenses** and:<br>1. compare with previous period;<br>2. vouch material items to source documentation; and<br>3. consider the reasonableness of other items. | Existence<br>Completeness |
| Extract as necessary and agree **intra-group or related company balances** to the other party's accounts, or obtain written confirmation of agreement between the companies, and ensure disclosed.<br>Obtain financial statements for group and related companies. Confirm by reference to the financial statements that intra-group or related company balances are recoverable. Obtain alternative confirmations or audit evidence if the financial statements show deficits or other difficulties in repaying the loans. Consider the adequacy of this evidence. | Existence<br>Completeness<br>Presentation and Disclosure |
| Confirm that intra-group or related company balances are properly presented in the correct part of the balance sheet. | Presentation and Disclosure |
| Identify any **loans due from directors** and ensure adequate disclosure of these is made in the financial statements.<br>(In respect of the Republic of Ireland: specifically consider compliance with sections 238–240 CA 2014.) | Presentation and Disclosure |
| **Disclosures** | |
| Review the disclosure requirements under IAS 1 and IFRS 15 where they relate to the client entity, ensure that they have been adequately presented and disclosed in line with those standards. | Classification<br>Presentation and Disclosure |

## 13.8  SUBSTANTIVE TESTING PROCEDURES FOR REVENUE AND RECEIVABLES

The substantive testing audit programme in **Example 13.2** outlined the principal procedures involved in testing revenue and receivables. In this section we will look at each of these in more detail:

1. Initial procedures:
   (a) Opening balances
   (b) Accuracy of schedules provided by management
   (c) Prepare the lead schedules
   (d) Analytical review.
2. Revenue and revenue deductions through tests of details:
   (a) Testing recorded revenue through tests of details
   (b) Testing revenue returns through tests of details
   (c) Testing revenue discounts through tests of details.
3. Receivables balance through test of details:
   (a) Receivables circularisations
   (b) Post-year-end cash receipts testing.
4. Revenue transactions and receivables balances – substantive analytical procedures
5. Other considerations:
   (a) Reasonableness of the doubtful debts provision
   (b) Cut-off procedures
   (c) Post-year-end returns.

### Initial Procedures

#### *Opening Balances and Accuracy of Schedules*

Before commencing further audit procedures, evidence must be obtained as to the accuracy of the opening balances of revenue and receivables. The reason for this is twofold:

1. it confirms that the comparative figures in the financial statements (which must be included in the current year's financial statements) agree to the final accounts of the prior year; and
2. it highlights any final entries (last-minute adjusting journal entries) of the prior year not correctly carried forward, which may indicate an error in the current year's financial statement figures.

The auditor should obtain the detailed **aged receivables listing** for the entity, gain comfort over its mathematical accuracy. At least one item should be selected from the schedule and traced to its respective source data to validate the accuracy of the schedule before further testing is performed on it and then perform the following:

- agree the current period's opening balance to the closing audited balances in the prior year's audit working papers or signed financial statements;
- agree the balance as per the aged receivables listing to the balance as per the trial balance and trace to the financial statements. Reconciling items should be tested in order to obtain the desired level of assurance and agreed to supporting documentation;

- review the aged receivables listing for any unusual balances, such as large balances, credit balances and old balances;
- test the reliability of the aged receivables listing by selecting a single customer and agreeing ageing to original invoice dates or, alternatively, recreate the aged receivables listing from the nominal listing (using Excel or audit application, such as ACL);
- obtain a copy of the sales nominal listing, test its mathematical accuracy and vouch it to the trial balance and trace to the financial statements – review its contents for any unusual items.

The auditor will also need to give consideration to the approach of auditing opening balances where it is an initial engagement; this is considered in **Chapter 6**, Section 6.9.

### *Prepare the Lead Schedules*

A lead schedule should be prepared to summarise all trade and other receivables balances for the prior year as well as the current year. This allows the auditor to ensure that they obtain evidence for all balances during the audit, thus providing some control over the performance of audit procedures. A typical lead schedule of the receivables area is included below in **Example 13.3** (relating to Large Company Limited – see **Appendix B**).

A lead schedule should also be prepared for revenue, which may be made up of a number of nominal listings, including revenue, discounts, etc. It too would be compared with the prior year to see if the difference is in line with expectations. Ratios, such as receivables days and ROCE, would be calculated for each year and the movement commented upon.

EXAMPLE 13.3: RECEIVABLES LEAD SCHEDULE (LARGE COMPANY LIMITED)[2]

| **Large Company Limited** | **Audit Materiality** | | | €3,642,500 |
|---|---|---|---|---|
| **31 December 2018** | **Performance Materiality** | | | €2,731,875 |
| | | | **Initials** | **Date** |
| | **Prepared by:** | | | |
| **Lead Schedule – Receivables** | **Reviewed by:** | | | |
| **Receivables – amounts falling due within one year** | | | | |
| | | **31 December 2018** | **31 December 2017** | |
| | | **€000** | **€000** | |
| Trade receivables | | 3,750 | 4,850 | |
| Provision for doubtful debts | | (500) | (750) | |
| Loan notes | | 1,500 | 1,500 | |

---

[2] Source: based on *Procedures for Quality Audit 2010* (© Chartered Accountants Ireland, 2010), H- and updated by the authors in December 2017.

| | | |
|---|---:|---:|
| Other receivables | 750 | 600 |
| Prepayments and accrued income | 1,000 | 1,050 |
| | 6,500 | 7,250 |

## Receivables – amounts falling due after one year

| | 31 December 2018 | 31 December 2017 |
|---|---:|---:|
| | €000 | €000 |
| Loan notes | 6,000 | 8,000 |
| Called-up share capital not paid | 685 | 875 |
| Prepayments and accrued income | 0 | 0 |
| Pension prepayment | 65 | 25 |
| Other prepayments | 1,950 | 1,350 |
| | 8,700 | 10,250 |

## Prepayments and accrued income

| | 31 December 2018 | 31 December 2017 |
|---|---:|---:|
| | €000 | €000 |
| Insurance | 200 | 500 |
| Rent | 500 | 0 |
| Supplier prepayment (bespoke goods) | 300 | 550 |
| | 1,000 | 1,050 |

## Movement in doubtful debts provision

| | 31 December 2018 | 31 December 2017 |
|---|---:|---:|
| | €000 | €000 |
| Opening balance | 750 | 700 |
| Increase in provision | 450 | 150 |
| Doubtful debt write-off | (700) | (100) |
| Closing balance | 500 | 750 |

## Trade receivables aged Analysis

| | 31 December 2018 | 31 December 2017 |
|---|---:|---:|
| | €000 | €000 |
| Current (within credit terms) | 3,100 | 4,250 |
| 30–60 days | 420 | 350 |
| 60–90 days | 150 | 140 |
| Greater than 90 days | 80 | 110 |
| | 3,750 | 4,850 |

## *Analytical Review*

An **analytical review** (see **Chapter 5**, Section 5.4) is usually performed at the start of each substantive procedure relating to each balance or class of transactions. Calculating ratios and analysing results against industry information, prior-year results, budgets, etc. allows the auditor to gain a better understanding for the movements in the year and to make comparisons against norms. It therefore provides the auditor with additional insights into the client entity and the industry it operates in, and better prepares them for the audit programme.

At the close of their substantive procedures the auditor aims to ensure that they can comment on all movements and key ratios with supporting explanations. If the auditor cannot explain any element, then this will highlight the need to perform additional substantive procedures. The analytical review performed here differs from a substantive analytical procedure in that the auditor's aim is not to substantiate the balance (i.e. prove the assertions), but rather to better understand the movements and relationships when performing substantive procedures.

While an analytical review will not provide any further comfort over financial statement assertions, it will provide an overview of the reasons for the movements in balances and should corroborate the auditor's findings noted through performance of substantive procedures.

The analytical review of revenue and receivables, performed as part of initial substantive procedures, can include calculations such as:
- receivables days ratio (receivables/credit sales × 365), i.e. the average number of days receivables are outstanding from customers;
- gross and net profit margins – these are common measures of revenue and costs (at both cost of sales and operating cost level) in order to determine the efficiency of the entity at generating margins;
- return on capital employed (ROCE), which measures the ratio of earnings before interest and tax (EBIT) to capital – a measure of how efficient the assets are at generating revenue.

The ratios are meaningless without comparison against prior-year results, industry norms or budgeted ratios. Wherever a change in relationships cannot be readily understood or an unusual pattern is uncovered, auditors should seek explanations from management and corroborate the explanation received by performing additional tests of details.

**Example 13.4** below shows an analytical review relating to revenue and receivables.

Having performed the initial procedures, the auditor must then commence more specific audit procedures relating to revenue and receivables (i.e. to test the classes of transactions and balances in the current year), starting with the audit procedures normally carried out in relation to revenue (class of transactions).

## EXAMPLE 13.4: ANALYTICAL REVIEW – REVENUE AND RECEIVABLES (LARGE COMPANY LIMITED)

**Trade Receivables**

|  | 2018 €000 |  | 2017 €000 |  |
|---|---|---|---|---|
| Trade receivables | 3,750 |  | 4,850 |  |
| Provision for doubtful debts | (500) | –13% | (750) | –15% |
|  | 3,250 |  | 4,100 |  |

**Revenue Analysis (obtained from the client)**

|  | 2018 €000 |  | 2017 €000 |  |
|---|---|---|---|---|
| Revenue (cash sales) | 237,750 | 85% | 129,500 | 65% |
| Revenue (credit sales) | 42,500 | 15% | 69,000 | 35% |
|  | 280,250 | 100% | 198,500 | 100% |

**Trade Receivables Aged Analysis**

|  | 2018 €000 |  | 2017 €000 |  |
|---|---|---|---|---|
| Current (within credit terms) | 3,100 | 83% | 4,250 | 88% |
| 30–60 days | 420 | 11% | 350 | 7% |
| 60–90 days | 150 | 4% | 140 | 3% |
| Greater than 90 days | 80 | 2% | 110 | 2% |
|  | 3,750 | 100% | 4,850 | 100% |

| Receivables days ratio | = (3,750 ÷ 42,500) × 365 | = (4,850 ÷ 69,000) × 365 |  |
|---|---|---|---|
| (trade receivables ÷ credit | 32.2 | 25.7 | **+6.5** |
| sales × 365) |  |  | **days** |

Total revenue has increased by €81,750,000 (41%) due to a new line of furniture that has broken into the luxury market, as well as an increase in foreign sales. Both of these factors pose increased inherent risks and have been taken into account in the audit strategy and the audit plan. While cash sales have increased by 84%, reducing the level of credit sales to just 15% of revenue compared to 53% of revenue in the prior year, the collectability of debtors appears to be reducing, with receivables days increased by approximately 6.5 days. The increase in cash sales has increased inherent risk, which has to be taken into account in the audit strategy and the audit plan.

### Testing of Revenue and Revenue Deductions through Tests of Details

As discussed at the outset of this chapter, 'revenue' represents sales made by the entity during the period by way of the supply of goods or services. If the auditor has tested the client entity's revenue and receivables controls and found them to be effective, resulting in a low **control risk**, they may decide to test the revenue figure using a substantive analytical procedure. This method of testing usually takes less time to carry out than substantive tests of details. If, however, the entity's controls proved to be weak, the auditor is required to perform focused substantive tests in the form of tests of details.

We will first consider the testing of recorded revenue using **tests of details**.

### *Testing Recorded Revenue through Tests of Details*

In this context, tests of details involve the selection of a sample from the total revenue population (sampling is discussed in **Chapter 6**, Section 6.8) and the vouching of that sample to supporting documentation. This type of testing addresses the occurrence, rights and obligations, recording and completeness assertions.

When testing revenue the auditor should trace the figure for revenue from the financial statements to the trial balance and then obtain the nominal listings that make up the revenue total as it appears in the trial balance. Having checked the mathematical accuracy of the nominal listing and vouched its total back to the trial balance, the auditor should then select a random sample of revenue transactions and:

1. trace the transaction to the sales invoice – re-total the invoice. A sales invoice should include the name of the client entity, the date of the invoice, the gross value, VAT and net value of the invoice, and the quantity and description of the goods sold.
2. Trace the details from the invoice to the signed goods dispatch note (or service delivery note) vouching that the details contained on each document agree. For example, the GDN is on the client entity's headed paper, the customer's name and account is the same on both the invoice and the GDN, the quantity is the same and the date on the GDN supports the period in which the transaction was recorded.
3. Trace the unit amount charged on the invoice to the client entity's price list.
4. Vouch any discounts noted on the invoice to client entity's price list, agreed customer discounts or management approval.
5. Ensure the GDN is signed by the customer as acceptance of the receipt of goods/service (proof of delivery).
   Items 1.–5. address various assertions: the customer-signed GDN proves occurrence; the date on the GDN supports cut-off; the vouching of quantities delivered to the quantities on the invoice along with the tracing of the unit price charged to the client entity's price list supports recording; and the client entity being named on the GDN and invoice supports rights and obligations.
6. Trace the receipt from the customer to the customer's remittance and on to the bank statement. Tracing to the bank validates occurrence, rights and obligations and recording.

As item 6. was performed from financial statements to source documents, only the occurrence assertion is validated. To validate completeness, the test now needs to be performed in the opposite direction. So, taking a sample of goods dispatched from the warehouse, trace them to signed GDNs, then to the customer invoice, then to transaction, nominal ledger, trial balance and finally to the financial statements. Although this direction of testing tests completeness (and not occurrence), it is also a dual test as it provides evidence of the rights and obligations, recording and cut-off assertions, for the same reasons noted above.

## Testing Revenue Returns through Tests of Details

When testing revenue the auditor needs also to consider revenue returns. Revenue returns represent goods returned by customers that are refunded. As with recorded revenue (above), tests of details of revenue returns address the occurrence, rights and obligations, recording and completeness assertions.

When testing total sales returns recorded by the client in the period, the auditor should consider:
- the mathematical accuracy of sales returns credit notes;
- check pricing by matching credit notes to sales invoices;
- ensuring that the credit note was approved by an individual authorised to issue credit notes;
- ensuring that the credit note has been correctly posted to the receivables ledger and the customer's account; and
- verification that output VAT has been calculated properly on sales returns credit notes.

## Testing Revenue Discounts through Tests of Details

Revenue discounts relate to discounts offered to the client entity's customers. The auditor will mainly be concerned with the **authorisation** of discounts. Again, tests of details address the occurrence, rights and obligations, recording and completeness assertions.

Where the client issues discounts to customers, the auditor should perform testing to validate:
- that any sales discount has been approved by an individual authorised to do so;
- that where the discount has been issued due to damaged inventory, the facts surrounding the discount should be validated through inspection of appropriate information held on file by the client; and
- that the granting of discounts complies with company policy.

### Receivables Balance

Having tested the classes of transactions that make up revenue, the auditor must then focus on the receivables balance. The most common method of testing the receivables balance is by way of **receivables circularisation**. Other typical methods include review of post-year-end cash/bank receipts and substantive analytical procedures. We will discuss these in more detail below.

## *Receivables Circularisations*

A receivables circularisation is a form of **external confirmation** (see **Section 6.6**), i.e. a request to a third party to divulge information to the auditor, and is one of the most reliable forms of audit evidence because it is independent, obtained directly by the auditor and exists in documentary form. The receivables confirmation requests confirmation directly from the client entity's customer of the existence of the year-end balance on the client entity's receivables ledger, and whether or not they agree with this balance. Circularisations therefore address the existence and rights and obligations assertions and, to some degree, the valuation assertion.

The use of receivables circularisations to test the year-end receivables balances has a number of **advantages**, including:

- direct external, third-party evidence that provides high-quality evidence over the existence and ownership of the debt and also the accuracy of the recorded amount due;
- confirmation of the effectiveness of the client entity's internal control system;
- assistance in determining cut-off procedures by identifying invoices in transit over the year end; and
- providing evidence of items in dispute, e.g. where the amount stated by the customer differs from the amount recorded in the books of the client entity.

Using such circularisations also has its **disadvantages**, however, which include:

- where the client entity's customers are small businesses or private individuals, they are less likely to maintain accurate ledger balances to provide a reliable response;
- customers may be less likely to admit to owing more than is shown on the confirmation letter;
- many trivial differences are likely to be reported as a result of cash/goods in transit; and
- the non-response rate may be high.

As discussed in **Chapter 6**, Section 6.6, there are two methods of circularisation:

1. **Negative circularisation** – where the customer is requested to respond only if they are not in agreement with the balance stated.

   The problem with this is that it may be impossible to tell whether the customer agrees with the year-end balance stated or whether there is simply a failure on their part to reply. It can be concluded that negative confirmations provide less persuasive audit evidence than positive confirmations.

   ISA 505, paragraph 15, does permit the use of negative confirmations (as the sole substantive procedure), but only if the auditor is satisfied that: internal controls are operating effectively; risk of material misstatement is low; the population to be circularised consists of a large number of small account balances; very few exceptions are expected; and the auditor has no reason to believe the recipients of the letters will disregard the confirmation request. This form of circularisation is rarely used due to the risks connected to it.

2.  **Positive circularisation** – where the customer is asked to reply whether they agree with the balance or not. In some cases, customers are asked to supply the balance themselves.

    The positive form is used when planned **detection risk** is low or individual customer balances are relatively large. In general, as long as non-responses are verified by other means, this method provides statistically valid evidence. While positive circularisation tends to be the favoured method over negative circularisation, a combination of the two may be used in a single audit engagement.

The following should be considered when performing a receivables circularisation:

- **Control of external confirmation process** The auditor must remain in control of the external confirmation process, meaning that they must select the customers to be contacted, prepare and send the confirmation requests and ensure that the responses are sent directly to the auditor and not through the client.

- **Timing in sending external confirmations** The receivables circularisation process should be carried out a suitable length of time prior to the commencement of the audit fieldwork to allow customers time to respond.

- **Stratification of ledger to ensure sufficient value of the ledger is circularised** The auditor should target high-value balances on the year-end receivables ledger in order to gain high assurance over the total balance. *Do not, however, omit nil balances, credit balances or accounts written off in the period.*

- **Investigation into differences between responses and client balances** If a customer's response is not in agreement with the balance in the client entity's receivables ledger, appropriate investigation into the difference should be conducted by the auditor, with appropriate journal adjustments proposed, if necessary, to correct the balance in the client entity's ledger.

- **Non-responses** Where responses are not returned, the auditor should ordinarily consider contacting the customer by telephone to obtain a response. If this fails to elicit a response, alternative procedures should be performed to confirm the year-end balance per the receivables ledger (see below).

- **Management refusal to permit circularisation** Where the client entity's management request the auditor not to perform a receivables circularisation, the auditor must consider if there are valid grounds for such a request – and obtain audit evidence to support the validity of management's request. The auditor should adopt an attitude of **professional scepticism** to management's request and consider if it raises any questions around their integrity or if it indicates the possibility of fraudulent behaviour within the entity.

If the auditor agrees to management's request and does not perform the circularisation, the auditor should apply alternative audit procedures to obtain **sufficient appropriate**

**audit evidence** regarding the year-end receivables balance (discussed below). If the auditor does not accept the validity of management's request and is prevented from carrying out the confirmations, there has been a **limitation of scope** and there is a possible impact on the auditor's report (see **Chapter 19**).

- **Responses sent to the client entity** Where responses are returned to the client entity directly, these cannot be accepted as audit evidence on the grounds that the client may have manipulated the response.

With regard to responses received, the auditor should be aware of the following possible issues:

- **Collectability** If the customer confirms the balance due to the client entity, although this confirms to the auditor the accuracy of the recorded balance, it does not confirm the collectability and the valuation of the balance, i.e. is recoverability of the balance likely? The auditor must consider this further when testing the **doubtful debt provision** (see below).
- **Customer disagrees with balance** If the customer is not in agreement with the balance in the client entity's records, the auditor must attempt to reconcile the difference. Differences can be due to:
  - timing differences, for example:
    - the customer has sent a cheque payment to the client entity, which has not been received at the time of preparation of the receivables circularisation;
    - goods were recently delivered and signed for, but the customer is waiting on the invoice to record the transaction;
    - goods are in transit;
    - the client entity has credited the customer's account with a discount for prompt payment, but the customer has not yet received the credit note and updated its records;
  - permanent differences, for example:
    - the client entity has posted an invoice incorrectly to the customer's account, either for the wrong amount or to the wrong customer account entirely;
    - the customer has not posted a legitimate invoice to its system.

The auditor must carry out appropriate work to reconcile any differences arising.

The auditor must summarise findings from the receivables circularisation in a suitable manner. The audit working paper should list each account selected for confirmation and the results obtained from each request, cross-referenced to the actual circularisation response. Differences should be investigated and discussed with management when deemed to be material. A possible means of documenting audit work is shown in **Example 13.5** below.

EXAMPLE 13.5: RECEIVABLES CIRCULARISATION SUMMARY

| Customer Name/Code | Balance per Client Entity Ledger | Balance Confirmed by Customer | Difference Arising | Further Audit Work Performed on Difference Arising |
|---|---|---|---|---|
| Customer I I001 | €400,000 | €375,000 | €25,000 | Confirmed client entity had posted three invoices totalling €25,000 to Customer I in error – invoices should have been posted to Customer L. Inspected invoices and confirmed are in the name of Customer L (not Customer I). |
| Customer C C001 | €596,000 | €550,000 | €46,000 | Relates to cash in transit – received and banked 2 Jan. 2018. |
| Customer D D001 | €364,000 | €364,000 | €0 | |
| Customer F F001 | €4,000 | No Response | N/A | Follow up on non-response – discovered customer is in liquidation. Was included in doubtful debt provision. |
| Customer N N001 | €30,000 | No Response | N/A | Alternative procedures performed at Working Paper Reference [XX]. |

In the case where no responses are received, **alternative procedures** should be performed. The two main alternative procedures are:
- examining post-year-end cash/bank receipts; and
- vouching unpaid invoices to other supporting documentation (similar to the test described above under revenue test of details, where invoices are traced to signed GDNs).

### Post-year-end Cash Receipts Testing

Testing post-year-end cash/bank receipts can be the first option in testing the receivables balances, or it can be an alternative testing procedure where a receivables circularisation is either: (a) not returned; (b) compromised; or (c) does not agree with the balance per the **aged receivables listing**.

The most logical way to confirm **money outstanding** (i.e. a **receivables balance**) at the year end is to see if it was paid after year end. The performance of post-year-end cash receipts testing addresses the existence/occurrence, completeness and valuation assertions.

Performing this test correctly involves:
- Obtaining a detailed breakdown of the sales invoices that make up the year-end balance per the receivables ledger for each customer.
- Obtaining details of cash received from selected customers post-year end with details of the sales invoices to which the receipts relate.
- Vouching cash receipts to remittances or bank statements.
- Where cash has not been received post-year end from the customer, the auditor should vouch the year-end receivables balance to supporting documentation, such as invoices, goods dispatch notes and customer orders, to confirm the occurrence of the sale.
- It is important to determine the invoices outstanding at the year end in order to confirm that post-year-end cash payments relate to invoices that have been included on the ledger at the year end. If post-year-end cash receipts that relate to pre-year-end invoices that are not outstanding on the ledger are discovered, a **cut-off error** has occurred and the receivables ledger is understated. It will be necessary to propose an adjusting journal to correct for material pre-year-end sales invoices not included on the receivables ledger.

It should be noted that the direction of the test is again important. Tracing from the receipts in the bank statement to recorded receivables at year end tests for the completeness of receivables, whereas testing from the receivables listing to the receipts post-year end tests for the existence of the recorded receivables.

## The Use of CAATs

When performing tests of details, sample sizes can be high due to the materiality of revenue and receivables figures in the financial statements. CAATs can be used to reduce the number of items selected for sample testing while still ensuring a representative sample is selected. This is achieved by stratifying the customer balance to maximise the effectiveness of testing (see **Example 13.6**).

EXAMPLE 13.6: STRATIFICATION OF THE RECEIVABLES BALANCE (LARGE COMPANY LIMITED)

Taking the aged receivables listing, the auditor can stratify the balances into categories according to the value owing by each customer. This allows the auditor to ensure that they test the highest values and, in doing so, reduce the materiality of the remaining balance – thereby reducing the sample size required in the remaining balance.

|  | >€500 €000 | €99–€500 €000 | <€100 €000 | Total €000 |
|---|---|---|---|---|
| Total balance | 2,031 | 1,414 | 305 | 3,750 |

| No. of accounts | 3 | 5 | 10 | 18 |
|---|---|---|---|---|
| % of total balance | 54% | 38% | 8% | 100% |
| % of no. of accounts | 17% | 27% | 56% | 100% |

So, instead of calculating a sample size on the total of €3,750,000, the auditor fully tests the three customers at a value of €2,031,000 (54% of the total balance is now validated). They can then calculate a sample size on the remaining value of €1,719,000. This provides the auditor with a more efficient (in that the ultimate number of items tested will be reduced) and effective (in that a larger percentage of the total value will be covered) method of auditing.

### Revenue Transactions and Receivables Balances – Substantive Analytical Procedures

Thus far we have discussed only the tests of details approach to substantively testing revenue and receivables. The other type of substantive testing frequently used for revenue and receivables (particularly when the controls environment is strong) is **substantive analytical procedures**. This type of substantive procedure addresses the existence/occurrence, completeness, rights and obligations, recording/valuation and cut-off assertions.

Substantive analytical procedures can be used as the main test for revenue or receivables or they can be used in conjunction with substantive tests of details. If the controls surrounding revenue and receivables have been tested and a strong control environment exists, the auditor can use substantive analytical procedures and avoid tests of details relating to the above assertions. (The background to the approach of the performance of substantive analytical procedures has been discussed in **Chapter 6**.)

### *Performing Substantive Analytical Procedures Relating to Receivables*

As outlined in **Chapter 6**, Section 6.5, when performing substantive analytical procedures the following four steps should be performed:

1. Calculate a 'threshold level', based on performance materiality, which represents the maximum monetary value the auditor is willing to accept when comparing the expected result to the actual figures, i.e. those in the financial statements.
2. Calculate an 'expectation' of the current-year receivables balance, explaining the basis of the calculation and an assessment of the reliability of the data used. (Remember, before building the expectation the auditor should consider the practicality of doing so – is it going to be possible to calculate an expected value or are there too many variables making up the value that the auditor is trying to prove?)
3. Calculate the deviation between the actual figures and the 'expectation'. If the deviation is below the threshold level, no additional substantive testing is required.
4. If the deviation is above the threshold level, perform further substantive testing to provide sufficient appropriate audit evidence around the unexpected deviation.

### *Performing Substantive Analytical Procedures Relating to Revenue*

Substantive analytical procedures for revenue will follow the basic four-step approach above. When calculating the expectation for current-period revenue, the following can be used:

- results for the prior period;
- current-period revenue budget as developed by management (provided that the budgetary process has been tested by the auditor and is found to be robust);
- market expectations for the industry within which the business operates.

When developing an independent expectation for current-period results, the auditor must consider if there were any significant changes in the client entity's operations during the period under review (compared to the prior period) that impacted on the revenue level for the current period. Consideration should be given to the following:

- Is the duration of the period under review in line with the duration of the prior period?
- Have any new divisions opened (e.g. a new store) during the period under review?
- Have any divisions been discontinued during the period under review?
- Have any new products been introduced?
- Have any products been discontinued?
- Has the client entity's competitive environment changed?
- Has the macroeconomic environment changed, e.g. have consumer spending habits altered?
- Have new sales personnel been employed during the period under review, potentially impacting on trading results?
- Have selling prices been increased during the period under review?
- How does current-period gross margin compare to prior-period margin?
- After review, how do daily/weekly/monthly revenue figures for the current period compare to the same period in the prior year?

Depending on the answers to the questions above, the auditor must:

- consider how they might impact on the calculation of an expectation for current-period revenue;
- obtain relevant, reliable substantive evidence to support and/or quantify the known changes; and
- build in the effects of such changes on revenue within the current-period expectation.

As with the substantive analytical procedures for revenue, for receivables the auditor also needs to consider any significant changes in the client entity's operations during the period under review. Considerations should be given to the following:

- Has the company expanded significantly, resulting in increased revenue and a corresponding increase in the period-end receivables balance?
- Has the company reduced operations significantly, resulting in reduced revenue and a corresponding decrease in period-end receivables balance?

- Have normal payment terms for customers been changed during the period, e.g. from 30 days to 45 days, i.e. a change in the receivables days ratio?
- Have any one-off sales contracts been taken on and completed during the period and remain due at the period end?
- Has the macroeconomic environment changed, e.g. have consumer spending habits changed?

Depending on the answers to the questions above, the auditor must:
- consider how they might impact on the calculation of an expectation for period-end receivables balance; and
- build in the effects of the known changes within the current-period expectation.

**Example 13.7** below provides an illustration of the procedures outlined above for both revenue and receivables.

EXAMPLE 13.7: WORKED EXAMPLE – SUBSTANTIVE ANALYTICAL
PROCEDURES FOR REVENUE AND RECEIVABLES

You are undertaking the audit of the revenue and receivables area for your client, Holiday Heaven Ltd. You are at the phase of the audit where substantive analytical procedures are being performed. You have ascertained the following information from the work carried out by the audit team to date:
(a) Revenue levels for existing products have remained reasonably in line with the prior period.
(b) No products have been discontinued in the period.
(c) Two new sales contracts have been won during the period, these are one-off contracts, details as follows as agreed to signed contracts:
   (i) Contract 1 commenced 1 February 2018 contracting the client to produce and supply the customer with goods totalling €100,000 (sales value) per month;
   (ii) Contract 2 commenced 1 October 2018 contracting the client to produce and supply the customer with goods totalling €45,000 (cost price) per month. Gross profit margin on this contract is expected to be 40%.
(d) The selling price for all items (except new contracts in the year) increased by 5% on 1 September 2018 – corroborated through inspection of a letter sent out to customers in August 2018 outlining the above.
(e) Normal credit terms have increased from 30 days in the prior period to 35 days in the current period – corroborated through inspection of a letter sent out to credit customers in January 2018 stating this.
(f) A dispute is ongoing with one customer for payment of €300,000, which is nine months outstanding at the period end. This was a new customer accepted in the period under review. The audit team inspected invoices issued to the customer and letters sent to it demanding payment. The dispute is confirmed as now being with the legal representatives.

**Other required information:**
- Current period: 12 months to 31 December 2018
- Current-period revenue: €6,690,000
- Period-end receivables balance: €930,000
- Threshold for further investigation: 75% of planning materiality of €25,000, i.e. €18,750
- Prior period: 15 months to 31 December 2017
- Prior-period revenue: €6,575,000
- Prior period-end receivables balance: €540,410.

## Substantive analytical procedure for revenue

### 1. Develop expectation

| | |
|---|---|
| Prior-period revenue | = €6,575,000 over 15 months |
| Prior-period monthly revenue | = €6,575,000/15 |
| | = €438,333 |

Expected revenue for current period using prior-period monthly revenue value
$$= (€438,333 \times 8) + (€438,333 \times 1.05 \times 4) \text{ [W1]}$$
$$= €3,506,667 + €1,840,999$$
$$= €5,347,666$$

Adjustment for additional revenue won during the year:
Additional revenue from Contract 1 = €1,100,000 [W2]
Additional revenue from Contract 2 = €225,000 [W3]

**Total expected revenue for current period = €5,347,666 + €1,100,000 + €225,000**
$$= €6,672,666$$

### 2. Outline threshold for further investigation
From information above, deviation threshold is €18,750.

### 3. Compare actual result to expectation and calculate deviation

| | |
|---|---|
| Actual revenue | = €6,690,000 |
| Total expected revenue for current period | = €6,672,666 |
| Deviation from expectation | = €17,334 |

### 4. Perform further investigation where deviation is above threshold for further investigation
As deviation is below the threshold for further investigation, no further work is deemed necessary.

[W1]: Being eight months' revenue at the average monthly revenue of the prior period + 4 months' revenue adjusted for 5% price increase in September 2018.
[W2]: Being €100,000 per month over 11 months.
[W3]: Being revenue of €75,000 over 3 months.

| | |
|---|---|
| Cost price | = €/£45,000 |
| Gross margin | = 40% |

Cost price      = 60%
Revenue         = 100% being (€45,000/60) × 100 = €75,000 per month
Contract Value = (€75,000 × 3 mths) = €225,000.

## Substantive analytical procedure for receivables

### 1. Develop expectation
Expectation to be developed using the information ascertained in relation to debtor credit terms and ongoing dispute with customer – assuming that sales are spread evenly throughout the year.

Credit terms are 35 days, as corroborated above.
Actual sales are €6,690,000.
Expectation can be developed using this information and the receivables days ratio (assuming sales are spread evenly throughout the year):

$$\frac{Receivables}{Revenue} \times 365 = Receivables\ days$$

$$\frac{Receivables}{€6,690,000} \times 365 = 35$$

$$Receivables = (35/365) \times €6,690,000$$
$$= €641,507$$

Add increase in period-end receivables due to customer dispute: €300,000

**Expected receivables = €641,507 + €300,000 = €941,507**

### 2. Outline deviation for further investigation
From information above, deviation threshold is €18,750.

### 3. Compare actual result to expectation and calculate deviation
Expected receivables          = €941,507
Actual receivables            = €930,000
Deviation from expectation    = €11,507

### 4. Perform further investigation where deviation is above threshold for further investigation
As the deviation is below threshold for further investigation, no further work is deemed necessary.

## Other Considerations

Having performed audit procedures on the revenue-related figures and on the receivables balance, the auditor will now have to consider:
- the reasonableness of the **doubtful debts provision** (which confirms the valuation assertion for the receivables balance);
- cut-off procedures relating to revenue and receivables; and
- post-year-end returns.

### Reasonableness of the Doubtful Debts Provision

On the face of the statement of financial position, the figure for receivables is net of the doubtful debts provision. As such, in confirming that the valuation of the receivables number is correct, the auditor must consider the reasonableness of the provision for doubtful debts. Provisions may be made by the client entity for a variety of reasons, including: the customer has gone into liquidation; the customer is disputing the balance; the customer's balance is significantly aged. The auditor will seek to verify the reason surrounding the provision.

Most entities determine the doubtful debts provision by:
• making a general provision, which is usually determined by applying a percentage to balances overdue by more than a specified period; or
• making a specific provision, which involves identifying customers that are known to be in financial difficulties or where payment is in dispute.

The doubtful debt provision is an estimate (see **Chapter 6**, Section 6.10), meaning, therefore, that ISA 540 applies. The auditor is required to adopt one or more of the following approaches:
• reviewing and testing the process used by management;
• using an independent estimate;
• reviewing subsequent events.

The first approach, usually adopted for verifying general provisions, is to:
• obtain the client entity's procedures for determining the doubtful debts provision estimate and to consider the reliability and reasonableness of these procedures;
• ensure that the procedures have been followed and have been appropriately approved;
• consider the reasonableness of assumptions used in the calculation of the doubtful debts provision; and
• check calculations and consider the reliability of prior-year provisions.

Approaches usually adopted when considering specific doubtful debt provisions include examining correspondence from customers, reviewing customer credit reports and financial statements, and discussing collectability of debts with management.

The risk of doubtful debts occurring is a common risk for most businesses. The auditor must exercise caution and assess the ageing of the balances outstanding on the year-end receivables ledger and consider if a doubtful debt provision has been made by the client entity. If not, the auditor must consider if a provision is necessary. This assessment is crucial for the overall valuation of the receivables balance included within the financial statements. If the auditor feels the provision is under-provided, they should request the client entity to increase the provision or take any shortfall to the schedule of unadjusted misstatements (errors schedule) for consideration at the close of the audit.

The auditor should also consider the following:
• the adequacy of the internal control system relating to approval of credit terms and follow-up of overdue debts;
• the period of credit allowed and taken;

- whether or not balances have been settled post-year end;
- whether or not an account is made up of specific items, e.g. customer paying amounts on account, such as round sum amounts off the total balance rather than paying specific invoices – this could indicate that the customer has cash-flow difficulties and is, potentially, a doubtful debt;
- whether or not an account is within the approved maximum credit limit;
- reports on major receivables from collectors, agencies, etc.;
- any legal proceedings and the legal status of receivables, e.g. customers in liquidation are unlikely to be able to pay amounts owed to their suppliers and should therefore be written off rather than simply provided for; and
- the ageing of receivables can be an indication that the amount due from the customer is not collectible and therefore indicates that a provision might be required for the potential non-receipt of the amount due.

The auditor should perform the following:
- review the **aged receivables listing** for debts aged 60–90 days and older. The auditor should also at this point review a sample of sales invoices included on the period-end ledger to assess the reasonableness of the ageing of the invoices by the system on the period-end ledger;
- confirm and verify if such balances have been paid post-year end;
- where balances have not been settled post-year end, the auditor should inquire from management if there are any circumstances surrounding the non-payment of the balance, such as a dispute between the customer and the entity, the customer being declared bankrupt or experiencing cash-flow difficulties;
- where receipt of the balance outstanding on the aged receivables listing at the year end is deemed unlikely after the above testing is performed, the auditor should consider if the client has a doubtful debt provision for the balance; and
- where the client has not provided for the balance and the auditor deems that a provision is necessary, then an adjusting journal should be proposed.

The doubtful debts provision created by the client entity is known as an **accounting estimate** as the final payment amount that will be received from the customer is not known with certainty. It is the role of the auditor to assess the facts surrounding the aged balances and to determine if the provision appears reasonable based on what is known.

Where the client entity has included a general provision in the accounts (i.e. a provision that is general in nature and not established in respect of a specific customer and balance), the auditor should understand the basis of the provision and inspect corroborating information to determine the reasonableness of the provision.

### Cut-off Procedures Relating to Revenue and Receivables

Cut-off ensures that items sold (and having met the revenue recognition criteria) in the first few days of the new period are not recorded in the year-end revenue. Additionally, cut-off ensures that items sold (and having met the revenue recognition criteria) in the period prior to the year end are not recorded in the revenue of the next period. Cut-off, therefore, also helps to address the completeness and occurrence assertions.

In summary, cut-off errors can arise when either of the following occurs:
- a pre-year end dated sales invoice is not posted to the receivables ledger until post-year end; or
- a post-year end dated sales invoice is posted to the receivables ledger before the year end.

When either of the above occurs, the sale in question will have been recorded in the incorrect period in the financial statements of the client entity.

In order to determine whether the client has undertaken appropriate cut-off procedures at the year end, the auditor should perform appropriate tests. The auditor should:
- assess the high-risk period, i.e. the dates around the year end where the risk of a cut-off error occurring is deemed greatest – this could be the final week of trade pre-year end and the first week of trade post-year end;
- target invoices posted to the receivables ledger during the high-risk periods; and
- inspect the chosen sales invoices and the corresponding delivery documents to confirm that the sales have been recorded in the correct period.

### Post-year-end Returns

It is important for the auditor to consider post-year-end credit notes issued by the client to ensure that no major sales values need to be reversed due, say, to faulty goods being dispatched throughout the final month of the year. The auditor should consider:
- any significant post-year-end credit notes raised have been accounted for in the correct period, e.g. if a credit note has been raised post-year end in relation to a pre-year-end sales invoice, then the credit note has not been accounted for in the correct period and an adjusting journal will be necessary;
- the level of credit notes raised post-year end. Where there are unusual amounts of high-value credit notes issued early in the new accounting period in relation to pre-year-end sales invoices, the auditor should consider the legitimacy of the sales invoices issued pre-year end and consider the possibility of a cut-off error arising;
- the reason for the returns and the credit notes being issued; and
- any journal adjustments that may be proposed to correct for post-year-end credit notes raised relating to pre-year-end invoices.

## 13.9 DISCLOSURE REQUIREMENTS

Finally, with regard to revenue and receivables, the auditor will consider the adequacy of the disclosures. The auditor needs to consider the requirements of IFRS 15 and IAS 1 to ensure that all disclosures are:
- complete (i.e. no revenue- and receivables-related disclosures are missing – the auditor can use IFRS 15 and IAS 1 as a checklist);
- accurate (reflect the actual transactions and information relating to events surrounding revenue and receivables);
- relate to events that actually occurred; and
- are properly presented (i.e. in a manner expected by IFRS 15 and IAS 1).

Specific disclosure considerations relating to revenue and receivables include:

- auditors must be aware of the disclosure requirements for trade receivables and revenue under the applicable financial reporting framework;
- distinction between receivables amounts due within one year and those falling due after one year;
- review of receivables ledger may indicate amounts owed from employees, officers, other group companies and related parties, which should be specifically disclosed if found to be material;
- credit balances included in the receivables ledger may, if found to be material, require reclassification to current liabilities;
- evidence of other activities requiring disclosure may be obtained through the review of minutes from board of directors' meetings and from inquiry of management;
- obtain management's representations on these matters in writing in a representation letter; and
- the disclosure objective specified by IFRS 15, paragraph 110, requires "an entity to disclose sufficient information to enable users of financial statements to understand the nature, amount, timing and uncertainty of revenue and cash flows arising from contracts with customers." Therefore, "an entity shall disclose qualitative and quantitative information about all of the following:
  (a) its contracts with customers ...;
  (b) the significant judgments, and changes in the judgments, made in applying this Standard to those contracts ...; and
  (c) any assets recognised from the costs to obtain or fulfil a contract with a customer".

## 13.10 CONCLUSION

When the auditor has performed controls testing, substantive analytical review and substantive tests of details, it must be considered if sufficient appropriate audit evidence has been obtained over revenue and receivables, which would give the appropriate level of assurance over the assertions stated at the outset, these being:

- completeness;
- classification/recording or valuation;
- existence/occurrence;
- cut-off;
- rights and obligations; and
- presentation and disclosure.

The auditor must also consider if the testing performed has appropriately addressed the key risks identified in the revenue and receivables cycle, and hence reduced the risk of material misstatement to a suitably low level.

The auditor must consider the impact of their testing on revenue and receivables on the **audit opinion**. This is acheived by considering whether any misstatements, found either individually or in aggregate (when combined with other misstatements detected throughout the audit), will result in the financial statements being materially misstated. As such, all misstatements found are taken to the auditor's errors schedule for consideration at the audit completion stage (discussed in detail in **Chapter 18**). The auditor's report on financial statements is considered in detail in **Chapter 19**.

## SUMMARY OF LEARNING OBJECTIVES

**Learning Objective 1**   Understand what is included in the audit of revenue and receivables.

In the financial statements of an entity, the revenue figure represents the income earned by the business in return for the passing of title on goods or services. The receivables balance arises as a result of sales made and represents money due to the business from customers for those sales.

**Learning Objective 2**   Be able to identify the risks and audit objectives applicable to revenue and receivables.

The primary risks associated with revenue and receivables relate to:
1. existence of trade receivables balances; and
2. collectability of receivables.

The audit objectives for revenue are that revenue transactions actually occurred, are complete, pertain to the entity (rights and obligations), are correctly recorded (accurate) and cut-off, and adequately classified, presented and disclosed in line with the applicable financial reporting framework.

The audit objectives for receivables are that the receivables balances exist, are complete, reasonably valued, that the client entity has the rights and obligations to the debt and that it is adequately classified, presented and disclosed in the financial statements.

**Learning Objective 3**   Be able to determine an appropriate audit strategy for revenue and receivables, taking into consideration the specific risks and audit objectives (management assertions).

With respect to revenue, the auditor seeks to prove that revenue recorded in the financial statements relates to events that occurred and that it has been recorded accurately and only relates to transactions where risks and rewards of items have passed to the buyer.

When auditing the receivables balance, the auditor seeks to confirm their existence and the entity's right to collect receivables (rights and obligations) and to gain assurance over the collectability of the receivables balance (i.e. valuation). They also seek to prove that they are properly classified and disclosed in the financial statements.

**Learning Objective 4**   Be able to develop an audit programme that addresses all the audit objectives (management assertions) for revenue and receivables.

Where the revenue and receivables balances are not material to the financial statements, limited controls and substantive testing will be performed. However, revenue and receivables are usually material figures and transactions tend to be high in volume; for this reason the auditor usually takes a controls approach when testing revenue and receivables in order to reduce the level of detailed substantive testing.

**Learning Objective 5**   Be able to describe and apply specific substantive testing procedures relating to the audit of revenue and receivables.

The principal document when auditing revenue and receivables is the aged receivables listing. Other documents that may form part of audit evidence connected to revenue and receivables include:

- sales invoices;
- goods dispatch notes (GDNs);
- proof of delivery notes (PDNs);
- customer statements; and
- customer remittances.

**Key Substantive Testing Procedures Connected to Revenue**  The auditor may carry out detailed testing of the revenue balance by vouching transactions included in the revenue general ledger to source documents, confirming their occurrence and accuracy. Additionally, they will seek to gain assurance over completeness by tracing from documents of first entry to entries in the revenue ledger.

Alternatively, if controls have tested as strong and reduced substantive procedures are being performed, the auditor may carry out substantive analytical procedures (proof in total).

**Key Substantive Testing Procedures Connected to Receivables**  For the receivables balance the auditor may:

- Circularise customers to confirm that the balance exists and is accurately recorded at year end (or apply alternative procedures, such as substantive analytical procedures or tracing of receivables to post-year-end receipts in the bank statement).
- Review valuation by reference to a review of the doubtful debts provision set by management and by reviewing the aged receivables listing and post-year-end receipts.

The auditor will also assess the adequacy of disclosure notes relating to revenue and receivables.

**Learning Objective 6**   Understand the role CAATs can play when auditing revenue and receivables.

The auditor may use a combination of audit software, data analysis tools and other applications, such as Excel, when auditing the area of revenue and receivables.

**Learning Objective 7**   Understand the auditor's approach relating to the disclosures of revenue and receivables.

The auditor should seek to ensure that all disclosures relating to receivables are complete, accurate, pertain to the entity and adequately presented in line with applicable international reporting standards.

## QUESTIONS

### Self-test Questions

13.1   What benefits are derived from an aged receivables listing?

13.2   Discuss an audit procedure that should be performed to test the receivables balance.

13.3   How might the auditor use substantive analytical procedures in the audit of revenue and receivables?

13.4   Which procedures should an auditor perform when testing total revenue?

13.5   List the two methods of confirming receivables balances, and discuss the benefits of each method.

13.6   Explain the advantages and disadvantages relating to receivables circularisation.

13.7   Explain the four steps an auditor should consider when performing substantive analytical procedures.

13.8   How do most entities determine the provision for doubtful debts?

13.9   Why must an auditor review the aged receivables listing for debts aged 60–90 days and older?

13.10  What procedures will an auditor perform to test cut-off?

### Review Questions

(See Suggested Solutions to Review Questions in **Appendix C**.)

### *Question 13.1*

You are a newly appointed audit senior in Burns & Burns Chartered Accountants, working on the audit of SuperSmart Ltd, an Irish wholesale chain. You have just commenced the year-end statutory audit for SuperSmart. The assessed materiality for the year ended 31 December 2018 amounts to €/£ 1,395,000 on the basis of 5% of profit before tax.

It is now February 2019 and you are given the results of audit procedures conducted around receivables during the interim audit (for the 11-month period to 30 November 2018) (Appendix 1).

As a follow-up procedure to the receivables confirmation process conducted during the interim audit, you have asked SuperSmart to conduct an accounts receivable roll-forward from 30 November 2018 to 31 December 2018. The results of the final audit for receivables (for the year ended 31 December 2018) are set out in Appendix 2.

#### APPENDIX 1: RESULTS OF INTERIM AUDIT

As part of the interim audit work, receivables confirmations as at 30 November 2018 were sought as per the five balances below (selected at random from the listing of trade receivables).

| Customer Name | Balance per Receivables Listing at 30 Nov. 2018 £/€ | Balance per Confirmation Received £/€ | Comments |
|---|---|---|---|
| AIM | 230,000 | 226,166 | Difference represents a foreign exchange difference. AIM has used an FX rate of 1 : 1.18, while SuperSmart translated at the rate on the date of the transaction, which was 1 : 1.2. SuperSmart confirmed that it will re-translate all FX balances at year end. |
| Davitt | 456,900 | 400,000 | Difference relates to an invoice for goods collected by Davitt on 29 November 2018, Davitt had not yet received the invoice and so has not yet posted the invoice. |
| Finn | 136,098 | 120,000 | Difference relates to a payment by Finn on 29 November that did not reach SuperSmart's bank until 4 December. |
| Sloan | 457,900 | 427,900 | Sloan dispute the value on one invoice, which they believe should be £/€167,000 and not £/€197,000 as per the contract agreed. They claim SuperSmart are not giving them credit for a once-off rebate of £/€30,000 noted in the contract for first-time orders over £/€100,000. |
| Doyle's | 345,780 | N/A | No response. |

### APPENDIX 2: ROLL-FORWARD PREPARED BY FINANCE MANAGER OF SUPERSMART AUDITED BY THE AUDIT JUNIOR

| Opening Receivables Balance | £/€ | Audit Work Performed |
|---|---|---|
| Debtors balance at 30 November 2018 | 34,876,908 | Agreed to receivables listing at 30 November 2018. |
| Revenue: 1 December to 31 December 2018 | 10,786,987 | Amount includes £/€567,000 of revenue recognised for a long-term contract with a key supplier. The contract was signed in December and represents (a) £/€230,000 for strategic product-placing during the Christmas period; (b) £/€230,000 for strategic product-placing during Q1 2019; and (c) £/€107,000 for listing two of the supplier's new product lines to be launched in February 2019. Otherwise sales occurred evenly throughout the month. |

| Cash receipts: received between 1 December and 31 December 2018 | (11,286,897) | Amount posted to bank in the general ledger. £/€10,987,897 was received in respect of trade debtor payments, the balance represented a receipt for the sale of a piece of plant and machinery that had a carrying value of £/€200,000. No transaction has been posted to dispose of the asset due to the funds being received late in December and being placed as a sundry receipt against receivables. |
|---|---|---|
| Credit notes issued in December | (186,897) | Amounts are in line with prior years and usually arise within one month of sales and usually represent approx. 1.8% of monthly sales. |
| Bad debts | (76,098) | Agreed to letter from liquidator confirming zero payment would be received for a specific receivable from a related party of SuperSmart. |
| Debit balances transferred from payables listing | 160,789 | A number of accounts (gas and electricity) set up for direct debit and invoices not received until the following month, resulting in payment being taken before the invoice/expense is posted. |
| Net FX gains taken to P&L | 87,000 | Recalculated a sample of FX exchange gains and losses and validated rates used – no issues noted. |
| **Revenue at 31 December 2018** | **34,361,792** | Confirmed mathematical accuracy and agreed to financial statements. |

## Requirement

(a) In respect of the receivables confirmation process conducted as part of the interim audit procedures at 30 November 2018, set out:
   (i) any further audit procedures you will perform in relation to each customer circularised;
   (ii) any adjustments required in relation to the outcome of the interim testing.
(b) In respect of the follow-up procedures conducted as part of the year-end audit of revenue and receivables at 31 December 2018, set out:
   (i) the additional audit procedures you would request your audit junior to conduct on the accounts receivable roll-forward (consider each of the items in Appendix 2);
   (ii) a summary of adjustments required.
(c) Outline what audit procedures you might follow to audit the valuation assertion associated with receivables. You should discuss the potential circumstances giving rise to the need to provide for specific receivables and how the auditor might validate those circumstances.

You can ignore VAT and tax.

## Question 13.2

You are given the following information regarding total revenue for Football Crazy Ltd:

| | FY 2018<br>(1 Jan–31 Dec 2018)<br>€000 | FY 2017<br>(1 Jan–31 Dec 2017)<br>€000 |
|---|---|---|
| DVDs* | 335 | 227 |
| Sweatshirts ** | 55 | 37 |
| Magazines*** | 178 | 198 |
| | 568 | 462 |

* Five new DVDs have been brought to the market during the financial year to 2018, details as follows:

| DVD | Introduced to Market | Selling Price | Budgeted Monthly Sales Volume (Units) |
|---|---|---|---|
| 1 | Feb 2018 | €10 | 250 |
| 2 | April 2018 | €17 | 300 |
| 3 | July 2018 | €12 | 485 |
| 4 | September 2018 | €15 | 245 |
| 5 | November 2018 | €22 | 165 |

Two DVDs were discontinued in January 2018 due to poor revenue in the prior year, details as follows:

| DVD | Selling Price | Prior Year Annual Sales Volume (Units) |
|---|---|---|
| 1 | €22 | 565 |
| 2 | €19 | 500 |

** The sweatshirt range for adults has remained the same; however, a new range for children was introduced during the 2018 financial year, details as follows:
- new sweatshirt range introduced for children for the final two months of the 12-month period under review;
- selling price range of sweatshirts on sale is €12–€15;
- based on market research, expected monthly sales of sweatshirts is 650 per month.

*** During financial year 2018 the company was forced to reduce magazine selling prices due to growing competition from competitors:

| Magazine | Prior-year Selling Price | Prior-year Sales Volume | Prior-year Sales Revenue | New Reduced Price | Month of Price Cut |
|---|---|---|---|---|---|
| 1 | €2.50 | 20,000 | €50,000 | €2.30 | Jan 2018 |
| 2 | €2.00 | 13,500 | €27,000 | €1.80 | Jan 2018 |
| 3 | €4.75 | 10,000 | €47,500 | €4.45 | March 2018 |
| 4 | €3.50 | 11,000 | €38,500 | €3.10 | Jan 2018 |
| 5 | €1.25 | 28,000 | €35,000 | €1.10 | June 2018 |
| | | | €198,000 | | |

**Requirement**

(a) Use the information above to develop an expectation for total sales revenue for the 2018 financial year, showing the overall expectation and an expectation for each individual revenue stream.

(b) Outline for each particular sales component what additional information you would require in order to determine the reliability of the information used when developing the expectation above.

(c) Explain briefly the remaining three parts of the four-step approach which should be considered by the auditor when performing substantive analytical procedures.

# 14

# THE AUDIT OF BANK AND CASH

LEARNING OBJECTIVES

Having studied this chapter on the audit of bank and cash, you should:
1. understand what is included in the audit of bank and cash;
2. be able to identify the risks and audit objectives (management assertions) applicable to bank and cash;
3. be able to determine an appropriate audit strategy for bank and cash, taking into consideration the specific risks and audit objectives (management assertions);
4. be able to develop an audit programme that addresses all the audit objectives (assertions) for bank and cash;
5. be able to describe and apply specific substantive testing procedures relating to the audit of bank and cash;
6. understand the role CAATs can play when auditing bank and cash; and
7. understand the auditor's approach relating to the disclosures of bank and cash.

## CHECKLIST OF RELEVANT STANDARDS

The relevant standards, in both the RoI and the UK/NI, covered in this chapter are:
- ISA 315 *Identifying and Assessing the Risks of Material Misstatement through Understanding the Entity and its Environment*
- ISA 330 *The Auditor's Responses to Assessed Risks*
- ISA 500 *Audit Evidence*
- ISA 505 *External Confirmations*
- ISA 510 *Initial Audit Engagements – Opening Balances*
- ISA 530 *Audit Sampling*
- IAS 7 *Statement of Cash Flows*

Note, in general when referring to ISAs, it should be understood as referring to the UK and Ireland versions, unless otherwise specified as either ISA (UK) or ISA (Ireland). See the Introduction for an extant list of auditing standards for the RoI and the UK/NI.

## KEY TERMS AND DEFINITIONS FOR THIS CHAPTER

**Bank and Cash** Represents the bank balances and cash on hand included within current assets, and the bank overdrafts and bank loans included within the entity's current and non-current liabilities.

**Bank Confirmation** A letter requested by the auditor and sent directly from the bank to the auditor that discloses cash on deposit, loans and details of all accounts in the name of the client entity at the balance sheet date.

**Bank Reconciliation** An internal control performed by the client entity that reconciles the balance per the bank statement to the balance per the ledger (accounting records).

**Cash on Hand** Cash held by the client that has not yet been lodged (this could include petty cash).

**'Window Dressing'** A strategy used by management near the year end to manipulate the appearance of the financial statements (e.g. where profit has performed poorly in the year, management might overinflate the revenue by including some of January's sales in December's revenue).

## 14.1 INTRODUCTION

The objective of substantive testing is to validate the transactions, balances and disclosures at the assertion level in response to identified risks (inherent, control and detection risks as discussed in **Chapters 7** and **8**). The auditor commences substantive testing by focusing on the risk of material misstatement within the transactions and balances being tested, and then identifying the assertions impacted by these risks and then identifying substantive audit procedures that will best test the existence of material misstatement driven by the identified risks.

**Sections 14.2–14.8** of this chapter consider how the auditor addresses the substantive testing of bank and cash. In doing so, this chapter deals with how the auditor:
- identifies audit risks and audit objectives (management assertions) for bank and cash;
- develops an audit plan for bank and cash and refines this into an audit programme;
- designs specific tests associated with bank and cash; and
- checks the adequate presentation and disclosure in the financial statements relating to bank and cash.

Throughout the chapter it is highlighted where CAATs can be used by the auditor in assisting with ensuring the effective and efficient audit of bank and cash.

Finally, in **Section 14.9** we consider the auditor's approach when auditing the reasonableness of disclosures relating to bank and cash.

## 14.2 WHAT IS BANK AND CASH?

Bank and cash represents the bank balances and **cash on hand** included within current assets, and the bank overdrafts and loans included within current and non-current liabilities (i.e. both positive and negative bank balances). Bank and cash also incorporates balances relating to cash on deposit.

The auditor is predominantly concerned with the existence and completeness of all bank and cash balances.

The auditor will need to ensure that debit and credit balances relating to bank and cash are not netted against one another, but instead disclosed separately under assets and liabilities as appropriate.

## 14.3 RISKS ASSOCIATED WITH BANK AND CASH

In **Chapter 7** we discussed the topic of risk and considered how the auditor should go about detecting risks. We also discussed how the auditor should consider these risks when designing the nature, timing and extent of further audit procedures relative to each financial cycle. As such, before developing the audit plan the auditor needs to consider a number of risks that may be associated with bank and cash. These can include:
- the reliability of the entity's cash-recording system;
- the frequency of bank reconciliations (i.e. how often does the client entity receive bank statements and when are the reconciliations prepared?);
- physical controls over cash and its susceptibility to theft;
- risk due to fraud. For example, false bank accounts, fraudulent or erroneous payments, rights over bank accounts (e.g. does the client entity own the account or does it belong to another company within the group?), and whether the company has rights to all of the cash in the bank account;

- cut-off – whether the payments and receipts have been recorded in the correct period); and
- other transactional risks that could result in a material misstatement if not mitigated, e.g. credit card transactions.

## 14.4 AUDIT OBJECTIVES/MANAGEMENT ASSERTIONS FOR BANK AND CASH

As discussed in **Chapter 6**, it is necessary for the auditor to obtain sufficient appropriate audit evidence to satisfy all of the audit objectives and to eliminate the possibility of any of the risks outlined above going undetected. The auditor must design tests to address these assertions and thereby address the identified risks. The auditor must design tests to address these assertions and thereby address the identified risks. In **Chapter 4** we introduced audit objectives (management assertions) and explained their generic meanings, before reintroducing the topic again throughout **Chapter 8**, making management assertions specific to each financial cycle. **Table 14.1** recaps the audit objectives as they relate to balances for bank and cash.

Note that there are no management assertions (audit objectives) relating to transactions and events for bank and cash. This is because movements in bank and cash in the year will be captured during the testing of other substantive areas. For example, the receipt and payment of cash would fall under revenue and receivables and purchases and payables, respectively.

TABLE 14.1: BANK AND CASH – AUDIT OBJECTIVES

| Management Assertion/Audit Objective | Control Objective for Account balance |
|---|---|
| Existence | To ensure that recorded bank and cash balances exist at the date of the SOFP. |
| Completeness | To ensure that all bank and cash balances that exist are fully recorded at the date of the SOFP. |
| Rights and Obligations | To ensure the entity has the rights and any related obligations to all bank and cash balances shown in the SOFP. |
| Valuation | To ensure bank and cash balances are properly valued and a provision has been made for any balances that may not be recoverable. |
| Cut-off | All transactions have been accounted for in the correct accounting period. |
| Presentation and Disclosure | To ensure bank and cash balances are properly classified and disclosed in the SOFP and that lines of credit, loan guarantees and other restrictions on bank and cash balances are appropriately disclosed. |

Now that we understand the objectives of the auditor with regard to bank and cash, in the sections to follow let us consider how he addresses these objectives through substantive testing.

## 14.5  DEVELOPING THE AUDIT PLAN FOR BANK AND CASH

Before the audit of bank and cash is undertaken, an assessment of the audit risk must be completed. As discussed in detail in **Chapter 7**, audit risk is made up of three components: inherent risk; control risk; and detection risk.

Cash is inherently risky because it is liquid, and therefore highly susceptible to theft. If the client entity operates a cash business, this will be recognised as an **inherent risk**.

Generally, when it comes to cash and cash equivalents, the most efficient method of testing is focused substantive procedures. **All bank accounts must be tested substantively**, regardless of the outcome of controls testing, which usually means the auditor will not test the controls unless to gain a greater understanding of the management and control of cash in a predominantly cash business (e.g. retail business, where all customer transactions are in cash).

## 14.6  AUDIT TRAIL FOR BANK AND CASH

Before commencing substantive procedures, it is important for the auditor to have an appreciation of the key documents involved. To appreciate the role of the auditor in validating transactions, classes of transactions or balances at the assertion level it is important to first understand the audit trail associated with the relevant cycle. **Figure 14.1** below outlines an audit trail that could be followed when validating the various management assertions associated with bank.

It is essential that the **direction** of the test is appropriate to the assertion being tested. So, when testing for occurrence/existence, the auditor will start with the financial statements and trace back through the trial balance, etc. to the source documents. However, when testing for completeness the auditor will always start with the source documents and trace upwards to the financial statements. Whatever the direction of the test, the source document data is used to validate whether the transaction has been appropriately recorded/valued and that it proves the entity's rights and obligations assertion over the transaction/balance. Sometimes a blend of source documents will be required to validate all assertions, while in other instances a single source document will validate a number of assertions.

In the figure, a transaction as it appears on the bank statement is entered on the client entity's accounting system by way of a journal entry (transaction). Each journal entry that impacts on the bank will attach itself to the nominal listing for bank. The nominal listing then shows a summary of all payments and receipts from the bank. From the bank statement (source document) the balance is €16,886.50, but on the extract from the nominal ledger (and therefore the trial balance and the financial statements) the balance is €12,700 – reflecting any number of reconciling items that the auditor can validate through the bank reconciliation prepared by the client (see further below).

When it comes to bank and cash, the auditor is interested in the following key documents:
1. **Bank Reconciliation** The bank reconciliation is performed by the client entity and reconciles the balance per the bank statement to the balance per the ledger (accounting records).

## FIGURE 14.1: BANK AUDIT TRAIL

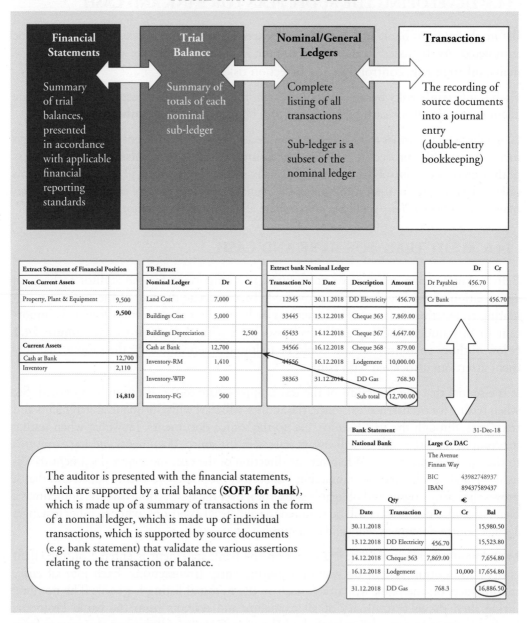

2. **Bank Confirmation** The bank confirmation is written confirmation from the client entity's bank disclosing the client entity's cash on deposit, loans and details of all accounts in the name of the client entity at the balance sheet date.

3. **Bank Mandates** A written instruction to a bank, asking it to make regular payments or to open a new account, usually includes signatories.

4. **Loan Agreements** An agreement (usually in the form of a contract) detailing particulars such as the contractual parties, the amount of the loan, the interest rate and repayment details and any related covenants.

**5. Debt Covenants** Formal agreement between the bank and the client entity with regard to conditions that will be met to maintain debt.

The bank confirmation (another example of an **external confirmation**) is requested by the auditor directly from the client entity's bank, and the confirmation is returned directly to the auditor. The confirmation provides the auditor with independent, reliable **audit evidence** (see **Chapter 6**). Bank confirmations can be subdivided into two categories:
- standard information (e.g. the bank balances); and
- supplementary information relating to trade finance and derivative and commodity trading.

The use of bank confirmations in the substantive testing procedures is discussed later at **Section 14.8**.

## 14.7 SUBSTANTIVE AUDIT PROGRAMME FOR BANK AND CASH

An audit programme records the specific details of tests to be performed by the auditor. The audit programme becomes a guide for the **audit engagement team** on the work to be performed in a particular area. As work is completed, a reference is included on the audit programme showing the location in the audit file where details of the tests performed are included. The audit programme for any cycle will vary from entity to entity, but in **Example 14.1** we consider the typical tests the auditor would include in the audit programme for bank and cash. Students should note that in a real-life scenario, each test would be referenced to the location in the audit working file where the test is actually performed.

EXAMPLE 14.1: AUDIT PROGRAMME FOR BANK AND CASH[1]

| Large Company Limited December 2018 | Audit Materiality | | €3,642,500 |
|---|---|---|---|
| | Performance Materiality | | €2,731,875 |
| | | Initials | Date |
| | Prepared by: | | |
| | Reviewed by: | | |
| **Bank Balances and Cash on Hand Audit Programme** | | | |
| **Initial Procedures** | | | |
| Assess the appropriateness of the accounting policy and the accounting estimates method for this area. Ensure that the accounting policy is in accordance with accounting standards and applicable law, and that the methods used for making the accounting estimates are appropriate. | Existence Completeness Rights and Obligations Valuation Presentation and Disclosure | | |

---

[1] Source: based on *Procedures for Quality Audit 2010* (© Chartered Accountants Ireland, 2010) I1 and updated by the authors December 2017.

| | |
|---|---|
| Agree opening balances to prior-year working papers. | Presentation and Disclosure |
| Obtain or prepare a lead schedule and agree to financial statements. | Completeness<br>Existence<br>Valuation |
| **Bank Reconciliation** | |
| Obtain or prepare reconciliations of all accounts held. Check outstanding items to post-period-end bank statements.<br><br>Inquire into any items un-presented for a significant period of time. | Completeness<br>Existence<br>Valuation<br>Presentation and Disclosure |
| **Bank Confirmations** | |
| Obtain standard bank confirmation and check to reconciliations as per ISA 505:<br>1. in the case of each non-response, perform alternative audit procedures to obtain relevant and reliable audit evidence (ISA 505, para 12);<br>2. if it is determined that a response to a bank confirmation request is necessary to obtain sufficient appropriate audit evidence, alternative audit procedures will not provide the audit evidence required. If such confirmation is not obtained, determine the implications for the audit and the auditor's opinion in accordance with ISA 505 (para 13). | Completeness<br>Existence<br>Valuation<br>Presentation and Disclosure |
| **Other Considerations** | |
| Consider whether **window dressing** has taken place. In particular:<br>1. check that all payments recorded prior to the period end were dispatched before that date;<br>2. review cash book and statements for significant movements around the year end; and<br>3. verify any significant reconciling items reversed in the subsequent period. | Completeness<br>Existence<br>Valuation<br>Presentation and Disclosure |

| | |
|---|---|
| Where possible, verify material amounts of cash on hand. Consider whether there have been significant cash movements in the period and what further verification work is needed. | Occurrence/Existence Valuation |
| Review cash book during the period and highlight significant and unusual entries. Investigate any such items found. Consider checking analysis. | |
| Ensure that disclosure is made of all bank security. <br>(a) Review covenants in place in relation to bank facilities. Document situations where these have been breached in the period, commitments and security given and implications for the audit. <br>(b) Ensure adequate disclosure of commitments, security and covenants in place, including any breach of covenants noted. | Occurrence/Existence Rights and Obligations |

## 14.8 SUBSTANTIVE TESTING PROCEDURES FOR BANK AND CASH

The substantive testing audit programme in **Example 14.1** above outlined the principal procedures involved in testing revenue and receivables. In this section we will look at each of these in more detail:

1. Initial procedures:
   (a) Opening balances
   (b) Accuracy of schedules provided by management
   (c) Prepare the lead schedule
   (d) Analytical review.
2. Bank and cash balances:
   (a) Examination of bank reconciliations
   (b) Bank confirmations
   (c) Cash balances.
3. Other considerations:
   (a) Valuation assertion
   (b) Ownership assertion
   (c) Completeness assertion
   (d) Audit of Statement of Cash Flows.

## Initial Procedures

### Opening Balances

Before commencing further audit procedures, evidence must be obtained as to the accuracy of the opening balances of bank and cash. The reason for this is twofold:

1. it confirms that the comparative numbers in the financial statements (which must be included in the current year's financial statements) agree to the final accounts of the prior year; and

2. it highlights any final entries (last-minute adjusting journal entries) of the prior year not correctly carried forward, which may indicate an error in the current year's financial statement figures.

The auditor verifies opening balances as follows:

- Agree the opening balances to the prior-year audit working papers and signed financial statements. This may highlight an opening balance in the current year's accounts that does not agree to the closing balance per the prior year's financial statements – in which case a change would be made to the opening balance of the current year, which would impact the closing balance of the current year. This usually arises due to final adjustments in the prior year that are not reflected in the actual accounts (nominal and general ledgers).

- If this is the first year of the audit engagement, the auditor will still need to establish that the opening balances are materially correct, which can pose difficulties if either the client entity was exempt from audit in the prior year or a predecessor auditor carried out the audit. The audit of opening balances in such instances is discussed in detail in **Chapter 6**, Section 6.9.

### Accuracy of Schedules

All bank reconciliations should be tested for their mathematical accuracy and should be agreed to the schedule of bank balances that tie in with the trial balance and on into the financial statements. At least one item should be selected from the schedule and traced to its respective source data to validate the accuracy of the schedule before further testing is performed on it.

### Prepare the Lead Schedule

The **lead schedule** acts as a summary of the balances and transactions to be audited relating to a particular class of transaction and balances. It allows the auditor to control the procedures by referencing each balance or transaction to the audit working paper that records the audit tests that have been performed. An example of a lead schedule for bank and cash is shown below at **Example 14.2**.

## EXAMPLE 14.2: BANK AND CASH LEAD SCHEDULE
## (LARGE COMPANY LIMITED)[2]

| Large Company Limited 31 December 2018 | Audit Materiality | | €3,642,500 |
|---|---|---|---|
| | Performance Materiality | | €2,731,875 |
| | | Initials | Date |
| | Prepared by: | | |
| Bank Balances and Cash on Hand | Reviewed by: | | |
| | | 31/12/2018 | 31/12/2017 |
| | | €000 | €000 |
| **Receivables Balances: Bank and Cash** | | | |
| Current account | | 9,199 | 20,528 |
| Deposit account | | 95,000 | 85,000 |
| Petty cash | | 1 | 2 |
| | | 104,200 | 105,530 |
| | | | |
| **Payables Balances: Amounts payable within one year** | | | |
| **Current** | | | |
| Galway bank loan | | 1,000 | 1,000 |
| Dublin bank loan | | 3,250 | 8,650 |
| | | 4,250 | 9,650 |
| **Amounts payable after one year** | | | |
| Non-current Eurobond | | 3,750 | 350 |
| Galway bank loan | | 14,000 | 15,000 |
| Dublin bank loan | | 2,600 | 12,210 |
| | | 20,350 | 27,560 |
| **Total Bank Loans** | | **24,600** | **37,210** |

## Analytical Review

An analytical review (see **Chapter 5**, Section 5.4) is usually performed at the start of each substantive testing of a balance or class of transactions. Calculating ratios and analysing results against industry information, prior-year results, budgets, etc. allows the auditor to better understand the movements in the year and to make comparisons against norms.

---

[2] Source: based on *Procedures for Quality Audit 2010* (© Chartered Accountants Ireland, 2010) I and updated by the authors December 2017.

It therefore provides the auditor with additional insights into the client entity and the industry it operates in, and better prepares them for the audit programme.

A typical ratio used in the bank and cash cycle is 'interest cover', which expresses interest relative to earnings before interest and tax (EBIT) – basically showing how many times EBIT could cover interest charges. Other calculations used in bank and cash substantive procedures could include debt ratios, such as debt to equity. **Example 14.3** below illustrates the types of ratio and comparison the auditor might perform in relation to bank and cash.

EXAMPLE 14.3: ANALYTICAL REVIEW – BANK AND CASH (LARGE COMPANY LIMITED)

|  | 2018 €000 | 2017 €000 | Change €000 |
|---|---|---|---|
| **Receivables Balances: Bank and Cash** | | | |
| Current account | 9,199 | 20,528 | (11,329) |
| Deposit account | 95,000 | 85,000 | 10,000 |
| Petty cash | 1 | 2 | (1) |
| | **104,200** | **105,530** | **(1,330)** |

Cash reserves have decreased due to repayment of loans.

**Payables Balances: Amounts payable within 1 year**

|  | 2018 | 2017 | Change |
|---|---|---|---|
| Current account | 4,250 | 9,650 | (5,400) |
| Amounts payable after 1 year | 20,350 | 27,560 | (7,210) |
| Total bank loans | **24,600** | **37,210** | **(12,610)** |

Both short- and long-term borrowing has decreased due to the repayment of the Dublin loan facilitated by the significant surge in cash revenue.

|  | 2018 | 2017 | Change |
|---|---|---|---|
| **Interest cover = EBIT ÷ interest** | = 73,400 ÷ 550 | = 24,610 ÷ 550 | |
| | 133 | 45 | 88 |

Expectation would be for interest costs to decrease due to the repayment of the Dublin loan; however, it was not repaid until the year end, meaning similar interest charges were still incurred.

With the improvement in profit, interest cover has improved greatly.

## Bank and Cash Balances

Having performed the initial procedures, now let us consider the specific audit procedures the auditor might carry out in relation to the bank and cash balances, which essentially includes: the examination of bank reconciliations; review of bank confirmations; and the review of cash balances.

## *Examination of Bank Reconciliations*

The client entity should prepare bank reconciliations for every bank account included within the bank and cash balances on the financial statements. The auditor is required to review all bank reconciliations by performing the following:

- Obtaining a copy of all bank reconciliations in respect of all bank accounts held at the date of the SOFP and and identify both who performed and who reviewed the reconciliations – without this information the reconciliations would not constitute sufficient appropriate audit evidence.
- Obtain explanations for any large or unusual reconciling items.
- Agreeing the total as per the reconciliation to the bank/cash account in the nominal ledger, the bank confirmation and the bank statements.
- Recalculating the totals in the reconciliation to ensure their mathematical accuracy.
- Tracing any outstanding cheques at the date of the SOFP to post-year-end bank statements. In the case of outstanding cheques taking a longer than expected time to clear after the year end, obtain explanations as to the delay and ensure that the cheques were actually issued by the client prior to the date of the SOFP and not after the date of the SOFP. Depending on the number of outstanding cheques and lodgements, a sample of outstanding items may be tested.
- Tracing outstanding lodgements to post-year-end bank statements.
- Agreeing a sample of lodgements from the bank statements to the lodgement book.
- For a sample of receipts and payments taken from the cash receipts/cheque payments book, checking that items selected are either included on the bank statements prior to year end or included on the list of outstanding lodgements/cheques.
- Examining the cash receipts book for evidence of reversals of lodgements subsequent to the year end.
- Reviewing the bank statements, cash receipts book and cheque payments book for any large or unusual items.
- Ensuring interest payable on loans is properly accrued and included in the financial statements.
- For a sample of items included within outstanding cheques and lodgements, the auditor should test to ensure that the items have been treated appropriately in the year-end receivables and payables, i.e. items included in outstanding lodgements have been removed from the receivables ledger, and items included within outstanding cheques have been removed from the payables ledger.
- Obtaining post-year-end bank statements and tracing all prior-year-dated cheques to outstanding cheques listed on the bank reconciliation (this could assist in finding prior-year cheques not included as outstanding on the bank reconciliation). If uncleared cheques are material, it might indicate '**window dressing**' – where cheques are written on the last day of the year but not mailed for several weeks until there are funds in the account to meet these payments. The entity will not usually delay in lodging cheques received and as such the auditor should expect outstanding lodgements on the bank reconciliation to clear the bank within one week of

the year end. Make inquiries of management if the delay in presentation of cheques is greater than two weeks.

- Tracing deposits in transit on the bank reconciliation to deposits on the post-year-end bank statement (these should be one of the first items shown on the post-year-end bank statement; if not, inquire into the reason for the time lag and corroborate explanation – significant delays in depositing receipts could indicate fraudulent practice of 'teeming and lading'). Scan the statement for unusual items, such as unrecorded bank debits/credits, bank errors and corrections.

## Bank Confirmations

Bank confirmations should be sent by the auditor on the auditor's letterhead and clearly identify all of the information required. It is important that the auditor maintains complete control over the process. The bank confirmation is a very important part of the audit of bank and cash as it provides the auditor with **independent third-party audit evidence**.

ISA 505, paragraph 7, states:

"When using external confirmation procedures, the auditor shall maintain control over external confirmation request, including:

(a) Determining the information to be confirmed or requested;

(b) Selecting the appropriate confirming party;

(c) Designing the confirmation requests, including determining that requests are properly addressed and contain return information for responses to be sent directly to the auditor; and

(d) Sending the requests, including follow-up requests when applicable, to the confirming party."

The confirmation of other arrangements with the banks should also be conducted through the bank confirmation process. When returned, the bank confirmation should confirm:

- guaranteed loans to third parties;
- bills discounted with recourse;
- details of any contingent liabilities of which the bank may be aware;
- details of the existence of any other banking relationships with the client entity of which the recipient bank may be aware; and
- any unused facilities (e.g. bank overdrafts).

The bank confirmation should be signed or stamped by the bank and be returned directly to the auditor. **Example 14.4** below gives a sample of a bank confirmation request provided by the Banking & Payments Federation Ireland.

It is important to note that bank confirmation request letters cannot be relied upon entirely. Such confirmations include a disclaimer in favour of the bank and, in essence, the bank cannot be held liable if it provides incomplete/inaccurate information.

EXAMPLE 14.4: BANK CONFIRMATION REQUEST LETTER[3]

**STANDARD FORM OF REQUEST**

This form has been approved by Banking & Payments Federation Ireland and
The Consultative Committee of Accountancy Bodies – Ireland (CCAB-I).

Name _____          (Auditor)

Address _____          Date _____

_____          Our Ref _____

_____

Customer/Client Name _____

Address _____

Account number/Holding branch _____

_____

I/We have read this document and I/We authorise you to provide the information
requested herein in respect of the accounts of the above-name customer and also to disclose the number of joint accounts, if any, to which the above-named customer is party.

Please send this information to our auditor(s),

Yours faithfully

_____

**Authorised Signature(s)**

Dear Sir

We report that at the close of business on   /   /   the records of this branch showed:

1. BANK ACCOUNTS

| Description of a/cs (including deposit a/cs) | S/SX Note A | Date of last letter outlining terms/ conditions of borrowing | Balance | Dr/ Cr | Amounts accrued but not posted at above date (Note B) | |
|---|---|---|---|---|---|---|
| | | | | | Est. Interest Dr/Cr | Est. Current Account Fees & other charges |
| | | | | | | |
| | | | | | | |

---

[3] Source: Banking & Payments Federation Ireland, see www.bpfi.ie/customer-assist/business-customers/
bank-report-for-audit-purposes/

***Note A***: Where a specific letter of set-off for principal exists affecting any of the above accounts, please indicate this by adding 'S' to the account title. If the set-off refers to accounts other than those being reported on use 'SX'. (Other set-off may arise either at law or on foot of a bank security document).

***Note B***: The provision of this information may entail work and cost. If the information is not essential this request should be deleted.

2. FULL TITLES AND DATES OF CLOSURE OF ALL ACCOUNTS CLOSED DURING PERIOD:

3. CUSTOMER'S ASSETS
   Nature of security held directly from customer (e.g. Deeds, Stocks, Shares, etc.). Amount only of any guarantees held for the benefit of the customer.

4. CONTINGENT LIABILITIES
   All known contingent liabilities

|     |                                                                                                          | Date(s) | Amount |
| --- | -------------------------------------------------------------------------------------------------------- | ------- | ------ |
| (a) | Total of Bills discounted for your customer, with recourse                                               |         |        |
| (b) | Amounts and dates of each Guarantee, (excluding Acceptances) Bond or Indemnity given to you by the customer. |         |        |
| (c) | Amounts and dates of each Guarantee, (excluding Acceptances) Bond or Indemnity given by you on behalf of your customer. |         |        |
| (d) | Total of Bills drawn on and accepted by Bank on behalf of customers (excluding (f) hereunder)            |         |        |
| (e) | Total Forward Foreign Contracts                                                                          |         |        |
| (f) | Total of Outstanding Liabilities under Documentary Credits                                                |         |        |
| (g) | Others – Please give details                                                                             |         |        |

The information available at branch contained herein is given in confidence for your use only, in your capacity as Auditor(s) and without responsibility on the part of the Bank or any of its officials.

***Note***: No information can or will be given which would disclose confidential information regarding other customers.

Signed  ..........................................................  Manager

  ..........................................................  Date

## Cash Balances

Bank reconciliations and bank confirmations relate to the audit of bank balances, we now need to consider how the auditor goes about substantively testing cash balances included within the financial statements.

Where cash transactions are significant and therefore **inherent risk** is high, the auditor should:
- Consider if internal controls surrounding cash receipts and payments are sufficient.
- Where the SOFP cash balance is **material**:
  - review the operation of the cash system (how cash is collected, reconciled to till receipts, lodged and reconciled to the bank account);
  - count the cash, either at the year end or by performing a surprise cash count at a randomly selected point during the audit;
  - during the cash count, ensure that full control exists over all cash simultaneously to prevent cash from being swapped from one count to another; perform the count in the presence of independent client entity personnel (not those in regular custody of cash); list details of notes and coins and ensure IOUs are recorded and collectable and that they are made according to the client entity's policy guidelines.
- Reconcile the cash counted to the petty cash records, and investigate any differences.
- Have the cashier perform and initial the reconciliation as evidence of agreement.

## Other Considerations

Having performed the substantive procedures relating to bank and cash balances, there are some other matters the auditor must consider before the substantive procedures relating to bank and cash can be considered adequately completed.
- **Test the valuation assertion** – the auditor should review relevant loan agreements or board minutes to determine whether there are any restrictions on the availability or use of bank balances or cash.
- **Test the ownership assertion** – the auditor should:
  - obtain sufficient audit evidence in relation to bank balances from bank confirmations; and
  - check that all bank statements are in the name of the client entity.
- **Test the completeness assertion** – the auditor should:
  - carry out an analytical review of the balances and obtain explanations for any large or unusual variations;
  - review the bank confirmations, minutes of board meetings and inquire of management if any new accounts were opened during the period;
  - investigate whether separate bank accounts exist for the payment of payroll or petty cash, and ensure that all bank accounts are included at the date of the SOFP.
- **Audit the statement of cash flows** – the movement in the balance of cash and cash equivalents for the period is shown in the statement of cash flows The statement of cash flows is one of the primary statements within the financial statements. It shows how cash and cash equivalents have flowed in and out of the entity by category – operating, investing and financing – over the reporting period. The auditor should obtain **sufficient appropriate audit evidence** to support the figures included in the statement of cash flows and ensure they are consistent with the other primary statements in the financial statements.

Additionally, the auditor should ensure that all disclosures, as required by IAS 7 *Statement of Cash Flows*, are included in the notes to the financial statements. Financial ratios that employ cash-flow measures can be used to evaluate the company's going concern assumption, therefore the auditor should seek to use the information contained in the statement of cash flows to evaluate the client entity's liquidity status and abilities.

- **Holds on assets** – the auditor will be particularly interested in possible holds on assets resulting from loans, and to gain assurance that the disclosures surrounding any holds on assets are complete the auditor should verify the bank confirmation to the loan agreement.
- **Interrogation of bank transactions** – online banking facilities are such that a download of transactions for the period can readily be obtained and interrogated. The auditor can use CAATs to search for:
  - duplicate payments;
  - payments to related parties;
  - large-scale payments or payments over a certain value;
  - specific transactions to support other audit procedures; or
  - to analyse transactions around the year end date.

## 14.9 DISCLOSURE REQUIREMENTS

Finally, with regard to bank and cash the auditor will consider the adequacy of the disclosures in the client entity's financial statements. In doing so, the auditor aims to ensure that disclosures relating to bank and cash are:
- complete (no bank-related disclosures are missing);
- accurate (reflect the actual transactions and information relating to events surrounding bank and cash);
- relate to events that actually occurred or existed at the year end; and
- are properly presented in line with international financial reporting standards.

The **bank confirmation** is the key document that the auditor will use to assist with supporting some of the above requirements. The bank confirmation will:
- indicate to the auditor the existence of contingent liabilities (discussed further in **Chapter 18**) that may need to be disclosed;
- provide the auditor with details of the bank's interest charges on any loans to the client entity that may need to be disclosed; and
- facilitate the preparation of notes relating to monies due within one year and after more than one year.

## 14.10 CONCLUSION

When the auditor has performed controls testing (see **Chapter 8**) and all the substantive procedures discussed above, it must be considered if sufficient appropriate audit evidence has been obtained over bank and cash balances to give the appropriate level of comfort required over the assertions stated at the outset, these being:
- completeness;
- valuation;

- existence/occurrence;
- cut-off;
- rights and obligations; and
- presentation and disclosure.

The auditor must also consider if the testing performed has appropriately addressed the key risks identified around bank and cash, and has reduced the risk of material misstatement to a suitably low level.

The auditor must consider the impact of their testing on bank and cash on the **audit opinion**. This is achieved by considering whether any misstatements found, either individually or in aggregate (when combined with other misstatements detected throughout the audit), will result in the financial statements being materially misstated. All misstatements found are taken to the auditor's errors schedule for consideration at the audit completion stage (discussed in detail in **Chapter 18**). The auditor's report on financial statements is considered in detail in **Chapter 19**.

## SUMMARY OF LEARNING OBJECTIVES

**Learning Objective 1** Understand what is included in the audit of bank and cash.

Bank and cash represent the bank balances and cash on hand included within current assets, and the bank overdrafts and loans included within current and non-current liabilities.

**Learning Objective 2** Be able to identify the risks and audit objectives (management assertions) applicable to bank and cash.

The primary risks associated with bank and cash relate to:
- physical controls over cash/susceptibility to theft;
- fraud; and
- cut-off.

The auditor is seeking to ensure that:
- all bank balances (positive and negative) are included and are therefore complete;
- all bank balances that are included relate to real balances that exist;
- all positive and negative bank balances are owned by the client entity, i.e. it has the rights and obligations to those balances;
- they are reasonably and accurately valued; and
- they are classified, presented and disclosed in line with applicable international financial reporting standards.

**Learning Objective 3** Be able to determine an appropriate audit strategy for bank and cash, taking into consideration the specific risks and audit objectives (management assertions).

The auditor seeks to gain assurance that the bank and cash balances exist and are accurate; that all bank and cash balances are included and appropriately classified, presented and disclosed on the statement of financial position.

**Learning Objective 4** Be able to develop an audit programme that addresses all the audit objectives (management assertions) for bank and cash.

Due to the fact that all bank and cash balances need to be validated by the auditor, it is rare to rely on the client entity's internal controls, therefore the auditor will perform focused substantive testing.

**Learning Objective 5** Be able to describe and apply specific substantive testing procedures relating to the audit of bank and cash.

The bank confirmation, bank statements and bank reconciliations are the key documents of interest to the auditor. Other documents that may form part of audit evidence connected to bank and cash include:
- bank mandates;
- loan agreements; and
- debt covenants.

The main audit procedures surrounding bank and cash relate to:
- **bank confirmations** – which cover the existence, valuation, rights and obligations and completeness assertions;
- reperformance/review of **bank reconciliations**;
- reviews to ensure '**window dressing**' has not taken place; and
- attendance at the physical count of cash balances (where material).

**Learning Objective 6** Understand the role CAATs can play when auditing bank and cash.

The auditor may use a combination of audit software, data analysis tools and other applications, such as Excel, when auditing the area of bank and cash.

**Learning Objective 7** Understand the auditor's approach relating to the disclosures of bank and cash.

The auditor needs to consider the disclosure requirements necessary for bank and cash by ensuring they are: complete; accurate; relate to events that actually occurred; and are properly presented in line with applicable international reporting standards.

## QUESTIONS

### Self-test Questions

14.1 What audit benefits are derived from a bank confirmation?

14.2 Why is it important to check outstanding cheques at the year end?

14.3 What steps should the auditor take if there is evidence of 'window dressing' at the year end?

14.4 List three key risks associated with the audit of the bank and cash balances.

14.5 List the four key management assertions associated with the bank and cash balances. For each one, list at least one audit procedure that should be performed to address it.

14.6 As part of the audit of bank and cash, what should the auditor prepare and send in order to obtain independent reliable audit evidence about an entity's year-end bank balances?

## Review Questions

(See Suggested Solutions to Review Questions in **Appendix C**.)

### Question 14.1

You are the audit senior on Jackson Ltd a company established in 1975 specialising in the manufacture of mining equipment. Your audit junior has emailed you a copy of the audit working papers for the substantive audit work performed on bank and cash (see below).

---

Subject: Jackson Ltd – audit of bank and cash

Dear Audit Senior,

Please find attached my working papers, showing the work I have carried out on the area of bank and cash assigned to me. I am sorry that my working papers are not complete, but I need some guidance on how to proceed.

Noted below, National Bank is marked as not responded, however please note that this was received by the financial controller of Jackson and he said he will send it on to me.

---

| Bank Name | BIC/IBAN | Balance per bank confirmation £/€000 | Balance per trial balance £/€000 |
|---|---|---|---|
| Union Bank | IE3837383739383839 IE373683 | 6,850 | 6,850.00 |
| Bank of Europe | HF373826393873938 HF383838 | (7,000) | 1,367.87 |
| National Bank | UY784374893284389 UY478383 | No response | 98,765.50 |
| United Finance | UF489327483278438 UF837933 | No response | 9,098.00 |
| HGF Finance | HG347832784397438 HG837498 | No confirmation sent (balance immaterial) | 9.18 |

**Requirement**

In response to the email received from the audit junior:

(a) Outline why it is important to confirm all bank accounts held and operated by the entity during the year.

(b) From the information given, outline for your audit junior the further activities to be performed to complete testing on the bank confirmations.

## Question 14.2

You are the audit senior on JAG Limited, a company that manufactures large aeroplane parts, which prepares financial statements to 31 December. You are completing the filing work for the audit for 31 December 2018. Due to illness, one of your audit juniors will not be able to complete the audit engagement and has sent you an email with the unfinished working papers on the cash flow statement (see below). You will have to reassign this work to another audit junior.

| | £/€000 | Substantive audit procedure |
|---|---|---|
| **Cash Flow from Operating Activities** | | |
| Profit before taxation | 10,078 | → Agreed to SOCI |
| Depreciation | (1,204) | → Agreed to depreciation charge on SOCI |
| Interest expense | (789) | → Agreed to interest charge on SOCI |
| Profit on sale of PPE | 570 | → Agreed to working papers within PPE where profit on sale of PPE was recalculated |
| | **8,655** | → Check mathematical accuracy |
| **Working capital movements** | | |
| Decrease in trade and other receivables | 1,750 | |
| Decrease in inventories | (1,205) | |
| Increase in trade payables and accruals | 980 | |
| Taxation paid | (1,850) | |
| Interest paid | (720) | |
| **Net inflow from operating activities** | **7,610** | |
| **Cash Flow from Investing Activities** | | |
| Amount received on sale of PPE | 2,100 | |
| **Net inflow from investing activities** | **2,100** | |

**Cash Flow from Financing Activities**

| | |
|---|---:|
| Dividends paid | (1,200) |
| Loan repayment | (700) |
| **Net outflow from financing activities** | **(1,900)** |

| | |
|---|---:|
| **Net cash inflow** | 7,810 |

## Requirement

In assigning the work to the new audit junior outline:

(a)  the importance of the audit of the cash flow statement; and

(b)  the procedures to complete the unfinished audit work on the cash flow statement.

# 15

# THE AUDIT OF INVESTMENTS

LEARNING OBJECTIVES

Having studied this chapter on the audit of investments you should:
1.  understand what is included in the audit of investments;
2.  be able to identify the risks and audit objectives applicable to investments;
3.  be able to determine an appropriate audit strategy for investments, taking into consideration the specific risks and audit objectives (assertions);
4.  be able to develop an audit programme that addresses all the audit objectives (assertions) for investments;
5.  be able to describe and apply specific substantive testing procedures relating to the audit of investments;
6.  understand the role CAATs can play when auditing investments; and
7.  understand the auditor's approach relating to the disclosures of investments.

## CHECKLIST OF RELEVANT STANDARDS

The relevant standards, in both the RoI and the UK/NI, covered in this chapter are:
- ISA 315 *Identifying and Assessing the Risks of Material Misstatement through Understanding the Entity and its Environment*
- ISA 330 *The Auditor's Responses to Assessed Risks*
- ISA 500 *Audit Evidence*
- ISA 505 *External Confirmations*
- ISA 510 *Initial Audit Engagements – Opening Balances*
- ISA 520 *Analytical Procedures*
- ISA 550 *Related Parties*
- IAS 27 *Separate Financial Statements*
- IAS 28 *Investments in Associates and Joint Ventures*
- IAS 32 *Financial Instruments: Presentation*
- IAS 40 *Investment Property*
- IFRS 7 *Financial Instruments: Disclosures*
- IFRS 9 *Financial Instruments*
- IFRS 10 *Consolidated Financial Statements*
- IFRS 12 *Disclosure of Interests in Other Entities*

Note, in general when referring to ISAs, it should be understood as referring to the UK and Ireland versions, unless otherwise specified as either ISA (UK) or ISA (Ireland). See the Introduction for an extant list of auditing standards for the RoI and the UK/NI.

## KEY TERMS AND DEFINITIONS FOR THIS CHAPTER

**Amortisation**    The reduction in the value of an intangible asset over its useful life.
**Debenture**    Debt instrument in the form of an unsecured loan issued by a company, which is generally backed by the issuer's creditworthiness rather than by physical assets.
**Diminution in Value**    The decrease (impairment) in the value of an asset. For example, economic conditions cause some investments to devalue and the client entity is required to measure the value lost in the asset.
**Investment Schedule**    List of all investments currently held by the client entity.

## 15.1 INTRODUCTION

The objective of substantive testing is to validate the transactions, balances and disclosures at the assertion level in response to identified risks (inherent, control and detection risks as discussed in **Chapters 7** and **8**). The auditor commences substantive testing by focusing on the risk of material misstatement within the transactions and balances being tested, and then identifying the assertions impacted by these risks and then identifying substantive audit procedures that will best test the existence of material misstatement driven by the identified risks.

**Sections 15.2–15.8** outline the requirements of the relevant ISAs, International Financial Reporting Standards (IFRSs) and International Accounting Standards (IASs) with respect to the audit of investments by the external auditor. These sections consider how the auditor:

- identifies audit risks and audit objectives (management assertions) for investments;
- develops an audit plan for investments and refines this into an audit programme;
- designs specific tests associated with investments; and
- ensures adequate presentation and disclosure in the financial statements relating to investments.

Throughout the chapter it is highlighted where CAATs can be used by the auditor in assisting with ensuring the effective and efficient audit of the area of investments.

Finally, in **Section 15.9** we consider the auditor's approach when auditing the reasonableness of disclosures relating to investments.

## 15.2  WHAT ARE INVESTMENTS?

Investment balances constitute ownership of securities issued by other entities and these may be in the form of certificates of deposit, shares, debentures or government bonds.

Investments are normally held for one of two reasons:
1. to achieve capital gain – the client entity expects or hopes that the fair value of the investment will increase, thereby providing the client entity with a capital gain when sold;
2. to generate income through interest or dividends earned on investments.

An entity generally holds investments for a long period of time (greater than one year).

Money held on deposit does not constitute an investment from an audit testing point of view and instead would be covered under bank and cash (see **Chapter 14**). Investments broadly relate to two categories:
1. financial instruments; and
2. investments requiring consideration of consolidation.

### Financial Instruments

Investments in financial instruments represent financial assets in the hands of the entity that owns them. The accounting requirements for such investments are determined by IFRS 7, IFRS 9 and IAS 32.

Investments are initially measured at cost, but should be subsequently re-measured. IFRS 9 outlines the requirements for the recognition and measurement of financial assets. The accounting requirements for subsequent re-measurement of the four categories of financial assets as defined by IFRS 9 are:
1. **Loans and receivables not held for trading** – amortised cost using the effective interest method subject to impairment.
2. **Held-to-maturity investments** – amortised cost using the effective interest method subject to impairment.

3. **Financial assets measured at fair value through profit or loss** – fair value, with value changes recognised through profit or loss.
4. **Available-for-sale assets and others not falling into any of the above categories** – measured at fair value in the statement of financial position (SOFP), with value changes recognised in other comprehensive income as an unrealised gain or loss, subject to impairment testing. If the fair value cannot be reliably measured, the asset is carried at cost.

### Investments requiring Consolidation Considerations

Investments can also be held for the purpose of acquiring influence or control over another entity and must be considered by the auditor. Such investments must be classified as subsidiaries, associates or joint ventures and are accounted for under IFRS 10, IAS 27 or IAS 28. Investments in such entities, depending on the degree of control or percentage of ownership, require consolidation and the generation of group financial statements.

The main audit considerations related to consolidated financial statements are explained in **Section 15.8**, but at this point a basic understanding of how such investments are presented in the financial statements is needed:
- a subsidiary's financial statements are consolidated;
- an associate's financial results are shown in the entity's SOFP (under non-current assets and referred to as 'Investment in associate') and in its SOCI as a share of profits/losses in the associate or profits/losses on the sale of an associate;
- financial investments are shown in the entity's SOFP (under non-current assets as 'Investments') and in its SOCI (as 'Finance income');
- investments that are not subsidiary, associate or joint arrangements are accounted for under IAS 39 and referred to as 'Investment interests').

When the auditor is dealing with a client entity that is a parent company, they will need to consider the requirements for group audits (see **Chapter 20**).

## 15.3 RISKS ASSOCIATED WITH THE AUDIT OF INVESTMENTS

In **Chapter 7** we discussed the topic of risk and we considered how the auditor should go about detecting risks. We also discussed how the auditor should consider these risks when designing the nature, timing and extent of further audit procedures relative to each financial cycle. As such, before developing the audit plan, the auditor needs to consider a number of risks that may be associated with investments.

According to ISA 315, the auditor should use professional judgement to assess the risk of material misstatement. Risk factors relating to investments include:
- the reliability of the investment recording system;
- physical controls over investments held and the susceptibility to theft of investments physically held by the client entity or by an independent custodian. If the investment certificates are held by the client entity, the auditor should ensure that they are adequately stored (i.e. in a securely locked safe);

- risk due to fraud, for example, false investments and rights over investments (the auditor must check that the investments are in the client entity's name or held in the name of a director or another entity). Does the client entity hold the risks and rewards relating to the investments recognised in its financial statements?;
- risk due to complicated accounting treatment involved in consolidations, which may lead to errors or be seen as an opportunity to conceal fraud; and
- risk of **diminution in value** not being adequately recorded in the financial statements.

## 15.4 AUDIT OBJECTIVES/MANAGEMENT ASSERTIONS FOR INVESTMENTS

As discussed in **Chapter 6**, it is necessary for the auditor to seek **sufficient appropriate audit evidence** to satisfy all of the audit objectives and to eliminate the possibility of any of the risks outlined above going undetected. The auditor must design tests to address these assertions and thereby address the identified risks. In **Chapter 4** we introduced audit objectives (management assertions) and explained their generic meanings, before reintroducing the topic throughout **Chapter 8**, making management assertions specific to each financial cycle. **Table 15.1** recaps the audit objectives as they relate to investment income and expenses (transactions) and investment balances.

TABLE 15.1: INVESTMENTS – AUDIT OBJECTIVES

| Management Assertion/Audit Objective | Control Objective for Transaction Class | Control Objective for Account Balance |
|---|---|---|
| **Existence or Occurrence** | Recorded investment revenues, gains and losses are the result of transactions and events that occurred during the period. | Recorded investment balances represent investments that exist at the date of the SOFP. |
| **Completeness** | All investment transactions and events are included in the statement of comprehensive income. | All investments that exist at the date of the SOFP are recorded in the SOFP. |
| **Rights and Obligations** | The entity has rights and obligations associated with the investment income, profits and losses recorded during the period. | All recorded investments are owned by the client entity, which hold the risks and rewards associated with them. |
| **Classification/ Recording (accuracy) or Valuation** | Investment revenues, gains and losses are accurately recorded. | Investments are stated at valuation as appropriate for the particular types of investment held. |

| Cut-off | Investment revenues, gains and losses are recorded in the correct period (particularly those around the year end date). | |
| --- | --- | --- |
| **Presentation and Disclosure** | Appropriate disclosures in the financial statements are made concerning: 1. related party investments; 2. the bases for valuing investments; and 3. the pledging of investments as collateral and any other disclosures as required under the applicable reporting standards. | Investment balances are properly identified, presented and disclosed in the financial statements in line with the the applicable financial reporting standards. |

## 15.5 DEVELOPING THE AUDIT PLAN FOR INVESTMENTS

Before the audit of investments is undertaken, an assessment of the audit risk must be completed. As discussed in detail in **Chapter 7**, audit risk is made up of three components: inherent risk; control risk; and detection risk.

Investment transactions and balances are an **inherent risk** due to their complicated accounting treatment. Purchases and sales of investments are often processed separately from all other purchases and sales, which can represent a **control risk** in that entities that hold substantial investments often adopt specific control procedures over them, or else process them ad hoc as they arrive, and as a result they are treated as non-routine transactions. The volume of investment transactions, however, is generally low and so, from a **detection risk** point of view, the auditor would usually take a focused substantive approach and not test the controls.

Where an investment relates to entities requiring consideration of consolidation, the auditor will need to consider the need for a group audit (see **Chapter 20**).

## 15.6 AUDIT TRAIL FOR INVESTMENTS

To appreciate the role of the auditor in validating transactions, classes of transactions or balances at the assertion level it is important to first understand the audit trail associated with the relevant cycle. **Figure 15.1** below outlines an audit trail that could be followed when validating the various management assertions associated with investments.

FIGURE 15.1: INVESTMENTS AUDIT TRAIL

| Financial Statements | Trial Balance | Nominal/General Ledgers | Transactions |
|---|---|---|---|
| Summary of trial balances, presented in accordance with applicable financial reporting standards | Summary of totals of each nominal sub-ledger | Complete listing of all transactions<br><br>Sub-ledger is a subset of the nominal ledger | The recording of source documents into a journal entry (double-entry bookkeeping) |

**Extract Statement of Financial Position**

| | |
|---|---|
| **Non Current Assets** | |
| Property, Plant & Equipment | 9,500 |
| Investments | 34,700 |
| | **44,200** |
| **Current Assets** | |
| Cash at Bank | 1,410 |
| Inventory | 700 |
| | 2,110 |

| TB-Extract | Dr | Cr |
|---|---|---|
| Land Cost | 7,000 | |
| Buildings Cost | 5,000 | |
| Buildings Depr | | 2,500 |
| Investments | 34,700 | |
| Inventory-RM | 1,410 | |
| Inventory-WIP | 200 | |
| Inventory-FG | 500 | |

| Transaction No. | Date | Description | Value |
|---|---|---|---|
| | 01.01.2018 | Opening Balance | 12,400 |
| 12345 | 12.06.2018 | Associate Investment | 12,000 |
| 33445 | 13.12.2018 | Government Bonds | 10,000 |
| 65433 | 14.12.2018 | 5 Year Savings Investment | 5,000 |
| 34566 | 16.12.2018 | Cash in of 10 Year Investment | 5,500 |
| 46373 | 31.12.2018 | Share of profit in Associate | 800 |
| | | Sub total | **34,700** |

| | Dr €000 | Cr €000 |
|---|---|---|
| Dr Investment in associate | 12 | |
| Cr Bank | | 12 |

**Stock Certificate**

THIS IS TO CERTIFY THAT
*Large Company Limited*
IS THE OWNER OF _1,000_ SHARES OF STOCK
OF _Hampbell Products Limited_
ON THIS _15_ DAY OF _June_ IN THE YEAR _2018_
AT: _A purchase price of €/€12.00 per share_
SIGNED _W O Hughes_  Being _8% of Total Shares at that date_

The auditor is presented with the financial statements, which are supported by a trial balance (**SOFP for investments**), which is made up of a summary of transactions in the form of a nominal ledger, which is made up of individual transactions, which is supported by source documents (e.g. bank statement) that validate the occurrence/existence of the transaction or balance.

It is essential that the **direction** of the test is appropriate to the assertion being tested. So, when testing for occurrence/existence, the auditor will start with the financial statements and trace back through the trial balance, etc. to the source documents. However, when testing for completeness the auditor will always start with the source documents and trace upwards to the financial statements. Whatever the direction of the test, the source document data is used to validate whether the transaction has been appropriately recorded/valued and that it proves the entity's rights and obligations assertion over the transaction/balance. Sometimes a blend of source documents will be required to validate all assertions, while in other instances a single source document will validate a number of assertions.

The type of documents held by entities will vary depending on the type of investment in question. If they relate to bonds or deposits, **investment certificates** will be requested by the auditor as evidence to support testing. Alternatively, the auditor could seek any ownership document that can prove occurrence/existence and valuation.

Entities that hold large volumes of investments will have **investment schedules** detailing their investment portfolio and identifying the investment type (listed, unlisted or other; and subsidiary, joint venture, associate or other). Where there is an investment schedule, it will be the primary document of interest to the auditor. It provides a summary of the client entity's investments, which can be reconciled to the financial statements. The investment schedule will not be the only verification needed, further documents, such as share/savings/bond certificates and dividend counterfoils will also be required to support audit objectives relating to the existence and valuation assertions.

## 15.7 SUBSTANTIVE AUDIT PROGRAMME FOR INVESTMENTS

An audit programme records the specific details of tests to be performed by the auditor. The audit programme becomes a guide for the audit engagement team on the work to be performed in a particular area. As work is completed, a reference is included on the audit programme, showing the location in the audit file where details of the tests performed are included. The audit programme for any cycle will vary from entity to entity, but in **Example 15.1** below we consider the typical tests the auditor would include in the audit programme for investments. Students should note that in a real-life scenario, each test would be referenced to the location in the audit working file where the test is actually performed.

EXAMPLE 15.1: AUDIT PROGRAMME FOR INVESTMENTS[1]

| Large Company Limited | Audit Materiality | | €3,642,500 |
|---|---|---|---|
| 31 December 2018 | Performance Materiality | | €2,731,875 |
| | | Initials | Date |
| | Prepared by: | | |
| | Reviewed by: | | |
| Investments Audit Programme | | | |
| Accounting Policy | | | |
| Assess the appropriateness of the accounting policy and the accounting estimates method for this area. Ensure that the accounting policy is in accordance with accounting standards and applicable law, and that the methods used for making the accounting estimates are appropriate. | | | |

---

[1] Source: based on *Procedures for Quality Audit 2010* (© Chartered Accountants Ireland, 2010), F1 and updated by the authors in December 2017.

| **Initial Procedures** | |
| --- | --- |
| Vouch **opening balances** to prior-year working papers | Presentation and Disclosure |
| Obtain or prepare lead schedules and agree to financial statements, distinguishing between:<br>1. investments listed on a stock exchange;<br>2. other investments; and<br>3. unlisted investments. | Existence<br>Completeness<br>Rights and Obligations |
| Ensure that the schedule also correctly distinguishes subsidiaries, associated companies and joint ventures and that it provides a sufficient audit trail. Agree to nominal ledger. | |
| Obtain or prepare separate schedules of additions and disposals and vouch as appropriate, confirming that recognition has taken place in the correct period. | Existence<br>Completeness<br>Rights and Obligations |
| **Test Valuation** | |
| Obtain and disclose market value at the date of the SOFP of all listed investments.<br><br>Agree valuation of investments to an authoritative source.<br><br>Confirm that the book value/carrying value of **unlisted** investments is not stated in excess of net realisable value. Obtain supporting evidence for the carrying value by obtaining and reviewing recent financial statements for the investment. Consider permanent diminution in value of investments. | Valuation |
| **Transactions on the Statement of Comprehensive Income (SOCI)** | |
| Check with an authoritative source that all bonus and rights issues have been accounted for. | Completeness |
| Vouch profits and losses on disposals, confirming that recognition has taken place in the correct period. | Occurrence<br>Cut-off<br>Classification and Recording (accuracy) |
| Recalculate all investment revenue, vouch to supporting documentation and trace to bank receipts. | Occurrence<br>Recording (accuracy)<br>Rights and Obligations |

| Assess the investment schedule and determine if income has been generated in the period in relation to each investment, recalculate the income due to the client entity and trace to the trial balance and financial statements. | Completeness Cut-off |
|---|---|
| **Other Considerations** | |
| Examine share certificates to ensure good title (and test a sample, if appropriate). Obtain confirmation (ISA 505) from third parties holding certificates of title, details of joint venture arrangements, etc.<br>* To some degree. | Existence Rights and Obligations Valuation* |
| Ensure investments are correctly analysed between current and non-current asset investments and investments are prepared in line with IFRS 12 for disclosures regarding investments in other entities; in line with IFRS 9 for disclosures relating to financial assets; and in line with IAS 32 in relation to presentation of financial assets. Use the standards as a checklist to ensure presentation and disclosure are adequate and complete. | Presentation and Disclosure |

## 15.8 SUBSTANTIVE TESTING PROCEDURES FOR INVESTMENTS

The substantive testing audit programme in **Example 15.1** outlined the principal procedures involved in testing investments. In this section we will look at each of these in more detail:

1. Initial procedures:
   (a) Opening balances
   (b) Accuracy of schedules provided by management
   (c) Prepare the lead schedule
   (d) Analytical review.
2. Substantive testing of movements of investments in the period:
   (a) Additions and disposals
   (b) Investment income.
3. Investment balance:
   (a) Ownership and existence
   (b) Valuation.
4. Other considerations:
   (a) Investments held in foreign currencies
   (b) Cut-off
   (c) Consolidation.

## Initial Procedures

### *Opening Balances*

Before commencing further audit procedures, evidence must be obtained as to the accuracy of the opening balance of investments. The reason for this is twofold: first, it confirms that the comparative numbers in the financial statements (which must be included in the current year's financial statements) agree to the final accounts of the prior year; and, secondly, it highlights any final entries (last-minute adjusting journal entries) of the prior year not correctly carried forward, which may indicate an error in the current year's financial statements' figures. The auditor checks opening balances as follows:

- Agree the opening balances to the prior-year audit working papers and signed financial statements. This may highlight an opening balance in the current year's accounts that does not agree with the closing balance per the prior year's financial statements – in which case a change would be made to the opening balance of the current year, which would impact the closing balance of the current year. This usually arises due to final adjustments in the prior year that are not reflected in the actual accounting records (nominal and general ledgers).

- If this is the first year of the audit engagement, the auditor will still need to establish that the opening balances are materially correct, which can pose difficulties if either the client entity was exempt from audit in the prior year or a predecessor auditor carried out the audit. The audit of opening balances in such instances is discussed in detail in **Chapter 6**, Section 6.9.

### *Accuracy of Schedules*

All schedules provided by the client entity, such as the investment schedule, should be totalled and cross-totalled to ensure their mathematical accuracy. Additionally, they should be agreed to the financial statements' balances and transactions that they support. At least one item should be selected from the schedule and traced to its respective source data to validate the accuracy of the schedule before further testing is performed on it. The auditor should review the activity in the investment-related accounts to identify entries that are unusual.

### *Prepare the Lead Schedule*

Prepare or obtain from the client entity a lead schedule that agrees to the investments (financial assets) note in the financial statements. The lead schedule for investments should provide a summary of the:

- cost at the start of the year, movements in cost (including additions, disposals and **diminution in value**) and cost at the end of the period; and
- net book value (NBV) (carrying amount) of investments (financial asset) at the start and end of the year.

An example of an investments lead schedule is given at **Example 15.2** below.

EXAMPLE 15.2: INVESTMENTS LEAD SCHEDULE (LARGE COMPANY LIMITED)

| Large Company Limited 31 December 2018 | | Audit Materiality | €3,642,500 |
| | | Performance Materiality | €2,731,875 |
| | | Initials | Date |
| | Prepared by: | | |
| Investments Lead Schedule | Reviewed by: | | |
| | Investment Properties €000 | Available-for-sale Investments €000 | Total €000 |
| **Cost** | | | |
| 1 January 2018 | 100,000 | 10,500 | 110,500 |
| Additions | 0 | 23,700 | 23,700 |
| Diminution in value | (20,000) | 0 | (20,000) |
| Disposals | 0 | (1,700) | (1,700) |
| 31 December 2018 | **80,000** | **32,500** | **112,500** |
| **Provision for diminution in value** | | | |
| 1 January 2018 | 0 | 300 | 300 |
| Additions | 0 | 0 | 0 |
| Disposals | 0 | 0 | 0 |
| 31 December 2018 | **0** | **300** | **300** |
| **Net book value** | | | |
| **31 December 2018** | **80,000** | **32,200** | **112,200** |
| **31 December 2017** | 100,000 | 10,200 | 110,200 |

## Analytical Review (Initial)

The auditor will perform an analytical review (see **Chapter 5**, Section 5.4) to ensure completeness and obtain explanations for any material variances. Analytical procedures can be applied to comparisons of receipts of interest and dividends to investment balances. In assessing investments, the auditor may look to calculate such ratios as **investment yield**, which is the percentage return on an investment (calculated by the income earned from the investment divided by the investment amount) and which can be compared year on year. The **return on capital employed** (ROCE) can be calculated to include or exclude investments in associates and its related share in profits to determine the impact of the associate on ROCE. Unexpected differences should be investigated as they could indicate misstatements. An example of an analytical review the auditor might carry out is included at **Example 15.3**.

## EXAMPLE 15.3: ANALYTICAL REVIEW – INVESTMENTS
## (LARGE COMPANY LIMITED)

|  | 2018 €000 | 2017 €000 | Movement €000 |
|---|---|---|---|
| Investment properties | 80,000 | 100,000 | (20,000) |
| Available-for-sale investments | 32,200 | 10,200 | 22,000 |
| Income from investment properties | 10 | 9 | 1 |
| Income from available-for-sale investments | 210 | 209 | 1 |
| Return on investment properties | 0.01% | 0.01% | 0% |
| Return on available-for-sale investments | 0.65% | 2.05% | (1.4%) |

Neither category of investments yields a large return and the return on available-for-sale investments fell by over 50%. Discussions with management reveal that these are strategic investments and are not currently held for immediate returns. The fall in investment properties relates to a diminution in value.

## Substantive Testing of Movements of Investments in the Period

Having performed the initial procedures, now let us consider the specific audit procedures the auditor might carry out in relation to the movements of investments in the period, which essentially involves: additions and disposals; and investment income.

### Additions and Disposals

Where investments have been acquired or disposed of during the year, the auditor should:
- ensure additions and disposals of investments have been authorised and approved;
- agree the cost of investments to supporting documents (contract notes or similar documentation);
- for listed investments, check the market value to the stock exchange daily list (as reported in the *Financial Times* or other reliable pricing source);
- for unlisted investments, if the valuation has been undertaken by the directors, discuss the basis of the valuation with the client in order to ascertain whether it has been made on the basis of reasonable criteria. The auditor may consider the need to acquire the advice of an expert; and
- check the profits or losses on the disposals of a sample of investments and ensure they have been correctly posted.

### Investment Income

The auditor should perform a check of the reported investment income to the **investment schedule** to ensure that all income due has been recorded and received. The investment schedule should act as a checklist for the auditor, allowing them to ensure that all investment income expected to be received has been received. The auditor can do this by vouching dividend/interest receipts to the remittance advices accompanying each payment. Additionally, to ensure that all of the expected interest due has been received, the auditor should recalculate the interest received by multiplying the par value of the debt by the interest rate. Alternatively, the auditor could confirm the amount of the interest receipt with the issuer. Finally, with respect to investment income, the auditor should view the investees' financial statements in order to verify the dividends received.

To ensure correct classification (as either interest/dividends, or profit/loss on disposal), the auditor should also check the posting of income to the correct account in the nominal ledger.

## Investment Balance

Having obtained evidence for the management assertions related to the movements of investments, the auditor must be satisfied as to the continued existence of the investments and their valuation included in the statement of financial position.

When it comes to auditing the investment balance, the auditor is predominantly interested in validating the ownership, existence and valuation assertions. Ownership and existence are normally covered in the same tests as the source documents that tend to support existence also confirm ownership, e.g. investment certificates.

### Ownership and Existence

Where securities (tradable financial assets that are typically divided into debt and equity securities) are held at the audited entity's premises, these should be inspected and counted at the same time as the auditor performs the cash count (if applicable). The auditor should ensure that:
- the custodian of the securities is present at the time of the inspection and count;
- a receipt is signed when the securities are returned; and
- the securities are adequately safeguarded until the inspection and count are complete.

Where securities are held by the bank for safekeeping, the auditor should ensure that the bank seals the boxes on the date of the inspection and count; and obtain confirmation from the bank that there will be no access to the box (other than by the auditors) until the inspection and count have been completed to ensure that there is no adding or removing of documents during the inspection.

Where the inspection and count take place on a date other than the date of the SOFP, a reconciliation should be performed between the date of the inspection/count and the date of the SOFP. All movements between these dates should be reviewed by the auditor.

When inspecting securities, the following information should be observed and verified:
- the certificate number on the document, that it agrees to the investment schedule;
- the name of the owner, that it pertains to the entity;
- the description of the security, that it agrees to the investment schedule and is adequately disclosed in the financial statements;
- the number of shares/debentures, that it agrees to the investment schedule;
- the face value of shares/debentures, that it agrees to the investment schedule; and
- the name of the issuer.

Further procedures that should be carried out by the auditor include:
- Obtaining direct external confirmation of investments held on behalf of the client entity, and inspection of the documents of title.
- Obtaining confirmation of securities held by third parties for safekeeping, which outlines the securities held by that entity at the year end date.
- Reviewing board minutes and obtaining representations from management to ascertain whether or not investments have been pledged as collateral or security for liabilities.
- Obtaining direct external confirmation from borrowers in respect of loans made to them by the client entity.

Remember, external confirmations (see **Chapter 6**, Section 6.6), as guided by ISA 505 *External Confirmations*, must be under the direct control of the auditor and the third-party's response must be made directly to them.

### Valuation

Having obtained evidence relating to the existence and rights and obligations assertions relating to investment balances, the auditor must now obtain evidence relating to the valuation assertion. The tests of valuation in an audit of investment include:
- Consideration of whether the value of any investments should be reduced to recognise a permanent **diminution in value**. The auditor should discuss any such diminution with management and obtain independent information to support the revaluation.
- If an investment was written down in previous years and the reasons for the write-down no longer apply, the auditor should check that the write-down has been reversed.
- Where financial assets are valued on the basis of **amortised cost**, consider recalculation tests based on cash flows and the interest rate used to discount the cash flows. Consider the appropriateness of the discount factor used. Also, consider the need for adjustments due to the diminished recoverability of the asset (and other factors) that give rise to impairment.
- Audited financial statements of the entity in which the investments are held can be used to assist in the valuation of unquoted shares, debentures and similar investments.
- Check that the basis of the valuation is consistent with the basis used in previous years. If there are any changes in the basis of the valuation, the auditor should discuss this with management, and ensure that the basis of valuation is reasonable and in line with the appropriate laws and regulations.
- Check market value calculations for listed investments to published prices, e.g. prices published by the *Financial Times*, Bloomberg, Reuters, etc. or prices obtained from independent stockbrokers. For infrequently traded securities, it may be necessary to seek advice from an independent stockbroker as to the estimated market value at the date of the SOFP.
- Confirm that directors' valuations of unlisted investments are reasonable. For each valuation the auditor should obtain independent support or written representations from management to support their valuations.

- Obtain evidence about the ability of the client entity to hold the investments on a long-term basis. Written representations from management indicating its intention to hold the investments on a long-term basis must be obtained.
- Review subsequent events to identify any changes in circumstances surrounding investments that may impact on the disclosure of such investments at the year end.
- In respect of investments in the form of loans, check that repayments are being made on time and that interest payments are being made.
- Discuss with management the recoverability of loans; obtain independent confirmation from those entities to which loans have been made of the value of and repayments on the loans.

## Other Considerations

Having performed the substantive procedures relating to investment movements and investment balances, there are some other matters the auditor must consider before adequately completing the substantive procedures relating to investments. These include: investments held in foreign currencies; cut-off; and consolidation (for group audits).

### Investments Held in Foreign Currencies

For investments held in foreign currencies, the auditor must ensure that the translations into the domestic currency are correct. This can be done by independently obtaining appropriate foreign exchange rates and recalculating the translations, ensuring there is no material difference in the rates used.

### Cut-off

For a sample of additions and disposals during the period, the auditor should check that they are accounted for in the correct accounting period.

### Consolidation

The individual accounts of a parent company do not adequately present its real economic activities and financial position. As such, consolidated financial statements are required where a parent entity controls another entity (in the form of a subsidiary, associate or joint venture). Control is defined by the ability of the parent entity to direct power over the accounting and financial policies of another entity. The parent entity that controls one or more other entities must prepare consolidated financial statements in line with IFRS 10 *Consolidated Financial Statements*. This single consolidation model (IFRS 10) is supported by a suite of standards designed to address the treatment of all types of business combination. These standards include:

- IAS 27 *Separate Financial Statements*
- IAS 28 *Investments in Associates and Joint Ventures*
- IFRS 11 *Joint Arrangements*
- IFRS 12 *Disclosure of Interests in Other Entities* (disclosure requirements used to be detailed within the standard relating to the particular investment type; however, disclosure requirements are now dealt with under IFRS 12).

Part V of Ciaran Connolly's *International Financial Accounting and Reporting*, 6th Edition (Chartered Accountants Ireland, 2015), provides an excellent overview of the accounting and financial reporting of business combinations. This textbook is not intended to assist with the study of consolidations, but instead addresses how the auditor considers whether the requirements laid down in the relevant standards have been adhered to by the client entity when preparing its financial statements.

In order to review the adequacy of the presentation of the financial statements relating to consolidation, the auditor must first understand the 'control' relationship between the parent entity and the entity in which it holds an interest. Control under IFRS 10 can exist when an investor holds power over an investee, which can present itself in a number of ways. The auditor must ask, "Does the parent entity have the rights to direct the relevant activities of the investee?". If the answer is "Yes", then the parent entity must present its investment by way of consolidation (i.e. the investee is a subsidiary of the parent company). If an investee is not a subsidiary, it must be defined as either: an 'associate interest'; a 'joint arrangement'; or an 'investment interest' (i.e. a 'financial instrument' under IAS 39).

The audit of consolidated accounts is a complex task and is discussed in more detail in **Chapter 20**.

## 15.9 DISCLOSURE REQUIREMENTS

Finally, with regard to investments, the auditor will consider the adequacy of the disclosures. The auditor needs to consider the requirements of IFRS 12 *Disclosure of Interests in Other Entities* and IFRS 7 *Financial Instruments: Disclosures* to check that all disclosures are:

- complete (no investment-related disclosures are missing; the auditor can use IFRS 12 and IFRS 7 as a checklist);
- accurate (reflect the actual transactions and information relating to events surrounding investments);
- relate to events that actually occurred; and
- are properly presented (in line with applicable financial reporting standards).

The investment-related disclosure requirements are included in IFRS 12 and include requirements relating to:
"• ... information about significant judgements and assumptions it has made (and changes in those judgements and assumptions) in determining:
  (a) that it has control of another entity ...
  (b) that it has joint control of an arrangement or significant influence over another entity; and
  (c) the type of joint arrangement (ie joint operation or joint venture) when the arrangement has been structured through a separate vehicle." (IFRS 12, para 7);
- information about interests in subsidiaries sufficient to enable the users of consolidated financial statements to, for example, understand the composition of the group (IFRS 12, para 10);

- information about interests in unconsolidated subsidiaries (where exceptions to consolidation are invoked) (IFRS 12, para 19A);
- information about interests in joint arrangements and associates, such as the nature, extent and financial effects of such interests (IFRS 12, para 20);
- significance of financial instruments (IFRS 7);
- information about hedge accounting (IFRS 7); and
- nature and extent of exposure to risks arising from financial instruments (IFRS 7).

The auditor will also need to consider the requirements of ISA 550 *Related Parties*, which is covered in more detail in **Chapter 18**.

## 15.10 CONCLUSION

Once the auditor has completed their substantive testing, they must consider whether **sufficient appropriate audit evidence** has been obtained for the investment balances and transactions, which give the appropriate level of assurance required over the assertions stated at the outset.

The auditor must also consider if the testing performed has appropriately addressed any key risks identified by the auditor around investments, and reduced the risk of material misstatement to a suitably low level.

When testing the area of investments, the auditor is most concerned with the valuation assertion due to the risk associated with **diminution in value**.

The auditor must consider the impact of their testing on investments on the **audit opinion**. This is achieved by considering whether any misstatements found, either individually or in aggregate (when combined with other misstatements detected throughout the audit), will result in the financial statements being materially misstated. As such, all misstatements found are taken to the auditor's errors schedule for consideration at the audit completion stage (discussed in detail in **Chapter 18**). The auditor's report on financial statements is considered in detail in **Chapter 19**.

Summary of Learning Objectives

**Learning Objective 1** Understand what is included in the audit of investments.

Investment balances constitute ownership of securities issued by other entities and these may be in the form of certificates of deposit, shares, debentures or government bonds. Such securities represent financial assets in the hands of the entity that owns them. Investments can also take the form of subsidiary investments, investments in associates and joint ventures or investment interests.

**Learning Objective 2** Be able to identify the risks and audit objectives applicable to investments.

The primary risks associated with investments relate to:
- diminution in value;
- reliability of investment recording system;
- complications surrounding consolidation and other complex accounting treatments; and
- validating fair value (where the investment is not listed).

The auditor's objectives are to validate: the occurrence and completeness of investment income, profit and losses; the existence and completeness of investments at the date of the SOFP; the rights and obligations of the client entity with regard to investment income, profit and losses as well as investment balances at the date of the SOFP; the accurate classification, recording and cut-off of investment income, profit and losses and valuation of investments at the date of the SOFP; and the accurate and adequate presentation and disclosure of investments in the financial statements in line with applicable financial reporting standards.

**Learning Objective 3** Be able to determine an appropriate audit strategy for investments, taking into consideration the specific risks and audit objectives (management assertions).

The auditor seeks to ensure that the investment balances exist and are accurate; that all investment balances are included and appropriately classified, presented and disclosed on the statement of financial position.

**Learning Objective 4** Be able to develop an audit programme that addresses all the audit objectives (management assertions) for investments.

The volume of transactions is generally low and so the auditor will usually take a focused substantive approach and not test the client entity's internal control system. This will not be the case where the investment requires consolidation, which is considered in more detail in **Chapter 20**.

**Learning Objective 5** Be able to describe and apply specific substantive testing procedures relating to the audit of investments.

Documents of interest to the auditor could include:
- investment schedules;
- share certificates;
- saving certificates; and
- bond certificates.

The main audit procedures surrounding investments relate to:
- confirming the existence of investments to authoritative sources;
- confirming the valuation of investments to authoritative sources;
- considering the requirement for consolidation; and
- considering permanent diminution in value.

**Learning Objective 6** Understand the role CAATs can play when auditing investments.

The auditor may use a combination of audit software, data analysis tools and other applications, such as Excel, when auditing the area of investments.

**Learning Objective 7**  Understand the auditor's approach relating to the disclosures of investments.

The auditor has a wide range of disclosure requirements to consider relating to investments and so should dedicate sufficient time to this area where significant investments are held. The aim is to check that disclosures are complete, accurate, pertain to the entity and that the financial statements are adequately presented in line with applicable international reporting standards.

## QUESTIONS

### Self-test Questions

15.1  List the different types of investment an entity might hold.

15.2  What valuation method should be used for trade investments?

15.3  What type of documentation might the auditor obtain as audit evidence when testing investments?

15.4  Identify the main steps an auditor adopts in order to assess the risk of a material misstatement in the investments balance.

### Review Questions

(See Suggested Solutions to Review Questions in **Appendix C**.)

### Question 15.1

Meridian Ltd is a large company with a number of financial investments in entities domestically and internationally. You have been assigned to the investments section of the audit engagement and a member of the client entity's finance team has provided you with the following schedule.

| Name of Investment | Investment €000 | Market Value €000 |
|---|---|---|
| Rainbow | 1,243 | 1,721 |
| Lilly | 936 | 1,321 |
| Golden | 1,654 | 1,320 |
| Yellow | 1,111 | 300 |
| Grenadier | 1,879 | 2,012 |
| **Total investments** | **6,823** | **6,674** |

The following information has also been provided:
• the investment in Rainbow was acquired during the year, and the Yellow investment was sold before the year end for €300,000;

- the investments' total balance in the draft financial statements is €6,823,000. Meridian Ltd has a policy of recognising its investments at cost with any gains/losses only recognised on disposal.

**Requirement**

(a) Describe the general and specific audit work you would plan in order to be able to form an opinion on the investment account balance of Meridian.

(b) From the information above, list the potential audit issues in Meridian and state the additional audit work that you would perform.

(c) Assuming the information included in the schedule is correct and the client has no further information to provide, outline the adjustments to the investment balance that you would recommend to your audit partner.

*Question 15.2*

You have been assigned to the audit of Wilcox Ltd, a successful property development company. The audit area for which you will have direct responsibility is that of current assets. Your audit manager has informed you that the prior-year audit file did not contain a detailed audit plan for current assets, but that he would like one prepared prior to the commencement of the current year's audit. You note from the prior-year audit file that the audit materiality figure was €100,000 and that the current assets at the previous year end were made up as follows:

|                               | **€000** |
|-------------------------------|----------|
| Trade investments (listed)    | 500      |
| Trade investments (unlisted)  | 800      |
| Prepayments                   | 100      |
| Bank balances                 | 950      |
| Cash balances                 | 100      |
|                               | **2,450** |

**Requirement** Set out the procedures that you would adopt in order to obtain the required assurance concerning the standard audit objectives for the current assets detailed above. You should assume that the current asset balances for the current year are expected to be at a similar level to those of the prior year.

# 16

# THE AUDIT OF PURCHASES AND PAYABLES

## LEARNING OBJECTIVES

Having studied this chapter on the audit of purchases and payables you should:
1.  understand what is included in the audit of purchases, payables and payroll;
2.  be able to identify the risks and audit objectives (management assertions) applicable to purchases, payables and payroll;
3.  be able to determine an appropriate audit strategy for purchases, payables and payroll, taking into consideration the specific risks and audit objectives (management assertions);
4.  be able to develop an audit programme that addresses all the audit objectives (assertions) for purchases, payables and payroll;
5.  be able to describe and apply specific substantive testing procedures relating to the audit of purchases, payables and payroll;
6.  understand the role CAATs can play when auditing purchases and payables; and
7.  understand the auditor's approach relating to the disclosures of purchases and payables.

## CHECKLIST OF RELEVANT STANDARDS

The relevant standards, in both the RoI and the UK/NI, covered in this chapter are:
- ISA 315 *Identifying and Assessing the Risks of Material Misstatement through Understanding the Entity and its Environment*
- ISA 330 *The Auditor's Responses to Assessed Risks*
- ISA 500 *Audit Evidence*
- ISA 505 *External Confirmations*
- ISA 510 *Initial Audit Engagements – Opening Balances*
- ISA 520 *Analytical Procedures*
- ISA 530 *Audit Sampling*
- IAS 1 *Presentation of Financial Statements*
- IAS 37 *Provisions, Contingent Liabilities and Contingent Assets*

Note, in general when referring to ISAs, it should be understood as referring to the UK and Ireland versions, unless otherwise specified as either ISA (UK) or ISA (Ireland). See the Introduction for an extant list of auditing standards for the RoI and the UK/NI.

## KEY TERMS AND DEFINITIONS FOR THIS CHAPTER

**Accrued Liability** Expenses for goods or services received that have not yet been paid for and for which no invoice has been received from the supplier.

**Aged Payables Listing** A full list of individual supplier balances that can be reconciled to the payables figure in the financial statements and analysed to assess the existence of supplier balances. It shows each supplier by reference to the length of time the payable balance has existed (usually broken down into payable within 30 days, 60 days, 90 days, and greater than 90 days).

**Earnings Management** The use of certain techniques to produce financial statements that portray a desired (rather than **true and fair**) picture of an entity's statement of comprehensive income.

**Search for Unrecorded Liabilities** Techniques used by the auditor to identify understatement of liabilities.

**Supplier Reconciliation** When a client entity reconciles the balance on its supplier's statement to the supplier's balance showing on its ledger.

## 16.1 INTRODUCTION

The objective of substantive testing is to validate the transactions, balances and disclosures at the assertion level in response to identified risks (inherent, control and detection risks as discussed in **Chapters 7** and **8**). The auditor commences substantive testing by focusing on the risk of material misstatement within the transactions and balances being tested, and then identifying the assertions impacted by these risks and then identifying substantive audit procedures that will best test the existence of material misstatement driven by the identified risks.

**Sections 16.2–16.8** outline the requirements of the international accounting standards with respect to the recording of purchases and payables. They consider how the auditor:

- identifies audit risks and audit objectives (management assertions) for purchases and payables;
- develops an audit plan for purchases and payables and refines this into an audit programme;
- designs specific tests associated with purchases and payables; and
- ensures adequate presentation and disclosure in the financial statements relating to purchases and payables.

Throughout the chapter it is highlighted where CAATs can be used by the auditor in assisting with ensuring the effective and efficient audit of the area of purchases, payables and payroll.

Finally, in **Section 16.9** we discuss the auditor's approach when auditing the reasonableness of disclosures relating to purchases and payables.

## 16.2 WHAT ARE PURCHASES AND PAYABLES?

Purchases are the goods and services obtained by an entity in the course of running its operations, and include all expense-type items relating to inventory, light and heat, rent, wages and salaries, consultancy expenses, and so on. Every business incurs costs in the process of generating goods and services, which it subsequently sells to its customers. For example, an entity involved in the manufacture of shoes will have to purchase leather in order to make shoes; and might employ the services of an advertising agency to promote its finished products. When such transactions are not settled immediately by cash payments, they give rise to **trade payables**. Such trade payables meet the definition of liabilities as set out in IAS 37 *Provisions, Contingent Liabilities and Contingent Assets,* which at paragraph 10 states:

"A liability is a present obligation of the entity arising from past events, the settlement of which is expected to result in an outflow from the entity of resources embodying economic benefits."

It is the auditor's duty to gain assurance that both purchases and trade payables have been reflected appropriately in the company's year-end financial statements. Payables include both trade payables (amount owed to suppliers supported by invoices) and accruals, which represent a recognition of a liability where an invoice has not yet been received.

In simple terms, all goods and services that a company has received during the financial year should be recorded within its financial statements as purchases in the statement of comprehensive income. Where amounts due to suppliers relating to purchases have not been settled at the year end, they should be recorded as **liabilities** in the statement of financial position. These are included either within trade payables, where an invoice has been received; or within accruals when the goods or services have been received but the invoice was not received from the supplier before the year end.

## 16.3  RISKS ASSOCIATED WITH PURCHASES AND PAYABLES

In **Chapter 7** we discussed the topic of risk and considered how the auditor should go about detecting risks. We also discussed how the auditor should consider these risks when designing the nature, timing and extent of further audit procedures relative to each financial cycle. As such, before developing the audit plan, the auditor needs to consider a number of risks that may be associated with purchases and payables. Risks associated with purchases and payables can include:

- inappropriate/fraudulent payments recorded in the purchases ledger due to weaknesses in internal controls in the purchases system (see **Chapter 8** for a full discussion of internal controls);
- misstatement of year-end payables and accruals due to incorrect **cut-off** procedures being applied (i.e. transactions occurring pre-year end not being recorded until the following period and, conversely, transactions occurring post-year end being incorrectly recorded in the current period);
- understatement of year-end payables and accruals due to failure to record all outstanding liabilities because of fraud or error;
- purchases not incurred for the purpose of the client entity's business – a lack of **segregation of duties** can pose a real risk that bogus purchases will be made. For example, an employee may hire a company to install a kitchen in their house and have it invoiced to the client entity with the description 'office shelving'. Without the requirement for approval of a purchase order (PO) and a goods receipt by someone independent of the requisitioner, it is entirely possible that an invoice for an activity that does not relate to the client entity is paid;
- fictitious supplier accounts represent a significant risk where there are insufficient controls and segregation of duties around suppliers' **master data.** Supplier accounts may be added to the master data of the client entity and fictitious invoices and payments made against that 'supplier'.

The auditor must consider the client entity's internal controls in determining how much substantive testing should be carried out on purchases and payables. The results of **inherent risk** and **control risk** assessments will help to establish the extent of substantive testing required.

## 16.4  AUDIT OBJECTIVES/MANAGEMENT ASSERTIONS FOR PURCHASES AND PAYABLES

Having established the risks associated with purchases and payables, the auditor must now ascertain the related audit objectives (management assertions). As discussed in **Chapter 6**, it is necessary for the auditor to obtain **sufficient appropriate audit evidence** to satisfy all of the audit objectives and to eliminate the possibility of any of the risks outlined above going undetected. The auditor must design tests to address these assertions and thereby address the identified risks. In **Chapter 4** we introduced audit objectives (management assertions) and explained their generic meanings, before reintroducing the topic throughout **Chapter 8**, making management assertions specific to each financial cycle. **Table 16.1** below recaps the audit objectives as they relate to purchases and payables.

TABLE 16.1: PURCHASES AND PAYABLES – AUDIT OBJECTIVES

| Management Assertion/Audit Objective | Control Objective for Transaction Class | Control Objective for Account Balance |
|---|---|---|
| | **Purchases and Payroll Expenses** | **Payables and Payroll Accruals** |
| **Existence or Occurrence** | • Recorded purchases transactions represent goods and services received.<br>• Recorded payment transactions represent payments made to suppliers and payables.<br>• Recorded payroll expenses relate to employee services received. | • Recorded trade payables represent amounts owed by the entity at the date of the SOFP.<br>• Accrued payroll liability balances represent amounts owed at the date of the SOFP. |
| **Completeness** | • All purchases/payment transactions that occurred have been recorded.<br>• Payroll expenses include all such expenses incurred. | • Trade payables include all amounts owed by the entity to suppliers of goods and services at the date of the SOFP.<br>• Accrued payroll liabilities include all amounts in respect of payroll and payroll deductions at the date of the SOFP. |
| **Rights and Obligations** | Recorded purchases and payroll transactions represent the liabilities of the entity. | Trade payables and accrued payroll liabilities are liabilities of the entity at the date of the SOFP. |
| **Classification/ Recording (accuracy) or Valuation** | Purchases/payment transactions and payroll transactions are correctly recorded in the accounting systems. | • Trade payables and accrued payroll liabilities are stated at the correct amount owed.<br>• Related expense balances conform with applicable accounting standards. |
| **Cut-off** | All purchases/payment and payroll transactions are recorded in the correct accounting period. | |
| **Presentation and Disclosure** | The details of purchases/ payments and payroll transactions support their presentation in the financial statements, including their classification and disclosure. | • Trade payables, accrued payroll liabilities and related expenses are properly identified and classified in the financial statements.<br>• Disclosures pertaining to commitments, contingent liabilities and related party payables are adequate. |

Having discussed the objectives of the auditor with regard to purchases and payables, we now consider how the auditor addresses these objectives through **substantive testing**.

## 16.5  DEVELOPING THE AUDIT PLAN FOR PURCHASES AND PAYABLES

Before the audit of purchases and payables is undertaken, an assessment of the audit risk must be completed. As discussed in detail in **Chapter 7**, audit risk is made up of three components: inherent risk; control risk; and detection risk. We will consider these components specifically as they relate to purchases and payables.

In **Chapter 8** we discussed whether or not controls around purchases and payables should be tested. Remember: where the purchases and payables balances are not material to the financial statements, limited controls testing and substantive testing will be performed. However, purchases and payables are usually a material figure and transactions tend to be high in volume. For this reason the auditor usually takes a controls approach when testing this area in order to reduce the level of detailed substantive testing.

When developing the audit plan relating to purchases and payables, a few general rules can be applied:
• Where the purchases figure and payables balance are not material to the financial statements, limited controls testing and substantive testing will be performed.
• Where a significant risk has been identified in relation to the purchases and payables cycle, the level of substantive testing to be performed will be higher.
• Where a strong control environment has been identified, the level of substantive testing to be performed will be much lower; where a weak control environment has been identified, more substantive testing will be required.

Generally, a controls testing approach is the most productive (effective and efficient) approach when testing the area of purchases and payables. Remember: as detailed in **Chapter 8**, Section 8.6, the auditor can decide to take a controls approach in relation to only certain assertions and then perform focused substantive testing on the other assertions. With respect to the completeness assertion, the auditor will quite often choose to take a wholly substantive approach due to the associated risks, i.e. focused substantive procedures (substantive tests of details) will be performed around the search for unrecorded liabilities.

## 16.6  AUDIT TRAIL FOR PURCHASES AND PAYABLES

To appreciate the role of the auditor in validating transactions, classes of transactions or balances at the assertion level it is important to first understand the audit trail associated with the relevant cycle. **Figure 16.1** below outlines an example of the audit trail the auditor might follow when validating the various management assertions associated with purchases and payables.

## FIGURE 16.1: PURCHASES AND PAYABLES AUDIT TRAIL

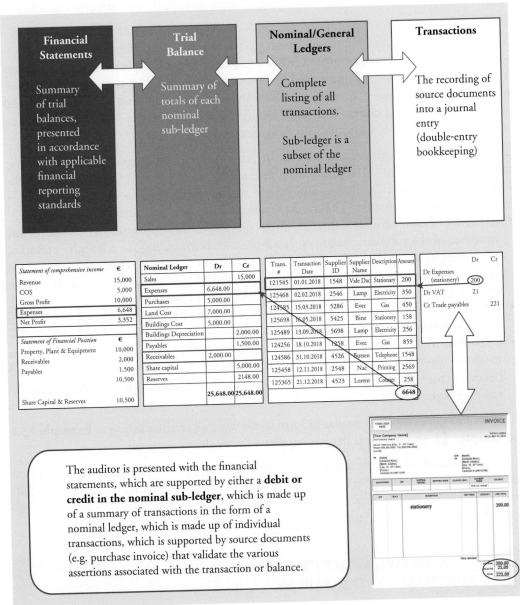

It is essential that the **direction** of the test is appropriate to the assertion being tested. So, when testing for occurrence/existence, the auditor will start with the financial statements and trace back through the trial balance, etc. to the source documents. However, when testing for completeness the auditor will always start with the source documents and trace upwards to the financial statements. Whatever the direction of the test, the source document data is used to validate whether the transaction has been appropriately recorded/valued and that it proves the entity's rights and obligations assertion over the transaction/balance. Sometimes a blend of source documents will be required to validate all assertions, while in other instances a single source document will validate a number of assertions.

The most obvious source document relating to purchases is the purchase invoice, which is supported by a goods receipt note (GRN), a purchase order (PO) and in some instances a purchase requisition. In **Figure 16.1** the invoice shows that 100 pens were purchased, which should be vouched to a signed GRN showing that 100 pens were delivered and accepted by the client entity. The GRN should be vouched to the PO and/or purchase requisition, which have authorised the purchase and cost.

The primary document of interest relating to payables is the **aged payables listing**, which is a full list of all individual supplier balances that exist at the date of the statement of financial position, and which can be reconciled to the payables figure in the financial statements. The aged payables listing also provides the auditor with:

- an ageing of each supplier's amount due – this allows the auditor to better analyse the existence of the suppliers' balances. If a balance is outstanding for a lengthy period of time without proceedings for collection, it may be an indication either that it does not exist or that it is genuine but the client entity has liquidity problems, i.e. the client entity might be delaying payment because it does not have the cash;
- a list from which to select a sample to perform substantive tests of details or perform reviews on **supplier reconciliations**; and
- if received in Excel (or a similar format), the list can be manipulated by the auditor to show top-value supplier balances, debit balances, round-sum balances and nil balances (nil balances are of interest in the search for unrecorded liabilities), which may highlight risks.

The aged payables listing is similar in form to the aged receivables listing at **Example 13.1** in **Chapter 13**, except that it depicts suppliers rather than customers.

Other documents of interest to the auditor will be the supplier reconciliations – the client entity's tracing of the supplier's balance on its statement to the balance on the corresponding client entity's ledger. This reconciliation supports the completeness, existence and valuation assertion assertions (audit objectives).

## 16.7 SUBSTANTIVE AUDIT PROGRAMME FOR PURCHASES AND PAYABLES

An audit programme records the specific details of tests to be performed by the auditor. It becomes a guide to the **audit engagement team** on the work to be performed in a particular area. As work is completed, a reference is included on the audit programme, showing the location in the audit file where details of the tests performed are included. While the audit programme for any cycle will vary from entity to entity, in **Example 16.1** below we consider the typical tests the auditor would include in the audit programme for purchases and payables. Students should note that in a real-life scenario, each test would be referenced to the location in the audit working file where the test is actually performed.

EXAMPLE 16.1: AUDIT PROGRAMME FOR PURCHASES AND
PAYABLES AND PAYROLL (LARGE COMPANY LIMITED)[1]

| Large Company Limited<br>31 December 2018 | Audit Materiality | | €3,642,500 |
|---|---|---|---|
| | Performance Materiality | | €2,731,875 |
| | | Initials | Date |
| | Prepared by: | | |
| | Reviewed by: | | |
| **Purchases and Payables and Payroll Audit Programme** | | | |
| **Accounting Policy** | | | |
| Assess the appropriateness of the accounting policy and the accounting estimates method for this area. Ensure that the accounting policy is in accordance with accounting standards and applicable law, and that the methods used for making the accounting estimates are appropriate. | Occurrence/ Existence Completeness Rights and Obligations Recording (accuracy) Classification | | |
| **Initial Procedures** | | | |
| Vouch opening balances to prior-year working papers. | Recording Presentation and Disclosure | | |
| Obtain or prepare lead schedules showing:<br><br>• amounts falling due within one year and after more than one year in the SOFP,<br>• cost of sales and expenses in the SOCI,<br>• payroll in the SOCI,<br><br>and prepare a commentary explaining the composition of transactions and balances, comparing them with prior periods and auditor expectations. | Occurrence/ Existence Completeness Rights and Obligations Recording (accuracy) Classification | | |
| Obtain a copy of the purchases and payroll general ledger, payables sub-ledger and agree cost of sales and other expenses to the trial balance and on into the financial statements (lead schedule).<br>Check accuracy of the document and review its contents for any unusual items. (e.g. debit balances). | Existence Completeness Recording (accuracy) | | |

---

[1] Source: Based on *Procedures for Quality Audit 2010* (© Chartered Accountants Ireland, 2010) and updated by the authors December 2017.

| Purchases Transactions | |
| --- | --- |
| **Tests of Details** | |
| • Select a sample of transactions from the purchases nominal ledger and trace them to the supplier invoice, GRN and PO (and/or purchase requisition if applicable) | Occurrence<br>Rights and Obligations<br>Recording (accuracy)<br>Classification |
| • Select a sample of purchase order transactions and trace to their related GRN, supplier invoice and posting to the purchases ledger that has been agreed to the trial balance and financial statements. | Completeness<br>Rights and Obligations<br>Recording (accuracy)<br>Classification |
| Alternatively, where the controls environment has been tested as effective, perform substantive analytical procedure on purchases, which usually takes the form of a comparison of costs to prior year (taking into consideration any expected deviations). If differences are within a tolerable threshold then no further procedures are required. | Occurrence<br>Completeness<br>Rights and Obligations<br>Recording (accuracy)<br>Classification |
| **Payables Balance** | |
| Obtain a copy of the aged payables listing, or from the payables sub-ledger prepare one using CAATs.<br>1. Select a sample from the payables listing and compare with supplier statements received by the client entity (or circularise the suppliers to obtain a statement showing all amounts outstanding from the client entity at the year end date).<br>2. Where differences are identified, determine if they are timing differences or represent something under- or over-stated by the client.<br>3. Query reconciling items with the client entity.<br><br>* Partially covers completeness assertion, in that it confirms for the recorded suppliers that all invoices are recorded but does not confirm that all suppliers are included (due to direction of the test). | Existence<br>Rights and Obligations<br>Valuation<br>Classification<br>Completeness* |
| Alternatively, obtain a copy of the aged payables listing, select a sample from the payables listing and trace the individual invoices outstanding to a copy of the invoice and then vouch the details to a signed GRN, PO (and/or purchase requisition where applicable).<br><br>* Shows original transaction was correctly recorded but not necessarily that it is correctly valued (e.g. it may have incurred interest since original recording due to late payment for example. | Existence<br>Rights and obligations<br>Recording (accuracy)* |
| **Search for Unrecorded Liabilities** | |
| Review post-period-end cash book, bank payments, purchase invoices and vouchers to identify any un-provided payables and/or accruals. | Completeness<br>Valuation<br>Rights and Obligations |

| | |
|---|---|
| Review open purchase orders report and query aged items. Review goods received and invoices not received, report and query any aged items. | Completeness Valuation Rights and Obligations |
| For the period after the SOFP date to the end of the fieldwork, scrutinise the following for payables omitted:<br>• purchase day book or invoice listing;<br>• invoices in the process of being passed for payment;<br>• cash book;<br>• correspondence with suppliers and inquire of the client entity's staff. | Completeness Valuation Rights and Obligations |
| Test cut-off procedures to ensure a liability is recorded for all inventory items received on credit (whether or not an invoice has been received). | Cut-off |
| **Other Considerations** | |
| **Sale or Return**<br>Inquire into correct treatment of inventory held on sale or return. | Occurrence Completeness |
| **Directors' Loans and Shareholders' Loans**<br>Prepare detailed schedules of movements on directors' loan accounts and shareholders' loan accounts. Obtain directors'/shareholders' own written confirmation of movements and balances. | Existence Presentation and Disclosure |
| **VAT (input credits and balance)**<br>1. Review VAT returns and reconcile a sample to the accounting records.<br>2. Test-check recording of VAT when testing sales and purchases.<br>3. Test to ensure VAT returns are completed correctly and accurately and submitted in a timely manner. Review most recent return to ascertain whether returns are up to date.<br>4. Consider whether any interest or penalties may be due and that they have been correctly recorded.<br>5. Review any correspondence with customs and excise authorities.<br>6. Reconcile the period-end VAT figure.<br>7. Test for payment or receipt of the balance post-period end.<br>8. Agree revenue payments/refunds to the relevant tax authority. | Occurrence/ Existence Completeness Rights and Obligations Recording (accuracy)/Valuation |
| **Accruals (charges to SOCI and balance in SOFP)**<br>1. Obtain or prepare a schedule of accruals.<br>2. Compare with previous year's schedule.<br>3. Vouch material items.<br>4. Consider the reasonableness of other items.<br>5. Vouch any material other payables to supporting documentation. | Occurrence/ Existence Completeness Rights and Obligations Recording (accuracy)/Valuation |

| | |
|---|---|
| **Inter-company balances**<br>Extract as necessary and agree group or inter-company balances to the other party's accounts, or obtain written confirmation of agreement between the companies.<br>Confirm that group or inter-company balances shown as due after more than one year are subject to at least 12 months' notice of repayment. | Valuation<br>Classification<br>Presentation and Disclosure<br>Recording (accuracy) |
| **Capital commitments**<br>Identify, schedule and check disclosure of capital commitments not provided for and which:<br>1. are contracted for; and<br>2. are committed but not contracted. (See also the PPE Audit Programme, in **Example 11.1** in Chapter 11). | Presentation and Disclosure |
| **Payroll** | |
| **Test of Details**<br>1. Obtain the payroll nominal listing and select a sample of payroll weeks or months to substantiate.<br>2. Trace and vouch the journals from the nominal listing to the payroll **control reports**, and in turn trace the figures from the payroll control reports to the payroll **'Gross to Net'**.<br>3. From the payroll gross to net select a number of employees and vouch the variable elements making up the gross payroll to supporting documentation (e.g. select number of hours paid to clock in reports).<br>4. Vouch rate of pay per hour or salary to employee contract from human resources.<br>Recalculate the payroll taxes and vouch other deductions to supporting documentation (e.g. union subscriptions).<br>5. Trace the gross amount paid to the bank. | Occurrence<br>Rights and Obligations<br>Recording (accuracy)<br>Classification |
| **Substantive Analytical Procedures**<br>If the client entity's controls surrounding payroll have been proven by the auditor to be strong, then apply substantive analytical procedures by calculating the expected payroll cost of the entity and comparing to its actual payroll costs. Substantiate all figures used to prepare the substantive analytical review. Calculate a tolerance threshold and if the difference between the expectation and the actual amount are within the threshold no further procedures are required. | Occurrence<br>Completeness<br>Rights and Obligations<br>Recording (accuracy)<br>Classification |
| **Employee Benefits**<br>Recalculate a sample of employee benefits validating to source documents (e.g. bonuses, share options, commissions). | Occurrence<br>Rights and Obligations<br>Recording (accuracy)<br>Classification |

| | |
|---|---|
| **Non-standard Payments Post-year End**<br>Review non-standard payments made to employees in January and determine to which period the payment relates. Ensure an accrual was made for payments relating to the period up to the year end. | Completeness<br>Recording (accuracy)<br>Classification |
| **Cut-off**<br>Consider the timing of preparation and payment of the payroll to ensure adequate accrual of payrolls not yet calculated and paid by year end. | Cut-off |
| **IAS 19 *Employee Benefits***<br>Consider the requirements of IAS 19 to ensure all necessary accruals, presentation and disclosures are adequate. | Existence<br>Completeness<br>Rights and Obligations<br>Recording<br>Classification |
| **Disclosure Requirements**<br>Review disclosures made in relation to directors' emoluments ensuring they are in line with reporting standards and legislation (RoI: CA 2014, Chapter 6, section 305, Disclosure of directors' remuneration and transactions; and UK: CA 2006, Chapter 4, sections 412 and 413, Information about directors' benefits). | Presentation and Disclosure |

## 16.8 SUBSTANTIVE TESTING PROCEDURES FOR PURCHASES AND PAYABLES

The substantive testing audit programme in **Example 16.1** outlined the principal procedures involved in testing purchases and payables and payroll. In this section we will look at each of these in more detail:

1. Initial procedures:
    (a) Opening balances
    (b) Accuracy of schedules provided by management
    (c) Prepare the lead schedules
    (d) Analytical review.
2. Purchases transactions:
    (a) Tests of details
    (b) Substantive analytical procedures.
3. Payables balance:
    (a) Supplier reconciliations
    (b) Search for unrecorded liabilities
4. Other considerations:
    (a) Sale or return
    (b) VAT (input credits and balance)

    (c)  Accruals (charges to SOCI and balance in SOFP)
    (d)  Inter-company balances
    (e)  Provisions.
5.  Payroll transactions.

## Initial Procedures

### *Opening Balances*

Before commencing further audit procedures, the auditor must obtain evidence as to the accuracy of the opening payables balance. The reason for this is twofold:
1.  it confirms that the comparative numbers in the financial statements (which must be included in the current year's financial statements) agree to the final accounts of the prior year; and
2.  it highlights any final entries (last-minute adjusting journals) of the prior year not correctly carried forward, which may indicate an error in the current year's financial statements' figures.

The auditor checks opening balances as follows:
- Agree the opening balances to the prior-year audit working papers and signed financial statements. This may highlight an opening balance in the current year's accounts that does not agree to the closing balance per the prior year's financial statements – in which case a change would be made to the opening balance of the current year, which would impact on the closing balance of the current year. This usually arises due to final adjustments in the prior year that are not reflected in the actual accounts (nominal and general ledgers).
- If this is the first year of the audit engagement, the auditor will still need to establish that the opening balances are materially correct, which can pose a difficulty if either the client entity was exempt from audit in the prior year or a predecessor auditor carried out the audit. The audit of opening balances in such instances is discussed in detail in **Chapter 6**, Section 6.9.

### *Accuracy of Schedules*

The auditor should obtain the detailed **aged payables listing** and gain comfort over its accuracy by selecting at least one item and tracing it to its respective source data for validation before further testing is performed on it. The following should then be performed:
- agree the balance per the aged payables listing to the balance per the trial balance and the balance per the statement of financial position. Reconciling items should be investigated by the auditor in order to obtain the desired level of assurance and agree to supporting documentation;
- review the aged payables listing for any unusual balances, such as large balances, debit balances, old balances, nil balances and round-sum balances;
- test the reliability of the aged payables listing by selecting one supplier and agreeing ageing to the original invoices' dates.

## *Prepare the Lead Schedules*

The **lead schedule** can be used to summarise all trade and other payables balances for the prior year as well as the current year. This allows the auditor to ensure that they obtain evidence for all balances during the audit, thus providing some control over the performance of audit procedures. Typical lead schedules for payables and purchases are given below in **Example 16.2** and **Example 16.3**.

### EXAMPLE 16.2: PAYABLES LEAD SCHEDULE (LARGE COMPANY LIMITED)[2]

| Large Company Limited | Audit Materiality | | €3,642,500 |
|---|---|---|---|
| 31 December 2018 | Performance Materiality | | €2,731,875 |
| | | Initials | Date |
| | Prepared by: | | |
| Payables Lead Schedule | Reviewed by: | | |

| | 31/12/2018 €000 | 31/12/2017 €000 |
|---|---|---|
| Payables – Amounts falling due within one year | | |
| Bank and other loans (**tested in Bank and Cash Lead Schedule**) | 4,250 | 9,650 |
| Obligations under finance leases and hire-purchase contracts (**tested under PPE**) | 2,500 | 4,000 |
| Derivative financial instruments | 120 | 80 |
| Trade payables | 109,320 | 114,650 |
| Tax payables | 2,690 | 2,740 |
| Other payables | 16,300 | 10,730 |
| Accruals and deferred income | 500 | 750 |
| | 135,680 | 142,600 |
| **Note:** amounts included in trade payables where suppliers claim reservation of title. | 20,000 | 21,000 |
| **Note:** all payables greater than one year for Large Company Limited relate to areas captured under other lead schedules, such as bank and cash and investments. | | |

---

[2] Source: based on *Procedures for Quality Audit 2010* (© Chartered Accountants Ireland, 2010), J- and updated by the authors in December 2017

EXAMPLE 16.3: PURCHASES LEAD SCHEDULE (LARGE COMPANY LIMITED)

| Large Company Limited 31 December 2018 | Audit Materiality: | | €3,642,500 |
|---|---|---|---|
| | Performance Materiality: | | €2,731,875 |
| | | Initials | Date |
| | Prepared by: | | |
| Payables Lead Schedule | Reviewed by: | | |

| | 31/12/2018 €000 | 31/12/2017 €000 |
|---|---|---|
| Cost of sales | 410,250 | 120,800 |
| Distribution costs | 23,000 | 20,000 |
| Administration expenses | 35,000 | 34,000 |

## Analytical Review

An analytical review (see **Chapter 5**, Section 5.4) is usually performed at the start of substantive testing in each audit area. Calculating ratios and analysing results against industry information, prior-year results, budgets, etc. allows the auditor to understand the nature of the movements during the year and to make comparisons against norms. It therefore provides the auditor with additional insights into the client entity and the industry it operates in, and better prepares them for the audit programme.

**Examples 16.4** and **16.5** below show the types of ratio and comparison the auditor might perform in relation to trade payables and purchases, including the commentary that might be made. These ratios include:

- trade payables days – showing the average number of days it takes the entity to pay its suppliers;
- gross margin – shows gross profit as a percentage of revenue to determine if revenue and costs are rising or falling at the same rate;
- operating costs as a percentage of sales – shows their relative size to sales, but also gives a guide with regard to reasonableness when compared with prior year.

Having carried out the initial procedures, the auditor must commence testing of movements during the period (i.e. the purchases figures in the statement of comprehensive income and payments made throughout the period) and balances (i.e. payables and accruals balances). We will first consider the substantive testing of the transaction classes relating to purchases.

EXAMPLE 16.4: ANALYTICAL REVIEW – PAYABLES (LARGE COMPANY LIMITED)

| Large Company Limited 31 December 2018 | Audit Materiality | | €3,642,500 |
|---|---|---|---|
| | Performance Materiality | | €2,731,875 |
| | | Initials | Date |
| | Prepared by: | | |
| | Reviewed by: | | |

**Payables Analytical Review**

| | 31/12/2018 €000 | 31/12/2017 €000 | Change €000 | % |
|---|---|---|---|---|
| Bank and other loan notes | 4,250 | 9,650 | (5,400) | (56) |
| Obligations under finance leases and HP contracts | 2,500 | 4,000 | (1,500) | (38) |
| Derivative financial instruments | 120 | 80 | 40 | 50 |
| Trade payables | 109,320 | 114,650 | (5,330) | (5) |
| Tax payables | 2,690 | 2,740 | (50) | (2) |
| Other payables | 16,300 | 10,730 | 5,570 | 52 |
| Accruals and deferred income | 500 | 750 | (250) | (33) |
| | 135,680 | 142,600 | (6,920) | (4.9) |

*Note:* bank loans are tested under bank and cash testing area. Obligations under finance leases and HP contracts are considered under non-current fixed assets.

**Commentary on movement following investigation**

The rent accrual has been omitted, resulting in the 33% decrease in accruals (this has been taken to the errors schedule). Other payables include a €5 million settlement provision set aside for a legal case won by a customer in late December 2018 and payable by 31 January 2019; this represents the majority of the 52% increase. A discussion of the fall in relation to payables is included below.

**Key Ratios**

$$\text{Trade payable days} = \frac{\text{Trade payables}}{\text{Cost of sales}} \times 365$$

| **2018** | **2017** | **Change** |
|---|---|---|
| $= \dfrac{109,320}{140,250} \times 365$ | $= \dfrac{114,650}{120,800} \times 365$ | |
| $= 284.5$ | $= 346.4$ | –61.91 days |

The payables days shows how many days, on average, it takes for the entity to pay its trade payables. From discussions with management, it was noted that the trade payables figure includes plant and machinery purchased in December 2018 for €82,250 and in December 2017 for €85,600. Below are the payables days recalculated, excluding PPE-related payables. The credit terms being taken were excessive in 2017 and suppliers had threatened to cease supply if improvements were not made, resulting in a reduction in payables days in 2018.

| 2018 | 2017 | Change |
|---|---|---|
| $= \dfrac{109,320-82,250}{140,250} \times 365$ | $= \dfrac{114,650-85,600}{120,800} \times 365$ | |
| $= 70.4$ | $= 87.8$ | $-17.4$ days |

EXAMPLE 16.5: ANALYTICAL REVIEW – PURCHASES (LARGE COMPANY LIMITED)

| Large Company Limited 31 December 2018 | Audit Materiality | | €3,642,500 |
|---|---|---|---|
| | Performance Materiality | | €2,731,875 |
| | | Initials | Date |
| | Prepared by: | | |
| | Reviewed by: | | |

**Purchases Analytical Review**

| | 2018 | 2017 | Change | |
|---|---|---|---|---|
| | €000 | €000 | €000 | % |
| Cost of sales | 140,250 | 120,800 | 19,450 | 16% |
| Gross profit % | 50% | 39% | | 11% |
| Distribution costs | 23,000 | 20,000 | 3,000 | 15% |
| Administration expenses | 35,000 | 34,000 | 1,000 | 3% |
| | 58,000 | 54,000 | 4,000 | 7% |
| Operating expenses as % of sales | 41% | 45% | | -3% |

While the cost of sales has increased by 16%, prior-year revenue has increased by 41%, resulting in an increase in gross margin of 11%. Large Company Limited has introduced a new high-end range of furniture, on which they are achieving greater margins.

Distribution and administrative costs are also both up on prior year. The rise of 15% in distribution costs is in line with expectations considering the increase in foreign sales. Administration costs have risen only marginally considering the high rise in other areas.

While the explanations obtained around the movements in costs appear reasonable, there appears to be a risk associated with completeness, therefore focused substantive testing will be performed on this assertion.

## Substantive Testing of Purchases Transactions in the Period

We have already established in **Section 16.2** what constitutes purchases, in that every business incurs costs in the process of generating goods and services, which it subsequently sells to its customers. For example, an entity will purchase goods for resale or raw materials to use in the manufacturing process (i.e. cost of sales purchases). Additionally, 'purchases' include all expense type items relating to light and heat, rent, wages and salaries (be it production, sales or administration related), consultancy expenses, etc. Having learnt about the audit objectives in **Table 16.1**, we now consider the types of substantive audit procedure the auditor might use to address these audit objectives. These procedures include **tests of details** and **substantive analytical procedures**.

### Purchases – Tests of Details

Tests of details over purchases are those audit procedures used to substantiate the purchases figure in the financial statements. In regard to purchases they are used to obtain audit evidence regarding the occurrence, completeness, recording, classification and rights and obligations assertions (audit objectives). Where the auditor does not feel that **sufficient appropriate audit evidence** over purchases can be obtained from substantive analytical procedures alone, they may choose to perform additional substantive tests of details.

When using tests of details for purchases the auditor obtains a soft copy of the purchases nominal ledger, totals it and traces it to the respective amounts included in the trial balance and the financial statements. From the nominal listing the auditor then selects a sample of transactions and traces these to the supplier invoices. The auditor will typically find the following information on the invoice:

- the client entity's name, which supports the **rights and obligations** assertion;
- the date, which validates the period in which the transaction is **recorded**;
- the description of the goods (or services) purchased, which validates the **classification** of the purchase item; and
- the quantity and price per unit of the goods, which equates to the total value charged to the client entity (excluding VAT) and which validates the **recording** assertion.

The auditor should re-total the invoice amounts and vouch them to those in the nominal ledger. The auditor should then trace the invoice to its related goods receipt note (GRN), which will include date the goods/services were delivered, the name of the client entity and the description and quantity of goods purchased; this corroborates the information validated on the invoice but also supports the occurrence assertion as proof that the goods/services were actually received. The GRN should then be traced and vouched to the purchase order (and/or purchase requisition), which further supports occurrence and rights and obligations assertions as it confirms that the good/service was approved for purchase and therefore purchased for a valid business purpose relating to the client entity. This single test, therefore, covers multiple assertions.

The only assertion remaining is the completeness assertion, which can be validated by changing the direction of the test, i.e. selecting a sample of purchase orders and tracing them to their GRNs, supplier invoices, nominal ledger, trial balance and the financial statements. Additional assurance over the completeness of purchases can be obtained from the performance of **unrecorded liabilities** testing, which is discussed below.

The auditor will often use sampling (see **Chapter 6**) as a method of generating an appropriate sample size. The auditor can use CAATs to assist in selecting the sample.

## Purchases – Substantive Analytical Procedures in Testing

Substantive analytical procedures (see **Chapter 5**, Section 5.4) are designed to substantiate predictable relationships among both financial and non-financial data. They are most applicable to large volumes of transactions that tend to be predictable over time.

Within the context of the audit of purchases, substantive analytical procedures are most suitable in gaining audit evidence for the purchases figure in the financial statements. A substantive analytical procedure can provide evidence to support the occurrence, completeness, classification, recording and rights and obligations assertions – if the auditor can conclude that their calculated expectation, supported by the substantive review of variable data used, is correct, they can therefore conclude that these assertions are also correct.

The purchases figure consists of a large volume of routine transactions that tend to be predictable over the course of a financial year. (Tests of details are more commonly used within the audit of trade payables and accruals balances.) When performing substantive analytical procedures the auditor must review their understanding of the client entity to establish whether changes to the purchases figure are to be expected. Significant changes in amounts between the current year and the prior year should be identified. Ratios, such as the gross profit margin ratio, should be calculated, and trends identified and analysed.

The auditor performs substantive analytical procedures by developing an expectation of the level of purchases in the year based upon key factors affecting the performance and operation of the business in that period. This could include:

- prior-year volumes of purchasing;
- movements in cost prices of key supplies;
- inflation; and
- movements in levels of demand for the finished goods produced.

The auditor will seek to quantify and substantiate the effects of each of these factors by obtaining documentary and other evidence where available. For example:

- prior-year purchase and sales volumes could be verified to prior-year audit working papers;
- movements in cost prices of key supplies could be verified by comparing current-year and prior-year supplier invoices; and
- movements in demand levels for finished goods could be verified by comparing current-year and prior-year sales reports.

Once the auditor has developed an expectation for the current-year purchases figure, it can be compared to the actual figure reported in the financial statements. This allows assurance to be gained over the completeness, existence and accuracy assertions of the purchases figure by confirming that their original expectation is within a predefined acceptable range (**tolerable error** or threshold) of the actual figure reported in the financial statements. Though this acceptable range is a matter of professional judgement, a commonly used range is a reported purchases figure within 5% of that expected.

Analysis of expense accounts is also important. This is usually undertaken by comparing the ratio of each expense to sales in the current and prior periods. An unusually low expense may indicate unrecorded liabilities. Wherever a change in relationships cannot be readily explained, the auditor must seek an explanation from management and corroborate it, usually by conducting additional tests.

## Substantive Testing of Trade Payables and Accruals Balances

Where purchase transactions are not settled immediately with cash payments, they give rise to **trade payables**.

Specific substantive testing over trade payables and accruals will tend to vary, depending upon the nature of the client entity's operations. However, there are a number of key substantive tests that are common to the audit of the majority of entities. These generally take the form of substantive tests of details, rather than substantive analytical procedures, and are summarised below along with the assertions that each test addresses.

### Reperformance of Supplier Statement Reconciliations

Where the client entity receives monthly statements from its suppliers, the auditor will seek to gain audit evidence over the completeness, existence, rights and obligations and valuation assertions of the trade payables balance by reconciling amounts appearing on year-end supplier statements to corresponding balances appearing on the payables ledger.

The supplier statements are evidence from a source other than the client entity, and therefore provide reliable audit evidence as to the accuracy of year-end supplier balances. Photocopied or faxed copies of supplier statements should not be used in testing; instead, the auditor should either request a copy of the statement from the supplier or confirm the balance directly with the supplier.

In selecting the supplier account balances for testing, the focus should not centre on the year-end supplier balance (or the highest value balances) but, instead, should centre on those suppliers with which the entity has had the greatest volume of business during the year – as the auditor is concerned with the risk that the recorded payables balance might be understated or omitted.

Differences between supplier statements and the recorded year-end trade payables balances should be investigated. The main reasons for differences are either goods/cash in transit or disputed amounts between the client entity and the supplier.

The auditor may choose to request **external confirmation** from suppliers regarding the balance outstanding from them to the client entity (see **Chapter 6**, Section 6.6). However, confirmation of trade payables is not often a method adopted by the auditor because:

- it offers no assurance that unrecorded liabilities will be discovered; and
- external evidence, such as invoices/supplier statements, should already be available to substantiate the balances.

It is recommended to confirm trade payables through circularisation of suppliers only when:

- the level of **detection risk** is low; and
- the suppliers being confirmed are those with which the company engaged in a substantial level of business and which do not issue monthly statements and/or the statement is not available at the date of the statement of financial position.

If external confirmations obtained through circularisation of suppliers are used to confirm trade payables, the auditors must be in direct control of the process – the request must be sent directly from the auditor, and responses returned directly to the auditor.

The request should be a **positive circularisation** (positive and negative confirmations are discussed in **Chapter 13**, Section 13.8), i.e. the amount due at the reporting date should not be stated on the request, instead the supplier should specify the amount due to them as recorded in their own records. The supplier should also be requested to provide details regarding purchase commitments and any collateral on the amount due.

It should be noted that when the auditor chooses a sample of trade payables balances from the payables listing and reviews the supplier statement reconciliation or requests confirmations from suppliers, it is only obtaining evidence on the completeness assertion – it is confirmation that the recorded suppliers, included on the payables, are complete but not that all suppliers are included on the payables listing. For example, if the auditor selects two suppliers from a list of 10 and validates the amounts outstanding to them as recorded on the payables listing to their respective supplier statements without any differences, then it is reasonable to conclude that the sample represents the total population of 10 suppliers. They can then conclude that each of the 10 suppliers are complete with regard to the amounts outstanding to them. It does not, however, prove that there is not an eleventh or twelfth supplier that is missing from the payables listing. For this reason further work is always performed on the completeness assertion in the form of a **search for unrecorded liabilities**.

## Tests of Details of Transactions Making up the Balance

Where the client entity does not receive or retain supplier statements, and the auditor cannot retrieve or obtain them, the amount owed to the supplier can be tested by tracing the transactions that make up the balance to their supporting documentation (in the same way as outlined under **Purchases – Tests of Details** above). This will also test the existence, rights and obligations and valuation assertions, provided the auditor reviews payments to suppliers in the intervening period to ensure the amounts have not already been paid. The auditor can do this by tracing amounts paid to the supplier from the bank statement to the specific payment proposal showing the transactions that the amount relates to. Again, with regard to completeness, further audit procedures are required in the form of a search for unrecorded liabilities.

## Search for Unrecorded Liabilities

The search for unrecorded liabilities is a fundamental substantive test of details over the completeness of trade payables and accruals common to almost every audit. The objective of the test is to gain assurance that all of a client entity's liabilities that were in existence at the year end were recorded in the statement of financial position.

Intentional understatement of year-end liabilities is a key technique that could be used by client entities engaging in '**earnings management**', i.e. by recording current-year expenditure in the following period, current-year costs are reduced with the result that profits are overstated. The auditor searches for unrecorded liabilities by examining various sources of evidence to identify the occurrence of events pre-year end that commit the client entity to the outflow of economic benefits. The auditor then checks that any such pre-year-end events are appropriately included in the year-end financial statements. The main sources of evidence are:

- **post-year-end payments** – identified from bank statements. Payments made in January usually relate to purchases of an earlier period, so the auditor selects a sample of payments made in January and requests a list of invoices that make up those payments, these can then be traced to the physical invoices and GRNs to determine when the event occurred (i.e. the goods/services were received) to ensure they are recorded in the right period;
- **post-year-end invoices received** – invoices received in January usually relate to purchases of an earlier period, so the auditor will trace the invoice back to its respective GRN and, if dated pre-year end, will ensure that it is recorded in the balances on the payables listing (or that it is accrued);
- **unmatched GRNs** – those that have not been matched to invoices (i.e. the goods were received but the invoices were not and therefore the amounts on the purchase order should be accrued at the year end;
- **open purchase orders** – significantly aged purchase orders indicate that items for which a purchase order was raised may have been received but not recognised as being received in the accounting records, as such no accrual would be recognised for the related expense (nor would the inventory (if an inventory-related purchase) have been included in the accounting records at year end); and
- **cut-off tests** – see below.

As an example, for a client entity with a 31 December year end: from a review of post-year-end bank statements the auditor identifies a significant payment of €100,000 made on 10 January. Upon investigation it is established that this payment relates to an invoice that was received on 3 January. On further examination the auditor finds that this invoice has been matched to a GRN dated 31 December. As the goods were received pre-year end and included in inventory, the transaction should be recorded in the current year's purchases and accruals. If this is not the case, the purchases and year-end accruals figures will be understated (i.e. not complete).

Substantive analytical procedures may also help identify unexpected differences between the current and prior year's liability figures, which could indicate the presence of unrecorded liabilities.

An examination of **contractual commitments** (conditions within a contract that oblige the organisation to transfer economic benefits under certain circumstances) may also indicate the existence of unrecorded liabilities, such as progress payments on long-term contracts. In addition, the performance of a subsequent events and contingent liabilities review may also contribute to uncovering unrecorded liabilities (see **Chapter 18**, Section 18.7).

### Cut-off Testing

Another key test performed in almost every audit of purchases is the performance of purchases cut-off testing. The objective of this test is to ensure that purchases close to the year end are recorded in the appropriate accounting period. Unlike sales, it may take several weeks for transactions that have occurred before the year end date to be invoiced by suppliers. Many entities do not have sufficient controls in place to ensure accurate distinction between the recording of transactions before and after the year end.

Purchases cut-off testing is generally performed by examining GRNs arising close to the year end and confirming that they are appropriately recorded in the financial statements of the period under review. Remember: a liability is recognised once an event takes place (occurs) that may result in the passing of economic benefits (requirement to pay for the goods/service received) that requires the entity to record the accrual at the time of receiving the goods/service and not at the time the invoice arrives.

To ensure that GRNs issued in the days prior to the statement of financial position have been recorded pre-year end, the date may be traced to purchase journal entries or to purchase accruals. In addition, GRNs dated after the year end date will be traced to the nominal ledger to ensure they have been recorded after the year end.

The number of GRNs to be examined is a matter of judgement, however, typically the auditor will examine the last 10 pre-year-end GRNs and the first 10 post-year-end GRNs. Details of the last pre-year-end GRNs can also be obtained by attendance at the year-end inventory count. The auditor can then identify the first post-year-end GRNs by following the numerical sequence.

## Other Considerations

### Sale or Return

The primary assertion being tested with regard to sale or return purchase transactions is **rights and obligations**. If the client entity has purchased goods on a sale-or-return basis, the auditor should examine the terms of the agreement and determine how much of the inventory was sold pre-year end and how much was returned post-year end. Technically, the stock that was returned post-year end should not be included as inventory (and, therefore, as purchases and payables) as the client entity had no obligation to transfer economic benefits in relation to the goods received and returned.

## Directors' and Shareholders' Loans

The auditor must be mindful of the client entity's legislative obligations to adequately disclose directors' and shareholders' loans. To gain assurance in this regard a schedule of amounts owing to directors and shareholders should be obtained and validated against source documents. This could include an examination of the documentation giving rise to the loan and a review of amounts paid to the directors and shareholders in the period to ensure that these amounts have been adequately deducted. The auditor is testing the occurrence, rights and obligations, completeness and valuation assertions.

CAATs can be used to search for instances of payables included in the payables listing, matching directors' names, or companies for whom the directors are associated, to ensure that disclosures are complete.

## VAT and Tax

The auditor should seek to ensure that the tax balance exists, is complete and accurately valued. The tax figure payable in the financial statements is made up largely of the opening balance, the payments made to, or receipts from, tax authorities in the period and the tax charge for the period. The auditor should carry out the following procedures on each:

- **opening balance** – agree to prior-year signed financial statements;
- **payments to/receipts from tax authorities** – a schedule of payments and receipts should be obtained from the client entity and traced to the bank statement;
- **tax charge** – the current-year tax charge should be agreed to the current-year statement of comprehensive income (which in turn should have been agreed to supporting documents on the composition of the tax charge).

VAT transactions will have been tested indirectly when using tests of details of purchases and revenue, thereby testing the occurrence, rights and obligations, classification, recording and, to some degree, completeness assertions. The VAT balance should be traced to the VAT return made to the relevant authorities after the year end. The composition of the return (i.e. a summary of the input and output VAT) should be examined and agreed to the details on the nominal listing, and the amount paid should be traced to the post-year-end bank statement.

The auditor should also consider if any penalties or interest were incurred on these returns and review the correspondence with customs and excise. VAT and other tax liabilities are required to be disclosed separately and the auditor should ensure that adequate disclosures are made.

## Accruals Substantive Tests of Details

The auditor can obtain audit evidence over the existence and valuation assertions of year-end accruals by recalculating a sample of accruals appearing on the year-end schedule of accruals. These calculations can be performed with the help of supporting documentation used by the client entity in its own calculation. For example, for an entity with a 31 December year end there may be an accrual for electricity costs for December (when the previous bill related to the quarter ending 30 November) and the next expected bill covers the period 1 December to 28 February. The auditor may recalculate the year-end accrual by dividing the previous quarterly bill by three.

The auditor will have already tested for the completeness of accruals by a search for unrecorded liabilities, but the auditor can also use substantive analytical procedures to validate the existence, completeness, rights and obligations and valuation assertions.

## Accruals Substantive Analytical Procedures

Some accruals are relatively consistent in that they are accrued every year and usually at the same rate, they therefore lend themselves well to be tested using substantive analytical procedures. For example, an entity will always have utility invoices that they have not received at the year end, but they will have used, say, gas and electricity for which they must accrue an expense. Generally speaking, the period of the accrual is the same every year and therefore, in the absence of unusual circumstances, the amounts to be accrued should be more or less the same year on year.

The auditor can compare the prior-year accruals listing to the current-year accruals listing to establish whether or not they appear reasonable. By comparing the year-on-year data, the auditor is not just looking for differences, they are also looking for instances where no difference exists when, given the circumstances, differences would be expected. For example, if in the prior year there was an electricity accrual for €500,000, and in the current year it is the same except that the client entity changed providers and instead of receiving invoices monthly it now receives them bi-monthly, then the auditor would expect that the electricity accrual should have been doubled.

In addition, the auditor should perform an **analytical review** of expenses included in the statement of comprehensive income to highlight any inconsistencies that could relate to under- or over-accruals (the completeness and existence assertions).

## Inter-company Transactions and Balances

Inter-company transactions relate to the purchase and sales between related companies; inter-company balances refer to the amounts owed to and from related companies. Inter-company payables can be tested for existence and completeness, valuation and rights and obligations by:
1. obtaining a list of inter-company payables and agreeing to the general ledger;
2. obtaining inter-company loan agreements;
3. validating that loan agreements were approved by board of directors;
4. agreeing interest rate to loan agreements;
5. obtaining a list of all inter-company balances from each legal entity and agree to individual ledgers in the corresponding entities.

The auditor should ensure that instances of foreign currency balances are adequately valued to address the valuation assertion.

Further considerations on consolidation to ensure adequate disclosure and valuation include:
- ensuring that inter-company balances net to zero on consolidation;
- if any inventory that has been sold between group entities with a margin remains in stock, ensure any margin on the inventory at year end is eliminated; and
- consideration of the existence of possible reversals of inter-company provisions for debit balances to be written back on consolidation.

## Provisions

Provisions will be discussed in more detail in **Chapter 18**, but at this point it should be noted that they are normally included within short- or long-term payables and as such audited alongside them. However, due to their nature the auditor is more concerned with undisclosed provisions, contingent liabilities and contingent assets.

Where disclosed, the auditor seeks to validate their existence by seeking documentation that supports their inclusion and valuation in the financial statements in accordance with IAS 37 *Provisions, Contingent Liabilities and Contingent Assets*. This evidence can exist in various forms depending on the type of provision, liability or asset.

## Payroll

### Payroll – Tests of Details

Tests of details are required where the entity's internal controls are either not assessed or if the auditor's testing finds them to be strong. If a strong control environment exists for payroll, i.e. there is good **segregation of duties**, the auditor will normally opt to use substantive analytical procedures. Tests of details will provide the auditor with assurance over the occurrence, rights and obligations, recording and classification assertions. Before commencing payroll testing the auditor will have gained an understanding of the frequency and number of payroll runs. For example, some entities have many payrolls that may include a monthly management run, a monthly non-management run, and one for employees paid weekly. The auditor will be required to perform substantive audit procedures on each of the payrolls run by the client entity.

Once the auditor has an understanding of the number and frequency of payrolls, a sample of payroll runs can be selected from which to choose a sample for testing. The auditor will start with the payroll nominal listing(s) and select a sample.

Once the auditor chooses the sample, a copy of the gross to net report for each sample chosen will be requested. The **gross to net report** shows the gross amount being paid to the employee less any deductions, which might include employee and employer payroll deductions (taxes), union subscriptions, etc. The auditor will tot the gross to net amounts and agree it to the payroll nominal listing and trace the total amount noted as net pay to employees to the bank statement to show that it has been paid. Once this is validated, the auditor will select a sample of employees and trace the variable elements of the gross make-up of their salary/wage and any deductions as follows:

- Trace each amount that makes up the gross pay to source documents. The gross pay may include a number of elements and each element needs to be validated by the auditor. Examples of payroll gross elements and their source documentation include:
  - **basic pay (salary)** – basic pay should be traced to an original copy of the employee contract, duly signed by the client entity and the employee.
  - **Basic pay (hourly wage)** – similar to above, the hourly rate should be traced to an original copy of the employee contract. The hourly rate, however, is only one

component – the number of hours worked by the employee must also be considered to validate the amount paid to the employee. The number of hours worked can be validated by checking the client entity's time reporting/clock-in records.

- ◆ **Commission/bonuses** – any commission or bonus elements should be recalculated based on the source document outlining the condition under which they are due.
- ◆ **Back pay** – any noted back pay should be traced to supported calculations and the reason why it is being paid.
- Trace the details from the gross to net report to the employee payslip and recalculate the employee's net pay.
- Trace any deductions to the relevant source documents, e.g. for voluntary deductions the approval given by the employee for the amount to be deducted.

### Payroll – Substantive Analytical Procedure

As previously mentioned, substantive analytical procedures are designed to substantiate predictable relationships among both financial and non-financial data, and are mostly applied to large volumes of transactions that are predictable over time. Payroll, therefore, lends itself well to substantive analytical procedures. In performing a substantive analytical review the auditor can gain assurance over occurrence, completeness, rights and obligations, recording and classification.

Payroll tends to be broadly similar year on year, or at least it should be relatively reasonable for the auditor to predict any movement and to value that movement. In creating their expectation of what the payroll cost should be, the auditor usually starts with the prior year's figure (which would be agreed to the prior year's financial statements). From here the auditor can determine factors that would indicate a change in payroll value, such as the inclusion of new employees and the exclusion of former employees, pay increases, or an increase in commission based on an increase in sales or a change to the terms of payment. Having identified the factors that might cause an increase or decrease in the cost of payroll, the auditor will seek to validate each variable. The following procedures are used, many of which can be performed using CAATs:

- Obtain a list of new employees and their start dates and, using functionality such as Excel, verify the employee's pay rate/salary in the HR records. The auditor can then estimate the cost of new employees, which can be added to the prior year's payroll cost. If the new employees are paid on an hourly basis, the auditor should obtain a report from the time reporting/clocking-in system to show all hours worked by employees in the period and verify the information to value the potential salary of hourly paid employees.
- Obtain a list of employees who ceased employment with the client entity and their end dates, and using functionality such as Excel, verify the employee pay rate/salary in the HR records. An estimate of the cost of these employees in the period can be calculated, which can be deducted from the prior year's payroll cost.
- Obtain information on pay increases, including approval by management and communication to the employee, and apply it to data and apply to the prior year's payroll.

- Obtain information about changes in commission structure and apply to date. If using Excel, this can be performed using formulas to show the impact of the change. If the change in commission is due to an increase in sales, the auditor should apply the increased percentage as an estimate of the impact on commissions.

Once each amount has been determined and validated to its source documents, the auditor will have an expectation of what can be reasonably assumed to be the payroll costs for the period. This figure is then compared to the actual figure included in the financial statements. The difference will then be compared to the threshold (**tolerable difference**) and if it is within this threshold no further procedures are required.

When the recorded payrolls are validated the auditor will need to pay attention to the completeness assertion and disclosure requirements.

### *Payroll – Non-standard Payments Post-year End and Cut-off*

The auditor will usually seek to perform additional tests to gain further assurance with regard to the completeness. The best way to do this is to review activities post-year end. With regard to payroll, the auditor can start with the bank payments relating to payroll paid post-year end, and trace them back to **gross to net reports**. The gross to net reports, and related control reports for the period, should be obtained as soft copies to allow the auditor to interrogate them.

Remember that the gross to net report shows the gross amount of pay and deductions. In analysing this, the auditor would search for unusual gross pay amounts, and would probably benefit from using a tool such as VLOOKUP in Excel to compare the gross salaries of each employee from the year-end month (e.g. December) to the following month (i.e. January). This would highlight any significant increases in payment, which should be further investigated to understand why the payment was made and if the payment relates to activities performed by the employee in the period up to the year end.

A similar exercise should be performed on the report that shows the composition of gross pay (i.e. the various elements that make up an employee's gross pay, including basic pay, bonuses, commission, etc.). In this report the auditor can identify bonus and commission payments made in January that likely relate to the prior period (usually bonus or commission received in January would relate to performance of a prior period). The auditor would then trace these amounts to ensure they were accrued at the year end. The auditor could also search for key words in this document, including 'back pay', 'pay correction' and so on; or create a pivot table showing all gross pay elements, thereby quickly highlighting the gross pay elements and their value and allowing the auditor to get a quick assessment of the overall value of each pay element to determine if those, that would by their nature be related to the prior period, have been accrued at the year end.

## IAS 19 Employee Benefits *and Disclosure Requirements*

There are significant disclosure requirements around payroll. The auditor should consider in particular the requirements of IAS 19 *Employee Benefits* and the legislative requirements with regard to the disclosure of directors' emoluments. The auditor should determine if the disclosure requirements are relevant to the entity and, where they are, ensure that the entity has fully disclosed payroll in line with those requirements. The disclosure requirements in relation to directors are laid down in the RoI in the Companies Act 2014, Chapter 6, section 305, 'Disclosure of directors' remuneration and transactions'; and in the UK/NI in the Companies Act 2006, Chapter 4, sections 412 and 413, 'Information about directors' benefits'.

Whether purchases and payables or payroll, the auditor will either use tests of details or substantive analytical procedures to carry out their testing. **Tests of details** tend to provide assurance over **occurrence**, **rights and obligations**, **recording** and **classification** and **completeness** only insofar as the auditor changes the direction of tests (testing from the source payroll documents, such as timesheets, back to the recorded data in the nominal ledgers and trial balance). Tests of details are required where the control environment is assessed as being weak. Substantive analytical procedures are popular with regard to these classes of transactions and balances due to their more predictive nature, generally speaking. Substantive analytical procedures provide assurance over **occurrence**, **completeness**, **rights and obligations**, **recording** and **classification**.

Whether testing using tests of details or substantive analytical procedures, the auditor should always seek to perform additional completeness testing by analysing events and transactions after the year end date to identify both cut-off errors and potential **earnings management** that attempt to delay costs to the next financial period. Finally, the auditor should carry out procedures to identify the required disclosures and ensure the entity has adequately disclosed all items in line with both the relevant standards and legislative requirements.

## 16.9 DISCLOSURE REQUIREMENTS

Finally, with regard to purchases and payables, the auditor will consider the adequacy of the disclosures. Disclosures relating to liabilities are covered throughout the international accounting standards (IASs), although particular attention should be paid to IAS 1 *Presentation of Financial Statements* and IAS 37 *Provisions, Contingent Liabilities and Contingent Assets*. The auditor aims to ensure that all disclosures are:

- complete (no disclosures relating to purchases, payables or payroll are missing. The auditor can use IAS 1 and IAS 37 as a checklist);
- accurate (reflect the actual transactions and information relating to events surrounding purchases and payables and payroll);
- relate to events that actually occurred; and
- are properly presented (in a manner expected by international accounting standards).

The auditor should assess the purchases and payables disclosure requirements as follows:

- obtain an understanding of the disclosure requirements for trade payables and purchases and payroll under the applicable financial reporting framework;
- review the payables ledger, which may indicate amounts owed to employees, directors, other group companies and related parties – these should be specifically disclosed if they are material;
- identify debit balances included in the payables ledger that may, if found to be material, require reclassification to current assets;
- review minutes from board of directors' meetings and from inquiries of management to identify any contingent liabilities that may need to be provided for or disclosed;
- review management meeting minutes, open purchase orders, significant contracts and post-year-end events to identify capital commitments or other material purchase commitments that may require disclosure. Ensure the necessary disclosures are made relating to directors' emoluments as required under the Companies Act 2014 and the Companies Act 2006 in the RoI and UK/NI, respectively.

## 16.10 CONCLUSION

When the auditor has performed controls testing, substantive analytical review and substantive tests of details, it must be considered if **sufficient appropriate audit evidence** has been obtained over purchases and payables to provide the appropriate level of assurance required over the assertions stated at the outset, these being:

- completeness;
- valuation;
- existence/occurrence;
- cut-off; and
- rights and obligations.

The auditor must also consider if the testing performed has appropriately addressed any key risks identified in the purchases and payables cycle, and therefore reduced the risk of **material misstatement** to a suitably low level.

When testing the area of purchases and payables, the auditor is most concerned with the **completeness** assertion, due to the risk associated with fraudulent financial reporting to reduce payables, resulting in an increase in profit.

When testing payroll, the auditor should be cognisant of the possibility of fictitious employees or unauthorised payroll variables (e.g. bonus or commission) and that, on termination of employment, those employees were removed from the payroll.

The auditor must consider the impact of their testing of purchases, payables and payroll on the **audit opinion**. This is achieved by considering whether any misstatements found, either individually or in aggregate (when combined with other misstatements detected throughout the audit), will result in the financial statements being materially misstated. As such, all misstatements found are taken to the auditor's errors schedule for consideration at the audit completion stage (discussed in detail in **Chapter 18**). The auditor's report on financial statements is considered in detail in **Chapter 19**.

## SUMMARY OF LEARNING OBJECTIVES

**Learning Objective 1** Understand what is included in the audit of purchases, payables and payroll.

Every business incurs costs in the process of generating the goods and services it subsequently sells to its customers. Where such transactions are not settled immediately through cash payments, they give rise to **trade payables**. Such trade payables meet the definition of liabilities as set out in IAS 37, paragraph 10.

Employee costs represent a significant portion of the expenses associated with any organisation, and the auditor is concerned with ensuring all employees' hours worked, or monies due for performance, in the period are fully recorded.

**Learning Objective 2** Be able to identify the risks and audit objectives (management assertions) applicable to purchases, payables and payroll.

The primary risks associated with purchases and payables relate to:
- completeness of payables; and
- inappropriate and fraudulent payments.

The auditor aims to prove that recorded purchases and payroll relate to goods/services received, and that payables and accruals exist; that all goods/services received and their related payables balances are recorded (complete); are accurately recorded in terms of value at the date of transaction and at the date of the SOFP; are accurately cut-off; that the entity holds the rights and obligations to the transactions and balances; and, finally, that they are presented and disclosed in line with applicable reporting standards.

The primary risks associated with payroll are those related to occurrence and recording, i.e. only work/performance by genuine employees is recorded as a cost and recorded at the amounts as agreed within the terms of the individual's contract. The auditor will be particularly alert to the existence of fictitious employees and to the lack of segregation of duties.

**Learning Objective 3** Be able to determine an appropriate audit strategy for purchases, payables and payroll, taking into consideration the specific risks and audit objectives (management assertions).

With respect to purchases, the auditor seeks to prove that the purchases recorded in the financial statements relate to events that occurred and that they are recorded accurately, completely and only relate to transactions that pertain to the entity.

When auditing the payables balance, the auditor seeks to confirm their existence and accuracy (valuation) as well as their completeness and that they are appropriately classified and disclosed.

When auditing payroll, the auditor will frequently test the controls surrounding payroll processes as payroll costs generally represent a material figure in the financial statements. Validating a strong control environment will allow the auditor to perform substantive analytical procedures, which can be a very effective and efficient way to test payroll.

**Learning Objective 4** Be able to develop an audit programme that addresses all the audit objectives (management assertions) for purchases, payables and payroll.

Purchases and payables are usually a material figure and transactions tend to be high in volume; thus, the auditor usually takes a **controls approach** when testing this area in order to reduce the level of detailed substantive testing.

**Learning Objective 5** Be able to describe and apply specific substantive testing procedures relating to the audit of purchases, payables and payroll.

The **aged payables listing** is the key document of interest to the auditor. Other documents that may form part of audit evidence connected to purchases and payables include:
- supplier statements and reconciliations;
- supplier invoices;
- open purchase order listing;
- goods received invoice not received report (GRIR);
- purchase orders (POs); and
- signed customer proof-of-delivery (POD) notes.

Regarding purchases, the auditor seeks to prove that recorded purchases in the financial statements relate to events that occurred, that they have been recorded accurately and only relate to transactions where risks and rewards (economic benefits) of items have passed to the buyer. The auditor will also seek to ensure that all purchase transactions are recorded (completeness).

When testing payroll, the auditor will usually perform substantive analytical procedures to validate the payroll costs. As part of the tests of details, the auditor will select a number of weeks/months from the gross to net reports and trace them to (a) the bank, to confirm payment to employees; (b) to time records to confirm hours worked; and (c) to employment contracts to confirm salary/wage rates. The auditor will be particularly interested in non-routine payroll amounts, such as bonuses, commission, etc. to ensure they are correctly authorised and in line with the employee's contractual terms or documented organisational policies.

When auditing the payables balance, the auditor seeks to confirm their existence, accuracy (valuation) and completeness by reperforming or reviewing supplier reconciliations. The auditor will pay particular attention to the **completeness assertion** by performing a number of audit procedures connected to the **search for unrecorded liabilities** (including post-year-end payments, review of open PO reports, etc.). The auditor will also seek to ensure the **completeness of accruals** by performing **substantive analytical procedures** (comparison with prior-year accruals to identify under-accruals).

**Learning Objective 6** Understand the role CAATs can play when auditing purchases and payables.

The auditor may use a combination of audit software, data analysis tools and other applications, such as Excel, when auditing the area of purchases, payables and payroll.

**Learning Objective 7** Understand the auditor's approach relating to the disclosures of purchases and payables.

The auditor aims to ensure that the disclosures relating to purchases and payables are complete, accurate, pertain to the entity and are adequately disclosed in line with related international accounting standards.


## QUESTIONS

### Self-test Questions

16.1   Define liabilities as set out in IAS 37, paragraph 10.

16.2   What benefits can be derived from an aged payables listing?

16.3   What are the key audit risks associated with purchases and payables?

16.4   List the key audit procedures performed to test accruals.

16.5   When is it recommended that an auditor should confirm trade payables? Discuss the method that should be used.

16.6   Explain why an auditor performs the search for unrecorded liabilities.

16.7   Discuss four methods the auditor might use to search for unrecorded liabilities.

16.8   How could an auditor test cut-off for purchases?

16.9   What nature of substantive procedures is the auditor most likely to adopt with regard to the substantive testing of payroll?

16.10  Describe the types of documents the auditor will consider when testing payroll?

16.11  What specific disclosure requirements will the auditor be interested in with regard to payroll?

16.12  Describe how the auditor might use substantive analytical procedures to test payroll expenses in the SOCI.

### Review Questions

(See Suggested Solutions to Review Questions in **Appendix C**.)

## Question 16.1

You are the audit junior for Hall Ltd, a company that supplies bathroom furniture, and have been assigned the audit of payables. For the four suppliers selected from the trade payables listing for sample testing, you have obtained the following three supplier reconciliations from the client (see below). No supplier statement was received from your fourth sample, Jackson Ltd, so the client could not carry out the supplier reconciliation.

### Hall Ltd – Supplier reconciliations

|  | £/€ |
|---|---|
| **Dock Ltd** |  |
| Balance per supplier statement | 10,870 |
| Invoices on statement, not on ledger | (2,900) |
| Balance per ledger | 7,970 |
|  |  |
| Exchange rate (£/€ : $) | 0.79 |
| Balance per ledger ($) | 6,296 |
|  |  |
| **Dino Ltd** |  |
| Balance per supplier statement | 22,300 |
| Invoices on ledger, not on statement | 2,500 |
| Balance per ledger | 24,800 |
|  |  |
| **Gino Ltd** |  |
| Balance per supplier statement | 72,900 |
| Disputed invoice* | 31,200 |
| Balance per ledger (€/£) | 41,700 |

*Hall Ltd insist goods not received.

You note on the payables listing that there are three suppliers who have debit balances.

### Requirement

(a) Outline the substantive audit procedures you will perform on each of these supplier reconciliations.

(b) Outline further substantive audit procedures you will perform in relation to Jackson Ltd.

(c) Outline the risks you would be concerned about with regard to the debit balances appearing on the payables listing.

(d) Outline the substantive audit procedures you would carry out to obtain assurance over the completeness of payables.

## Question 16.2

You are a new audit junior and have been assigned to the audit of Amber Facilities Ltd, which sells cleaning products. You are auditing the financial statements for the year ended 31 December 2018 and are assigned to the substantive audit of payroll.

You have selected a number of 'gross to net' reports to test and having agreed their totals to the payroll nominal ledger and to the bank, you have now selected a number of employees for detailed substantive testing. An extract from the respective gross to net reports and gross make-up reports are included below.

### GROSS TO NET EXTRACTS FOR SELECTED EMPLOYEES

| Employee Name | Gross Pay £/€ | Employee Payroll Taxes £/€ | Employee Payroll Insurance £/€ | Union Subs £/€ | Holiday Savings £/€ | Pension £/€ | Salary/ Wage Advance £/€ | Net Pay £/€ |
|---|---|---|---|---|---|---|---|---|
| James Dunne | 5,000 | 1,000 | 100 | 80 | | 250 | 4,000 | (430) |
| Jack Dean | 6,780 | 1,356 | 136 | | 800 | 339 | | 4,149 |
| Sarah Young | 3,500 | 700 | 70 | 80 | | 175 | | 2,475 |
| Donal Casper | 7,600 | 1,520 | 152 | | | 380 | | 5,548 |
| Dee O'Reegan | 3,450 | 690 | 69 | 80 | | 173 | | 2,438 |

### GROSS PAYROLL COMPONENTS EXTRACT FOR SELECTED EMPLOYEES

| Employee Name | Monthly Salary £/€ | Weekly Wages (based on hours worked) £/€ | Commission £/€ | Bonus Advance £/€ | Back Pay /Payroll Correction £/€ | Gross Pay £/€ |
|---|---|---|---|---|---|---|
| James Dunne | 5,500 | | | | (500) | 5,000 |
| Jack Dean | 5,000 | | | 1,780 | | 6,780 |
| Sarah Young | | 3,000 | 500 | | | 3,500 |
| Donal Casper | 5,700 | | | 1,900 | | 7,600 |
| Dee O'Reegan | | 3,000 | 300 | | 150 | 3,450 |

**Requirement**
(a) On initial review of the information obtained, outline two risks.
(b) From the information above, describe the substantive tests of details you would perform for **each employee**, for **each component** of the individual gross to net and gross make-up reports.
(c) Outline in what circumstances the auditor might choose to perform a substantive analytical procedure to validate the payroll expense in the financial statements.
(d) Describe a specific substantive analytical procedure, noting how each figure used is validated and how CAATs might aid the calculation of the expectation.

# 17

# THE AUDIT OF SHARE CAPITAL AND RESERVES

## LEARNING OBJECTIVES

Having studied this chapter on the audit of share capital and reserves you should:
1. understand what is included in the audit of share capital and reserves;
2. be able to identify the risks and audit objectives applicable to share capital and reserves;
3. be able to determine an appropriate audit strategy for share capital and reserves, taking into consideration the specific risks and audit objectives (management assertions);
4. be able to develop an audit programme that addresses all the audit objectives (management assertions) for share capital and reserves;
5. be able to describe and apply specific substantive testing procedures relating to the audit of share capital and reserves;
6. understand the role CAATs can play when auditing share capital and reserves; and
7. understand the auditor's approach relating to the disclosures of share capital and reserves.

## Checklist of Relevant Standards

The relevant standards, in both the RoI and the UK/NI, covered in this chapter are:
- ISA 315 *Identifying and Assessing the Risks of Material Misstatement through Understanding the Entity and its Environment*
- ISA 330 *The Auditor's Responses to Assessed Risks*
- ISA 500 *Audit Evidence*
- ISA 505 *External Confirmations*
- ISA 510 *Initial Audit Engagements – Opening Balances*
- ISA 520 *Analytical Procedures*
- ISA 530 *Audit Sampling*
- IAS 1 *Presentation of Financial Statements*
- IAS 8 *Accounting Policies, Changes in Accounting Estimates and Errors*
- IAS 33 *Earnings per Share*
- IFRS 2 *Share-based Payment*
- IFRS 9 *Financial Instruments*

Note, in general when referring to ISAs, it should be understood as referring to the UK and Ireland versions, unless otherwise specified as either ISA (UK) or ISA (Ireland). See the Introduction for an extant list of auditing standards for the RoI and the UK/NI.

## Key Terms and Definitions for this Chapter

**Articles of Association**   A legal document that controls the internal management of the business, and the policies made to guide the execution of the objects as set out in the memorandum of association.

**Equity**   Residual value of assets after deduction of liabilities representing the monies owed by an entity back to shareholders.

**Financial Liability**   Present obligation of an entity arising from past events, the settlement of which is expected to result in an outflow of the entity's resources.

**Memorandum of Association**   A legal document that defines the capacity of a company's activities and governs the relationship between the company and the outside world. It includes such items as: company name; type of company (e.g. limited or private); company objective; and intended powers of the company.

**Trust Deeds**   A legal document that transfers to a trustee the title to property.

**Share Register**   A list of all the current shareholders of a company updated on an ongoing basis.

## 17.1 INTRODUCTION

The objective of substantive testing is to validate the transactions, balances and disclosures at the assertion level in response to identified risks (inherent, control and detection risks as discussed in **Chapters 7** and **8**). The auditor commences substantive testing by focusing on the risk of material misstatement within the transactions and balances being tested, and then identifying the assertions impacted by these risks and then identifying substantive audit procedures that will best test the existence of material misstatement driven by the identified risks.

**Sections 17.2–17.8** outline the requirements of the international accounting standards, specifically those of IFRS 2 *Share-based Payment* and IAS 33 *Earnings per Share*, with respect to share capital and reserves, and then considers how the auditor:

*   identifies audit risks and audit objectives (management assertions) for share capital and reserves;
*   develops an audit plan for share capital and reserves and refines this into an audit programme;
*   designs specific tests associated with share capital and reserves; and
*   checks adequate presentation and disclosure in the financial statements relating to share capital and reserves.

Throughout the chapter it is highlighted where CAATs can be used by the auditor in assisting with ensuring the effective and efficient audit of the area of share capital and reserves.

Finally, in **Section 17.9** we consider the auditor's approach when auditing the reasonableness of disclosures relating to share capital and reserves.

## 17.2 WHAT IS SHARE CAPITAL AND WHAT ARE RESERVES?

Share capital is the investments made in the entity by its shareholders (i.e. the company's owners) at the time(s) the shares were issued. Both called-up share capital (shares issued to investors on the understanding that they will pay for them at a later date (possibly in instalments)) and called-up share capital not paid must be disclosed on the statement of financial position.

Reserves are the profits retained in the business and not distributed to the shareholders. Reserves include, for example, retained earnings and revaluation reserves. The Companies Act 2014 (RoI) and the Companies Act 2006 (UK/NI) require disclosure of the following categories of reserves:

*   profit or loss account;
*   share premium account;
*   revaluation reserve; and
*   other reserves, e.g. capital redemption reserve.

## 17.3  RISKS ASSOCIATED WITH SHARE CAPITAL AND RESERVES

In **Chapter 7** we discussed the topic of risk and we considered how the auditor should go about detecting risks. We also discussed how the auditor should consider these risks when designing the nature, timing and extent of further audit procedures relative to each financial cycle. As such, before developing the audit plan, the auditor needs to consider a number of risks that may be associated with share capital and reserves.

The risks associated with share capital and reserves mainly revolve around **presentation and disclosure**. Although in practice this section of the audit usually requires the least amount of time, it is an important part of the audit. It is good practice for the auditor to conduct a search on the client entity through either Companies House (in the UK/NI) or the Companies Registration Office (in the RoI) in order to verify information such as the existence of the company, its shareholders, directors and registered charges.

## 17.4  AUDIT OBJECTIVES/MANAGEMENT ASSERTIONS FOR SHARE CAPITAL AND RESERVES

As discussed in **Chapter 6**, it is necessary for the auditor to seek **sufficient appropriate audit evidence** to satisfy all of the audit objectives and to eliminate the possibility of any of the risks outlined above going undetected. The auditor must design tests to address these assertions and thereby address the identified risks. In **Chapter 4** we introduced audit objectives (management assertions) and explained their generic meanings before reintroducing the topic again throughout **Chapter 8**, making management assertions specific to each financial cycle. **Table 17.1** and **Table 17.2** below recap the audit objectives as they relate to share capital and reserves.

TABLE 17.1: SHARE CAPITAL AND RESERVES BALANCES – AUDIT OBJECTIVES

| Audit Objective/ Management Assertion | Objective of Audit Evidence |
| --- | --- |
| Existence | To ensure the company is in existence and is operating in line with its Memorandum and Articles of Association (its 'constitution'). |
| Completeness | To ensure any movement in the share capital account has been recorded in the year under review. To ensure opening reserves are accurately stated and tie into the prior-year closing reserves as per the last audited financial statements. |
| Rights and Obligations | The entity has an obligation to the recorded equity holders (shareholders). |
| Valuation | To ensure share capital is included in the financial statements at the correct value; often shares are allotted at a premium. |

| | |
|---|---|
| **Classification, Presentation and Disclosure** | To check that reserves are correctly disclosed in the financial statements and that provisions in the Articles of Association are adhered to. To check that share capital is appropriately disclosed in the financial statements. This includes disclosing: <br> • authorised share capital; <br> • issued share capital; and <br> • directors' and company secretary's interests in the share capital of the company or parent undertaking. <br> To check that share capital is presented correctly in the financial statements. In accordance with IAS 32, each class of shares must be appropriately disclosed as equity or a financial liability. <br> To check that dividends are not paid from capital. |

TABLE 17.2: SHARE CAPITAL AND RESERVES MOVEMENTS –
AUDIT OBJECTIVES

| Management Assertion / Audit Objective | Objective of Audit Evidence |
|---|---|
| **Occurrence** | All recorded movements in the statement of changes in equity are supported by events that occurred. |
| **Completeness** | All events that occurred in the period giving rise to movements in the statement of changes in equity have been included (i.e. they are complete). |
| **Recording (accuracy)** | All movements in equity and reserves are recorded at their correct value in line with applicable financial reporting standards |
| **Cut-off** | Transactions related to equity and reserves are recorded in the correct period. |
| **Rights and Obligations** | The client entity has the rights and obligations to the recorded equity and reserves. |
| **Classification, Presentation and Disclosure** | The classification, presentation and disclosures surrounding equity and reserves are in line with applicable financial reporting frameworks. |

## 17.5 DEVELOPING THE AUDIT PLAN FOR SHARE CAPITAL AND RESERVES

Before the audit of share capital and reserves is undertaken, an assessment of the audit risk must be completed. As discussed in detail in **Chapter 7**, audit risk is made up of three components: inherent risk; control risk; and detection risk.

The auditor will rarely test controls around share capital and reserves and instead will adopt a wholly substantive approach. This is because, usually, there are a limited number of transactions relating to share capital and reserves, and normally corroborating evidence has been obtained during other substantive procedures that support balances in the share capital and reserves accounts (e.g. revaluation of property and movement disclosed in the statement of comprehensive income).

## 17.6 AUDIT TRAIL FOR SHARE CAPITAL AND RESERVES

To appreciate the role of the auditor in validating transactions, classes of transactions or balances at the assertion level, it is important to first understand the audit trail associated with the relevant cycle. The nature, and therefore the types of source document, of share capital and reserves can vary hugely. As such, the audit trail will be very different depending on the specifics of the transaction or balance in question.

The auditor has been presented with the financial statements, which are supported by a trial balance. Each trial balance item is made up of a summary of transactions in the form of a nominal ledger. The nominal ledger is made up of individual transactions that are further supported by source documents, which validate the occurrence/existence of the transaction or balance. These source documents also provide evidence with regard to the correct recording and valuation of transactions and balances and that the entity had the rights and obligations to the transaction. If the auditor starts with the source documentation and traces it toward the trial balance then they will be able to test for the completeness assertion.

For example, if the auditor sees that the number of shares in issue are up by 1,000, it would be expected that there is a **share register** that supports the purchase of 1,000 shares and that selecting a sample of these will lead to share certificates, which will indicate who purchased them, how many were purchased and for what value. This information therefore validates that the transaction occurred, was recorded at the right amount and correctly classified and that the entity had the rights and obligations to the transaction.

With respect to share capital and reserves, the auditor is predominantly concerned with the examination of documentation pertaining to rights, preferences or restrictions that may be imposed by various authorities, agreements or legal requirements. Documents of interest to the auditor include:
- ordinary or preference share registers;
- ordinary or preference share certificates;
- **Memorandum of Association** and **Articles of Association**;
- trust deeds;
- documents pertaining to rights to acquire share capital (share options); and
- company search with the Companies Registration Office (CRO) in the RoI or with Companies House in the UK/NI.

## 17.7 SUBSTANTIVE AUDIT PROGRAMME FOR SHARE CAPITAL AND RESERVES

An audit programme records the specific details of tests to be performed by the auditor. The audit programme becomes a guide to the audit engagement team on the work to be done in a particular area. As work is completed, a reference is included on the audit programme showing the location in the audit file where details of the tests performed are included. The audit programme for any financial cycle will vary from entity to entity and, as such, in **Example 17.1** below we consider the typical tests the auditor might include in the audit programme for share capital and reserves. Students should note that in a real-life scenario, each test would be referenced to the location in the audit working file where the test is actually performed.

EXAMPLE 17.1: AUDIT PROGRAMME FOR SHARE CAPITAL & RESERVES[1]

| Large Company Limited 31 December 2018 | Audit Materiality: | | €3,642,500 |
|---|---|---|---|
| | Performance Materiality: | | €2,731,875 |
| | | Initials | Date |
| | Prepared by: | | |
| | Reviewed by: | | |
| **Share Capital and Reserves Audit Programme** | | | |
| Ensure the audit plan is reflected in the following tests. The following steps are suggestions only and should be removed or added to as necessary to address the risks of material misstatement identified at the risk assessment stage. | | | |
| **Accounting Policy** | | | |
| Assess the appropriateness of the accounting policy and the accounting estimates method for this area. Ensure that the accounting policy is in accordance with accounting standards and applicable law, and that the methods used for making the accounting estimates are appropriate. | Occurrence/Existence Completeness Rights and Obligations Recording (accuracy) Classification | | |
| **Initial Procedures** | | | |
| Vouch opening balances to prior-year working papers. | Recording (accuracy) Presentation and Disclosure | | |

---

[1] Source: based on *Procedures for Quality Audit 2010* (© Chartered Accountants Ireland, 2010), M1 and updated by the authors in December 2017.

| | |
|---|---|
| Obtain or prepare lead schedules showing the elements making up the share capital and reserves section in the SOFP, agree the details to the related nominals, trial balance, SOFP and statement of changes in equity (SOCE). Obtain the nominal listings and schedules that support the transactions and balances, total them and agree these to the trial balance (e.g. share listing, revaluations schedule, etc.). | Occurrence/Existence Completeness Rights and Obligations Recording (accuracy) Classification |
| Prepare an analytical review showing the movements from the prior period to the current period and calculate related ratios. | Existence Completeness Recording (accuracy) |
| **Review of Statement of Changes in Equity** | |
| *Movements in Share Capital* Obtain the nominals that support the share capital movements and trace these to supporting documentation (share certificates/cash receipts/board minutes). | Occurrence Recording (accuracy) Cut-off Rights and Obligations |
| *Profit or Loss and Other Comprehensive Income taken Directly to Reserves* Obtain a schedule showing the make-up of movements on reserve accounts (e.g. revaluation reserve and retained earnings). Trace profit or loss movement to SOCI, trace other movements to supporting documentation. | Occurrence Recording (accuracy) Cut-off Rights and Obligations |
| **Share Capital Balance** | |
| *Public Record Documents* Perform a company search with the Companies Registration Office (CRO) in the RoI or Companies House in the UK/NI and validate the details to the financial statements. | Existence Completeness Rights and Obligations |
| *Changes in Share Capital* The company search will give details of any changes to the share capital. Such changes include the issuing of shares, the redemption of shares, bonus shares, options taken up or issued, share splits and rights issues. It is important to check that these transactions are appropriately disclosed in the financial statements. | Existence Completeness Rights and Obligations |
| *Memorandum of Association and Articles of Association* Review to ensure appropriate disclosure of shares. | Presentation and Disclosure |

## 17.8 SUBSTANTIVE TESTING PROCEDURES FOR SHARE CAPITAL AND RESERVES

The substantive testing audit programme in **Example 17.1** outlined the principal procedures involved in testing share capital and reserves. In this section we will look at each of these in more detail:

1. Initial procedures:
   (a) Opening balances
   (b) Accuracy of schedules provided by management
   (c) Prepare the lead schedule
   (d) Analytical review.
2. Review of statement of changes in equity:
   (a) Movements in share capital
   (b) Profit or loss and other comprehensive income taken directly to reserves.
3. Share capital balance:
   (a) Public record documents
   (b) Changes in share capital
   (c) Memorandum of Association and Articles of Association.
4. Other considerations:
   (a) Financial liabilities versus equity instruments
   (b) Minutes of shareholders' meetings
   (c) Earnings per share.

### Initial Procedures

#### Opening Balances

Evidence must be obtained as to the accuracy of the opening balances. The reason for this is twofold:

1. it confirms that the comparative figures in the financial statements (which must be included in the current year's financial statements) agree to the final accounts of the prior year; and
2. it highlights any final entries (last-minute adjusting journal entries) of the prior year not correctly carried forward, which may indicate an error in the current year's financial statement figures.

The auditor tests opening balances by:
• agreeing the opening balances to prior-year audit working papers and signed financial statements. This will highlight any adjustments relevant to the prior-year financial statements that need to be carried forward into the current year's opening balances;
• if this is the first year of the audit engagement, a copy of the previous auditor's working papers (if possible) should be obtained and opening balances agreed to these working papers along with the prior-year signed financial statements. See **Chapter 6**, Section 6.9.

### Accuracy of Schedules

All schedules provided by the client entity, which in the case of share capital and reserves will be the shares register, should be totalled and cross-totalled to check their mathematical accuracy. Additionally, they should be agreed to the financial statements, balances and transactions that they support. At least one item should be selected from the schedule and traced to its respective source data to validate the accuracy of the schedule before further testing is performed on it.

### Prepare the Lead Schedule

The lead schedule acts as a summary of the balances and transactions to be audited relating to a particular class of transactions and balances. It allows the auditor to control the audit procedures by referencing each balance or transaction to the audit working paper that records the audit tests performed. For share capital and reserves, the lead schedule is similar to the share capital and reserves note in the financial statements (as can be seen in **Appendix B**, Note 28). An example of a lead schedule for share capital and reserves is included below at **Example 17.2**.

EXAMPLE 17.2: SHARE CAPITAL AND RESERVES LEAD
SCHEDULE (LARGE COMPANY LIMITED)[2]

| Large Company Limited 31 December 2018 | | | |
|---|---|---|---|
| | Audit Materiality | | €3,642,500 |
| | Performance Materiality | | €2,731,875 |
| | | Initials | Date |
| | Prepared by: | | |
| | Reviewed by: | | |
| Statutory Matters, Share Capital and Reserves Lead Schedule | | | |

| | 31/12/2018 €000 | 31/12/2017 €000 |
|---|---|---|
| **Authorised:** | | |
| 100,000,000 ordinary shares @ €1 | 100,000 | 100,000 |
| 5,000,000 10% redeemable preference shares @ €1 | 5,000 | 5,000 |
| | | |
| **Allotted, called-up and fully paid:** | | |
| 2018: 84,050,000 @ €1 ordinary shares @ €1 | 84,050 | |
| 2017: 78,160,000 ordinary shares @ €1 | | 78,160 |
| 3,000,000 10% redeemable preference shares @ €1 | 3,000 | 3,000 |

---

[2] Source: based on *Procedures for Quality Audit 2010* (© Chartered Accountants Ireland, 2010), M1 and updated by the authors in December 2017.

## Analytical Review

An analytical review (see **Chapter 5**, Section 5.4) is usually performed at the start of each substantive procedure relating to each balance or class of transactions. Calculating ratios and analysing results against industry information, prior-year results, budgets, etc. allows the auditor to get a feel for the movements in the year and to make comparisons against norms. It therefore provides the auditor with additional insights into the client entity and the industry it operates in, and better prepares them for the audit programme.

The analytical review performed here differs from a substantive analytical procedure in that the auditor's aim is not to substantiate the balance (i.e. prove the assertions), but rather to understand the movements and relationships and to assist in performing substantive procedures.

Specific ratios of interest to the auditor in relation to share capital and reserves include:
- earnings per share (EPS) – net income (less preference dividends) divided by the weighted average of ordinary shares;
- dividend yield – share dividend expressed as a percentage of the current share price;
- price/earnings (P/E) ratio – current market price divided by EPS, represents the price paid for each £/€1 of the client entity's profit; and
- debt to equity ratio – relative proportion of shareholders' equity to debt.

## Review of Statement of Changes in Equity

The statement of changes in equity (SOCE) shows the change in the shareholders' equity over an accounting period. It presents the opening balances, movements and closing balances associated with equity and reserve items, such as:
- increases and decreases in share capital (ordinary shares, preference shares and share premium);
- profit or loss for the period;
- comprehensive income taken directly to reserves;
- dividends paid and proposed for the period; and
- the impact of prior-year corrections or changes in policy (IAS 8 *Accounting Policies, Changes in Accounting Estimates and Errors*).

The auditor should commence testing by first vouching the opening balances to the closing balances in the statement of changes in equity in the prior year's signed financial statements. The auditor should then assess the movements within each of the equity and reserve accounts.

## Movements in Share Capital

Movements in share capital can include, for example, sale of additional shares, bonus issues, rights issues or redemption of shares. The auditor should obtain a copy of the share capital and share premium general ledger accounts and agree the movements to the difference between opening and closing balances on the financial statements. Once validated, the auditor should:

- scan the activity in the share capital and share premium account for large or unusual transactions;
- confirm the total number of shares issued, dividends paid or payable, and other pertinent information directly with the independent registrar or transfer agent; and
- vouch transfers to the share register and share transfer forms.

Having obtained evidence to support the opening balance and any movements, the auditor indirectly obtains evidence regarding the closing balance of **retained earnings** and the **revaluation**. Below we discuss in more detail the activities that should be carried out by the auditor in relation to the client entity's share capital.

### Profit or Loss and Other Comprehensive Income taken Directly to Reserves

The most prominent movement in retained earnings is the profit and loss for the period, which the auditor will have validated through various other audit procedures discussed in previous chapters. The auditor should also vouch that the amount included as profit or loss in the SOCE agrees to the profit or loss showing in the statement of comprehensive income. Other movements in retained earnings include dividends paid and proposed, which should be validated against the board minutes approving them and checked to ensure that they are compliant with legal regulations.

The auditor should review any changes in accounting policy and prior-year errors to determine whether: (a) those included are supported by relevant supporting documentation, and decisions taken are in line with applicable financial reporting standards; and (b) that all events representing a change in accounting policy or prior-year error requiring adjustment are included in the SOCE.

Movements in relation to revaluation reserves should be tested at part of PPE, outlined in **Chapter 11**.

### Share Capital Balance

Share capital is primarily audited by obtaining **external confirmations**. Below we discuss some of the records available and the substantive procedures that should be carried out by the auditor in relation to same.

### Public Record Documents

The auditor should perform a company search with the Companies Registration Office (CRO) in the RoI or Companies House in the UK/NI. The company search will detail all the documents filed and available on public record for the entity.

Once the search has been conducted, the auditor should review all documents filed during the period under review and, where necessary, request copies of them. The most common documents include the annual return, a change of registered office amendments or changes to the **Memorandum of Association** and the **Articles of Association**, changes in directors or company secretary and any changes to the share capital. It is important to check that any changes reflected in these documents are verified to board-approving minutes and that they are correctly updated and disclosed in the financial statements.

### Changes in Share Capital

The company search will give details of any changes to the share capital. Such changes include the issuing of shares, the redemption of shares, bonus shares, options taken up or issued, share splits and rights issues. It is important to check that these transactions are appropriately disclosed in the financial statements.

The auditor should check the consideration received for any shares issued and agree any amounts called up but not paid. In addition, the legality of any share repurchases should be investigated. The auditor also needs to determine whether or not a provision for premiums payable on redemption is required.

The authorised and issued share capital must be agreed to the company's annual return. The authorised share capital should also be agreed to the Memorandum and Articles of Association.

### Memorandum of Association and Articles of Association

The Memorandum of Association and the Articles of Association must be reviewed to gain an understanding of the rights attaching to each class of share. As per IAS 32 *Financial Instruments: Presentation*, consideration must be given to how equity instruments are treated, i.e. as liabilities or as equity. Authorised and issued share capital should be analysed in the financial statements by each class of shares. The auditor should examine significant shareholdings; in particular, the register of members should be vouched to issued share capital, and the auditor should check that correct disclosure of the directors' shareholdings has been made.

### Other Considerations

### Financial Liabilities versus Equity Instruments

The critical feature in differentiating a financial liability from an equity instrument is the existence of a contractual obligation of one party to the financial instrument to either deliver cash or another financial asset to the other party or to exchange another financial instrument with the holder under conditions that are potentially unfavourable. Put simply:
- if a contractual obligation exists, the instrument is a financial liability;
- if the instrument is redeemable at the option of the holder, it is a financial liability;
- if no contractual obligation exists, it is an equity instrument; and
- if the instrument is redeemable at the option of the company, it is considered an equity instrument.

**Examples 17.3** and **17.4** below consider the classification under a financial liability and under equity.

EXAMPLE 17.3: CLASSIFICATION UNDER FINANCIAL LIABILITY

Company A has issued preference shares that carry rights to cumulative fixed net dividends and repayment of share price on redemption (redeemable at the option of the holder). Should this be classed as a liability or equity?

Look at the substance of the arrangement:

Two obligations are attached to the preference shares **and** they are redeemable at the option of the holder – therefore they are classified as a financial liability.

EXAMPLE 17.4: CLASSIFICATION UNDER EQUITY

Company B has issued redeemable shares. Company B may redeem all or part of the shares at any time; holders are not entitled to payment of a dividend.

Again, look at the substance of the arrangement:

No obligations are attached to the preference shares **and** they are redeemable at the option of the company – therefore, they are classified as equity.

## Minutes of Shareholders' Meetings

It is a requirement under company law (in both the RoI and the UK/NI) that companies hold shareholder meetings and maintain minutes. A review of these minutes (along with any changes to the Memorandum and Articles of Association) should be part of the audit procedures. As discussed above, the auditor should examine documentation pertaining to rights, preferences or restrictions that may be imposed by various authorities, agreements or legal requirements. This includes:

- **trust deeds**;
- voting rights;
- preference shares and other preferences;
- dividend arrears; and
- rights to acquire share capital.

## Earnings per Share

IAS 33 *Earnings per Share* requires an entity to disclose its current and prior-year earnings per share (EPS), and diluted EPS where appropriate, and defines how EPS is calculated. The auditor should ensure that the EPS disclosed in the financial statement is in line with IAS 33. The EPS calculation is complicated and therefore is subject to **inherent risk**.

## 17.9 DISCLOSURE REQUIREMENTS

Finally, with regard to share capital and reserves, the auditor will consider the adequacy of the disclosures. The auditor needs to consider the requirements of international accounting standards to ensure that all disclosures are:

- complete (no share capital- and reserves-related disclosures are missing);
- accurate (reflect the actual transactions and information relating to events surrounding share capital and reserves);
- relate to events that actually occurred; and
- are properly presented (in line with applicable international accounting standards).

Specifically, when auditing the adequacy of presentation and disclosure of share capital and reserves, the auditor will:

- check that directors' and company secretary's interests in shares of the company disclosed in the directors' report agree with the information extracted from the register of directors' interests during the audit of share capital and reserves;
- check that each class of share is appropriately presented as equity and/or a financial liability in accordance with the requirements of accounting standards;
- check that proper disclosures of the accounting policies and methods adopted for equity instruments have been made;
- consider whether disclosure of non-distributable reserves is required in order to give a true and fair view;
- inquire from management as to the name of the entity's controlling party and, if different, its ultimate controlling party and agree details to the register of shareholdings and other corroborating evidence; and
- check that earnings per share (EPS) has been appropriately disclosed in accordance with IAS 33 *Earnings per Share*.

## 17.10 CONCLUSION

When the auditor has completed their substantive tests in the area of share capital and reserves, they must consider whether or not **sufficient appropriate audit evidence** has been obtained over share capital and reserves balances and transactions to provide the appropriate level of assurance over the audit objectives/management assertions stated, these being:

- completeness;
- existence/occurrence;
- cut-off;
- recording and valuation;
- rights and obligations; and
- classification, presentation and disclosure.

Additionally, the auditor must consider if the audit testing performed has appropriately addressed any key risks surrounding share capital and reserves that were identified during the course of the audit. They must also consider whether the risk of material misstatement arising as a result of key risks has been reduced to a suitably low level.

When testing the area of share capital and reserves, the auditor is most concerned with the presentation and disclosure of audit objectives/management assertions due to the regulatory requirements relating to this area.

The auditor must consider the impact of their testing of share capital and reserves on the audit opinion. This is achieved by considering whether any misstatements found, either individually or in aggregate (when combined with other misstatements detected throughout the audit), will result in the financial statements being materially misstated. As such, all misstatements found are taken to the auditor's errors schedule for consideration at the audit completion stage (discussed in detail in **Chapter 18**). The auditor's report on financial statements is considered in detail in **Chapter 19**.

## SUMMARY OF LEARNING OBJECTIVES

**Learning Objective 1** Understand what is included in the audit of share capital and reserves.

Share capital is the amount paid into the company by the shareholders (i.e. the owners) at the time(s) the shares were issued. Both called-up share capital and called-up share capital not paid must be disclosed on the statement of financial position.

Reserves are the profits retained in the business and not distributed to the shareholders.

**Learning Objective 2** Be able to identify the risks and audit objectives applicable to share capital and reserves.

The risks associated with share capital and reserves revolve mainly around presentation and disclosure.

With regard to equity and reserves, the auditor aims to ensure all transactions and balances: represent events that occurred and exist at the date of the statement of financial position; are complete; represent transactions for which the entity has the rights and obligations to; are recorded correctly in terms of value in line with applicable financial reporting standards and are properly classified, presented and disclosed.

**Learning Objective 3** Be able to determine an appropriate audit strategy for share capital and reserves, taking into consideration the specific risks and audit objectives (management assertions).

The auditor seeks to ensure that the share capital and reserves balances exist and are accurate; and that all share capital and reserve balances are included and appropriately classified, presented and disclosed on the statement of financial position.

**Learning Objective 4** Be able to develop an audit programme that addresses all the audit objectives (management assertions) for share capital and reserves.

The auditor will rarely test controls around share capital and reserves and instead will adopt a wholly substantive approach.

**Learning Objective 5** Be able to describe and apply specific substantive testing procedures relating to the audit of share capital and reserves.

Documents of interest to the auditor include:
- ordinary or preference share registers;
- ordinary or preference share certificates;
- Memorandum of Association and Articles of Association (its 'constitution');
- trust deeds;
- documents pertaining to rights to acquire share capital (share options); and
- company search and inspection of annual return.

The main audit procedures surrounding share capital and reserves relate to confirming the existence of shares by reference to share registers and ensuring the adequate disclosure and presentation of share capital and reserves in the financial statements. The auditor should also test the movements of share capital and reserves in the period. For share capital this will involve testing the additions and disposals of shares in the period.

**Learning Objective 6** Understand the role CAATs can play when auditing share capital and reserves.

The auditor may use a combination of audit software, data analysis tools and other applications, such as Excel, when auditing the area of share capital and reserves.

**Learning Objective 7** Understand the auditor's approach relating to the disclosures of share capital and reserves.

The auditor must consider if the disclosures included in the entity's financial statements are complete, accurate, pertain to the entity and are adequately disclosed in line with applicable international accounting standards.

The auditor should be mindful of the financial reporting standards, including IAS 1 *Presentation of Financial Statements*, which outlines the requirements of the inclusion of a SOCE, IAS 8 and IAS 33.

## QUESTIONS

### Self-test Questions

17.1 What is the difference between share capital and reserves?

17.2 List four categories of reserves.

17.3 List seven key documents of interest to the auditor when auditing share capital and reserves.

17.4 Explain how the audit of reserves is performed.

17.5 Discuss how a company search can benefit an auditor.

17.6 Explain what determines whether a financial instrument is classified as either a liability or as equity.

### Review Questions

(See Suggested Solutions to Review Questions in **Appendix C**.)

## Question 17.1

You are the audit senior on Printer Ltd for the year ended 31 December 2018. Following your review of the company search and the documents filed during the year, you note that 50 shares were issued at €2 each during the year. The nominal price per share is €1. The issue of the shares has not been reflected in the draft financial statements provided to you by Printer Ltd.

**Requirement** Outline the audit procedures you would undertake to audit the above.

## Question 17.2

You are auditing the equity of Martins plc and have been presented with the following information:

STATEMENT OF CHANGES IN EQUITY (EXTRACT)
FOR THE YEAR ENDED 31 DECEMBER 2018

|  | Share capital €/£000 | Share premium €/£000 | Revaluation reserve €/£000 | Retained earnings €/£000 | Total €/£000 |
|---|---|---|---|---|---|
| Opening balance | 200 |  | 450 | 560 | 1210 |
| Change in accounting policy |  |  |  | (45) | (45) |
|  | 200 |  | 450 | 515 | 1,165 |
| SOCI |  |  | 340 | 135 | 475 |
| Dividends |  |  |  | (40) | (40) |
| Share issue | 100 | 400 |  |  | 500 |
| Closing balance | 300 | 400 | 790 | 610 | 2,100 |

**Total Comprehensive Income** Profit for the year amounted to €/£135,000 and movement of €/£340,000 has been recorded in Other Comprehensive Income (in respect of a revaluation surplus on PPE).

**Share Capital** Share capital consists of 200,000 ordinary shares of €/£1 each as at 31 December 2017. On 5 May 2018, 500,000 ordinary shares of €/£1 each were issued and fully paid up.

**Dividends** Dividends for the year amount to €/£0.133 per share, and were approved by the directors on 20 December 2018.

**Requirement** Arising from your review of the information provided, set out the additional audit procedures you would request your audit assistant to perform.

## CHALLENGING QUESTIONS FOR PART III

These challenging questions aim to test your knowledge of **Chapters 11–17**. The challenging questions are intended to test your practical application of what you have learned in these chapters and so you are presented with a case study on which you are asked to deliver on a number of requirements.

(Suggested solutions to challenging questions are available through your lecturer.)

### Question III.1

You are a member of the engagement team on the audit of Large Company Limited. It is February 2019 and you have been assigned the area of non-current assets and have been provided with the following information:

- the non-current assets note as per the draft financial statements (see **Appendix B**, Note 13);
- Mastersons & Associates carried out the revaluation on the freehold land and buildings based in Dublin city centre. Mastersons & Associates are a UK company. Management has the document, prepared by Mastersons & Associates, outlining the findings and recommended valuation.
- the non-current asset value as per the statement of financial position in the draft financial statements is €140,500, the value per the Non-current Asset Register is €145,500 (the non-current asset register, which includes accumulated depreciation charges to date and date of purchase/disposal, is available in Excel).
- the non-current asset additions listing was received in Excel. A junior member of the audit team checked the mathematical accuracy of these schedules, which showed additions of €75,500,000 relating to plant and machinery and €35,000,000 relating to motor vehicles. The listing was sorted according to value, and the following were the items purchased for the lowest values:

### Plant and Machinery Additions

|  | € | € | € |
|---|---:|---:|---:|
| Pallet count reader | 500 | | |
| Fittings to Repair Line 1 | 1,200 | | |
| New conveyor belt | | 5,000 | |
| Improvement to Line 2 | 5,800 | | |
| New fork-lift trucks | | 11,500 | |
| New fork-lift trucks | | 15,000 | |
| New palletiser | | 16,000 | |
| Additions to Line 3 | | 22,000 | |
| | | | 77,000 |

### Motor Vehicle Additions

|  | € | € | € |
|---|---:|---:|---:|
| Install 5 car-phone kits | 1,200 | | |
| Volkswagen Passat (05D21256) | 8,900 | | |
| Toyota Avensis (06D21587) | 9,200 | | |
| | | | 19,300 |

- The company's accounting policies with regard to property, plant and equipment are included in the draft accounts of Large Company Limited (see **Appendix B**, Statement of Accounting Policies).
- The audit team performed controls testing on the non-current assets area at the interim audit carried out in November and found the controls around non-current assets to be effective.

## Requirement

(a) Your audit manager, John Doe, wants to be confident that you know how to substantively test the area of non-current assets. He asks you to send him a memo outlining:
  (i) the initial audit procedures you intend to perform on non-current assets. He notes that you should include at least **three** initial procedures **and** identify any **immediate issues noted** from the information obtained to date.
  (ii) the substantive audit procedures you intend to perform on additions, giving **specifics** relevant to the information obtained to date.
(b) You are running short of time and so are delegating the audit of depreciation and the revaluation to a more junior member of the audit team. You advise them to choose the most efficient method of testing depreciation. Your audit junior asks for clarification on the methods to test depreciation and how one can be more efficient than the other. You are therefore required to:
  (i) draft an e-mail to the audit junior, outlining two substantive testing procedures to audit depreciation;
  (ii) critique each method with regard to its efficiency; and
  (iii) outline two tests with regard to the revaluation carried out by Mastersons & Associates.

## Question III.2

You are a member of the engagement team on the audit of Large Company Limited. It is February 2019 and you have been assigned the area of receivables and have been provided with the following:
- Extract from the Receivables Lead Schedule prepared by the audit manager.
- Extract from the Aged Receivables Listing showing the make-up of the 'greater than 90 days' figure of €80,000.
- Extract from a meeting held with the credit controller.
- Analytical review performed by a junior member of the audit engagement team.

EXTRACT FROM RECEIVABLES LEAD SCHEDULE

| **Large Company Limited** **31 December 2018** | Audit Materiality | | €3,642,500 |
|---|---|---|---|
| | Performance Materiality | | €2,731,875 |
| | | Initials | Date |
| | Prepared by: | MM | 15/02/2019 |
| **Receivables Lead Schedule** | Reviewed by: | | |

**Receivables – amounts falling due within one year**

|                                 | 31 December 2018 | 31 December 2017 |
|---------------------------------|-----------------:|-----------------:|
|                                 | €000             | €000             |
| Trade receivables               | 3,750            | 4,850            |
| Provision for bad debts         | (500)            | (750)            |
| Loan notes                      | 1,500            | 1,500            |
| Other receivables               | 750              | 600              |
| Prepayments and accrued income  | 1,000            | 1,050            |
|                                 | 6,500            | 7,250            |

**Movement in bad debts provision**

|                                  | 31 December 2018 | 31 December 2017 |
|----------------------------------|-----------------:|-----------------:|
|                                  | €000             | €000             |
| Opening balance                  | 750              | 700              |
| Increase/(decrease) in provision | 450              | 150              |
| Bad debt write-off               | (700)            | (100)            |
| Closing balance                  | 500              | 750              |

**Trade Receivables Aged Analysis**

|                             | 31 December 2018 | 31 December 2017 |
|-----------------------------|-----------------:|-----------------:|
|                             | €000             | €000             |
| Current (within credit terms) | 3,100          | 4,250            |
| 30–60 days                  | 420              | 350              |
| 60–90 days                  | 150              | 140              |
| Greater than 90 days        | 80               | 110              |
|                             | 3,750            | 4,850            |

EXTRACT FROM AGED RECEIVABLES LISTING

| Customer | Name | Location | Total | Current | 30–60 | 60–90 | >90 |
|----------|------|----------|------:|--------:|------:|------:|----:|
|          |      |          | €000  | €000    | €000  | €000  | €000 |
| 1256325  | Downs Ltd    | UK  | 1   | –  | –  | –  | 1 |
| 1256327  | Marks Ltd    | RoI | 1   | –  | –  | –  | 1 |
| 1256358  | Avondale Ltd | UK  | 8   | 3  | 2  | 2  | 1 |
| 1258945  | Tuffy's Ltd  | RoI | 64  | 49 | 13 | –  | 2 |
| 1259687  | Bons Ltd     | NI  | 18  | –  | –  | 15 | 3 |
| 1259865  | AFG Ltd      | RoI | 185 | 80 | 60 | 40 | 5 |
| 1254587  | Dunner Ltd   | RoI | 7   | –  | 0  | 0  | 7 |

| 1254875 | Hogan Ltd | UK | 8 | – | – | – | 8 |
|---|---|---|---|---|---|---|---|
| 1254786 | Bernstein Ltd | UK | 18 | 10 | –2 | –2 | 12 |
| 1256985 | Jack Ltd | NI | 45 | 35 | 10 | –15 | 15 |
| 1256489 | Josh Ltd | RoI | 25 | – | – | – | 25 |
| | | | **3,750** | **3,100** | **420** | **150** | **80** |

## Minutes of Meeting regarding Bad Debt Provision

**Minutes of Meeting with Jean Kelly (Credit Controller) and Kate Louis (CFO)**

**In attendance**        **John Keane (Smith & Reilly)**
                         **Jean Kelly (Large Company Ltd)**
                         **Kate Louis (Large Company Ltd)**

**Re:**          **Bad debts provision**

**John Keane** – I see the bad debt provision is €500,000, yet the amount owing for more than 90 days is only €80,000. What makes up most of the provision?

**Kate Louis** – In November a very large customer (Gone Ltd) went into liquidation owing us €450,000. At present we are unsure if any of this is collectable as there is no indication how much creditors will receive. We expect to get nothing of this €450,000.

**John Keane** – This means that just €50,000 is assigned to all other balances, is that right?

**Kate Louis** – That is correct.

**John Keane** – The provision in the prior year was €750,000. Why was it so high?

**Kate Louis** – A similar situation arose at the end of last year, except the amount owing was €500,000, none of which we collected. Additionally, we had a lot of really old balances dating back a few years that we wrote off during the period on the advice of the debt collection agency. In total, bad debts written off were €700,000 and we increased the provision by €450,000 to account for the large bad debt at the end of 2018.

**John Keane** – Is the rest of the provision made up of 90+ days debts?

**Kate Louis** – Yes, we haven't provided for Josh because, although they've gone into liquidation, there is nothing available for unsecured creditors. One of our directors knows the liquidator and he is going to make sure we get the €25,000 back. He's doing the same for a big retailer who went into liquidation owing €300,000 from December 2018 (Away Ltd). We also haven't provided for AFG – the €5,000 relates to goods they say we didn't deliver. We can't find the POD, but we know the name of the person who the driver gave them to, so we are not letting this one go. We've provided for all the other balances greater than 90 days old as these have all either gone out of business or are likely to.

**John Keane** – Have you considered the possibility of debt less than 90 days being uncollectable?

**Kate Louis** – No, we only review them when they hit 90 days.

**John Keane** – The Jack Ltd debt appears to have been paid but just not allocated, is this correct?

**Jean Kelly** – Yes, that's correct, I forgot to allocate that.

**Kate Louis** – But it will just cover something else in case we've missed anything.

### ANALYTICAL REVIEW PERFORMED BY A JUNIOR MEMBER OF THE AUDIT ENGAGEMENT TEAM

| Accrual Item | 2018 €000 | 2017 €000 | Comment |
|---|---|---|---|
| Rent | 150 | 350 | Rent for Dublin premises is under accrued by €200,000 and rent of UK and NI offices has been omitted (being €200,000) |
| Electricity | 90 | 100 | Reviewed post-year-end invoice – accrual reasonable |
| Phone | 30 | 30 | Reviewed post-year-end invoice – accrual reasonable |
| Repair of building | 150 | 0 | Not applicable in prior year |
| Expenses not yet claimed | 70 | 60 | Reviewed payroll expenses claimed – reasonable |
| Unused holidays | 10 | 60 | The €10,000 represents unused holidays outstanding since 2017. No provision has been made for holidays outstanding from 2018, which are estimated to be approx. €70,000 |
| Bonuses due for 2018 (payable 2019) | 0 | 150 | Bonus accrual was omitted and is expected to be approx. €150,000 for 2018 |
| | 500 | 750 | |

### Requirement

(a) Your audit manager has asked you to:
   (i) Perform a review of the bad debt provision performed by management, prepared in audit working paper format, noting any items that you believe should be taken to the error schedule; and
   (ii) outline any further audit procedures you believe are necessary to conclude on the valuation of receivables.

(b) From the analytical review carried out by a junior member of the audit engagement team, she is unsure how to create the correction journal entry needed to adjust for the omissions of accruals and asks you to help her prepare it.

(c) The audit partner feels, with so much having been omitted from accruals, that there is a high risk that there are further unrecorded liabilities and asks you to outline further audit procedures to be carried out by the audit junior in order to conclude on the completeness assertion for payables and accruals.

### Question III.3

You are a member of the engagement team on the audit of Large Company Limited. It is February 2019 and you have been assigned to perform substantive testing on the revenue and cost areas of the Statement of Comprehensive Income. The following information is made available to you.

## Revenue

The company's principal activity is the manufacture of furniture. Revenue has increased in excess of 41% from €198 million in 2017 to €280 million in 2018. €42 million of this increase is attributable to an increase in sales to the UK (Large Company Limited is an Irish company using the euro as its functional currency). Sales to the UK are made in Sterling, and then converted to euro at a rate of €1 to £0.79 (the rate configured in the computer system when it was set up). A summary of the UK revenue transactions and the actual average monthly exchange rates are included below.

### SUMMARY OF UK REVENUE TRANSACTIONS

| Date of revenue transaction | Date shipped | Description | Sterling value of invoice £ | Euro value recorded in books € |
|---|---|---|---|---|
| 20/06/2018 | 18/06/2018 | Luxury Dining Suite | 1,580,000 | 2,000,000 |
| 20/07/2018 | 15/07/2018 | Suzzie Suite | 4,937,500 | 6,250,000 |
| 21/08/2018 | 15/08/2018 | Luxury Dining Suite | 4,147,500 | 5,250,000 |
| 30/09/2018 | 15/09/2018 | Bespoke Design Suite | 4,424,000 | 5,600,000 |
| 15/10/2018 | 10/10/2018 | High Harry Dining Chairs | 2,607,000 | 3,300,000 |
| 16/11/2018 | 10/11/2018 | Bespoke Design | 5,925,000 | 7,500,000 |
| 20/12/2018 | 10/12/2018 | High Harry Dining Chairs | 790,000 | 1,000,000 |
| 31/12/2018 | Not yet shipped | Bespoke Design | 4,345,000 | 5,500,000 |
| 31/12/2018 | Not yet shipped | Bespoke Design | 4,918,750 | 6,225,000 |
| | | | **33,674,750** | **42,625,000** |

### ACTUAL AVERAGE STERLING TO EURO RATE – JUNE TO DECEMBER 2018

| Month | Sterling Rate |
|---|---|
| June | 0.85 |
| July | 0.85 |
| August | 0.85 |
| September | 0.82 |
| October | 0.82 |
| November | 0.82 |
| December | 0.80 |

The two transactions recorded at 31 December 2018 relate to two contracts signed pre-31 December 2018. The first is for Luxury Direct Ltd and the goods are complete and were ready to ship on the 15 December 2018, but the customer requested that the invoice be sent but the goods be held until they could make room in their warehouse, which wouldn't be until January. The second relates to a contract signed on 20 December 2018 with Excellence Furniture. While the design is complete and the raw materials have been purchased, production will not commence until January 2019. An extract of the contract is included below.

CONTRACT BETWEEN EXCELLENCE FURNITURE AND
LARGE COMPANY LIMITED (EXTRACT)

**Date:** 20/12/2018

**Pricing**

A total sum of £4,918,750 will be payable as follows:

1. £500,000 on completion of designs;
2. £1,000,000 on purchase of specialised raw materials as detailed in the design; and
3. balance on completion of production.

**Cost**

Included within the cost of sales is an amount of €2,200,000, which relates to a provision for unusable raw materials. A recent change in legislation has rendered the raw materials unusable in production as they contain a toxic oil component.

**Requirement**

(a) Outline the audit procedures you would perform to validate the UK revenue transactions.
(b) Summarise any misstatements noted from your testing of the UK revenue.
(c) Discuss the audit procedures you would consider necessary in light of the provision made for unusable raw materials.

## Question III.4

You are the audit senior on the audit of Large Company Limited for the year ending 31 December 2018. You have been assigned to plan all aspects of the audit of the year-end physical inventory count. Inventory is a material figure in Large Company Limited's statement of financial activities.

From reading last year's audit file you are aware that Large Company Limited has inventory at its main production location, and also has inventory of finished goods at its branch location in Northern Ireland (Wood Kit) and in England (Wood Fit). The value of inventory at each of these locations at the end of 2018 is estimated to be €3 million each. Inventory is transferred to the branches at the cost of production. On sale they are invoiced at the company's normal selling prices. The inventory of Large Company Limited is valued on a standard cost basis.

In order to promote sales, Large Company Limited offers goods on a sale-or-return basis to two of its key customers. On an ongoing basis, the sales value of such inventory is estimated to be approx. €1 million. The gross profit margin on such sales is 40%.

**Requirement**
(a)  Detail the audit procedures to be followed at the year-end inventory count and the information you will need to prepare the audit plan. Assume that your client has told you that there is no need for your staff to attend the inventory counts at the branch locations.
(b)  Outline the principal risks that could lead to an incorrect inventory count at Large Company Limited.
(c)  Outline the circumstances under which standard cost would be a suitable method of valuing inventory.
(d)  Describe the audit procedures you would perform to be satisfied that the standard costs have been properly determined by Large Company Limited.
(e)  Discuss briefly what action you would take if you were to discover that there are significant variances between actual and standard values for inventory.

# PART IV

# THE AUDIT AND ASSURANCE PROCESS: COMPLETION PROCEDURES AND REPORTING

# THE AUDIT AND ASSURANCE PROCESS

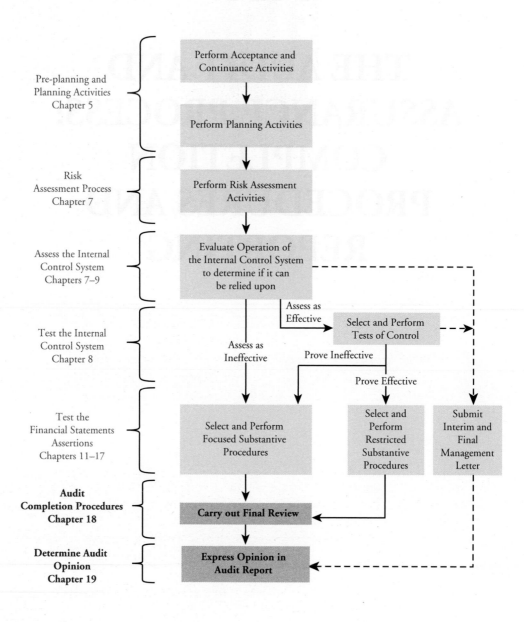

# 18

# AUDIT COMPLETION PROCEDURES

LEARNING OBJECTIVES

Having studied this chapter on audit work conclusions you should:
1. have a clear understanding of final analytical procedures and their importance in the conclusion of an audit;
2. be able to consider the misstatements taken to the schedule of unadjusted differences (errors schedule) when concluding on whether or not the financial statements are materially misstated;
3. understand the auditor's responsibility regarding subsequent events for the different time periods highlighted in ISA 560 *Subsequent Events*;
4. be able to discuss the requirements of the auditor regarding the assessment of the going concern assumption;
5. understand the content of written representations and the role that they play;
6. understand the auditor's approach to reviewing the classification of provisions, contingent liabilities and contingent assets;
7. understand the importance of the final review of the audit working papers;
8. be able to discuss the form of other reports directed at those charged with governance; and
9. understand the considerations of the auditor regarding related parties.

## CHECKLIST OF RELEVANT STANDARDS

The relevant standards, both in the RoI and the UK/NI, covered in this chapter are:

ISA 260 *Communication with Those Charged with Governance*
ISA 320 *Materiality in Planning and Performing an Audit*
ISA 450 *Evaluation of Misstatements Identified During the Audit*
ISA 501 *Audit Evidence – Specific Considerations for Selected Items*
ISA 520 *Analytical Procedures*
ISA 550 *Related Parties*
ISA 560 *Subsequent Events*
ISA 570 *Going Concern*
ISA 580 *Written Representations*
IAS 2 *Inventories*
IAS 10 *Events after the Reporting Period*
IAS 37 *Provisions, Contingent Liabilities and Contingent Assets*

Note, in general when referring to ISAs, it should be understood as referring to the UK and Ireland versions, unless otherwise specified as either ISA (UK) or ISA (Ireland). See the Introduction for an extant list of auditing standards for the RoI and the UK/NI.

## KEY TERMS AND DEFINITIONS IN THIS CHAPTER

**Analytical Procedures**   Defined in ISA 520, paragraph 4, as "evaluations of financial information through analysis of plausible relationships among both financial and non-financial data".

**Arm's-length Transaction**   A transaction conducted on such terms and conditions as between a willing buyer and a willing seller which are unrelated and are acting independently of each other and pursuing their own best interests.

**Going Concern**   The going concern assumption focuses on the client entity being able to continue in business for the foreseeable future without an intention to liquidate or cease the entity, or that there are no conditions that might not allow it to continue (e.g. a changing business environment or significant litigation that could impact on the future of the business).

**Letter of Representation**   ISA 580, paragraph 15, states: "written representations shall be in the form of a representation letter addressed to the auditor". See also **Written Representation**.

**Management**   "The person(s) with executive responsibility for the conduct of the entity's operations. For some entities in some jurisdictions, management includes some or all of those charged with governance, for example, executive members of a governance board, or an owner-manager." (ISA 260, paragraph 10) References to 'management' in this chapter and throughout include, where appropriate, "those charged with governance".

**Misstatement**   Defined in ISA 450, paragraph 4, as "A difference between the reported amount, classification, presentation, or disclosure of a financial statement item and the amount, classification, presentation, or disclosure that is required for the item to be in accordance with the applicable financial reporting framework. Misstatements can arise from fraud or error."

**Subsequent Events** "Events occurring between the date of the financial statements and the date of the auditor's report, and facts that become known to the auditor after the date of the auditor's report." (ISA 560, paragraph 5(e))

**Written Representation** "A written statement by management provided to the auditor to confirm certain matters or to support other audit evidence. Written representations in this context do not include financial statements, the assertions therein, or supporting books and records." (ISA 580, paragraph 7)

## 18.1  INTRODUCTION

As the audit draws to a conclusion, the auditor performs audit procedures to obtain further audit evidence in order to draw conclusions and finalise the audit process. The auditor will perform the following when concluding on an entity's financial statements:

1. final analytical procedures;
2. evaluation of misstatements identified during the audit;
3. subsequent events review;
4. evaluation of the going concern assumption;
5. management written representations (letter of representation);
6. review of provisions, contingent liabilities and contingent assets;
7. final review of working papers;
8. communication with those charged with governance; and
9. conclusion on related parties.

Each of these procedures will be discussed in turn in this chapter.

## 18.2  FINAL ANALYTICAL PROCEDURES

### Introduction

Final analytical procedures are similar to the preliminary analytical procedures performed at the planning stages of the audit covered in **Chapter 5**, Section 5.4, and again in **Chapter 7** (**Example 7.1**). They allow the auditor to review the financial statements in their entirety in order to highlight any unusual balances or relationships (gross profit movements) that may not have been noted in the audit.

In concluding on the audit work performed, the auditor should complete final analytical procedures to form an overall opinion on the financial statements. ISA 520 *Analytical Procedures*, paragraph 6, states:

"The auditor shall design and perform analytical procedures near the end of the audit that assist the auditor when forming an overall conclusion as to whether the financial statements are consistent with the auditor's understanding of the entity."

Performing final analytical procedures allows the auditor not only to see if the financial statements 'make sense' and if any unusual or unexpected relationships exist, but also whether the results are consistent with other information obtained by the auditor.

## The Benefits of Final Analytical Procedures

The performing of final **analytical procedures** offers a number of benefits:
- During the course of the audit a previously unidentified risk of material misstatement may arise. Final analytical procedures help reduce **detection risk** by providing the auditor with an opportunity to ensure they understand all movements in the financial statements.
- Unusual fluctuations or unexpected results that are inconsistent with other audit evidence will be highlighted.
- An opportunity to ensure conclusions formed during the audit of the financial statements can be supported.
- The auditor can conclude on the reasonableness of the financial statements with added assurance and support.

## Identification of New Risks during Final Analytical Procedures

In performing the final analytical procedures, if the auditor identifies new risks it may be necessary to re-evaluate the audit procedures performed. Prior to conducting additional procedures, the auditor should evaluate the misstatements identified and assess whether these misstatements have a material impact on the financial statements. In making this assessment, the possibility of similar undiscovered misstatements that may require further investigation should be considered. ISA 520, paragraph 7, states:

> "If analytical procedures performed in accordance with this ISA … identify fluctuations or relationships that are inconsistent with other relevant information or that differ from expected values by a significant amount, the auditor shall investigate such differences by:
> (a) Inquiring of management and obtaining appropriate audit evidence relevant to management's responses; and
> (b) Performing other audit procedures as necessary in the circumstances."

## Use of Benchmarks

Final analytical procedures may be performed by comparing current-year figures to prior-year financials or through **using external knowledge sources as a benchmark**. Based on the auditor's understanding of the client entity and its market, the auditor should identify an accurate and **comparable benchmark**. For example, if the client entity is a medium-sized hardware store, a large multinational hardware store should not be used for comparison purposes. It is important to remember to use **an appropriate benchmark** when performing final analytical procedures. The following are examples of instances of the use of benchmarks during final analytical procedures:
- customer acquisition – benchmark to compare how many new customers have been acquired during the financial year;

- customer retention – benchmark to compare how many customers have been retained during the financial year;
- sales growth – compare sales growth to the benchmark during the financial year;
- selling and marketing activities – compare selling and marketing activities to the benchmark;
- determine the key performance measures that capture the business activities so that actual key performance figures can be benchmarked against those budgeted.

In summary, final analytical procedures conducted by the auditor supplement the other audit procedures conducted during the course of the audit. They provide a comparison to the relative industry and an overall assessment of the client entity's performance. However, it is important to stress that final analytical procedures **supplement** other audit procedures and are not effective in any way on their own.

## 18.3 EVALUATION OF MISSTATEMENTS IDENTIFIED DURING THE AUDIT

### Introduction

ISA 450 *Evaluation of Misstatements Identified During the Audit*, paragraph 1, states that the auditor has a "responsibility to evaluate the effect of identified misstatements on the audit and of uncorrected misstatements, if any, on the financial statements". At the final stages of the audit, the auditor needs to summarise all misstatements found during the course of the audit. This is referred to as the **schedule of unadjusted differences** (or more commonly as 'the error schedule').

In addition, ISA 200, *Overall Objectives of the Independent Auditor and the Conduct of an Audit in Accordance with International Standards on Auditing*, paragraph 3, states:
"The purpose of an audit is to enhance the degree of confidence of intended users in the financial statements. This is achieved by the expression of an opinion by the auditor on whether the financial statements are prepared, in all material respects, in accordance with an applicable financial reporting framework."

During the course of the audit the auditor may note **misstatements** (whether material or not) in the accounts of the client entity that were not corrected by **management** and that should be included in the schedule of unadjusted differences (error schedule) if, after discussions with management, they are to remain uncorrected. It is important to consider **materiality** and **tolerable error** when examining the unadjusted differences. Once these have been set, the auditor should evaluate the effect of the uncorrected misstatements, both individually and in aggregate, on the financial statements.

If there are uncorrected misstatements carried over from the prior-year audit, these need to be assessed to determine if they continue to be a misstatement in the current year's financial statements. For example, an unrecorded liability recorded as an error in the prior year would not be an error in the current year provided it is now recorded. However, if an uncorrected liability relates to, for example, a legal claim that continues to be uncorrected, then the uncorrected error of the prior year remains an error in the current year. If a material misstatement is found in the current year that should have been recorded in the prior year, the auditor will need to consider if a prior-year adjustment is required to correct the opening balances.

Materiality is set at the **planning stage** of the audit. However, it should be reassessed throughout the audit. Generally, materiality is set as a percentage of either revenues, profit before tax or net assets. In practice, a lower level of materiality is often used when including misstatements in the schedule of unadjusted differences. A full discussion of the calculation and use of materiality is contained in **Chapter 5**, Section 5.4.

The auditor should take into account any uncorrected misstatements from the prior period as this may increase the risk of the current-period financial statements being materially misstated. The **overall materiality level (rather than performance materiality)** is then used to decide those adjustments that need to be made to the client's accounts. **Performance materiality**, as introduced in **Chapter 5**, Section 5.4, is used throughout the audit process to reduce the aggregation risk (i.e provide a margin of error) and ensure all potential material misstatements are captured. Now that the auditor is at the completion stage, all misstatements included in the schedule of unadjusted differences are compared against overall materiality.

## Misstatements Requiring Adjustment

Qualitative factors must also be taken into account when posting adjustments, for example classification errors that, if not rectified, could be in contravention of a financial reporting standard (e.g. misclassification of goods for resale as fixed assets is in contravention of IAS 2). A discussion should be held with management regarding the posting of adjustments to the accounts and, if the client refuses to adjust, the auditor must consider the effect on the auditor's report.

Some examples of why adjustments may be required include:
- a mistake in gathering or processing information from which the financial statements are prepared;
- the omission of an amount or disclosure, e.g. if a new asset was purchased during the year and not included in the **fixed asset register (FAR)**;
- an incorrect accounting estimate arising from overlooking or clearly misinterpreting facts, e.g. if the accountant has omitted significant details that may impact on a provision in the accounts, such as bad debts, inventory obsolescence, etc.;
- management's judgements concerning accounting estimates or the selection and application of accounting policies, which the auditor considers unreasonable or inappropriate; or
- an inappropriate classification, aggregation or disaggregation of information.

A single misstatement in itself may not be material; however, an accumulation of misstatements noted by the auditor could result in an overall material difference. During the course of the audit, the schedule of unadjusted differences will be kept as part of the **audit working papers**. At the final phase of the audit, the auditor must conclude on the cumulative effect of misstatements and their impact on the financial statements of the entity. An example of a schedule of unadjusted differences is set out below at **Figure 18.1**.

## FIGURE 18.1: SCHEDULE OF UNADJUSTED DIFFERENCES ('ERROR SCHEDULE')

| | | Adjusted (Yes/No) | Statement of Comprehensive Income | | Statement of Financial Position | |
|---|---|---|---|---|---|---|
| | | | Dr € | Cr € | Dr € | Cr € |
| Dr | Capital Expense | | X | | | |
| Cr | Fixed Assets | | | | | X |
| (Being the write-off of incorrectly capitalised assets) | | | | | | |

**Example 18.1** below is a worked example of the preparation and evaluation of the schedule of unadjusted differences. This example illustrates the types of misstatement the auditor may have encountered during the audit process. Remember: misstatements will have been included in the schedule of unadjusted differences, whether material or not, so that the auditor can consider if the aggregate effect of misstatements constitutes an overall material misstatement in the financial statements.

## EXAMPLE 18.1: EVALUATION OF MISSTATEMENTS INCLUDED IN THE SUMMARY OF UNADJUSTED DIFFERENCES

It is May 2019 and you are auditing Rapid Ltd for the year ended 31 December 2018. Rapid Ltd is a logistics company based in the Republic of Ireland that distributes throughout Europe. You have asked a member of the audit team to compile a list of all issues noted during the audit. The following is what you have been provided with:

- The bad debt provision provided by the directors is a general provision of €100,000 relating to all debtors greater than 90+ days, plus two specific provisions relating to Chairs.com and Sofa Express Ltd for €25,000 and €30,000, respectively. The general provision has been tested as adequate; however, your junior heard on the radio on his way to work this morning that Sofa Express have gone into liquidation with insufficient funds to pay creditors. Sofa Express Ltd owed €75,000 at 31 December 2018 and has paid €15,000 year-to-date 2019. The dispute with respect to Chairs.com, which relates to damage of property while being delivered costing €25,000, is ongoing.
- On auditing depreciation, it was noted that it was understated by €100,000.
- The solicitor's confirmation letter (which is covered under ISA 505 *External Confirmations*) returned from the solicitor outlines the likely value of a claim relating to an employee accident to be €75,000; there is no provision in the accounts relating to this.
- A payment of €150,000 made to a supplier in 2019 was recorded as being made in 2018.
- Cut-off tests revealed that a delivery that occurred in 2019, valued at €15,000, was included in the revenue for 2018. The client, however, has adjusted for this.

The schedule of unadjusted differences is set out to show the adjustments required to the statement of financial position (SOFP) and the statement of comprehensive income (SOCI). This facilitates a more effective and accurate evaluation of whether or not the financial statements are materially misstated.

| | SOFP | | SOCI | |
|---|---|---|---|---|
| | Dr € | Cr € | Dr € | Cr € |
| Dr Bad debt provision movement (SOCI) re. Sofa Express Ltd | | | 30,000 | |
| Cr Bad debt provision (SOFP) | | 30,000 | | |
| *Being correction of bad debt provision understatement (See Working)* | | | | |
| Dr Depreciation charge (SOCI) | | | 100,000 | |
| Cr Depreciation (SOFP) | | 100,000 | | |
| *Being correction of depreciation understatement* | | | | |
| Dr Claims provision movement (SOCI ) | | | 75,000 | |
| Cr Provision for legal claims (SOFP) | | 75,000 | | |
| *Being correction of legal claim understatement* | | | | |
| Dr Bank (SOFP) | 150,000 | | | |
| Cr Payables (SOFP) | | 150,000 | | |
| *Being correction of classification error on bank and payables* | | | | |
| **Summary** | **150,000** | **355,000** | **205,000** | – |

**Net impact (SOCI) €205,000 (Dr)**

**Note**: the cut-off error was adjusted by the client and so is not included in the schedule of unadjusted differences.

Working – Bad Debt Provision Understatement: Sofa Express Ltd

| | € |
|---|---|
| Owed at year end | 75,000 |
| Paid since year end | (15,000) |
| Still outstanding at time of liquidation | 60,000 |
| Required bad debt provision | 60,000 |
| Actual bad debt provision | (30,000) |
| **Understatement of bad debt provision** | **30,000** |

The schedule of unadjusted differences shows that the accounts are potentially materially misstated. While the net impact on the SOCI remains under the €270,000 overall materiality, the liabilities on the SOFP, in aggregate, are understated by €355,000. Assets are understated by €150,000, and therefore overall net assets are overstated by €205,000, which is below materiality. Errors must be considered both individually and in aggregate. While no one error is material, when all are considered together, a material error exists.

If the client entity were to amend the classification error of €150,000 between payables and bank, the aggregate error would then be:

| | SOFP | | SOCI | |
|---|---|---|---|---|
| | **Dr** | **Cr** | **Dr** | **Cr** |
| | € | € | € | € |
| Summary | – | 205,000 | 205,000 | – |
| Net impact (SOCI) | | 205,000 | 205,000 | |

A material misstatement would therefore not exist within any individual account balance or when considered in aggregate if this adjustment were to be made.

In conclusion, the auditor must document the significance and severity of the misstatements. The **schedule of unadjusted differences** allows the auditor to consider the **cumulative effect of the errors** and their impact on the financial statements. This summary should include misstatements that are not individually material but may be material when aggregated with other misstatements. At audit completion, the auditor is concluding on the cumulative effect of errors and whether or not they have a material impact on the financial statements. Where *unadjusted* material misstatements exist, the auditor should consider the implications for the audit report (see **Chapter 19**).

The auditor should request of management that all errors included in the schedule of unadjusted differences be corrected. Should management decide not to adjust for material errors, the auditor should seek **written representation** from **those charged with governance** explaining their reasons for non-adjustment and that they believe the uncorrected misstatements are immaterial to the financial statements. However, ISA 450, paragraph A24, notes that: "Obtaining this representation does not, however, relieve the auditor of the need to form a conclusion on the effect of uncorrected misstatements."

## 18.4 SUBSEQUENT EVENTS REVIEW

### Introduction

The auditor must consider whether events that occur after the reporting date have an impact on the financial statements. The auditor's responsibility with regard to subsequent events varies depending on the timing of the event. ISA 560 *Subsequent Events*, paragraph 5(e), defines **subsequent events** as:

> "Events occurring between the date of the financial statements and the date of the auditor's report, and facts that become known to the auditor after the date of the auditor's report."

Paragraph 2 of the standard also states that:

> "Financial statements may be affected by certain events that occur after the date of the financial statements. Many financial reporting frameworks specifically refer to such events. Such financial reporting frameworks ordinarily identify two types of events:
> (a) Those that provide evidence of conditions that existed at the date of the financial statements; and
> (b) Those that provide evidence of conditions that arose after the date of the financial statements."

IAS 10 *Events after the Reporting Period* outlines conditions pertaining to adjusting or non-adjusting events. It also states that, ideally, the date the financial statements are approved and signed by the board of directors and the date the auditor's report is approved and signed should be the same date.

The auditor must ensure that there are no events post-year end that will materially impact the financial statements:

> "The auditor shall perform audit procedures designed to obtain sufficient appropriate audit evidence that all events occurring between the date of the financial statements and the date of the auditor's report that require adjustment of, or disclosure in, the financial statements have been identified." (ISA 560, paragraph 6)

**Table 18.1** below outlines the key dates defined by ISA 560, and shows how the auditor's responsibilities regarding the detection, review and consideration of subsequent events vary depending on the timing of the event. Three time periods are recognised:
1. events occurring **between** the date of the financial statements (the year end date) and the date of the auditor's report;
2. facts that become known to the auditor **after** the date of the auditor's report but **before** the date the financial statements are issued; and
3. facts that become known to the auditor **after** the financial statements have been issued.

Let us now consider the approach of the auditor within each time period.

### Events Occurring between Date of the Financial Statements and Date of the Auditor's Report

The auditor has an active role in understanding management's approach to identifying subsequent events as well as performing audit procedures in order to identify subsequent events. ISA 560, paragraph 7, states that such procedures should include:

> "(a) Obtaining an understanding of any procedures management have established to ensure that subsequent events are identified.
> (b) Inquiring of management ... as to whether any subsequent events have occurred which might affect the financial statements.

(c) Reading minutes, if any, of meetings … held after the date of the financial statements and inquiring about matters discussed at any such meetings for which minutes are not available.

(d) Reading the entity's latest subsequent interim financial statements, if any."

If no interim financial statements are available (as suggested by item (d)), paragraph A7 advises that the auditor could inspect "available books and records, including bank statements".

TABLE 18.1: DEFINITION OF KEY DATES AS PER ISA 560

| Key Date | Definition | Responsibility of Auditor |
|---|---|---|
| **1. Events occurring between date of financial statements and date of auditor's report** | | |
| **Date of the financial statements** | The date of the end of the latest period covered by the financial statements. | The auditor has an active role in understanding management's approach to identifying subsequent events, as well as performing audit procedures in order to identify subsequent events. |
| **Date of approval of the financial statements** | The same date as that on which all the statements that comprise the financial statements, including related notes, have been prepared and those with the recognised authority have asserted that they have taken responsibility for those financial statements. The audit report is signed on that date. | |
| **2. Facts that become known after date of auditor's report but before date financial statements are issued** | | |
| **Date of the auditor's report** | The date the auditor signs the report on the financial statements in accordance with ISA 700. | The auditor need only consider the impact of facts/events that become known to them (i.e. there is no obligation to perform further audit procedures regarding subsequent events). |
| **Date the financial statements are issued** | The date that the auditor's report and audited financial statements are made available to third parties. | |
| **3. Facts that become known after financial statements have been issued** | | |
| **Date the financial statements are issued** | The date the auditor's report and audited financial statements are made available to third parties. | The auditor need only consider the impact of facts/events that become known to them (i.e. there is no obligation to perform further audit procedures regarding subsequent events). |

## Facts that become known to the Auditor after the Date of the Auditor's Report but before the Date Financial Statements are Issued

The auditor need only consider the impact of facts/events that become *known* to them after the date of the auditor's report, i.e. there is no obligation to perform further audit procedures regarding subsequent events. If an event/fact becomes known that would have resulted in a modified audit opinion, then the auditor should:

- discuss it with **management**;
- determine if the financial statements should be amended;
- inquire if management intend to amend the misstatement in light of the subsequent event:
  - if an amendment is made, it should be restricted to the subsequent event and the auditor should perform audit procedures to gain **sufficient appropriate audit evidence** on the amendment and issue a new report if necessary;
  - if no amendment is made by management, the auditor should instruct management not to issue the financial statements in their present form and to include a modified opinion report (i.e. qualifying the opinion); or
  - if no amendment is made and the auditor's instruction to management not to issue the financial statements is ignored, the auditor should then take appropriate action to seek to prevent reliance on the auditor's report. Such action might include attendance at the AGM or, if considered serious enough, resignation from the audit (in accordance with section 400 CA 2014 or section 519 CA 2006).

## Facts that become known to the Auditor after the Financial Statements have been Issued

ISA 560, paragraph 14, states: "After the financial statements have been issued, the auditor has no obligation to perform any audit procedures regarding such financial statements."

If, however, the auditor becomes aware of an event that would have required an amendment to the financial statements, the matter should be discussed with management, including an inquiry as to how they intend to address it. If the financial statements are amended and reissued, the auditor shall perform audit procedures on the amendment to be satisfied that the audit report is still appropriate and, if it is not, issue an amended audit report.

If no amendment is made to the financial statements by management, the auditor should take appropriate action to seek to prevent reliance on the auditor's report, which could include attending and speaking at the AGM.

## Adjusting and Non-adjusting Events

Once the auditor determines that an event has taken place subsequent to the date of the financial statements, they will need to consider if it is an adjusting or a non-adjusting event. This will determine whether or not a misstatement exists in the financial statements.

**Adjusting events** provide evidence of conditions that existed at the year end date and allow a more accurate valuation of balances and events at that date. These events must be reflected in the financial statements of the entity. IAS 10 *Events after the Reporting Period*, paragraph 9, gives examples of such events as:

- the settlement of a court case that confirms the entity has a present obligation at the reporting date;

- the receipt of information after the date of the SOFP that indicates an asset was impaired at that date;
- the determination, after the date of the SOFP, of the cost of assets purchased or proceeds of assets sold before that date;
- details of fraud or errors which mean that the financial statements are incorrect.

**Non-adjusting events** are not required to be reflected in the financial statements of the entity as they do not provide additional evidence of events that existed at the reporting date. There are, however, many non-adjusting events that *do* need to be disclosed – by way of a note to the financial statements – due to their materiality. For example:

- the discontinuance of an operation after the reporting date;
- major restructuring plans;
- a major business combination after the balance sheet date;
- an issue of shares after the balance sheet date.

Further examples of non-adjusting events are given in IAS 10, paragraphs 21–22.

## Audit Procedures to Identify Subsequent Events

As noted above, between the date of the financial statements and the date of signing of the auditor's report, the auditor has an active role in identifying subsequent events that may provide evidence of conditions that existed at the reporting date. This active role can be discharged by performing some of the following audit procedures:

- review of original signed minutes of meetings held by management, shareholders and those charged with governance;
- inquiring of the client entity's legal counsel;
- inquiring of management about:
  - new commitments or borrowings entered into;
  - major sales or acquisitions planned;
  - any increase in capital or debt instruments;
  - any assets appropriated or destroyed by fire, flood, etc.;
  - any developments in risk areas or where contingent liabilities were identified;
  - any events that call into question the appropriateness of the accounting policies utilised;
- reviewing latest management accounts, budgets, cash flows, etc. for unusual trends;
- investigating risk areas and contingencies arising from the nature of the business;
- calculating the current cash position and comparing it to the overdraft limit and cash-flow forecast and analysing movements since the year end;
- following up on any matters cleared tentatively or on the basis of inconclusive inform-ation during the detailed fieldwork;
- investigating unusual transactions occurring shortly before or after the year end date;
- reviewing journal entries to ensure that material adjusting events have been properly processed;
- agreeing details of material non-adjusting events with the notes to the financial statements.

For any subsequent events that have been identified, the auditor should ensure that they have been appropriately disclosed and accounted for by management. If management are unwilling to amend the financial statements for the effect of a material and/or pervasive subsequent event, the auditor must consider the potential impact on their audit opinion. This will be discussed further in **Chapter 19**.

## 18.5  GOING CONCERN

### Introduction

The going concern assumption focuses on the client entity being able to continue in business for the foreseeable future, without an intention to liquidate the entity or that there are no conditions that might not allow it to continue (e.g. a changing business environment or significant litigation that could impact on the future of the business).

As introduced in **Chapter 5**, ISA 570 *Going Concern*, paragraph 9, states that one of the objectives of the auditor is to "obtain sufficient appropriate audit evidence regarding, and concluded on, the appropriateness of management's use of the going concern basis of accounting in the preparation of the financial statements".

The primary responsibility for assessing the appropriateness of the **going concern** assumption (i.e. the basis on which the financial statements are prepared) rests with **those charged with governance** of the entity. The auditor has a secondary responsibility in that they must ensure the validity of management's assumptions. As part of the audit completion procedures, the auditor must reconsider their initial assessment of the going concern basis for the preparation of the financial statements, and revise it if necessary. It is recommended that there are early meetings between management and the auditor to discuss the assessment of going concern and any relevant disclosures.

The going concern assumption is a fundamental principle in the preparation of the financial statements. The auditor must ensure that the financial statements have been presented on a going concern basis only if assessments indicate that the entity will in fact continue in its present capacity for the foreseeable future (at least 12 months from the date of the audit report).

While going concern is considered initially at the planning stage, it is during the completion stage of the audit that the auditor makes a final decision on the going concern assumption of the entity. In order to conclude on whether or not the client entity is a going concern, the auditor will consider:
- the factors impacting the judgement of going concern;
- the assessment period for going concern; and
- the specific substantive audit procedures to assess the going concern assumption.

These are considered in turn below.

## Factors Impacting the Judgement of Going Concern

The auditor should remain alert to factors that may raise any doubts over the entity's ability to continue as a going concern. According to ISA 570, paragraph 5, the following factors are relevant:

"• The degree of uncertainty associated with the outcome of an event or condition increases significantly the further into the future an event or condition or the outcome occurs. ...

• The size and complexity of the entity, the nature and condition of its business and the degree to which it is affected by external factors affect the judgment regarding the outcome of events or conditions.

• Any judgment about the future is based on information available at the time at which the judgment is made. Subsequent events may result in outcomes that are inconsistent with judgments that were reasonable at the time they were made."

During the course of the audit the **audit engagement team** will gain an understanding of the organisation, and through the performance of controls testing and substantive procedures may obtain audit evidence to suggest that the entity may not be able to continue as a going concern. The engagement partner and engagement manager must ensure that the members of the engagement team are mindful of the factors outlined above and to alert the engagement manager if such evidence is discovered. This will ensure that all factors are considered at a senior level within the engagement team.

## Assessment Period for Going Concern

Generally, management will assess going concern for a period from one year from the date of approval of the financial statements. Where the period under consideration is less than one year, the auditor should disclose the following in the financial statements:
• the time period being considered by management, e.g. seven months; and
• the reason(s) why they believe the period being considered is appropriate.

## Specific Substantive Audit Procedures to Assess the Going Concern Assumption

### Audit Procedure 1 – Consideration of Management's Assessment of Going Concern

It is the auditor's responsibility to consider the appropriateness of management's (or those charged with governance) going concern assumption in the preparation of the financial statements (ISA 570, paragraph 6). This is usually achieved by:
• evaluating the means by which management have satisfied themselves that the going concern basis of preparation is appropriate;
• judging the adequacy of the length of the period management have assessed (it should be at least 12 months from the date of approval of the financial statements), and the systems by which they have identified warnings of future risks and uncertainties;
• examining all appropriate audit evidence utilised in making the assumption, e.g. reviewing board minutes, cash flows, loan agreements, budgets, management accounts and other reports of recent activities, etc.;
• assessing the sensitivity of the audit evidence to events and conditions both inside and outside the control of the entity;

- concluding on whether or not the auditor is of the same opinion as management, based on evidence available and reasonable assumptions about the outcome of future events;
- assessing management's plans for resolving any matters on the going concern assumption;
- assessing management's consideration of future periods.

### Audit Procedure 2 – The Auditor's Assessment of Going Concern

In considering the entity's ability to continue as a going concern, the auditor should be mindful of the following:
- the auditor's knowledge of the client entity and its operating characteristics, e.g. its business, products, competitors, environment, etc.;
- the industry and the economic conditions it operates in;
- management's assessment of the client entity's ability to continue as a going concern;
- the possibility of any legal cases involving the entity;
- any undisclosed arrangements or events that may hinder the entity's ability to continue as a going concern;
- any events or conditions that, individually or collectively, may have an impact on the going concern of the entity.

**Table 18.2** below provides examples of events or conditions that may indicate that an entity does not have the ability to continue as a going concern. These events or conditions are considered under three categories: financial; operating; and other.

TABLE 18.2: EXAMPLES OF EVENTS OR CONDITIONS THAT MAY IMPACT (INDIVIDUALLY OR COLLECTIVELY) ON THE GOING CONCERN ASSUMPTION OF AN ENTITY

| Financial | Operating | Other |
|---|---|---|
| • Entity has not met necessary borrowing agreements.<br>• Indication of the withdrawal of financial support by creditors.<br>• Unable to pay creditors on the appropriate due dates.<br>• Loan facilities up for renewal within 12 months from date of approval of financial statements.<br>• Inability to finance new products and product development.<br>• Substantial operating losses.<br>• Net liability or net current liability position. | • Loss of key management or staff.<br>• Labour difficulties and a shortage of key suppliers.<br>• Loss of a major market or loss of a key supplier.<br>• Fundamental changes in the marketplace or in technology to which the entity cannot respond.<br>• Excessive dependence on a few products where the market is depressed. | • Non-compliance with capital or other statutory requirements.<br>• Changes in legislation or government policy which may adversely affect the business.<br>• Pending legal claims against the company which cannot be met.<br>• Non-compliance with capital or other statutory requirements.<br>• Legislative changes that will adversely impact the entity. |

## *Audit Procedure 3 – Conclude on Going Concern Assumption*

Finally, the auditor should prepare appropriate documentation to show the **audit evidence and conclusions** reached on the going concern assumption. Any implications for the **audit report** should be considered based on circumstances presented. These could include:

1. The auditor concurs with management's assessment that the entity is a going concern – no modification of the audit opinion is required regarding going concern.
2. The auditor considers that there are uncertainties connected to the going concern assumption that will not be known until the occurrence of future events. However, the auditor is satisfied that all necessary provisions and disclosures are made based on the evidence available at the time of the fieldwork (and reassessed in line with responsibilities associated with subsequent events, as outlined in **Section 18.4**). In this instance, the auditor will issue an **unmodified opinion** and in the audit report will include a separate section under the heading 'Material Uncertainty Related to Going Concern'. This section should draw attention to the disclosure note outlining the details of the material uncertainty, and state that the auditor's opinion is not modified in respect of this matter. (Previously, this would have been noted under an **emphasis of matter** paragraph.)
3. The auditor considers that there are uncertainties connected to the going concern assumption that will not be known until the occurrence of future events and is not satisfied that all necessary provisions and disclosures are made based on the evidence available at the time of the fieldwork (and reassessed in line with responsibilities associated with subsequent events, as outlined in **Section 18.4**). In this instance, the auditor disagrees with the financial statements and may issue a **qualified opinion** ('except for') or an **adverse opinion**, as appropriate. This is in line with ISA 705. In the 'Basis for qualified/adverse opinion' section of the auditor's report, it must state that a material uncertainty exists that calls in to question the entity's ability to continue as a going concern and the fact that the financial statements do not disclose this matter.
4. The auditor disagrees with the going concern assumption and as such disagrees with the financial statements, and issues an **adverse opinion**. An adverse opinion is generally the outcome of a disagreement on going concern due to the gravity of the misstatement, be it financial or non-financial (i.e. disclosure-related).
5. Should the period considered by management be less than 12 months from the date of approval of the financial statements and management refuses to extend the period of assessment, the auditor should disclose this fact in the audit report in the section headed 'Conclusions relating to going concern'. This does not prevent the auditor from carrying out audit procedures to determine if they believe the entity to be a going concern, although the reluctance of management to extend their period of assessment may raise concerns for the auditor that could give rise to previously unforeseen risks. The auditor should, even if the period assessed by management is adequate, inquire of management if they are aware of any events or conditions beyond the period assessed that could impact on the entity's ability to continue as a going concern.

A summary of the above discussion is included at **Table 18.3** below.

TABLE 18.3: CONCLUDING ON THE GOING CONCERN ASSUMPTION

| Type of Disclosure | Type of Audit Report |
|---|---|
| 1. The auditor concludes that there are no concerns surrounding the use of the going concern assumption and thereby agrees with the basis on which the financial statements are prepared. | An **unqualified, unmodified** opinion is issued. |
| 2. Adequate evidence exists regarding an **uncertainty** over the going concern assumption. That is, the auditor does not conclude that entity is not a going concern, but that an uncertainty exists, which cannot be concluded upon right now as the outcome will be determined by an event that is to occur in the future, the outcome of which may lead to the entity not being able to continue as a going concern. This uncertainty has been **fully disclosed by management in the financial statements by way of a disclosure note.** | An **unqualified opinion**, including an explanatory 'material uncertainty related to going concern' paragraph in the 'Basis for opinion' section. |
| 3. Adequate evidence is available to the auditor, yet **uncertainty** exists over the going concern assumption, which is *not* fully disclosed by the directors in the financial statements. | A **qualified opinion** of an 'except for' type, due to disagreement over adequacy of disclosures. |
| 4. Financial statements are found to be prepared on a going concern basis; however, audit evidence suggests that the entity is not a going concern. | An **adverse opinion** should be issued as the financial statements do not give a **true and fair** view. |
| 5. Management have not fully considered the going concern assumption for at least one year following the approval of the financial statements. | If full disclosures of facts concerning the period under review are provided by management and the auditor has no concerns regarding going concern, then no reference to the matter is made in the audit report. If inadequate disclosures are made, then the period reviewed should be noted in the 'Basis for opinion' section of the report, noting the period of going concern considered by management. The audit report, however, will not be qualified unless the auditor disagrees that the client entity is a going concern. |

The auditor should also always include a note with respect to going concern in management's **letter of representation**, which will require the directors to confirm their assumptions and, if necessary, their understanding of uncertain events and their possible impact.

## *Audit Procedure 4 – Subsequent Events and Going Concern Uncertainties*

Under items 2. and 3. above, where there are uncertain future events that may provide evidence of conditions that existed at the reporting date, then the auditor should, prior to the signing of the financial statements, consider if any further evidence is available that will provide a more accurate picture of necessary provisions and disclosures relating to going concern.

## Concluding on a Going Concern Uncertainty Disclosure Note

When concluding on the adequacy of, or requirement for, a financial statement disclosure related to uncertainties as to the continued existence of the entity as a going concern, the auditor considers whether the financial statements:

- adequately describe the principal events or conditions that give rise to the significant doubt on the entity's ability to continue in operation, and management's plans to deal with these events or conditions; and
- whether there is a "material uncertainty" related to events or conditions that may cast significant doubt on the entity's ability to continue as a going concern and, therefore, that it may be unable to realise its assets and discharge its liabilities in the normal course of business (ISA 570, paragraph 19).

**Table 18.3** below summarises the types of audit opinion that the auditor may issue when concluding on going concern, taking into account the different types of concerns that may arise as well as considering management's response to those concerns. These requirements specifically relate to entities that are required, or those that choose voluntarily, to report on their compliance with the *UK Corporate Governance Code*.

The first reporting requirement relates to the period used by those charged with governance in assessing going concern and requires the auditor to disclose in the audit report if this period is less than one year.

The second requirement is aimed at improving overall reporting quality for the user. According to the *UK Corporate Governance Code* (discussed in **Chapter 2**), those charged with governance are required to report on how they have complied with the Code or to explain why they have not. The auditor is required to read this report and, taking into account the knowledge gained and work carried out relating to going concern, consider the adequacy of assertions made in this report by the directors. Specifically, the auditor is asked to consider:

- the robustness of risk assessment, including future performance, solvency and liquidity;
- whether these risks are adequately disclosed, including a description of how they are being managed;

- the directors' statement relating to the ability to continue as a going concern and the period considered in concluding on the going concern assumption, including consideration of any material uncertainties;
- the directors' statement relating to how they have carried out their assessment, why they felt the period reviewed to be appropriate and their expectation that they consider the entity to continue to be able to meet its liabilities over the period assessed.

Where the auditor feels that further disclosures are required, they may need to consider including these in the audit report in accordance with the requirements of ISA 700.

(**Chapter 19** discusses the types of audit report in more detail; and **Appendix 19.3** depicts the auditor's decision-making process when considering the reporting implications for going concern.)

### Communication with Regulators/the Audit Committee

When the auditor of a regulated entity considers that it may be necessary to include a reference to going concern matters in the auditor's report, the auditor may have a duty to communicate with the relevant regulatory, enforcement or supervisory authorities.

In the case of PIEs, the auditor is **required** to report to the relevant regulatory, enforcement or supervisory authority. With PIEs, the auditor is required to explain judgements or events that cast significant doubt about the entity's ability to continue as a going concern and, if this constitutes a material uncertainty, it must also be included in the additional report to the audit committee (see **Section 18.9** below).

## 18.6 WRITTEN REPRESENTATIONS

### Introduction

The auditor will hold a number of meetings with the client entity's management throughout the audit, during which management will make a number of oral representations regarding various matters in connection with the financial statements. Management's representations are required to be formalised in a **letter of representation** (written representations), addressed by management to the auditors. **Written representations** represent audit evidence in which management acknowledges its responsibility for the fair presentation of the financial statements in accordance with the applicable financial reporting framework and that it has approved the financial statements. Additionally, written representations allow the auditor to confirm and solidify the oral representations made by management, summarising the points made and having management sign the document acknowledging the accuracy of the statements made.

ISA 580 *Written Representations*, paragraph 6, requires the auditor to "obtain written representations from management and, where appropriate, those charged with governance that they believe that they have fulfilled their responsibility for the preparation of the financial statements and for the completeness of the information provided to the auditor". A sample of a letter of representation is included at **Appendix 18.1**.

Written representations are recognised as being an appropriate and important method of obtaining audit evidence. By receiving such evidence in writing, the auditor ensures that there is no conflict as to what was originally said and leaves little room for misinterpretation or misunderstanding. Written representations also complement other audit procedures, such as the going concern review.

Importantly though, matters relating to representations made by management should be material in nature and should not deter the auditor from seeking all other possible evidence to support their conclusions. That is, written representations are not a substitute for other evidence that the auditor could reasonably expect to be available; rather, they serve to corroborate other evidence (albeit, it being recognised that in some instances written representations may be the only source of audit evidence available).

The auditor should assess the reasonableness of the representations on material matters by:
- obtaining corroborative evidence from inside or outside the entity;
- assessing the representations for inconsistency with other evidence obtained; and
- considering whether those who made the representations can be expected to be well-informed on the matter.

## General and Specific Representations

Written representations can be either general or specific. **General representations** are a matter of course (generic) and are included in all letters of representation. The auditor may in some instances require additional **specific representations** to corroborate other audit evidence and ensure that evidence obtained is complete. Examples of both general and specific representations are included in **Table 18.4** below.

TABLE 18.4: GENERAL AND SPECIFIC WRITTEN REPRESENTATIONS

**General Representations**
- All transactions have been recorded and are reflected in the financial statements.
- Management have fulfilled its responsibility for preparing and presenting the financial statements as set out in the audit engagement letter, and the financial statements are prepared and presented in accordance with the applicable financial reporting framework.
- Management have provided the auditor with all relevant accounting records and information as agreed in the audit engagement letter, and as required by the Companies Act 2014 (RoI) and Companies Act 2006 (UK/NI).
- Management acknowledges its responsibility for the design and implementation of internal controls to prevent and detect error.

- Management believes that the effects of those uncorrected misstatements found by the auditor during the audit are immaterial, both individually and in aggregate, to the financial statements taken as a whole. (A summary of such items should be included in or attached to the written representations.)

- All subsequent events to the approval of the financial statements requiring adjustment or disclosure have been adjusted or disclosed.

- All information pertaining to related party relationships and transactions is complete and has been accounted for and disclosed.

- The selection and application of accounting policies is appropriate.

**Specific Representations**

- Any subsequent events and their effect on the entity are noted.

- The basis of estimates or provisions where evidence to support them is not considered sufficient and the amounts included in the financial statements are based on management's judgements or averages.

- The goodwill of the entity is considered to be impaired and the value has been written down.

- A legal claim has been settled and management does not anticipate any further action in this instance.

- Any other representations relevant to the particular audit, e.g. inventory obsolescence or bad/doubtful debts provisions.

## Other Issues Relating to Written Representations

### Preparation

It is generally the auditor who drafts the representations on behalf of the client entity. However, management should be encouraged to participate in drafting the written representations. The auditor should not leave it until the end of the audit process to draft the **letter of representation**; instead, any matters that may warrant inclusion in the letter should be noted in the audit working papers throughout the audit process.

The letter must be on the client entity's own letterhead, signed and dated by an appropriate member of management and approved on a date as close as possible to, but not after, the signing of the auditor's report on the financial statements, and not before the subsequent events (see **Section 18.4**) review has been concluded.

### Refusal by Management to Sign the Written Representations

In cases where management refuse to co-operate in providing the necessary written representations, the auditor should discuss the matter further with management or, where relevant, the audit committee. The integrity of management must be evaluated, and the effect of their refusal to sign on the sufficiency, appropriateness and reliability of audit evidence should be considered. The auditor may conclude that not all the information deemed necessary has been obtained, which would constitute a **limitation of scope**. Should the client entity's management refuse to sign any representations (including those outlined in paragraphs 10 and 11 of ISA 580), the auditor should issue a **disclaimer of opinion**.

### Written Representations and PIEs

ISA 580, paragraph A22-2, refers to specific requirements relating to PIEs. stating that "the written representations requested from those charged with governance are relevant to the auditor's communications in the additional report to the audit committee that all requested explanations and documents were provided by the entity."

## 18.7  PROVISIONS, CONTINGENT LIABILITIES AND CONTINGENT ASSETS

At the final stage of the audit, the auditor must also consider the **adequacy and completeness of provisions, contingent liabilities and contingent assets**.

### Provisions

IAS 37 *Provisions, Contingent Liabilities and Contingent Assets*, paragraph 14, states that a provision should only be recognised when:
"(a)  an entity has a present obligation (legal or constructive) as a result of a past event;
(b)  it is probable that an outflow of resources embodying economic benefits will be required to settle the obligation; and
(c)  a reliable estimate can be made of the amount of the obligation."

Essentially, a provision is recognised when the entity deems it likely to have to pay amounts as a result of an event that occurred prior to (or at) the date of the SOFP. The entity must be able to reliably estimate the value of the amount to be transferred in the future. This amount is then included under liabilities within the statement of financial position.

The auditor will measure the provision by reference to the guidance above. Additionally, the auditor must ensure that the disclosure of a provision is adequate to allow the user of the financial statements to understand:
• the nature of the obligation;
• the expected timing of any resulting transfers of economic benefits; and
• the uncertainty surrounding the amount and timing of any transfers.

When auditing the estimate of the provision provided by the entity, the auditor will refer to ISA 540 *Auditing Accounting Estimates, Including Fair Value Accounting Estimates, and Related Disclosures*. The requirements of the auditor under ISA 540 are discussed in **Chapter 6**, Section 6.10.

If the event does not meet the criteria for a provision (i.e. there is no present obligation, no probable transfers of economic benefits and it is not possible to evaluate the timing and amount of the obligation), it may, however, be classified as a **contingent liability**.

## Contingent Liabilities and Contingent Assets

A 'contingency' is a possible asset or liability that arises from past events, the existence of which will be confirmed only by the occurrence or non-occurrence of one or more uncertain future events not wholly within the control of the entity. In line with IAS 37 *Provisions, Contingent Liabilities and Contingent Assets*, a contingent liability is recognised and disclosed in the accounting records when the contingency is **probable** and the amount of the liability can be **reasonably estimated**. Contingent assets are assessed continually and should only be disclosed when an "inflow of economic benefits is **probable**", and are recognised in the financial statements when the inflow of economic benefits is "virtually certain".

Contingent liabilities are more of a concern for auditors than contingent assets because management may not be inclined to disclose them in the financial statements and because the events generally lie outside the accounting period. Examples would include pending litigations, disputes, etc.

As discussed in **Chapter 16**, as part of the substantive procedures the auditor will have validated the existence and valuation of disclosed contingencies. However, when performing the final audit procedures, the auditor should be searching for any undisclosed liabilities. The most common ways to obtain such information is to:
- review subsequent events up to the date of approval of the financial statements;
- inquire of management of any unresolved legal disputes and obtain an estimate of claims to be paid (this information should also be disclosed in the **letter of representation**);
- inquire of the entity's legal counsel and banks;
- review the entity's solicitor's fees on its supplier account;
- review bank letters and other related correspondence;
- review original signed minutes of board and management meetings;
- review contracts and loan agreements entered into by the entity;
- review current and previous years' tax returns;
- request written confirmation from the entity's solicitors, etc. of any known existing, pending or expected contingent liabilities.

ISA 501 *Audit Evidence – Specific Considerations for Selected Items,* paragraph A21, states that:
"Direct communication with the entity's external legal counsel assists the auditor in obtaining sufficient appropriate audit evidence as to whether potentially material litigation and claims are known and management's estimates of the financial implications, including costs, are reasonable."

Having reviewed all evidence available, the auditor must assess whether or not a contingent liability or a contingent asset exists. The client entity should not recognise a monetary amount in the statement of comprehensive income or the statement of financial position regarding a contingent asset or liability. It is essential that the auditor ascertains the nature of matters with respect to management's treatment as a provision or contingent liability.

A matter subsequently treated as a contingent liability may be recognised as a provision only when:
- it can be reliably measured;
- it is probable the future event will occur; and
- the transfer of economic benefits is probable.

If none of these characteristics exists, the auditor must disclose the contingent liability, which must therefore be disclosed in the notes to the financial statements, providing the following information:
- an estimate of its financial effect;
- an indication of uncertainties relating to the amount or timing of the outflow of economic benefits; and
- the possibility of reimbursement.

If the uncertainty identified is adequately disclosed, an **unqualified audit report** should be issued. If the uncertainty identified is considered significant, the auditor should disclose such information in the 'material uncertainty relating to going concern' paragraph of the audit report without qualifying the audit opinion. However, where the auditor considers that the disclosure made by management is insufficient, they must qualify their opinion ('except for disagreement') or issue an adverse audit report. Again, this will be discussed in greater detail in **Chapter 19**.

## 18.8  FINAL REVIEW OF AUDIT WORKING PAPERS

### Introduction

The file is now ready for review by the **audit engagement partner**. The partner examines the audit working papers and the information gathered over the course of the audit. The objective of the audit review is to evaluate the evidence obtained during the course of the audit and whether it constitutes **sufficient appropriate audit evidence**, as well as assessing the conclusions reached by the person preparing the working papers.

Whether "sufficient appropriate audit evidence has been obtained to support the conclusions reached and for the auditor's report to be issued" will depend on a number of factors:
- significance of the potential misstatements in the assertions and the likelihood of their having a material effect, individually or aggregated with other potential misstatements, on the financial statements;
- effectiveness of management's responses and controls to address risks;
- experience gained during previous audits with respect to similar potential misstatements;
- results of audit procedures performed, including whether specific instances of fraud or error were identified;

- source and reliability of the available information;
- persuasiveness of the audit evidence;
- understanding of the client entity and its environment, including its internal controls.

In reviewing the audit work, the partner thus ensures that:

- sufficient appropriate audit evidence has been obtained in each area of the audit process;
- the work performed by the auditor and the final financial statements are in compliance with statutory requirements (e.g. Companies Act 2014 (RoI), Companies Act 2006 (UK/NI)), with accounting and auditing standards (e.g. IASs, IFRSs, ISAs, FRSs, etc.) and with other relevant regulations (e.g. the *UK Corporate Governance Code*);
- the work completed by audit staff is accurate, thorough and in accordance with the audit programme;
- the judgements exercised by audit staff during the course of the audit were reasonable and appropriate and have been properly documented;
- all audit work has been completed in accordance with the conditions and terms specified in the **letter of engagement**;
- the audit staff have properly resolved any significant accounting, auditing and reporting questions raised during the audit;
- the audit work is properly performed, documented in working papers and supports the audit opinion (see **Chapter 19**);
- accounting policies adopted are in accordance with the applicable financial reporting framework, are appropriate to the entity and are applied consistently;
- the presentation of the final financial statements is appropriate in form, content and manner; and
- finally, the review should ensure that the audit working papers have been documented in accordance with the International Standards on Auditing and that the firm's quality control policies and procedures have been met (see the discussion on International Standard on Quality Control 1 *Quality Control for Firms that Perform Audits and Reviews of Financial Statements, and other Assurance and Related Services Engagements* (ISQC 1) in **Chapter 2**, Section 2.8).

Paragraph 14 of ISA 230 *Audit Documentation* notes that: "The auditor shall assemble the audit documentation in an audit file and complete the administrative process of assembling the final audit file on a timely basis after the date of the auditor's report." Paragraph 15 also states that: "After the assembly of the final audit file has been completed, the auditor shall not delete or discard audit documentation of any nature before the end of its retention period."

Checklists are common practice for ensuring that all aspects of the financial statements are covered, not only by the engagement partner but also by the audit team and audit manager. As well as facilitating the review of the audit work performed, they act as evidence in showing a review has been carried out. The final analytical procedures and going concern analysis performed at the final phase of the audit will allow the auditor to make an informed conclusion on financial statements produced by the client entity.

## 18.9 COMMUNICATION WITH THOSE CHARGED WITH GOVERNANCE

The final step the auditor should undertake before formulating the audit opinion is to communicate to those charged with governance any significant issues identified during the audit process that have impacted on the audit process and procedures (ISA 260 *Communication with Those Charged with Governance*). The standard defines **those charged with governance** as including directors (executive and non-executive) of the company and the members of an audit committee, where one exists, or equivalent individuals for other types of entities. Some of the significant issues that may be considered for communication include:

- difficulties in carrying out audit procedures, e.g. incomplete accounting records (**limitation of scope**);
- views on accounting policies, estimates and financial statement disclosures;
- material unadjusted misstatements;
- summary of representations to be agreed by management;
- review of the going concern assumption and any related concerns;
- expected modifications to the audit report; or
- any fraudulent activities identified or non-compliance with regulations.

Some key communications are required relating to entities that are required to, or those that choose voluntarily to, report on their compliance with the *UK Corporate Governance Code*.

ISA 260, paragraph 16-1, requires the auditor to communicate with the audit committee information they believe to be relevant to the board's and the audit committee's fulfilment of certain provisions of the Code. Along with the items noted above as standard communication points for all entities, the auditor is specifically required to communicate:

- the business risks taken into account for the purpose of the audit and the implications of these risks on the overall scope and materiality of the audit;
- significant accounting policies;
- valuations of material assets and liabilities;
- effectiveness of the entity's system of internal control, to the extent that it was reviewed as part of the audit;
- robustness of management's risk assessment activities; and
- any other matters identified as relevant to the audit committee in carrying out its function.

This communication should inform the audit committee of the matters required to be reported on by the auditor under the extended audit reporting requirements introduced in ISA 700 (as discussed in **Chapter 19**).

**Table 18.5** below shows the reporting treatment of matters identified based on their level of significance.

TABLE 18.5: COMMUNICATION OF AUDIT ISSUES

| Level of Matter Identified | Communicating Body |
| --- | --- |
| Significant | Written and verbal communication to audit committee or governing body. |
| Less significant | Verbal discussion and/or written communication with management having the authority to take appropriate action. |

Another form of communication is the **management letter**, which is generally sent to those charged with governance at the end of the audit. It outlines the key weaknesses identified by the auditor, the associated risks and the remedial action required by the client entity (see **Chapter 8**, Section 8.10).

### Report to the Audit Committee

For audits relating to the financial statements of **a public interest entity (PIE)**, ISA 260 now requires an additional report from the auditor to the audit committee of the entity. The report should be in writing and signed and dated by the audit firm, and be submitted not later than the date of the audit report. This additional report is intended to provide the audit committee with the results of the audit work carried out as well as more detailed information about the outcome of the audit. Its purpose is to enhance communication between the auditor and the client entity's audit committee.

The objective of the report is to allow the audit committee to better carry out its new responsibility with regard to the monitoring of the statutory audit, and the performance and independence of the auditor. If the PIE does not have an audit committee, the additional report is still required and should be submitted to the body performing equivalent functions within the entity. ISA 260, paragraph 16R-2, outlines the auditor's responsibility with regard to the additional report and identifies the minimum contents it should include. The auditor must, at the request of the audit committee, be prepared to discuss in detail any matter addressed within the additional report.

The report is made directly to the audit committee and is not available to the general public, unless the PIE is subject to a request under freedom of information principles in which case it may be released.

## 18.10 RELATED PARTIES

ISA 550 *Related Parties*, paragraph 3, states that "the auditor has a responsibility to perform audit procedures to identify, assess and respond to the risks of material misstatement arising from the entity's failure to appropriately account for or disclose related party relationships, transactions or balances in accordance with the requirements of the framework".

Accordingly, the auditor pays particularly close attention to these relationships due to the fact that fraud may be more easily committed through related parties and the opportunity for collusion is greater.

Related party relationships arise due to the existence of a control relationship, or a common control relationship, between the client entity and another party. ISA 550, paragraph 10, offers a more extensive definition of what constitutes a related party.

During the risk assessment, discussed in **Chapter 7**, the auditor will have designed procedures to obtain information relevant to identifying the risks of material misstatement arising from related parties. In order to gain an understanding of related parties, the auditor should: inquire of management; maintain alertness for related party information when reviewing records or documents; and share related party information with the engagement team to ensure all members are aware of any related party relationships that exist.

With regard to the first of these measures – inquiring of management – the auditor should request of management a schedule of related parties, including any transactions that occurred during the period under review and/or balances that exist at the date of the statement of financial position. This will allow the auditor to ensure those transactions and balances are adequately disclosed in line with IAS 24 *Related Party Disclosures*. A risk still exists with regard to possible related parties not disclosed to the auditor.

ISA 550, paragraph 5, reminds the auditor of the need to understand if the "entity's related party relationships and transactions is relevant to the auditor's evaluation of whether one or more fraud risk factors are present as required by ISA 240 [UK and Ireland], because fraud may be more easily committed through related parties". **Table 18.6** below outlines common examples of fraud associated with related parties and audit procedures to identify them.

Should the auditor, during the course of the audit, identify related parties not previously disclosed by management, this may indicate intentional concealment of instances of fraud. In such cases the auditor should:

- promptly communicate the information to the engagement team;
- inform management and request that they identify all transactions and balances relating to the newly identified related party;
- inquire of management why the internal controls of the entity did not identify the related party;
- perform appropriate audit procedures on the newly identified related party;
- consider the risk that further unidentified related parties exist; and
- consider whether the omission by management is intentional or unintentional. If considered intentional, the auditor should consider the implications for the audit opinion.

TABLE 18.6: IDENTIFYING FRAUDULENT RELATED PARTY TRANSACTIONS OR BALANCES

| Type of Transaction/Balance | Fraud Risk | Audit Procedures |
|---|---|---|
| Purchases/Sales | • Purchase/sales transactions or loan interest are not at arm's length, to the detriment of one or other party.<br>• Potentially no goods or services have actually been transferred and so there is no event to support the transaction.<br>• Transactions are not adequately authorised (particularly for the entity negatively impacted by transactions that are not at arm's length). | Use data analysis tools to search for significantly low- or high-cost goods purchased/sold relative to standard or average costs/ sales price from other suppliers/customers.<br><br>Use data analysis software to search for various permutations of related parties' names to identify potentially undisclosed transactions arising within the purchases/revenue nominal ledgers. |
| Loans | | Use data analysis tools to search for permutations of the related parties' names in accounts payable and receivable listings (including the transactions therein) to identify potential undisclosed loans. |

Where the auditor identifies significant transactions and balances that are outside the normal course of business, the underlying contracts and/or agreements that support the transactions should be obtained. The terms of the transactions should be understood to ensure that they are appropriately accounted for and disclosed in the financial statements. If management account for and disclose related party transactions as occurring in the normal course of business (arm's-length transaction), the auditor should obtain sufficient appropriate audit evidence to support this assertion.

When concluding on related party relationships, transactions and balances, the auditor should conclude whether or not they have been appropriately accounted for and disclosed and ensure that they do not prevent the fair presentation of the financial statements. Finally, the auditor should obtain **written representations** from management stating that they have disclosed all related party relationships and transactions of which they are aware and that they have been appropriately accounted for.

## 18.11 CONCLUSION

The auditor has now reached the audit reporting stage. They have completed the planning activities, performed controls assessment and testing where applicable, concluded on all substantive testing and, finally, as discussed throughout this chapter, performed all concluding activities required to be able to form an opinion on the financial statements.

The audit procedures discussed throughout this chapter cover areas not contained within specific financial cycle testing and are intended to allow the auditor to:

- Address issues that cannot be concluded on until the end of the audit, including:
  - concluding on going concern, for which evidence will have been gathered throughout the audit;
  - ensuring that no subsequent events have occurred that need further substantive procedures; and
  - concluding on the classification of provisions, contingent liabilities and contingent assets.
- Reflect on the audit evidence collected through:
  - the performance of final analytical procedures;
  - the performance of a final review of the audit working papers; and
  - the evaluation of misstatements taken to the schedule of unadjusted differences (error schedule) in order to conclude on whether or not a material misstatement exists in the financial statements.
- Obtain written representations from management to confirm statements they have made both implicitly and explicitly.

Next, the auditor considers the implications of the conclusions for the **audit report**, which will be the focus of **Chapter 19**. The auditor must examine details of evidence obtained and ensure that the following are appropriately addressed:

1. disagreement over amount of an account value or relating to the adequacy of a disclosure;
2. limitation of scope, where evidence ought reasonably to be available to the auditor but is unavailable;
3. significant uncertainty, where the auditor is required to make a professional judgement based on evidence available.

## SUMMARY OF LEARNING OBJECTIVES

**Learning Objective 1** Have a clear understanding of final analytical procedures and their importance in the conclusion of an audit.

The auditor performs final analytical procedures in order to ensure that they fully understand all relationships and movements in the financial statements; and that they can comment on these relationships and movements, which are supported by the audit evidence obtained throughout the audit.

**Learning Objective 2** Be able to consider the misstatements taken to the schedule of unadjusted differences (error schedule) when concluding on whether or not the financial statements are materially misstated.

An adjustment in itself may not be material; however, an accumulation of misstatements noted by the auditor could result in an overall material difference. The auditor should record a schedule of unadjusted differences in the audit working papers during the course of the audit. During the final phase of the audit, the auditor must conclude on the cumulative effect of misstatements and their impact on the financial statements.

**Learning Objective 3** Understand the auditor's responsibility regarding subsequent events for the different time periods highlighted in ISA 560 *Subsequent Events.*

The auditor has an active role in identifying subsequent events up to the point that the audit opinion is signed. After the date of signing of the financial statements, the auditor has no active role in identifying adjusting subsequent events. However, should they become aware of events that impact on conditions that existed at the date of the SOFP, then it should be discussed with management whether the accounts need to be amended:

• If amended – the auditor reviews the amendment and confirms that the audit opinion remains appropriate.
• No amendment – the auditor disagrees with financial statements and issues modified/adverse audit opinion.

**Learning Objective 4** Be able to discuss the requirements of the auditor regarding the assessment of the going concern assumption.

The primary responsibility for assessing the appropriateness of the going concern assumption in which the financial statements are prepared rests with management. There is a secondary responsibility in respect of the going concern assumption used in the preparation of the financial statements in that the auditor must ensure the validity of management's assumptions.

When concluding on the adequacy of, or requirement of, a financial statement disclosure related to uncertainties as to the continued existence of the entity, the auditor considers whether the financial statements:

• adequately describe the principal events or conditions that give rise to the significant doubt on the entity's ability to continue in operation, and management's plans to deal with these events or conditions; and
• whether there is a "material uncertainty" related to events or conditions that could cast significant doubt on the entity's ability to continue as a going concern and, therefore, that it may be unable to realise its assets and discharge its liabilities in the normal course of business (ISA 570, paragraph 18).

**Learning Objective 5** Understand the content of written representations and the role that they play.

ISA 580 requires the auditor to obtain written representations from management with appropriate responsibilities for the financial statements and knowledge of the matters concerned.

Written representations are not a substitute for other audit procedures available to the auditor, but rather serve to corroborate such evidence and eliminate any misunderstandings in oral representations that may have been made by management.

**Learning Objective 6** Understand the auditor's approach to reviewing the classification of provisions, contingent liabilities and contingent assets.

The client entity must ensure that matters are adequately classified as provisions, contingent liabilities or contingent assets, as outlined in IAS 37. A liability can only be recognised in the accounts if there is a probable transfer of economic benefits that can be reliably measured and is likely to occur.

**Learning Objective 7** Understand the importance of the final review of the audit working papers.

Checklists are common practice in ensuring that all aspects of the financial statements are covered, not only by the reporting partner but also by the audit team and audit manager. As well as facilitating the review of the audit work performed, they also act as evidence in showing a review has been carried out.

**Learning Objective 8** Be able to discuss the form of other reports directed at those charged with governance.

Before formulating an opinion, the auditor is required to communicate to the entity and to management any significant issues identified during the audit process that impacted on the audit process and procedures (ISA 260).

**Learning objective 9** Understand the considerations of the auditor regarding related parties.

The auditor should aim to ensure that all related parties have been identified and appropriately accounted for and disclosed. If accounted for as arm's-length transactions, then the auditor should obtain sufficient appropriate audit evidence to support this.

## QUESTIONS

### Self-test Questions

18.1    What are the benefits of performing final analytical procedures?

18.2    What key document is used by the auditor when evaluating the misstatements identified during the audit?

18.3   What is the purpose of the schedule of unadjusted differences?

18.4   What are the three key time periods relevant to the auditor when considering subsequent events?

18.5   What are the auditor's responsibilities with regard to subsequent events occurring between the date of the financial statements and the date of the auditor's report?

18.6   Name five audit procedures an auditor might carry out to identify subsequent events.

18.7   What is meant by the term 'going concern'?

18.8   Name two financial, two operational and two other examples of events that may have an impact on the going concern of a client entity?

18.9   What is a written representation?

18.10  Name five matters that the auditor might include in a written representation.

18.11  What is a contingent liability?

## Review Questions

(See Suggested Solutions to Review Questions in **Appendix C**.)

### *Question 18.1*

You are the audit senior on Monitor Ltd, a security company. This is one of your firm's largest and most successful clients with annual fee income (audit, tax and other services) in excess of €150,000 in each of the last three years.

The company, established in 1978, is owned 50:50 by two directors, Mike Greenwood and Dominic Clarke. You have been informed that Dominic Clarke is the brother-in-law of one of the tax partners in your firm, but that taxation services are provided by a different partner in the firm.

The 2018 audit fieldwork was completed one month ago, but the financial statements have not yet been approved by the directors due to the absence on leave of one of the directors. You understand that the financial statements are now due to be signed at the end of the week and have arranged a meeting with the financial controller. At the meeting the financial controller informed you of the following matters:

- one of the customers covered by the doubtful debts provision has gone into liquidation. However, Monitor had ceased trading with this customer just after the year end and the debt due at the year end had been provided for in full;

- subsequent to the audit fieldwork, the company has changed all its banking arrangements to another bank that was offering lower overdraft rates. You are informed that in the current difficult trading environment the company is undertaking a review of all of its significant contracts;

- the company is considering a sale and leaseback of its premises to raise finance to repay certain commitments;

- it is hoped to pay the final balance of 20% of the previous year's audit fee within the next two months, with the current year's fee to be paid when the re-financing is put in place.

**Requirement** Draft a file note, under the heading 'Subsequent Events Procedures', which outlines the matters that have come to your attention since the completion of the audit fieldwork. The note should address each of the following:

- further verification work required;
- any other procedures which, based upon the above information, you consider may need to be carried out.

## Question 18.2

Your audit of Santa Ltd has uncovered the following:

1. Prepayments of €50,000 have been included within the trade payables balance in the trial balance, due to a mis-posting by the accountant.
2. Your payroll testing has identified bonus payments, in respect of the financial year, of €175,000 paid to staff subsequent to the year end. However, the year-end bonus accrual was only €25,000.
3. You have recalculated the depreciation charge as €364,000, which compares with the balance of €320,000 included in the accounts.
4. You were unable to agree the opening revenue reserves in the trial balance to the opening revenue reserves in the financial statements. This has been explained to you as being adjustments, which were processed through the prior year's financial statements, but which were posted into the accounting system in the current year.

The above matters have been brought to the attention of your client. However, no adjustments have been made to the accounts.

### Requirement

(a) State what further audit work (if necessary) you would carry out in respect of each of the above matters.
(b) Draft the schedule of unadjusted differences (errors schedule) in respect of the above matters for review by the audit partner.
(c) Set out the factors that should be taken into account by the audit partner in their review of the schedule of unadjusted differences.

## Question 18.3

It is May 2019 and you are auditing Express Ltd for the year ended 31 December 2018. Express Ltd is a logistics company based in the Republic of Ireland that distributes throughout Europe.

You are at the close of the audit and, as audit senior, you are performing a final review of all audit working papers and issues noted. While you review the working papers, you have asked a member of the audit team to compile a list of all issues noted. You have been provided with the following:

- The doubtful debt provision provided by the directors is a general provision of €100,000 relating to all debtors greater than 90+ days, plus two specific provisions relating to Sofas. com and Beds Express Ltd for €25,000 and €30,000, respectively. The general provision has been tested as adequate, however your junior heard on the radio on his way to work

this morning that Beds Express Ltd has gone into liquidation with insufficient funds to pay creditors. Beds Express Ltd owed €75,000 at 31 December 2018 and has paid €15,000 to date. The dispute with respect to Sofas.com, which relates to damage of property while being delivered costing €25,000, is ongoing.
- On auditing depreciation, it was noted that it was understated by €100,000.
- The solicitor's letter returned outlines the likely value of a claim relating to an employee accident to be €75,000. The client's accounts, however, have no provision relating to this.
- A payment of €150,000 made to a supplier in 2019 was recorded as being made in 2018.
- Cut-off tests revealed that a delivery that occurred in 2019, valued at €15,000, was included in revenue of 2018. The client, however, has adjusted for this.

During your review of the working papers you note that all assertions with respect to payables have been covered except completeness. You additionally note that while the calculations and assumptions for the revaluation of property have been adequately performed and found to be reasonable, you do not see any information with respect to the valuer.

### Requirement
(a) Prepare an error schedule summarising all of the unadjusted errors noted throughout the audit.
(b) Considering that materiality is €270,000,
  (i)  are these accounts materially misstated?
  (ii) if the client did not want to make too many changes to the financial statements, what single adjustment could be made to bring the errors within materiality?
(c) Outline two other types of adjusting events (subsequent events).
(d) Name two matters that the auditor should confirm with respect to the valuer who provided a valuation on the property.

## APPENDIX 18.1: ILLUSTRATIVE REPRESENTATION LETTER[1]

[Entity's Letterhead]

(To Auditor)

(Date)

This representation letter is provided in connection with your audit of the financial statements of ABC Company for the year ended 31 December 20XX for the purpose of expressing an opinion as to whether the financial statements are presented fairly, in all material respects (or *give a true and fair view*), in accordance with International Financial Reporting Standards.

We confirm that, to the best of our knowledge and belief, having made such inquiries as we considered necessary for the purpose of appropriately informing ourselves:

### Financial Statements

- We have fulfilled our responsibilities, as set out in the terms of the audit engagement dated [insert date], for the preparation of the financial statements in accordance with International Financial Reporting Standards; in particular the financial statements are fairly presented (or *give a true and fair view*) in accordance therewith.
- Significant assumptions used by us in making accounting estimates, including those measured at fair value, are reasonable. (ISA 540)
- Related-party relationships and transactions have been appropriately accounted for and disclosed in accordance with the requirements of International Financial Reporting Standards. (ISA 550)
- All events subsequent to the date of the financial statements and for which International Financial Reporting Standards require adjustment or disclosures have been adjusted or disclosed. (ISA 560)
- The effects of uncorrected misstatements are immaterial, both individually and in the aggregate, to the financial statements as a whole. A list of the uncorrected misstatements is attached to the representation letter. (ISA 450)
- [Any other matters that the auditor may consider appropriate (see paragraph A10 of ISA 580).]

### Information Provided

- We have provided you with:
  - access to all information of which we are aware that is relevant to the preparation of the financial statements, such as records, documentation and other matters;
  - additional information that you have requested from us for the purpose of the audit; and

---

[1] Source: based on Appendix 2 to ISA 580 *Written Representations*.

- ◆ unrestricted access to persons within the entity from whom you determined it necessary to obtain audit evidence.
- All transactions have been recorded in the accounting records and are reflected in the financial statements.
- We have disclosed to you the results of our assessment of the risk that the financial statements may be materially misstated as a result of fraud. (ISA 240)
- We have disclosed to you all information in relation to fraud or suspected fraud that we are aware of and that affects the entity and involves:
  - ◆ management;
  - ◆ employees who have significant roles in internal control; or
  - ◆ others where the fraud could have a material effect on the financial statements. (ISA 240)
- We have disclosed to you all information in relation to allegations of fraud, or suspected fraud, affecting the entity's financial statements communicated by employees, former employees, analysts, regulators or others. (ISA 240)
- We have disclosed to you all known instances of non-compliance or suspected non-compliance with laws and regulations whose effects should be considered when preparing financial statements. (ISA 250)
- We have disclosed to you the identity of the entity's related parties and all the related-party relationships and transactions of which we are aware. (ISA 550)
- [Any other matters that the auditor may consider necessary (see paragraph A11 of ISA 580).]

Management

# 19

# AUDIT REPORTS

LEARNING OBJECTIVES

Having studied this chapter on audit reports you should:
1. be able to describe the principles underpinning the form and content of audit reports with reference to the relevant standards and legislation;
2. be able to explain the different types of audit opinion and how they impact on the audit report;
3. be able to identify when a modified opinion might be issued;
4. understand the auditor's responsibility with regard to comparative information and other information included with the financial statements;
5. understand the other reporting matters to be considered by the auditor; and
6. understand the considerations of the auditor in respect to their responsibility to communicate key audit matters in the audit report.

## Checklist of Relevant Standards

The relevant standards, both in the RoI and the UK/NI, covered in this chapter are:

ISA 250 *Section A – Consideration of Laws and Regulations in an Audit of Financial Statements*

ISA 450 *Evaluation of Misstatements Identified During the Audit*

ISA 570 *Going Concern*

ISA 700 *Forming an Opinion and Reporting on Financial Statements*

ISA 701 *Communicating Key Audit Matters in the Independent Auditor's Report*

ISA 705 *Modifications to the Opinion in the Independent Auditor's Report*

ISA 706 *Emphasis of Matter Paragraphs and Other Matter Paragraphs in the Independent Auditor's Report*

ISA 710 *Comparative Information – Corresponding Figures and Comparative Financial Statements*

ISA 720 *The Auditor's Responsibilities Relating to Other Information*

Note, in general when referring to ISAs, it should be understood as referring to the UK and Ireland versions, unless otherwise specified as either ISA (UK) or ISA (Ireland). See the Introduction for an extant list of auditing standards for the RoI and the UK/NI.

## Key Terms and Definitions in this Chapter

**Adverse Opinion**   An audit opinion given when, due to an uncorrected disagreement on a material and pervasive matter, the auditor concludes that the financial statements do **not** give a **true and fair view**.

**Disagreement**   When audit evidence proves that there is a **material misstatement** in the financial statements and management will not make a correction.

**Disclaimer of Opinion**   An audit opinion given when, due to a **limitation in scope** in relation to a matter that is **material and pervasive**, the auditor cannot determine whether the financial statements give a true and fair view.

**Emphasis of Matter Paragraph**   "A paragraph included in the auditor's report that refers to a matter appropriately presented or disclosed in the financial statements that, in the auditor's judgment, is of such importance that it is fundamental to users' understanding of the financial statements." (ISA 706, paragraph 7(a))

**Key Audit Matters**   "Those matters that, in the auditor's professional judgment, were of most significance in the audit of the financial statements of the current period." (ISA 701, paragraph 8)

**Limitation of Scope**   Inability to obtain sufficient appropriate audit evidence on which to conclude an opinion.

**Modified Opinion**   In the audit report, an opinion given when: 1. it is concluded that, based on the audit evidence obtained, the financial statements as a whole are not free from material misstatement; or 2. the auditor is unable to obtain sufficient appropriate audit evidence to conclude that the financial statements as a whole are free from material misstatement.

**Other Matter Paragraph**   "A paragraph included in the auditor's report that refers to a matter other than those presented or disclosed in the financial statements that, in the auditor's judgment, is relevant to users' understanding of the audit, the auditor's responsibilities or the auditor's report." (ISA 706, paragraph 7(b))

**Pervasive**   Term used to describe the extent of the impact of a single misstatement, or the cumulative impact of multiple misstatements, on the financial statements. A pervasive misstatement impacts on many elements of the financial statements, resulting in the financial statements not presenting a true and fair view.

**Qualified Opinion**   Where either: 1. a material misstatement occurs due to disagreement; or 2. a limitation of scope has been imposed on a matter that is material but is not pervasive and so a **qualified (except for) opinion** is issued (i.e. the auditor's opinion on the financial statements is that they give a true and fair view *except for* an isolated material matter).

**Unqualified Opinion**   A 'clean' audit opinion, i.e. the financial statements give a true and fair view.

## 19.1 INTRODUCTION

While the content of this chapter on audit reports is very technical, it is also very logical. For a good understanding of the material, it is essential to carefully study both the technical guidance and the examples given.

First, we set the scene by examining the legislative environments that govern audit reports in the UK and in the RoI **(Section 19.2)**. Then, in **Section 19.3**, we consider the actual contents of an audit report, section by section, as prescribed by ISA 700 *Forming an Opinion and Reporting on Financial Statements*.

The auditor's primary task is to report to the shareholders on the truth and fairness of the financial statements prepared by the client entity's management. The independent auditor's report is the end product of any audit engagement. It contains the auditor's opinion on the financial statements – an opinion that is based on the auditor's overall assessment – taking into account evidence obtained during each phase of the audit process. In **Section 19.4** we look in detail at the different opinions that the auditor may issue.

Audit reports are governed by a number of International Standards on Auditing (ISAs), as issued by the Irish Auditing & Accounting Supervisory Authority (IAASA) in the RoI and in the UK/NI by the Financial Reporting Council (FRC), as well as by company law (see **Chapter 1**). Also in Chapter 1, we discussed the EU Audit Regulation and Directive (ARD), which brought about important changes to all areas of audit regulation, including the oversight of auditors, quality and standard application, competition in the market, auditor selection and the independence of the auditor. You will recall that one of the most significant changes affecting the regulation of audit was the requirement for each EU Member State to appoint a single competent authority (either the IAASA or the FRC), tasked with the oversight of the auditing profession, including the setting of auditing and ethical standards and the regulation, monitoring and enforcement of the statutory audit environment.

Essentially, there are six key standards specifically dedicated to audit reports. The first four deal with the format, content and opinion of the audit report:
- ISA 700 *Forming an Opinion and Reporting on Financial Statements*
- ISA 701 *Communicating Key Audit Matters in the Independent Auditor's Report*
- ISA 705 *Modifications to the Opinion in the Independent Auditor's Report*
- ISA 706 *Emphasis of Matter Paragraphs and Other Matter Paragraphs in the Independent Auditor's Report.*

The two remaining standards address the auditor's responsibility with respect to comparative information, other information and the directors' report:
- ISA 710 *Comparative Information – Corresponding Figures and Comparative Financial Statements*
- ISA 720 *The Auditor's Responsibilities Relating to Other Information.*

Complications may arise when the auditor has significant or material issues relating to the financial statements being audited. To help gain an understanding of these complications, decision trees have been used to outline the thought processes and the options open to the auditor.

It is important to note from the outset that the auditor's opinion is on the current and comparative period information presented in the financial statements. This is addressed in ISA 710 and discussed in **Section 19.5** below.

Under ISA 720 the auditor's responsibility with respect to 'other information' in the financial statements is clarified and examined in **Section 19.6**.

We will start our discussion with the requirements of company law and its impact on the audit report.

## 19.2  COMPANY LAW

In both the Republic of Ireland and the UK, company law requires the auditor to provide an opinion as to whether or not the financial statements of the entity being audited have been prepared in accordance with the requirements of company law. The auditor's statutory report and the function of the auditor are covered in the RoI under Part 6, Chapters 10 and 11 of the Companies Act 2014 (CA 2014) and in the UK under Part 16, Chapter 3 of the Companies Act 2006 (CA 2006).

The principal duty of the auditor is to report to the members (of the entity to whom they have been appointed auditor) on the statutory financial statements laid before the members as examined by them. This requirement is laid down in the RoI by section 391 CA 2014; and in the UK by section 495 CA 2006. As outlined in **Chapter 1**, Section 1.4, company law in both jurisdictions imposes similar requirements relating to the auditor, as set out in section 336 CA 2014 in the RoI and in the UK/NI in sections 498–502 CA 2006.

In addition, the auditor shall, if requested to do so, provide evidence of their approval under law to act as auditor, as required by EU Directive 2006/43/EC.

At all times the auditor has a duty to carry out all audits with professional integrity. In preparing the audit report, the auditor must exercise the skill, care and caution of a reasonably competent, careful and cautious auditor. Directive 2006/43/EC requires that "Statutory auditors should adhere to the highest ethical standards. They should therefore be subject to professional ethics, covering at least their public-interest function, their integrity and objectivity and their professional competence and due care." If negligent in their duties, the auditor may be liable for damages incurred by the client entity under contract law and/or to the members of the entity, and in some limited circumstances to prospective shareholders.

In order to ensure the auditor is adequately equipped to carry out their duties, company law provides for the following rights:
- The auditor has the right to access all accounting records and any information or explanation that is necessary for the performance of their role (RoI: section 386 CA 2014; UK: section 499 CA 2006). Any breaches, such as making a false statement to an auditor, are an indictable offence.
- The auditor shall be entitled to be notified of, attend and be heard at a general meeting (GM) (RoI: section 180(6) CA 2014; UK: section 502 CA 2006).

Company law also imposes more specific requirements with respect to the audit report, which are summarised in **Table 19.1** below. The table highlights the need for the auditor to be mindful not only of the requirements contained within international standards on auditing but also of company law as it relates to the auditor's report. In the RoI, company law is enforced by the Office of the Director of Corporate Enforcement (ODCE), which is given powers under section 47 of S.I. No. 312 of 2016 (see www.odce.ie). In the UK, company law is enforced by the Department for Business, Energy & Industrial Strategy (DBEIS), which does so through The Insolvency Service (see www.gov.uk/government/organisations/department-for-business-energy-and-industrial-strategy).

TABLE 19.1: COMPANY LAW REPORTING REQUIREMENTS
(REPUBLIC OF IRELAND AND NORTHERN IRELAND)

| Republic of Ireland<br>Companies Act 2014, Chapter 11 | Northern Ireland/UK<br>Companies Act 2006, Chapter 3 |
|---|---|
| **Introduction paragraph** – identify the entity's financial statements and, where appropriate, the group financial statements that are subject to the audit and the financial reporting framework that has been applied in their preparation. | **Introduction paragraph** – identify the entity's financial statements, and where appropriate the group financial statements, that are subject to the audit and the financial reporting framework that has been applied in their preparation. |
| **Respective responsibilities of directors and auditors/scope of the audit of the financial statements** – a description of the scope of the audit identifying the auditing standards in accordance with which the audit was conducted. | **Respective responsibilities of directors and auditors/scope of the audit of the financial statements** – a description of the scope of the audit identifying the auditing standards in accordance with which the audit was conducted. |
| **Opinion paragraph** – give a clear expression of the truth and fairness of the entity's SOFP, assets, liabilities and financial position at the financial year end and of the profit and loss of the entity for the financial year. The report should clearly state whether the opinion is qualified or unqualified, adverse or a disclaimer. | **Opinion paragraph** – give a clear expression of the truth and fairness of the entity's SOFP, assets, liabilities and financial position of the company at the financial year end and of the profit and loss of the entity for the financial year. |
| **Opinion paragraph** – whether the financial statements are prepared in accordance with the relevant financial reporting framework and the Companies Act 2014. | **Opinion paragraph** – whether the financial statements are prepared in accordance with the relevant financial reporting framework and the Companies Act 2006. |
| **Statement under 'Opinions on other matters prescribed by the Companies Act 2014'** – whether the auditor has obtained all the information and explanations that they consider necessary for the purposes of the audit. | **'Report by exception'** – where the auditor has not received all the information and explanations they require for their audit. |
| **Statement under 'Opinions on other matters prescribed by the Companies Act 2014'** – whether in the auditor's opinion the accounting records of the company were sufficient to permit the financial statements to be readily and properly audited. | **'Report by exception'** – where adequate accounting records have not been kept, or returns adequate for their audit have not been received from branches not visited by them. |

**Statement under 'Opinions on other matters prescribed by Companies Act 2014'** – whether in the auditor's opinion the financial statements are in agreement with the accounting records.

**Statement under 'Opinions on other matters prescribed by the Companies Act 2014'** – whether in the auditor's opinion the information given in the directors' report is consistent with the financial statement in accordance with CA 2014.

**'Report by exception'** – where, in the auditor's opinion, the disclosures of directors' remuneration and transactions specified by law are not made.

**Name, signature and date** – requirement for the auditor/audit firm to state their name and for the senior statutory auditor (partner) to sign the audit report.

**'Report by exception'** – where the financial statements and the audited part of the directors' remuneration report are not in agreement with the accounting records and returns.

**Statement under 'Opinions on other matters prescribed by the Companies Act 2006'** – whether the information given in the directors' report and the strategic report (if any) for the financial year for which the financial statements are prepared is consistent with the financial statements (section 496 CA 2006).

**'Report by exception'** – where, in the auditor's opinion, certain disclosures of directors' remuneration specified by law are not made.

**Name, signature and date** – requirement for the auditor/audit firm to state their name and to sign the audit report.

## 19.3 BASIC CONTENTS OF THE AUDIT REPORT

### Introduction

The auditing standards are prescriptive with respect to the contents of audit reports. ISA 700 *Forming an Opinion and Reporting on Financial Statements* establishes standards on the form and content of the auditor's report. In ISA 700, reference to "financial statements" means a complete set of general purpose financial statements (i.e. financial statements prepared in accordance with a general purpose framework). ISA 700 promotes consistency in the auditor's report, but recognises the need for flexibility to accommodate particular circumstances of individual jurisdictions. ISA 700 establishes standards on the form and content of the auditor's report. **Figure 19.1** below demonstrates the broad framework imposed by the auditing standards and company law on the format and contents of audit reports. The figure is based on ISA 700, paragraphs 21–49, which lists the basic elements that should appear in the independent auditor's report. All elements of this figure are essential requirements, including the title and addressee at the outset and the closing elements. Each element is then discussed in detail.

FIGURE 19.1: OUTLINE OF AN AUDIT REPORT

Title **(a)** [ISA 700, paragraph 21]

Addressee **(a)** [ISA 700, paragraph 22]

- Auditor's opinion (separate opinion) **(b)** [ISA 700, paragraphs 23–27]
- Basis for opinion **(c)** [ISA 700, paragraph 28]
- Conclusions relating to going concern **(d)** [ISA 700, paragraph 29]
- Key audit matters (relevant for PIEs) **(e)** [ISA 700, paragraph 30–31]
- Other information **(f)** [ISA 700, paragraph 32]
- Opinions on other matters prescribed by the Companies Act 2014/Companies Act 2006 **(g)** [CA 2014/CA 2006]
- Matters on which we are required to report by exception **(h)** [CA 2014/CA 2006]
- Respective responsibilities of those charged with governance and auditors **(i)** [ISA 700, paragraphs 33–42]
- Other reporting responsibilities **(j)** [ISA 700, paragraphs 43–45]

Closing elements **(k)** [ISA 700, paragraphs 46–49]

## (a) Title and Addressee

The required title is 'Independent Auditor's Report'. Using the word 'independent' distinguishes it from other reports issued and included with the financial statements. The title is required under ISA 700, paragraph 21, as well as by legislation (CA 2014/CA 2006).

The independent auditor's report, referred to here for ease as the auditor's report, is usually addressed to the entity's shareholders (members) in both the UK and the RoI, as the audit is undertaken on their behalf. The addressee is required under ISA 700, paragraph 22, as well as by CA 2014/CA 2006.

## (b) Auditor's Opinion

The opinion paragraph should be clearly headed "Opinion" and should, in accordance with ISA 700, paragraph 24:
"(a) Identify the entity whose financial statements have been audited;
 (b) State that the financial statements have been audited;
 (c) Identify the title of each statement comprising the financial statements;
 (d) Refer to the notes, including the summary of significant accounting policies; and
 (e) Specify the date of, or period covered by, each financial statement comprising the financial statements."

Within the opinion paragraph, the auditor must clearly state the financial reporting framework used to prepare the financial statements. The opinion paragraph must then clearly state whether, in the auditor's opinion, the financial statements give a true and fair view (in all material respects) in accordance with the stated financial reporting framework (e.g. FRS 102 or IFRSs issued by the International Accounting Standards Board).

Once again, it should be noted that only matters material to the financial statements are considered by the auditor. If the opinion is **unqualified**, the auditor must clearly state that **"the financial statements give a true and fair view"**.

Should the auditor be engaged to express an opinion on the compliance of the financial statements with an additional financial reporting framework (e.g. IFRS as adopted by the European Union), then that second opinion shall be clearly separated from the first opinion under a heading 'Opinion in Respect of an Additional Financial Reporting Framework'.

## (c) Basis for Opinion

The basis for opinion paragraph is placed directly below the opinion paragraph and must:
(a) Refer to the fact that the audit was conducted in accordance with ISAs (either Ireland or the UK) and applicable law, a requirement of CA 2014/CA 2006.
(b) Refer to the section of the auditor's report that describes the auditor's responsibilities under ISAs (either Ireland or the UK).
(c) Make a clear expression of independence and the framework under which that independence is measured.

   ISA (Ireland) 700, paragraph 28(c) instructs that: "In Ireland, auditors are subject to ethical requirements from two sources: the IAASA's Ethical Standard [for Auditors (Ireland) 2017] concerning the integrity, objectivity and independence of the auditor, and the ethical pronouncements established by the auditor's relevant professional body. When identifying the relevant ethical requirements in the auditor's report, the auditor indicates that these include the IAASA's Ethical Standard, applied as required for the types of entity determined to be appropriate in the circumstances."

   The corresponding paragraph in ISA (UK) 700 (paragraph 28(c)) differs only in that it is the FRC's Ethical Standard that is cited.
(d) State whether they believe that the audit evidence obtained by them during the course of the audit is "sufficient and appropriate to provide a basis for the auditor's opinion".

## (d) Conclusions Relating to Going Concern

Where applicable, the auditor shall report in accordance with ISA 570 *Going Concern* whereby the auditor is required to draw the user's attention to:
• the directors' statement regarding going concern and their explanation of how they have assessed the prospects of the group, including over what period they have done so;

- the directors' statement relating to going concern, required under the Listing Rules in accordance with Listing Rule 9.8.6R(3), is materially inconsistent with knowledge obtained in the audit.

Furthermore, the auditor should specifically state whether or not they have anything to report with regard to the appropriateness of the use of the going concern basis.

## (e)  Key Audit Matters

ISA 701 *Communicating Key Audit Matters in the Independent Auditor's Report* applies to audits of "listed entities and circumstances when the auditor otherwise decides to communicate key audit matters in the auditor's report". In general, unless "required by law or regulation", there is no requirement to include a key audit matters section (ISA 701, paragraph 5). The "law or regulation" stipulation relates to audits of **public interest entities (PIEs)** or entities that choose to voluntarily report on how they have applied the *UK Corporate Governance Code* (and in the RoI, the Irish Corporate Governance Annex (the 'Irish Annex')).

The financial crisis of 2008 put corporate governance back in the limelight, with shareholders concerned about the effectiveness of company stewardship and the perceived lack of opinion offered by the auditor in relation to this effectiveness. As such, concerns were raised over the format of the audit report being so prescriptive that it prevented the auditor from providing adequate transparency and insights about the company. This resulted in the FRC updating the *UK Corporate Governance Code* to respond to some of the concerns, backed up by changes to ISA 700 and ISA 701, both revised by the FRC in June 2016, which gave rise to 'extended audit reports'. IAASA subsequently adopted the revised versions of ISA 700 and ISA 701.

Where an entity is required to (due to its listing requirement under law or regulation or due to its status as a PIE), or voluntarily chooses to, report on how it has applied the *UK Corporate Governance Code*, or to explain why it has not, then the auditor is required to include the following in their audit report:
- a description of the key **risks** impacting on the audit strategy;
- the threshold used for **materiality** and how the auditor applied the concept of materiality in planning and performing the audit; and
- a description of the **scope** of the audit and how that scope addressed the noted risks and how it was influenced by the application of materiality.

ISA 701 encourages auditors to be specific in their explanations and avoid "abstract matters expressed in standardised language", which would result in generic inherent risks being reported, rather than those with substance specific to the entity. Furthermore, the standard advises the auditor to ensure their explanations enable the user to understand the significance in the context of the audit of the financial statements as a whole.

Provision C.3.8 of the *UK Corporate Governance Code* requires the **audit committee** to describe its work in discharging its duties in a separate section of the financial statements and the auditors are asked to co-ordinate with this report so as to avoid duplication, but to be mindful at the same time of the separate duties of the two parties.

It should be noted that the 'key audit matters' paragraph is not a substitute for expressing a modified opinion.

### (f) Other Information

ISA 720 *The Auditor's Responsibilities Relating to Other Information* deals with 'other information', which is discussed in detail below at **Section 19.6**.

### (g) Opinions on Other Matters Prescribed by the Companies Act 2014/Companies Act 2006

#### *Republic of Ireland*

As discussed in **Section 19.2**, and required by Part 6, Chapter 11 CA 2014, the auditor is required to express an opinion as to whether:
- the auditor has obtained all the information and explanations that they consider necessary for the purposes of the audit;
- in the auditor's opinion, the accounting records of the company were sufficient to permit the financial statements to be readily and properly audited;
- in the auditor's opinion, the financial statements are in agreement with the accounting records; and
- in the auditor's opinion, the information given in the directors' report is consistent with the financial statements.

#### *UK/Northern Ireland*

As discussed in **Section 19.2**, and required by Part 16, Chapter 3 CA 2006, the auditor is required to express an opinion as to whether the information given in the directors' report and the strategic report for the financial year for which the financial statements are prepared is consistent with the financial statements.

### (h) Matters on which the Auditor is Required to Report by Exception

#### *Republic of Ireland*

As discussed in **Section 19.2**, paragraph 336(8), Part 6, Chapter 6 CA 2014 requires the auditor to report by exception where, in the auditor's opinion, certain disclosures of directors' remuneration and transactions specified by law are not made.

## *UK/Northern Ireland*

As discussed in **Section 19.2**, under Part 16, Chapter 3 CA 2006, the following items are required to be reported by exception:

- where the auditor has not received all the information and explanations they require for their audit;
- where adequate accounting records have not been kept, or returns adequate for their audit have not been received from branches not visited by them;
- where the financial statements and the audited part of the directors' remuneration report are not in agreement with the accounting records and returns;
- where, in the auditor's opinion, certain disclosures of directors' remuneration specified by law are not made.

### (i)  Respective Responsibilities of Those Charged with Governance and Auditors

It is important that the user of the financial statements understands the respective responsibilities of those involved in the financial statements, i.e. senior management of the entity and the auditor.

As such, the auditor is required to outline the responsibilities of both parties. Specifically, the auditor's report shall include a statement that those charged with governance are responsible for the preparation of financial statements that give a true and fair view.

The auditor must also state that they are required to comply with either IAASA's Ethical Standard for Auditors (Ireland) 2017 or, in the UK, the FRC's Ethical Standard (2016) (discussed throughout **Chapter 2**).

The directors' responsibilities statement can be included within the directors' report contained within the financial statements and, this being the case, the auditor can then refer to the page containing the directors' responsibilities. The description of the auditor's responsibilities shall be included in either:

(a) the written body of the auditor's report; or

(b) within an appendix to the auditor's report; or

(c) by referencing the applicable version of a 'Description of the Auditor's Responsibilities for the Audit of the Financial Statements' that is maintained on the website of the appropriate authority.

### (j)  Other Reporting Responsibilities

As newly required under the Audit Regulation Directive (ARD) (see **Chapter 1**, Section 1.5) and in accordance with ISA 700, paragraph 45R-1, for audits of public interest entities (PIEs) the audit report must include:

- details of who appointed them as the auditor (audit firm);
- the date of the appointment;

- the expectation of how effective the audit will be in "detecting irregularities, including fraud";
- confirmation that "the audit opinion is consistent with the additional report to the audit committee";
- declaration that the auditor (audit firm) "remained independent" during the audit and did not perform any non-audit services for the entity; and
- disclosure of any additional services that were provided to the entity and its controlled undertakings and which were not disclosed in its management/annual report or financial statements.

## (k)  Closing Elements

Applicable in both the RoI and the UK/NI, the audit report must conclude with:
- the name of the audit engagement partner;
- the signature of the auditor;
- the date of the auditor's report; as stated in paragraph 49-1: "The date of an auditor's report on an entity's financial statements shall be the date on which the auditor signed the report expressing an opinion on those financial statements." (ISA 700, paragraph 49-1); and
- the location in the jurisdiction where the auditor practices (i.e. the auditor's address).

## Illustrative Example of a Standard Unqualified Audit Report

As outlined above, for most entities the form and content of an auditor's report is standard, as dictated by legislative and regulatory requirements. For PIEs, however, the content of the auditor's report can be more extensive. **Examples 19.1** and **19.2**, show illustrative unqualified audit reports for a listed company that is a PIE for use in the RoI and the UK/NI, respectively. The examples demonstrate the full format requirements in each jurisdiction, including the additional requirements as they relate to listed companies and PIEs (or other companies that must, or choose to, report under the *UK Corporate Governance Code*) (and the Irish Corporate Governance Annex in the RoI).

EXAMPLE 19.1: ILLUSTRATIVE UNQUALIFIED AUDIT REPORT (RoI)[1]

### INDEPENDENT AUDITOR'S REPORT TO THE MEMBERS OF XYZ PLC

**Opinion**

We have audited the financial statements of [*name*] ('the Company') and its subsidiaries ('the Group') for the [*year/period*] ended [*date*], which comprise the [*insert names of each statement comprising the financial statements*] and notes to the financial statements,

---

[1] Source: TA 02/2017 – *Guidance on the new ISAs (Ireland) Auditing Standards issued by the Irish Auditing & Accounting Supervisory Authority,* 'Example 3 Auditor's report on financial statements of Irish Company – Listed PIE' (Chartered Accountants Ireland, 2017).

including the summary of significant accounting policies set out in note [ ]. The financial reporting framework that has been applied in their preparation is Irish Law and International Financial Reporting Standards (IFRS) as adopted by the European Union and, as regards the Company financial statements, as applied in accordance with the provisions of the Companies Act 2014.

In our opinion:
- the Group financial statements give a true and fair view of the assets, liabilities and financial position of the group as at ............... and of its profit [loss] for the year then ended;
- the Company statement of financial position gives a true and fair view of the assets, liabilities and financial position of the Company as at ..........;
- the Group financial statements have been properly prepared in accordance with IFRS as adopted by the European Union;
- the Company financial statements have been properly prepared in accordance with IFRS as adopted by the European Union as applied in accordance with the provisions of the Companies Act 2014; and
- the Group financial statements and Company financial statements have been properly prepared in accordance with the requirements of the Companies Act 2014 and, as regards the Group financial statements, Article 4 of the IAS Regulation.

## Basis for opinion

We conducted our audit in accordance with ISAs (Ireland) and applicable law. Our responsibilities under those standards are further described in the *Auditor's Responsibilities for the Audit of the Financial Statements* section of our report. We are independent of the Group and Company in accordance with ethical requirements that are relevant to our audit of financial statements in Ireland, including the Ethical Standard as applied to public interest entities issued by the Irish Auditing & Accounting Supervisory Authority (IAASA), and we have fulfilled our other ethical responsibilities in accordance with these requirements.

We believe that the audit evidence we have obtained is sufficient and appropriate to provide a basis for our opinion.

## Key audit matters

Key audit matters are those matters that, in our professional judgment, were of most significance in our audit of the financial statements of the current period and include the most significant assessed risks of material misstatement (whether or not due to fraud) that we identified, including those which had the greatest effect on: the overall audit strategy, the allocation of resources in the audit; and directing the efforts of the engagement team. These matters were addressed in the context of our audit of the financial statements as a whole, and in forming our opinion thereon, and we do not provide a separate opinion on these matters.

*[Provide a description of each key audit matter in accordance with ISA (Ireland) 701]*

## Our application of materiality

*[Provide an explanation of how the auditor applied the concept of materiality in planning and performing the Group and Company audit. This is required to include the threshold used by the auditor as being materiality for the Group and Company financial statements as a whole but may include other relevant disclosures]*

## An overview of the scope of our audit report

*[Provide an overview of the scope of the Group and Company audit including an explanation of how the scope addressed each key audit matter and was influenced by the auditor's application of materiality.]*

*[Explanation as to what extent the audit was considered capable of detecting irregularities, including fraud]*

## Conclusions relating to principal risks, going concern and viability statement

We have nothing to report in respect of the following information in the annual report, in relation to which the ISAs (Ireland) require us to report to you whether we have anything material to add or draw attention to:

- the disclosures in the annual report [set out on page] that describe the principal risks and explain how they are being managed or mitigated;
- the directors' confirmation [set out on page] in the annual report that they have carried out a robust assessment of the principal risks facing the group and the parent company, including those that would threaten its business model, future performance, solvency or liquidity;
- the directors' statement [set out on page] in the financial statements about whether the directors considered it appropriate to adopt the going concern basis of accounting in preparing the financial statements and the directors' identification of any material uncertainties to the group's and the parent company's ability to continue to do so over a period of at least twelve months from the date of approval of the financial statements;
- whether the directors' statement relating to going concern required under the Listing Rules in accordance with Listing Rule 9.8.6R(3) is materially inconsistent with our knowledge obtained in the audit; or
- the directors' explanation [set out on page] in the annual report as to how they have assessed the prospects of the group and the parent company, over what period they have done so and why they consider that period to be appropriate, and their statement as to whether they have a reasonable expectation that the group and the parent company will be able to continue in operation and meet its liabilities as they fall due over the period of their assessment, including any related disclosures drawing attention to any necessary qualifications or assumptions.

## Other information

The directors are responsible for the other information. The other information comprises the information included in the [annual report][other title] other than the financial statements and our auditor's report thereon. Our opinion on the financial statements does not cover the other information and, except to the extent otherwise explicitly stated in our report, we do not express any form of assurance conclusion thereon.

In connection with our audit of the financial statements, our responsibility is to read the other information and, in doing so, consider whether the other information is materially inconsistent with the financial statements or our knowledge obtained in the audit or otherwise appears to be materially misstated. If we identify such material inconsistencies or apparent material misstatements, we are required to determine whether there is a material misstatement in the financial statements or a material misstatement of the other information. If, based on the work we have performed, we conclude that there is a material misstatement of this other information, we are required to report that fact.

We have nothing to report in this regard.

In this context, we also have nothing to report in regard to our responsibility to specifically address the following items in the other information and to report as uncorrected material misstatements of the other information where we conclude that those items meet the following conditions:

- *Fair, balanced and understandable* – [the statement given/the explanation as to why the annual report does not include a statement] by the directors that they consider the annual report and financial statements taken as a whole is fair, balanced and understandable and provides the information necessary for shareholders to assess the group's and the parent company's performance, business model and strategy, is materially inconsistent with our knowledge obtained in the audit; or
- *Audit committee reporting* – [the section describing the work of the audit committee does not appropriately address matters communicated by us to the audit committee] [the explanation as to why the annual report does not include a section describing the work of the audit committee] is materially inconsistent with our knowledge obtained in the audit; or
- *Directors' statement of compliance with the UK Corporate Governance Code* – the parts of the directors' statement required under the Listing Rules relating to the company's compliance with the *UK Corporate Governance Code* containing provisions specified for review by the auditor in accordance with Listing Rule 9.8.10R(2) do not properly disclose a departure from a relevant provision of the *UK Corporate Governance Code*.

### Opinions on other matters prescribed by the Companies Act 2014

Based solely on the work undertaken in the course of the audit, we report that:
- in our opinion, the information given in the directors' report is consistent with the financial statements; and
- in our opinion, the directors' report has been prepared in accordance with [applicable legal requirements][the Companies Act 2014]

We have obtained all the information and explanations which we consider necessary for the purposes of our audit.

In our opinion the accounting records of the Company were sufficient to permit the financial statements to be readily and properly audited and the Company statement of financial position is in agreement with the accounting records.

## Matters on which we are required to report by exception

Based on the knowledge and understanding of the group and the parent company and its environment obtained in the course of the audit, we have not identified material misstatements in the directors' report.

The Companies Act 2014 requires us to report to you if, in our opinion, the disclosures of directors' remuneration and transactions required by sections 305 to 312 of the Act are not made. We have nothing to report in this regard.

The Listing Rules of the Irish Stock Exchange [and/or UK Listing Authority] require us to review:
- the Directors' statement, [set out [on page ...]], in relation to going concern and longer term viability;
- the part of the Corporate Governance Statement on pages [ ] relating to the Company's compliance with the provisions of the UK Corporate Governance Code [*ISE only*: and the Irish Corporate Governance Annex] specified for our review; and
- certain elements of disclosures in the report to shareholders by the Board of Directors' remuneration committee.

## Respective responsibilities

### *Responsibilities of directors for the financial statements*

As explained more fully in the directors' responsibilities statement set on page [ ], the directors are responsible for the preparation of the financial statements and for being satisfied that they give a true and fair view, and for such internal control as they determine is necessary to enable the preparation of financial statements that are free from material misstatement, whether due to fraud or error.

In preparing the financial statements, the directors are responsible for assessing the Group and the parent Company's ability to continue as going concerns, disclosing, as applicable, matters related to going concern and using the going concern basis of accounting unless management either intends to liquidate the Group or the parent Company or to cease operations, or has no realistic alternative but to do so.

### *Auditor's responsibilities for the audit of the financial statements*

Our objectives are to obtain reasonable assurance about whether the financial statements as a whole are free from material misstatement, whether due to fraud or error, and to issue an auditor's report that includes our opinion. Reasonable assurance is a high level of assurance, but is not a guarantee that an audit conducted in accordance with ISAs (Ireland) will always detect a material misstatement when it exists. Misstatements can arise from fraud or error and are considered material if, individually or in the aggregate, they could reasonably be expected to influence the economic decisions of users taken on the basis of these financial statements.

[*Explanation as to what extent the audit was considered capable of detecting irregularities, including fraud*]

Further details relating to our work as auditor is set out in the Scope of Responsibilities Statement contained in the appendix of this report, which is to be read as an integral part of our report.

[*Or alternatively to the above*]

**Option A** – A further description of our responsibilities for the audit of the financial statements is located on the IAASA's website at: http://www.iaasa.ie/getmedia/b2389013-1cf6-458b-9b8f-a98202dc9c3a/Description_of_auditors_responsibilities_for_audit.pdf. This description forms part of our auditor's report.

**Option B** – [*Include the full detail of the appendix to the report within the report here.*]

**Other matters which we are required to address**

We were appointed by [*state by whom or which body the auditor was appointed*] on [*date*] to audit the financial statements for the year ending [date] and subsequent financial periods. The period of total uninterrupted engagement including previous renewals and reappointments of the firm is [*X*] years.

The non-audit services prohibited by IAASA's Ethical Standard were not provided to the group and we remain independent of the group in conducting our audit. [*Indicate any services, in addition to the audit, which were provided by the firm to the group that have not been disclosed in the financial statements or elsewhere in the annual report.*]

Our audit opinion is consistent with the additional report to the audit committee.

**The purpose of our audit work and to whom we owe our responsibilities**

Our report is made solely to the Company's members, as a body, in accordance with section 391 of the Companies Act 2014. Our audit work has been undertaken so that we might state to the Company's members those matters we are required to state to them in an auditor's report and for no other purpose. To the fullest extent permitted by law, we do not accept or assume responsibility to anyone other than the Company and the Company's members, as a body, for our audit work, for this report, or for the opinions we have formed.

Signature:

*A Partner* [*printed name*]
for and on behalf of [*audit company name*]
Chartered Accountants, Statutory Audit Firm
[*Address*]
[*Date*]

EXAMPLE 19.2: ILLUSTRATIVE UNQUALIFIED AUDIT REPORT (UK/NI)[2]

## INDEPENDENT AUDITOR'S REPORT TO THE MEMBERS OF XYZ PLC

### Opinion

We have audited the financial statements of XYZ Plc (the 'parent company') and its subsidiaries (the 'group') for the year ended [date] which comprise [specify the titles of the primary statements] and notes to the financial statements, including a summary of significant accounting policies. The financial reporting framework that has been applied in the preparation of the group financial statements is applicable law and International Financial Reporting Standards (IFRSs) as adopted by the European Union.

In our opinion the financial statements:
- give a true and fair view of the state of the group's and of the parent company's affairs as at [date] and of the group's and of the parent company's [profit/loss] for the year then ended;
- have been properly prepared in accordance with [IFRSs as adopted by the European Union]; and
- have been prepared in accordance with the requirements of the Companies Act 2006; and, as regards the group financial statements, Article 4 of the IAS Regulation.

### Separate opinion in relation to IFRSs as issued by the IASB

As explained in note [X] to the group financial statements, the group in addition to complying with its legal obligation to apply IFRSs as adopted by the European Union, has also applied IFRSs as issued by the International Accounting Standards Board (IASB).

In our opinion the group financial statements give a true and fair view of the consolidated financial position of the group as at [date] and of its consolidated financial performance and its consolidated cash flows for the year then ended in accordance with IFRSs as issued by the IASB.

### Basis for opinion

We conducted our audit in accordance with International Standards on Auditing (UK) (ISAs UK) and applicable law. Our responsibilities under those standards are further described in the Auditor's Responsibilities for the Audit of the Financial Statements section of our report. We are independent of the group in accordance with the ethical requirements that are relevant to our audit of the financial statements in the UK, including the FRC's Ethical Standard as applied to listed public interest entities, and we have fulfilled our other ethical responsibilities in accordance with these requirements. We believe that the audit evidence we have obtained is sufficient and appropriate to provide a basis for our opinion.

---

[2] Source: *Compendium of illustrative auditor's reports on United Kingdom private sector financial statements for periods commencing on or after 17 June 2016*, Appendix 6 (FRC, October 2016).

### Conclusions relating to principal risks, going concern and viability statement

We have nothing to report in respect of the following information in the annual report, in relation to which the ISAs (UK) require us to report to you whether we have anything material to add or draw attention to:

- the disclosures in the annual report [set out on page ...] that describe the principal risks and explain how they are being managed or mitigated;
- the directors' confirmation [set out on page ...] in the annual report that they have carried out a robust assessment of the principal risks facing the group, including those that would threaten its business model, future performance, solvency or liquidity;
- the directors' statement [set out on page ...] in the financial statements about whether the directors considered it appropriate to adopt the going concern basis of accounting in preparing the financial statements and the directors' identification of any material uncertainties to the group and the parent company's ability to continue to do so over a period of at least twelve months from the date of approval of the financial statements;
- whether the directors' statement relating to going concern required under the Listing Rules in accordance with Listing Rule 9.8.6R(3) is materially inconsistent with our knowledge obtained in the audit; or
- the directors' explanation [set out on page ...] in the annual report as to how they have assessed the prospects of the group, over what period they have done so and why they consider that period to be appropriate, and their statement as to whether they have a reasonable expectation that the group will be able to continue in operation and meet its liabilities as they fall due over the period of their assessment, including any related disclosures drawing attention to any necessary qualifications or assumptions.

### Key audit matters

Key audit matters are those matters that, in our professional judgment, were of most significance in our audit of the financial statements of the current period and include the most significant assessed risks of material misstatement (whether or not due to fraud) we identified, including those which had the greatest effect on: the overall audit strategy, the allocation of resources in the audit; and directing the efforts of the engagement team. These matters were addressed in the context of our audit of the financial statements as a whole, and in forming our opinion thereon, and we do not provide a separate opinion on these matters.

*[Description of each key audit matter in accordance with ISA (UK) 701.]*

### Our application of materiality

*[Explanation of how the auditor applied the concept of materiality in planning and performing the group and parent company audit. This is required to include the threshold used by the auditor as being materiality for the group and parent company financial statements as a whole but may include other relevant disclosures.]*

### An overview of the scope of our audit report

*[Overview of the scope of the group and parent company audit, including an explanation of how the scope addressed each key audit matter and was influenced by the auditor's application of materiality.]*

*[Explanation as to what extent the audit was considered capable of detecting irregularities, including fraud.]*

## Other information

The other information comprises the information included in the annual report [set out on pages ...][, including [*specify the titles of the other information*] [set out on pages ...]], other than the financial statements and our auditor's report thereon. The directors are responsible for the other information. Our opinion on the financial statements does not cover the other information and, except to the extent otherwise explicitly stated in our report, we do not express any form of assurance conclusion thereon.

In connection with our audit of the financial statements, our responsibility is to read the other information and, in doing so, consider whether the other information is materially inconsistent with the financial statements or our knowledge obtained in the audit or otherwise appears to be materially misstated. If we identify such material inconsistencies or apparent material misstatements, we are required to determine whether there is a material misstatement in the financial statements or a material misstatement of the other information. If, based on the work we have performed, we conclude that there is a material misstatement of this other information, we are required to report that fact.

We have nothing to report in this regard.

In this context, we also have nothing to report in regard to our responsibility to specifically address the following items in the other information and to report as uncorrected material misstatements of the other information where we conclude that those items meet the following conditions:

- *Fair, balanced and understandable* – [the statement given/the explanation as to why the annual report does not include a statement] by the directors that they consider the annual report and financial statements taken as a whole is fair, balanced and understandable and provides the information necessary for shareholders to assess the group's performance, business model and strategy, is materially inconsistent with our knowledge obtained in the audit; or
- *Audit committee reporting* – [the section describing the work of the audit committee does not appropriately address matters communicated by us to the audit committee/ the explanation as to why the annual report does not include a section describing the work of the audit committee] is materially inconsistent with our knowledge obtained in the audit; or
- *Directors' statement of compliance with the UK Corporate Governance Code* – the parts of the directors' statement required under the Listing Rules relating to the company's compliance with the UK Corporate Governance Code containing provisions specified for review by the auditor in accordance with Listing Rule 9.8.10R(2) do not properly disclose a departure from a relevant provision of the UK Corporate Governance Code.

## Opinions on other matters prescribed by the Companies Act 2006

In our opinion the part of the directors' remuneration report to be audited has been properly prepared in accordance with the Companies Act 2006.

In our opinion, based on the work undertaken in the course of the audit:
- the information given in the strategic report and the directors' report for the financial year for which the financial statements are prepared is consistent with the financial statements and those reports have been prepared in accordance with applicable legal requirements;
- the information about internal control and risk management systems in relation to financial reporting processes and about share capital structures, given in compliance with rules 7.2.5 and 7.2.6 in the Disclosure Rules and Transparency Rules sourcebook made by the Financial Conduct Authority (the FCA Rules), is consistent with the financial statements and has been prepared in accordance with applicable legal requirements; and
- information about the company's corporate governance code and practices and about its administrative, management and supervisory bodies and their committees complies with rules 7.2.2, 7.2.3 and 7.2.7 of the FCA Rules.

### Matters on which we are required to report by exception

In the light of the knowledge and understanding of the group and the parent company and its environment obtained in the course of the audit, we have not identified material misstatements in:
- the strategic report or the directors' report; or
- the information about internal control and risk management systems in relation to financial reporting processes and about share capital structures, given in compliance with rules 7.2.5 and 7.2.6 of the FCA Rules.

We have nothing to report in respect of the following matters in relation to which the Companies Act 2006 requires us to report to you if, in our opinion:
- adequate accounting records have not been kept by the parent company, or returns adequate for our audit have not been received from branches not visited by us; or
- the parent company financial statements and the part of the directors' remuneration report to be audited are not in agreement with the accounting records and returns; or
- certain disclosures of directors' remuneration specified by law are not made; or
- we have not received all the information and explanations we require for our audit; or
- a corporate governance statement has not been prepared by the parent company.

### Responsibilities of directors

As explained more fully in the directors' responsibilities statement [set out on page ...], the directors are responsible for the preparation of the financial statements and for being satisfied that they give a true and fair view, and for such internal control as the directors determine is necessary to enable the preparation of financial statements that are free from material misstatement, whether due to fraud or error.

In preparing the financial statements, the directors are responsible for assessing the group's and the parent company's ability to continue as a going concern, disclosing, as applicable, matters related to going concern and using the going concern basis of accounting unless the directors either intend to liquidate the group or the parent company or to cease operations, or have no realistic alternative but to do so.

**Auditor's responsibilities for the audit of the financial statements**

Our objectives are to obtain reasonable assurance about whether the financial statements as a whole are free from material misstatement, whether due to fraud or error, and to issue an auditor's report that includes our opinion. Reasonable assurance is a high level of assurance, but is not a guarantee that an audit conducted in accordance with ISAs (UK) will always detect a material misstatement when it exists. Misstatements can arise from fraud or error and are considered material if, individually or in the aggregate, they could reasonably be expected to influence the economic decisions of users taken on the basis of these financial statements.

A further description of our responsibilities for the audit of the financial statements is included in appendix [X] of this auditor's report. This description, which is located at [*indicate page number or other specific reference to the location of the description*], forms part of our auditor's report.

**Other matters which we are required to address**

Following the recommendation of the audit committee, we were appointed by [*state by whom or which body the auditor was appointed*] on [*date*] to audit the financial statements for the year ending [*date*] and subsequent financial periods. The period of total uninterrupted engagement is [*X*] years, covering the years ending [*date*] to [*date*].

The non-audit services prohibited by the FRC's Ethical Standard were not provided to the group or the parent company and we remain independent of the group and the parent company in conducting our audit.

[*Indicate any services, in addition to the audit, which were provided by the firm to the group that have not been disclosed in the financial statements or elsewhere in the annual report.*]

Our audit opinion is consistent with the additional report to the audit committee.

[*Signature*]
*A Partner* [*printed name*]
for and on behalf of [*audit company name*]
Chartered Accountants, Statutory Audit Firm
[*Address*]
[*Date*]

Examples of private company audit reports and public non-PIE entity audit reports, for use in the RoI, can be found in the Chartered Accountants Ireland, Technical Alert TA 02/2017 *Guidance on the new ISAs (Ireland) Auditing Standards issued by the Irish Auditing and Accounting Supervisory Authority*. For use in the UK/NI, the FRC's October 2016 bulletin, *Compendium of illustrative auditor's reports on United Kingdom private sector financial statements for periods commencing on or after 17 June 2016*, provides further examples of unqualified audit reports.

There have been a series of changes to the format of the report, which is now less prescriptive than the format of audit reports of the past. The new format requires the auditor to give the user of the financial statements a much greater insight into the audit engagement process, the regulatory and legal environments, the key risks addressed during the audit and how these impacted the conduct of the audit, as well as specifically addressing the issue of going concern in a more direct fashion than before. All of these measures should enhance users' understanding of the audit process, including critical judgements made during the audit.

## 19.4 THE AUDIT OPINION

### Introduction

In **Chapter 18**, the auditor performed the concluding procedures in order to form the audit opinion. ISA 700, paragraphs 10–15, contain guidance on forming an audit opinion on the financial statements. Below we will consider the types of audit opinion that the auditor may reach.

There are essentially two categories of opinion that an auditor can issue: **unqualified** or **modified**.

1. An unqualified opinion is a 'clean' audit opinion, essentially stating that "the financial statements give a true and fair view". An unqualified opinion may include additional communication in the form of an **emphasis of matter paragraph** or an **other matter paragraph** (ISA 706) – but the opinion remains unqualified, i.e. there are no material misstatements.
2. A modified opinion indicates that a material misstatement exists (or could exist) in the financial statements, which has arisen either as a result of:
   (a) **disagreement**; or
   (b) **limitation of scope**.

ISA 705 establishes three types of modified opinion: a qualified opinion; an adverse opinion; and a disclaimer of opinion. **Figure 19.2** below illustrates the different audit opinions by way of a decision tree.

FIGURE 19.2: TYPES OF AUDIT OPINION

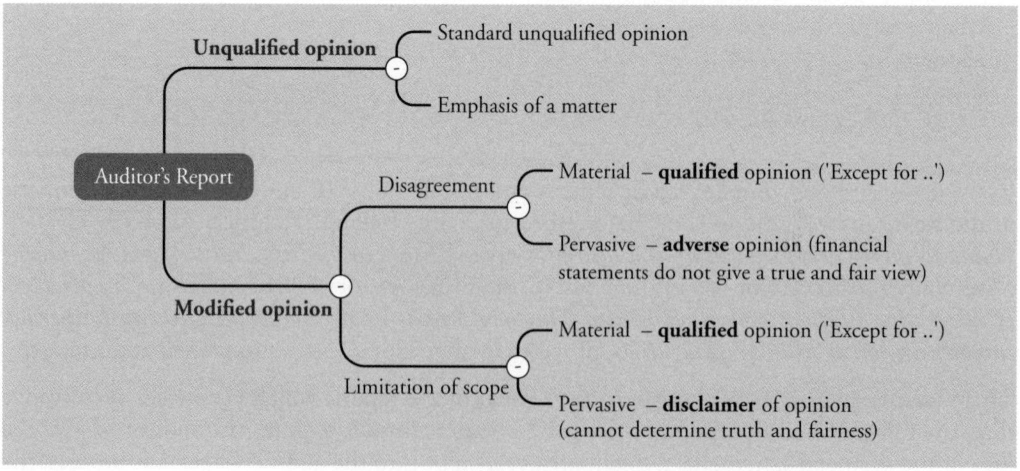

## Unqualified Opinion

### *Standard Unqualified Opinion*

A standard unqualified opinion is the audited entity's desired outcome, as it is a 'clean' audit opinion with no modifications required, i.e. "the financial statements give a true and fair view". **Example 19.1** and **Example 19.2** above are illustrative examples of standard unqualified audit reports (for RoI and UK/NI, respectively).

### *Unqualified Opinion – Emphasis of Matter or Other Matter Paragraphs*

As noted above, an unqualified opinion can include additional communication in the form of **emphasis of matter** or **other matter** paragraphs (see **Table 19.2**).

TABLE 19.2: UNQUALIFIED OPINION – ADDITIONAL COMMUNICATIONS

**Emphasis of Matter Paragraph** "A paragraph included in the auditor's report that refers to a matter appropriately presented or disclosed in the financial statements that, in the auditor's judgment, is of such importance that it is fundamental to users' understanding of the financial statements." (ISA 706, paragraph 7(a))

**Other Matter Paragraph** "A paragraph included in the auditor's report that refers to a matter other than those presented or disclosed in the financial statements that, in the auditor's judgment, is relevant to users' understanding of the audit, the auditor's responsibilities or the auditor's report." (ISA 706, paragraph 7(b))

ISA 706 provides guidance specifically for the additional communication of emphasis of matter and other matter paragraphs, but other standards are also relevant: ISA 701 around key audit matters and ISA 570 around going concern.

An emphasis of matter arises where, in the auditor's opinion, the matter in question is **not materially misstated** and is **adequately presented and disclosed** in the financial statements, but is of such importance that it is **fundamental to users' understanding** of the financial statements and therefore that attention should be drawn to it. The auditor does not qualify their opinion with respect to the matter, as **sufficient appropriate audit evidence** that the matter is not materially misstated has been obtained, and they are satisfied that it is adequately presented and disclosed in the financial statements.

The emphasis of matter paragraph is included immediately after the **basis for opinion paragraph** in the audit report and is headed 'Emphasis of Matter'. The paragraph should:
(a) clearly state that the auditor's **opinion is not modified in respect of the matter** being emphasised; and
(b) make clear reference to the **location of the disclosure note** in the financial statements that fully describes the matter being emphasised.

ISA 706, paragraph A5, provides the following as examples of circumstances that may give rise to an emphasis of matter paragraph:

"• An uncertainty relating to the future outcome of exceptional litigation or regulatory action.

• A significant subsequent event that occurs between the date of the financial statements and the date of the auditor's report.

• Early application (where permitted) of a new accounting standard that has a material effect on the financial statements.

• A major catastrophe that has had, or continues to have, a significant effect on the entity's financial position."

An illustrative example is given in **Example 19.3** below, demonstrating how the emphasis of matter paragraph would be included in the auditor's report. (This example is based on Note 34 to the financial statements of Large Company Limited, **Appendix B**.) As you can see, management has included a note relating to a contingent liability and we will assume that the auditor feels that this disclosure is adequate to address the issue. As such the auditor feels that the issue is adequately presented in the financial statements, but feels that it is very important to the users' understanding of the financial statements and therefore draws their attention to the note using an emphasis of matter paragraph.

EXAMPLE 19.3: EXTRACT FROM THE INDEPENDENT AUDITOR'S REPORT OF LARGE COMPANY LIMITED ILLUSTRATING 'EMPHASIS OF MATTER'

### INDEPENDENT AUDITOR'S REPORT TO THE MEMBERS OF LARGE COMPANY LIMITED (EXTRACT)

**Opinion and Basis for Opinion paragraphs**

[No change to that of an unqualified opinion.]

**Emphasis of Matter – Possible Outcome of a Lawsuit**

In forming our opinion on the financial statements, **which is not modified**, we have considered the adequacy of the disclosure made in Note 34 to the financial statements concerning the possible outcome of a lawsuit alleging the sale of faulty furniture resulting in an injury incurred on a customer's premises. The ultimate outcome of the matter cannot be determined at present, and no provision for any liability that may result has been made in the financial statements based on the advice of the company's solicitors that the action is unlikely to succeed. A successful outcome for the plaintiff, however, could cost up to €6,000,000, which is 8.2% of 2018 profit before tax.

**Opinions on Other Matters Prescribed by the Companies Act [2014 or 2006]**

Based solely on the work …

For illustrative examples of auditor's reports with modified opinions relating to going concern, see the Appendix in ISA 570 *Going Concern*. These examples illustrate the requirements where the auditor is required to modify their opinion or to report that a material uncertainty exists. In the RoI, ISA (Ireland) 570 does include the Appendix, but with the caveat that the examples have not been tailored for Ireland.

## Modified Opinion

As noted above, a modified opinion indicates that a material misstatement exists, or could exist. A modified opinion can be damaging to an audited entity as the user's attention is brought to an issue in the financial statements or to the auditor's ability to complete the audit. The normal assurance provided by the external auditor's report is therefore not possible, which could affect the decisions of the users of the financial statements.

ISA 705 *Modifications to the Opinion in the Independent Auditor's Report* gives guidance on the expression of modified opinions on the financial statements. It aims to ensure that the auditor's assessment giving rise to the modified opinion is appropriate and that it is expressed when:

(a) **disagreement** arises: "The auditor concludes, based on the audit evidence obtained, that the financial statements as a whole are not free from material misstatement" (ISA 705, paragraph 4(a)); or

(b) there has been a **limitation of scope**: "The auditor is unable to obtain sufficient appropriate audit evidence to conclude that the financial statements as a whole are free from material misstatement." (ISA 705, paragraph 4(b))

ISA 450 *Evaluation of Misstatements Identified During the Audit* defines a **misstatement** as: "A difference between the reported amount, classification, presentation, or disclosure of a financial statement item and the amount, classification, presentation, or disclosure that is required for the item to be in accordance with the applicable financial reporting framework." (ISA 450, paragraph 4(a))

ISA 705 outlines what circumstances might give rise to a material misstatement, including:

1. **The appropriateness of the selected accounting policies** The auditor needs to ask:
   (a) Are the selected accounting policies in line with the applicable financial reporting framework?
   (b) Do the transactions and events that underlie the financial statements achieve fair presentation when selected accounting policies are applied?
   (c) Are changes in accounting policies in line with the applicable financial reporting framework?

2. **The application of the selected accounting policies** The auditor needs to consider:
   (a) Are all transactions and events applied in line with selected accounting policies?
   (b) Have the accounting policies been applied consistently?

3. **The appropriateness or adequacy of disclosures in the financial statements** The
   auditor needs to ask:
   (a) Have all necessary disclosures been included in line with the applicable financial
       reporting framework?
   (b) Are all disclosures that are included in the financial statements in line with the
       applicable financial reporting framework?
   (c) Are the disclosures made sufficient to achieve fair presentation?

Once the auditor has determined that there is a **misstatement**, or a potential misstatement
due to disagreement or limitation of scope, and concludes that the misstatement is
**material**, a modified opinion will be issued. The auditor then needs to determine how
material the misstatement is or could be. A material misstatement can either be:

1. material but not pervasive – while the item is material, it is **not** so material that the
   entire set of financial statements does not give a true and fair view; or
2. material and pervasive – the item is so material and pervasive that the entire set of
   financial statements does not give a true and fair view.

These are now considered in detail below.

ISA 705, paragraph 5(a), states that "Pervasive effects on the financial statements are those
that, in the auditor's judgment:

   (i)   Are not confined to specific elements, accounts or items of the financial statements
         [for example, if efforts have been made to increase profit by applying incorrect cut-
         off to revenue, by understating accruals or by capitalising revenue expenditure];
   (ii)  If so confined, represent or could represent a substantial proportion of the
         financial statements [for example, if the value of the misstatement is 50% of
         profit]; or
   (iii) In relation to disclosures, are fundamental to users' understanding of the financial
         statements [for example, if the directors have failed to include a note with respect
         to the possible outcome of a legal claim that, while not requiring provision in the
         accounts has the potential to result in a significant settlement that could pose cash-
         flow problems for the entity and therefore impact on its ability to continue as a
         going concern]."

Essentially, pervasive effects are not isolated, are well in excess of materiality or relate
to the inadequacy of disclosures seen to be fundamental to the user of the financial
statements.

It is important that the auditor adequately assesses the level of materiality as being either
'material and not pervasive' or 'material and pervasive' because very different opinions
are issued based on the assessed level of pervasiveness. Once a misstatement is considered
material, a modified opinion will be required. However, the level of materiality will further
impact on the type of modification (see below). To further support your understanding,
refer to **Appendix 19.1** of this chapter, which illustrates the auditor's decision-making
process when deciding on the audit opinion that will be issued.

## *Modified Opinion – Disagreement*

A **disagreement** arises when the auditor concludes that a material misstatement exists in the financial statements and the client entity is not willing to correct it.

Having determined that there is a material misstatement due to a disagreement, the auditor must assess the level of materiality outlined above, i.e.:

1. is it material but not pervasive?; or
2. is it material and pervasive?

The level of materiality will determine the type of modified opinion that should be reported:

1. if it is material but not pervasive – a **qualified opinion**, "except for ...", would be appropriate;
2. if it is material and pervasive – an **adverse opinion** would be reported.

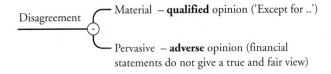

Disagreement
- Material – **qualified** opinion ('Except for ..')
- Pervasive – **adverse** opinion (financial statements do not give a true and fair view)

**Example 19.4** below is a worked example of the auditor's decision in relation to a disagreement leading to a qualified opinion. It illustrates the auditor's consideration of the level of materiality to be applied and the form of the audit opinion. Included in the example are extracts from the auditor's reports for the RoI and for the UK/NI to demonstrate how the audit opinion would impact on the form and content of the auditor's report.

EXAMPLE 19.4: ASSESSMENT OF LEVEL OF MATERIALITY WHERE
DISAGREEMENT – QUALIFIED OPINION "EXCEPT FOR ..."

**Materiality for Large Company Limited is €3,642,500** (i.e. overall materiality determined in **Chapter 5,** Section 5.4).

A cut-off error occurred in relation to two transactions around the year end. The transactions related to the manufacture of luxury furniture for an overseas customer. According to the contract, the customer took rights to the furniture on delivery to the customer's premises in Japan. The transactions were recognised as sales when dispatched on 31 December 2018. The furniture was not signed for by the customer until arrival in Japan on 15 February 2019. The gross profit value of the transactions was €3,715,200. The balance of cut-off testing showed that all other transactions were appropriately accounted for in the correct accounting period.

**What type of opinion will the auditor issue if the client does not correct the financial statements?**

This gives rise to a disagreement as the treatment of these two transactions is not in line with IFRS 15 *Revenue from Contracts with Customers* because revenue on these two transactions is recognised before the transfer of control to the buyer.

The item is material because it exceeds the performance materiality of €3,642,500. However, it is not pervasive – it does not impact on the *entire* set of financial statements. One could say that **'the financial statements give a true and fair view except for these two transactions'**.

The auditor would issue a qualified opinion, 'except for ...'

The correction of this error would require the following journal entry:

|  | Dr € | Cr € |
|---|---|---|
| SOCI (Profit before tax) | 3,715,200 | |
| SOFP (Net impact on inventory and receivables) | | 3,715,200 |
| VAT payable | | – |
| Income tax | | 464,400 |
| Tax payable | 464,400 | |
|  | 4,179,600 | 4,179,600 |

*Being correction of cut-off error*

***Note***: there is no VAT on non-domestic revenue; assumes an income tax rate of 12.5%.

Extracts from the independent auditor's report illustrating the expression and presentation of the qualified opinion in this scenario are given below. Separate extracts for the Republic of Ireland and the UK/Northern Ireland reflect the legislative and regulatory differences in each jurisdiction.

### REPUBLIC OF IRELAND

## INDEPENDENT AUDITOR'S REPORT
## (EXTRACT – QUALIFIED OPINION)

[Students should note that the overall format of the auditor's report remains unchanged other than relating to this extract and, more specifically, to the italicised text.]

### Qualified opinion

We have audited the financial statements of Large Company Limited as at 31 December 2018, which comprise the Statement of Financial Position, the Statement of Comprehensive Income, the Statement of Cash Flows and the Statement of Changes in Equity for the year then ended, and the related Notes 1–35, including a summary of significant accounting policies.

The financial reporting framework that has been applied in their preparation is applicable law and International Financial Reporting Standards (IFRSs) as adopted by the European Union.

In our opinion, except for the effects of the matter described in the 'Basis for qualified opinion' section of our report:
• the Group financial statements give a true and fair view of the assets, liabilities and financial position of the Group as at 31 December 2018 and of its profit for the year then ended;

- the Company statement of financial position gives a true and fair view of the assets, liabilities and financial position of the Company as at 31 December 2018;
- the Group financial statements have been properly prepared in accordance with IFRS as adopted by the European Union;
- the Company financial statements have been properly prepared in accordance with IFRS as adopted by the European Union as applied in accordance with the provisions of the Companies Act 2014; and
- the Group financial statements and Company financial statements have been properly prepared in accordance with the requirements of the Companies Act 2014 and, as regards the Group financial statements, Article 4 of the IAS Regulation.

## Basis for qualified opinion

*Included in the revenue shown on the statement of comprehensive income is an amount of €3,715,200 relating to two transactions that occurred in 2019. This does not comply with IFRS 15 Revenue from Contracts with Customers in that, according to the contract, control did not transfer to the buyer until delivery to the buyer's premises, which did not occur until February 2019. Accordingly, net profit before tax should be reduced by €3,715,200 and tax should be reduced by €464,400, resulting in a reduction of profit and retained earnings of €3,250,800.*

We conducted our audit in accordance with International Standards on Auditing (Ireland) (ISAs (Ireland)) and applicable law. Our responsibilities under those standards are further described in the 'Auditor's responsibilities for the audit of the financial statements' section of our report. We are independent of the Group and Company in accordance with the ethical requirements that are relevant to our audit of the financial statements in the Republic of Ireland, including the Ethical Standard issued by the Irish Auditing & Accounting Supervisory Authority, and we have fulfilled our other ethical responsibilities in accordance with these requirements. We believe that the audit evidence we have obtained is sufficient and appropriate to provide a basis for our opinion.

## Opinions on other matters prescribed by the Companies Act 2014

[Unchanged from unqualified opinion]

## Matters on which we are required to report by exception

[Unchanged from unqualified opinion]

### UK/NORTHERN IRELAND

## INDEPENDENT AUDITOR'S REPORT
## (EXTRACT – QUALIFIED OPINION)

[Students should note that the overall format of the auditor's report remains unchanged other than relating to this extract and, more specifically, to the italicised text.]

## Qualified opinion

We have audited the financial statements of Large Company Limited as at 31 December 2018, which comprise the Statement of Financial Position, the Statement of Comprehensive Income, the Statement of Cash Flows, the Statement of Changes in Equity and the related Notes 1–35, including a summary of significant accounting policies. The financial reporting framework that has been applied in their preparation is applicable law and International Financial Reporting Standards (IFRS) as adopted by the European Union.

*In our opinion, except for the effects of the matter described in the 'Basis for qualified opinion' paragraph, when reporting in accordance with a fair presentation framework the financial statements:*
- *give a true and fair view of the state of the company's affairs as at 31 December 2018 and of its profit for the year then ended;*
- *have been properly prepared in accordance with IFRSs as adopted by the European Union;*
- *have been prepared in accordance with the requirements of the Companies Act 2006.*

## Basis for qualified opinion

*Included in the revenue shown on the statement of comprehensive income is an amount of £3,715,200 relating to two transactions that occurred in 2019. This does not comply with IFRS 15 Revenue from Contracts with Customers in that, according to the contract, control did not transfer to the buyer until delivery to the buyer's premises, which did not occur until February 2019. Accordingly, net profit before tax should be reduced by £3,715,200 and tax should be reduced by £464,400, resulting in a reduction of profit and retained earnings of £3,250,800.*

We conducted our audit in accordance with International Standards on Auditing (UK) and applicable law. Our responsibilities under those standards are further described in the 'auditor's responsibilities for the audit of the financial statements' section of our report. We are independent of the company in accordance with the ethical requirements that are relevant to our audit of the financial statements in the UK, including the FRC's Ethical Standard (2016), and we have fulfilled our other ethical responsibilities in accordance with these requirements. We believe that the audit evidence we have obtained is sufficient and appropriate to provide a basis for our opinion.

## Opinions on other matters prescribed by the Companies Act 2006

In our opinion the information given in the directors' report for the financial year for which the financial statements are prepared is consistent with the financial statements.

## Matters on which we are required to report by exception

[Unchanged from unqualified opinion]

**Example 19.5** considers a similar example to that of **Example 19.4**, but where the facts lead to an adverse opinion.

### EXAMPLE 19.5: ASSESSMENT OF LEVEL OF MATERIALITY WHERE DISAGREEMENT – ADVERSE OPINION

**Materiality for Large Company Limited is €3,642,500** (i.e. Overall Materiality determined in **Chapter 5**, Section 5.4).

Cut-off testing has revealed that the **client entity** applied inappropriate revenue recognition rules in that all furniture sales revenue was recognised on dispatch rather than on delivery (according to the contract with the customers, ownership passed on arrival of the furniture in the customer's premises). Seven transactions that occurred prior to the year end, while dispatched in 2018, did not arrive to customers until 2019. The net profit before tax value of these transactions was €7,982,800.

Additionally, in December the client commenced a new sales strategy with all domestic customers whereby the customers could buy on a sale-or-return basis. The sale-or-return term was for a period of 30 days. Five customers took up the offer and took delivery of the goods between 20 and 30 December 2018. The net profit before tax value of these transactions was €22,200,600.

**Should the transactions be considered material but not pervasive or material and pervasive?**

The above scenario would be considered pervasive due to the value of the error. The combined error is €30,183,400, which is 50% of profit. Therefore its correction would result in pre-tax profits of €30,210,600 instead of the €60,394,000 currently reported. In this instance, it is correct to say that **the financial statements do not give a true and fair view**.

The auditor would issue an **adverse opinion**.

The correction of this error would require the following journal entry:

|                                  | Dr €        | Cr €        |
| -------------------------------- | ----------- | ----------- |
| Net profit before tax            | 30,183,400  |             |
| SOFP (inventory and receivables) |             | 30,183,400  |
| Income tax                       |             | 3,772,925   |
| Tax payable                      | 3,772,925   |             |
|                                  | 33,956,325  | 33,956,325  |

*Being correction of incorrect application of revenue recognition rules under IFRS 15*

**Note:** Ignore VAT; assumed income tax rate of 12.5%.

Let us now consider how the issuing of an adverse opinion would be reflected in the independent auditor's report for the Republic of Ireland and for the UK/Northern Ireland.

REPUBLIC OF IRELAND

# INDEPENDENT AUDITOR'S REPORT
# (EXTRACT – ADVERSE OPINION)

[Students should note that the overall format of the auditor's report remains unchanged other than relating to this extract and, more specifically, to the italicised text.]

## Adverse opinion

We have audited the financial statements of Large Company Limited as at 31 December 2018, which comprise the Statement of Financial Position, the Statement of Comprehensive Income, the Statement of Cash Flows and the Statement of Changes in Equity for the year then ended, and the related Notes 1–35, including a summary of significant accounting policies. The financial reporting framework that has been applied in their preparation is applicable law and International Financial Reporting Standards (IFRS) as adopted by the European Union.

*In our opinion, because of the significance of the matter described in the 'Basis for adverse opinion' section of our audit report, the financial statements do not give a true and fair view of the assets, liabilities and financial position of the company,* in accordance with IFRSs as adopted by the European Union, of the state of the company's affairs as at 31 December 2018 and of its profit for the year then ended.

In all other respects, in our opinion, the financial statements have been properly prepared in accordance with the requirements of the Companies Act 2014.

## Basis for adverse opinion

*Incorrect revenue recognition has been applied to a number of transactions. Net profit of €7,982,000 was recognised for goods where control had not yet transferred to the buyer, which is not in line with IFRS 15 Revenue from Contracts with Customers. A further net profit of €7,200,600 was recognised in relation to goods sold on a sale-or-return basis where the return period had not ceased prior to the year end; this is not in line with IFRS 15. If revenue recognition had been applied according to IFRS 15 the effect on the Statement of Comprehensive Income would result in a reduction of €15,183,400 and €1,897,925 to profit before tax and income tax, respectively, resulting in a reduction in profit for the year and retained earnings of €13,285,475.*

We conducted our audit in accordance with International Standards on Auditing (Ireland) (ISAs (Ireland)) and applicable law ... provide a basis for our adverse opinion.

## Opinions on other matters prescribed by the Companies Act 2014

*Notwithstanding our adverse opinion on the financial statements:* Based solely on the work undertaken in the course of this audit, we report that ... is in agreement with the accounting records.

## Matters on which we are required to report by exception

Based on our knowledge ... to report in this regard.

UK/NORTHERN IRELAND

# INDEPENDENT AUDITOR'S REPORT
## (EXTRACT – ADVERSE OPINION)

[Students should note that the overall format of the auditor's report remains unchanged other than relating to this extract and, more specifically, to the italicised text.]

### Adverse opinion

We have audited the financial statements of Large Company Limited as at 31 December 2018, which comprise the Statement of Financial Position, the Statement of Comprehensive Income, the Statement of Cash Flows and the Statement of Changes in Equity for the period then ended, the related Notes 1–35, including a summary of significant accounting policies. The financial reporting framework that has been applied in their preparation is applicable law and International Financial Reporting Standards (IFRSs) as adopted by the European Union.

*In our opinion, because of the significance of the matter described in the 'Basis for adverse opinion' section of our report, when reporting in accordance with a fair presentation framework the accompanying financial statements do not give a true and fair view of the company's affairs as at 31 December 2018 and of its profit for the year then ended, and have not been properly prepared in accordance with IFRSs as adopted by the European Union.*

### Basis for adverse opinion

*Incorrect revenue recognition has been applied to a number of transactions. Net profit of €7,982,000 was recognised for goods where control had not yet transferred to the buyer, which is not in line with IFRS 15 Revenue from Contracts with Customers. A further net profit of €7,200,600 was recognised in relation to goods sold on a sale-or-return basis where the return period had not ceased prior to the year end; this is not in line with IFRS 15. If revenue recognition had been applied according to IFRS 15, the effect on the Statement of Comprehensive Income would result in a reduction of €15,183,400 and €1,897,925 to profit before tax and income tax, respectively, resulting in a reduction in profit for the year and retained earnings of €13,285,475.*

We conducted our audit in accordance with International Standards on Auditing (UK) and applicable law. Our responsibilities under those standards are further described in the 'auditor's responsibilities for the audit of the financial statements' section of our report. We are independent of the company in accordance with the ethical requirements that are relevant to our audit of the financial statements in the UK, including the FRC's Ethical Standard, and we have fulfilled our other ethical responsibilities in accordance with these requirements. We believe that the audit evidence we have obtained is sufficient and appropriate to provide a basis for our adverse opinion.

### Opinions on other matters prescribed by the Companies Act 2006

*Notwithstanding our adverse opinion on the financial statements,* in our opinion the information given in the directors' report for the financial year for which the financial statements are prepared is consistent with the financial statements.

### Matters on which we are required to report by exception

We have nothing to report in respect of ...

In summary, from the extracts from the independent auditor's report shown above in **Example 19.4** and **Example 19.5**, the auditor is required to:

- outline a clearly headed 'Opinion' paragraph, which immediately indicates to the user whether the opinion is qualified and, if so, what form the qualification takes;
- provide an example of the financial effects and a brief description of the matter giving rise to the disagreement in the 'Basis for opinion' paragraph; and
- for omitted disclosures, include the **omitted information where practicable** (i.e. the information is available and not too lengthy for the auditor's report).

---

*Note:* even though the opinion was qualified/adverse in the scenarios above, this does not exclude the need to include an '**Emphasis of matter**' paragraph where required.

---

**Table 19.3** below suggests some common examples of situations that could give rise to a disagreement leading to a qualified opinion ('except for ...') or an adverse opinion.

TABLE 19.3: COMMON EXAMPLES OF SITUATIONS THAT
COULD GIVE RISE TO DISAGREEMENT

| Audit opinion | Examples where it might apply |
|---|---|
| Qualified opinion, 'except for ...' | • Inadequate provision for doubtful debts.<br>• Non-disclosure in accounts of going concern problems (which could also give rise to an adverse opinion).<br>• Disagreement over the value of some inventory. |
| Adverse opinion | • Failure to comply with Companies Acts 2014/Companies Act 2006, accounting standards, etc. without acceptable reason.<br>• Significant concern about the company's ability to continue as a going concern, which is not adequately disclosed in the financial statements.<br>• Significant uncertainties regarding the existence, ownership, valuation or recording of assets and liabilities. |

### Modified Opinion – Limitation of Scope

A **limitation of scope** (also referred to as a limitation on the scope of an audit) arises where the auditor fails to obtain sufficient appropriate audit evidence, preventing them from concluding on the truth and fairness of a particular matter **or** on the truth and fairness of the entire set of financial statements. ISA 705, paragraph A8, outlines three instances that may give rise to a limitation of scope:

"(a) Circumstances beyond the control of the entity [for example the entity's records were destroyed in a fire or the entity's controls are ineffective and the auditor determines that performing substantive procedures alone is not sufficient to conclude on an opinion];

(b)  Circumstances relating to the nature or timing of the auditor's work [for example, the auditor was appointed after the year end date and was unable to attend the physical counting of inventories and no alternative audit procedures were available]; or

(c)  Limitations imposed by management [for example, management prevent the auditor from circularising the bank or customers]."

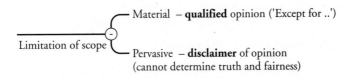

Limitation of scope
Material – **qualified** opinion ('Except for ..')
Pervasive – **disclaimer** of opinion (cannot determine truth and fairness)

If a limitation of scope arises, and it is determined that it is a **material misstatement**, it is again a question of the level of materiality: is it material but not pervasive?; or is it material and pervasive?

As with the discussion on **disagreement** above, if the limitation of scope is material but not pervasive, then a qualified opinion, "except for ...", would be issued. If, however, the limitation of scope is material and pervasive, a **disclaimer of opinion** would be issued. By issuing a disclaimer of opinion, the auditor is reporting that they are unable to form an opinion on the financial statements and that they do not know if they give a true and fair view or not.

Remember, if the limitation of scope is not material, then an **unqualified opinion** would be issued.

**The Requirement for the Auditor to Identify Alternative Audit Procedures**   It is important to note at this point that where a limitation of scope is imposed, the auditor should seek to apply alternative audit procedures, and if other procedures are not considered adequate, the implications for the audit report should be considered. For example, where a limitation is imposed on the attendance at the physical inventory count (i.e. the entity refuses to allow the auditor to attend), the auditor should attempt to count the stock at a later date and perform a roll-back to the year-end, provided the controls in the organisation are such that this would be practicable and reliable.

ISA 705, paragraph A9, also notes that "Limitations imposed by management may have other implications for the audit, such as the auditor's assessment of fraud risks and consideration of engagement continuance."

**Example 19.6** considers a scenario where there is a limitation of scope that is material but not pervasive.

EXAMPLE 19.6: ASSESSMENT OF LEVEL OF MATERIALITY AND TYPE OF QUALIFICATION WHERE: LIMITATION OF SCOPE – QUALIFIED OPINION "EXCEPT FOR ..."

**Materiality for Large Company Limited is €3,642,500** (i.e. overall materiality determined in **Chapter 5**, Section 5.4).

The auditor was not made aware of one of the locations where a physical inventory count took place on 31 December 2018. The value of inventory held on the premises not attended by the auditor was €3,972,500. The auditor has exhausted other audit procedures but, due to a lack of controls, cannot carry out alternative procedures to determine the existence, condition and quantity of inventory in question at the year end.

**What type of opinion will the auditor issue?**

This will give rise to a limitation of scope imposed by management, resulting in the auditor being unable to obtain **sufficient appropriate audit evidence** relating to the existence of an element of inventory at 31 December 2018.

The item is material because it exceeds the materiality of €3,642,500. However, it is not pervasive – it does not impact on the entire set of financial statements. One would say that the financial statements give a true and fair view **except for** this matter.

The auditor would issue a qualified opinion, 'except for ...'.

Extracts from the independent auditor's report illustrating the expression and presentation of the qualified opinion in this scenario are given below. Separate extracts for the Republic of Ireland and the UK/Northern Ireland reflect the legislative and regulatory differences in each jurisdiction.

REPUBLIC OF IRELAND

## INDEPENDENT AUDITOR'S REPORT (EXTRACT – QUALIFIED OPINION)

[Students should note that the overall format of the auditor's report remains unchanged other than relating to this extract and, more specifically, to the italicised text.]

### Qualified opinion

We have audited the financial statements of Large Company Limited as at 31 December 2018 ..... International Financial Reporting Standards (IFRSs) as adopted by the European Union.

*In our opinion, except for the possible effects of the matter described in the 'Basis for qualified opinion' section of our report:*
• the Group financial statements give a true and fair view of the assets, liabilities and financial position of the group as at 31 December 2018 and of its profit [loss] for the year then ended;

- the Company statement of financial position gives a true and fair view of the assets, liabilities and financial position of the Company as at 31 December 2018;
- the Group financial statements have been properly prepared in accordance with IFRSs as adopted by the European Union;
- the Company financial statements have been properly prepared in accordance with IFRSs as adopted by the European Union as applied in accordance with the provisions of the Companies Act 2014; and
- the Group financial statements and Company financial statements have been properly prepared in accordance with the requirements of the Companies Act 2014 and, as regards the Group financial statements, Article 4 of the IAS Regulation.

### Basis for qualified opinion

*With respect to a quantity of inventory having a carrying amount of €3,972,500 (being 8% of total carrying value of inventory of €49,774,000), the audit evidence available to us was limited because we did not observe the physical inventory count as at 31 December 2018 as management did not make us aware of its existence at the time of physical counting. Owing to the nature of the company's records, we were unable to obtain sufficient appropriate audit evidence regarding the inventory quantities and condition by using other audit procedures.*

We conducted our audit in accordance with International Standards on Auditing (Ireland) and applicable law … provide a basis for our opinion.

### Opinions on other matters prescribed by the Companies Act 2014

Based solely on the work undertaken … the Companies Act 2014.

*In respect solely of the limitation on our work relating to inventory described above:*
- *we have not obtained all the information and explanations that we consider necessary for the purpose of our audit; and*
- *we were unable to determine whether proper accounting records have been kept as they were not sufficient to permit the financial statements to be readily and properly audited.*

### Matters on which we are required to report by exception

Based on our knowledge … to report in this regard.

UK/NORTHERN IRELAND

## INDEPENDENT AUDITOR'S REPORT
## (EXTRACT – QUALIFIED OPINION)

[Students should note that the overall format of the auditor's report remains unchanged other than relating to this extract and, more specifically, to the italicised text.]

### Qualified opinion

We have audited the financial statements of Large Company Limited as at 31 December 2018 … International Financial Reporting Standards (IFRSs) as adopted by the European Union.

*In our opinion, except for the possible effects of the matter described in the 'Basis for qualified opinion' section of our report the financial statements when reporting in accordance with a fair presentation framework:*

- *give a true and fair view of the state of the company's affairs as at 31 December 2018 and of its profit for the year then ended;*
- *have been properly prepared in accordance with IFRSs as adopted by the European Union; and*
- *have been prepared in accordance with the requirements of the Companies Act 2006.*

In all other respects, in our opinion the financial statements have been properly prepared in accordance with the requirements of the Companies Act 2006.

### Basis for qualified opinion

*With respect to a quantity of inventory having a carrying amount of £3,972,500 (being 8% of total carrying value of inventory of £49,774,000), the audit evidence available to us was limited because we did not observe the physical inventory count as at 31 December 2018 as management did not make us aware of its existence at the time of physical counting. Owing to the nature of the company's records, we were unable to obtain sufficient appropriate audit evidence regarding the inventory quantities and condition by using other audit procedures.*

We conducted our audit in accordance with International Standards on Auditing (UK) and applicable law … provide a basis for our opinion.

### Opinions on other matters prescribed by the Companies Act 2006

In our opinion the information given in the directors' report for the …

### Matters on which we are required to report by exception

*In respect solely of the limitation on our work relating to inventory described above:*
- *we have not obtained all the information and explanations that we considered necessary for the purpose of our audit; and*
- *we were unable to determine whether adequate accounting records had been kept.*

We have nothing to report in respect of …

**Example 19.7** below considers a limitation of scope that results in a disclaimer of opinion.

EXAMPLE 19.7: ASSESSMENT OF LEVEL OF MATERIALITY WHERE:
LIMITATION OF SCOPE – DISCLAIMER OF OPINION

**Materiality for Large Company Limited** is €3,642,500 (i.e. overall materiality determined in **Chapter 5**, Section 5.4).

Management of the client entity refused to allow the auditor to attend at the physical inventory count (inventory for Large Company Limited is €49,774,000) or to permit circularisation to confirm customer balances (trade receivables for Large Company Limited is €3,250,000). No explanations were provided by management for the imposed limitations.

## What type of opinion will the auditor issue?

The above scenario gives rise to a limitation of scope imposed by management. The scenario would be considered as pervasive due to the level of the possible error and the fact that it is not confined to specific balances in the financial statements. The combined balance represents €53,024,000 (13%) of the statement of financial net asset position.

The auditor would issue a disclaimer of opinion.

Let us now consider how the issuing of a disclaimer opinion would be reflected in the independent auditor's report for the Republic of Ireland and for the UK/Northern Ireland.

REPUBLIC OF IRELAND

# INDEPENDENT AUDITOR'S REPORT
# (EXTRACT – DISCLAIMER OPINION)

[Students should note that the overall format of the auditor's report remains unchanged other than relating to this extract and, more specifically, to the italicised text.]

### Disclaimer of opinion

*We were engaged to audit the financial statements of Large Company Limited as at 31 December 2018,* which comprise the Statement of Financial Position, the Statement of Comprehensive Income, the Statement of Cash Flow and the Statement of Changes in Equity for the year then ended, and the related Notes 1–35, including a summary of significant accounting policies. The financial reporting framework that has been applied in their preparation is applicable law and International Financial Reporting Standards (IFRSs) as adopted by the European Union.

*Due to the significance of the matters described in the 'Basis for disclaimer of opinion' section of our report, we have not been able to obtain sufficient appropriate audit evidence to provide a basis for an audit opinion. Accordingly, we do not express an opinion on the accompanying financial statements.*

### Basis for disclaimer of opinion

*The audit evidence available to us was limited because we were unable to observe the counting of the physical inventory, having a carrying value of €49,774,000, and we were unable to send confirmation letters to trade receivables, having a carrying value of €3,250,000, due to limitations placed on the scope of our audit work by the directors of the company. As a result of this, we have been unable to obtain sufficient appropriate audit evidence concerning both inventory and trade receivables.*

We conducted our audit in accordance with International Standards on Auditing (Ireland) and applicable law. *We do not believe that the audit evidence we have obtained is sufficient and appropriate to provide a basis for an opinion.*

### Opinions on other matters prescribed by the Companies Act 2014

*Notwithstanding our disclaimer of an opinion on the financial statements,* in our opinion the information given in the directors' report for the financial year for which the financial statements are prepared is consistent with the financial statements.

**Matters on which we are required to report by exception**

*Arising from the limitation of our work referred to above:*
- *we have not obtained all the information and explanations that we consider necessary for the purpose of our audit; and*
- *we were unable to determine whether proper accounting records have been kept.*

**Auditor's responsibilities for the audit of the financial statements**

*The auditor's responsibility is to conduct an audit of the entity's financial statements in accordance with ISAs (Ireland) and to issue an auditor's report, however, because of the matter(s) described in the 'Basis for disclaimer of opinion' section of our report, we were unable to obtain sufficient appropriate audit evidence to provide a basis for an audit opinion on the financial statements.*

UK/Northern Ireland

### INDEPENDENT AUDITOR'S REPORT
### (EXTRACT – DISCLAIMER OPINION)

[Students should note that the overall format of the auditor's report remains unchanged other than relating to this extract, and more specifically to the italicised text.]

**Disclaimer of opinion**

*We were engaged to audit the financial statements of Large Company Limited as at 31 December 2018*, which comprise the Statement of Financial Position, the Statement of Comprehensive Income, the Statement of Cash Flow and the Statement of Changes in Equity for the period then ended, and the related Notes 1–35, including a summary of significant accounting policies. The financial reporting framework that has been applied in their preparation is applicable law and International Financial Reporting Standards (IFRSs) as adopted by the European Union.

*Due to the significance of the matters described in the 'Basis for disclaimer of opinion' section of our report, we have not been able to obtain sufficient appropriate audit evidence to provide a basis for an audit opinion. Accordingly, we do not express an opinion on the accompanying financial statements.*

**Basis for disclaimer of opinion**

*The audit evidence available to us was limited because we were unable to observe the counting of the physical inventory, having a carrying value of £49,774,000, and we were unable to send confirmation letters to trade receivables, having a carrying value of £3,250,000, due to limitations placed on the scope of our audit work by the directors of the company. As a result of this, we have been unable to obtain sufficient appropriate audit evidence concerning both inventory and trade receivables.*

We conducted our audit in accordance with International Standards on Auditing (UK) and applicable law. *We do not believe that the audit evidence we have obtained is sufficient and appropriate to provide a basis for an opinion.*

### Opinions on other matters prescribed by the Companies Act 2006

Notwithstanding our disclaimer of an opinion on the financial statements, in our opinion the information given in the directors' report for the financial year for which the financial statements are prepared is consistent with the financial statements.

### Matters on which we are required to report by exception

Arising from the limitation of our work referred to above:
• we have not obtained all the information and explanations that we consider necessary for the purpose of our audit; and
• we were unable to determine whether proper accounting records have been kept.

We have nothing to report in respect of the following matters where the Companies Act 2006 requires us to report to you if, in our opinion:
• returns adequate for our audit have not been received from branches not visited by us; or
• the financial statements are not in agreement with the accounting records and returns; or
• certain disclosures of directors' remuneration specified by law are not made.

### Auditor's responsibilities for the audit of the financial statements

*The auditor's responsibility is to conduct an audit of the entity's financial statements in accordance with ISAs (UK) and to issue an auditor's report, however, because of the matter(s) described in the 'Basis for disclaimer of opinion' section of our report, we were unable to obtain sufficient appropriate audit evidence to provide a basis for an audit opinion on the financial statements.*

**Table 19.4** provides further examples of situations that could give rise to a limitation of scope.

TABLE 19.4: FURTHER EXAMPLES OF SITUATIONS
WHERE A LIMITATION OF SCOPE MAY ARISE

| Audit opinion | Examples where it might apply |
|---|---|
| Qualified opinion, 'except for ...' | • Limited evidence available for cash purchases, which are material but not pervasive.<br>• Some records lost due to accidental flooding/fire. |
| Disclaimer of opinion | • Appointed as auditors after year end and unable to attend year-end physical inventory count where inventory is a very material balance in the financial statements (e.g. 50% of total assets).<br>• Directors deny access to information regarding significant claims against the company.<br>• No cash-flow forecasts/cash budgets prepared, so the going concern assumption cannot be considered. |

## Withdrawal from Engagement – Limitation of Scope

There may be instances where, due to a limitation of scope imposed, the auditor deems it necessary to withdraw from the engagement. ISA 705, paragraph13(b), states that:

"If the auditor concludes that the possible effects on the financial statements of undetected misstatements, if any, could be both material and pervasive so that a qualification of the opinion would be inadequate to communicate the gravity of the situation, the auditor shall:

(i)  Withdraw from the audit, where practicable and possible under applicable law or regulation; or

(ii) If withdrawal from the audit before issuing the auditor's report is not practicable or possible, disclaim an opinion on the financial statements."

Should the auditor decide to withdraw from the engagement, before doing so they are required to "communicate to those charged with governance any matters regarding misstatements identified during the audit that would have given rise to a modification of the opinion" (ISA 705, paragraph 14).

A decision tree is included at **Appendix 19.2** as an aid to understanding the auditor's decision-making process when considering a **limitation of scope**.

## Summary – The Audit Opinion

Audit opinions can be:
1.  unqualified:
    * standard unqualified opinion – financial statements give a true and fair view;
    * unqualified with an emphasis of matter/other matter paragraph – financial statements give true and fair view, but contain a matter of such importance to the users' understanding of the financial statements that the auditor wishes to draw attention to it (matter is not materially misstated and is adequately presented and disclosed);
2.  modified:
    * disagreement – financial statements are not in accordance with the applicable financial reporting framework:
        ♦ qualified opinion, 'except for …' – except for the particular material matter with which the auditor disagrees, the financial statements give a true and fair view (material but not pervasive);
        ♦ adverse opinion – the financial statements do not give a true and fair view (material and pervasive);
    * limitation of scope – auditor's work has been limited in some way:
        ♦ qualified opinion, 'except for …' – except for the particular material matter to which the auditor's scope has been limited, the financial statements give a true and fair view (material but not pervasive);
        ♦ disclaimer opinion – due to limitation of scope, the auditor cannot determine whether the financial statements give a true and fair view or not (material and pervasive).

## 19.5  COMPARATIVE INFORMATION – CORRESPONDING FIGURES

In line with IAS 1 *Presentation of Financial Statements*, prior-year comparative figures are required to be included in a set of financial statements, they therefore form part of the financial statements. The auditor, therefore, cannot express an opinion on the financial statements without obtaining assurance over the comparative figures. ISA 710 *Comparative Information – Corresponding Figures and Comparative Financial Statements* offers the auditor guidance with regard to their review of comparative information, although it should be noted that in the RoI and the UK, the "corresponding figures" method is the required method of presentation and, as such, paragraphs 15–19 on comparative financial statements do not apply.

ISA 710, paragraph 6, defines the key terms as follows:

**Comparative Information**   "The amounts and disclosures included in the financial statements in respect of one or more prior periods in accordance with the applicable financial reporting framework."

**Corresponding Figures**   "Comparative information where amounts and other disclosures for the prior period are included as an integral part of the current period financial statements, and are intended to be read only in relation to the amounts and other disclosures relating to the current period (referred to as 'current period figures'). The level of detail presented in the corresponding amounts and disclosures is dictated primarily by its relevance to the current year's comparative financial figures."

As **comparative information** forms an integral part of any set of financial statements, it is not surprising that the auditor has a responsibility with respect to corresponding figures. We can see from **Section 19.3** that the auditor makes no reference to comparative figures in the audit report (unless that reference forms part of a necessary modification); nonetheless, the audit opinion is deemed to include the current and comparative period figures.

With regard to prior-period financial statements audited by a predecessor auditor (introduced in **Chapter 5**), ISA 710, paragraph A7-1, states that:

" … the incoming auditor does not refer to the predecessor auditor's report on the corresponding figures in the incoming auditor's report for the current period. The incoming auditor assumes audit responsibility for the corresponding figures only in the context of the financial statements as a whole. The incoming auditor reads the preceding period's financial statements and, using the knowledge gained during the current audit, considers whether they have been properly reflected as corresponding figures in the current period's financial statements."

This means that for entities where an auditor did not audit the financial statements in the prior period, they still need to gain assurance over the **comparative figures**.

### Modified Opinion by Incoming Auditor on Corresponding Figures

Having carried out audit procedures relating to comparative figures, the auditor may find that material misstatements exist with regard to comparative figures. It may be necessary, therefore, for the auditor to modify the audit opinion or to include an other matter paragraph in relation to comparative figures where:

- The prior-year financial statements were subject to a qualified opinion and the qualification has not yet been resolved. For example, where a provision for a legal claim, which the client entity's solicitors determine is likely to materialise, continues to be omitted from the financial statements.
- The client entity was audit-exempt in the prior year and so the corresponding figures are unaudited. ISA 510 *Initial Audit Engagements – Opening Balances* provides the auditor with guidance in these circumstances; however, ISA 710, paragraph 14, states: "If the prior period financial statements were not audited, the auditor shall state in an Other Matter paragraph that the corresponding figures are unaudited. Such a statement does not, however, relieve the auditor of the requirement to obtain sufficient appropriate audit evidence that the opening balances do not contain misstatements that materially affect the current period's financial statements";
- During the course of the audit, the auditor discovers a **material misstatement** that relates to the corresponding figures. For example, if the auditor determines that an asset in use in the prior year has not been depreciated and management continue not to depreciate, then the auditor would qualify the audit report referring to both prior- and current-year figures.

    In this example, if management have properly stated the corresponding figures and corrected the error in the current year, meaning that depreciation is now correct, then the auditor may refer to the prior-year misstatement in an **emphasis of matter paragraph**.

For audits of financial statements of **public interest entities** (PIEs), the incoming auditor may become aware of a possible material misstatement of corresponding figures as part of the requirement in ISA 510 to obtain an understanding of the methodology used to carry out the audit in the preceding period.

If the auditor is unable to obtain sufficient appropriate audit evidence regarding the opening balances due to unaudited financial statements from the prior year, the auditor is required by ISA 705 to express either a qualified opinion or a disclaimer of opinion, as appropriate.

## 19.6 THE AUDITOR'S RESPONSIBILITIES RELATING TO OTHER INFORMATION

ISA 720 *The Auditor's Responsibilities Relating to Other Information*, paragraph 12(c), defines other information as "Financial or non-financial information (other than financial statements and the auditor's report thereon) included in an entity's annual report".

For private companies the term 'annual report' will typically include the directors' report, the directors' statement of responsibilities, the independent auditor's report and the audited financial statements (including the statement of accounting policies). For public companies, public interest entities (PIEs), charities, etc., 'annual report' will usually mean the inclusion of additional reports regarding the activities of the entity and governance issues.

In the absence of a specific requirement in the particular circumstances of the audit engagement, the auditor has no specific responsibility to determine whether or not other information is properly stated. Likewise, the audit opinion does not extend to other information. The auditor does, however, have a responsibility to read the other information in the annual report for "material inconsistency" with the audited financial statements, and for any information that appears to be "materially misstated" (ISA 720, paragraph 11).

## Inconsistent or Misstated Other Information

ISA 720 **requires** the auditor to read the other information in the annual report before signing off on the audit report. The existence of **material inconsistency** or **material misstatement** between the audited financial statements and the other information could potentially:

1. "undermine the credibility" of the audit report and/or the audit opinion; and
2. cause a user to doubt the reliability of the audit report and/or the audit opinion, or "inappropriately influence the economic decisions of the user".

Where the auditor becomes aware of a material inconsistency or misstatement, it is necessary to consider whether it is the financial statements themselves or the other information that requires revision. Either way, the matter will need to be discussed with **management**. If it is the financial statements that require revision, and management refuse to make the necessary revisions, then either a **qualified opinion** ('except for …') or an **adverse opinion** should be expressed, depending on how material and pervasive the matter is.

If it is the other information that requires revision and management refuse to revise, the auditor should consider including an **other matters paragraph** to describe the material inconsistency or misstatement. The auditor could also use their right to address shareholders at the annual general meeting, but legal advice as to the possible consequences of doing so should always be sought beforehand. As a last resort the auditor should resign and use their resignation statement to the shareholders (as required by sections 400–402 CA 2014 in the RoI and by sections 519–525 CA 2006 in the UK).

Under UK and Irish company law,[3] if the directors' report is inconsistent with the financial statements, the auditor must make reference to these inconsistencies in the audit report. As a specific statutory obligation this assumes greater importance than the non-statutory requirements of ISA 720.

This modification is made in the 'Opinions on other matters' paragraph prescribed by CA 2014/ CA 2006, where the auditor must expressly state whether, in their opinion, the information given in the directors' report is consistent with the financial statements. The auditor can expand upon this modification in an other matters paragraph, which should be included directly below the opinion paragraph, or an emphasis of matters paragraph, where applicable.

---

[3] In the UK, section 496 CA 2006; in the RoI, section 336(5) CA 2014.

## 19.7 COMMUNICATION WITH THOSE CHARGED WITH GOVERNANCE

Having considered all comparative figures in the financial statements, as well as the consistency of other information contained in other reports and, specifically, in the directors' report, the auditor is now in a position to form an opinion. In practice, while the audit has been performed on behalf of the members, the auditor does not now issue the report without first discussing it with the client entity's management (those charged with governance).

Prior to issuing the audit report, the auditor should make the intended opinion clear to those charged with governance. If a **modified opinion** is being issued, its proposed wording should clearly demonstrate to management the reasons or circumstances giving rise to the **disagreement** or **limitation of scope** (see **Section 19.4**), and act as a confirmation of those circumstances. Informing those charged with governance of the audit opinion before the audit report is issued provides management with the opportunity to either:

1. remove the limitation of scope (if practicable), i.e. identify alternative methods of testing that would address the assertion; or
2. correct the material misstatement giving rise to the disagreement.

## 19.8 OTHER REPORTING MATTERS

### Modified Audit Opinion and Dividends

Where a modified audit opinion has been given on the previous year's annual financial statements, the client entity's ability to make a distribution by reference to those financial statements could be in doubt unless it receives a statement from the auditor, in accordance with CA 2014/CA 2006, concerning the client entity's ability to make a distribution.

In the RoI, section 121(3)(c) CA 2014 states that "if, by virtue of anything referred to in that report, the report is not an unqualified report, the statutory auditors shall also have stated in writing (either at the time the report was made or subsequently) whether, in their opinion, that thing is material for the purpose of determining, by reference to the relevant items as stated in those financial statements, whether that distribution would be in contravention of section 117 [profits available for distribution]."

Similarly in the UK, section 837(4)(a) CA 2006, where an audit report is qualified, "the auditor must have stated in writing (either at the time of his report or subsequently) whether in his opinion the matters in respect of which his report is qualified are material for determining whether a distribution would contravene this Part [Distributions]." It also requires that a copy of that statement be circulated to members.

## Subsequent Events and Revised Accounts

Where a material misstatement is discovered after the financial statements and audit report have been issued, revised financial statements may have to be issued. In this case the auditor will need to issue a new audit report on the revised financial statements (unless the original financial statements were audit-exempt and the revision does not change this). Where the revision of the original financial statements results in a loss of audit exemption, the auditor will prepare a revised audit report giving an opinion as to whether:

- the revised financial statements have been properly prepared;
- a true and fair view, as at the date of the original financial statements, is given;
- in the auditor's opinion, the original financial statements failed to comply with the legislative requirements with reference to the directors' statements of responsibilities;
- the information contained in the directors' report (or revised directors' report) is consistent with the revised financial statements.

Where the original financial statements were audited and only the directors' report is revised, the auditor will issue a new report to include an opinion on whether the information given in the revised report is consistent with the original statutory financial statements.

## Summary Financial Statements, Interim Reports and Preliminary Announcements

Auditors may be involved in issuing other reports, such as summary financial statements, which are issued in some countries by large quoted companies. Some listed companies may also issue interim financial statements and may request the auditors to carry out a review of the interim financial information and provide a conclusion on it. The auditor has no statutory responsibility for the interim financial reports. Accordingly, ISA 720 does not apply to preliminary announcements of financial information, or to securities-offering documents, including prospectuses. However, the FRC has issued an International Standard for Review Engagements (ISRE) (UK and Ireland) 2410, which applies to the auditor reviewing interim financial information issued by the entity.

Where the client entity's management wish to announce preliminary results, the auditors are required to communicate their consent to the publication.

## 19.9 EFFECT OF A MODIFIED OPINION

Generally, auditors believe that issuing a **modified opinion** is a last resort. In order to avoid doing so, they will discuss the **disagreements** and **limitations of scope** at great length with management. In most cases, management are prepared to adjust the financial statements for any material errors or omissions that the auditor brings to their attention, as they would be keen to ensure the accuracy of the financial statements.

Management will also be aware that a modified opinion could have serious consequences for the entity:

- it could affect shareholders' confidence in the company and its management;
- it could discourage potential investors;
- it could affect the willingness of lenders to continue offering a facility to the company; or
- it could affect the company's creditworthiness with its suppliers.

However, if the auditor feels a modified opinion is appropriate, they must be able to justify the basis for the modification and explain it in the audit report.

The auditor must use their professional judgement to decide how serious are the issues involved, i.e. are they material but not pervasive or material and pervasive, as this will influence the form of qualification that will be included in the audit report.

The auditor must decide how seriously the issue/issues affect the truth and fairness of the financial statements.

Should the auditor fail to conclude on an **appropriate** audit opinion, this can also have serious consequences, such as:

- current or potential investors/shareholders (members) may make inappropriate investment decisions based on the financial statements and supported by an unqualified audit opinion, but which in fact contain material misstatements (albeit it should be noted that the auditor's legal liability is to the shareholders).
- In relation to going concern, by not issuing an appropriate opinion the auditor is preventing users of the financial statements from being fully aware that the entity may not be a going concern. By highlighting the issue, in whatever format of audit report is appropriate in the circumstances, while the entity may still not be a going concern the earlier recognition of this fact may allow time for a receiver to be appointed and to avoid substantial further losses by suppliers, lenders, etc.
- The auditor could be subject to litigation if damages are suffered.
- The profession at large comes under increased pressure where an audit fails to highlight material misstatements to the users of financial statements, calling into question the credibility of the profession.

## 19.10 CONCLUSION

The independent auditor's report is the end result of an audit engagement and provides the auditor's opinion on the financial statements, an opinion that is based on their overall assessment, taking into account evidence gained during each phase of the **audit process**.

The audit opinion is contained in a separate paragraph within the body of the auditor's report. Guidance on what is required to be included in the audit report is found within six specific International Standards on Auditing (ISAs), as well as within the Companies Acts in force in each jurisdiction.

ISA 700 outlines the basic format of a 'clean' (unqualified) audit opinion, while ISA 705 and ISA 706 address modified opinions. Modified, or qualified, opinions result from either:

- disagreement, which produce either an 'except for ...' qualification or an adverse opinion, depending on the materiality of the matter; or
- a limitation of scope, which is either an 'except for ...' qualification or a disclaimer of opinion.

Additionally, ISA 710 and ISA 720 cover the auditor's responsibility in relation to comparative information and other information.

Together with the ISAs, the auditor is required to comply with company law requirements with regard to audit reports. Within the RoI, this takes the form of the Companies Act 2014 and related legislation; for the UK/NI it refers to the Companies Act 2006.

Before concluding on the opinion, the auditor should be confident that they have carried out the **audit conclusion** tasks as outlined in **Chapter 18**, and so be confident that an appropriate opinion is being issued.

## SUMMARY OF LEARNING OBJECTIVES

**Learning Objective 1**  Be able to describe the principles underpinning the form and content of audit reports with reference to the relevant standards and legislation.

There are six standards dealing directly with audit reports and the audit opinion:
- ISA 700 *Forming an Opinion and Reporting on Financial Statements*
- ISA 701 *Communicating Key Audit Matters in the Independent Auditor's Report*
- ISA 705 *Modifications to the Opinion in the Independent Auditor's Report*
- ISA 706 *Emphasis of Matter Paragraphs and Other Matter Paragraphs in the Independent Auditor's Report*
- ISA 710 *Comparative Information – Corresponding Figures and Comparative Financial Statements*
- ISA 720 – *The Auditor's Responsibilities Relating to Other Information*.

ISA 700 and relevant company legislation (RoI: CA 2014 and UK/NI: CA 2006) prescribe the form and content of an audit report.

**Learning Objective 2**  Be able to explain the different types of audit opinion and how they impact on the audit report.

Where the auditor believes the financial statements give a true and fair view, an **unqualified** opinion is issued.

ISA 706 deals with instances where the auditor believes the financial statements give a true and fair view, but feels that a particular matter that is **not materially misstated** and is **adequately presented and disclosed** in the financial statements is significant enough that the users' attention should be drawn to it. In these instances an unqualified audit opinion is issued but with an **emphasis of a matter** or **other matter** paragraph. This refers the user to the disclosure note describing the circumstances surrounding the issue.

If the auditor's opinion is that the accounts do not give a true and fair view, or that something has prevented the forming of an opinion on all or part of the financial statements, then a **modified** opinion will be issued (ISA 705).

**Learning Objective 3**   Be able to identify when a modified opinion might be issued.

There are two main types of modified opinion:
* **disagreement** – where the auditor disagrees with the financial statements prepared by the client:
  * **qualified opinion** ('except for ...') – where the auditor concludes that misstatements, individually or in the aggregate, are material but not pervasive to the financial statements;
  * **adverse** – where the effects of the disagreement are so material and pervasive that the auditor concludes that an 'except for ...' opinion is not adequate to disclose the misleading or incomplete nature of the financial statements.
* **limitation on scope** – where the auditor is unable to form an opinion on the financial statements due to a limitation being imposed, resulting in
  * **qualified opinion** ('except for ...') – where the auditor concludes that the possible effects of undetected misstatements, if any, on the financial statements could be material but not pervasive;
  * **disclaimer of opinion** – where the limitation is so material or pervasive that it prevents the auditor from forming any opinion on the financial statements.

**Learning Objective 4**   Understand the auditor's responsibility with regard to comparative information and other information included with the financial statements.

ISA 710 outlines the auditor's responsibility with respect to corresponding figures and comparative information in the financial statements and states that while the audit report does not make any specific reference to the corresponding figures in the financial statements, the audit opinion is deemed to include both years.

ISA 720 requires the auditor to read all **other information** presented along with the financial statements to ensure that there are no material inconsistencies or misstatements between other information and the audited financial statements. Where a material inconsistency or misstatement exists and is uncorrected by management, the auditor will consider the impact on the audit report.

**Learning Objective 5**   Understand the other reporting matters to be considered by the auditor.

When concluding on an audit opinion, it is essential that **those charged with governance** are informed of the decision and the contents of the audit report to:

1. confirm their agreement with the situation; and
2. give them the opportunity to change the outcome, should it be practicable.

Other issues relating to audit reports include:
- impact on distribution of **dividends**; and
- involvement in **summary financial statements, interim reports** and **preliminary announcements**.

While the consequences of an incorrect modification are serious, so too are the consequences of an unqualified opinion where a modified one was warranted and, as such, the auditor needs to be confident that they have carried out all the steps outlined in **Chapter 18** so that they can be satisfied that sufficient and appropriate audit evidence has been obtained to support their opinion.

**Learning Objective 6**   Understand the considerations of the auditor in respect to their responsibility to communicate key audit matters in the audit report.

Key Audit Matters (where the entity is a public interest entity (PIE), a listed entity or one that voluntarily chooses to report on its compliance (or non-compliance) with the *UK Corporate Governance Code*) require the auditor to give details of the assessed risks, how the level of materiality was determined, and how the scope of the audit was planned and performed, taking into account the assessed risks and materiality.

## QUESTIONS

### Self-test Questions

19.1   What governs the contents of an audit report?

19.2   Which standards cover the contents of the audit report?

19.3   In relation to the Republic of Ireland, what does the Companies Act 2014 require to be included in the audit report?

19.4   In relation to Northern Ireland/UK, what does the Companies Act 2006 require to be included in the audit report?

19.5   What are the key contents of an audit report?

19.6   What is the difference between an unqualified opinion and a modified opinion?

19.7   What is meant by the term 'disagreement' with respect to audit reports?

19.8   What is meant by the term 'limitation of scope' with respect to audit reports?

19.9   If a limitation of scope exists in relation to a material matter, which two types of opinion might the auditor issue?

19.10   If a disagreement exists in relation to a material matter, which two types of opinion might the auditor issue?

19.11   What is an 'emphasis of matter paragraph'?

19.12   Name three instances where an auditor might include an emphasis of matter paragraph.

19.13 What are the key paragraphs that are impacted on by a modification resulting from an 'except for ...' qualification relating to limitation of scope?

19.14 What are the key paragraphs that are impacted on by a modification resulting from an 'except for ...' qualification relating to disagreement?

19.15 Name four circumstances that might give rise to a disclaimer of opinion.

19.16 Name four circumstances that might give rise to an adverse opinion.

19.17 What is the auditor's responsibility with regard to other information included with a set of financial statements?

19.18 What is the auditor's responsibility with regard to the directors' report?

19.19 Where within the audit report would the auditor report on a material inconsistency between other information and the audited financial statements?

## Review Questions

(See Suggested Solutions to Review Questions in **Appendix C**.)

### *Question 19.1*

GreenTech Ltd is an Irish-owned drinks manufacturer for whom you are concluding the audit for the year ended 31 December 2018. During your audit of GreenTech Ltd, which has reported an after-tax profit of €6,500,000 and has been assigned an overall audit materiality level of €500,000, the following errors were identified:

- Trade receivables of €100,000 have been included within the trade payables balance in the trial balance, due to a mis-posting by the accountant.
- Your accruals testing has identified rent payments, in respect of the financial year under review, of €350,000 paid to the landlord subsequent to the year end. However, the year-end rent accrual was only €300,000.
- You have recalculated the bad debt provision as €750,000 (which would result in a €300,000 charge to the income statement). This compares with an actual charge of €50,000 currently recorded in the draft financial statements.
- During sample testing of revenue, two invoices could not be traced to signed delivery documents. This arose because GreenTech invoice on dispatch of the goods rather than on receipt of confirmation of acceptance of the goods. Due to this, it had not been noticed that the goods were not accepted by the customer and were instead returned to inventory. The two invoices had a combined value of €35,000 and were part of a sample test of 20 invoices that had a total value of €1,110,000. Total recorded revenue in the period was €50,000,000. *The inventory value included in the draft financial statements is reflective of physical inventory count procedures, so the resulting error does not impact on inventory and cost of sales.*

### Requirement

(a) Draft the schedule of unadjusted errors (errors schedule) in respect of the above matters for review by the audit partner.

(b) Does any one individual error result in a material misstatement?

(c) Are the financial statements as a whole materially misstated?

The directors of GreenTech disagree with your assessment of the potential misstatement contained within revenue and on that basis refuse to make any amendments to the accounts. You are satisfied with your testing and maintain that the likely error is a fair reflection of the potential misstatement of revenue.

**Requirement**
(d) What will be the impact of the directors' decision on your audit report?
(e) Draft an extract from the auditor's report reflecting the opinion you have chosen for (d) above. The extract should include the basis for opinion and opinion paragraphs only.

Having considered the impact on the audit report, the directors of GreenTech agree to make the necessary amendments to the financial statements, having devised a method of reliably valuing the error arising from invoicing on dispatch. You are now satisfied that the schedule of unadjusted errors does not contain any material misstatements. However, during the course of your consideration of the going concern assumption, you note that GreenTech has applied for a substantial loan in order to upgrade their production facility, due to the introduction of a new law requiring certain food standards to be met. The decision on the loan facility will not be determined until after you have signed the audit report. Should the loan not be granted, the company will not be able to meet the legal requirements and as such may need to cease production.

**Requirement**
(f) Outline how, or if, the above will impact on the audit report if the directors **do not agree** to include a note to the financial statements regarding the uncertainty surrounding going concern.
(g) Outline how, or if, the above will impact on the audit report if the directors **agree** to include a note to the financial statements regarding the uncertainty surrounding going concern.

## Question 19.2

(a) Explain **four** audit procedures an auditor can perform to assess the reasonableness of the going concern assumption.
(b) Explain the various implications for the audit report where there are uncertainties surrounding the going concern assumption.
(c) Discuss the potential impact of an auditor issuing an incorrect opinion on a set of financial statements that **should not** have been prepared on a going concern basis.

## APPENDIX 19.1: AUDIT OPINION DECISION TREE

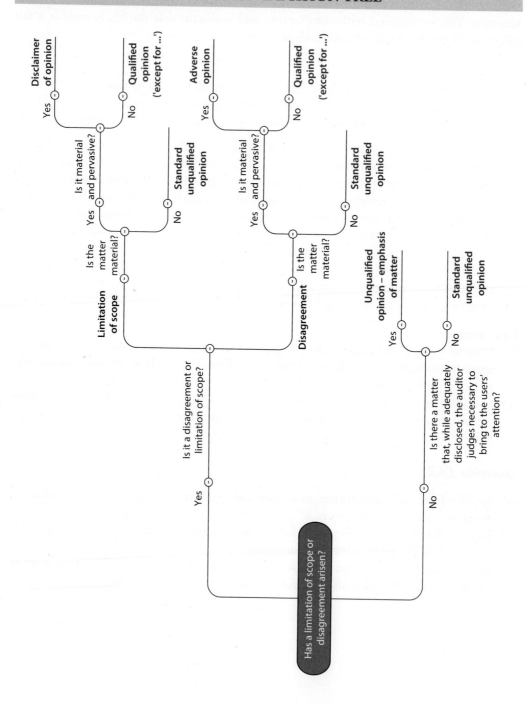

## APPENDIX 19.2: DECISION TREE FOR CONCLUDING ON LIMITATION OF SCOPE IMPOSED BY MANAGEMENT

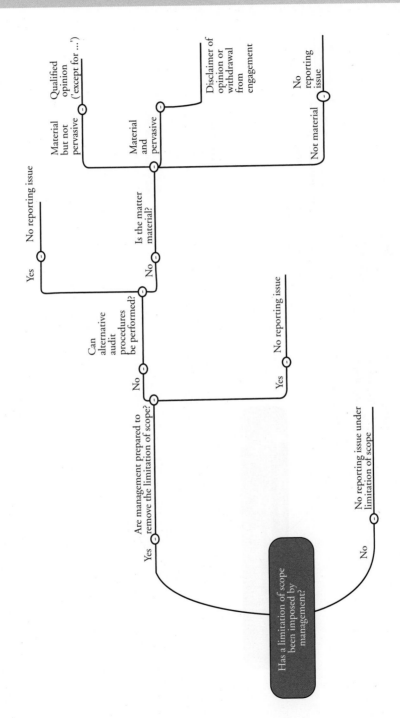

## APPENDIX 19.3: DECISION TREE FOR CONCLUDING ON GOING CONCERN

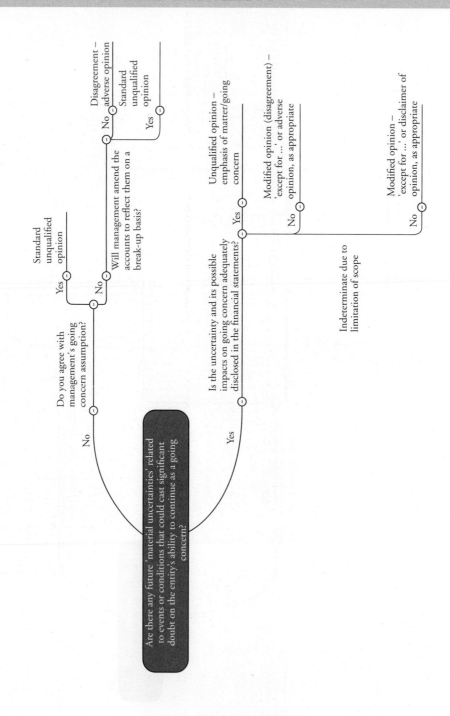

# 20

# GROUP AUDITS

LEARNING OBJECTIVES

Having studied this chapter on group audits you should:
1. understand the additional considerations with regard to acceptance and continuance of group audits;
2. understand the requirements of ISA 600 with regard to risk assessment procedures and the communication of group audit instructions to component auditors;
3. be able to identify the considerations of the auditor with regard to group components, component auditors and materiality when performing an audit of group financial statements;
4. understand the importance of the scoping of significant and non-significant components;
5. know the auditor's responsibilities with regard to materiality when auditing group financial statements; and
6. understand the concluding activities required by the group auditor prior to the issue of an opinion.

## CHECKLIST OF RELEVANT STANDARDS

The relevant standards, both in the RoI and the UK/NI, covered in this chapter are:
ISA 220 *Quality Control for an Audit of Financial Statements*
ISA 600 *Special Considerations – Audits of Group Financial Statements (Including the Work of Component Auditors)*
IAS 27 *Separate Financial Statements*
IAS 28 *Investments in Associates and Joint Ventures*
IFRS 3 *Business Combinations*
IFRS 10 *Consolidated Financial Statements*
IFRS 11 *Joint Arrangements*
IFRS 12 *Disclosure of Interests in Other Entities*

Note, in general when referring to ISAs, it should be understood as referring to the UK and Ireland versions, unless otherwise specified as either ISA (UK) or ISA (Ireland). See the Introduction for an extant list of auditing standards for the RoI and the UK/NI.

## KEY TERMS AND DEFINITIONS IN THIS CHAPTER

**Component**   "An entity or business activity for which a group or component management prepares financial information that should be included in the group financial statements." (ISA 600, paragraph 9)

**Component Auditor**   "An auditor who, at the request of the group audit engagement team, performs work on financial information related to a component for the group audit." (ISA 600, paragraph 9)

**Component Management**   "Management responsible for the preparation of the financial information of a component." (ISA 600, paragraph 9)

**Component Materiality**   "The materiality for a component determined by the group engagement team." (ISA 600, paragraph 9)

**Group Audit**   "The audit of group financial statements." (ISA 600, paragraph 9)

**Group Auditor vs. Component Auditor**   The group auditor (also referred to as the principal auditor, or the parent company auditor) has responsibility for reporting on the group financial statements. The component auditor has responsibility for reporting on an individual component of the group.

**Scoping**   A term used to describe the exercise carried out to determine which components will undergo full audit procedures (scoping in) and which will be considered insignificant and be subject to a reduced level of testing (scoping out).

**Significant Component**   "A component identified by the group engagement team (i) that is of individual financial significance to the group, or (ii) that, due to its specific nature or circumstances, is likely to include significant risks of material misstatement of the group financial statements." (ISA 600, paragraph 9).

## 20.1 INTRODUCTION

This chapter outlines the requirements for a **group audit** and describes the audit process involved. International accounting standards (IFRS and IAS), as well as company law in the Republic of Ireland and the UK/NI, require the preparation and audit of consolidated (group) financial statements when a group exists. A group is deemed to exist when a parent company owns one or more subsidiaries and/or holds investments in associates and joint ventures.

It is important to note that the principles of auditing a group are the same as the audit of a single entity and that all of the ISAs are relevant to a group audit. ISA 600 *Special Considerations – Audits of Group Financial Statements (Including the Work of Component Auditors)* deals with the specific issues of group audit.

Group audits have a number of unique features, such as:
- the requirement for complicated consolidation adjustments;
- the need to ensure compliance with a number of complex financial reporting standards;
- the entities that comprise the group (the components) may be audited by firms of auditors other than the principal auditor (group auditor);
- the planning and organising of a group audit is usually complex, e.g. the components can be based in several different countries.

When group financial statements are required to be audited, it is common for the **group auditor** (the principal auditor named on the audit engagement document) to require the assistance of other auditors, referred to as **component auditors**. For example, as the larger corporates, such as Kerry Group plc or CRH plc in the RoI, or the Marks and Spencer Group plc in the UK, continue to expand into more far-reaching geographical areas, the complexity of the financial statements, and thus the audits thereon, also become increasingly challenging.

The roles, responsibilities and competencies of the group auditor and component auditors involved in a group audit are clearly stated in ISA 600, paragraph 4:
> "the group engagement partner is required to be satisfied that those performing the group audit engagement, including component auditors, collectively have the appropriate competence and capabilities. The group engagement partner is also responsible for the direction, supervision and performance of the group audit engagement."

This inevitably places a significant amount of responsibility and risk on the group audit engagement partner (and the related firm), which will require the audit partner to have an active part in communicating with the client entity on a regular basis.

We have already discussed **audit risk** in detail (see **Chapter 7**) and appreciate that it relates to the risk that:
(a) the financial statements contain a material misstatement/error; and
(b) the auditor does not detect that material misstatement/error.

When dealing with groups, audit risk becomes more complicated as it relates to the risk that:
(a) the financial statements contain a material misstatement/error; and
(b) the **component auditor** fails to detect that material misstatement/error; and
(c) the **group auditor** fails to detect that the component auditor failed to detect the material misstatement/error.

Ultimate responsibility lies with the group auditor, hence they must be satisfied as to the competence of the component auditor to reduce the risk they are taking in relying on that component auditor's work.

In practical terms, when an audit firm engaged in a group audit requires the use of component auditors, it will usually look to member affiliates of its firm. For instance, if there is an overseas **component**, the audit firm will naturally tend to engage its overseas affiliate as the component auditor. When, due to the need for additional expertise or geographical or jurisdictional constraints, they need to engage the services of non-affiliated firms, the emphasis on component auditor quality will tend to increase – the group auditor may not be familiar with the quality of that audit firm's work.

(*Note*: **joint audits** are not discussed in this chapter as the audit process involved is similar to any audit, except in that the audit is carried out jointly by two audit firms and they give a joint audit opinion – two firms sign the audit report.)

## 20.2  GROUP AUDIT FIRM ACCEPTANCE AND CONTINUANCE CONSIDERATIONS

In **Chapter 5** we outlined the factors that an auditor should consider before accepting (or continuing) an audit engagement. A group audit engagement will entail some additional considerations, including:
1. **Considerations relating to adequacy of the group audit firm's resources** Along with the standard acceptance and continuance considerations, the group auditor needs to ask: 'Does the group audit engagement team have the necessary resources to competently perform the group audit to the extent necessary to obtain sufficient appropriate audit evidence?' Remember: the engagement team must not only perform audit procedures on its own assigned components but also on:
   (a) the competence of the component auditors; and
   (b) a portion of the component auditor's work in order to minimise audit risk.
2. **Considerations as to the adequacy of the group audit firm's internal policies and procedures to sufficiently address the requirements of ISA 600**
   (a) the assessment of risks for the group;
   (b) the assignment of instructions/communication with component auditors;
   (c) the consolidation process; and
   (d) the evaluation of the sufficiency of audit evidence obtained from component auditors.

## 20.3  THE GROUP AUDIT PROCESS

As already noted, the principles of auditing a group are the same as the audit of a single entity and all of the ISAs are applicable to a group audit. However, key differences arise in relation to the planning, monitoring, supervision and review required by the group auditors in ensuring **sufficient appropriate audit evidence** has been obtained, at a group level, to support the audit opinion of the group auditor.

**Figure 20.1** sets out a comparison of the typical audit process for a single entity (performed by a component auditor) and the additional features of the group audit process.

You will see that the group audit instructions are a significant additional aspect of the group audit. There is particular emphasis placed on risk assessment and the determination of materiality for the group and the component auditors. The close involvement between the group auditor and the component auditors manifests itself particularly in relation to the systems

FIGURE 20.1: THE GROUP AUDIT PROCESS

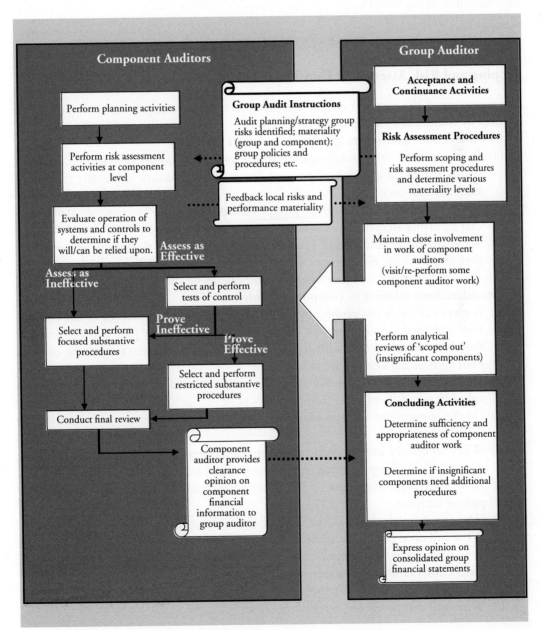

and substantive testing of the operations and controls in the components. The extent of involvement depends on the significance to the group results of any particular component and the outcome of the **scoping** exercise carried out by the group auditor (discussed below).

At the conclusion of the audit process, each component auditor must formally report to the group auditor, giving an opinion on the financial information of the component being consolidated into the group financial statements. This opinion is in the form of a **clearance opinion** stating either that there are no material matters affecting the component financial information or, if there are, then the component auditor will provide full information relating thereto.

## 20.4 GROUP AUDIT FIRM SCOPING AND RISK ASSESSMENT

### Scoping and Risk Assessment Considerations

Having accepted the engagement for the group audit, the engagement team now has a number of additional considerations, including:

1. **Considerations relating to group components**
   (a) Is there a sufficient understanding of the group, its components, their environments and the consolidation process? This will be necessary to identify the risk of material misstatement of the group's financial statements.
   (b) What components make up the group? **Components** may be operational or financial reporting structures and not necessarily legal structures.
   (c) What are the significant and insignificant components of the group, and who will perform the audit engagement activities on those components?
   (d) How will insignificant (immaterial) components be treated?
2. **Considerations relating to component auditors**
   (a) Is there sufficient understanding as to the professional competence of the component auditors? Considering the importance of the role they play and the onus on the group audit partner with regard to their opinion, understanding the component auditor is a key requirement.
   (b) Do the component auditors possess the necessary understanding of auditing and other standards applicable to the group audit?
   (c) Do the component auditors comply with the ethical requirements relevant to the group audit?
   (d) What regulatory environment does the component auditor operate within? Are the standards of regulation acceptable to the group auditor?
   (e) Have there been any negative regulatory investigation findings against the component auditor?
   (f) How much involvement in the work of the component auditors will be needed?
   (g) What will need to be communicated to the component auditors in order for them to audit the assigned component?
3. **Considerations relating to materiality**
   (a) What will group materiality be set at?
   (b) What will component materiality be set at?

(c) Will different materiality levels be required for certain transactions or balances that are considered more risky?

(d) What level of error/misstatement will be considered as clearly trivial to the group financial statements?

## Scoping of Significant and Insignificant Components

A significant component is defined as: "(i) that is of individual significance to the group, or (ii) that, due to its specific nature or circumstances, is likely to include significant risks of material misstatement of the group financial statements" (ISA 600, paragraph 9(m)).

ISA 600, paragraph A5, states:

"The group engagement team may apply a percentage to a chosen benchmark as an aid to identify components that are of individual financial significance. Identifying a benchmark and determining a percentage to be applied to it involve the exercise of professional judgment. Depending on the nature and circumstances of the group, appropriate benchmarks might include group assets, liabilities, cash flows, profit or turnover. For example, the group engagement team may consider that components exceeding 15% of the chosen benchmark are significant components. A higher or lower percentage may, however, be deemed appropriate in the circumstances."

There may be hundreds of components that make up the financial statements of a large group. The auditor does not have to perform focused substantive procedures on all components if they are **insignificant** to the group as a whole, because they are:

(a) individually financially insignificant; and

(b) pose no significant risk of material misstatement due to their specific nature or circumstances.

For insignificant components the auditor can perform **analytical procedures** at the group level. However, a word of warning: although individual components may be insignificant, the aggregate effect of all insignificant components may be too material to warrant their exclusion. For this reason, some seemingly insignificant components may need to be 'scoped back in' for more focused substantive procedures in order to gain **sufficient appropriate audit evidence** on the group as a whole. This is explained further by way of **Example 20.1** below.

EXAMPLE 20.1: SCOPING OF SIGNIFICANT AND INSIGNIFICANT COMPONENTS

A group audit engagement team has identified components with revenue of €10 million or less as being **insignificant** (provided no specific risks have been identified within those components). The group audit is required to perform greater than 90% coverage of all revenue. A group audit partner is reviewing the scoping exercise (scoping exercise 1) performed by the group audit engagement team and determines that while all components scoped out do meet the laid-down criteria, the coverage required to obtain sufficient appropriate audit evidence for revenue is not achieved if all insignificant components are scoped out. Therefore, scoping exercise 2 is performed.

| Component | Revenue €000 | Scoping Exercise 1 | Scoping Exercise 2 |
|---|---|---|---|
| 1 | 70,000 | Scope in | Scope in |
| 2 | 25,000 | Scope in | Scope in |
| 3 | 10,000 | Scope out | **Scope in** |
| 4 | 15,000 | Scope out | **Scope in** |
| 5 | 2,000 | Scope out | Scope out |
| 6 | 1,000 | Scope out | Scope out |
| 7 | 80,000 | Scope in | Scope in |
| 8 | 2,000 | Scope out | Scope out |
| 9 | 3,000 | Scope out | Scope out |
| 10 | 2,000 | Scope out | Scope out |
| 11 | 1,000 | Scope out | Scope out |
| 12 | 500 | Scope out | Scope out |
| 13 | 1,000 | Scope out | Scope out |
| 14 | 3,000 | Scope out | **Scope in** |
| 15 | 2,000 | Scope out | Scope out |
| 16 | 2,500 | Scope out | Scope out |
| 17 | 200 | Scope out | Scope out |
| 18 | 500 | Scope out | Scope out |
| 19 | 700 | Scope out | Scope out |
| Total group revenue | 221,400 | | |
| Total scoped in | | 175,000 | 203,000 |
| Total scoped out | | 46,400 | 18,400 |
| % Scoped in | | 79% | 92% |

For demonstration purposes, the scoping is based on revenue only; in practice it will include an assessment of other key balances in the financial statements of the component.

## Understanding the Environment of the Group and its Components

Gathering audit evidence and engaging in the risk assessment process (see **Chapter 6** and **Chapter 7**, respectively) is an integral part of the group audit engagement team's processes. Based on the results, it will issue **group audit instructions** to the component auditors. The group audit instructions deal principally with such matters as:
• the financial reporting standards applicable to the financial statements of the component to be audited;
• group accounting policies, which should be consistent throughout the group;
• foreign currency exchange rates, which should be applied consistently throughout the group;

- risks identified at the group level that relate to the group as a whole or are component-specific (e.g. a component operating in a poorly regulated economy will be deemed to have a higher risk of fraud than other components);
- related parties identified at a group level for the purpose of disclosing related party year-end balances and transactions during the year;
- guidance with regard to the role of internal audit and internal controls (usually relating to the requirements of the Sarbanes–Oxley Act 2002 (SOX)). This is discussed in **Chapter 2**, Section 2.7. Where the company is required to be SOX-compliant, significantly more work will be required on the area of fraud – particularly for companies listed on the New York Stock Exchange, where compliance with the Foreign Corrupt Practices Act (FCPA) will be required to be considered;
- procedures for reconciling and confirming inter-company balances between the parent and components and between components;
- the need for components to comply with additional laws and regulations that may not be in operation in their local environment.

Other additional detailed instructions include:
- a template **schedule of unadjusted differences** – to capture all errors/misstatements noted on the component audit;
- a template for disclosure deficiencies – to report disclosures required for consolidation purposes;
- a template for control deficiencies – to report any internal control weaknesses that need to be brought to the attention of those charged with governance.

Practically speaking, such instructions can be quite extensive for large, complex groups. Thus, their preparation (and the information-gathering in order to prepare them) can be an ongoing task for the group audit engagement team.

### Obligations on the Component Auditor to follow Group Audit Instructions

The effectiveness and efficiency of the group audit consolidation process depends very much on the co-operation of component auditors. Hence, the planning and group audit instructions given to component auditors must be clear, unambiguous and precise. The group audit engagement team will have issued a strict set of deadlines by which information must be supplied to them. A 'group consolidation pack', for completion by each component auditor, will have been issued by the group audit engagement team and will include such matters as:
- confirmation of performance of the component audit by reference to group financial reporting policies;
- response to all risks identified by the group audit engagement team – if those risks apply to the component;
- communication of any additional risks identified at a local level only;
- confirmation of details of relevant related parties' disclosure information;
- details of the extent of use (if any) of internal audit by the **component management**;

- notification of any breaches of laws and regulations by the component;
- notification of any evidence of management bias in the financial reporting by the component;
- completed schedules, e.g. schedule of unadjusted differences, disclosure of internal control deficiencies, etc.;
- an audit clearance report (the component auditor's opinion on the component's audited financial information for consolidation in the group financial statements).

## Group Materiality

The setting of materiality levels in a group audit is complex and involves setting a **group materiality** figure. This represents the value at which an item's omission or inclusion will impact materially on the decisions of users of the group financial statements. However, the group auditor needs to consider the aggregate impact of undetected misstatements/errors and must therefore set materiality for each component lower than that of the overall group materiality, albeit still relevant to the significance of the component.

FIGURE 20.2: SETTING MATERIALITY FOR A GROUP AUDIT

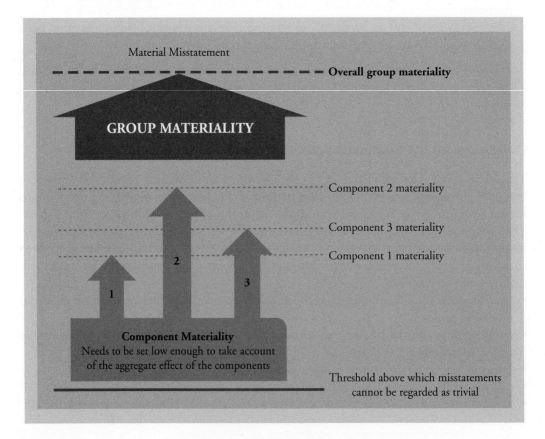

Once **component materiality** has been set, the component auditor will set performance materiality; however, the group audit team will evaluate the appropriateness of this. Component materiality in respect of significant components is generally determined by the group audit team.

## 20.5  GROUP AUDIT CONCLUDING ACTIVITIES

As the group audit process reaches its final stages, there are still important audit concluding activities to take place. The group auditor must assess if **sufficient appropriate audit evidence** has been obtained from all components. Any material matters to be brought to the attention of **those charged with governance** must be collated and assessed. While the process of consolidating all of the component financial information will have been completed, technical issues regarding accounting treatment or disclosures could arise and will need to be addressed. Each of these possible concluding activities are now outlined.

In the following discussion it is important to remember that it is the group audit engagement partner who is responsible for the audit opinion on the group accounts, regardless of the presence of group entities that may have different component auditors.

### Review of Sufficiency and Appropriateness of Component Auditor Work

Throughout the audit, it will have been necessary for the group auditor to maintain a close involvement in the work of the component auditors. This may include a review of their files or a reperformance of some of the audit activities (facilitated by an on-site visit should the review of electronic files be deemed insufficient). This will be particularly necessary should the group auditor determine that there are significant risks relating to the component; or, for whatever reason, there are concerns regarding the component auditor. If it is determined that the component auditor has not provided **sufficient appropriate audit evidence**, then the group audit engagement team should perform additional audit procedures.

### Communication with Those Charged with Governance

The group auditor is required to discuss not only the issues arising in the components directly audited by the group audit engagement team, but also those arising with regard to the individual components audited by other component auditors. Such issues noted should include non-compliance with laws and regulations, instances of perceived management bias, unadjusted misstatements/errors (shown by components), significant system or control deficiencies, etc. All of these items will be collated through the group audit engagement team's review of the group consolidation packs.

### The Consolidation Process

For most groups, the consolidation process will be a complicated one. Ideally, the group will operate a group-wide enterprise resource planning (ERP) system (see **Chapter 9**), which reports the individual components in the same format. This will greatly reduce the work of the group auditor. However, in the absence of such a system, the group audit engagement team will have an onerous task in checking that:

- all components are included in the consolidated financial statements;
- all necessary consolidation adjustments have been accounted for, as per IFRS 10 *Consolidated Financial Statements*, and consistent accounting policies have been applied; and
- all intergroup balances and transactions have been disclosed and eliminated, where appropriate, on consolidation.

Common consolidation adjustments that the auditor is likely to encounter include: intra-group eliminations (e.g. intergroup sales and cost of sales, unrealised profit, interest paid and received and payables and receivables); alignment of accounting policies; foreign exchange to functional currency; or adjustments for non-coterminous year ends. The auditor must design procedures to ensure that all necessary adjustments are made and are done so correctly and consistently.

Consolidation will be one of the key areas where the group auditor will use **computer-assisted audit techniques (CAATs)** – see **Chapter 9**.

## 20.6 IMPORTANCE OF COMMUNICATION IN GROUP AUDITS

Co-ordinating the audit process in any audit can be difficult, even for a straightforward audit, so when it comes to the audit of a complex group, e.g. with multiple worldwide locations, etc., the importance of communication is critical. Effective communication and co-ordination will ensure that the audit is planned and performed efficiently, and is completed:

- within specified timeframes;
- within specified requirements (applicable financial reporting standards, consistent group accounting policies and legal and regulatory requirements); and
- in compliance with ethical requirements and applicable auditing standards.

The timeframe of a group audit commences with the planned date for the issue of the audited financial statements, as agreed with the client group's management. Working backwards from this date, the group auditor can plan out the group audit. Once the timeframe is determined it needs to be communicated – this can be achieved through a combination of group audit instructions, on-site visits to component auditors or conference calls and video-conferencing or the use of virtual meeting technology, such as Skype.

It is essential that the group auditor maintains a **control checklist** of the issue of the group audit instructions to each component, as well as the return receipt of the responses, and that these are documented on the audit file. Additionally, meetings held with the component auditors should be documented and recorded in the audit file.

## 20.7 CONCLUSION

The principles and procedures of auditing a group are the same as for the audit of a single entity, and all of the ISAs are equally applicable. However, the process of managing a group audit is very different and poses its own set of challenges and risks to the group audit firm.

The overriding point is that the group audit partner holds ultimate responsibility for the audit opinion expressed on the group financial statements, and for this reason must be confident with regard to:

- adequate scoping of components;
- adequate review of component auditor competency and eligibility; and
- adequate review of a component auditor's work.

## SUMMARY OF LEARNING OBJECTIVES

**Learning Objective 1** Understand the additional considerations with regard to acceptance and continuance of group audits.

The group auditor must consider whether the audit firm has sufficient resources to manage a group audit, which requires the audit of components as well as component auditor reviews. It must also be considered if the firm has adequate policies and procedures to deal with the requirements of ISA 600.

**Learning Objective 2** Understand the requirements of ISA 600 with regard to risk assessment procedures and the communication of group audit instructions to component auditors.

A comprehensive assessment of audit risk is necessary. A thorough understanding of the group, its components and the environment they operate in is vital for this assessment. Key risks identified will be notified to all component auditors.

**Learning Objective 3** Be able to identify the considerations of the auditor with regard to group components, component auditors and materiality when performing an audit of group financial statements.

From the outset, it is essential to establish the scope of the group audit (what components are included) and carry out an assessment of the professionalism and competency of the component auditors.

**Learning Objective 4** Understand the importance of the scoping of significant and non-significant components.

The auditor must give consideration to the scoping in and scoping out of significant and insignificant components, ensuring that there is adequate coverage of key balances in the financial statements.

**Learning Objective 5** Know the auditor's responsibilities with regard to materiality when auditing group financial statements.

Determining audit materiality for the group and for each of its components is critical to the group audit process. This information needs to be clearly communicated to the component auditors.

**Learning Objective 6** Understand the concluding activities required by the group auditor prior to the issue of an opinion.

The auditor has a considerable task in checking the consolidation of the financial statements of a group: checking that **all components have been consolidated** with **consistent accounting policies** and that **all inter-company items have been eliminated**.

Prior to issuing the audit opinion, the group auditor needs to ensure: the **adequate scoping of components**; an **adequate review of component auditor competency and eligibility**; and an **adequate review of a component auditor's work**. All of this is necessary to ensure that the group auditor issues the appropriate audit opinion on the group financial statements.

Additionally, the group auditor must ensure **adequate documentation** is maintained with regard to component auditor communication.

## QUESTIONS

### Self-test Questions

20.1   What is a component of a group?

20.2   What is a component auditor?

20.3   Is it correct that the group auditor can rely on the opinion of the component auditor?

20.4   Is the process of a group audit entirely different from that of a non-group audit?

20.5   What additional acceptance and continuance considerations might the auditor have in relation to a group?

20.6   What deems a component 'insignificant'?

20.7   What audit procedures must the group auditor perform on insignificant components?

20.8   Why is setting materiality for a group more difficult than for a single entity?

20.9   Name eight items that might be included in a set of group audit instructions.

20.10  Why might an insignificant component need to be scoped back in for full audit procedures?

20.11  Why does the group auditor need to consider the appropriateness of a component auditor's work if the component auditor has said they carried out all audit procedures and no material errors/misstatements exist?

20.12  Why is communication so important for group audits?

20.13  What should the auditor take into consideration at the consolidation stage of the audit?

## Review Questions

(See Suggested Solutions to Review Questions in **Appendix C**.)

### Question 20.1

Jupiter plc is a long-established major international group involved in the manufacture and supply of children's toys. Jupiter has an extensive store network operating in 17 countries. It has been expanding rapidly over the past number of years, and to date operates from 1,100 locations throughout western Europe, the USA, Canada, South America, Australia and China.

You are a member of the group audit engagement team of McDonald & Co., a global Chartered Accountants and Registered Auditors firm. The firm have been the auditors of Jupiter plc for the past five years and the group audit planning is taking place for the year ending 31 December 2018.

In the last year, five key acquisitions were made, all 100% subsidiaries, as part of the group's strategic plan to enter the eastern European market. The following details are provided.

| Company acquired | Location | Principal activity | Auditor |
|---|---|---|---|
| Aladdin | Croatia | Children's toys | McDonald & Co. – affiliate audit firm |
| My Toy Shop | Hungary | Children's toys | Audit Sense – local audit firm |
| Treasure Trove | Poland | Children's toys | McDonald & Co. – affiliate audit firm |
| All Sports Wear | Russia | Adult sportswear | McDonald & Co. – affiliate audit firm |
| Games'R'Us | Serbia | Children's toys | Corey & Sons – local audit firm |

Notes from a meeting with senior management of each subsidiary highlighted the following issues:
- The previous auditors of My Toy Shop, Reilly & Co., resigned in 2018. No further details have been provided.
- The acquisition of All Sports Wear represents a diversification away from the key activities of the group. However, Jupiter hopes to benefit from significant economies of scale over the next 5–10 years.
- Aladdin and Treasure Trove are subsidiary companies and process the purchase invoices through a local shared service centre based in Croatia.
- The majority of the acquired subsidiaries report under the same financial reporting framework as Jupiter, however local rules apply and various accounting packages are used.

### Requirement
(a)  Describe **six** matters of significance that you would include in the group audit planning document for Jupiter plc.

(b) Discuss **four** considerations of the group audit firm in respect of the use of component auditors.

## Question 20.2

Conrad plc is a long-established global player involved in the manufacture and supply of household appliances. Conrad has been expanding rapidly over the past number of years and to date operates in 23 countries through 1,200 locations.

You are a member of the group audit engagement team of White & Co., a global Chartered Accountants and Registered Auditors firm.

During 2018, Conrad acquired Wilson, a 100% subsidiary, as part of its strategic plan to dominate the South American market. Goodwill on the acquisition of Wilson is recognised in the consolidated Statement of Financial Position at €1,700,000 (converted to euro from Peruvian Sol). The calculation provided to you by the client is shown below.

| Cost of Investment | € million |
|---|---|
| Cash consideration | 5.8 |
| Deferred consideration payable 31 October 2019 | 1.6 |
| Share issue | 0.2 |
| Incidental costs of acquisition (legal fees, stamp duty, etc.) | 0.3 |
| **Total** | **7.9** |
| Net assets acquired | (6.1) |
| **Goodwill** | **1.8** |

## Requirement

(a) Analyse **four** matters that should be considered, and the evidence required, in respect of the carrying value of the cost of the investment of Wilson in the financial statements of Conrad.
(b) Set out your understanding of the role of the group audit partner in the audit of Conrad plc.
(c) Outline **four** additional areas for consideration in a group audit engagement.

## CHALLENGING QUESTIONS FOR PART IV

(Suggested Solutions to Challenging Questions are available through your lecturer.)

These challenging questions aim to test your knowledge of **Chapters 18–20**, relating to audit work conclusion, audit reports and group audits. They are intended to test your practical application of what you have learned in these chapters and so you are presented with a case study on which you are asked to deliver on a number of requirements.

## Question IV.1

You have reached the completion stage of the audit of Large Company Limited and, as audit senior, you are carrying out the audit procedures relating to audit work conclusions.

## Requirement

(a) Going concern is one of the key principles on which a set of financial statements is based and as such the audit manager wants to be sure you are aware of the respective responsibilities relating to going concern. Outline the responsibilities in the form of a memo, including:
   (i)   the directors' and auditor's responsibilities with respect to going concern;
   (ii)  the basic steps required by the auditor under ISA 570 *Going Concern*; and
   (iii) a list of financial and operational events that may impact on the going concern assumption.
(b) A junior member of the audit team asks if, during an audit, they note that there is a future event that could result in the company no longer being a going concern, what type of audit opinion should be issued. Advise the audit junior of the possible opinions.
(c) The completeness assertion is always the most difficult to prove for the auditor, particularly when it comes to provisions and contingent liabilities. Outline how the auditor might search for unrecorded liabilities.

## Question IV.2

The audit manager of Large Company Limited has performed a final review of the audit working papers and identified the following areas that have not yet been tested. She sends you an email (see below) asking you to complete the substantive procedures for a number of areas.

---

**Email: 21 March 2019**

Please note I have performed a review of the audit working papers for Large Company Limited and noted that the following areas do not have adequate audit evidence:

1. **Taxation** – the taxation figure outstanding at 31 December 2018 is €2,310,000. Please complete the audit working papers for this taking the following into account:

---

> Opening balance (relating to 2017)   €2,280,000
> Tax payments made during the year   €12,426,000
> Tax charge for the period   €12,456,000
> Closing balance   €2,310,000
>
> 2. **Intangible assets** – the intangible assets of €1.15 million on the SOFP are made up of patents obtained by the client during 2017. This is disputed by Leisure Furniture, a major competitor.
>
> 3. **Subsequent events** – there do not appear to be any audit procedures relating to subsequent events.
>
> 4. **Related parties** – there is no mention of related parties in the audit file. Have they been considered?
>
> 5. **Other information** – there is no indication that a review has been performed on the other information included alongside the financial statements in the annual report.
>
> Please note that we are approaching 30 March 2019 and the client has indicated that it will not provide us with any further audit evidence after this date so you need to carry out these activities as quickly as possible.

**Requirement**

(a) Outline the audit procedures you would perform to complete the substantive testing of taxation and in doing so identify any misstatements requiring correction (including the correction journal).

(b) Outline the audit procedures you would undertake to audit the patent rights dispute.

(c) Outline the audit procedures that should be carried out with respect to the period between when the audit fieldwork was performed and the signing of the auditor's report.

(d) Outline why an auditor is interested in related party transactions. List five substantive audit procedures that an auditor will follow to obtain information relevant to identifying the risks of material misstatement arising from related party transactions.

(e) Discuss the auditor's responsibilities relating to 'other information' included alongside the financial statements in the Annual Report.

(f) Discuss the potential implications for the audit report regarding the deadline for completion of the audit work.

## Question IV.3

It is March 2019 and you have performed all the procedures for the audit work conclusion, except for the finalisation and review of the schedule of unadjusted differences. A summary of all the errors collected throughout the audit is given below.

### SUMMARY OF MISSTATEMENTS/ERRORS FOUND DURING THE AUDIT

**Error 1** – The review of management's doubtful debt provision revealed that it was understated by €315,000. Additional audit procedures performed revealed a further understatement of €450,000.

**Error 2** – Analytical procedures performed on accruals revealed an omission of accruals to the value of €670,000. Further procedures revealed a further omission of €800,000 (all expense-related).

**Error 3** – Stock was overvalued by €150,000 due to the incorrect application of bill of material (BOM) values – this was attributed to a lack of controls in the area.

**Error 4** – Revenue recognition issues considered:

- Goods sold on a sale-or-return basis in December 2018, where the return period did not end until February 2019, were recognised as sales in 2018. The value of the sale was €550,000.
- Goods dispatched on 31 December 2018 did not arrive at the customer's premises until 4 January 2019 were included in revenue in 2018. The contract stipulated that ownership passed on arrival of the goods at the customer's premises. The value of the sale was €1,500,000.
- Goods dispatched on 31 December 2018 did not arrive at the customer's premises until 4 January 2019 were included in revenue in 2018. The contract stipulated that ownership passed on dispatch of the goods and payment was received on date of dispatch. The value of the sale was €800,000.
- A customer balance showing a credit balance of €300,000 was included within trade receivables.

### Requirement

(a) Based on the misstatements/errors outlined, provide the audit manager with a summary, in tabular form, to show the impact on the statement of comprehensive income and on the statement of financial position. Assume all transactions are VAT-exempt and ignore tax.

(b) Considering the schedule of unadjusted differences that you have prepared, are these financial statements materially misstated? (Performance materiality is €2,731,875 and overall materiality is €3,642,500.)

(c) If management refuse to amend the financial statements, what type of an audit opinion would you issue?

(d) Draft the 'Basis for opinion' and 'Opinion' paragraphs to support the opinion you believe is necessary.

### Question IV.4

Discuss the possible implications of issuing an unmodified audit opinion on a large public interest entity that is not a going concern, and is liquidated within 12 months of the signing of the audit report.

# Appendix A

# PAST EXAM[1] QUESTIONS REFERENCE LIST

| Paper | Question | Topic Examined |
|---|---|---|
| Summer 2013 | 1(a) | Substantive audit procedures – receivables circularisation and alternative procedures |
| | 1(b) | Substantive audit procedures – receivables observations from testing |
| | 1(c) | Substantive audit procedures – receivables existence and post-year-end cash testing |
| | 2(a) | Ethical issues |
| | 2(b) & (c) | Substantive audit procedures – inventory |
| | 2(d) | Audit report implications |
| | 3(a) | Audit completion procedures – going concern |
| | 3(c) | Audit completion procedures – going concern (audit report implications) |
| | 3(d) | Substantive audit procedures – finance costs |
| | 4(a) | Corporate governance and the audit committee |
| | 4(b) | Substantive audit procedures – cash flow |

---

[1] Chartered Accountants Ireland.

| | 1(a) | Controls testing – recommendation report contents, limitations and timing |
|---|---|---|
| | 1(b) | Substantive audit procedures – receivables/inventory/PPE |
| | 1(c) | Substantive audit procedures – foreign currency balances |
| | 2(a) | Substantive audit procedures – legal proceedings/PPE revaluation |
| | 2(b) | Ethical issues |
| Autumn 2013 | 3(a) | Controls testing – control deficiencies, risks and recommendations – payables |
| | 3(b) | Substantive audit procedures – payables |
| | 4(a) | Substantive audit procedures – inventory physical count differences |
| | 4(b) | Substantive audit procedures – inventory existence and completeness |
| | 4(c) | Substantive audit procedures – inventory valuation |
| | 1(a)i | Controls testing – inventory existence |
| | 1(a)(ii) & (iii) | Substantive audit procedures – inventory |
| | 1(b) | Substantive audit procedures – tax |
| | 1(c) | Audit completion procedures |
| | 1(d) | Ethical issues |
| Summer 2014 | 2(a)–(c) | Substantive audit procedures – receivables |
| | 3(a) | Audit report implications |
| | 3(b) | Using the work of others |
| | 4(a) | Substantive audit procedures – inventory physical count |
| | 4(b) | Summary of uncorrected misstatements |
| | 4(c) | Substantive audit procedures – bank confirmations |
| | 4(d) | Substantive audit procedures – PPE capitalisation |
| | 4(c) | Substantive audit procedures – payables credit balances |

| | | |
|---|---|---|
| **Autumn 2014** | 1(a) | Substantive audit procedures – inter-company balances |
| | 1(b) | Substantive audit procedures – provisions |
| | 1(c) | Substantive audit procedures – SOFP |
| | 1(d) | Ethical issues |
| | 2(a) | Substantive audit procedures – share capital and reserves |
| | 2(b) | Audit completion procedures – subsequent events |
| | 3(a) | Controls testing – PPE additions |
| | 3(b) | Substantive audit procedures – PPE additions |
| | 3(c) | Audit report implications |
| | 4(a) | Interim audit testing |
| | 4(b) | Substantive audit procedures – inventory physical count |
| | 4(c) | Audit planning – materiality |
| | 4(d) | Audit completion procedures – communication with management |
| | 4(a) | Audit planning – revenue and receivables risks |
| | 4(b) | Controls testing – revenue controls weaknesses |
| | 4(c) | Substantive audit procedures – receivables |
| | 4(d) | Substantive audit procedures – inventory |
| | 4(e) | Ethical issues |
| **Summer 2015** | 1(a) | Audit planning – risk (inventory) |
| | 1(b) | Controls testing – revenue controls weaknesses |
| | 1(c) | Substantive audit procedures – receivables |
| | 1(d) | Substantive audit procedures – inventory |
| | 1(e) | Ethical issues |
| | 2(a) | Audit report implications |
| | 2(b) | Substantive audit procedures – provisions |
| | 2(c) | Substantive audit procedures – bank confirmations |
| | 3(a) | Substantive audit procedures – payables |
| | 3(a) | Substantive audit procedures – payables |
| | 3(c) | Audit completion procedures – statement of uncorrected misstatements |
| | 3(d) | Audit completion procedures – related parties |
| | 4(a) | Controls testing |
| | 4(b) | Substantive audit procedures – intangible assets |
| | 4(c) | Using the work of others |
| | 4(d) | Substantive audit procedures – receivables valuation |
| | 4(e) | Audit planning – sampling |

| | | |
|---|---|---|
| Autumn 2015 | 1(a) | Audit planning – risk |
| | 1(b) | Substantive audit procedures – revenue (substantive analytical procedure) |
| | 1(c) | Audit planning – risk |
| | 1(d) | Substantive audit procedures – related parties |
| | 1(e) | Ethical issues |
| | 2(a) | Substantive audit procedures – PPE and provisions |
| | 2(b) | Audit report implications |
| | 2(c) | Audit completion procedures – statement of uncorrected misstatements |
| | 2(d) | Audit report implications |
| | 3(a) | Substantive audit procedures – receivables |
| | 3(b) & (c) | Audit completion – subsequent events |
| | 3(d) | Audit completion – going concern |
| | 4(a) | Audit planning |
| | 4(b) | Substantive audit procedures – legal claims (provisions) |
| | 4(c) | Substantive audit procedures – inventory held by a third party |
| | 4(d) | Audit considerations – refusal to allow confirmation |
| | 4(e) | Ethical issues |
| Summer 2016 | 1(a) | Ethical issues |
| | 1(b) | Substantive audit procedures – non-current assets |
| | 1(c) | Substantive audit procedures – receivables dispute |
| | 1(d) | Audit completion procedures – going concern |
| | 1(e) | Audit report implications |
| | 2(a) | Substantive audit procedures – deferred tax, non-current assets, revenue |
| | 2(b) | Audit completion procedures – statement of uncorrected misstatements |
| | 3(a) | Audit evidence – external confirmation requests |
| | 3(b) | Substantive audit procedures – receivables |
| | 3(b) | Substantive audit procedures – receivables (debtors circularisation) |
| | 4(a) | Management responsibilities |
| | 4(b) | Controls/substantive audit procedures – inventory count instructions |
| | 4(c) | Substantive audit procedures – revenue |
| | 4(d) | Audit completion procedures – management representation letter |

| | | |
|---|---|---|
| | 1(a) | Ethical issues |
| | 1(b) | Audit planning – risk |
| | 1(c) | Controls testing – revenue and receivables |
| | 1(d) | Substantive audit procedures – non-current assets |
| | 1(e) | Audit report implications |
| Autumn 2016 | 2(a) | Substantive audit procedures – cash |
| | 2(b) | Audit completion – statement of uncorrected misstatements |
| | 3(a) & (b) | Substantive audit procedures – inventory physical count |
| | 4(a) | Controls testing – control environment |
| | 4(b) | Audit evidence – relevant evidence |
| | 4(c) | Audit report implications |

# Appendix B

# LARGE COMPANY LIMITED[1]

## Extracts from the *Directors' Report and Financial Statements*
## year ended 31 December 2018

(Note: these financial statements are for illustrative purposes only and are NOT intended as the study source for financial reporting.)

---

[1] Source: based on *Pro Forma Financial Statements 2011 (Republic of Ireland)* (© Chartered Accountants Ireland, 2011) and updated by the authors December 2017.

# LARGE COMPANY LIMITED

## Directors' Report and Financial Statements

## CONTENTS

## DIRECTORS' REPORT

The directors present their report and audited financial statements for the year ended 31 December 2018.

### Principal Activities and Review of the Business

The company's principal activity continued to be the manufacture of furniture.

Revenue has increased by 41% to €280,250,000. The directors believe that this trend will continue for the foreseeable future as a new line of furniture has effectively broken into the luxury market. Demand for this range has also increased in foreign countries, with €42,625,000 of the increase being attributable to exports.

All other ranges are selling successfully and are expected to do so for the coming year.

### Future Developments

The directors are hopeful that the new line of furniture will expand into the United States. At present all sales are either in Ireland or in the United Kingdom. Market research has indicated that turnover could as much as double in the next three years if the major retail outlets in the United States accept the range. Negotiations are ongoing and should be completed by July.

### Results and Dividends

|  | €000 |
|---|---|
| Profit for the financial year | 60,394 |
| It is recommended that this be dealt with as follows: | |
| Ordinary dividends | |
| – dividends paid [*State date*] 2018 of 30.34c per share | (25,500) |
|  | 34,894 |
| Statement of comprehensive income at beginning of year | 50,360 |
| Statement of comprehensive income at end of year | 85,254 |

## Research and Development

The company is involved in the development of two new ranges of furniture for future commercial production. These ranges are the "Authentic Mexican Pine range" and the "Mahogany Cast Iron range". An additional employee has been employed to investigate these designs and to develop accompanying accessories.

## Branch Operations

The company has overseas branch operations as follows:

| Name of branch | Country of operation |
| --- | --- |
| Wood kit | Northern Ireland |
| Wood fit | England |

## Directors

The present membership of the Board is set out in the schedule of Directors, Advisors and Other Information. Details of directors' shareholdings, related interests and transactions are provided in Note 6 to these financial statements.

Mr Kevin Byrne and Ms Linda Connolly retire from the board by rotation in accordance with the Articles of Association and, being eligible, offer themselves for re-election. Ms Deirdre Hogan was appointed to the board during the year and, in accordance with the Articles of Association, retires and offers herself for election. Mr John Hogan retired from the board during the year and the directors express their sincere appreciation for his contribution to the company over the many years he served as a director.

## Political Donations

The company made the following disclosable political donations in the current year:

- Party A       –       €60,000
- Party B       –       €60,000
- Party C       –       €5,500

## Principal Risks and Uncertainties

### Financial Risk Management Objectives and Policies

The company uses financial instruments throughout its business. It uses derivatives to manage interest rate and currency exposures and to achieve a desired profile of borrowings. All transactions in derivatives are designed to hedge against risks without engaging in speculative transactions. The core risks associated with the company's financial instruments (i.e. its interest-bearing loans and debt, cash and cash equivalents, short-dated liquid investments and finance leases, on the operational level trade receivables and payables) are currency risk, interest rate risk, credit risk and liquidity risk. The board reviews and agrees policies for the prudent management of these risks as follows.

### Currency Risk

The company's activities in the UK are conducted primarily in Sterling, this results in low levels of currency transaction risk, variances affecting operational activities in this regard are reflected in operating costs or in cost of sales in the statement of comprehensive income in the years in which they arise. The principal foreign exchange risk is translation-related, arising from fluctuations in the euro value of the company's net investment in Sterling. The company manages its borrowings, where practical and cost-effective, to partially hedge the foreign currency assets. Hedging is done using currency borrowings in sterling (same currency as the assets), or by using currency swaps.

### Finance and Interest Rate Risk

The company's objective in relation to interest rate management is to minimise the impact of interest rate volatility on interest costs in order to protect recorded profitability. A long-term strategy for the management of the exposure considers the amount of floating rate debt that is anticipated over the period and the sensitivity of the interest charge on this debt to changes in interest rates, and the resultant impact on reported profitability. The company has a mix of fixed and floating rate debt, and uses interest rate swaps to exchange at predetermined intervals the difference between fixed and floating interest rates by reference to a predetermined notional principal. The majority of these swaps are regarded as hedging financial instruments.

### Liquidity and Cash Flow Risk

The company's objective is to maintain a balance between the continuity of funding and flexibility through the use of borrowings with a range of maturities. The company's policy is to ensure that sufficient resources are available either from cash balances, cash flows and near-cash liquid investments to ensure all obligations can be met when they fall due. To achieve this the company ensures that its liquid investments are in highly rated counterparties; when relevant, it limits the maturity of cash balances and borrows the majority of its debt needs under term financing.

## *Credit Risk*

The fair value of the company's financial assets are provided in the following table.

|  | 2018 | 2017 |
| --- | --- | --- |
|  | €000 | €000 |
| Cash and cash equivalents | 104,200 | 105,530 |
| Trade and other receivables | 15,200 | 17,500 |
| Derivative financial instruments | 2,290 | 1,630 |
| Other financial assets | 36,400 | 15,300 |
|  | 158,090 | 139,960 |

Other financial assets includes holdings in listed and unlisted share capital.

The company's credit risk is predominantly attributable to its trade receivables. Provisions for bad debts are made based on historical evidence and any new events which might indicate a reduction in the recoverability of cash flows. The company's receivables are made up of a large number of customers and hence the risk of default is reduced. In addition, the company uses credit insurance when allowing credit to more risky customers, requests letters of credit, parent company guarantees or cash collateral.

The company may be exposed to credit-related loss in the event of non-performance by counterparties in respect of cash and cash equivalents and derivative financial instruments. However, the company considers the risk to be negligible as it only transacts with financial institutions that are rated as investment grade or above. Information on the derivative financial instruments is provided in Note 25 to these financial statements.

## Payment of Payables

The directors acknowledge their responsibility for ensuring compliance with the provisions of the EC (Late Payment) Regulation 2012. Procedures have been implemented to identify the dates upon which all invoices fall due for payment and to ensure that payments are made by such dates. Such procedures provide reasonable assurance against material non-compliance with the regulations.

## Books of Account

The measures taken by the directors to ensure compliance with the requirements of Section 282 of the Companies Act 2014, regarding proper books of account, are: the implementation of necessary policies and procedures for recording transactions; the employment of competent accounting personnel with appropriate expertise; and the provision of adequate resources to the financial function. The books of account of the company are maintained at [*address/es*].

## Events After the Reporting Period

Details of important events affecting the company which have taken place since the end of the financial year are given in Note 31 to these financial statements.

## Auditors

In accordance with Section 383(2) of the Companies Act 2014, the auditors, Opinion & Co., Chartered Accountants, will continue in office.

On behalf of the board

Thomas Hogan          Mark Hogan          [*state date*] 2019
*Director*                *Director*

## DISCLOSURE NOTES: STATEMENT OF ACCOUNTING POLICIES (EXTRACT)

The following accounting policies have been applied consistently in dealing with items which are considered material in relation to the company's financial statements.

### Basis of Preparation

The financial statements have been prepared on the going concern basis and in accordance with IFRS as adopted by European Union (additionally Large Company Limited has applied IFRS, as issued by the International Accounting Standards Board (IASB) and Irish statute comprising the Companies Act 2014). Accounting Standards generally accepted in Ireland in preparing financial statements giving a true and fair view are those published by Chartered Accountants Ireland and issued by the Financial Reporting Council.

### Revenue Recognition

Revenue is stated net of trade discounts, VAT and similar taxes and derives from the provision of goods falling within the company's ordinary activities.

### Investment Properties

Investment properties are recognised using the fair value model, revalued annually and are not depreciated or amortised. This treatment is a departure from the requirement of company law to provide depreciation on all fixed assets which have a limited useful life. However, these investment properties are not held for consumption but for investment. The directors believe that the policy of not providing depreciation is necessary in order for the financial statements to give a true and fair view, since the current value of investment properties, and changes to that current value, are of prime importance rather than the calculation of annual depreciation.

Changes in fair value are recognised in the comprehensive income statement.

### Property, Plant and Equipment

All tangible fixed assets are initially recorded at historic cost. Freehold land and buildings (all non-specialised properties) are revalued on the basis of fair values.

Revaluation gains are recognised in other comprehensive income.

Revaluation losses caused by a clear consumption of economic benefits are recognised in other comprehensive income to the extent that there is a revaluation surplus relating to the asset. Beyond this the loss is recognised as an expense in the comprehensive income statement.

Finance costs directly attributable to the construction of freehold buildings are capitalised as part of the cost of these assets. The capitalisation rate used is the weighted average rate of general borrowing outstanding during the period. Only capital items with a net of VAT cost in excess of €1,000 are capitalised.

## Depreciation

Depreciation is provided on all property, plant and equipment other than freehold land and investment properties, at rates calculated to write off the cost or valuation, less estimated residual value, of each asset systematically over its expected useful life, as follows:

| | | |
|---|---|---|
| Freehold buildings | – | straight-line over 22 years |
| Leasehold land and buildings | – | straight-line over the term of the lease |
| Plant and machinery | – | straight-line over 3 years |
| Motor vehicles | – | straight-line over 4 years |

The carrying values of tangible fixed assets are reviewed annually for impairment in periods if events or changes in circumstances indicate the carrying value may not be recoverable. A full year's depreciation is charged in the year of addition and in the year of disposal.

## Inventories

Inventory is stated at the lower of cost and net realisable value. In the case of finished goods and work in progress, cost is defined as the aggregate cost of raw material, direct labour and the attributable proportion of direct production overheads based on a normal level of activity. Net realisable value is based on normal selling price, less further costs expected to be incurred to completion and disposal.

## Leasing and Hire-purchase Commitments

Assets held under finance leases and hire-purchase contracts are capitalised in the balance sheet and are depreciated over their useful lives, with the corresponding lease or hire-purchase obligation being capitalised as a liability. The interest element of the finance lease rentals is charged to the comprehensive income statement over the period of the lease and represents a constant proportion of the balance of capital repayments outstanding.

Operating lease rentals are charged to the comprehensive income statement on a straight-line basis over the lease term.

## Provisions for Liabilities

Provisions for the expected legal costs are charged against profits when an action against the company commences. The effect of the time value of money is not material, therefore the provisions are not discounted.

## Foreign Currencies

### Functional and Presentation Currency

Items included in the financial statements are presented in euro, the currency of the primary economic environment in which the entity operates (the "functional currency").

The principal exchange rates used for the translation of results, cash flows and balance sheets into euro were as follows:

|  | 2018 | 2017 |
| --- | --- | --- |
|  | €1=Stg£ | €1=Stg£ |
| Average | 0.810 | 0.867 |
| Year end | 0.816 | 0.835 |

### Transactions and Balances

Transactions in foreign currencies are recorded at the rate ruling at the date of the transaction. Monetary assets and liabilities denominated in foreign currencies are retranslated at the rate of exchange ruling at the date of the statement of financial position or the contracted rate. All differences are taken to the statement of comprehensive income. Translation differences are disclosed separately in a "foreign currency reserve", within equity reserves.

## Dividends

Dividends to the company's equity shareholders (holders of ordinary shares) are recognised as a liability of the company when approved by the company's shareholders. Preference share dividends are cumulative and cannot be waived, therefore they are treated in the same manner as debt interest and are accrued for, if not paid when due.

## Capital Instruments

Shares are included in shareholders' funds. Other instruments are classified as liabilities if not included in shareholders' funds and if they contain an obligation to transfer economic benefits. The finance cost recognised in the comprehensive income statement in respect of capital instruments other than equity shares is allocated to periods over the term of the instrument at a constant rate on the carrying amount.

### Issue Costs of Capital Instruments

The cost of issue of preference shares and debentures are charged to the comprehensive income statement on a straight-line basis over the life of the instrument. A corresponding amount is transferred from reserves to the share premium account.

# LARGE COMPANY LIMITED

## STATEMENT OF COMPREHENSIVE INCOME

for the year ended 31 December 2018

|  | Notes | 2018 €000 | 2017 €000 |
|---|---|---|---|
| Revenue |  | 280,250 | 198,500 |
| Cost of sales |  | (140,250) | (120,800) |
| Gross profit |  | 140,000 | 77,700 |
| Other operating income |  | 750 | 700 |
| Investment revenue | 3 | 350 | 330 |
| Distribution costs |  | (23,000) | (20,000) |
| Administration costs |  | (35,000) | (34,000) |
| Profit/(loss) on sale of tangible fixed assets | 2 | 420 | (120) |
| Loss on disposal of available-for-sale investments | 2 | (120) | – |
| Impairment of investment property | 2 | (10,000) | – |
| Finance costs | 4 | (550) | (550) |
| **Profit before tax** |  | 72,850 | 24,060 |
| Income tax expense |  | (12,456) | (8,500) |
| **Profit for the year** | 29 | 60,394 | 15,560 |

| **Other Comprehensive Income** |  |  |  |
|---|---|---|---|
| Unrealised surplus on revaluation of investment property |  | – | 10,000 |
| Impairment of revalued investment property |  | (10,000) | – |
| Unrealised deficit on revaluation of freehold property |  | (17,200) | – |
| Actuarial gain on market value of the defined benefit pension scheme's assets and liabilities |  | 200 | 80 |
| Currency translation effects on foreign borrowings |  | (200) | 150 |

| | | |
|---|---:|---:|
| Fair value movement on effective cash flow financial instruments | 100 | (200) |
| Income tax on other comprehensive income | – | – |
| **Other comprehensive income net of tax** | (27,100) | 10,030 |
| **Total comprehensive income for the year** | 33,294 | 25,590 |

Approved by the directors on [*state date*] 2019

On behalf of the board:

| | |
|---|---|
| Thomas Hogan | Mark Hogan |
| Director | Director |

## STATEMENT OF FINANCIAL POSITION

### as at 31 December 2018

| | Notes | 2018 | 2017 |
|---|---|---:|---:|
| **ASSETS** | | **€000** | **€000** |
| **Non-current Assets** | | | |
| Property, plant and equipment | 13 | 130,050 | 140,500 |
| Other intangible assets | | 1,150 | 1,140 |
| Derivative financial instruments | | 1,900 | 1,460 |
| Financial assets | 14 | 112,200 | 110,200 |
| Pension asset | | 1,200 | 1,000 |
| | | 246,500 | 254,300 |
| **Current Assets** | | | |
| Inventories | 15 | 49,774 | 35,020 |
| Trade and other receivables | 16 | 15,200 | 17,500 |
| Derivative financial instruments | | 390 | 170 |
| Available-for-sale investments | | 4,200 | 5,000 |
| Cash and other cash equivalents | | 104,200 | 105,530 |
| | | 173,764 | 163,220 |
| **Total assets** | | **420,264** | **417,520** |

| | | 2018<br>€000 | 2017<br>€000 |
|---|---|---|---|
| **EQUITY AND LIABILITIES** | | | |
| **Equity Attributable to Owners** | | | |
| Capital and Reserves | | | |
| Share capital | 28 | 84,050 | 78,160 |
| Share premium account | 29 | 2,990 | 570 |
| Retained earnings | 29 | 85,254 | 50,360 |
| Other components of equity | 29 | 1,600 | 28,700 |
| **Total equity** | | **173,894** | **157,790** |
| | | | |
| **Non-current liabilities** | | | |
| Long-term borrowing | 20 | 20,350 | 27,560 |
| Other liabilities | 20 | 89,590 | 89,070 |
| Long-term provisions | 24 | 750 | 500 |
| **Total non-current liabilities** | | **110,690** | **117,130** |
| | | | |
| **Current Liabilities** | | | |
| Trade and other payables | 19 | 109,320 | 114,650 |
| Short-term borrowing | 19 | 4,250 | 9,650 |
| Other | 19 | 19,420 | 15,560 |
| Current tax payable | 19 | 2,690 | 2,740 |
| **Total current liabilities** | | **135,680** | **142,600** |
| | | | |
| **Total liabilities** | | **246,370** | **259,730** |
| | | | |
| **Total equity and liabilities** | | **420,264** | **417,520** |

Approved by the directors on [*state date*] 2019

On behalf of the board:

Thomas Hogan      Mark Hogan
Director            Director

## STATEMENT OF CHANGES IN EQUITY

### for the year ended 31 December 2018

|  | Share Capital €000 | Share Premium €000 | Other Components of Equity €000 | Retained Earnings €000 | Total Equity €000 |
|---|---|---|---|---|---|
| **At 1 January 2018** | **78,160** | **570** | **28,700** | **50,360** | **157,790** |
| **Comprehensive Income:** | | | | | |
| Profit for year | | | | 60,394 | 60,394 |
| **Other Comprehensive Income:** | | | | | |
| Impairment of investment property | | | (10,000) | | (10,000) |
| Deficit on revaluation of freehold property | | | (17,200) | | (17,200) |
| Actuarial gains on defined benefit pension scheme | | | 200 | | 200 |
| Exchange adjustment | | | (200) | | (200) |
| Fair value gains on cash flow hedge | | | 100 | | 100 |
| **Transactions with Owners:** | | | | | |
| Share issue | 5,890 | | | | 5,890 |
| Share premium | | 2,420 | | | 2,420 |
| Equity dividends paid | | | | (25,500) | (25,500) |
| **At 31 December 2018** | **84,050** | **2,990** | **1,600** | **85,254** | **173,894** |

## NOTES TO THE FINANCIAL STATEMENTS (EXTRACT)

### 2.  Exceptional Items

|  | 2018 | | 2017 |
|---|---|---|---|
|  | €000 | €000 | €000 |
| Recognised in arriving at operating profit | | | |
| Bad debts | | (1,000) | – |
| | | | |
| Recognised below operating profit | | | |
| Profit/(loss) on sale of property, plant and equipment | 420 | | (120) |
| Impairment of investment property | (10,000) | | |
| (Loss) on disposal of available-for-sale investments | (120) | | – |
| | | (9,700) | |
| | | (10,700) | (120) |

Details of the impairment of the investment property are disclosed in Note 14 to the financial statements.

The company also disposed of a rare cutting machine. This transaction resulted in the above exceptional gain of €420,000.

Shares costing €1,700,000 were also disposed of, resulting in an exceptional loss of €120,000.

### 3.  Investment Revenue

|  | 2018 | 2017 |
|---|---|---|
|  | €000 | €000 |
| Available-for-sale non-current asset investment income | 210 | 209 |
| Available-for-sale current asset investment income | 75 | 71 |
| Other investment income | 10 | 9 |
| Net return from defined benefit pension scheme | 20 | 11 |
| Bank interest receivable | 30 | 23 |

| | | |
|---|---:|---:|
| Other interest receivable and similar income | 5 | 7 |
| | 350 | 330 |
| Of which derived from listed investments | 215 | 205 |

## 4.  Finance Costs

| | 2018 | 2017 |
|---|---:|---:|
| | **€000** | **€000** |
| Bank loans, overdrafts and other loans wholly repayable within 5 years | 95 | 98 |
| Other loans | 15 | 19 |
| Mark to market of designated fair value hedges and related debt* | 5 | 8 |
| Finance lease interest on finance leases and hire-purchase contracts | 18 | 20 |
| Finance costs in respect of completed freehold building | 12 | 15 |
| Overdue tax | 5 | – |
| Dividends on preference shares | 300 | 300 |
| Additional finance costs of financial liabilities | 100 | 90 |
| | 550 | 550 |

* The company uses interest rate swaps to convert fixed rate debt to floating rate debt. Fixed rate debt which has been converted to floating rate debt using interest rate swaps is stated in the statement of financial position at adjusted fair value to reflect movements in the underlying interest rates. The movement in this adjustment, together with the offsetting movement in the fair value of the swaps, is taken to the statement of comprehensive income each year.

## 6.  Directors' Remuneration

Staff costs include the following in respect of directors of the company:

| | 2018 | 2017 |
|---|---:|---:|
| | **€000** | **€000** |
| **Fees** | 250 | 235 |
| Amounts paid to third parties for the services of directors | 25 | 20 |
| Company pension contributions to money purchase schemes | 45 | 36 |
| Pensions to former directors | 15 | 5 |
| Amounts receivable under long-term incentive schemes | 15 | 25 |
| Compensation for loss of office | 10 | – |
| | 360 | 321 |

|  | No. | No. |
|---|---|---|
| The number of directors for whom benefits accrued under the money purchase scheme during the year were: | 6 | 6 |
| The number of directors for whom retirement benefits are accruing under defined benefit schemes amounted to: | 1 | 1 |

## 7. Staff Costs

|  | 2018 €000 | 2017 €000 |
|---|---|---|
| Wages and salaries | 9,256 | 8,856 |
| Social security costs | 1,110 | 954 |
| Pension costs | 1,523 | 1,230 |
|  | 11,889 | 11,040 |

The average number of persons employed by the company (including executive directors) during the year, analysed by category, was as follows:

|  | 2018 No. | 2017 No. |
|---|---|---|
| Management | 39 | 37 |
| Administration | 56 | 54 |
| Production | 208 | 198 |
| Research and development | 7 | 3 |
| Sales | 23 | 18 |
|  | 333 | 310 |

## 11. Dividends

|  | 2018 €000 | 2017 €000 |
|---|---|---|
| *Equity Dividends on Ordinary Shares* |  |  |
| Dividend paid of 30.34c (2016: 12.79c) per share | 25,500 | 10,000 |
|  | 25,500 | 10,000 |

A dividend is proposed of €15,500 (18.44c per share); (2017: €23,714 (30.34c per share)).

## 13. Property, Plant and Equipment

| | Freehold Land and Buildings €000 | Plant and Machinery €000 | Motor Vehicles €000 | Total €000 |
|---|---|---|---|---|
| **Cost** | | | | |
| At 1 January 2018 | 400,000 | 113,625 | 28,800 | 542,425 |
| Additions | – | 82,250 | 35,000 | 117,250 |
| Deficit on revaluation | (355,000) | – | – | (355,000) |
| Disposals | – | (49,000) | (14,655) | (63,655) |
| *At 31 December 2018* | 45,000 | 146,875 | 49,145 | 241,020 |
| **Depreciation** | | | | |
| At 1 January 2018 | 319,800 | 61,725 | 20,400 | 401,925 |
| Charge for year | 18,000 | 48,705 | 14,500 | 81,205 |
| Elimination on revaluation | (337,800 | – | – | (337,800) |
| Disposals | – | (29,000) | (5,360) | (34,360) |
| At 31 December 2018 | – | 81,430 | 29,540 | 110,970 |
| **Net book value** | | | | |
| At 31 December 2018 | 45,000 | 65,445 | 19,605 | 130,050 |
| At 1 January 2018 | 80,200 | 51,900 | 8,400 | 140,500 |

### Freehold Land and Buildings

Freehold land (€15,000,000) which is not depreciated is included in land and buildings. On 31 December the land was valued at its original cost by the external surveyors (details in next paragraph).

The freehold buildings were valued at €30,000,000, being their value in use, in accordance with the Appraisal and Valuation Manual of the Royal Institution of Chartered Surveyors, on 31 December 2018 by external professional surveyors, Big Value Valuers and Co. Chartered Surveyors. The property had been revalued to €385,000,000, but by 31 December 2018 was depreciated to €47,200,000. The sudden decline in value of the freehold buildings was caused by the upsurge of political trouble and the exit of commercial businesses in the local area. The total reduction in the net book value is €17,200,000. The year-end valuation (€30,000,000) is not materially different from the open market value.

## Modified Historical Cost

Particulars relating to revalued land and buildings are given below:

|  | 2018 €000 | 2017 €000 |
|---|---|---|
| **Opening book amount** | 65,200 | 95,200 |
| Depreciation | (18,000) | (30,000) |
| **Adjusted book amount** | 47,200 | 65,200 |
| Revaluation gain/(loss) |  |  |
| Recognised in the statement of changes in equity | (17,200) | – |
| Closing book amount | 30,000 | 65,200 |

## Finance Costs

Where applicable, finance costs were capitalised at 10% (2017: 12%). The cost of freehold buildings includes €5,000,000 of finance costs that were capitalised in 2017. No finance costs were capitalised in 2018.

## Historical Cost Information for the Property included at Valuation

On the historical cost basis, land and buildings would have been included as follows:

|  | €000 |
|---|---|
| **Cost** |  |
| At 1 January 2018 and 31 December 2018 | 100,000 |
| **Cumulative depreciation based on cost** |  |
| At 1 January 2018 | 74,320 |
| Charge for the year | 6,500 |
| At 31 December 2018 | 80,820 |
| **Net book values** |  |
| At 1 January 2018 | 25,680 |
| At 31 December 2018 | 19,180 |

Other tangible fixed assets are included at cost.

## 14.  Financial Assets

| | Investment Properties €000 | Available-for-sale Investments €000 | Total €000 |
|---|---|---|---|
| **Fair value** | | | |
| At 1 January 2018 | 100,000 | 10,500 | 110,500 |
| Additions | – | 23,700 | 23,700 |
| Diminution in value | (20,000) | – | (20,000) |
| Disposals | – | (1,700) | (1,700) |
| At 31 December 2018 | 80,000 | 32,500 | 112,500 |
| **Provision for diminution in value** | | | |
| At 1 January 2018 | – | 300 | 300 |
| Charge for year | – | – | – |
| Disposals | – | – | – |
| At 31 December 2018 | | 300 | 300 |
| **Net book value** | | | |
| At 31 December 2018 | 80,000 | 32,200 | 112,200 |
| At 1 January 2018 | 100,000 | 10,200 | 110,200 |

### Non-current Asset Investments

The statement of financial position value of €112,200,000 reflects the market value of the company's investment properties and available-for-sale investments as at the year end (2017: €110,200,000). In accordance with the company's accounting policy, these assets are held at fair value. The available-for-sale investments represent an equity stake in an unlisted entity. The stake is classified as 'available for sale' as the company has no power to exercise any influence over the underlying entity.

### Investment Properties

The investment properties were valued at €80,000,000, being their fair value for existing use, in accordance with the Appraisal and Valuation Manual of the Royal Institution of Chartered Surveyors, on 31 December 2018 by Big Value Valuers and Co., Chartered Surveyors. This has resulted in an impairment in value to €10,000,000 below the original cost price.

The historical cost and aggregate depreciation based on historical cost calculated at a rate of 5% per annum are as follows:

|  | €000 |
| --- | ---: |
| **Cost** | |
| At 1 January 2018 and 31 December 2018 | 90,000 |
| **Cumulative depreciation based on cost** | |
| At 1 January 2018 | 18,000 |
| Charge for the year | 4,500 |
| At 31 December 2018 | 22,500 |
| **Net book values** | |
| At 1 January 2018 | 72,000 |
| At 31 December 2018 | 67,500 |

### True and Fair View Override

Had the investment properties been depreciated in accordance with companies legislation, the reported profit for the year would have been €4,500,000 less, and assets and reserves in the statement of financial position €12,500,000 lower.

## 15. Inventories

|  | 2018 €000 | 2017 €000 |
| --- | ---: | ---: |
| Raw materials and consumables | 9,320 | 7,770 |
| Work in progress | 12,530 | 10,750 |
| Finished goods and goods in transit | 27,924 | 16,500 |
|  | 49,774 | 35,020 |

## 16. Trade and Other Receivables

| Due after One Year | 2018 | 2017 |
|---|---|---|
| | €000 | €000 |
| Loan notes | 6,000 | 8,000 |
| Other receivables: | | |
|    Called-up share capital not paid | 685 | 875 |
| Prepayments and accrued income: | | |
|    Pension prepayment | 65 | 25 |
|    Other prepayments | 1,950 | 1,350 |
| | 8,700 | 10,250 |

| Due within One Year | 2018 | 2017 |
|---|---|---|
| | €000 | €000 |
| Loan notes | 1,500 | 1,500 |
| Trade receivables | 3,250 | 4,100 |
| Other receivables | 750 | 600 |
| Prepayments and accrued income | 1,000 | 1,050 |
| | 6,500 | 7,250 |

"Other receivables" include amounts advanced to finance the acquisition of shares in the company.

Trade receivables are stated net of a provision of €500,000 (2017: €750,000) for estimated bad debts based on historical experience.

| | 2018 | 2017 |
|---|---|---|
| | €000 | €000 |
| Opening balance | 750 | 700 |
| Increase in provision | 450 | 150 |
| Bad debts written off | (700) | (100) |
| Closing balance | 500 | 750 |

An aged analysis is utilised to determine the likelihood of payment default.

Aged analysis of trade receivables:

|                             | 2018 | 2017 |
|-----------------------------|------|------|
|                             | €000 | €000 |
| Current (within credit terms) | 3,100 | 4,250 |
| 30–60 days                  | 420  | 350  |
| 60–90 days                  | 150  | 140  |
| Greater than 90 days        | 80   | 110  |
|                             | 3,750 | 4,850 |

The directors consider the net trade receivable value to be representative of fair value.

## 19. Trade and Other Payables: Amounts Falling Due within One Year

|                                                              | 2018 | 2017 |
|--------------------------------------------------------------|------|------|
|                                                              | €000 | €000 |
| Bank and other loans                                         | 4,250 | 9,650 |
| Obligations under finance leases and hire-purchase contracts | 2,500 | 4,000 |
| Derivative financial instruments                             | 120  | 80   |
| Trade payables                                               | 109,320 | 114,650 |
| Bills of exchange payable                                    | 150  | 230  |
| Other payables                                               | 16,150 | 10,500 |
| Accruals and deferred income                                 | 500  | 750  |
|                                                              | 132,990 | 139,860 |
| **Tax payables**                                             |      |      |
| Corporation tax                                              | 2,310 | 2,280 |
| PAYE                                                         | 100  | 120  |
| VAT                                                          | 80   | 60   |
| Capital gains tax                                            | 120  | 80   |
| Other tax                                                    | 30   | 110  |
|                                                              | 2,640 | 2,650 |
| Social welfare (PRSI)                                        | 50   | 90   |
|                                                              | 2,690 | 2,740 |
|                                                              | 135,680 | 142,600 |

*Trade payables includes the following:*

| | | |
|---|---|---|
| Due at the year end to suppliers who claim reservation of title | 20,000 | 21,000 |

## 20. Payables: Amounts Falling Due after More than One Year

| | 2018 €000 | 2017 €000 |
|---|---|---|
| Bank and other loans | 20,350 | 27,560 |
| Obligations under finance leases and hire-purchase contracts | 85,000 | 85,000 |
| Preference shares | 3,000 | 3,000 |
| Derivative financial instruments | 70 | 50 |
| | 108,420 | 115,610 |

**Other payables**

| | | |
|---|---|---|
| Government grants | 1,308 | 808 |
| Pension commitments | 212 | 174 |
| Other | – | 38 |
| | 1,520 | 1,020 |
| | 109,940 | 116,630 |

## 24. Provision for Liabilities

| | Deferred Tax €000 | Legal Costs €000 | Post-retirement Benefits €000 | Total €000 |
|---|---|---|---|---|
| At 1 January 2018 | 250 | 15 | 235 | 500 |
| Charged to statement of comprehensive income account | 180 | 50 | 35 | 265 |
| Utilised during the year | – | (15) | – | (15) |
| At 31 December 2018 | 430 | 50 | 270 | 750 |

For details on the movements to the legal costs provision see Note 34.

## 26. Sensitivity Analysis – Financial Instruments

### Interest Rate Risk

At 31 December 2018, if interest rates had been 1% lower with all other variables held constant, post-tax profit for the year would have been €12,000 higher (in 2017 post-tax profits would have been €13,000 higher), arising mainly as a result of lower interest expense on variable borrowings, and other components of equity would have been €11,000 (2017: €11,800) higher, arising mainly as a result of an increase in the fair value of fixed rate financial assets classed as 'available for sale'.

If interest rates had been 1% higher with all other variables held constant, post-tax profits would have been €9,500 lower (in 2017 post-tax profits would have been €11,000 lower), arising mainly as a result of higher interest expense on variable borrowings, and other components of equity would have been €12,950 (2017: €11,500) lower, arising mainly as a result of an increase in the fair value of fixed rate financial assets. Profit is more sensitive to interest rate decreases than increases because of borrowings with capped interest rates. The sensitivity is lower in 2017 than in 2018 because of the increase in outstanding borrowings.

### Foreign Currency Exchange Rate Risk

At 31 December 2018, if the euro had weakened 10% against Sterling with all other variables held constant, post-tax profits for the year would have been €56,000 lower (in 2017 the post-tax profit would have been €21,000 lower), and other components of equity would have been €18,000 (2017: €17,000) higher.

Conversely, if the euro had strengthened 10% against Sterling with all other variables held constant, post-tax profits for the year would have been €56,000 higher (in 2017 the post-tax profit would have been €25,000 higher), and other components of equity would have been €18,000 (2017: €17,000) lower. The lower foreign currency exchange rate sensitivity in losses/profits in 2018 compared with 2017 is attributable to an increase in foreign denominated debt. Equity is more sensitive in 2018 than in 2017 because of the increased use of hedges of foreign currency purchases, offset by the increase in foreign currency debt.

## 28. Share Capital

| | 2018 €000 | 2017 €000 |
|---|---|---|
| **Authorised** | | |
| 100,000,000 A ordinary shares of €1 each | 100,000 | 100,000 |
| 5,000,000 10% redeemable preference shares of €1 each | 5,000 | 5,000 |
| **Allotted, called-up and fully paid** | | |
| 84,050,000 (2017: 78,160,000) ordinary shares of €1 each | 84,050 | 78,160 |
| 3,000,000 10% redeemable preference shares of €1 each | 3,000 | 3,000 |

## Preference Shares

The preference shares, which were issued at par, are redeemable on 31 December 2028 at par. They carry a dividend of 10% per annum, payable half-yearly in arrears on 30 June and 31 December. The dividend rights are cumulative.

## Share Issue

On 30 June 2018, 5,890,000 ordinary shares were issued at €1.40 each.

## 29. Share Premium, Other Components of Equity and Retained Earnings (Extract)

|  | Share Premium €000 | Other Components of Equity €000 | Retained Earnings €000 | Total €000 |
|---|---|---|---|---|
| At 1 January 2018 | 570 | 28,700 | 50,360 | 79,630 |
| Premium on share issue | 2,356 | – | – | 2,356 |
| Finance cost of share issue | (36) | – | – | (36) |
| Exchange difference on loan | – | (200) | – | (200) |
| Derivative financial instruments |  | 100 |  | 100 |
| Impairment of investment property |  | (10,000) | – | (10,000) |
| Revaluation of tangible assets | – | (17,200) | – | (17,200) |
| Actuarial gain on market value of defined benefit scheme's assets |  | 200 | – | 200 |
| Additional finance cost of preference shares to share premium account | 100 |  | – | 100 |
| Profit for the year | – | – | 60,394 | 60,394 |
| Dividends distributed in the year (Note 11) | – | – | (25,500) | (25,500) |
| At 31 December 2018 | 2,990 | 1,600 | 85,254 | 89,844 |

## Analysis of retained earnings:

|  | 2018 €000 | 2017 €000 |
|---|---|---|
| Retained earnings excluding pension asset | 84,054 | 49,360 |
| Pension reserve | 1,200 | 1,000 |
| Retained earnings | 85,254 | 50,360 |

## 30. Reconciliation of Movements in Total Equity

|  | 2018 €000 | 2017 €000 |
|---|---|---|
| Recognised gains and losses for the year | 33,294 | 25,590 |
| Dividends paid | (25,500) | (10,000) |
| New shares subscribed | 5,890 | – |
| Premium on new shares | 2,356 | – |
| Finance cost of issue | (36) | – |
| Additional finance cost of non-equity shares | 100 | 90 |
| Net increase in total equity | 16,104 | 15,680 |
| Opening total equity | 157,790 | 142,110 |
| Closing total equity | 173,894 | 157,790 |

## 31. Events After the Reporting Period

The company sold a franchise licence in Cork on 28 February 2019 and realised a gain on disposal of €10,000,000.

## 32. Capital Commitments

At the date of the statement of financial position the company had entered into contracts for future capital expenditure amounting to:

|  | 2018 €000 | 2017 €000 |
|---|---|---|
| Contracted | 3,000 | – |
| Authorised but not contracted | 750 | 500 |
|  | 3,750 | 500 |
| Government grants reclaimable in respect of the above future capital expenditure (estimated) | 1,500 | – |

## 34. Contingent Liability and Subsequent Provision

Karmax Ltd purchased furniture in 2018 has commenced an action against the company. Karmax Ltd claims that the furniture was defective, resulting in injury to one of their customers. The company's solicitors have advised that the action is unlikely to succeed. Therefore no provision for any liability has been made.

A provision of €65,000 for legal costs in connection with the defence has been provided for under other provisions (Note 24). €15,000 of this provision has been utilised in the year, leaving a closing balance on the provision account of €50,000.

It has been estimated that should the action be successful the maximum liability could be €6,000,000 to the plaintiff with an additional €500,000 in court costs. No provision has been made for these costs based on the solicitor's advice and the directors' judgement on the matter.

## 35. Approval of Financial Statements

The board of directors approved these financial statements for issue on [*state date*].

# Appendix C

# SUGGESTED SOLUTIONS TO REVIEW QUESTIONS

## QUESTION 1.1

In the case taken against Hanley & Burn, the judge will consider the following:

1. Did Hanley & Byrne owe a duty of care to the plaintiff? In this case the answer is yes – the auditor is appointed by the shareholders and the principal duty (as stated in company legislation) of the auditor is to report to the shareholders of Preston Ltd on the financial statements audited by them.

2. Was the auditor negligent in carrying out their duty? The auditor has a duty to exercise professional integrity and carry out audits with this in mind. In preparing their report, auditors must exercise the skill, care and caution of a reasonably competent, careful and cautious auditor.

   Hanley & Byrne will be required to demonstrate to the judge that they performed audit procedures in accordance with applicable accounting standards and that they have audit working papers to support the procedures performed and the audit opinion reached.

3. Was there a loss suffered due to reliance on the audit report? If the company collapsed during 2018, the shareholders inevitably lost a considerable amount of their investment and possibly received nothing on liquidation. It is likely that the shareholders did suffer a loss due to their reliance on the auditor's report.

4. Can the loss be quantified? The value of shares before the collapse versus money obtained (if any) after the collapse represents the loss suffered by the shareholder. The value of the loss attributable to the auditor will be determined by the judge after considering the existence of contributory negligence. Contributory negligence is a failure on the part of a plaintiff, in this case the client entity, to meet certain required standards of care. Together with the defendant's (auditor's) negligence, it contributes to bringing about the loss in question. In *AWA Ltd v. Daniels T/A Deloitte Haskins & Sells* (1992), the auditors failed to warn management of a control failing that they had discovered during their audit – the failing later caused loss to the company. The company was held to be partially responsible for not establishing adequate controls in the first place.

## QUESTION 1.2

The auditor expresses an opinion with reasonable assurance that the financial statements are free from material misstatement, whether due to fraud or error. Reasonable assurance is measured with reference to materiality. There are some inherent limitations of an audit that can result in the auditor issuing an inappropriate opinion, these include:

- **Sampling risk** – it would be impractical for the auditor to test 100% of all transactions and all items making up each balance, the auditor therefore selects a representative sample to test. This introduces a risk that either a single, or a series of, materially misstated item(s) will not be selected as part of the sample and will therefore go undetected by the auditor.
- **Non-sampling risk** – relates to inappropriate behaviour, usually associated with the competence of the auditor. For example, the auditor may test 100% of the population but the testing method may not be relevant to the assertion being tested, resulting in them inadvertently drawing an incorrect conclusion.
- **Auditor's judgement and professional scepticism** – some items cannot be measured or concluded upon definitively (e.g. provisions), for which the auditor must use their professional judgement (albeit adopting professional scepticism). There is, therefore, a risk of an incorrect conclusion on the item being considered (judged) and that a material misstatement/error exists. Audit evidence in these instances is said to be persuasive but not conclusive.

Furthermore, an inappropriate opinion may be issued due to a breach in the relevant Ethical Standard. For example, if the auditor or the audit firm have a self-interest in the client entity, an inappropriate opinion may be knowingly issued. The relevant Ethical Standard and the ISQC 1 are in place to assist the audit firm in safeguarding itself against such ethical issues arising.

## QUESTION 2.1

There are a number of threats to integrity, objectivity and independence arising in the case of Trafford Ltd.

- **Familiarity Threat** Your firm has been auditor of Trafford Ltd for 10 years, indeed the company has not had any other auditors. In addition, the audit partner appears to have a close relationship with the client's managing director and has been audit partner on the engagement for 10 years. All these factors indicate a familiarity threat that could potentially impact on your firm's ability to adequately challenge the client's management where required and increasing the risk of issuing an inappropriate audit opinion.
- **Intimidation Threat** The managing director of the client entity, Arnold Ferguson, appears to be a rather domineering figure and has shown tendencies towards intimidating members of the audit team in the past. This increases the risk that your firm may be pressurised into accepting his judgements, even where they may not be appropriate. This may result in your firm issuing an inappropriate audit opinion.

- **Self-interest Threat** The fees generated by the audit of Trafford Ltd are now extremely significant in the context of your firm's total income from audit activity – over 20% of total audit income. The loss of this audit client could have a serious impact on your firm's future income. The risk is that your firm will be reluctant to challenge the client's management on difficult issues for fear of displeasing them and the threat of the client changing auditors.
- **Self-review Threat** Arnold Ferguson has recently raised the idea that your firm may wish to perform internal audit services for Trafford Ltd. Should your firm accept this internal audit engagement, it may result in work performed by your firm in its capacity as internal auditor being relied upon by your firm in its capacity as external auditor. This is a clear self-review threat as the adequacy of internal audit work needs to be assessed by the external auditor prior to placing reliance on it.

**Action to be Taken** Prior to accepting the external audit engagement for the next financial year, your firm should assess whether adequate safeguards have been put in place to guard against each of the threats identified above, and reduce the threat to an acceptable level in accordance with the relevant Ethical Standard. In particular, the involvement of the current audit partner should be seriously considered. The long association is a real threat and could be resolved by appointing a new engagement partner. The domineering role of the client entity's managing director could have a pervasive effect on the organisation and raises the risk of financial mis-reporting and fraud. The continuation as auditor needs to be evaluated. The fees dependency issue needs to be tackled, and the audit firm should not take on additional work. The firm is now in breach of independence guidelines and there would be a clear conflict of interest if the firm took up the internal audit assignment.

## QUESTION 2.2

### Memorandum

To:      Mr Rick Parry, Istanbul Ltd
From:   XYZ Chartered Accountants
Subject: Corporate governance practices in listed companies

The standard for best practice in corporate governance is contained in the *UK Corporate Governance Code* (April 2016).
- If Istanbul Ltd is to become listed, it would be required under Stock Exchange Listing Rules to report its compliance with the requirements of this code in its annual financial statements.
- Some of the key structures/practices that the directors in Istanbul should consider implementing in advance of listing include:
  - undertake a thorough review of the effectiveness of its internal controls, and commit to future reviews on an annual basis;

- ◆ hold formal board meetings on a regular basis;
- ◆ appoint a number of non-executive directors to the company's board, ensuring that there is a reasonable balance between non-executive and executive directors;
- ◆ establish an audit committee to liaise with external and internal auditors and to manage the appointment of auditors. This committee should be chaired by an independent non-executive director;
- ◆ separate the roles of chairman and chief executive of the board;
- ◆ establish a formal, rigorous and transparent procedure for appointing new directors to the board;
- ◆ ensure all board members are supplied with information on a timely basis prior to board meetings; and
- ◆ establish a procedure whereby the board undertakes an annual review of its own performance.
- By establishing the above procedures and practices, corporate governance procedures will be enhanced and the transition to listed status will be eased.

## QUESTION 2.3

Whereas the ethical standards prescribe the rules and safeguards to protect the auditor's integrity, objectivity and independence, the ISQC 1 outlines the internal quality control systems that an audit firm should have in place to *support* the ethical behaviour of the auditor. These internal quality control measures should exist at the firm level as well as at the individual engagement level.

ISQC 1 outlines the following areas in which policies and procedures should be in place:
- leadership responsibilities – recognises the importance of quality and promotes the ethos of 'tone at the top';
- monitoring of quality control, including a clear process for the communication and remediation of deficiencies;
- monitoring of compliance with ethical standards;
- acceptance and continuance of audit engagements;
- engagement performance – to ensure that there is adequate ethical and quality considerations at the engagement level;
- human resources – staff are at the heart of any quality and ethical environment and policies should exist around recruiting competent and experienced personnel, providing necessary training, etc.

Clear policies and procedures in these areas will ensure that the audit firm is able to prevent, detect, correct and safeguard against threats to its independence, integrity, objectivity and deliver a high-quality engagement performance.

## QUESTION 3.1

### Audit Planning Memorandum – Qualitax Ltd: audit for year ending 31 December 2018

**Subject:** Key Requirements of ISA 240

First, it should be noted that for the purposes of the ISAs an auditor is concerned with fraud that causes a material misstatement in the financial statements. This can be broken down into fraudulent financial reporting and misappropriation of assets.

As auditors, we are responsible for obtaining reasonable assurance that the financial statements taken as a whole are free from material misstatement, whether caused by fraud or error.

We need to adopt an approach of professional scepticism throughout the audit, considering the potential for management override of controls and recognising the fact that audit procedures that are effective for detecting error may not be effective in detecting fraud.

Our objective is to identify and assess the risk of material misstatement of the financial statements due to fraud. We need to respond to those risks by performing appropriate audit procedures.

As an audit team we are required to discuss how and where the entity's financial statements may be susceptible to material misstatement due to fraud, including how fraud might occur.

We need to discuss the risk of fraud with management and those charged with governance.

Our audit procedures are likely to include:
- testing journal entries for validity;
- reviewing accounting estimates for reasonableness and lack of bias;
- scrutinising transactions outside the normal course of business and ascertaining their business rationale; and
- paying particular attention to the recognition of revenue.

At the conclusion of our audit we shall obtain written representations from management and those charged with governance regarding their knowledge of any allegations of fraud, or suspected fraud, affecting the entity's financial statements.

## QUESTION 3.2

(a) **The auditor's responsibility for detecting fraud**
   ISA 240 *The Auditor's Responsibilities Relating to Fraud in an Audit of Financial Statements* states that the primary responsibility for the prevention and detection of fraud rests with both those charged with governance of the entity and management.

The auditor is responsible for obtaining reasonable assurance that the financial statements taken as a whole are free from material misstatement, whether caused by fraud or error. Accordingly, the auditor should assess the risk of fraud and plan and perform appropriate audit procedures in order to have a reasonable expectation of detecting material fraud or error.

(b) **Whether fraud by management or employees (not in management positions) is more easily perpetrated**

In general it is easier for management to perpetrate fraud. Management is frequently in a position to directly or indirectly manipulate accounting records and thereby influence financial information drawn therefrom. Management may be in a position to override controls that otherwise seem to be operating effectively. There is also a greater possibility of collusion, either through the direct instruction of employees or the seeking of their co-operation in carrying out fraud.

## QUESTION 5.1

(a) **The procedures an auditor should adopt before accepting an appointment**

The prospective engagement partner should consider the following matters when deciding whether to accept a new client.

1. The integrity of the prospective client's management and its principal owners.
2. The legality of the entity's activities, and the entity's reputation.
3. The entity's business environment and who will use the financial statements.
4. The entity's financial position and prospects.
5. The likelihood that the scope of the audit will be restricted or subject to an unacceptable time constraint.
6. Any key accounting policy issues.

Before accepting a new engagement, the auditor should determine that a sufficient number of **competent staff** will be available to provide the services that the client has requested.

Before commencing any services on an engagement for a new client, the auditor should determine whether the audit firm is **independent** with respect to the client. It should also be confirmed that there are no potential conflict of interests.

Where a registered auditor is a corporate practice, it should obtain written confirmation from a potential audit client, or associated undertaking, that it **holds no interests** in the firm before accepting the audit appointment.

(b) **Matters that should be included in a letter of engagement**

*Addressee* For clients incorporated under CA 2014/CA 2006, the auditor should address the engagement letter to the directors of the company.

*Confirmation of the Terms of the Engagement* The auditor should always discuss the scope of the engagement with the client's management, and should then confirm the matters agreed in the engagement letter. In the case of a new engagement, the auditor should normally discuss and agree the contents of the engagement letter with the client's management before accepting the audit appointment.

The auditor should obtain the client's confirmation of the terms of the engagement by sending an additional copy of the engagement letter, asking the client to sign and return it.

In the case of a company, the auditor should request that the letter be tabled at a board meeting or, where the board delegates this responsibility, at a meeting of a suitable committee of the board, and for the approval of the letter to be minuted.

A copy of the engagement letter should be filed with the audit working papers.

*Contents of the Letter* Audit firms may wish to send their corporate clients an engagement letter covering additional services, e.g. corporate tax advice and assistance in preparing tax computations.

Other matters that may be dealt with in the engagement letter include:
- fees and billing arrangements;
- procedures in the event that the client has a complaint about the service;
- where appropriate, arrangements concerning the involvement of:
  - other auditors and experts in some aspect of the audit;
  - internal auditors and other staff of the entity;
- any restriction of the auditors' liabilities to the client;
- where appropriate, the country by whose laws the engagement is governed;
- a reference to any further agreements between the auditors and the client;
- a proposed timetable for the engagement.

## QUESTION 5.2

### ENGAGEMENT LETTER – LEOVILLE LTD

The Board of Directors,
Leoville Ltd

Date:

### Re: Proposed Presentation of Business Plan for Las Cases Ltd to your Bankers

Dear Sirs,

I refer to our recent meeting. It is our understanding that Leoville Ltd proposes to raise €4 million to fund its investment in Las Cases Ltd.

We further understand that your shareholding in Las Cases Ltd will be 50% of the share capital, with the balance of the share capital to be held by Poyferre Ltd.

The purpose of this letter is to set out the basis on which we are to assist Leoville Ltd in its formal presentation to your bankers of:

- a business plan for the new venture, Las Cases Ltd; and
- the preparation of management accounts of Leoville Ltd for the six months ended 30 June 2018.

### Leoville Ltd's Management Accounts for the Six Months Ended 30 June 2018

As directors of the company you are responsible for ensuring that the company maintains proper accounting records and for the preparation of the management accounts based on such accounting records.

Our responsibility is to **review** the accounts as prepared by you and to discuss any issues arising therein with the management of the company. We will not carry out an audit on the management accounts and, accordingly, we will **not** express an audit opinion.

We will review the statement of financial position and related statements of comprehensive income and cash flows and will report on this review to the directors of the company. Our report on the management accounts is at present expected to read as follows:

> "Our review consisted principally of obtaining an understanding of the process for the preparation of the financial statements, applying analytical procedures to the underlying financial data, assessing whether accounting policies have been consistently applied, and making enquiries of management responsible for financial and accounting matters. Our review excluded audit procedures, such as tests of control and verification of assets and liabilities and was, therefore, substantially less in scope than an audit performed in accordance with auditing standards. Accordingly, we do not express an audit opinion on the financial information.
>
> On the basis of our review,
> - we are not aware of any material modification that should be made to the financial information as presented; and
> - in our opinion the financial information has been prepared consistent with the accounting policies set out on pages — to —.
>
> Clearly, the limited nature of our review work will thus be conveyed to your bank, which will examine the management accounts of which our report will form a part."

### Business Plan for Las Cases Ltd

The drafting of a business plan and preparation of trading projections for this company for the period from 1 January 2019 to 31 December 2019 is a matter for which the directors of Las Cases Ltd are solely responsible. We further understand, from our recent discussions, that you will retain specialist textile industry consultants to advise on particular aspects of this new venture. Our responsibility will be to report to the directors of Leoville Ltd on our management of the plan's preparation. As the nature of the plan and the trading projections relate to a future accounting period, we clearly cannot offer any audit opinion on these matters.

The responsibilities of the directors of Las Cases Ltd are to make the underlying commercial assumptions that will form the basis of the plan. In this respect you will use the input of senior management of Leoville Ltd and Poyferre Ltd to assist you in the preparation of this plan and the related projections. You are also solely responsible for engaging the input of consultants and for deciding on the scope and nature of their engagement. Furthermore, your responsibility is to select appropriate accounting policies in line with generally accepted accounting principles and which reflect the activities of the proposed business.

Our report on the trading projections for the new venture is at present expected to read as follows:

"We have reviewed the accounting policies and the calculations for the trading projections of Las Cases Ltd for which the directors are solely responsible. In our opinion, the forecasts so far as the accounting policies and the calculations are concerned have been properly compiled on the basis of the assumptions made by the directors of the company. Also, the projections are presented, in our opinion, on a basis consistent with the accounting policies normally adopted by the company."

## Other Issues

Unless otherwise agreed, it will not be our responsibility to undertake or assist in the formal presentation to your bankers in relation to the application for finance.

Additionally, in order to ensure that the work we have agreed to can be done in sufficient time to enable the presentation to be made four weeks from now, we must have your agreement to the timetable set out in the Appendix to this letter. You should be aware that, without adhering to the numerous deadlines for information identified in this Appendix, it will not be possible to complete the assignment within the given timescale.

Our fees are based on the time required by the individuals assigned to the engagement, plus direct out-of-pocket expenses. Individual hourly rates vary according to the degree of responsibility involved and the experience and skill required.

We would be grateful if you would confirm in writing your agreement to these terms by signing and returning the enclosed copy of this letter to indicate that it is in accordance with your understanding of the arrangements in relation to the preparation of the business plan for the new venture and Leoville Ltd's management accounts for the six months ended 30 June 2018. Alternatively, you should inform us if your understanding of the proposed arrangement is not in accordance with the terms of the engagement as set out in this letter.

Yours faithfully,


We agree to the terms of this letter.

Signed for and on behalf of Leoville Ltd

## QUESTION 5.3

### Memorandum

To:      Audit trainees
From:  Audit senior

Re:      Planning, controlling and recording of an audit

In order to ensure an effective and efficient audit it is essential that the audit is properly planned, recorded and controlled. Auditors are required by professional standards and guidelines to adequately plan, control and record their work.

## Planning

The nature of the planning required will vary from audit to audit and will be dependent on the complexity of the client's business, the auditor's knowledge of the client and its business and the reporting requirements to which the audit is subject.

Adequate planning:
- establishes the intended means of achieving the audit objectives;
- assists in the direction and control of the work;
- helps to ensure that attention is devoted to the critical areas of the audit; and
- helps to ensure that the work is completed expeditiously.

### Business Review

One of the first stages of the audit planning process is to carry out a review of the client's business. This will comprise gaining an understanding of the business, carrying out a preliminary analytical review, reviewing significant accounting policies and making a preliminary assessment on materiality.

### Evaluating Audit Risk

Audit risk can be divided into two main categories:
1. **The risk of material misstatement** – the risk that items in the financial statements, either individually or in aggregate, will be materially misstated and that the client's controls may not be effective in detecting those misstatements.
2. **Detection risk** – the risk that misstatements will not be detected by the audit work.

The auditor can assess the risk of misstatement by an assessment of inherent risk and control effectiveness; detection risk can be controlled by varying the nature, extent and timing of audit tests.

Inherent risk is the susceptibility of an account balance or type of transaction to material misstatement through fraud or error, before taking into account the effectiveness of the client's internal controls.

The auditor should carry out a search for inherent risks, evaluate the significance of those risks and relate such risks to account balances, classes of transactions and the audit objectives. The auditor's assessment of these risks will form the basis of audit testing and will impact on the audit emphasis.

## Review of Internal Controls for Audit Strategy Purposes

A business must have some system of internal controls in order to function. The nature and complexity of these systems will vary from business to business and will depend on the complexity of the business. An internal control structure can be divided into three main categories:

1. the control environment;
2. the accounting system; and
3. the internal controls.

The control environment is the overall attitudes, abilities, awareness and actions of the individuals in the organisation, particularly those of management, concerning the importance of control and the emphasis attached to it.

Accounting systems normally comprise the financially significant computer applications and the computer environment within which these are developed, implemented, maintained and operated. These systems form the basis for the preparation of periodic financial statements and other information required by management to control the business.

Internal accounting controls are the specific procedures established by management to ensure that transactions are completely and accurately processed, transactions are recorded as authorised by management, assets are safeguarded and that the accounting systems are reliable and the account balances are correct.

The auditor's initial assessment of the control environment is crucial. If in their opinion the control environment is unfavourable, they are unlikely to carry out further procedures to assess the controls with a view to placing reliance on them in performing the audit.

Regardless of whether or not there is confidence in the internal controls system, the auditor must gain an understanding of the client's accounting systems. This enables the auditor to design audit tests to ensure an efficient and effective audit.

If the auditor decides to rely on the internal control system, they will need to make a detailed assessment of that system in order to design the tests of controls.

The review of the internal control system will influence the audit strategy and is therefore a crucial element of the audit planning stage.

## Determining Audit Strategy

The audit strategy sets out the principal features of the planned audit approach. The auditor develops the strategy by considering their knowledge of the client, together with more up-to-date information obtained through the business review and the preliminary assessment of internal controls.

## Substantive Testing Plan

Having determined the audit strategy the auditor can then develop the substantive testing plan. This forms the link between the audit strategy and the detailed tests to be performed during the audit.

For each audit area, the substantive testing plan should set out the following:
- the audit objectives relevant to the particular account balance or class of transactions;
- an evaluation of the inherent risks;
- a general assessment as to the extent to which control effectiveness reduces those risks and any specific control risks identified; and
- the nature, extent and timing of the substantive tests.

## Administrative Matters

For a new client it is necessary to ensure that all required steps regarding the firm's appointment have been carried out. This includes clearance from previous auditors and agreeing the terms of the engagement with the client.

The staff needed to carry out the audit must be assigned, ensuring that they have the experience required to carry out the engagement and that there is no conflict of interest.

Consideration needs to be given as to whether it will be necessary to engage the services of other experts and, if so, the timing and nature of their report.

The audit partner and manager will then set timetables and time and fee budgets.

Before the audit work is commenced, it is essential that all members of staff are properly briefed.

# Controlling

The audit partner needs to ensure that the audit work is being performed to an acceptable standard and that problems are quickly identified and brought to the attention of the partner or manager. The most important elements of control are the direction and supervision of audit staff and the review of their work.

## Roles of Partners and Managers

An audit team usually comprises people of different levels of experience and seniority. It is usual for all work to be reviewed by a person more senior than the person who performed the work. In some cases, for larger, high-risk clients it is usual to have a second partner review.

## Procedures

The nature of the procedures needed to control an audit, and the extent to which they need to be formalised, will depend on the organisation of the audit firm and the degree of delegation of the audit work. The procedures established should be designed to ensure:
- work is allocated to audit staff who have the appropriate training, experience and proficiency;

- audit staff of all levels clearly understand their responsibilities and the objectives of the procedures they are carrying out;
- the working papers provide an adequate record of the work done and the conclusion reached; and
- the work performed is reviewed by a more senior member of staff to ensure that the work was adequately performed and to confirm that the results obtained support the audit conclusions reached.

### Quality Assurance Inspection

Each registered auditor is required to establish and maintain quality control procedures appropriate to its circumstances. The audit firm's programme of quality assurance inspection has, as its main objective, to ensure that the audits are conducted in accordance with the relevant policies and procedures.

## Documenting

The quantity, type and content of audit working papers will vary with the circumstances, but they must meet the following overall objectives:
- assist in the efficient conduct of work;
- enable the work carried out to be independently reviewed; and
- demonstrate that the auditor has properly performed all the audit work necessary to enable an opinion to be formed on the financial statements.

For this reason the following procedures are important:
- remove all lists of outstanding work once the work required has been completed;
- record all relevant information received (and its source) when questions of principles or judgement arise;
- the working papers should be consistent with the financial statements and audit report given;
- each working paper should be: dated; record the preparer's initials; give the client's name; record the period covered by audit; detail the subject matter; and show evidence of review;
- no unnecessary information should be kept on file;
- appropriate conclusions on the result of work performed should always be recorded; and
- all working papers should be kept confidential.

## QUESTION 6.1

(a) Supplier statement reconciliations are a useful procedure as they verify each of the financial statement assertions:
- existence – that the liability exists at the year end;
- rights and obligations – that the liability pertains to the entity at the year end;
- occurrence – that the purchase pertains to the entity during the relevant period;
- completeness – that there are no unrecorded liabilities;
- valuation – that the liability is recorded at an appropriate carrying value; and

- classification/recording – that the creditor is recorded at the proper amount; and
- cut-off – the purchase is allocated to the correct period.

(b) Request the following from the audit junior:

- Supplier A – verify the actual reason for not recording the invoice and establish if there is a cut-off error.
- Supplier D – follow up as to the reason for not posting the credit note. If it is an error, it should be recorded on the schedule of unadjusted differences.
- Supplier R – add to schedule of unadjusted differences and no further work is necessary.
- Supplier W – establish why there is a delay in the posting of the October payment. This could have implications for the reliance the auditor places on the internal control system. Ensure the assistant enquires as to the present status of the discount claim. If there is no evidence that the discount is to be given, then bring it to the schedule of unadjusted differences as an error.

## QUESTION 6.2

| Transaction Class /Account Balance | Is the suggested test relevant to the assertion being tested? Why? |
|---|---|
| PPE | No – test proves that the asset exists but does not prove that the entity owns the asset. A better test would be to inspect the ownership document related to the asset (e.g. for vehicles, the registration certificate). |
| Inventory | Attendance at the physical inventory count will partially address the valuation assertion. While at the physical inventory count the auditor should also observe, for example, that damaged or short-dated goods are identified on the count sheets to ensure a provision is made against them later; and consider other possible indications of impairment, which may mean that the inventory is valued at an amount greater than NRV. |
| Payables | This only partially covers completeness – it will validate the completeness of suppliers already recorded (i.e. that all invoices owing to them are complete), but it will not give evidence with regard to missing suppliers. |
| Investments | No – test proves the occurrence and recording assertions and existence, but does not give an indication of the current valuation of the investment. |
| Purchases | Yes – tracing a sample from the nominal purchases ledger to the invoice, GRN and purchase order will prove that the transaction occurred. |
| Revenue | Yes – tracing a sample from the sales (revenue) ledger to the invoice, POD and sales order will prove that the transaction occurred. |
| Inventory | This only partially covers completeness – it will validate the completeness of inventory already recorded, but it will not provide evidence with regard to missing inventory. |

## QUESTION 7.1

(a) **Outline approach to address significant risk in relation to inventory**
  - Choose a sample of inventory items and test the post-period-end sale price of those items of inventory.
  - Inspect the sales invoice raised when these items were sold.
  - Consider whether the year-end valuation is appropriate based on inventory valued at the lower of cost or net realisable value (NRV).
  - Where the NRV is lower than the carrying value of stock items, year-end inventory has been overstated and a stock provision against these stock items will be necessary.
  - Calculate a reasonable inventory provision that will restate inventory at a value which is not overstated.
  - Adjust inventory for the provision.

(b) **Impact on the audit plan of the absence of key employee**
The five-month absence of supplier statements reconciliations and daily till reconciliations means that for the critical areas of accounts payable, purchases and sales, the controls around the completeness, classification/recording and existence/occurrence assertions have been compromised.

In the absence of adequate controls at the period end, accounts payable balances must be tested substantively through the performance of period-end supplier statement reconciliations. A greater amount of creditor balances may need to be reconciled in order to test the balance down to the materiality level, whereas if the control was operating effectively during the year, the level of substantive testing would be reduced.

As Oh So Chic is predominantly a cash business, in the absence of daily till reconciliations, gaining comfort over the completeness, accuracy and existence/occurrence of total sales figure per the financial statements may not be possible. The auditor may not be able to express an opinion on the financial statements given the inability to validate the assertions noted above in relation to cash sales. As a result, a qualified audit opinion may be issued.

(c) **Audit considerations if contract is to be agreed**
This will be a contract with a related party and therefore has inherent risk attached to it. As the company is experiencing a downturn in sales, the related party relationship with Gorgeous Shoes could be manipulated in order to improve the sales figures for Oh So Chic through sales invoices being raised at overstated amounts. When performing an audit with a related party, the auditor will have to inspect and review all sales invoices raised in respect of Oh So Chic and ensure that sales have been made on an arm's length basis, i.e. that they have neither been inflated – which would be likely in this scenario – or reduced to an unrealistic selling price due to the related party relationship.

The auditor must also ensure that the following are disclosed in the financial statements in relation to related parties:
  - the names of all related parties;
  - the basis of how the related party relationship has arisen; and
  - the nature and amount of transactions with related parties that took place during the period – together with period-end balances with those related parties.

## QUESTION 7.2

(a) The below is not an exhaustive list of the potential audit risks for TechMad Ltd – any relevant risk identified and correctly classified would be acceptable.

| Audit Risk | Audit Risk Component | Risk Level |
|---|---|---|
| Technological advancement in the software industry is high-risk – products may quickly be rendered obsolete. | **Inherent** – industry-related | Financial statements |
| Rapid growth may result in over-trading or an inability to control the entity due to the rapid increase in transactions and transaction types. | **Inherent** – rapid growth, over-trading **Control** – may not be able to introduce controls quickly enough to handle increased volume of transactions or new types of accounting complexity | Financial statements |
| Unqualified accounting staff – may not fully understand the requirements of accounting standards. | **Inherent** – inexperienced staff **Control** – may not be experienced enough to introduce relevant controls | Financial statements – as Mary has the ability to impact on all aspects of the financial statements |
| Revenue recognition – accounting rules can be difficult to apply with regard to long-term contracts. | **Inherent** – due to long-term contracts and complex accounting **Control** – one individual with responsibility and that individual is not qualified (may not fully understand how to apply the standard); also, no review of workings/ decisions | Class of transactions / account balance – revenue, receivables, inventory  Potentially financial statements too if not recognising costs associated with builds |
| Foreign exchange transactions – new to the company, FX accounting rules can be difficult to apply, plus unqualified accounting staff. | **Inherent** – complex accounting **Control** – no SOD (only one accounting staff) and no review | Class of transactions / account balance – revenue, receivables, FX gains and losses |

| Rapid increase in staff | **Inherent** – rapid increase in staff (lack of experience may lead to poor quality product) **Control** – employee starters and leavers is a difficult area to control | Financial statement – if poor quality products produced as a result, it could have detrimental impact on company and therefore its ability to continue as a going concern  Class of transactions / account balance – connected to payroll |
| New debt structure | **Inherent** – complex accounting concepts may be introduced around recognising interest or maintaining certain covenants. | Class of transactions / account balance – loan liability, interest in SOCI  Financial statements – if loan is recalled due to not meeting covenants, it could cause a going concern issue. |
| Lack of segregation of duties – one person in control of most of the finances | **Control** – lack of SOD | Financial statements |
| Lack of controls | **Control** | Financial statements |

(b) The numerous inherent risks suggest that the level of inherent risk is high. The high number of control risks and the fact that, effectively, there is no internal control system in place mean that the level of control risks is also high, i.e. it would not be worthwhile to test the controls.

With high inherent risk and high control risk, the auditor must ensure a low detection risk by carrying out focused substantive testing. This will alter the nature, timing and extent of the auditors substantive testing as follows:

- Nature – without being able to validate the existence of controls, the auditor will have to carry out detailed substantive testing rather than using substantive analytical procedures, which are only recommended when the control environment has been tested and proven to be strong. Tests of details testing can be considerably more time-consuming.

- Timing – in instances where the control environment has been tested and proven strong, the auditor will be able to perform more substantive audit testing in advance of the year end and then rely on the controls in the organisation to support roll-forward activities. In this case, where the control environment cannot be validated, the auditor must carry out all (or the majority) of the substantive testing at, or after, the year end.
- Extent – the volume of audit evidence required is greater where the detection risk is required to be low (e.g. sample sizes will be greater).

(c) **Business risk** – the existence of a risk that will impact on the client entity's goals and objectives, e.g. transacting in foreign exchange where rates are volatile may create unexpected losses that impact on the profitability objectives of the client entity.

**Audit risk** – the risk that the auditor will issue an inappropriate audit opinion. Audit risk is made up of: inherent risk, control risk and detection risk.

## QUESTION 7.3

To:     Audit partner
From:   Audit manager
Re:     Parallel Ltd – inherent and control risks identified during initial meeting with client for year ended 31 December 2018

As requested, please find below details of identified inherent and control risks noted during my discussion with management.

### Inherent Risks

- 80% of sales are to Irish supermarkets that are currently under pressure to reduce prices due to cross-border sales and the recessionary environment. This may put pressure on Parallel Ltd to reduce prices to allow the supermarkets to maintain margins and entice consumers to continue purchasing.
- Management are under pressure from the group company to reduce costs, which may indicate an incentive to under-record expenses.
- Inexperienced staff may have been carrying out tasks during the strike period.
- Impact on reputation/sales due to strike.
- Marketing costs have been cut by 60%, which may further impact the ability to sell.
- Replacement of financial controller will result in loss of knowledge. In addition, there was a month where no financial controller was in place.
- Management were reluctant to discuss reason for his departure, which in itself is concerning.

Overall the absence and turnover of key staff raises concerns with respect to the reliability of the accounting function throughout the year. The pressure to reduce costs and a difficult sales environment may be a motive for management to under-accrue expenses, and may also be indicative of a threat to the going concern.

**Control Risks**

- Controls around purchasing may be weak as a number of unexpected costs suddenly arose in the last two months of the prior year, further investigation may be required to see if these were unrecorded/un-accrued expenses that came to light late. In addition, pressure to keep costs low may motivate management to hide costs and override controls.
- Many of the members of staff on strike were from accounts receivable and payable functions – this may have affected the operation of the controls within these departments during this period.
- Many of the staff on strike were distribution-related and some of the signed PODs were not returned, meaning that sales were finalised without signed PODs – this may have an impact on the validity of sales.
- The payroll provider changed during 2018, which may have changed the control environment.

Overall, from a controls perspective, it may be wise to substantively test receivables, payables and payroll due to the possibility of control deficiencies in these areas. In the are of revenue, the occurrence assertion may also be a concern and focused substantive procedures should be performed in this area.

With the above notes in mind, the following questions should be raised with Parallel Ltd's management:

- Despite budgeted sales of just €4.8 million and pressures in the economy, the actual sales figure is €4.9 million. What factors have contributed to these higher than expected sales?
- Why has Material B cost 18% more than expected, despite only a 2% increase in sales?
- Why is factory electricity 6% higher than budget considering sales are just 2% higher than expected?
- Considering wage reductions (reason for strike), why are labour costs 22% greater than budget?
- Distribution and finance administration salaries are down just 2% despite wage reductions and a period of strike, why is this?
- Office rent is 52% lower than budgeted – it is unusual to be able to reduce a fixed cost by such a substantial amount, how was this achieved?
- During our discussions you indicated an intended 60% reduction in marketing costs, which are showing 40% lower than budgeted. How did you manage to maintain sales while cutting marketing?
- Budgeted receivables write off was €/£100,000 but actual is just €25,000, this seems unusual considering the environment. What is the reason for the difference?
- Depreciation of office equipment is 72% higher than budgeted, was there a significant purchase of office equipment during the year?

## QUESTION 8.1

(a) Weaknesses
1.  HR are not involved in the recruitment process.
    **Risks**
    - Recruitment may not have been authorised.
    - New employee's salary or rate decided by one person (may be excessive).
    - Bias or poor judgement may exist in the recruitment process without the independence and expertise of HR.
2.  Employee's details are provided to HR by the individual managers.
    **Risk**
    - The 'employee' may not exist and the bank details may be those of the manager or a connected person.
3.  There is a lack of segregation of duties as Terry, the payroll supervisor, enters the new starters into the payroll system.
    **Risks**
    - Terry could add an employee not included on the list and use his own or a connected person's bank account details.
    - Terry could input the incorrect salary or hourly rate.
4.  There is a lack of segregation of duties as Terry, the payroll supervisor, is the only person with access to remove employees from the payroll system.
    **Risk**
    - Terry could avoid removing an employee for a period of time, change their payroll details and process wages for himself.
5.  No review is performed to match the entries made by James, the payroll assistant, to the spreadsheets sent by the individual managers.
    **Risks**
    - Data entry errors could go undetected – employees could be underpaid/overpaid.
    - James could add additional hours for colleagues – fraudulent overpayment.
6.  No independent review is carried out on the gross to net reports or any payroll reports prior to the instruction being given to the bank to pay employees.
    **Risk**
    - Fraud and error in the payroll processing would go unnoticed.
7.  Only one authorisation is required to pay 1,000 employees.
    **Risk**
    - Additional payrolls may be processed.
    - Errors may go unnoticed.

(b)
- HR should sign off on all new hire requirements to confirm valid business need.
- HR should be part of the interview process to ensure the best candidate is hired and no bias exists in the interview process.
- HR should sign off on wage/salary rate.
- HR should obtain bank details directly from the new recruit.

- HR, not Terry, should be responsible for inputting new recruits into the payroll system as Terry has too many other payroll tasks.
- If HR does not input new recruits, they should review the exception report generated by the system and compare it to the authorised list sent to Terry.
- HR, not Terry, should remove all leavers directly in the payroll system as Terry has too many other payroll tasks.
- If HR does not remove leavers in the system, they should review the exception report generated by the system and compare it to the authorised list sent to Terry.
- Terry should review inputs by James by using batch totals at the end of each manager's spreadsheet to ensure that the total number of basic, overtime and holidays hours entered for each manager equal those on the payroll spreadsheet.
- Alternatively, each manager should be given their exception report showing summary hours, holidays, etc. per the payroll system and be requested to sign off. This will also ensure that leavers and new starts are captured.
- A reconciliation of the headcount per the payroll system and the headcount per HR should be performed periodically.
- There should be two authorised individuals required to sign off on the file before it is sent to the bank for payment (similar to cheques).

(c)

|     | Cycle | Assertion | Suggested Test |
|-----|-------|-----------|----------------|
| (i) | Revenue | Occurrence | 1. Select a sample of invoices from the general ledger and trace them back to customer signed purchase order delivery dockets to confirm goods were delivered to support the transaction. |
| (ii) | Receivables | Valuation | **Any one of below**<br>1. Review the ageing of customer balances and enquire of any balances that are outside of customer agreed terms.<br>2. Review post-year-end receipts from customers. |
| (iii) | Fixed Assets | Existence | **Any one of below**<br>1. Observe fixed asset count at year end.<br>2. Compare listing of assets to insurance certs.<br>3. Compare listing of assets to ownership documents. |
| (iv) | Purchases | Completeness | **Any one of below**<br>1. Select a number of suppliers and review supplier reconciliation.<br>2. Review post-year-end invoices.<br>3. Review post-year-end payments.<br>4. Review debit balances on the supplier listing. |

## QUESTION 8.2

(a)

| Weakness | Recommendation |
|---|---|
| Lack of policies and procedures, including inventory count procedures, and related accounting policies surrounding the inventory cycle, which may result in inconsistent application of policies and lack of adherence to desired procedures. | Policies and procedures and related accounting policies should be drafted by management. Accounting policies should be in accordance with accounting standards and applicable laws. |
| Inventory and purchases cut-off may not be accurate. Pearl imports materials from China that can be in transit for up to three months. As inventory is accounted for on receipt, at year end only goods that are received into the warehouse should be included in the inventory balance and a respective payables balance recognised. | Year-end cut-off should be monitored to ensure that only goods that have been physically received into the warehouse are included in the inventory balances and the corresponding payables balance recognised. |
| Credit period has been extended for Bathrooms Unlimited. There is an increased risk as balances outstanding become older that they may become irrecoverable. | Strict credit control procedures should be implemented for all customers. Where credit limits are extended for certain customers, these should be approved by the credit controller and monitored closely on a monthly basis. |
| A timetable of counts should be maintained and regularly reviewed to ensure that all sections are counted at least once in the year. If perpetual inventory counts are not complete and accurate there is a risk that inventory may be over- or under-stated. | • The inventory counts should cover all sections. If any areas of the warehouse are not counted, then these should be counted at the year end.<br>• A log of when each section was last counted should be maintained.<br>• Inventory counts should cover all the inventory lines. If any areas of the warehouse are not counted, then this will need to be done at the year end to ensure completeness and accuracy of the records. |
| There is only one inventory count team at each count. | A second independent team should check the counts performed by the inventory team. Counting the inventory twice will help to ensure completeness and accuracy of the counts, and that any inventory adjustments are appropriate. |

| | |
|---|---|
| The inventory count team is made up of the warehouse supervisor and one other employee from the warehouse. The inventory count is not carried out by employees independent of the warehouse. | Ensure stock-take instructions exist and are documented to include count teams. The count should be performed by personnel who are independent of the warehouse function. (The auditor should attend a physical inventory count to ensure these instructions are adhered to.) |
| Inventory descriptions and quantities as per the ERP system are noted on the inventory count sheets, which are then used by the members of the count team. The inventory count is not performed 'blind' (i.e. the expected results of the count should not be known to the counters). | Ensure stock-take instructions exist and are documented to include blind inventory count sheets. |
| The inventory count team is only comparing the ERP records to the warehouse floor, this simply ensures that the inventory exists, not that it is complete. | • To address the completeness assertion, the warehouse floor quantities should also be compared back to the ERP system. This will identify any inventory physically present but not included in the records.<br>• A second count team should be established to compare results and investigate differences.<br>(The auditor should attend a physical inventory count to ensure these instructions are adhered to.) |
| Differences between physical and ERP records are not investigated. Differences are simply adjusted in the system by the warehouse supervisor. | Inventory adjustments arising from the counts must be verified and updated by an appropriate member of the finance team to ensure that the records are accurate. All differences should be investigated. Unsolved differences between the physical count and perpetual records should be written off following authorisation from management. |
| Damaged and obsolete materials are stored in the warehouse beside useable materials. Third-party inventory is stored amongst the bathroom accessories. | Damaged and obsolete materials should be segregated from useable materials, and third-party inventory held in a separate location. All inventory should be held in an environment that prevents deterioration. The status of inventory should be known at all times. |

| | |
|---|---|
| Damaged and obsolete materials are recorded on the inventory count sheet as 'in stock and available for use'. | Damaged and obsolete materials should be identified and removed from the useable material area of the warehouse and written off. All write-offs should be adequately approved by an appropriate member of the finance team. Disposal records should be maintained. |
| Inventory continues to move in and out of the warehouse during the stock count. | Movements of inventory should be stopped from the designated areas during the perpetual inventory count. Inventory records could be under-/over-stated if product lines are missed or double counted due to movements in the warehouse. |
| Inventory records are adjusted by a member of the count team, the warehouse supervisor, three days after the count is performed. Due to the constant movement of inventory, this does not allow the immediate investigation of any differences. | Immediately after the count, the count sheets should be compared to the inventory records, any adjustments should be investigated and, if appropriate, the records updated in a prompt manner by an authorised person, independent of the count. |
| Write-offs are not approved as adjustments are simply overwritten by the warehouse supervisor when inputting results. | • All write-offs should be adequately investigated immediately after the inventory count and appropriately approved by the finance team. Disposal records should be maintained for all write-offs.<br>• A reconciliation should be performed between the inventory sub-ledger and general ledger. |
| All employees at each location have access to the warehouse at all times of the day. Inventory is not safeguarded and may be subject to misappropriation. | Access to the warehouse should be restricted to appropriate employees only – access cards should be implemented. |
| In previous years the auditor has not been allowed to attend the year-end stock count. | The auditor should request from management or those charged with governance to attend the year-end inventory count to ensure that inventory count procedures are being followed and that recommendations have been implemented. |

(b)

| Test of control | Assertions |
|---|---|
| **General**<br>Assess the appropriateness of the accounting policies and procedure documentation and the accounting estimates method for inventories. Ensure that the accounting policy is in accordance with accounting standards and applicable laws. | Valuation / occurrence / completeness / rights and obligations / cut-off |
| Obtain a report from the system outlining who in the organisation has access to which functions in the inventory system. Review the report to ensure that no segregation of duties issues exist (e.g. individuals with access to physical inventory should not have access to perform inventory write-offs). | Valuation / occurrence / completeness / rights and obligations |
| **Inventory status**<br>During your attendance at the physical inventory count, identify damaged and obsolete inventory, obtain a status inventory report and compare a sample to ensure appropriate status is recorded. Additionally, ensure that inventories held for third parties, if any, are segregated from the client entity records. | Occurrence / valuation / rights and obligations |
| During your attendance at a physical inventory count, observe the segregation of damaged, obsolete and third-party inventory. | Valuation |
| **Inventory counts**<br>Ensure stock count instructions exist and are documented and attend a physical inventory count to ensure they are adhered to. | Existence / valuation |
| Select a random sample of X months and request physical inventory count records to confirm physical inventory counts are taking place as prescribed and inspect reconciliations between count records and perpetual inventory records. | |
| **Inventory write-offs**<br>Select a sample of X write-offs of inventory to ensure they were adequately approved. Ensure disposal records exist for the selected inventory. | Occurrence / accuracy |

| | |
|---|---|
| **Standard costing**<br>Request a sample of X standard cost variance reviews to ensure they are taking place periodically and to ensure there is evidence of management's investigation of differences. | Valuation |
| **Inventory safeguarding**<br>Observe physical securities. | Existence |
| **Inventory reconciliations**<br>Request and inspect a sample of X months' randomly selected reconciliations between the inventory sub-ledger and the general ledger. | Completeness / existence / valuation |

(c) Risk factors:
  • Reliability of recording system for inventory
  • Timing of inventory counts and reliability of roll-forward procedures
  • Location of inventory
  • Controls over inventory
  • Fluctuation in inventory levels
  • Nature of inventory and specialist knowledge needed
  • Susceptibility of inventory to obsolescence
  • Risk due to fraud.

## QUESTION 9.1

(a) The use of computers is embedded in the financial reporting and control environment of client entities, and the auditor must use CAATs to conduct an efficient and effective audit.

CAATs provide the auditor with significantly improved efficiency by reducing the time needed to perform more mundane and routine tasks (a simple example would be the totting of manual ledgers, or the identification of unusual items within a manual ledger). This enables the auditor to devote more time to the issue of risk and the investigation of unusual transactions or balances identified. CAATs will also perform tasks with a greater degree of accuracy, increasing audit quality (effectiveness).

CAATs can be used to improve the efficiency and effectiveness of substantive audit procedures by:
  • controlling the audit using specialist audit software;
  • obtaining electronic copies of client reports for analysis; and
  • assisting with sample selection.

CAATs also offer the ability to test the reliability of client software, e.g. the IT application controls or security controls, the results of which can then be used to assess control risks and to design further audit procedures.

There are disadvantages to using CAATs, including:
- specialist knowledge or training required to fully understand the outcomes presented (specialist IT staff may even be required);
- can be expensive and time-consuming to set up – software must either be purchased or designed, so the auditor will need to carry out a cost–benefit analysis to determine if the use of CAATs is appropriate in the given circumstances, including the cost of specialist staff, if applicable;
- the audit team may not have sufficient IT skills and knowledge to create the complex data extracts and programming required;
- a risk that data can become corrupted or lost when using CAATs.

For the most part, however, the benefits of CAATs well exceed the associated costs and are becoming increasingly a part of regular auditing procedures.

(b) The below is not an exhaustive list of possible software functions and their uses but shows a range of possible answers.

| Function | Use (example) |
|---|---|
| Data queries – ability to search for data with specific criteria (e.g. invoices greater than a specific value). | Obtain the debtors listing and write a query to extract:<br>• all credit balances;<br>• all balances exceeding a certain value. |
| Data stratification – ability to divide data into categories defined by the user. | Obtain debtors listing and stratify the listing into groups:<br>• customer balances <€5,000;<br>• customer balances between €5,000 and €25,000;<br>• customer balances > €25,000.<br><br>Allows different sampling methods to be applied to each category of receivable, ensuring maximum value of receivables tested in the most efficient manner. |
| Missing sequence identification – the ability to sort by sequence and so identify missing sequence numbers. | Download all receivables invoices issued in the period, sort according to invoice number to identify if not in sequence, i.e. potential missing invoice(s). |
| Sum totals – ability to total large volumes of data. | Obtain the aged receivables listing and total all invoices due at the year end. Compare the result to the balance on the trial balance. |

| | |
|---|---|
| VLOOKUP – ability to combine data from two sheets/databases using a common file on both sheets / databases. | Obtain the receivables listing summarised by customer. Obtain the credit limits assigned to each customer. VLOOKUP the customer number from one file to another and retrieve the credit balance so that it shows against the balance outstanding. Helps to identify all instances where the customer owes in excess of their credit limit and assists with the evaluation of the valuation assertion. |
| Pivot tables – the ability to quickly summarise data into a more meaningful and concise report for analysis/review. | Obtain a list of all sales by sales category for the current period and the prior period on one file. Create a pivot to present the information showing each revenue type and the respective revenue for each year. Allows an analytical procedure to be performed on the year-on-year variance. |
| Word template letters. | Creating receivables letters for circulation. |

(c)  IT security measures:

- **Logical access controls** – IT systems should be secured with the use of passwords and other suitable security parameters. These measures should be regularly reviewed to ensure that they remain effective.
- **User access management** – an organisation should ensure that appropriate controls are in place to govern access to its IT systems. In particular, a process should be established to ensure that the granting of user access is appropriately approved and that accounts are removed when staff leave employment or change roles.
- **System security** – ensuring that antivirus software is up-to-date and that there is adequate protection for the system through use of firewalls, etc. Entities should ensure that all employees who use the systems are provided with guidance and policies in relation to the use of e-mails, internet access and other business tools.
- **Physical security** – in addition to good logical security settings, an entity should also ensure that physical access to its IT systems is appropriately restricted, particularly with respect to the server room, where even the climate is of key importance to the operational effectiveness of the computer systems, therefore strict access controls are essential.

## QUESTION 9.2

Processing invoices, and other finance support functions, are likely to see jobs replaced by automated functionality, however there will always need to be someone overseeing these functions. Computers can only do what they are programmed to do and will still need human intervention to facilitate review and to ask is it reasonable by applying professional scepticism – which is beyond the capability of a computer.

The growth in AI Accountants will likely mean that the auditor will spend less time recording what happened and instead use their time to analyse the data captured by automated processes. The accountant/auditor will have more time to perform more value-added tasks, such as offering insights to support decision-making. To some extent this is true already – the use of CAATs has enabled the auditor to focus more on data analysis than on the procedures themselves. Increasingly, accountants and auditors are required to have 'big data' and data analytics skills.

While accountants and auditors will be required to upskill technically to support such a technological environment, their new role in analysing data and communicating this analysis to senior management will require more 'soft' skills, calling for a broader skill set. The education of the accountant/auditor is likely to evolve to equip them with a more multi-disciplined education, incorporating technical accounting skills and a greater degree of IT skills, as well as more sophisticated soft skills.

Specifically with regard to auditing, the use of sample data will become less prevalent as specialised audit software allows 100% of the data to be tested. AI tries to perform tasks that normally require human intelligence – this is the continuing advancement of the knowledge-based systems of which we are familiar – but can it ever really replace the professional scepticism required of the auditor? It is unlikely, but it may aid it.

The profession of auditing continues to grow and more focus than ever is given to the role of the auditor. The increasing ability of technology to help with the detection of fraud will reduce audit risk and improve the quality and efficiency of audits. In turn, this will result in better outcomes for the audited client and for the entity's shareholders/members, improving capital markets in the process. Technology offers efficiencies for auditing without jeopardising audit quality (in fact, it increases it) and will increase audit profitability if it is embraced as an opportunity rather than as a threat.

## QUESTION 9.3

(a) When conducting an audit of an e-commerce organisation, the steps outlined below should be completed.
   1. **Map flow of transactions and data** – e-commerce can increase the complexity of processes. In order to identify key risks and controls, auditors should consider using process or data flow diagrams to map the flow of transactions.
   2. **IT general controls** – testing should be completed for applications and infrastructures. Interfaces from externally facing websites and internal systems should be tested to obtain assurance that all data transferred is complete and accurate.
   3. **Key application controls** – data input controls are typical of the application controls that should be tested as part of an e-commerce audit.
   4. **Network controls** – as key elements of the IT environment are externally facing, the auditor should consider engaging the services of IT security specialists to perform a penetration test of websites and mobile applications. A penetration test is where the actions of a computer hacker are simulated in order to identify security vulnerabilities or weaknesses. Firewalls are used by organisations to

separate external internet traffic from internal network traffic. The firewalls in place between externally facing technology and other internal systems are key controls. The processes in place for managing firewall rules should be tested as part of an e-commerce audit.

(b) The key control considerations for the finance director centre on completeness, accuracy and reliability of the processing of transactions. Each element of the provision of services online needs to examined in detail and measured against the objectives of completeness, accuracy and reliability.

In relation to security in an online environment, the need for appropriate security is vitally important. The e-commerce enabled website is equivalent to a shop and should be secured appropriately. Businesses will typically be responsible for collecting sensitive information, such as credit card numbers and personal details, and will need to ensure that these are not lost or accessed by intruders.

## QUESTION 10.1

- There is a need to evaluate and perform audit procedures to confirm their adequacy for the external auditor.
- Establish if the internal auditor has adequate technical training/proficiency and determine if the work of assistants is supervised/reviewed/documented.
- Ensure sufficient appropriate audit evidence has been obtained to be able to draw reasonable conclusions therefrom.
- Determine the conclusions reached are appropriate in the circumstances and any reports prepared are consistent with the results of the work performed.
- Ensure any exceptional/unusual matters disclosed by the internal auditor are properly resolved.

It is difficult to determine until the above is complete whether or not the internal audit carried out will reduce the work of the external auditor – the external auditor cannot simply take the work at face value. The external auditor has sole responsibility for the audit opinion expressed and while there may be a need to obtain expert advice, it is done so knowing that sufficient appropriate audit evidence must be obtained, including not only with regard to the subject matter but also to the calibre of the appointed expert.

## QUESTION 10.2

Dear John,

I felt I had to write to you and express my concerns about your plans to reduce the time on your upcoming audit engagement. I think it is admirable that you are taking the training so seriously and trying to increase the margins for our firm, but some of your intentions are of concern to me.

Before I discuss these with you, there is one resounding issue regarding an auditor's responsibility when issuing an audit opinion on the financial statements. While the auditor may call on various sources to assist in concluding an audit opinion, it is the auditor who holds sole responsibility for that opinion. No reference is made, therefore, to the use of the service auditor, the internal auditor or the auditor's expert in the audit report. Doing so would be perceived as an attempt to diminish the auditor's own responsibility with respect to the conclusion drawn.

For this reason, when using the work of others the auditor must be satisfied as to the adequacy of the qualifications, expertise and competence of individuals involved. In addition, the auditor must be satisfied as to the reasonableness, accuracy, relevance and completeness of the conclusions drawn by others.

**Internal audit** Before you proceed with the work of the internal auditor you will need to satisfy yourself with regard to the competence, experience and quality of the internal audit team's work.

ISA 610 *Using the Work of Internal Auditors* will help you when deciding on whether or not to use the work of the internal auditor. It outlines the following audit procedures that may be carried out by the external auditor prior to relying on the work of the internal audit team. These include:
- examination of items already examined by the internal auditors;
- examination of other similar items; and
- observation of procedures performed by the internal auditors.

**Service organisation Type 1 and Type 2 reports** A Type 1 report is the use of a service auditor to report on the description and design of the service provider's controls with respect to the client entity. It does not make any reference to the operation and effectiveness of the controls; to gain assurance around the operation and effectiveness of the controls you will need to obtain a Type 2 report. The principal auditor remains responsible for the opinion provided on the financial statements, and for this reason must be satisfied that the Type 2 report constitutes sufficient appropriate audit evidence with respect to the competence and professionalism of its preparer and its form and content. ISA 402 *Audit Considerations Relating to an Entity Using a Service Organisation* offers further guidance on your responsibility when the client entity uses a service organisation.

**Using the work of an auditor's expert** Before engaging the work of the expert, the auditor is responsible for evaluating the necessary qualifications, competence, capabilities and objectivity of the expert. The auditor cannot simply accept a second opinion on a valuation and perform no further work. The auditor is not the expert and therefore cannot judge the assumptions and methods used, but they should seek to gain an understanding of them to be able to consider their reasonableness. This will involve discussions with the expert as well as with the client.

## QUESTION 10.3

The IIA's Code of Ethics are principles relevant to the profession and practice of internal auditing; its Rules of Conduct describe the behaviour expected of internal auditors. The Code of Ethics applies to providers of internal audit services. Its purpose is to promote an ethical culture in the global profession of internal auditing.

Being independent, however, is somewhat more difficult for the internal auditor due to their direct employment by the entity. The internal auditor faces the same issues and threats to independence as the external auditor, although they present themselves in different ways. For example:

1. **Self-interest threat** The internal auditor's remuneration package is agreed within the organisation. Quite often the individual to whom the internal auditor reports will influence, if not dominate, the performance reviews of the internal auditor. For this reason it is essential that the head internal auditor report directly to the audit committee. Consider a situation where the internal auditor, who reports directly to the CFO, identifies a control failing and potential fraud in the CFO's department. A self-interest threat arises due to the internal auditor's concern for their remuneration, or possibly their employment, if they were to report these failings.

2. **Intimidation threat** The head of internal audit will often sit on the line below senior management and may be intimidated by more senior management into not reporting certain instances of fraud or error. The audit committee should ensure the entity enforces a whistleblowing hotline to permit the anonymous reporting of concerns over fraud or error.

## QUESTION 11.1

(a) In auditing additions the auditor should ensure all additions are capitalised in line with IAS 16.

  (i) The freehold land and buildings addition item selected is described as Building 1 expansion, the invoice however describes the activity as "Roofing Repairs". If the work carried out was to expand the existing building this could be classified as a capital addition; the invoice, however, suggests otherwise and indicates that the item should be expensed. As such, the error would be noted for consideration against other errors to see if, when taken in aggregate, they represent a material error.

   **Correction Journal**

   |  | DR € | CR € |
   |---|---|---|
   | Dr  Expenses – repairs and maintenance | 15,000 | |
   | Cr  Freehold land and buildings cost | | 15,000 |
   | Dr  Depreciation – SOFP | 500 | |
   | Cr  Depreciation – SOCI | | 500 |

   *Being correction of repairs item classified as capital cost under PPE and related depreciation*

(ii) While the industrial drilling machine appears to be a legitimate capital item the recording of the transaction is incorrect as the amount capitalised includes VAT. The VAT element should be noted as an error and considered with other errors to see if, in aggregate, they represent a material error.

**Correction Journal**

|  | DR € | CR € |
|---|---|---|
| Dr  VAT – SOFP | 1,000 | |
| Cr  Plant and machinery cost | | 1,000 |
|  |  |  |
| Dr  Depreciation – SOFP | 100 | |
| Cr  Depreciation – SOCI | | 100 |

*Being correction of recording of VAT as cost within PPE and related depreciation*

(iii) The purchase of the vehicle is a genuine capital item, however, it was purchased in December and the registration of the vehicle indicates that it will not be registered until January 2019. Therefore the entity will not hold risks and rewards until January. This being the case, the item cannot be capitalised in the period and the transaction should be reversed. It should be noted that this item exceeds materiality and if not corrected in the financial statements could lead to a qualified opinion.

**Correction Journal**

|  | DR € | CR € |
|---|---|---|
| Dr  Payables (supplier account Dino Cars Direct) | 92,000 | |
| Cr  VAT | | 17,000 |
| Cr  Motor vehicles cost | | 75,000 |
|  |  |  |
| Dr  Depreciation – SOFP | 9,375 | |
| Cr  Depreciation – SOCI | | 9,375 |

*Being correction of asset capitalised incorrectly and related depreciation*

(iv) Both the asset description on the invoice "drilling parts" and the client entity's capitalisation policy indicate that this item should not be capitalised. Drilling parts indicates a consumable item rather than a capital item, and therefore should be expensed. Furthermore, the client entity's own PPE policy states that assets are capitalised where they exceed €3,000. The error should be noted by the auditor and considered with other errors to ensure that in aggregate they do not exceed materiality.

If the item was still in stock it could be classified as inventory, however, considering they were bought in August this is unlikely.

**Correction Journal**

|  | DR € | CR € |
|---|---|---|
| Dr  Expenses | 1,500 | |
| Cr  Plant and machinery cost | | 1,500 |
| | | |
| Dr  Depreciation – SOFP | 150 | |
| Cr  Depreciation – SOCI | | 150 |

*Being correction of expense item capitalised*

The errors found in relation to additions are high, therefore testing should be expanded to reflect the risk that further additions errors could have occurred. It may be that the volume of PPE additions are not high enough to allow for full testing of the additions population in order to sufficiently reduce the risk of undetected material misstatements.

Furthermore, the total of PPE at cost or valuation as at 31 December 2018 of €3,557,000 is mathematically incorrect and should in fact be €3,057,000. This item should be discussed with management and the reason for the difference investigated further.

(b) When auditing revaluations it is likely that the auditor will need to use an expert in the valuation of land and building. In doing so the auditor should consider the requirements of ISA 620 *Using the Work of an Auditor's Expert*.

When using an auditor's expert, the auditor must always be mindful that full responsibility for the audit opinion expressed is theirs and should therefore take necessary steps, as deemed appropriate, to ensure:

- the relevance and reasonableness of the expert's findings and their consistency with other audit evidence collected by the auditor;
- the relevance and reasonableness of the assumptions and method used by the expert, which may include items such as assumption of planning permission attached to the property that the auditor must validate to be factual; and
- all source data used by the expert is relevant to the client entity and the property in question.

Furthermore, the auditor must consider the expert being used, ensuring the expert is sufficiently independent of the client entity and is sufficiently experienced and qualified to value the property. The auditor should also ensure that all assets within that class have been revalued in line with IAS 16. Finally, the entity's defined PPE policy (as per its financial statements) should be inspected to ensure the client entity is acting in accordance with it.

(c) In general, with regard to valuation, the auditor should always re-total all schedules provided by the client entity to ensure there are no simple mathematical errors. The total on the schedule does not total correctly and should be discussed with management. Furthermore, the auditor should ensure that the opening balances of the current year agree with the closing balances of the prior-year signed financial statements. Performing an analytical review will also provide an indication of risks associated with valuation, which may require more investigation. Some more specific procedures the auditor should carry out include:

**Valuation – Freehold land and buildings** The auditor should review the fixed assets register to see what makes up the full freehold land and buildings carrying value. A portion of the freehold land and buildings was revalued during the period. For the remaining properties the auditor should consider whether there are indications these could be impaired. This might include recent downturns in property valuations where the properties are located or, with regard to buildings, physical inspection of the sites may indicate that buildings are physically impaired below their carrying value. Note, once a policy exists to revalue, all assets within that class must be revalued.

**Plant and machinery and motor vehicles** While the useful lives of plant and machinery appear reasonable, the useful lives of motor vehicles appears excessive at eight years. A review should be performed to assess how long motor vehicles are held before disposal to determine if the average use from vehicles is eight years. A similar exercise could be carried out for more material items of plant and machinery.

A selection of assets from the fixed assets register should be physically inspected to ensure their condition does not indicate impairment and to ensure that they are in use. Consideration should also be given to other factors that could indicate the impairment of PPE, such as a discontinued product line that might render an item of plant and machinery obsolete.

(d) CAATs and the substantive testing of depreciation charged in the period:
- substantive analytical procedure – taking the cost of each category of asset and applying the respective useful economic lives would give an expected depreciation charge that could be compared to the actual charge in the financial statements. If the difference is within a calculated threshold it could be considered to be correctly recorded. The auditor would have to use the depreciation policy to deal with anomalies such as ensuring a full year's depreciation is charged for current-year additions and none for current-year disposals, and to remove fully depreciated assets.
- Alternatively, the auditor could use Excel (for example) to test 100% of the depreciation transactions by reperforming the depreciation calculation for each asset. This could be facilitated by downloading the FAR into Excel and, using a combination of cost, useful economic lives and date of purchase, applying a formula to accurately calculate the charge on an asset-by-asset basis.

## QUESTION 11.2

(a) **Indication of impairment – discontinuance of product line resulting in non-use of related manufacturing assets**   According to the planning notes the client entity is no longer manufacturing carpets, therefore the looms were not in use at the year end. There is an intention for the carpet looms to be sold in 2019 and therefore should be classified as 'assets held for sale' and shown under current assets in the SOFP. The assets should be shown at their expected fair value (expected sales value less any costs to sell), if this value is less than the carrying value the difference should be taken to the profit and loss statement for the period ended 31 December 2018. For the asset to be permitted to be carried as an asset held for sale the entity must show active efforts to sell.

**Application of policy against IFRS** If a policy exists to revalue assets, the entity must revalue **all** assets in that class. The entity states in its PPE policy that only land located in Dublin is revalued – therefore, either the entity must revalue all land or carry all land at cost. If the decision is to carry all land at cost the revaluation amount of €800,000 must be reversed.

(b) In carrying out this substantive analytical procedure it is important to note that each variable used in the calculation has been substantively tested. This analytical procedure has been performed excluding the impact of the carpet looms, which are considered separately.

| | Freehold Land and Buildings €000 | Plant and Machinery €000 | Motor Vehicles €000 | Substantive test performed | Source |
|---|---|---|---|---|---|
| Cost at 1 Jan 2018 per Note | 1,500 | 1,233 | 500 | Vouched against prior-year signed financial statements | Prior-year audit |
| Plus: additions in the period | 150 | 309 | 98 | Validated through substantive procedures performed on additions | Full year's depreciation in year of purchase (per policy) |
| Less: value of land | (900) | | | Traced to FAR – substantive analytical procedures carried out on FAR to validate completeness and existence of assets | No depreciation charged on land; land is 60% of cost at 1 Jan 2018 |

| | Freehold Land and Buildings €000 | Plant and Machinery €000 | Motor Vehicles €000 | Substantive test performed | Source |
|---|---|---|---|---|---|
| Less: assets disposed in period | – | (203) | (57) | Validated through substantive procedures performed on disposals | Nil charge in year of disposal per policy |
| Value of fully depreciated assets | – | (250) | (100) | Traced to FAR | Value fully depreciated per Note |
| **Value of assets to be depreciated for 1 Jan–31 Dec 2018** | **750** | **1,089** | **441** | | |
| Useful life (years) | 50 | 10 | 5 | Assessment of reasonableness of useful lives, e.g. asset turnover and condition relates to useful life | Useful lives as per policy |
| **Expected depreciation charge** | **15** | **109** | **88** | | |

| | |
|---|---|
| Actual depreciation charge | €240,000 |
| Expected depreciation charge | €212,000 |
| Difference | (€28,000) |
| Threshold | €10,000 |

**Conclusion of testing**

Difference between expected depreciation charge and actual depreciation charge is greater than the threshold. Further substantive procedures will be required to determine why the difference exists. As land and buildings and motor vehicles appear to be reasonable to the expectation, further testing should concentrate on the depreciation charge for plant and machinery.

## QUESTION 12.1

| Product | Current unit selling price £/€ | Revised selling price less 2% disc. £/€ | Cost £/€ | NRV greater than cost? | Provision required £/€ |
|---|---|---|---|---|---|
| Bedside locker | 150 | 125 – 2.50 = 122.50 | **125** (150/120 × 100) | No | **2,250** (125 – 122.50) × 900 |
| Double bed | 110 | 90 – 1.80 = 88.20 | **91.7** (110/120 × 100) | No | **3,850** (91.70 – 88.20) × 1,100 |
| Wardrobe | 210 | 175 – 3.50 = 171.50 | **175** (210/120 × 100) | No | **21,000** (175 – 171.50) × 6,000 |

**Substantive procedures**

- Current selling price – agreed current sales price to previous sales lists/sales invoices.
- Revised selling price – vouched revised sales price to supporting documentation (minutes of meetings approving the reduction/revised sales lists/communications on prices with customers).
- Cost – agreed cost of each of the items to purchase invoices.
- Checked accuracy of the mark-up by recalculation based on known sales and cost prices – discussed with management whether there were variances as there may be other components included in cost other than direct cost of purchasing if differences are noted.
- Agreed quantities on hand at year end to the inventory listing.
- Checked audit notes from year-end physical inventory count.
- Identified whether there were any further costs expected to be incurred in selling these products, such as promotional expenses, that would need to be taken into account in the NRV exercise above.
- Based on the above, an inventory provision of €27,100 is required. This should be included in the schedule of unadjusted differences to be considered with other errors found to ensure that in aggregate they do not exceed overall materiality.

## QUESTION 12.2

(a) Before attendance at the physical inventory count, prepare by gaining a better understanding of the inventory with regard to inventory types, materiality of different products, materiality of inventory held at different locations and any previously noted audit risks or risks identified during planning. With regard to Tulla:
  - As there is a number of locations in Northern Ireland and the RoI, planning will need to ensure that all locations are attended by the auditor. Priority should be given to the most material locations (based on value, not volume) and care should be taken not to exclude material locations.

- It intends to hold the physical inventory count three days prior to year end – although it notes that movement will be minimal, care will need to be taken to ensure that the count instructions are adequate to deal with cut-off.
- The count procedures should be received in advance of the count and reviewed to ensure they are adequate to ensure inventory quantity can be correctly quantified. If any concerns are noted, they should be brought to the attention of Tulla in advance of the inventory count and in enough time to correct and communicate any change in procedure.
- 10% of the inventory held by Tulla represents approximately 80% of the final inventory value – it is important for the auditor to familiarise themselves with inventory to be confident that material inventory items are given sufficient attention during the physical count.

During the count the following procedures should be adhered to at each site:
- Ensure the warehouse floor is sufficiently tidy and organised to facilitate a reliable count.
- Ensure a system of controlling inventory count sheets is in place.
- Ensure damaged, short-dated or obsolete inventory items are separately stored and marked to avoid counting with good stock.
- Ensure no movement of inventory during the count.
- Ensure there are teams of two counting and that they are performing blind counts.
- Ensure each member of the count team performs an independent count and a comparison is completed at the end, with any variances between individual count sheets being investigated. The counts sheets should be signed on completion.
- A sample of inventory items should be taken from the completed physical inventory count sheets and traced to the quantity on the warehouse floor (sheet-to-floor) to test for the existence of the inventory items recorded on the count sheets. A sample of inventory items should be taken from the warehouse floor to the physical inventory count sheets (floor-to-sheet) to test for the completeness of inventory items recorded on the count sheets.
- Copies of last and first goods received and dispatched dockets should be taken to facilitate testing of cut-off during the audit field work.
- Inventory items that were planned for dispatch to customers between 28 and 31 December should have been ready for dispatch and clearly marked to avoid any cut-off errors.

(b)
   (i) **Purchases cut-off:** select the last GRNs for goods delivered pre-physical inventory count and check that they have been recorded in the recorded stock before the physical inventory count. Also, select a sample of GRNs for stock received after the physical inventory count and ensure they were not recorded in the stock system until after the physical inventory count.

      Select the last and first 10 goods received transactions from the system and trace to signed GRNs to ensure recorded in correct period.

(ii) **Sales cut-off:** select the last dispatch dockets for goods dispatched pre-physical inventory count and ensure the sale has been recorded before the physical inventory count. Select the first dispatch dockets for goods dispatched after physical inventory count and ensure the sale has been recorded after the physical inventory count.

Select the last and first 10 goods dispatch transactions from the system and trace to signed goods dispatch note to ensure recorded in correct period.

Close attention should be paid to how the planned deliveries between 28 and 31 December were treated to ensure that if the deliveries took place, they were removed from inventory.

(c) To test the final inventory listing to validate quantities:
- Select a sample of inventory items from the physical inventory count sheets (copies of which were taken on the day) and trace quantities to the final inventory listing – tests for completeness.
- Select a sample of inventory items from the final inventory count sheet and trace the quantities to the physical inventory count sheets – tests for existence.
- Obtain explanations for any differences.
- Obtain confirmations of inventories held by third parties (if particularly material then attendance at a physical inventory count would have been required).
- Consider potential existence of other inventory items, e.g. consignment stock, stock sold on sale or return.

(d) During the physical inventory count, valuation can be considered as follows:
- Note stock segregated due to damage, obsolescence or nearing sell-by date and ensure these are not included in the count.
- Review good stock items during count to ensure there is no evidence of damage and, for perishable goods, review sell-by dates.
- Tulla will have acquired a lot of Christmas-branded stock, if this is still in stock at 28 December it is likely to need to be heavily discounted, therefore NRV may be below cost.

## QUESTION 13.1

(a) Further audit procedures and adjustments relating to receivables confirmations received.

**AIM** – SuperSmart are correct to record the transaction at the rate of the original transaction. At year end however, they should retranslate any FX debt using the rate at 31 December 2018. **No adjustment** required, but translation of FX balances should be tested as part of the year-end testing of receivables.

**Davitt** – SuperSmart have correctly recorded the goods collected as a sale in November and therefore receivable from Davitt. This is simply goods in transit and is a timing difference, which **does not require an adjustment.**

**Finn** – SuperSmart have correctly not recorded the receipt at 30 November (to make any adjustment would distort the roll-forward). **No adjustment necessary**.

**Sloan** – Sloan disagree with the balance owed due to a disagreement with regard to an invoice that they claim is overstated by £/€30,000. The contract needs to be examined, and if Sloan are correct an **adjustment as follows** is required and should be taken to the schedule of unadjusted differences:

|  |  | DR | CR |
| --- | --- | --- | --- |
|  |  | €/£ | €/£ |
| Dr | Revenue | 30,000 |  |
| Cr | Receivables (Sloan's account) |  | 30,000 |
| *Being overcharging of invoice XXXX* |  |  |  |

Note the value of VAT is not known and is not dealt with in this journal.

**Doyle's** – due to the non-response from Doyle's, further audit procedures are required to validate the existence and rights and obligations of the receivable. This can be done by reviewing the receivables listing at 31 December 2018 to determine if Doyle's have paid, which can be traced to the December bank statement, validating if the amount was owed or not at the end of December. At this point no adjustment is required until further testing is completed.

(b)
- **Receivables balance at 30 November 2018** – no further testing required.
- **Revenue 1 November to 31 December 2018** – the long-term contract was all recognised up-front and does not follow revenue recognition rules according to IFRS 15 *Revenue from Contracts with Customers*. Of the £/€567,000, it would appear that only £/€230,000 has been earned by 31 December 2018 as the other two elements relate to activities that will be performed by SuperSmart in the period after 31 December 2018.

Adjustment required:

|  |  | DR | CR |
| --- | --- | --- | --- |
|  |  | €/£ | €/£ |
| Dr | Revenue | 337,000 |  |
| Cr | Receivables (Sloan's Account) |  | 337,000 |
| *Being overcharging of invoice XXXX* |  |  |  |

- **Cash receipts** – of the £/€11,286,897 received, only £/€10,987,897 relates to trade receivables. The balance (£/€299,000) relates to monies received from the sale of PPE. This receipt is used to calculate the profit or loss on disposal of the asset as follows:

| | | DR | CR |
|---|---|---|---|
| | | €/£ | €/£ |
| Cr | PPE | | 200,000 |
| Dr | PPE – disposal | 200,000 | |
| Dr | Receivables (Sloan's account) | 299,000 | |
| Cr | PPE – disposal | | 299,000 |
| Cr | Profit on sale of fixed asset | | 99,000 |
| Dr | PPE – disposal | 99,000 | |

*Being correction of cash receipt to reflect sale of asset*

- **Credit notes issued in December** – if credit notes issued in each month represent approximately 1.8% of revenue of the previous month, there should be a provision in respect of December 2018 to allow for expected credit notes that are likely to be issued in January 2019.

Adjustment required:

| | | DR | CR |
|---|---|---|---|
| | | €/£ | €/£ |
| Cr | Provision for credit notes | | 194,166 |
| Dr | Revenue | 194,166 | |

*Being provision for credit notes in respect of December revenue*

- **Bad debts** – while the transaction appears correct and is validated by the liquidator's letter, the debt being written off is in relation to a related party – the auditor therefore needs to further review the relationship and the circumstances giving rise to the original transaction and the events that have caused the debt to be written off. Related parties require separate disclosure in the financial statements and the auditor should ensure that the necessary disclosures are made in relation to the transactions and write off. No adjustments are noted at this point.
- **Debit balances transferred from payables listing** – the fact that suppliers were paid by direct debit for services received but not posted indicates that there are missing expense transactions (payables are not complete) and an adjustment is required to post these transactions.

Adjustment required:

| | | DR | CR |
|---|---|---|---|
| | | €/£ | €/£ |
| Cr | Receivables | | 160,789 |
| Dr | Payables | 160,789 | |

*Being reversal of debit balances transferred to receivables*

|  | DR | CR |
|---|---|---|
|  | €/£ | €/£ |
| Cr    Accruals |  | 160,789 |
| Dr    Expenses | 160,789 |  |

*Being accrual of expenses paid by direct debit*

(c) Review of clients bad debt provision:
- Obtain an analysis of the bad debt provision to show which customer balances have been provided for by the client.
- Obtain an analysis of the invoice numbers, invoice dates and invoice amounts that have been provided for.
- Discuss with management how provision amounts have been determined and assess reasonableness and basis of provision amounts.

It will be important for the auditor to confirm any of the circumstances above in order to validate the need for the provision amount. Attention should be given to the following when considering the amount provided for by the client and if it is necessary or adequate:
- Has the customer gone bankrupt? If so, the total customer balance on the ledger at year end should be provided for in full. **Confirmation**: bankruptcy should be known publicly and can be easily validated.
- Is there a dispute over a balance which has been provided for? **Confirmation**: inspect correspondence (letters, e-mails, etc.) with the customer discussing the dispute.
- Is the customer experiencing financial difficulties? **Confirmation**: review of customer's payment patterns may indicate cash flow problems. For example, if the customer is making round sum payments on a timely basis, such as €/£1,000 each month, this could suggest that the customer is experiencing difficulties and may cast doubt over the recoverability of the balance and confirm the need for a provision.
- How long has the balance which has been provided for been outstanding? **Confirmation**: inspect invoices that have been provided for and confirm their age.
- How recent was the last payment received from the customer? The greater the length of time, the greater the risk that future payments will not be received. **Confirmation**: inspect customer's accounts and cash receipts book, verify the date of the final payment made.
- Is the customer account on hold or is the client still trading with the customer? **Confirmation**: inspect accounting system to confirm if the customer account is on hold or if it remains active.
- Is the client actively chasing the debt? **Confirmation**: inspect correspondence (letters, e-mails, etc.) with the customer requesting payment for aged balances.

In order to review the completeness of the provision, the auditor should also obtain a copy of the aged receivables listing and consider if further balances exist, which, while being old, have not been provided for by the client. Obtain explanations from the client as to why no provision has been made.

In view of information obtained from testing, the auditor must consider if the provision is adequate, i.e. has an over-/under-provision been made? The auditor should consider if correcting audit adjustments are necessary.

## QUESTION 13.2

(a) **Total sales revenue expectation (2018)**

|  | € |  |
| --- | --- | --- |
| Total sales to 31/12/2018 | 462,000 |  |
| Increase in revenue due to new DVDs brought to market | 130,280 | See (i) below |
| Decline in revenue due to DVDs discontinued | (21,930) | See (ii) below |
| Increase in revenue due to introduction of children's sweatshirt range | 17,550 | See (iii) below |
| Decline in revenue due to reduction in magazine prices | (16,050) | See (iv) below |
| **Total revenue expectation for sales to 31/12/18** | **571,850** |  |

| **Expected Sales FY 2018** | |
| --- | --- |
|  | **€** |
| DVDs | 335,350 |
| Sweatshirts | 54,550 |
| Magazines | 181,950 |
| Total | 571,850 |

(i) New DVDs

| DVD | Number of Months on the Market | Expected Revenue (No. of months on market × selling price × budgeted monthly sales) |
| --- | --- | --- |
| 1 | 11 | 11 × €10 × 250 = €27,500 |
| 2 | 9 | 9 × €17 × 300 = €45,900 |
| 3 | 6 | 6 × €12 × 485 = €34,920 |
| 4 | 4 | 4 × €15 × 245 = €14,700 |
| 5 | 2 | 2 × €22 × 165 = €7,260 |
| **Expected increase in revenue** | | **€130,280** |

(ii)  Discontinued DVDs

**DVD 1**

Lost revenue = €22 × 565

= €12,430

**DVD 2**

Lost revenue = €19 × 500

= €9,500

Total expected decline in revenue = **€21,930**

(iii)  Children's sweatshirts
Number of months on the market = 2
Average selling price = €13.50
Expected monthly sales = 650
Expected increase in revenue = 2 × €13.50 × 650
= **€17,550**

(iv)  Magazines

| Price Cut | No. of Months Price Cut in Operation | Prior-year Annual Sales Volume | Lost Revenue |
|---|---|---|---|
| €0.2 | 12 | 20,000 | €0.2 × 20,000 = €4,000 |
| €0.2 | 12 | 13,500 | €0.2 × 13,500 = €2,700 |
| €0.3 | 10 | 10,000 | €0.3 × 10/12 × 10,000 = €2,500 |
| €0.4 | 12 | 11,000 | €0.4 × 11,000 = €4,400 |
| €0.15 | 7 | 28,000 | €0.15 × 7/12 × 28,000 = €2,450 |

**Decline in revenue      €16,050**

(b)  Additional information to determine reliability:

(i)  New DVDs
- Determine the basis of budgeted figures, understand the budget and assess its robustness.
- Consider who prepares the budget.
- Consider who authorises the budget.
- Determine if actual results are traced to budget on a timely basis and if remedial action is taken.
- Understand why budgeted figures have not been achieved and validate the reasons for this.
- Confirm the month of introduction of new DVDs to the market, for example, by inspection of sales catalogue or sales records.
- Validate selling prices of DVDs, for example, by inspection of sales catalogues or sales invoices.

(ii)  Discontinued DVDs
- Confirm that selling prices for DVDs 1 and 2 were €22 and €19, respectively, for all of the prior year.

- Confirm the month of discontinuation of DVDs to the market, for example, by inspection of sales catalogues or sales records.

(iii) Sweatshirts
- Confirm month of introduction of children's sweatshirts to market, for example, by inspection of sales catalogues or sales records.
- Validate selling prices of children's sweatshirts, for example, by inspection of sales catalogues or sales invoices.
- Inspect market research and assess reliability of data to confirm expected monthly sales figure.
- Consider if average selling price is a reliable basis for use when determining expectation.

(iv) Magazines
- Assess reliability of using prior-year sales volume when determining expectation.
- View sales records to confirm selling price cut for amount of price cut and date of price cut, e.g. inspect invoice 'before' and 'after' date and confirm that price cut has taken place.

(c)  Completion of the four-step approach:

- Develop the threshold for further investigation based on the planning materiality of €10,000, for example, 75% of €10,000, i.e. €7,500.
- Compute the difference between expectation and the actual result:

|                | €       |
| -------------- | ------- |
| Expected sales | 571,850 |
| Actual sales   | 568,000 |
| Difference     | 3,850   |

- Where the difference is greater than the threshold, perform additional testing. In this case this is not deemed necessary as the difference is below the threshold for further investigation.

## QUESTION 14.1

**Subject:** Importance of confirming all bank accounts

Dear Audit Junior,

First, in general, external confirmation requests should be sent on the auditor's letterhead and should clearly identify all information required. It is important that the auditor maintain complete control over the process. The audit confirmation is a very important part of the audit of bank and cash as it provides the auditor with reliable independent third-party audit evidence. It should disclose cash on deposit, loans and details of all accounts in the name of the audit client at the date of the SOFP, and identify any accounts closed during the year.

**Further audit procedures on bank confirmations**

Please note that there is still considerable work to be performed with regard to the bank confirmations. Please perform the following activities:

- For bank confirmations received, where differences arise (Bank of Europe) you should review the bank reconciliation and validate the reconciling items that result in the bank overdraft being shown as a debit balance in the financial statements.
- For Union Bank and National Bank, you should also obtain a copy of the bank reconciliations and accompanying original bank statements and validate that the details therein match the confirmation.
- For HGF Finance, immediately send a bank confirmation, regardless of the value of the bank balance (even if it is nil). You must send a bank confirmation that outlines more detail than just the balance and any information that may indicate a significant value not reflected in the SOFP.
- Immediately follow up on bank confirmations not received and ensure control is maintained over the follow-up process going forward.

For each confirmation received you should ensure:

- all loans, guarantees, charges over assets and/or derivatives are fully complete in all sections;
- amounts are traced through the bank statement/bank reconciliation working paper;
- all matters noted in the confirmation are followed up; and
- interest provisions are provided for.

Further, with regard to the confirmation letter received directly by the CFO, you will discard this and contact the bank directly, requesting that the bank confirmation be sent to you directly.

Regards,
Audit Senior

## QUESTION 14.2

**Subject:** Audit of cash flow statement for JAG Limited

Dear Audit Junior,

Please note you are being assigned the audit of the cash flow statement of JAG Limited due to the illness of your colleague. First, I would like to impress upon you the importance of the audit in this area; and secondly to outline the procedures to complete the audit.

With regard to cash flow, it is essential that adequate substantive audit procedures are performed on the statement of cash flow because:

* it is a primary statement within the financial statements; and
* financial ratios that employ cash-flow measures can be used to evaluate a company's going concern assumption, therefore the auditor should seek to use the information contained in the SOCF to evaluate the client entity's liquidity status and abilities.

The following working paper is partially complete but includes the additional substantive audit procedures that you need to perform to complete the work on cash flow.

| | £/€000 | Substantive audit procedure | Further procedures required? |
|---|---|---|---|
| **CASH FLOW FROM OPERATING ACTIVITIES** | | | |
| Profit before taxation | 7,232 | → Agreed to SOCI | No |
| Depreciation | 1,204 | → Agreed to depreciation charge on SOCI | No |
| Interest expense | 789 | → Agreed to interest charge on SOCI | No |
| Profit on sale of PPE | (570) | → Agreed to working papers within PPE where profit on sale of PPE was recalculated | No |
| **Working capital movements** | **8,655** | → Check mathematical accuracy | Yes |
| Decrease in trade and other receivables | 1,750 | → Recalculate difference between opening and closing trade and other receivables on SOFP | Yes |
| Decrease in inventories | (1,205) | → Recalculate difference between opening and closing inventories on SOFP | Yes |
| Increase in trade payables and accruals | 980 | → Recalculate difference between opening and closing trade payables and accruals on SOFP | Yes |
| Taxation paid | (1,850) | → Obtain a listing of the amounts and dates of payments made to the tax authorities<br>Obtain an electronic copy of the bank statement and trace amounts noted as paid to the bank statement<br>Search for further tax authority payments not recorded | Yes |

| Interest paid | (720) | → Obtain a listing of the amounts and dates of payments made to all financial institutions<br>Obtain an electronic copy of the bank statements and trace amounts noted as paid interest to the bank statement<br>Using CAATs, search for further interest payments recorded on the bank statement but not included on the SOCF | Yes |
|---|---|---|---|
| **Net cash inflow from operating activities** | **7,610** | → Check mathematical accuracy | Yes |

## CASH FLOW FROM INVESTING ACTIVITIES

| Amount received on sale of PPE | 2,100 | → Trace to PPE working papers and trace amount received to bank statement | Yes |
|---|---|---|---|
| **Net inflow from investing activities** | **2,100** | → Check mathematical accuracy | Yes |

## CASH FLOW FROM FINANCING ACTIVITIES

| Dividends paid | (1,200) | → Obtain a listing of dividends paid and trace to bank statement | Yes |
|---|---|---|---|
| Loan repayment | (700) | → Obtain a listing of loan repayments making up the amount and trace to bank statement | Yes |
| **Net cash outflow from financing activities** | **(1,900)** | → Check mathematical accuracy | Yes |
| **Net cash inflow** | **7,810** | → Check mathematical accuracy<br>→ Compare the opening and closing cash and cash equivalents from the SOFP and ensure the difference is €7,810,000 | Yes |

## QUESTION 15.1

(a) Investment audit work:
- Vouch each of the investments to its supporting documentation.
- Verify that each of the investments is in the name of Meridian.
- Obtain copies of the investments' reports to confirm the net market values of each of the investments.

- Investigate where cost of investment is greater than market value, i.e. Golden and Yellow.
- Where the cost of the investment is greater than its market value, inquire from management if the investment has been impaired and assess the need for an impairment review.
- For any new investments, agree the purchase to its supporting documentation in the year of purchase; consideration paid should be agreed to bank statements.
- The Yellow investment should not have been included in the client schedule as it had been sold before year end – the schedule should only include investments still held.
- The sale of the Yellow investment should be vouched and the loss reviewed to ensure that it is appropriately calculated and correctly accounted for and disclosed.

(b) Potential audit issues:
- The market value of the investment in Golden equals €1,320,000, which is €334,000 lower than the cost of the investment; therefore an impairment of €334,000 exists.
- The impairment on investments may need to be adjusted for as the investment in Yellow is still appearing on the client's year-end schedule despite the fact that it was sold before the year end.
- The circumstances surrounding why Yellow is still appearing on the year-end schedule need to investigated and understood.

(c) Proposed adjustments:

|  | €000 | €000 |
|---|---|---|
| DR SOCI – loss on sale | 811 | |
| CR Investment Yellow – SOFP | | 811 |
| *Being the sale of the investment not recorded* | | |
| DR SOCI – impairment provision | 334 | |
| CR Investment Golden – SOFP | | 334 |
| *Being the recording of the investment at the lower of cost or market value* | | |

## QUESTION 15.2

Procedures to obtain the required assurance concerning the standard audit objectives for the current asset balances:

### Trade Investments (Listed and Unlisted)

### Completeness
- Sufficient assurance on the completeness objective for investments is normally obtained from work in conjunction with other objectives, particularly those relating to existence and rights and obligation.

- Recalculation of totals is an efficient method of auditing income from fixed-interest investments, such as loans, debentures, fixed-rate preference shares and government securities. The auditor should re-compute the total income by using the principal amount and a known interest rate.
- A substantive analytical review may, for example, be based on a comparison of the average recorded yield on the investment portfolio (or outstanding loans) with prior years and with budget. Alternatively, the auditor may develop an estimate by applying an average yield to the average market value of investments.

**Accuracy**
- The required assurance concerning the accuracy objective is obtained from work on the other objectives. For example, the work carried out to verify the existence and ownership of investments should provide secondary assurance that those investments have been accurately recorded. However, it is still necessary to check the following:
  - the control account reconciliation;
  - the carrying values of investments;
  - the classification of investments in subsidiaries and associates; and
  - that the amounts in the financial statements agree with the accounting records.
- Where there is an investment control account in the general ledger, check the reconciliation of the control account with the total of the individual investment balances by:
  - tracing the totals to the general ledger;
  - testing individual balances with the investment ledger (or equivalent records); and
  - checking the additions of the reconciliation.
- As part of the business review, review the client's accounting policies for determining the carrying value of investments, including checking that such policies conform with relevant legislation and accounting standards, that they are appropriate to the circumstances, and have been consistently applied.
- Examine supporting documents for additions (e. g. broker's contract notes), ascertain that the transaction was properly authorised and approved and trace the acquisition to the investment ledger or equivalent detailed record.
- Examine supporting documents, such as broker's contract notes, ensuring that disposals have been authorised and approved. The disposals should be checked to the investment ledger or equivalent detailed records. The correct calculation and recording of any gain or loss on disposals should also be checked. If only part of the investment has been sold, the auditor should check that the unsold balance is recorded correctly.
- It is not normally necessary to investigate the selling price if it is possible to rely on the independence of the broker who has originated the contract note. However, if there is any doubt about the independence of the broker, or if the investment is not listed, it is important to consider if the sale price appears reasonable. If necessary, reference to a stock exchange official list (if listed), or to audited financial statements or PE ratios of similar companies (if not listed).
- If there are any investments carried at a valuation, check the market value to the stock exchange daily list or the *Financial Times* (for listed investments). For unlisted

investments, the valuation by the directors is often based on the underlying net assets or a PE ratio of similar companies using reports or valuations made by experts. Discuss the basis of the valuation with the client, review the available financial statements, and inspect any reports of the experts on whom the directors have relied.

### Existence: Rights and Obligations

- The principal substantive test for the existence and ownership of investments is the inspection of documents of title, or confirmation from third parties (normally independent, reliable authorised custodians) that they are holding such documents on behalf of the client. The auditor should also obtain direct confirmation of loans.
- To ascertain whether investments have been pledged as collateral or as security for liabilities (of either the client or a third party), the auditor should make enquiries of the client's management, and review board minutes, loan agreements and other appropriate documentation.

### Cut-off

- Sufficient assurance relating to the cut-off objective is normally obtained from work carried out on the completeness, accuracy, existence and rights and obligations objectives. For example, work on additions and disposals will also provide evidence that purchases and sales of investments and income from investments have been recorded in the appropriate period.

### Valuation

- Clients may classify investments as either fixed assets or current assets and the treatment of any diminution in value will vary accordingly. In the case of fixed assets, provision is required for any permanent diminution in value whereas, for current assets carried at cost, provision is also required for any temporary diminution in value (i.e. so that the current asset is carried at the lower of cost and NRV).
- There are two complementary procedures that the auditor may use with regard to assessing any diminutions in value:
  - checking individual investments and making specific enquiries into their current status and prospects; and
  - reviewing the investment portfolio in the light of background knowledge of the client acquired during the business review, and discussing the portfolio with members of management who possess an adequate level of knowledge and seniority.
- For listed investments carried at cost, a significant decrease in the market value may suggest a permanent diminution in value. However, market value might not be an appropriate indicator if the market for the shares is small or infrequent, or if the dealings have been suspended. In these cases the auditor may need to follow the procedures relating to unlisted investments.
- Unlisted investments should be examined by reference to all the available information, such as recent audited financial statements, reports by independent accountants or investment advisers, and operating forecasts and budgets produced by the investee.

Consider the marketability of the investment and, in the case of overseas investments, any restriction on the remittances of funds.
- Management is frequently reluctant to recognise that an apparent reduction in the value of an investment is permanent, particularly if the client is committed to some form of continued support to the investee. While it is important to recognise that decisions concerning the permanent impairment of value involve judgement, the auditor should not accept unrealistic optimism on the part of management.

### Presentation and Disclosure
- To help achieve the objective the auditor should, at the end of the audit, review the financial statements and consider whether full and proper disclosure has been achieved.

### Prepayments
- Be aware that the prepayments balance in total only equals the audit materiality balance and, as such, only limited work should be carried out.
- Perform substantive analytical review of prepayments based on prior-period amounts adjusted for any relevant changes in the business. The auditor should be aware of the client's major items of income and expenditure from which prepayments, accrued income and other debtors might arise.
- Examination and checking of supporting documents should only be carried out where prepayments appear to be out of line with the expected amount and where the difference is material (e.g. one-third of the audit materiality level).

## Bank and Cash Balances

### Completeness
- The required assurance that all bank balances have been identified and accounted for is obtained principally from an understanding of the entity's business (the business analytical review).
- In particular, consider whether the number of bank accounts appears adequate for the level of business.
- Additional procedures may be appropriate, such as:
  - reviewing the list of balances at the previous balance sheet date and enquiring into any changes; and
  - scrutinising bank confirmations, cash books, bank statements and board minutes for evidence of accounts opened or closed during the period.

### Accuracy
- Detailed checking of the bank reconciliations should normally provide sufficient assurance that bank and cash transactions have been accurately processed. Check the bank reconciliation at the same date that confirmation of balances are obtained from the bank.

- Perform the following procedures:
    - check the balances on the reconciliations to the general ledger, the bank confirmations and the bank statements;
    - test the additions of the reconciliations, and of the lists of unpresented cheques and outstanding lodgements;
    - trace entries in the cash records before the substantive testing date to the bank statements or reconciliations;
    - check unpresented cheques and outstanding lodgements recorded in the bank reconciliation to the cash records and the bank statement; and
    - investigate and verify any other reconciled items.
- Select from the receipts and payments recorded in the cash records for the period before the substantive testing date to ensure that the items selected are either:
    - recorded on bank statements prior to the substantive testing date; or
    - included in the bank reconciliation as unpresented cheques or outstanding lodgements.
- Check that any material payments to creditors that were identified during creditors' reconciliations as not recorded on the creditors' statement at the reconciliation date are traced to the unpresented cheque listing.
- Review the detailed list of unpresented cheques for all large amounts (especially any large round-sum amounts) that have not been cleared by the bank since the substantive testing date, and trace to original documentation; discuss with the client why they have not been cleared.
- Any unpresented cheques not cleared by the time the audit procedures are carried out, the auditor should:
    - obtain explanations for any large or unusual items; and
    - investigate cheques outstanding for more than six months and consider whether they should be added back to the bank balance and payables.

**Existence**

- Sufficient evidence that recorded bank and cash balances exist is obtained by direct confirmation from the client's bankers. Confirmation should cover all banks with which the client held an account during any part of the period under audit, including payroll and dividend accounts, even though the account might have been closed before the year end date. This will identify possible unrecorded bank borrowings and contingent liabilities.
- Many clients' cash balances are immaterial and, depending on the assessment of the risk of misstatement, substantive testing may not be necessary. In the current circumstances, however, the cash balances are very material and the auditor will need to specifically address them.
- The auditor should attend the year-end cash count – unannounced. To avoid any possibility that a shortfall could be blamed on the audit staff, it is essential to count cash

in the custodian's presence, insist that he or she stays until the count is completed, and ask the custodian to sign the record of the amount counted to confirm acceptance of the findings. The auditor should check the amount counted to the general ledger and to the petty cash records.
- Cash funds often include cheques that have been cashed for directors or employees. However, shortages of cash are often concealed by the inclusion of fictitious, forged, or worthless cheques and IOUs in the funds. Therefore:
  - examine cheques carefully and ensure that they bear a recent date and are not post-dated;
  - check that they are subsequently banked and cleared; and
  - check that there is authority for the issue of IOUs and test that they are subsequently repaid.

## Cut-off
- Much of the required assurance concerning the cut-off of bank and cash balances is obtained from the work on bank reconciliations.
- Identify any significant transfers of funds between two or more of the company's bank accounts in the period prior to year end. In respect of such transfers, check that receipts and payments are recorded in the accounting records in the same accounting period and that any such items not reflected by the bank in the same accounting period appear in the appropriate bank reconciliation.
- Review the accounting records for evidence of the inclusion of lodgements that were physically received after the year end.
- Review the lapse of time between the date of issue of unrepresented cheques, as recorded in the accounting records, and the date of their subsequent presentation at the bank – consider if they might not have been released by the client until after the year end.

## Valuation
- If balances are held with reputable banks, the auditor should not need to question recoverability.
- If there are substantial balances in other countries or currencies, determine whether there are any restrictions on the transferability of funds that could affect the value of the asset or, for any other reason, should be disclosed in the financial statements.

## Rights and Obligations
- As a rule this objective should be accomplished through the normal bank confirmation procedures.

## Presentation and Disclosure
- Normally addressed at the end of the audit by reviewing the financial statements and considering whether full and proper disclosure has been achieved.

## QUESTION 16.1

(a) Supplier reconciliations:

|  | £/€ | Substantive audit procedure |
|---|---|---|

**Dock Ltd**

| Balance per supplier statement | 10,870 | → | Agree to supplier statement |
|---|---|---|---|
| Invoices on statement, not on ledger | 2,900 | → | Obtain copies of the relevant invoices and the related goods/services received note to establish when the goods/services were received. If received in the financial period under review, ensure the client has accrued them. If not accrued, investigate reasons for their exclusion and bring to the schedule of unadjusted differences as appropriate |
| Balance per ledger | 7,970 | → | Check mathematical accuracy |
| Exchange rate (£/€ : $)  0.79 | | → | Check rate to independent source as being the rate at the date of the SOFP |
| Balance per ledger ($)    6,296 | | → | Check mathematical accuracy |

**Dino Ltd**

| Balance per supplier statement | 22,300 | → | Agree to supplier statement |
|---|---|---|---|
| Invoices on ledger, not on statement | 2,500 | → | Obtain copies of the invoices making up the £/€2,500 and trace to related GRNs. Ensure the goods were received in the period to validate their inclusion |
| Balance per ledger | 24,800 | → | Check mathematical accuracy |

**Gino Ltd**

| Balance per supplier statement | 72,900 | → | Agree to supplier statement |
|---|---|---|---|
| Disputed invoice (Hall insist goods not received) | 31,200 | → | Request the supplier to provide POD or the contract in order to establish whether or not the goods/services were received in the period as stated on the GRN or in accordance with the contract |
| Balance per ledger (€/£) | 41,700 | → | Check mathematical accuracy |

(b) Further procedures for Jackson Ltd (statement not received) – identify the invoices making up the payables ledger balance and trace back to original invoice, from there:
   - trace from the invoice to the GRN to agree that stock items have been received and are recorded in the correct period;
   - confirm directly with supplier, if possible (permission obtained from client entity);
   - review post-year-end payments made by Hall and check which invoices are being paid; and
   - any invoices being paid not included in the year-end payables ledger balance, trace to GRN to check when the goods/services were received – if goods/services were received pre-year end ensure either on creditors' ledger or on the 'goods received not yet invoiced' report.

(c) Potential audit risks associated with debit balances on the creditors' ledger:
   - Risk of debit balances **and** reason for occurrence – for example, does the debit balance indicate weak controls around direct debits or unsupported payments?
   - Risk that the balance is not recoverable.
   - May have resulted from payments being made and related expense not recognised in the income statement (arises regularly with regard to utilities paid by direct debit where payment is made in advance and not always matched to the posting of an invoice).
   - Classification difference – may need to be reclassified to debtors.

(d) Search for unrecorded liabilities:
   - Review the post-year-end bank statement and select a sample of payments made post-year end. Note payments made post-year end normally relate to goods or services received pre-year end (to take account of credit periods allowed). Trace the sample of payments to their related invoices and GRNs to determine when the goods/services were received; if received pre-year end, has an accrual been posted and included in the financial statements?
   - Review invoices received post-year end and trace to GRNs to determine when received; if received pre-year end, ensure the client has adequately accrued them.
   - Perform analytical procedures to identify potential missing accruals. For example, electricity tends to be consistent year on year so performing an analytical review will identify any unusual/unexpected differences for investigation.
   - Perform cut-off procedures by inspecting GRNs posted in the days following the year end to determine if they actually relate to the prior period.
   - Review the open purchase order report and obtain explanations for significantly aged items that might indicate that goods were in fact received but not recorded as received and have therefore been accrued.
   - Review debit balances on the payables listing that may indicate missing postings.

## QUESTION 16.2

(a) Two risks identified:
- Back-pay/payroll correction – two incidents (James Dunne and Dee O'Reegan). The reason for how these arose should be queried with the payroll clerk and the possibility of further undetected payroll corrections should be assessed.
- James Dunne receives a payroll advance in excess of a full month's net pay – poses risks with regard to recovery. Payroll advances should be avoided where possible or strong controls should be in place to ensure timely repayment.

(b) For the gross to net report the following substantive tests of details will be performed:
- Recalculate the gross to net and gross components for mathematical accuracy and compliance with legislative income tax requirements relevant to each specific employee's circumstances (as outlined on their official tax certificate received from the government).
- Trace the union subscriptions and holiday pay to signed confirmation from the employee that these deductions may be deducted from his/her payroll.
- Recalculate pension contributions and agree to employee-signed pension documentation.
- Agree details to the employees' payslips.
- Compare the gross amount per the gross to net listing to the gross components report and investigate any differences.
- Query payroll advance, trace to approval and to company policy on payroll advances. Establish status of repayment of advance.

For the gross components report the following substantive tests of details will be performed:
- Recalculate the report for mathematical accuracy.
- Trace each monthly salary amount to the employee's signed contract (contract should be signed by both the client entity and the employee).
- For wages, trace the hours worked to the client entity's payroll time reporting system and agree wage rates to employee's signed contract (check mathematical accuracy to ensure hours by wage rate equate to amount noted on gross components report).
- Agree commission paid in line with the client entity's documented terms/policy and employee's signed contract; recalculate the commission payment and agree.
- Agree bonus payments to agreed-upon bonus structures as outlined in the employee's contract. Where performance-based/conditional, validate the targets/conditions were met to support payment.
- Investigate reasons for back pay/payroll corrections to understand whether or not the reasons given pose a risk of further undetected payroll corrections.

(c) Substantive analytical procedures are mostly applicable to large volumes of transactions that tend to be predictable over time. If there are too many variables or there are considerable unpredictable movements in payroll year on year, it may not be practical to perform substantive analytical procedures.

In performing a substantive analytical review, the auditor can gain assurance over occurrence, completeness, rights and obligations, recording and classification assertions – it can be an efficient test to perform, but will need to ensure that the control environment for the payroll cycle is strong if considering using substantive analytical procedures.

(d) In creating a payroll expectation the auditor usually starts with the prior-year figure and then determines factors that would indicate a change in payroll value, such as: new employees or leavers; payroll increases/decreases; or changes in bonus/commission terms. Each payroll element used needs to be validated by the auditor to truly substantiate the procedure. CAATs can be used as follows:

| Payroll element (variables) | Substantive test | Source and use of CAATs |
|---|---|---|
| Payroll expense for prior year | Validate against prior-year signed financial statements | |
| Add the value of new starters in the period | Substantiate against report from HR | HR report showing starters and their start date in the period. Separately, obtain the employee's master data, use VLOOKUP to check the salary of each new starter in the period and proportion the salary based on the period of time from their start date to the year end. For hourly paid employees, also obtain time recording reports for the period, using VLOOKUP to check the hourly rate from the employee's master data to calculate wages earned in the period. |
| Less the value of leavers in the period | Substantiate against report from HR | HR report showing leavers and their finish date in the period. Separately, obtain the employee's master data, use VLOOKUP to check the salary of each leaver and proportion the salary based on the period of time from their finish date to the year end. For hourly paid employees, also obtain time recording reports for the period, using VLOOKUP to check the hourly rate from the employee's master data to estimate what their pay would have been from the date of leaving to the year end. |

| Add salary increase | Substantiate against authorisation documents and communication to employees | Apply the percentage increase rate or increase per employee to the expectation as per documentation and communication. |
|---|---|---|
| Add/deduct increase/ decrease in bonuses and commissions | Substantiate increase/decrease to communicated bonus/ commission terms | Apply the change in bonus/commission terms to the expectation data created above. |

## QUESTION 17.1

As the new shares have been issued at a premium, the following should be completed.
1. Ensure the issue of share capital at a premium is in line with the provisions of Printer Limited's Memorandum and Articles of Association.
2. Determine the correct disclosure for the financial statements.
3. An audit adjustment is necessary to reflect the issue of the new shares.
4. Ensure the issue of shares at a premium is correctly disclosed in the financial statements.
5. Vouch the transaction and trace the cash receipt to the bank statement.
6. Inquire as to why the transaction was not included in the draft accounts.
7. Review board minutes for evidence of approval of new issue of shares.

## QUESTION 17.2

The additional audit procedures could include:
* **Opening balances**
  * Agree opening balances for 2018, to prior-year signed financial statements.
* **Retained earnings**
  * Review the change in accounting policy with reference to IAS 8 *Accounting Policies, Changes in Accounting Estimates and Errors* to ensure the change is applied appropriately to the retrospective period directly through the retained earnings account. Recalculate the related amounts and ensure the reason for the change in accounting policy is in line with IAS 8.
  * Agree profit figure to SOCI.
* **Revaluation reserve**
  * Ensure you reference the revaluation movement to the relevant section on the PPE file where it was tested.
* **Share capital**
  * Agree share capital details to CRO/Companies House annual return.
  * Agree issue of shares to board minutes.

- ◆ Agree payment received for issued shares to bank statements.
- ◆ Understand the rights, preferences and restrictions that might apply by reviewing Memorandum and Articles of Association.
- **Dividends**
  - ◆ Agree approval of dividends to board minutes.
  - ◆ Agree payment of dividends to bank statements.
  - ◆ Ensure there is appropriate level of reserves for making dividends.

## QUESTION 18.1

To:     Monitor Ltd
From:   A. Senior
Re:     Subsequent events procedures
Date:   01/07/2019

Following my meeting with the financial controller on 11 June 2019 the following subsequent events require attention.

### Customer gone into liquidation

Further verification work required:
1. Confirm that the debt was fully provided for and no further provision is required.
2. Inspect any liquidator's report to determine if the company is likely to recover any of the debt.
3. Consider if any further doubtful debt provisions are necessary in light of this customer going into liquidation.

Another procedure that may need to be carried out would be to evaluate the effect the loss of this customer will have on future trading and on the going concern assumption.

### Change of banking arrangements, review of contracts and proposed sale and leaseback

Further verification work required:
1. Inspect latest post-year-end management accounts.
2. In light of this new information, extend going concern audit procedures.
3. Inquire of management their exact intention regarding contracts and progress regarding the proposed sale and leaseback of premises.

Other procedures that may need to be carried out:
- Consider if there are any further going concern disclosures required in the accounts.
- Consider if there is any impact on the audit opinion based on the revised going concern review.
- Consider if there are any post-balance sheet disclosures required in the financial statements in accordance with IAS 10 *Events after the Reporting Period*.
- Consider the accounting impact the proposed sale and leaseback will have on next year's financial statements.

## Unpaid prior-year audit fee balance

Consider any ethical conflict arising because of the prior year's unpaid audit fee balance and the contingent nature of the audit fee payment for the 2018 audit.

## QUESTION 18.2

(a) Further audit work required:
1. No further audit work is required – bring the error straight to the schedule of unadjusted differences.
2. Verify that the bonus payments should have been accrued in full at the year end and, if this is the case, inquire as to why it was not. If there is an error, bring the error to the schedule of unadjusted differences.
3. Confirm that your calculation is correct, e.g. you may have included fully written down assets in your calculation in error. If there is an error, bring it to the schedule of unadjusted differences.
4. Verify adjustments to prior-year working papers, ensuring that closing reserves are correct and can be agreed to the closing trial balance.

(b) Schedule of unadjusted differences:

|  |  | SOFP | | SOCI | |
|---|---|---|---|---|---|
|  |  | DR | CR | DR | CR |
|  |  | € | € | € | € |
| Dr | Prepayments | 50,000 | | | |
| Cr | Trade payables | | 50,000 | | |
|  | *Being correction of mis-posting* | | | | |
| Dr | Staff bonus costs | | | 150,000 | |
| Cr | Accruals | | 150,000 | | |
|  | *Being correction of understatement of bonus costs* | | | | |
| Dr | Depreciation | | | 44,000 | |
| Cr | Fixed assets (accumulated depreciation) | | 44,000 | | |
|  | *Being correction of depreciation charge* | | | | |

(c) The audit partner will need to take the following into account when reviewing the schedule of unadjusted differences:
- Materiality of each error – if an individual item on its own is material the financial statements should be adjusted. Where a number of errors add up to a material amount then consideration will be required as to which item(s) to adjust for.

- The reason for the error in payroll – if there is evidence of fraud this should be reported to the directors and the auditor may have an obligation to report to a third-party regulator.
- The need for further investigation of any of the matters.
- Whether any of the errors found impact on other aspects of the audit, e.g. the reliance the auditor places on internal controls, the auditor's assessment of the integrity of management, etc.
- The year-on-year impact, i.e. the auditor may have to review the prior-year schedule of differences.
- The result of any discussion with the client and explanations received.

## QUESTION 18.3

(a) Schedule of unadjusted differences:

|  | SOFP | | SOCI | |
| --- | --- | --- | --- | --- |
|  | DR €| CR €| DR €| CR €|
| Dr Bad debt provision – expense |  |  | 30,000 |  |
| Cr Bad debt provision |  | 30,000 |  |  |
| *Being correction of bad debt provision understatement* |  |  |  |  |
| Dr Depreciation charge re. Beds Express Ltd |  |  | 100,000 |  |
| Cr Accumulated depreciation |  | 100,000 |  |  |
| *Being correction of depreciation understatement* |  |  |  |  |
| Dr Claims provision – expense |  |  | 75,000 |  |
| Cr Provision for legal claims |  | 75,000 |  |  |
| *Being correction of legal claim understatement* |  |  |  |  |
| Dr Bank | 150,000 |  |  |  |
| Cr Payables |  | 150,000 |  |  |
| *Being correction classification error on bank and payables* |  |  |  |  |
| **Summary** | 150,000 | 355,000 | 205,000 | – |
| **Net impact on the SOFP/SOCI** |  | 205,000 | 205,000 |  |

**Note:** the cut-off error was adjusted by the client and is not brought to the schedule of unadjusted differences.

Workings – Beds Express Ltd

|  | € |
|---|---|
| Owed at year end | 75,000 |
| Paid post-year end | (15,000) |
| Still outstanding at time of liquidation | 60,000 |
| Required bad debt provision | 60,000 |
| Actual bad debt provision | 30,000 |
| Understatement of bad debt provision | 30,000 |

(b)
  (i) Yes, these accounts are materially misstated. While the SOCI remains under the €270,000 materiality threshold, the liabilities on the SOFP in aggregate are €355,000 understated. Errors must be considered both individually and in aggregate. While no one error is material, when all are considered together a material error exists.
  (ii) The classification error of €150,000 is the most significant and if it were adjusted the liabilities would no longer be an aggregated material error. In addition, this adjustment would not change the SOCI.

(c) Adjusting subsequent events
  • The settlement of a court case confirming that the entity has a present obligation at the SOFP date.
  • The receipt of information after the SOFP date indicating that an asset was impaired at the SOFP date.
  • The determination after the SOFP date of the cost of assets purchased or proceeds of assets sold before the SOFP date.
  • Details of fraud or errors that show the financial statements are incorrect.

(d) Property valuer
  1. Check they are professionally qualified to undertake the valuation.
  2. Check they have the expertise and experience to undertake the valuation.

## QUESTION 19.1

(a) Schedule of unadjusted differences:

|  | SOCI | | SOFP | |
|---|---|---|---|---|
|  | DR (€) | CR (€) | DR (€) | CR (€) |
| Dr Trade receivables |  |  | 100,000 |  |
| Cr Trade payables |  |  |  | 100,000 |
| *Being correction of misclassification* |  |  |  |  |
| Dr Rent expense | 50,000 |  |  |  |
| Cr Rent accrual |  |  |  | 50,000 |
| *Being under accrual of rent* |  |  |  |  |

| | | | | |
|---|---|---|---|---|
| Dr Increase in doubtful debts provision (SOCI) | 250,000 | | | |
| Cr Increase in provision (SOFP) | | | | 250,000 |
| *Being under-provision of doubtful debt* | | | | |
| Dr Revenue | 35,000 | | | |
| Cr Receivables | | | | 35,000 |
| *Being known error relating to incorrect recording of revenue* | | | | |
| Dr Revenue | 1,540,035 | | | |
| Cr Receivables | | | | 1,540,035 |
| *Being likely error (extrapolated error) relating to incorrect recording of revenue\** | | | | |
| **Summary** | **1,875,035** | **0** | **100,000** | **1,975,035** |
| **Net impact on SOCI/SOFP** | **1,875,035** | | | **1,875,035** |

\* Working

Error rate = Errors found ÷ Population tested = €35,000 ÷ €1,110,000 = 3.15% (*rounded*)

Population not tested = €50,000,000 − €1,110,000 = €48,890,000

Likely error = Population not tested × Error rate

= €48,890,000 × 3.15%

= €1,540,035.

(b) Only the revenue errors totalling €1,575,035 are material. The auditor will be careful to ensure that they are satisfied with the testing and may consider further audit procedures to be satisfied that the likely error is a fair reflection of the potential size of the misstatements contained within revenue.

(c) Yes, the financial statements as a whole are materially misstated. Materiality is €500,000 and profit is overstated by €1.9 million.

(d) The auditor will issue a modified audit report based on the overstated revenue. The other errors are not material, either individually or when considered in aggregate, once the revenue error is removed.

1. The above scenario gives rise to a **disagreement** in that management believe the revenue figure is valid, while audit testing has revealed that revenue was recognised in advance of proof of delivery, resulting in a potential overstatement of revenue of almost €1.6 million (€1.54 million likely and €0.035 million known).

2. This is a material matter as it impacts revenue and receivables by €1.6 million. The before-tax profit is therefore overstated by €1.6 million, resulting in an after-tax impact of €1.4 million (after taking into consideration tax of 12.5% (€200,000)). Due to the fact that the matter is material, this leads to a **modified audit opinion**.

3. The item impacts revenue and receivables by almost three times the value of materiality and for that reason may be considered by the auditor to be so material that it warrants an **adverse opinion** (i.e. these financial statements do not give a true and fair view).

(e)

## INDEPENDENT AUDITOR'S REPORT TO THE MEMBERS OF GREEN TECH LTD (EXTRACT)

**Basis for adverse opinion**

Included in the revenue shown in the statement of comprehensive income is an amount of €1,575,035 relating to a known overstatement of €35,000 and a possible further overstatement of €1,540,035 (representing the extrapolated error) resulting from the early recognition of revenue due to the practice of invoicing on dispatch.

Accordingly, receivables and revenue should be reduced by approximately €1,575,035 **and** tax should be reduced by approximately €196,879, which would result in a reduction of profit and retained earnings of €1,378,156.

**Adverse opinion**

In our opinion, because of the significance of the matter described in the 'Basis for adverse opinion' paragraph, the financial statements do not give a true and fair view, in accordance with International Financial Reporting Standards (IFRSs) as adopted by the European Union, of the state of the company's affairs as at 31 December 2015 and of its profit for the year then ended.

(f)   This scenario gives rise to a fundamental uncertainty. While no provisions are required in the statement of financial position, a disclosure note would be required to disclose the material nature of the requirement to secure a loan. The item is deemed material due to the fact that failure to secure the loan will result in the company no longer being a going concern on the basis that it will have to cease production.

If the directors do not disclose this matter by way of note to the financial statements, then the auditor will disagree (disagreement) with the treatment of the fundamental uncertainty, giving rise to a modification in the form of an 'except for' qualification.

(g)   Should the directors fully disclose the matter it no longer gives rise to a disagreement. The auditor does not disagree with the financial statements as the primary statements and notes do give a true and fair view. The auditor will, however, need to modify the audit opinion by including an 'emphasis of matter' paragraph in accordance with ISA 705. This modification does not give rise to a qualification, but merely draws the users' attention to the note already disclosed by the directors in the financial statements.

## QUESTION 19.2

(a)   When assessing the reasonableness of the going concern assumption, the auditor should first look to the client entity's own assessment of going concern and in doing so should assess:
  • the length of the period assessed by management;
  • the systems by which they have identified warnings of future risks and uncertainties;
  • the reasonableness and extent of information, documentation and reports used by management in making their assessment. In doing so, the auditor should re-examine all material used by management in their assessment. The auditor should expect

that management has used a combination of the following in determining the reasonableness of the going concern assessment:

- ◆ cash flow projections and adverse key financial ratios – indicate an inability to meet borrowing arrangements, to finance new products and product development, or to pay suppliers when they become due. If these are of concern, then borrowing capacity should be reviewed to ensure the entity is able to obtain new financing;
- ◆ substantial and/or recurring operating losses;
- ◆ significant long-term contracts, with emphasis on measuring the cost incurred to date against percentage completion and expected profit.

If management have not reviewed the above, the auditor should do so in their own assessment of going concern, as well as taking into account other information discovered during the audit.

(b) Where the auditor assesses that there are uncertainties surrounding the going concern assumption, there are number of potential impacts on the audit report depending on the actions of management.

- Auditor considers there are uncertainties connected to the going concern assumption that will not be known until the occurrence of future events and **is satisfied** that necessary provisions and disclosures are made based on evidence available.

An **unqualified** audit report is issued, which includes an emphasis of matter paragraph directing the user to the disclosure note surrounding the matter of uncertainty.

- Auditor considers there are uncertainties connected to the going concern assumption that will not be known until the occurrence of future events and **is not satisfied** that provisions and disclosures are made based on evidence available.

A **qualified**, **modified opinion** is issued, disagreeing with the going concern assumption and thus with the financial statements:

- ◆ **adverse opinion** – where the uncertainty around going concern is a **disagreement** and is considered pervasive;
- ◆ **disclaimer of opinion** – where the auditor considers that they have not, and cannot, obtain all the information and explanations deemed necessary to make a decision around going concern (**limitation of scope**); again, it is considered **pervasive**.

Where a company is a public interest entity (PIE), or voluntarily chooses to comply with the *UK Corporate Governance Code*, the auditor (in accordance with ISA 700) is required to consider the adequacy of assertions made in the report by the directors outlining their assessment of going concern.

(c) The auditor's role is to offer some credibility to a set of financial statements, to address the separation of ownership and control and to reassure existing and potential investors as to the reasonableness of the financial statements. Users of financial statements can then rely on the information in the financial statements to make investment decisions. Albeit the auditor's remit is to the members (shareholders of a client entity), the audit report is relied upon by many other stakeholders.

The going concern assumption is obviously central to the users of financial statements (shareholders, potential investors, etc.). A failure to recognise that an entity's going concern assumption is not valid, i.e. that the entity is not actually a going concern, can have far-reaching repercussions. The failure of a company directly affects its employees, shareholders and investors, and the creditors that it owes money to, but it can also impact on the entity's business sector and related industries, on the audit firm and the profession itself and, in extreme circumstances, on the wider economy (national and international).

## QUESTION 20.1

(a) The following points would be of significance:
1. Risk identification, assessment and response to such audit risks
   - Group auditor to outline material risks identified and the assessment of these risks at group level that could impact on the group and local component entity accounts.
   - Group auditor to suggest audit procedures in response to the identified risk.
2. Materiality
   - Group auditor to set out overall audit planning materiality based on projected group results for the year under review.
   - Performance materiality for the group financial statements to be applied to specific transactions or balances.
   - Group component materiality to be set at a lower level than group materiality (60–75%) and communicated to component auditors.
   - Component auditors, if reporting separately for local statutory purposes, will set materiality for that purpose.
3. Response to audit risks
   - Group auditor to determine the audit procedures in response to the identified risks and communicate same to component auditors.
4. Use by the auditor of external experts
   - Group auditor to outline any planned use of external experts, e.g. actuaries.
5. Acquisition of subsidiaries in Eastern Europe and Russia and component auditors
   - Group audit to provide brief summary of financial position of new subsidiary to highlight any risks regarding local GAAP and any impact for consolidation.
   - May be need for audit visits as component auditors are not affiliates of parent audit firm.
   - Competence of component auditors.
   - Regulatory requirements of the components (and related component auditors) and whether they are acceptable to the group.
   - Involvement in the work of the component auditor.
   - Communications to the component auditors in order for them to audit the subsidiary in line with group audit requirement.

6. Communication with previous auditors
   - Jupiter, on behalf of Audit Sense and with permission from the management of My Toy Shop, should communicate with the outgoing auditors in compliance with the relevant ethical requirements and consider its 'Statement of Circumstances' outlining the reasons for the resignation (sent to the Registrar of Companies).
7. Audit timetable and logistics
   - Key milestone dates, such as commencement date of interim audit visits, date for issue of interim management letter, date that first draft management accounts will be available for audit, key deadlines for component auditors, etc., and audit billing dates.
   - Audit of the shared service centre for the purchase invoice processing process.
8. Consolidation process
   - Coterminous year end dates.
   - Systems in use by the newly acquired subsidiaries.
   - Foreign exchange rates.

(b) Considerations of the group audit firm when using component auditors include:
   1. Evaluation of the competence of the component auditors.
   2. Do the component auditors sufficiently understand the auditing and other standards applicable to the group audit?
   3. Do the component auditors comply with the ethical requirements relevant to the group audit?
   4. What regulatory environment does the component auditor operate within? Are the standards of regulation acceptable to the group auditor?
   5. Have there been any regulatory investigation findings against the component auditor?
   6. What level of involvement will the group audit firm have in the work of the component auditors?
   7. What needs to be communicated to the component auditors for them to audit the assigned component?
   8. Sufficient appropriate audit evidence is obtained from all components at the audit conclusion stage of the group audit work.
   9. The group auditor must maintain a close involvement in the work of the component auditors throughout the audit.
   10. Review of component auditors' files.
   11. Reperformance of some activities, e.g. electronic review or facilitated through an on-site visit (particularly if significant risks exist or there is concern regarding the component auditor).
   12. If the group auditor determines that the work of the component auditor does not present sufficient appropriate audit evidence, the group audit engagement team should perform additional audit procedures.

## QUESTION 20.2

(a)

1. Completeness
   - According to the schedule provided by the client, the cost of investment comprises four elements: cash, deferred consideration, share issue and incidental costs.
   - Consider whether the cost of investment is complete.
   - Incidental costs of acquisition (legal and professional fees) have been included in the cost of investment. This would appear to be appropriate. Fees and similar incremental costs incurred directly in making an acquisition should be included as per IFRS 3 *Business Combinations*.
2. Agree consideration to legal documentation
3. Agree cash consideration to bank statement
4. Deferred consideration – discounted per IFRS 3

   In relation to the cash, the only matter to consider is whether the cash has actually been paid. If it is the case that the amount had not been paid before the year end, the amount should be recognised within 'Payables: amounts falling due within one year' on the SOFP.

   However, this seems unlikely given that normally control of an acquired company only passes to the acquirer on cash payment. IFRS 3 states that the cost of investment should be recognised at fair value, which means that deferred consideration should be discounted to present value at the date of acquisition. If the consideration payable has not been discounted, the cost of investment, and the corresponding liability, will be overstated.

5. Recalculate
6. Agree reasonable discount factor used
7. Audit evidence
   - Agreement of the monetary value and payment dates of the consideration per the client schedule to legal documentation signed by vendor and acquirer.
   - Agreement of €5.8 million paid to Conrad's bank statement and cash book prior to year end. If payment occurs after year end, confirm that the amount has been accrued within 'Payables: falling due within one year' on the individual company and consolidated SOFP.
   - Board minutes approving the payment.
   - Re-computation of discounting calculations applied to deferred consideration.
   - Agreement that the discount rate used is pre-tax, and reflects current market assessment of the time value of money.

(b) ISA 600, paragraph 4, states the roles, responsibilities, competencies of the group auditors and component auditors involved in a group audit:
   - "the group engagement partner is required to be satisfied that those performing the group audit engagement, including component auditors, collectively have the

appropriate competence and capabilities. The group engagement partner is also responsible for the direction, supervision and performance of the group audit engagement."

- There is a significant amount of responsibility and risk on the group audit engagement partner (and the related firm), therefore the audit partner has an active role and should be in regular communication with the audit client.
- The group audit partner holds ultimate responsibility for the audit opinion expressed on the client entity's group financial statements and for this reason he must be confident with regard to:
  - ◆ adequate scoping of components;
  - ◆ adequate review of the component auditor's competency and eligibility; and
  - ◆ adequate review of the component auditor's work.

(c) Additional areas for consideration in a group audit engagement include:
1. Planning and organising a group audit is usually complex, e.g. components can be based in different countries.
   - Do the group auditors have the necessary resources (group engagement team) to competently perform the audit of the group to obtain sufficient appropriate audit evidence?
   - Apportion the component auditor's work to minimise the audit risk.
2. Ensure compliance with many complex accounting standards.
3. Considerations as to the adequacy of the group auditor's internal policies and procedures to sufficiently address the requirements of ISA 600:
   - assessment of risks for the group;
   - assignment of instructions/communications with component auditors;
   - consolidation process; and
   - evaluation of the sufficiency of the audit evidence obtained from component auditors.
4. Components may be audited by firms of auditors other than the group auditor (i.e. audit may not be carried out by the one firm). Considerations include:
   - Evaluation of the competence of the component auditors.
   - Do the component auditors sufficiently understand the auditing and other standards applicable to the group audit?
   - Do the component auditors comply with the ethical requirements relevant to the group audit?
   - What regulatory environment does the component auditor operate within? Are the standards of regulation acceptable to the group auditor?
   - Have there been any regulatory investigation findings against the component auditor?
   - What level of involvement will the group audit firm have in the work of the component auditors?
   - What needs to be communicated to the component auditors for them to audit the assigned component?

5. Complex consolidation adjustments – group auditors are required to evaluate the appropriateness, completeness and accuracy of consolidation adjustments, as well as to identify fraud risk factors and indicators of management bias.
   - Mechanical exercise of ensuring that routine consolidation adjustments have been made:
     - check that the audit packs have been reasonably completed;
     - matters identified within the audit packs have been included in the consolidation;
     - check the transcription of the audited financial statements of each component to the consolidation schedule;
     - check that adjustments made on consolidation are appropriate and consistent with prior years – adjustments could be permanent or current-year adjustments;
     - consolidation schedules should be checked for arithmetical accuracy;
     - tracing items through the consolidation process, checking ongoing adjustments to prior-year working papers and reconciling balances.
   - Determine whether the adjustments made are required and whether they are complete.
   - Determine how the consolidation process is actually performed, e.g. spreadsheets.
6. Materiality
   - What will group materiality be set at?
   - What will component materiality be set at?
   - Will different materiality levels be required for certain transactions or balances that are considered riskier?
   - What level of error will be considered as 'clearly trivial' to the group financial statements?
7. Scoping
   - Scoping is probably the single most critical element of a group audit.
   - The auditor does not have to perform focused substantive procedures on all components due to their insignificance to the group as a whole.
   - The aggregate effect of all insignificant components may be too material to warrant their exclusion, and for this reason some seemingly insignificant components will need to be scoped back in for more focused substantive procedures in order to gain sufficient appropriate audit evidence on the group as a whole.

# Glossary

**Accrued Liability**   Expenses for goods or services received that have not yet been paid for and for which no invoice has been received from the supplier.

**Adverse Opinion**   An audit opinion given when, due to an uncorrected disagreement on a material and pervasive matter, the auditor concludes that the financial statements do not give a true and fair view.

**Aged Inventory Listing**   Lists the total inventory balance broken down by the length of time the inventory has been on the entity's books.

**Aged Payables Listing**   A full list of individual supplier balances that can be reconciled to the payables figure in the financial statements and analysed to assess the existence of supplier balances. It shows each supplier by reference to the length of time the payable balance has existed (usually broken down into payable within 30 days, 60 days, 90 days, and greater than 90 days).

**Aged Receivables Listing**   A full list of individual customer balances that can be reconciled to the receivables figure in the financial statements. The balance for each customer is broken down by the length of time it has been outstanding (usually due within 30 days, 60 days, 90 days and greater than 90 days). Used to help assess the recoverability of amount receivable.

**Aggressive Earnings Management**   See **Earnings Management**.

**Amortisation**   The reduction in the value of an intangible asset over its useful life.

**Analytical Procedures**   Defined in ISA 520, paragraph 4, as "evaluations of financial information through analysis of plausible relationships among both financial and non-financial data".

**Analytical Review**   Comprises the analysis of movements and relationships between items of data. It involves the comparison of recorded values with expectations developed by the auditor.

**Application Controls**   An 'application' is a specific computer program, such as the payroll programme used to calculate wages and salaries. Application controls are the specific controls embedded in the application to ensure the integrity of input data, data processing and the output data. Also known as IT application controls.

**Arm's-length Transaction**   A transaction conducted on such terms and conditions as between a willing buyer and a willing seller which are unrelated and are acting independently of each other and pursuing their own best interests.

**Articles of Association**   A legal document that controls the internal management of the business, and the policies made to guide the execution of the objects as set out in the memorandum of association.

**Assertion Level**   In order to assess whether there are misstatements that materially impact on the financial statements as a whole, the auditor must consider risk at two levels; the financial statement level and the classes of transactions, account balances, disclosures and the related assertions level.

**Assertions**   "Representations by management, explicit or otherwise, that are embodied in the financial statements, as used by the auditor to consider the different types of potential misstatement that may occur." (ISA 315, paragraph 4(a))

**Assurance**   A statement that inspires confidence in the subject matter.

**Audit**   An audit (in the context of a financial audit) is an independent examination of an entity's financial statements in order to determine if they are reasonable and in accordance with applicable accounting standards.

**Audit Assurance Engagement**   The objective of an audit is to gain reasonable assurance about whether the financial statements as a whole are free from material misstatement, whether due to fraud or error, and to issue an auditor's report that includes an opinion.

**Audit Engagement**   When a company has to go through the audit process, an auditor may use the term 'audit engagement'.

**Audit Evidence**   All information used by the auditor in arriving at the conclusions on which the audit opinion is based, including the information contained in the accounting records underlying the financial statements and other information.

**Audit Opinion**   An expression of opinion on the truth and fairness of a company's set of financial statements.

**Audit Plan**   The audit plan is more detailed than the overall audit strategy. It includes the nature, timing and extent of audit procedures to be performed.

**Audit Programme**   Records the specific details of controls testing and substantive testing. It becomes a guide to the audit engagement team as to the work to be performed in a particular area.

**Audit Risk**   The risk that the auditor will fail to reach an appropriate conclusion about the entity and the accounting information on which they are reporting. In other words, an unqualified audit opinion may be issued when in fact a material misstatement exists in the financial statements; or the issuing of a qualified opinion when there is no material misstatement.

**Audit Strategy**   The audit strategy includes the more general audit requirements, such as the resources required, the budget, the timing and the management of how the audit is to be carried out.

**Audit Trail**   The electronic or paper trail that provides the auditor with audit evidence regarding the step-by-step documented history of a transaction.

**Audit Working Papers**   Documentation used to record the various tests that have been performed by the audit engagement team at each stage of the audit process, from the initial audit planning stage though to audit completion procedures and the issuing of the audit report. The working papers should demonstrate that the auditor has obtained sufficient appropriate audit evidence to support the audit opinion.

**Auditor's Expert**   If expertise in a field other than accounting or auditing is necessary to obtain sufficient and appropriate audit evidence, the auditor shall determine whether to use the work of an auditor's expert. For example, if the entity has revalued property in the period, the auditor will require the use of an expert in the form of a property valuer as the auditor is not an expert in this field.

**Automated Controls**   A type of internal control, those that are embedded within the client entity's computerised accounting system. In general, they make the processing of information more reliable.

**Bank and Cash**   Represents the bank balances and cash on hand included within current assets, and the bank overdrafts and bank loans included within the entity's current and non-current liabilities.

**Bank Confirmation**   A letter requested by the auditor and sent directly from the bank to the auditor that discloses cash on deposit, loans and details of all accounts in the name of the client entity at the balance sheet date.

**Bank Reconciliation**   An internal control performed by the client entity that reconciles the balance per the bank statement to the balance per the ledger (accounting records).

**'Bannerman Paragraph'**   A paragraph included in the auditor's report that seeks to protect auditors against exposure to third-party claims. Essentially, it informs third parties that the auditor does not accept any responsibility to those parties where they rely on the audited financial statements.

**'Big Data'**   As businesses grow in size, the volume of data collected expands exponentially. Computerised systems support large volumes of both structured and unstructured data, and accessing this data to add value to the business is strategically important.

**Bill of Material (BOM)**   A list of all components required to make a particular item of inventory, including quantities of each item needed to manufacture a finished product.

**Business Risk**   "A risk resulting from significant conditions, events, circumstances, actions or inactions that could adversely affect an entity's ability to achieve its objectives and execute its strategies, or from the setting of inappropriate objectives and strategies." (ISA 315, paragraph 4(b))

**Cash on Hand**   Cash held by the client that has not yet been lodged (this could include petty cash).

**Chart of Authority**   Dictates who in the organisation can perform certain transactions and activities and to what value, e.g. who can place a purchase order and to what value, and who can approve purchase orders.

**Circularisation**    The receiving of direct representation from a third party to verify information included in the financial statements. It is a very reliable method of obtaining audit evidence. A circularisation is usually in the form of letters requesting information from independent parties such as banks, customers (receivables), suppliers (payables) and solicitors.

**Classification**    A management assertion/audit objective for transactions and account balances requiring that they are categorised in accordance with financial reporting frameworks such as FRS and IFRS.

**Competent Authority**    The EU Audit Regulation and Directive (ARD) introduced the requirement for each EU Member State to appoint a single authority tasked with the regulation and oversight of the auditing profession. In the RoI, the Irish Auditing & Accounting Supervisory Authority (IAASA) is the appointed competent authority and in the UK it is the Financial Reporting Council (FRC).

**Complementary User Entity Controls**    Controls that the service organisation assumes, in the design of its service, will be implemented by user entities.

**Completeness**    Assurance is obtained whereby all account balance and transactions are included in the relevant accounting period.

**Component**    "An entity or business activity for which a group or component management prepares financial information that should be included in the group financial statements." (ISA 600, paragraph 9)

**Component Auditor**    "An auditor who, at the request of the group audit engagement team, performs work on financial information related to a component for the group audit." (ISA 600, paragraph 9)

**Component Management**    "Management responsible for the preparation of the financial information of a component." (ISA 600, paragraph 9)

**Component Materiality**    "The materiality for a component determined by the group engagement team." (ISA 600, paragraph 9)

**Computer-assisted Audit Techniques (CAATs)**    CAATs involve the use of IT systems by an auditor to support their testing of financial statements.

**Control Activity**    The policies and procedures by which the internal control system is enforced and implemented.

**Control Deviations**    Situations where actual events differ from those expected. For example, an auditor selects 200 invoices and traces them to customer-signed proof of delivery notes (PODs), but finds five deviations in that five of the customer PODs are not signed.

**Control Risk**    The risk that a material misstatement could occur in an assertion. Controls should be put in place to address risks and should prevent, detect or correct fraud or errors that may occur. Absence of these types of control increases control risk. For example, where cash **reconciliations** are not performed daily or if there is a lack of **segregation of duty**.

**Controls Activities**    Policies and procedures adopted by management of the entity to assist in ensuring the orderly and efficient conduct of its business, including adherence to internal policies, the safeguarding of assets, the prevention and detection of fraud or error, the accuracy and completeness of the accounting records and the timely preparation of reliable financial information.

**Controls Approach**    Having assessed the client entity's control environment and concluded that the internal control system is reliable, the auditor adopts a controls approach to test that the controls are functioning effectively. The alternative audit testing approach is substantive testing.

**Corporate Governance**    Is "the system by which companies are directed and controlled" (Cadbury Report 1992).

**Corrective Controls**    Control systems are designed to help prevent, detect and correct fraudulent transactions, errors and misstatements. A corrective control ensures that action is taken where necessary.

**Corroborative Evidence**    Evidence or information that strengthens or supports other evidence or information received.

**Covered Person**    Includes partners, principals, shareholders and employees of the audit firm who form part of the engagement team or the chain of command of the engagement, or are involved in non-audit services provided to the client entity.

**Cut-off**    A management assertion/audit objective for transactions and account balances requiring that they are included in the correct accounting period. For example, goods received by the year end are included in purchases and inventory in the correct accounting period.

**Cycle Counts**   An entity's performance of ongoing counts of its inventory throughout the year instead of a full inventory count at the year end.

**Data Analytics**   Accessing the strategic business value in 'big data' is an important feature of businesses. Sophisticated IT tools are used to analyse this data to create insightful reports that provide key business metrics when and where needed.

**Data Input Controls**   Controls designed to ensure that the data for input to a computerised system has been authorised appropriately, is complete and accurate.

**Data Output Controls**   Controls designed to ensure that the processing of transactions has been correctly carried out and that output reports are distributed to authorised personnel only.

**Data Processing Controls**   Controls designed to provide reasonable assurance that the computer processes have been performed as intended.

**Debenture**   Debt instrument in the form of an unsecured loan issued by a company, which is generally backed by the issuer's creditworthiness rather than by physical assets.

**Detection Risk**   The risk that the auditor will not detect a material misstatement that exists in an assertion.

**Detective Controls**   Controls to detect errors that have already occurred in the system, allowing their correction.

**Diminution in Value**   The decrease (impairment) in the value of an asset. For example, economic conditions cause some investments to devalue and the client entity is required to measure the value lost in the asset.

**Direct Control Activity**   A **control activity** that prevents unauthorised personnel from carrying out an activity, e.g. an unauthorised employee is prevented from approving a purchase order.

**Directional Testing**   Refers to the direction in which the auditor performs a test. For example, to test for completeness the auditor performs tests from source documents to the general ledger; whereas to test for occurrence, the auditor performs tests in the opposite direction, i.e. from the general ledger to source documents.

**Directors' Responsibility Statement**   Statement included in a set of financial statements that summarises the directors' responsibilities in relation to the preparation of the financial statements. It is usually included in the directors' report or immediately following it.

**Disagreement**   When audit evidence proves that there is a material misstatement in the financial statements and management will not make a correction.

**Disclaimer of Opinion**   An audit opinion given when, due to a limitation in scope in relation to a matter that is material and pervasive, the auditor cannot determine whether the financial statements give a true and fair view.

**Doubtful Debts Provision**   A credit balance set against receivables, representing the estimate of uncollectable amounts included in the trade receivables listing. The auditor will evaluate the adequacy of the doubtful debt provision when considering the valuation of receivables.

**Dual Test**   A test that can be used to support both controls testing and substantive testing procedures.

**Earnings Management**   The use of certain techniques to produce financial statements that portray a desired (rather than true and fair) picture of an entity's statement of comprehensive income.

**Emphasis of Matter Paragraph**   "A paragraph included in the auditor's report that refers to a matter appropriately presented or disclosed in the financial statements that, in the auditor's judgment, is of such importance that it is fundamental to users' understanding of the financial statements." (ISA 706, paragraph 7(a))

**Engagement Letter**   A written document, signed by the client and the audit firm, confirming the auditor's acceptance of the appointment and including a summary of the responsibilities of those charged with governance and of the auditor, the scope of the engagement and the form of any reports to be issued by the auditor.

**Engagement Partner**   The partner, or other person, in the firm responsible for the engagement and its performance, and for the report that is issued on behalf of the firm.

**Enterprise Resource Planning (ERP)**   A system used by organisations to manage multiple aspects of the business.

**Equity**   Residual value of assets after deduction of liabilities representing the monies owed by an entity back to shareholders.

**Errors Schedule**   See **Schedule of Unadjusted Misstatements**.

**Ethics Partner**   A partner in the firm "possessing the necessary seniority, relevant experience, authority and leadership levels ... as having the responsibility for ensuring the firm's compliance with supporting ethical provision 1.1." (Ethical Standard (RoI and UK versions), paragraph 1.12)

**Exception Report**   A report run from the client entity's computer system highlighting unusual activity. For example, within payroll, an exception report might be run for overtime in excess of 10 hours.

**Existence**   A management assertion/audit objective for transactions and account balances requiring that it is established that an asset or liability actually exists. The audit procedures applied will depend on the circumstances.

**External Audit**   A formal examination of a company's financial statements, with a formal conclusion on their truth and fairness in the form of an audit opinion expressed in an audit report.

**Familiarity Threat**   The threat to the auditor's objectivity and independence that arises when the audit firm or auditor accepts, or insufficiently questions, the client entity's point of view due to the close relationship held, usually as a result of long association (being the entity's auditor for many years).

**Final Inventory Listing**   Breaks down the inventory balance in the financial statements by inventory item, along with the quantity and unit price per inventory item. Its total should represent the carrying value of inventory in the financial statements.

**Financial Liability**   Present obligation of an entity arising from past events, the settlement of which is expected to result in an outflow of the entity's resources.

**Financial Reporting Council (FRC)**   UK authority that regulates auditors, accountants and actuaries. It issues financial reporting standards (FRSs) and the *UK Corporate Governance Code*. In the specific context of auditing, it is the **competent authority** in the UK, issuing the Ethical Standard, ISQC 1 and ISAs (UK).

**Financial Statements**   The financial statements of a client entity represent a compilation of individual reports and statements that show how it has used the funds entrusted by its shareholders and other stakeholders. A set of financial statements normally includes a directors' report, auditor's report, a statement of accounting policies, and primary financial statements with notes, such as the statement of comprehensive income, statement of financial position, statement of cash flows, etc.

**Fixed Asset Register (FAR)**   A asset-by-asset listing of all fixed assets owned by the client entity, setting out purchase details (cost, purchase date, description, etc.), asset category, applicable depreciation rates and charges, and net book values (NBVs).

**Forensic Audit**   A forensic audit involves the examination or investigation of an entity's (or individual's) financial information in order for it to be used as evidence in court. A forensic audit usually occurs as a result of allegations of fraud and its outcome forms part of the evidence for the prosecution.

**Fraud Risk Factors**   Events or conditions indicating an incentive or pressure to commit fraud or that provide an opportunity to commit fraud.

**General IT Controls**   Those controls that support the entire IT system. If an entity's general IT controls are weak, this will impact on its application controls.

**Going Concern**   A going concern is a business that operates without the threat of liquidation in the near future, must be evaluated for at least the next 12 months from date of signing of the financial statements. The directors of a client entity must perform an assessment of the going concern assumption to be satisfied that it is appropriate to prepare the financial statements on that basis. If a client entity is not a going concern, the financial statements should be prepared on a **break-up basis**.

**Governance**   The combination of processes and structures implemented by the board to inform, direct, manage and monitor the activities of the entity towards the achievement of its objectives.

**Gross to Net Report**   A summary report produced by an entity setting out the gross pay for each employee, less statutory and voluntary deductions to calculate the net pay due.

**Group Audit**   "The audit of group financial statements." (ISA 600, paragraph 9)

**Group Auditor vs. Component Auditor**   The group auditor (also referred to as the principal auditor, or the parent company auditor) has responsibility for reporting on the group financial statements. The component auditor has responsibility for reporting on an individual component of the group.

**Independence**   Defined as "freedom from conditions and relationships which, in the context of an engagement, would compromise the integrity or objectivity of the firm or covered persons." (Ethical Standard for Auditors (Ireland), paragraph 120; Ethical Standard (2016), paragraph 123)

**Indirect Control Activity**   A **control activity** that supports the controls within the internal control system. A **chart of authority** for example.

**Informed Management**   In regard to non-audit/additional services, a member of the client entity's management designated to make judgements or to authorise decisions.

**Inherent Risk**   The susceptibility of an assertion to a misstatement that could be material. Inherent risks exist due to the nature of the industry in which the client entity operates, product type or transaction types. For example, an entity that deals predominantly in cash is inherently risky, as is a company governed by management with a poor reputation.

**Integrity**   Defined as "being trustworthy, straightforward, honest, fair and candid; complying with the spirit as well as the letter of applicable ethical principles, laws and regulations; behaving so as to maintain the public's trust in the auditing profession; and respecting confidentiality except where disclosure is in the public interest or is required to adhere to legal and professional responsibilities." (Ethical Standard for Auditors (Ireland), paragraph 120; Ethical Standard (2016), paragraph 123)

**Interface Controls**   Controls designed to control the transfer of data from one system to another.

**Internal Audit**   The process designed, implemented and maintained by those charged with governance, management and other personnel to provide reasonable assurance about the achievement of an entity's objectives with regard to reliability of financial reporting, effectiveness and efficiency of operations and compliance with applicable laws and regulations.

**Internal Audit Activity**   "A department, division, team of consultants or other practitioner(s) that provides independent, objective assurance and consulting services designed to add value and improve an organizations' operations. The internal audit activity helps an organization accomplish its objectives by bringing a systematic, disciplined approach to evaluate and improve the effectiveness of governance, risk management and control processes." (Institute of Internal Auditors, *International Standards for the Professional Practice of Internal Auditing* (*Standards*), October 2017)

**Internal Audit Independence**   "... the freedom from conditions that threaten the ability of the internal audit activity to carry out internal audit responsibilities in an unbiased manner." (Institute of Internal Auditors, *International Standards for the Professional Practice of Internal Auditing* (*Standards*), October 2017)

**Internal Control**   "The process designed, implemented and maintained by those charged with governance, management and other personnel to provide reasonable assurance about the achievement of an entity's objectives with regard to reliability of financial reporting, effectiveness and efficiency of operations, and compliance with applicable laws and regulations. The term 'controls' refers to any aspects of one or more of the components of internal control." (ISA 315, paragraph 4(c))

**International Auditing and Assurance Standards Board (IAASB)**   An independent and international body setting standards in auditing and assurance and other related areas. The IAASB sets the International Standards on Auditing (ISAs) for adoption in local jurisdictions by a **competent authority**.

**International Ethics Standards Board for Accountants (IESBA)**   An independent body that sets robust internationally appropriate ethical standards, including auditor independence requirements, for professional accountants worldwide. These are compiled in the *Code of Ethics for Professional Accountants*.

**International Standard on Quality Control (ISQC)**   Standard issued by the FRC and the IAASA outlining an audit firm's responsibility with respect to a "System of Quality Control" for audits of financial statements and for review of the performance of that audit.

**Inventory**   Entities engaged in the sale of goods usually maintain a level of finished goods (product) to ensure an uninterrupted supply to its customers.

**Investment Schedule**   List of all investments currently held by the client entity.

**Irish Auditing & Accounting Supervisory Authority**   An independent body responsible for the supervision and regulation of accountancy bodies. In the auditing context, it is the competent authority in the RoI tasked with the oversight of the profession and the setting of standards.

**Irish Corporate Governance Annex**    The *UK Corporate Governance Code*, issued by the FRC, is recognised in the RoI as the framework for corporate governance. Companies listed on the Irish Stock Exchange (now trading as Euronext Dublin) are expected to follow the Code and is referred to in the *Main Securities Market Listing Rules* as 'Appendix 4 The Irish Corporate Governance Annex'.

**IT Controls**    The terms 'IT controls' and 'computer controls' are used interchangeably to describe controls operated by computers.

**Key Audit Matters**    "Those matters that, in the auditor's professional judgment, were of most significance in the audit of the financial statements of the current period." (ISA 701, paragraph 8)

**Knowledge-based Systems**    A knowledge-based system allows an auditor to design a questionnaire containing the most common questions related to a particular procedure and to support this with troubleshooting information that can help to guide them with respect to best practice.

**Lead Schedule**    Acts as a summary of the balances and transactions to be audited that relate to a particular class of transactions and balances. It allows the auditor to control the audit procedures by referencing each balance or transaction to the location in the audit file where the related testing can be found.

**Letter of Representation**    ISA 580, paragraph 15, states: "written representations shall be in the form of a representation letter addressed to the auditor". See also **Written Representations**.

**Limitation of Scope**    Inability to obtain sufficient appropriate audit evidence on which to conclude an opinion.

**Logical Security Controls**    Protection of computer software through the introduction of safeguards such as user identification (user name) and passwords or other authentication, firewalls or routers.

**Long Association**    See **Familiarity Threat**.

**Management**    "The person(s) with executive responsibility for the conduct of the entity's operations. For some entities in some jurisdictions, management includes some or all of those charged with governance, for example, executive members of a governance board, or an owner-manager." (ISA 260, paragraph 10)

**Management Assertions**    Explicit or implicit representations made by management in presenting a set of financial statements to the auditor. Management are saying, "We believe that these financial statements represent: transactions that occurred and balances that exist; are complete transactions and balances; accurately recorded transactions and correctly valued balances; transactions and balances that pertain to the entity; transactions that are recorded in the correct financial period; and are fairly classified, presented and disclosed." The objective of the auditor is to prove or disprove these assertions by obtaining evidence, and so they are also referred to as audit objectives.

**Management Letter**    Written communication from the auditor to the client entity's management or those charged with governance informing them of any significant issues identified during the audit process. For larger entities, where an interim audit visit occurs, it is likely that two management letters will issue, i.e. following the interim and final audit visits.

**Management Representations**    A written statement by management provided to the auditor to confirm certain matters or to support other audit evidence. See also **Written Representations**.

**Management's Expert**    "An individual or organization possessing expertise in a field other than accounting or auditing, whose work in that field is used by the entity to assist the entity in preparing the financial statements." (ISA 500, paragraph 5)

**Manual Controls**    Those internal controls of the client entity that are carried out by its employees (as opposed **to automated controls**). Examples include the performance of cash and bank reconciliations and the carrying out of credit checks. Manual controls are subject to human error. A cash business is likely to require more manual controls.

**Master Data**    Also known as 'standing data', master data relates to the information held by an entity that supports transactions. Customers' names and their bank account details are examples of master data. The integrity of master data is of utmost importance to any entity.

**Material Misstatement**    In simple terms, material misstatement is said to occur when an erroneous item's inclusion or omission in the financial statements could affect the economic decisions of the users of the financial statements.

**Materiality**    The magnitude of an omission or misstatement of accounting information that, in light of surrounding circumstances, makes it probable that the judgement of a reasonable person relying on the information would have been changed or influenced by the omission or misstatement. Essentially, it is the concept of significance to the users of financial statements.

**Memorandum of Association**   A legal document that defines the capacity of a company's activities and governs the relationship between the company and the outside world. It includes such items as: company name; type of company (e.g. public or private); company objective; and intended powers of the company.

**Misappropriation**   The dishonest use of the assets of the client entity, such as stealing inventory or abuse of a company phone.

**Misstatement**   Defined in ISA 450, paragraph 4, as "A difference between the reported amount, classification, presentation, or disclosure of a financial statement item and the amount, classification, presentation, or disclosure that is required for the item to be in accordance with the applicable financial reporting framework. Misstatements can arise from fraud or error." Misstatements may be classified as fraud (intentional); as other illegal acts, such as non-compliance with laws and regulations (intentional or unintentional); or as errors (unintentional).

**Modified Opinion**   In the audit report, an opinion given when: 1. it is concluded that, based on the audit evidence obtained, the financial statements as a whole are not free from material misstatement; or 2. the auditor is unable to obtain sufficient appropriate audit evidence to conclude that the financial statements as a whole are free from material misstatement.

**Multiple Control Activities**   A combination of control procedures – preventative, detective and corrective, both manual and automated – to address a risk.

**'Nature, Timing and Extent'**   The audit plan, which is more detailed than the overall audit strategy, determines the nature, timing and extent of audit procedures to be performed to gain sufficient appropriate audit evidence. 'Nature' refers to the purpose of the procedure; 'timing' refers to when it is performed; and 'extent' to the quantity to be performed, e.g. sample size.

**Net Realisable Value (NRV)**   The value of inventory based on sales price less the cost to completion, less sales, marketing and distribution costs. It may also be defined as the value the inventory would achieve in the open market in its present condition.

**Objectivity**   Defined as "acting and making decisions and judgments impartially, fairly and on merit (having regard to all considerations relevant to the task in hand but no other), without discrimination, bias, or compromise because of commercial or personal self-interest, conflicts of interest or the undue influence of others, and having given due consideration to the best available evidence." (Ethical Standard for Auditors (Ireland), paragraph 120; Ethical Standard (2016), paragraph 123)

**Occurrence**   A management assertion/audit objective for transactions and account balances requiring that all transactions have actually occurred, are genuine and free from fraud or misstatement.

**Organisational Structure**   The hierarchical arrangement of authority and rights and duties within an organisation.

**Other Matter Paragraph**   "A paragraph included in the auditor's report that refers to a matter other than those presented or disclosed in the financial statements that, in the auditor's judgment, is relevant to users' understanding of the audit, the auditor's responsibilities or the auditor's report." (ISA 706, paragraph 7(b))

**Persons Closely Associated**   Defined as: (a) a spouse (or equivalent); (b) a dependent child; (c) a relative who, during the engagement, has lived in the same household as the associated person for at least one year; (d) a firm whose managerial responsibilities are discharged by, or which is directly or indirectly controlled by, the firm / person with whom they are associated, or by any person mentioned in (a), (b) or (c) or in which the firm or any such person has a beneficial or other substantially equivalent economic interest; (e) A trust whose managerial responsibilities are discharged by, or which is directly or indirectly controlled by, or which is set up for the benefit of, or whose economic interests are substantially equivalent to, the firm / person with whom they are associated or any person mentioned in (a), (b) or (c).

**Pervasive**   Term used to describe the extent of the impact of a single misstatement, or the cumulative impact of multiple misstatements, on the financial statements. A pervasive misstatement impacts on many elements of the financial statements, resulting in the financial statements not presenting a true and fair view.

**Physical Controls**   Safeguards to prevent business assets, such as cash or inventory, from theft or misappropriation. They could also relate to the safeguarding of documents or computer installations.

**Physical Inventory Count Sheet**   A record of the physical inventory held on the entity's premises, completed during a physical count (stock-take).

**Policies and Procedures**   Policies outline the principles or rules that guide decisions within an organisation (e.g. it might be a company's policy to only accept return of goods within 28 days of sale). Procedures outline what action is to be taken or what steps are to be followed when performing a particular task (e.g. when a customer presents a return, the procedure might be to request a receipt or invoice and check that the date on the receipt or invoice is within 28 days; for returns over €100, contact a supervisor to approve the return).

**Presentation and Disclosure**   A management assertion/audit objective for transactions and account balances requiring that they comply with applicable legislation and financial reporting frameworks with regard to set-down formats and contents of financial statements, including disclosure notes.

**Preventative Controls**   Controls that help prevent an error occurring in the first place. For example, the inability to process a customer's order where it would cause the customer to exceed their credit limit.

**Professional Scepticism**   Refers to a particular state of mind that an auditor must maintain to conduct audit engagements appropriately. The 'scepticism approach' enables the auditor to recognise that circumstances may exist that cause the financial statements to be materially misstated. The auditor should, therefore, be alert and remain cautious about information and events that indicate the existence of material misstatement.

**Public Interest Entities (PIEs)**   In general terms (in both the RoI and the UK), a PIE is an entity "whose transferable securities [i.e. stocks , shares and debt] are admitted to trading on a regulated market" (ISA 220, paragraph 7(m)-1).

**Qualified Opinion**   Where either: 1. a material misstatement occurs due to disagreement; or 2. a limitation of scope has been imposed on a matter that is material but is not pervasive and so a qualified (except for) opinion is issued (i.e. the auditor's opinion on the financial statements is that they give a true and fair view except for an isolated material matter).

**Random Sampling**   The process of applying auditing procedures to less than 100% of a population, such that each unit has an equal chance of being selected.

**Real Time**   Transactions that occur in 'real time' are those that are completed without any delay or requirement for manual intervention (i.e. systems that respond to inputs immediately).

**Reasonable Assurance**   Providing a high degree of assurance but not an absolute assurance.

**Receivables Circularisation**   A letter sent to the client entity's customers by the auditor, the objective of which is to obtain independent evidence as to the existence and accuracy of the receivables balance in the financial statements. The auditor must receive permission from the client entity before circularising its customers.

**Recognised Accountancy Body (RAB)**   In the RoI, a body responsible for the supervision and monitoring of the audit profession and the issuing of qualifications. RABs are designated by the IAASA, in its role as the **competent authority** in the RoI. The Institute of Chartered Accountants in Ireland is a RAB. To act as an auditor in the RoI, authorisation to do so must be granted by the RAB.

**Recognised Qualifying Body (RQB)**   In the UK/NI, a body responsible for the issuing of audit qualifications, designated as such by the FRC in its role as the **competent authority** in the UK/NI. The Institute of Chartered Accountants in Ireland is a RQB (as appointed by the FRC).

**Recognised Supervisory Body (RSB)**   In the UK/NI, a body responsible for the supervision and monitoring of the audit profession, designated as such by the FRC in its role as the **competent authority** in the UK/NI. The Institute of Chartered Accountants in Ireland is a RSB (as appointed by the FRC). To act as an auditor in the UK/NI, authorisation to do so must be granted by the RSB.

**Reconciliation**   A very important control feature that involves the checking (reconciling) of an amount against its source. Examples are **bank reconciliations** and the reconciliation of receivables and payables ledger with the nominal/general ledger.

**Recording**    A management assertion/audit objective for transactions and account balances requiring that they are accurately recorded to provide a full audit trail through the accounting system. The recording of transactions should be complete, accurate and free from error, fraud and misstatement.

**Recurring Audit**    Long-standing audit client.

**Review and Authorisation**    An internal control to ensure that tasks performed are checked and approved in accordance with procedures. For example, the procedures to decide and assign a customer's credit limit.

**Rights and Obligations**    A management assertion/audit objective for transactions and account balances requiring that it is verified that an entity has recognised ownership/rights to an asset, and obligations for liabilities incurred.

**Roll-forward or Roll-back Procedures**    When the auditor is unable to attend the physical inventory count at year end, they may attend an earlier or later physical inventory count and, internal control procedures permitting, perform a roll-forward or roll-back to determine the existence of inventory at year end.


**Sample Population**    All of the items that make up the balance or transaction being tested by the auditor, e.g. the receivables balance population is made up of all the customers' individual balances.

**Schedule of Unadjusted Differences/Misstatements**    A summary of **all** misstatements, whether or not they are material, found during the course of the audit. The auditor considers the unadjusted misstatements in light of the audit planning materiality and a conclusion is drawn on the overall materiality of misstatements/errors found. This is also referred to as the 'errors schedule'.

**Scoping**    In group audits, a term used to describe the exercise carried out to determine which components will undergo full audit procedures (scoping in) and which will be considered insignificant and be subject to a reduced level of testing (scoping out).

**Search for Unrecorded Liabilities**    Techniques used by the auditor to identify understatement of liabilities.

**Segregation of Duties**    The division of key tasks in a transaction to ensure that no one individual can perform a transaction from beginning to end.

**Self-interest Threat**    A situation in which the auditor's decisions may be influenced by their own self-interest in the matter. For example, if the auditor holds shares in a client entity they may be reluctant to make a decision that will impact the opinion expressed in the auditor's report and thereby affect the value of shares.

**Self-review Threat**    Arises during an audit when the auditor is reviewing a non-audit service provided by the audit firm. For example, if the auditor is seconded to the client entity to assist with its payroll function and in the course of the audit, may need to re-evaluate the work performed in the non-audit service.

**Server Room**    A room that houses mainly computer servers. Climate is one of the factors that affects the energy consumption and environmental impact of a server room and so access to this area should be restricted to maintain required levels of control.

**Service Auditor**    An auditor who, at the request of the service organisation, provides an assurance report on the controls of that organisation.

**Service Organisation**    A third-party organisation (or element of a third-party organisation) that provides services to user entities that are part of those entities' information systems relevant to financial reporting.

**Share Register**    A list of all the current shareholders of a company updated on an ongoing basis.

**Significant Component**    "A component identified by the group engagement team (i) that is of individual financial significance to the group, or (ii) that, due to its specific nature or circumstances, is likely to include significant risks of material misstatement of the group financial statements." (ISA 600, paragraph 9)

**Significant Risks**    Those risks that have the potential to impact significantly on the financial statements and therefore need special audit consideration. Examples include revenue recognition and management override of controls.

**Subsequent Events**    "Events occurring between the date of the financial statements and the date of the auditor's report, and facts that become known to the auditor after the date of the auditor's report." (ISA 560, paragraph 5(e))

**Substantive Analytical Procedures**   Also known as a 'proof in total', a substantive analytical procedure is an audit procedure that is generally more efficient than **tests of details** and is permitted where a low level of inherent and control risks exist. It involves the auditor developing an independent calculation (expectation) of the balance being audited and comparing it with the actual balance as per the financial statements. If the auditor's independent expectation is within a threshold from the actual figure, then no further testing is required by the auditor in relation to the balance. (Other assertions, however, such as valuation, may still need to be considered.)

**Sufficient Appropriate Audit Evidence**   'Sufficient' refers to the quantity of evidence obtained; 'appropriate' refers to the requirement for evidence to be of a high quality and to be relevant to the objective of the audit procedure.

**Supplier Statement Reconciliation**   When a client entity reconciles the balance on its supplier's statement to the supplier's balance showing on its ledger.

**System Control**   A system control is one that is embedded into an entity's IT system. For example, the system can ensure the segregation of duty control requirement is met by ensuring that only those individuals with credit control rights can approve the opening of a new customer account on credit.

**Tests of Controls**   Audit procedure to test the effectiveness of a control used by the client entity to prevent or detect material misstatement.

**Tests of Detail**   A type of substantive procedure that refers to the selection of a sample and the tracing of each item selected to evidence that supports the assertion being tested.

**Third Party Test**   Consideration of whether the ethical outcomes required by the overarching principles and supporting ethical provisions have been met should be evaluated by reference to the perspective of an objective, reasonable and informed third party.

**Those Charged with Governance**   The person(s) with responsibility for overseeing the strategic direction of the entity and obligations related to the accountability of the entity. This includes overseeing the financial reporting process.

**Tolerable Misstatement**   The application of performance materiality to a particular sampling procedure. Tolerable misstatement may be the same amount or an amount lower than performance materiality. The auditor seeks assurance that the tolerable misstatement is not exceeded by the actual misstatement contained in the balance.

**'Tone at the Top'**   The words and actions of the directors and senior management of an organisation, in this case relating to internal controls and ethical values.

**'True and Fair View'**   In the auditor's report an opinion is given as to whether the financial statements give a "true and fair view". This term is not defined in legislation but is given to mean that the financial statements give an accurate, fair, unbiased view.

**Trust Deeds**   A legal document that transfers to a trustee the title to property.

***UK Corporate Governance Code*** The preeminent corporate governance code, setting out standards of good practice ('principles') in relation to board leadership and effectiveness, remuneration, accountability and relations with shareholders. First issued by the FRC in 2010 and regularly updated since.

**Unqualified Opinion**   A 'clean' audit opinion, i.e. the financial statements give a true and fair view.

**User Auditor**   An auditor who audits and reports on the financial statements of a user entity.

**User Entity**   A client entity is referred to as a user entity when it outsources a key function impacting on the financial statements (for example, when a client entity outsources its payroll function it is known as a user entity).

**Valuation**   A management assertion/audit objective for transactions and account balances requiring that they are recorded at the correct value. Financial statements are generally prepared under the historical cost convention, which means that transactions and balances are initially recorded at their original cost. However, certain transactions/balances may be recorded at a 'fair value' depending on the applicable financial reporting framework.

**Walkthrough Test**   The tracing of a single transaction from beginning to end ('cradle to grave') to establish if it operates as described in the policies and procedures of the client entity.

**'Window Dressing'**   A strategy used by management near the year end to manipulate the appearance of the financial statements (e.g. where profit has performed poorly in the year, management might over-inflate the revenue by including some of January's sales, i.e. post-year-end, in December's revenue).

**Written Representations**   "A written statement by management provided to the auditor to confirm certain matters or to support other audit evidence. Written representations in this context do not include financial statements, the assertions therein, or supporting books and records." (ISA 580, paragraph 7)

# Index